T0305278

SEWN IN COAL COUNTRY

SEWN IN COAL COUNTRY

An Oral History of the
Ladies' Garment Industry in
Northeastern Pennsylvania,
1945–1995

ROBERT P. WOLENSKY

The Pennsylvania State University Press
University Park, Pennsylvania

Additional credits: page ii, courtesy of the Northeastern Penn-sylvania Oral and Life History Collection, Eberly Family Special Collections Library, Penn State University; page vi, courtesy of Kheel Center, Cornell University.

Library of Congress Cataloging-in-Publication Data

Names: Wolensky, Robert P., editor.
Title: Sewn in coal country : an oral history of the ladies'
    garment industry in northeastern Pennsylvania, 1945–1995
    / [edited by] Robert P. Wolensky.
Description: University Park, Pennsylvania : The Pennsylvania
    State University Press, [2020] | Includes bibliographical
    references and index. | Summary: "A study of the ladies'
    garment industry in northeastern Pennsylvania between
    1945 and 1995, featuring sixteen selected oral histories
    conducted with workers, shop owners, and others with
    knowledge of the industry"—Provided by publisher.
Identifiers: LCCN 2019046995 | ISBN 9780271084909 (cloth)
    | ISBN 9780271084985 (paperback)
Subjects: LCSH: International Ladies' Garment
    Workers' Union—History. | Clothing workers—
    Pennsylvania—Interviews. | Women's clothing
    Industry—Pennsylvania—History—20th century. | Clothing
    trade—Pennsylvania—History—20th century. | Labor
    unions—Pennsylvania—History—20th century. | LCGFT:
    Oral histories. | Interviews.
Classification: LCC HD9940.U5 P35 2020 | DDC
    331.88/18709227482—dc23
LC record available at https://lccn.loc.gov/2019046995

The Pennsylvania State University Press is a member of the
Association of University Presses.

It is the policy of The Pennsylvania State University Press to
use acid-free paper. Publications on uncoated stock satisfy
the minimum requirements of American National Standard
for Information Sciences—Permanence of Paper for Printed
Library Material, ANSI Z39.48–1992.

To the people affiliated with the Wyoming Valley garment industry of northeastern Pennsylvania

and

To Min and Bill Matheson and the many other oral history subjects who have generously contributed interviews to the Wyoming Valley Oral History Project

---

History studies not just facts and institutions; its real subject is the human spirit.

—NUMA DENIS FUSTEL DE COULANGES, 1864

People are trapped in history, and history is trapped in them.

—JAMES BALDWIN, 1955

One has only to scratch the surface of memory and the stories gush out.

—ALESSANDRO PORTELLI, 2003

In the present and the future, there will certainly be thoughtful activists who—seeking resources for making sense of what is happening and for finding pathways to a better future—will want to know something of these insurgent experiences and ideas of the past.

—PAUL LE BLANC AND TIM DAVENPORT, 2015

Labour movements, whatever else they were, were also "cultural revolutions."

—ERIC HOBSBAWM, 1978

There is no higher religion than human service. Working for the common good is the greatest creed.

—MIN MATHESON, 1982

I have tried to be objective. I do not claim to be detached.

—RALPH MILIBAND, 1962

CONTENTS

ILLUSTRATIONS

GALLERY

Wherever men have lived there is a story to be told.

—HENRY DAVID THOREAU, 1861

Thoreau's comment notwithstanding, author Wallace Stegner contended that a place is not really a place until its stories have been told and remembered through literature, ballads, yarns, legends, and monuments.[1] In connecting place and story, one of the most compelling tales to come out of Pennsylvania during the middle years of the twentieth century occurred in the unique cultural landscape called the Wyoming Valley of Luzerne County, in the northeastern corner of the state.[2] The episode occurred during the Commonwealth's (and the nation's) transition from high industrialism to post-industrialism.

The principal actors were affiliated with the ladies' clothing industry. They included thousands of members in the International Ladies' Garment Workers' Union (ILGWU), as well as hundreds of apparel entrepreneurs, a small number of whom were alleged organized criminals. They were all connected directly or indirectly to the nation's sartorial center in New York, where garment making ranked as the city's largest manufacturing sector. It was very much a big city versus hinterland—a core versus periphery—saga built around one place's desire for low-cost production (the big city) and another's desperate need for jobs and income (the hinterland).[3] Unlike most garment-related studies, which have focused on large urban hubs, the chronicle presented here focuses primarily on small cities and towns, virtually all of which once made a living by mining coal.

The story began with a common practice within free enterprise economies, namely, capital mobility. Between the mid-1930s to the mid-1960s, hundreds of so-called runaway shops left New York City to establish operations in various areas of the northeastern United States. They were in search of lower costs, including cheap (read nonunion) workers as well as freedom from "interference" by organized labor. Northeastern Pennsylvania, a distressed region with a declining economy, emerged as a prime destination. The area's relative proximity to the garment district, abundant supply of women workers, and low real estate and rental prices proved irresistibly attractive.[4]

Parts of this story came to my attention during research on the Tropical Storm Agnes flood of 1972. As the nation's most destructive natural disaster to that point in time, Agnes struck several states along the Atlantic seaboard and inflicted the most severe damage in the Keystone State. The city of Wilkes-Barre (population approximately fifty-nine thousand in 1970) and the surrounding Wyoming Valley towns sustained the greatest losses—over $1 billion (equivalent to $5.96 billion in 2018)—when the Susquehanna River overflowed its banks at record levels. My research focused on community politics and decision making during the short-term (i.e., the first-year) recovery period. Along with conducting documentary research, I interviewed more than eighty flood victims, municipal and state government officials, and civic and business leaders.

I found that the catastrophe precipitated intense conflict between and among citizen groups, and between local citizens and state and federal agency officials.[5] A decade later, I undertook a second inquiry funded by the National Science Foundation focusing on the long-term (i.e., ten year) recovery. In that study, I learned that the near-term acrimony expanded through the decade and sparked a multidimensional citizens' movement that significantly shaped the rehabilitation process even as it shook the foundations of community power relationships.[6]

Minnie (Min) and Wilfred (Bill) Matheson figured prominently in both projects. Former area ILGWU leaders, they had returned from New York City to retire in early 1972. Although their residence lay outside the flood zone, the storm devastated their daughter's family dwelling as well as the homes of several friends and former union colleagues. Concern for flood victims prompted the couple and their daughter to establish the Flood Victims' Action Council (FVAC). I interviewed the Mathesons and their daughter and son-in-law (Betty and Larry Greenberg) in separate sessions, and I conducted thirty additional interviews with other FVAC members. I also reviewed the group's informally organized papers along with numerous newspaper accounts and state and federal government documents.

It became immediately clear that the Mathesons had established the FVAC to bring a union-activist organizing repertoire to the recovery process. With Min Matheson's charismatic leadership, Bill Matheson's strategizing abilities, and Betty Greenberg's knowledge of local political dynamics, they mobilized dozens of victims, staged several demonstrations, confronted various public officials, wrote countless letters, and organized sundry bus trips to Washington and Harrisburg. Their efforts helped individual sufferers as well as public and private organizations to secure unprecedented federal and state financial assistance. Just as important, the FVAC served as a watchdog to insure the "clean" distribution of recovery funds in a political culture well-known for governmental and corporate perfidy.[7]

During their interviews in 1973 and again during the second study in 1982, the Mathesons regularly diverged from Agnes-related topics to recall their days as the leaders of the Wyoming Valley District of the ILGWU. As their labor-related accounts grew ever more detailed and compelling, and as I learned that a good number of their fellow (now retired) ILGers were available and willing to talk, I decided to embark on an oral history project of union members and others associated with the garment sector.[8] The endeavor opened a realm of stories, problems, and questions that exceeded my expectations, and I soon realized that I had stumbled on to one of the region's most important industrial and working-class episodes.

Kenneth C. Wolensky and Nicole Wolensky Civettini later joined the project, the main result of which was *Fighting for the Union Label: The Women's Garment Industry and the ILGWU in Pennsylvania*, published by Penn State University Press in 2002. In writing the book, we relied on government and organization documents, newspaper reports, and forty-two audio-recorded oral history interviews, the great majority of them with union members.[9] As with most social historians, the manuscript presented, in chronological order, our interpretation of "the facts" through eight chapters, each one devoted to a separate aspect of the study. More than a few *Fighting* reviewers applauded the book for having "broken out of the New York–Chicago–Los Angeles approach to the industry"[10] and thereby having "integrated a 'non–New York' story into the canonical history of the ILGWU."[11] The reviewers further agreed that, while the voice of the individual manager, worker, and shop owner were present, the study offered mainly an institutional history.

The present volume differs from *Fighting* in three ways. First, individual narratives—drawn from an expanded pool of workers, shop owners, union managers, and others—stand at the core of this work. Although institutional history has not been forgotten, it is of secondary importance. Second, greater attention is devoted to the theoretical and practical concerns associated with the solidarity unionism that lay at the heart of the Mathesons' and the workers' union-building philosophy (and which, I learned, the Mathesons brought to the FVAC). Third, the final chapter focuses on the project's broader implications for the study of labor, working-class, gender, and oral history. As such, the book can serve as a companion to the traditional historiographical approach offered in *Fighting*.

Doing Oral History

The sixteen oral history narratives included in fifteen of these chapters (chapter 10 presents a joint interview) singly and collectively capture the life-changing effects the new industry brought to workers, families, workplaces, and communities.[12] Their "voices" were selected from among the sixty-three interview subjects who contributed eighty-four audio-recorded interviews to the ILGWU Garment Industry Collection within the Wyoming Valley Oral History Project, which, in turn, is part of the larger Northeastern Pennsylvania Oral and Life History Collection (NPOLHC) housed at Pennsylvania State University. Most were garment workers, but I also spoke to shop owners and managers as well as others having a direct association with the industry. For example, to understand the business point of view, I interviewed two shop proprietors whose oral histories are presented here. To explore the relationship between the ILGWU and the larger community, I interviewed the husband and wife owners of the union's official printing shop as well as the physician-director of the union's health center. Such ground-level experiences allowed the subjects to offer muntidimensional insights into a vanishing world of American working-class and industrial history.

Ideas and Motivations

In conceptualizing and orienting this work, I relied on a several thinkers. Some came from my own discipline of historical sociology. As the narrators take the reader on a journey into the fears, triumphs, failures, strategies, and conflicts that filled their memories, they also provide understandings of the larger cultural, political, economic, and institutional forces that framed their experiences. They accordingly demonstrate what sociologist C. Wright Mills referred to as the relationship between the personal and the social—two levels of experience that cannot be conceptually separated.[13] In a similar way, these voices offer a case study of what Ronald Berger and Richard Quinney called *Storytelling Sociology*, where individual narrative can divulge the process by which social structure and personal agency shape biography.[14]

Sociologist Pierre Bourdieu's concept of cultural capital was particularly helpful in my appreciating the Wyoming Valley as a traditionalistic society that presented challenges to garment workers and the ILGWU. Moreover, Bourdieu's idea of linguistic capital assisted my efforts to comprehend the gender-related effects of the union's educational, political, and leadership programs.[15] Bourdieu is again discussed in chapter 1.

My deliberations were also nourished by American labor historian Herbert Gutman's insistence that workers' personal decisions in the workplace, home, and locality should remain important subjects for scholarship *and* public education.[16] In a similar vein, I welcomed British labor historian E. P. Thompson's emphasis on lesser-known working-class events in out-of-the-way places for what they can reveal about the nuanced interactions between labor and management, labor and polity, and labor and community.[17] Both Gutman and Thompson stressed the criticality of individual agency by arguing that working people make their own history regardless of whether efforts succeed or disappoint. Moreover, they both stressed doing "history from below," which expresses a conceptual and methodological preference toward the lives and actions of "ordinary people" who had, in prior times, been excluded from the historical record.[18]

Two other labor writers, Staughton and Alice Lynd, co-authors of *Rank and File*, and Staughton Lynd, who penned *Solidarity Unionism*, stressed labor's efficacy at the grassroots level. In so arguing, the Lynds helped me answer a key question: What was the "secret" behind the achievements of the ILGWU in the Wyoming Valley? How did the union cultivate deep loyalty among members, cooperative associations with most owners, and a wide legitimacy in the community?[19] And how did the union and its members deal with the involvement of organized crime in the garment industry? The answer, I realized, could be found in the solidarity unionist approach to organizing and maintaining a labor association. On this topic, I also benefited from the scholarship of Elizabeth Faue, whose inquiries into labor history, particularly in Minneapolis during the first half of the twentieth century, made a strong case for solidarity unionism.[20]

When it came to oral history, literary scholar Alessandro Portelli offered several essential outlooks.[21] Portelli's research has pointed to the benefits as well as the difficulties associated with human memory and oral interviews. By focusing on the meanings that subjects construct out of everyday events, he argued that storytelling regularly bends to circumstance, role, ideology, and culture. A primary goal of the oral historian is to study the ostensible as well as the hidden meanings within a subject's words as they relate to memory and context.[22] This topic is further examined in the chapter 16, where the deeper meanings that the subjects brought to their garment industry experiences, including regular interactions with organized crime, are scrutinized.

Finally, the project was inspired and informed by the late historian Robert Zieger and his dedication to labor and working-class history. Through his example, Bob set a high bar for analytical and conceptual rigor, and he also provided early encouragement for my investigations into anthracite labor history.[23]

Plan of the Book

Following the introduction's overview of the topic and the region, chapters 1 through 15 offer one oral history each (except for chapter 10's joint interview). The final chapter discusses the implications of the volume for the four research areas mentioned above. Next follow three appendixes: appendix 1 explicates the oral history research and editing techniques; appendix 2 presents a glossary of terms, places, and events; and appendix 3 offers brief biographies of those persons mentioned in the volume, including the oral history subjects. I recommend that the reader examine each subject's biographical sketch before reading their chapters. I also recommend regular checks of appendix 2 and appendix 3 as the need arises. The final sections of the book include the notes and bibliography.

ROBERT P. WOLENSKY

Stevens Point and Madison, Wisconsin | Wilkes-Barre, Pennsylvania | September 29, 2019

ACKNOWLEDGMENTS

A volume such as this, more than four decades in the making, manages to accrue a large number of personal and institutional debts of gratitude.

On the personal side, I would like to express my deepest appreciation to the sixteen individuals who contributed the oral histories contained herein. An extraspecial recognition goes to Min and Bill Matheson for sparking my interest in the garment industry project during our first meeting in 1973. To paraphrase Augustine, these individuals may be gone but their legacy is still with us. This book is intended, in part, to help insure the remembrance of their difficulties, accomplishments, and philosophies.

Other people who were essential to the project in one way or another include Bill Best, Paul Boyer, Alice and Fred Brutko, Lucia Daily, Tom Dublin, John Dziak, Ron Faraday, Susan Stanford Friedman, Erica Funke, Richard Greenwald, Ruth and Jack Hagan, Ann and Max Harris, Judy Kelly, Chester Kulesa, Jack and Ann Larsen, Dave Lindberg, Tom Mackamans, Mary Jo and Richie McClain, Fran and Fred Moody, Bode Morin, Lynn Nyhart, Charlie Petrillo, Craig Robertson, Mary Ann Savakinas, Dan Sherman, Irene and Chas Siegal, Carl and Gail Siracuse, Ron and Jo Slusser, Lynn Vogel, Merry Weisner-Hanks, Dave Witwer, Carol Wolensky, Jack and Gigi Wolensky, Joseph Wolensky, Fr. Paul Wolensky, and Ann Wolensky. I thank them all very much.

At the University of Wisconsin–Stevens Point, I would like to recognize the vital contributions of Ally Burch, Mitchell Butalla, Chris Cirmo, Julia Delvaux, Kyle Ebelt, Erica Ede, Bob Enright, Emily Gostonczik, Karin Hyler, Christopher Legare, Ed Miller, Jasmine Ostrowski, Sue-Marie Rendall, Liane Schroeder, Ashley Walton, and Rebecca Wisniewski. Honors Interns Emily Cleaver, Amber Hederer, and Noah Pulsifer were especially energetic and innovative in assisting with the final draft of the manuscript, including the figures.

My research at Cornell University's Kheel Center for Labor-Management Documentation and Archives was greatly facilitated by administrative assistant Melissa Holland, research archivist Patrizia Sione, and director Cheryl Beredo.

The photographs in these pages are the result of the generous cooperation of the following persons and organizations: Steven Lukasik and William Lukasik, Sr., who were the official ILGWU Wyoming Valley District photographers for many years, and William Lukasik, Jr., who granted permission to use their images while providing important consultation in helping me find my way through the Lukasik Studio's many holdings; the Kheel Center, Cornell University; Mary Ann Moran-Savakinus, executive director of the Lackawanna Historical Society; Dave Janoski and the *Citizens' Voice* newspaper archives; the ILGWU Wyoming Valley District Archives (Kheel Center); the Library of Congress; Getty Images; the Hoover Institution Library and Archives (Stanford University); Min Matheson; Clementine Lyons; and John Landefeld and Katherine Burmaster.

A special note of gratitude to Betty Greenberg, who kindly offered time and insights in the form of two oral history interviews (one with her husband, Larry), and several phone conversations and informal meetings. Betty also provided important materials from her parents' informal archives. Many thanks also to Ken Wolensky for conducting a number of garment interviews on his own and with me, for bringing it all together in our first volume on the subject (*Fighting for the Union Label*), and for recently providing images and consultation. A similar wholehearted acknowledgment to Nicole Wolensky Civettini for her work on *Fighting*, especially the chapter on the strike of 1958, for her colleagueship, and for inspiring me to carry on with this research. I would have loved to have them both as co-authors, but life situations and circumstances did not cooperate. An extra thanks to Megan Hastie for lending her considerable editorial skills to a completed version of the manuscript, and for providing valuable criticisms of and recommendations to improve aspects of the arguments in the introduction and chapter 16. Megan learned much local history from her father, Bill Hastie, Sr., who has been a most kind and astute mentor in my studies of both coal mining and garment making in northeastern Pennsylvania. Bill celebrated his one hundredth birthday on May 28, 2019, and I thank him most sincerely for the continuing education and friendship.

On the institutional side, I am beholden to the following institutions for offering resources and support: the Center for the Small City, University of Wisconsin–Stevens Point; the Institute for Research in the Humanities, University of Wisconsin–Madison; the Kheel Center, Cornell University; the Eberly Family Special Collections Library, Pennsylvania State University; the Department of History, University of Exeter, UK; the Center for 21st Century Studies, University of Wisconsin–Milwaukee; the D. Leonard Corgan Library, King's College; the Eugene S. Farley Library, Wilkes University; the Weinberg Memorial Library, University of Scranton; the Osterhout Free Library, Wilkes-Barre; the Albright Memorial Library, Scranton; the Greater Pittston Historical Society; University of Exeter Forum Library; and the Anthracite Heritage Foundation, Wilkes-Barre.

At Penn State University Press, I would like to express my earnest appreciation to acquisitions editor Kathryn Yahner. It was a pleasure working with Kathryn, a true professional who provided full support and encouragement and who always found ways to get things done. Also at the press, I want to extend my sincere gratitude to editorial assistant Hannah Nicole Hebert copyeditor extraordinaire Nicholas Taylor, as well as Brian Beer, Laura Reed Morrison, and Regina Ann Starace. Elsewhere at Penn State University, I would like to highlight the cooperation of Jim Quigel and

Athena Jackson of the Eberly Family Special Collections Library for accommodating the Northeastern Pennsylvania Oral and Life History Collection, and for accommodating me during many weeks of archival research over the years.

Again, on a personal note, I would like to recognize my daughters, Meredith Hagan Jursnick and Nicole Wolensky Civettini (yet again), as well as my granddaughters, Lilia and Ruthie Civettini, for their enthusiasm, presence, and moral backing. In writing this book, I was partially motivated by the idea of helping them learn something about the garment-making world in which their grandmother and great-grandmother, Rosalie Wolensky; great-grandmother and great-great-grandmother, Catherine Wolensky; and many other relatives and friends lived and worked.

The most important and heartfelt gratitude goes to my wife, Molly Hagan Wolensky, who has encouraged, endured, and loved through all these many years of my researching, writing, traveling, and not sufficiently taking care of things around the house. In as much as she is the source of it all, this volume stands as monument to our love and certainly would not have been possible without her.

ABBREVIATIONS

ACWA   Amalgamated Clothing Workers of America

AFL   American Federation of Labor

AIM   Associate ILGWU Members

ARA   Area Redevelopment Administration

CIO   Congress of Industrial Organizations

CPUSA   Communist Party of the USA

FRTF   Flood Recovery Task Force

FVAC   Flood Victims' Action Council

ILGWU   International Ladies' Garment Workers' Union

NAA   Northeast Apparel Association

NAFTA   North American Free Trade Agreement

NLRA   National Labor Relations Act

NPOLHC   Northeastern Pennsylvania Oral and Life History Collection

NRA   National Recovery Act

PGMA   Pennsylvania Garment Manufacturers Association

PHMC   Pennsylvania Historical and Museum Commission

RICO   Racketeer Influenced and Corrupt Organization Act

TAA   Trade Adjustment Act of 1974

TRA   Trade Relief Agreement Act

UMWA   United Mine Workers of America

Introduction

Northeastern Pennsylvania and the Garment Industry

Is there any man so blind that he does not know why that anthracite region is dotted with silk mills? Why are they not on the prairies of the West? Why are they not somewhere else? Why is it that the men who make money that is spun from the lives of these little babes, men who use these children to deck their daughters and their wives—why is it that they went to Scranton and to all those towns? They went there because the miners were there. They went there just as naturally as a wild beast goes to find its prey. They went there as a hunter goes where he can find game.

—CLARENCE DARROW, *ATTORNEY FOR THE DAMNED*

For working women in northeastern Pennsylvania between 1940 and 1960, life was hard and choices were limited.

—BONNIE STEPENOFF, *THEIR FATHERS' DAUGHTERS*

Locational Foundations: Pennsylvania and New York

Situated in the central Appalachian range north of the Blue Mountains, northeastern Pennsylvania holds a ten-county expanse that once contained 95 percent of the Western Hemisphere's highest-quality carbon-based fuel—anthracite coal. Commonly known as "hard coal" because of its density and high ignition point, anthracite played

2

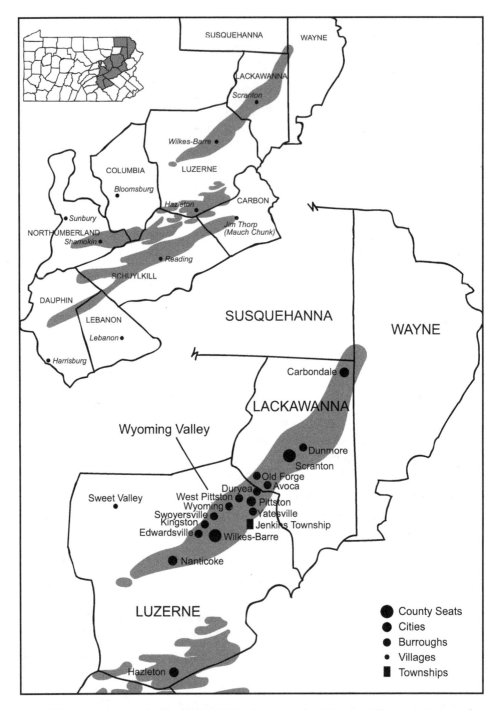

MAP 1 | The Pennsylvania anthracite fields, including the surrounding Wyoming Valley areas. Courtesy of the Center for the Small City, University of Wisconsin–Stevens Point.

the crucial role in lighting the fires of American industrial development during the early nineteenth century.[1] The coal seams metamorphosed into four geological sectors: the Southern field, headquartered at Pottsville; the Western-Middle field, between Mahanoy City and Shamokin; the Eastern-Middle field, around Minersville and Hazleton; and the Northern field, encompassing both Wilkes-Barre and the Wyoming Valley as well as Scranton and the Lackawanna Valley (map 1).

Proximity to consumers along the Eastern seaboard enhanced demand such that, by 1860, anthracite had become the country's leading energy source. However, the more plentiful bituminous or "soft coal," found in western and central Pennsylvania and thirty-five other states, soon assumed the dominant position. The escalating need for both types of energy meant that, by 1900, the United States had become the world's leading coal producer. For the hundred years between the 1820s and the 1920s, Pennsylvania ranked first in total tonnage output among U.S. states.

The largest deposits of anthracite were found in Carbon, Columbia, Lackawanna, Luzerne, Northumberland, and Schuylkill Counties.[2] By the outset of the Civil War, the canoe-shaped Northern field emerged as the most populated and productive quadrant. In 1900, the field employed some sixty-five thousand men and boys working above and below ground. The Wyoming Valley of Luzerne County, which includes the cities of Wilkes-Barre, Pittston, and Nanticoke along with numerous smaller towns, held the largest seams and the most productive collieries.[3]

The industry's growth required enormous capital investments along with scores of managers, workers, processors, shippers, and sellers. In maintaining the enterprise from miner to user, the companies had to cover substantial start-up and operating costs and, at the same time, meet stockholders' requirements for high returns. Because labor constituted up to 80 percent of the typical firm's operating expenditures, a plentiful supply of low-cost manpower became imperative.[4]

Skilled and unskilled immigrants from the British Isles (including Ireland) and Germany provided the labor force in the decades preceding the Civil War. But as these workers pushed for better wages and conditions, they became ever more committed to industrial unions. Following a series of postwar strikes during the 1870s—the most famous being under the banner of the Workingmen's Benevolent Association in 1875—the mine owners began recruiting eastern and southern Europeans who, they believed, would have little interest in organized labor. Company agents traveled to European countries to recruit workers with the promise of a transatlantic ticket, housing in a company-owned patch town, and a mining job. The inducements prompted tens of thousands from over two dozen countries to make the journey.[5] The mix of immigration, ethnicity, and religion within a relatively insular mining environment helped produce a unique cultural landscape often referred to as "the coal region" or, more pejoratively, "a state called anthracite."[6]

However, to the owners' dismay, the "greenhorns" learned about the benefits of industrial unions and, despite their diversity, cultivated a surprising level of solidarity in the march toward collective bargaining. Management had beaten back all unionization

4

FIG. 1 | The Huber coal breaker, Ashley, Pennsylvania, 2001. This breaker, the last one standing in the Wyoming Valley, was demolished in 2014. Photo courtesy of the Center for the Small City, University of Wisconsin–Stevens Point.

attempts between the 1840s and early 1890s until the United Mine Workers of America (UMWA) arrived on the scene in 1894. The nation's first comprehensive miners' organization proceeded to organize the vast majority of the 140,000 workers across the four anthracite fields. Dedication to the UMWA and its policies led to successful strikes in 1900 and 1902—historic shutdowns that marked the beginning of the area's broad-based and deeply rooted commitment to organized labor.[7]

Early Women's Employment: Silk and Lace

Yet anthracite mining was not the only local trade. As the coal counties' populations expanded to 1.4 million in 1920 and peaked at 1.5 million in 1930, silk and lace mill owners saw an opportunity in the plentiful supply of low-cost female labor. They began relocating from neighboring states, where labor unions had been organizing their factories.[8] Although women had always toiled inside the mine-working home, the men's paltry wages required that wives and daughters secure additional income in the mushrooming silk and lace mills. As an unintended consequence, women began assuming a more determined role within the family and the community. Susan Glenn studied such industrial gender transformations and characterized them as contributing to "the new womanhood."[9]

Bonnie Stepenoff studied the area's silk mills and found that, between 1880 and 1925, the industry bolstered a tenfold increase in statewide production. Between 1900 and 1910, Pennsylvania employed twenty-seven thousand of the nation's seventy-nine thousand silk workers.[10] By 1914, the state had the country's largest silk industry. Luzerne County's factories alone engaged nearly twelve thousand persons in 1914. Almost all of them were girls toiling for companies that had fled organized labor in Paterson, New Jersey—the epicenter of American silk manufacturing—following the strike of 1913, when some twenty-five thousand workers shut down three hundred plants and dye houses.[11]

Mill owner Samuel J. Aronsohn represented the typical silk entrepreneur. As the sole proprietor of Samuel J. Aronsohn Inc., a firm valued at $1 million at the turn of the century ($29.9 million in 2018 dollars), he transferred operations from Paterson, New Jersey to Scranton in order to avoid the union and gain cost advantages. Upon opening the new plant, he warned employees, "If the union gets into Scranton, I'll move my factory to another town." He fired one girl and threatened to discharge another for merely mentioning the word "union."[12] Other companies moved to Wilkes-Barre for the same reason, as Oscar J. Harvey and Ernest Gray Smith indicated in their classic 1909 work, A History of Wilkes-Barre: "The frequent labor strikes at Paterson, New Jersey, [have been] reacting to the benefit of Wilkes-Barre."[13]

To the migrating firms' dissatisfaction, however, labor organizers followed and workers joined. By the late nineteenth and early twentieth centuries, most firms were operating with a unionized workforce. For example, in 1900 and again in 1901, mill hands in Scranton and Carbondale took strike action under the direction of the United Textile Workers, an affiliate of the American Federation of Labor.[14] As a precursor to the Paterson strike of 1933, employees of the Wilkes-Barre Silk Mill Company walked off the job in 1929 when the Communist-led National Textile Workers Union called them out.[15] Women's activism in the silk industry resonated with the surges in mineworkers' militancy at the turn of the century and again during the 1920s and early 1930s.[16] To the benefit of the local economy, silk businesses and their unions continued to flourish, with forty-five operating plants in Luzerne County alone in 1922.[17]

Whereas silk manufacturers migrated into coal country, lace production was a homegrown enterprise. The Wilkes-Barre Lace Manufacturing Company opened Pennsylvania's first plant in 1886, a year in which the firm produced a quarter million pairs of Nottingham curtains. By 1899, output had climbed to nine hundred thousand pairs.[18] The Wyoming Valley Lace Mills Company began operations in 1892, making Wilkes-Barre one of the foremost lace-making towns, with two of the state's seven factories. In 1899, Scranton business leaders enticed a company from England to relocate to their city, and the Scranton Lace Manufacturing Company was born.[19] As had their counterparts in the silk trade, the lace workers forged an active labor movement that consisted of mainly of women.[20]

Various Northern-field coal towns also sprouted hosiery and knitting works: Wilkes-Barre had three such operations by 1899; Plymouth and Pittston, two each; and Scranton, one.[21] Women, again, constituted the bulk of the labor force.

The Ladies' Garment Industry

New York City had emerged as the nation's garment-making capital during the second half of the nineteenth century. Men, women, and children from Jewish, Italian, Polish, and other immigrant groups toiled in a production system structured around homeworking, sweatshops, and small- to medium-sized factories. Homeworking developed as a residence-centered, family-based work scheme whereby jobbers secured production contracts from manufacturers, then delivered unfinished goods to tenement-housed families and returned on a scheduled basis to collect the final product. The term "sweatshop" described a factory-based manufacturing system where the employers' profits were tied to the amount of effort they could squeeze, or "sweat," from their hirelings, who were typically younger women, children, and older adults.[22]

Toward the end of the century, some of the larger companies began "putting out" dress- and blouse-making orders to jobbers who, in turn, contracted with independent entrepreneurs (who were termed "contractors" or "subcontractors").[23] The arrangement gave the manufacturing houses greater flexibility by allowing them to rely on jobbers and contractors when demand was high and to terminate the relationships when orders slackened. Other advantages included the transfer of various responsibilities and risks to the jobbers and contractors, including wage fluctuations, capital investments, and—as important as any factor—confronting organized labor.[24]

To satisfy consumers' desire for ready-made clothing in the early twentieth century, manufacturers brought in the latest technologies, built new plants, and hired larger workforces. By the 1920s, factories ranged in size from a dozen employees in small contracting shops, to several hundred in medium-sized plants, to thousands in large plants. As the industry enlarged, it took on a pyramid shape: owners at the top, managers and jobbers in the middle, and employees on the bottom (fig. 2).[25]

However, the larger body of workers grew ever more resentful of the pressurized schedules, mounting income inequalities, and severe power imbalances, and they began to form localized labor unions. Then, in June 1900, delegates from a number of established groups united to form the International Ladies' Garment Workers' Union. The group affiliated with the American Federation of Labor and established a headquarters in New York.[26] The ILGWU developed a highly motivated corps of organizers and managers who recruited large numbers to the cause. By 1920, the union counted more than one hundred thousand members. However, when the pro-business, anti-union climate of the 1920s combined with the Great Depression after 1929, the rolls fell to thirty-one thousand in 1931. Fortunes changed with the national election of 1932, which brought the generally pro-union Franklin

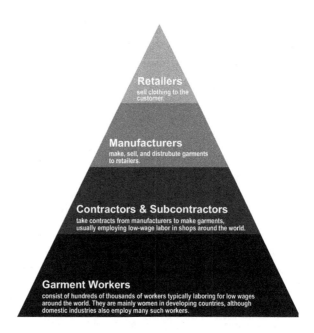

FIG. 2 | The garment industry pyramid. The pyramid is a representation of the number of people within each garment industry group as well as their relative power and control. Based on Miriam Ching Yoon Louie, *Sweatshop Warriors: Immigrant Women Workers Take on the Global Factory* (Cambridge, Mass.: South End Press, 2001), 4–5.

D. Roosevelt administration and his New Deal programs, including the National Recovery Act (NRA), which guaranteed an employee's right to join a labor union. In taking advantage of the law, the ILGWU expanded its organizing campaigns and realized a membership surge to 198,000 in 1933 (a year that also saw an industry-wide strike for better wages and benefits). By 1935, membership numbers climbed to nearly a quarter million.[27] Buttressed by strong leaders, a dedicated rank and file, and a commitment to solidarity and social unionism, the ILGWU became one of the nation's largest and most influential labor bodies.[28]

Organizing the Runaway Shops

During the second half of the 1920s, after decades of internecine conflict between coal operators and mineworkers as well as increasing competition from other fuels, anthracite began a steady decline. The Great Depression worsened already difficult circumstances, as did the out-migration of silk, lace, hosiery, and knitted goods plants to the American South. As the coal region's economic conditions deteriorated, garment producers in New York City—like the silk makers in Paterson, decades earlier—took notice.

Despite the ILGWU's growing prominence—and, indeed, because of it—a significant change in the economic geography of garment making took place in the 1930s. Large and small producers began seeking ways to circumvent the union's wage scales and shop controls, mainly through deals with jobbers who contracted with nonunion shops in the greater metropolitan zone.

When the union caught up with these businesses, jobbers encouraged their contractors to seek more remote locales that were within relatively easy reach of the Garment Center in New York.[29] The ILGWU's new president in 1933, David Dubinsky, understood the threat posed by the burgeoning "runaway shop" problem. He initiated a drive to unionize "scab" operations—many with organized crime affiliations—wherever their location. Northeastern Pennsylvania stood out as one of the more attractive destinations because of its favorable employment climate and its location about 140 miles from Manhattan. Yet, while the New York union moved to combat the trend, desperate coal-mining families welcomed the prospect of new jobs, despite the low pay, long hours, and poor working conditions.

In 1937, the ILGWU chose Scranton as the first regional outpost. By 1944, the flood of contractors required another office in Wilkes-Barre. President Dubinsky placed Bill Matheson in charge of the new bureau, a move that required the Matheson family to relocate from another distant station, in Sayre, Pennsylvania, where Mr. Matheson had been organizing that town's runaways. In 1942, his spouse, Min Matheson, had left her active union work in New York to join her husband in Sayre so they could begin a family. After a few years, her leadership abilities as the former chairlady of Local 22 and its thirty-two thousand members impelled Dubinsky to call her back into service in the Wyoming Valley.[30] She assumed the district manager's position in 1945, while her husband became the state education director. They settled in the centrally located borough of Kingston across the Susquehanna River from Wilkes-Barre.

When they arrived on the scene, the Mathesons found only a handful of unionized shops, which together comprised a total of eight hundred members. They discovered that working and living conditions were much worse than they had anticipated, especially in the city of Pittston, where a number of contractors dominated not only the workplace but various aspects of employees' private lives as well, including their political rights as citizens.[31] At the same time, however, the duo was pleased to learn that, although the workers came from numerous ethnic groups—Italian, Polish, Lithuanian, Slovak, and many others—in keeping with the mineworkers' traditions, they acted in solidarity when it came to forming and maintaining a labor union. Thus the ILGWU benefited from the legacy of UMWA president John Mitchell's call for ethnic solidarity during the strike of 1900, a value disposition that permeated multiple labor campaigns through the years:

> The coal you're mining is not Slavic coal. It's not Irish coal. It's not Polish coal. It's not Italian coal. It's coal. You're all working under the same working conditions and while you don't have to drink, if you're Irish, with Italians, but you work with them and to get anything done in the way of improvements in the work force at the job, at the job site, you've got to bury your antagonism temporarily and join with these people in a common effort. Otherwise, you know, you're just fodder, cannon fodder for capitalists.[32]

FIG. 3 | New York City rally against organized crime, 1953. ILGWU members protest the criminal element's influence within the garment industry. Photo courtesy of the Kheel Center, Cornell University.

Min Matheson was particularly distressed by the subordination and powerlessness faced by the local women. She recalled (chap. 3) that the female workers in Pittston, many of whom were of Italian ancestry, "did the cooking, and the cleaning, and the sewing, and the taking care of the lunches, and getting the children out to school and the husbands out to work in the mines," after which they went to the factories where the proprietors "paid them nothing for weeks" as part of a training period.[33] The instruction occurred despite the fact that many had learned sewing skills in school, at home, and in federal educational programs. The hours were long and the paychecks distressingly low: "There were laws in the land," she said, "but they [the owners] weren't carrying out any of the laws. They did what they wished and made it easy for the women to come in any time of the day or night. Double, triple shifts."[34]

Pittston's status as the region's seat of organized crime foretold the criminal element's involvement as shop owners, managers, and front men.[35] There, as in New York, Philadelphia, Reading, Pottsville, Scranton, and numerous other cities, organized criminals laundered money from gambling, prostitution, alcohol bootlegging, and other illegal enterprises into legitimate businesses such as garment making.[36] While the Mathesons gained some immediate organizing successes in

Wilkes-Barre, Kingston, Plymouth, and other towns, Pittston remained forcefully resistant. Several narrators in the following chapters recall the struggle to organize that town's legitimate shops as well as its mob-owned or -influenced plants. They also describe similarly difficult encounters with the criminally owned shops in Edwardsville and Sweet Valley.[37]

The Mathesons Are Transferred, the Industry Declines

Despite having spearheaded the unionization of 168 garment shops, comprising more than eleven thousand members (seven thousand of them in greater Pittston), in 1963 Dubinsky reassigned Min Matheson to direct the Union Label Department at the main office on Broadway. Bill Matheson went into retirement but continued as his wife's chief adviser. The couple did not welcome the move; nor did the Wyoming Valley membership or the larger community. According to the *Pittston Dispatch*, "Never has Greater Wilkes-Barre witnessed a demonstration such as the transfer of Mrs. Matheson evoked. The reaction attested to not only the loyalty she commanded from the rank and file but the esteem in which she was held in the community after two decades of service."[38] In a show of appreciation, more than seven hundred people—union members, shop owners, public officials, business leaders, and friends—attended a farewell dinner in the Mathesons' honor.

Once settled in Manhattan, Mrs. Matheson worked diligently on behalf of union-made ladies' clothing. She initiated one of the ILGWU's most successful promotional campaigns by redesigning the union label, arranging fashion shows to spotlight the latest wear, and initiating media advertising. The latter included a radio and television commercial featuring the "Look for the Union Label" song, which was broadcast nationwide.[39] A series of new managers served the Wyoming Valley District but, for circumstantial and personal reasons, none proved as determined and reliable, according to the interview subjects (see, e.g., Philomena Caputo, chap. 11). Certainly the precipitous falloff in demand for American-made apparel stood out as a paramount feature of the post-Matheson era. Beginning in the mid-1970s, imported goods began arriving in the United States, fueled by the manufacturers' pursuit of lower-cost international destinations. A new round of regional deindustrialization commenced in a pattern similar to that of the silk, lace, coal, shoe, cigar, hosiery, knit goods, and freight and passenger railroad industries in prior times.[40]

Needless to say, considerable economic hardship and social dislocation followed. Pearl Novak (chap. 14) recalls the ILGWU's final stand in 1995: a two-month strike against the Leslie Fay Company in a failed attempt to retain the Wyoming Valley's largest manufacturer. Internal fraud and unwise business decisions had resulted in the firm's bankruptcy, after which management decided to reorganize and shift production to Guatemala and other developing nations.

Leo Gutstein (chap. 13)—a shop owner whose father had "run away" from New York in the mid-1930s—followed the trend by opening what turned out to be an unsuccessful venture in the Dominican Republic. For his part, William Cherkes (chap. 2)—whose father had also left New York in the 1940s to open a business in Kingston—followed the example of most other small proprietors: he closed up and retired. Both Gutstein and Cherkes were eldest sons who had entered the business in their youth and eventually assumed ownership. They oversaw the loss of family enterprises that had flourished for the better part of the twentieth century. Like their employees, they were powerless to stop the collapse of the domestic industry in the face of immense capital movement abroad, facilitated by free trade and geopolitical strategies (discussed further in chap. 16).[41]

Importantly, the two owners' interviews also reveal that—despite stops and starts—they ultimately cooperated with the ILGWU and established good personal and working relationships with its representatives and members. Although they might have been, at root, objectively opposed to collective bargaining, both Cherkes and Gutstein respected their employees and actually spoke with some pride about their shops "being union." Through their thoughtful narratives, they recognize the profound meanings the industry and its workers held for them.

The end for one of the region's most successful business sectors was most severely felt by the thousands of working-class employees who depended on garment occupations. As their jobs disappeared, the union's bargaining position weakened, working conditions deteriorated, and union leaders became more compliant in dealing with management. Instances of minor corruption began to creep in, which marred the clean record the ILGWU had established in the Wyoming Valley. Indeed, the union experienced virtually no malfeasance or scandal under the Mathesons' leadership (unlike the regional office of the United Mine Workers of America during the same period).[42]

For over three decades, the ILGWU worked with the overwhelming majority of owners to create a stable business climate as well as a favorable work environment. In the process, the Wyoming Valley became one of the state's garment-producing hubs. The industry was so successful that, by the late 1950s, union leaders in New York were voicing concerns about the coal region's competitive advantage and potential power, an issue that led to persistent intra-union conflict, as the narratives by Min Matheson, John Justin (chap. 7), and others demonstrate.

Each narrator in the following pages uses his or her first-person voice to tell a worker's story or an owner's story that is also a Pennsylvania, a New York, or, in the end, an international story. The ILGers speak about the profound changes to their working and personal lives, from weakness and fear to enablement and dignity; the owners highlight a turn from conflict and uncertainty to cooperation and prosperity. Nevertheless, in the last frame, both the workers and the owners not only regretted their loss of livelihood but also winced at the irony of the economic logic—the profit motive and attendant desire to lower costs—that between the 1930s and 1960s had brought the apparel business to the Wyoming Valley, only to drive its migration to other sites around the world in later decades. Both groups could only try to endure the consequences of a radically globalizing, anti-union, and "race to the bottom" industry.[43]

1

Dorothy "Dot" Ney

Garment Worker, Union Organizer,
and Business Agent

Beginning in 1943 and continuing until her retirement in 1980, Dorothy Ney completed thirty-seven years in the garment industry. She spent two years on a sewing machine and thirty-five years as a union organizer and business agent in the Wyoming Valley. Although she had no prior union experience, she attributes her activist transformation to having "clicked" with, and believed in, the ILGWU district manager Min Matheson. Mrs. Ney exemplified the vital role women played in the union movement, including her having served as president of the Wilkes-Barre District Council in the late 1940s and early 1950s. Her interview highlights several organizing campaigns that required picket lines and strikes, especially against shops owned by alleged organized criminals such as Thomas "Three-Finger Brown" Lucchese, Angelo Sciandra, and Russell Bufalino. She also describes the grassroots, solidarity-based strategy through which the union recruited and cultivated members and expanded its involvement into community development and elective politics. Her narrative demonstrates that the ILGWU was not merely *in* the community, but *of* the community.

FIG. 4
Dorothy Ney, 1993.
Photo courtesy of the
Northeastern Pennsylvania
Oral and Life History
Collection, Pennsylvania
State University.

Dorothy Ney, from an audio-
recorded interview with Robert
P. Wolensky conducted at Mrs.
Ney's home in Wilkes-Barre,
Pennsylvania, on July 23, 1993.
The interview is included
in the Wyoming Valley Oral
History Project, which is one of
eight projects within the Northeastern Pennsylvania Oral and
Life History Collection housed
in the Eberly Family Special
Collections Library, Penn State
University Libraries.

DN: I started at Stella Dress, a factory on Market Street in Kingston in 1943.[1] I joined the union in 1945 when Min [Matheson] was in the area. She had just come in at that time and she was organizing. She came into the shop and spoke to us and we joined the union. I was elected chairlady at the shop after we joined.

Q: Was there any trouble making it a union shop?

DN: No, no. That was one of the best union shops in the Valley. I think the owner's name was Mr. Levine. He was from New York. Later on, he sold it to Mr. Carter. Mr. Levine was one of the best employers in this Valley. He had several shops, but he didn't have as many as Mr. Carter.

Q: What did your position as chairlady involve?

DN: Well, I took up the complaints and saw that the company lived up to the contract and did whatever they had to do, that they paid the right wages and honored holidays and everything like that. The wages weren't much, probably thirteen dollars a week at that time. I know the dues were fifty cents a month. We had a payroll deduction. That was in the contract that all the shops deducted [dues] from the paycheck and turned it over to the union.

I met Min, and Min and I clicked. We have been friends all these years. We organized an awful lot of shops because there were not many organized when she came here. Very few shops. When she left [in 1963], most of the shops in the Valley had been organized. We had some very, very bitter strikes [that] lasted a long time.

Q: Can you tell us about some of them?

DN: Well, the first strike I was ever on, I was working at Anita Dress in Edwardsville. We were not in the union at the time. That was a bitter strike. Some people [workers] were going into the shop and they kept working. They didn't all stay out. I don't know how long that strike went on [but] it came to a climax when the girls were in there working. We had this huge picket line—and not only a huge picket line, but everybody [strikers and townspeople] in Edwardsville used to congregate at that factory, every morning and every night at quitting time.

This one day a [U.S. Army] soldier went through the picket line. He said he was going to get his sister out. So he went in but we wouldn't let them out! . . . This was around six o'clock at night and the girls were still in there. When they did come out, there was a big riot. Everybody got into it because the soldier crossed the picket line. . . . They had to call in the police and everything. Shortly afterwards, that strike was settled. There was too much going on in Edwardsville—the police didn't like it, the mayor didn't like it, nobody liked it. That was the first real big strike that I was on.[2]

Q: How many people did you have on the line?

DN: Oh, god, at that time there were hundreds of people. Some may not have been on the line but they were around there, you know, watching. As I said, people used to congregate every morning and every quitting time to see what was going on. It was on the radio. It was publicized all over. That one day it was terrible. They said they called in the militia or something to restore order. It wasn't that only *we* were fighting. The citizens were fighting. Don't forget this was a "union valley." The Mine Workers [UMWA] were very strong at one time. Even in the forties they were still pretty strong.

I remember the union had a lawyer. The lawyer they had at that time—I'm not going to mention his name—he was a very fine lawyer but he was not a labor lawyer. So I said to Min, "There is a great lawyer in this valley and he's labor-minded. That's Dan Flood." So we called him and he came over to the police station. He became the lawyer for the union for many years. But [later] he didn't do much because his partner took care of everything, Jim Lenahan. I mean, Dan was mostly in Washington [after he was elected to the U.S. House of Representatives in 1945], but that was the first time Min met Dan Flood. I had known him from before, and I knew he was a good lawyer. I knew he was a good labor person.[3]

Q: What was Min Matheson like on the picket line?

DN: Very, very fiery. She made the best speeches. She could convince anybody to join the union. *(laughs)* Anybody. And she was very well liked and respected by the members. That was the important thing. She just called anybody up and they [would listen to her]. If I was working in a factory when a strike was going on and Min needed pickets, the girls would just get up and leave the factory. We'd be on the picket line from seven 'til eight in the morning and then we'd go to work. And then we'd quit work early and go back to the picket line, so we would be there when the scabs were coming out of the factory.

Q: Did you typically have workers from several shops participating on the picket lines?

DN: Oh, definitely. Min could always get pickets. They were very faithful. Good union people. When it got real bad [in Edwardsville], we had at least one hundred pickets there. In the beginning, it wasn't too bad. There were only a few people going in and out of the factory there. Most of the workers were picketing. There were only a few in there working, causing all this commotion. But when the soldier crossed the picket line, that took care of that.

Q: I gather you were trying to unionize that shop?

DN: Right. We had many strikes, many strikes. As I said, there were so few places organized when Min came here. But [most strikes] didn't amount to anything because they [the shop owners] quickly joined the union. They signed up and that was the end of it. Maybe we'd picket for a couple of days and that was it. Then the boss and the union would get together because they knew sooner or later they had to [cooperate].

We had a real tough one in Sweet Valley that lasted a long time. This was in the '58 strike, when everyone went out on strike. It was a general strike. The contract ran out and they [the owners] didn't sign the [new] contract so everybody was out on strike. Sooner or later they settled but [one shop in] Sweet Valley didn't settle. They were on strike for months after that because the owner was [alleged mobster] "Three-Finger Brown," Tommy Lucchese. He was out of New York. That was really a tough one.[4] Nobody was working there. They had dresses in there that they tried to get out. I mean the Teamsters would come [with trucks] and try to get them out.[5]

The one day, they [the truck drivers] came with a writ so we had to let them in. Lucchese's lawyer was there and the truckers were there. He showed me the writ and said, "Is it OK to go in, Dorothy?" I said, "Yes, you can go in, no problem, go ahead." We only had about maybe five or six pickets on the line. But we were expecting them, you know, we were expecting the truck. Usually we got tipped off when the trucks were coming. We actually had a lot of pickets but they were hiding up in the hills. They couldn't see them![6]

So we let them in. A couple [of deputies] from the sheriff's office were there. We let them all in, but we wouldn't let any of them out! All of a sudden, all these pickets came down from the hills and surrounded the place. We wouldn't let them out. They begged us to let them out. We wouldn't let them out. . . . We were supposed to abide by that writ, so we told them to go in—but we wouldn't let them out!. . . . Those sheriff's deputies, they were scared to death. They were afraid to come out. The sheriff went on the air that night, on TV, and blasted me. I was in charge of the picket line down there. I forget exactly what he said [about] breaking the law and all this. On the six o'clock news. Sheriff [Joseph] Mock, his name was. I called him at home and told him what I thought about him, because the things he said were not true. He called Min a couple days later [and] wanted to have lunch with us. We sat down and became friends.

That took care of that place. This lawyer that represented them, he's still here. I told him that this fella who owned the factory was with the Mafia in New York. "Oh, I don't believe that," he said. "His son is in military school or in one of the big schools, and he wouldn't be there if his father was in the Mafia." Then a year or so later [during the McClellan hearings] it all came out in the papers that he was tried and everything. I met that lawyer up in the courthouse and I told him about it. He said, "Dorothy, I never believed you, but I wish I believed you because I didn't want to get tangled up in anything like that." Someone eventually bought that shop. He [Lucchese] sold it and a pro-union person bought it and it became one of the very best shops around.[7]

Q: Did the gangsters have a lot of control in the dress industry?

DN: Oh, I guess they did at that. But only certain shops, not too many in this lower [Wilkes-Barre, Kingston, and Nanticoke] end of the Valley. Not too many around here. In Pittston [yes]. But not so much around here, outside that one in Edwardsville and that one out in the country, Sweet Valley. I don't remember having problems with any in Wilkes-Barre and the surrounding areas.

Q: So was it easier organizing in the Wilkes-Barre and Nanticoke areas?

DN: Yes, because most of the shops were owned by local people or people who came in from New York and made their homes here. But up in Pittston it was much,

much tougher. We had one tough one. I think that was the last shop that was organized in Pittston. That was the holdout. It was on the corner of Railroad and Main Street. Larry Sitzman owned [managed] it. Most of Pittston was organized by that time. This was probably after 1958, if I remember. Most of the shops were organized around here [Wilkes-Barre] much earlier than 1958. But that was the last big holdout in Pittston, because they [organized criminals] wouldn't let Sitzman have the union.

I know that we were abused on the picket line. The boss used to come out to sweep [the sidewalk] and he'd sweep the water on us, throw the water on us. All over our legs. But we wouldn't move. What happened there—I hate to keep saying the Mafia, but that's what they were—there were two of them that were always across the street. They used to say, "We won't harm the girls but don't bring any men up here, don't bring any men up here." So one morning the fellas from the Central Labor Council [i.e., the Greater Wilkes-Barre Labor Council] came to help us. There were quite a few fellas there. All the big shots that belonged to the Mafia were out of town that day and the only guys they had there were these two that were always across the street. We used to call them Murph and Blackie. . . . Their job was to scare us. Scare us!

But they never really scared us because we used to talk to them like I'm talking to you. They used to threaten us and we talked just like I'm talking to you. Not quite as nice but I mean we'd say hello, or if we passed them, we'd make some kind of remark or they'd make a remark, but they were doing what they were told to do. Those were their nicknames. I think their real names were Murph Loquasto and Blackie Salvo. They were tough, they were tough. . . . I never saw them with guns. Not them. Anyway, when the Central Labor Council guys came up, I called Min and said, "What are you going to do now that the men are here? The two tough guys are here, too—what will they do? Maybe there will be a few more of them." Well, there was a big riot in Pittston. There was a big fight on that picket line. I think one of the Teamsters [from the Labor Council] went to the hospital.

The next day we went on the same picket line. There wasn't a soul on the street, not a soul. It was so quiet. We went over to the coffee shop across the street from this factory, where we always went in the morning. He [the owner] wouldn't let us in. I said, "What's the matter?" He said, "Dorothy, just go home. Please leave and go home." So then, one of the Teamsters came down. He was driving a truck and he stopped. I told him what was going on. He went in there and [when he came out] he said, "They're all in there from out of town, the Mafia."

So what could you do? We continued to picket. See, we were stupid. We didn't know they were that powerful until they raided them up in New York that time [i.e., the Apalachin crime summit in 1957]. You know, we used to call them the Mafia but we really didn't know how powerful they were.

Then the tough guys came out and one or two were sitting next to the factory talking and in a roundabout way threatening us. "If you don't get away from there . . ." There was another fight on the picket line. I think the mayor [was there]. Larry Sitzman's lawyer came down, went in, and closed the shop. He said, "If we don't close this shop, there's going to be a murder here in Pittston today." "Now," he said, "I want this shop closed and I want you out of here." And that was the end of that.

Q: Did the shop reopen?

DN: Mr. Carter bought it. Mr. Carter bought a lot of these shops. *(laughs)* He was a good employer. . . .

Q: Were the Teamsters generally supportive?

DN: Yes. A lot of them wouldn't even stop [to pick up dresses]. They saw a picket line, they wouldn't stop. They used to come back and tell my husband [who] worked in the [Friedman's Express trucking company's] office [in Wilkes-Barre]. He was dispatcher. They used to come back and tell him they saw me on the picket line.[8] That's one thing about the unions around here—they supported each other. . . .

Q: Do you recall anything specific about Mrs. Matheson on that Pittston picket line?

DN: Oh, well, Min was right on the picket line with us. She went at six o'clock in the morning like we did and she was on the picket line most every morning unless she couldn't make it for some reason, [when] she had a meeting or something. Even that gang up there had a lot of respect for Min. They knew she was doing her job. They didn't want her there but they had a lot of respect for her. But it was tough organizing that shop. Now this fella [Sitzman] would have joined the union. I don't know whether he owned that shop or maybe ran it with somebody else. He would have joined but they [organized criminals] wouldn't let him. They wanted their one shop in Pittston they could control. . . .

That was the last holdout in Pittston until Dolly Falcone came along [in 1959] and ran [alleged organized crime boss] Russ[ell] Bufalino's shop on the upper end of the town. We picketed there for a long time. We had union members in there, don't forget. Eventually, after a long strike, she closed down. And that took care of Pittston. . . . I was on [administrative] staff when we had that strike. I went on the staff in '58. I became a business agent in 1958. I was an officer of the union. It was a full-time job and it was hard work but it was interesting.

Q: How many hours a day would you work?

DN: Oh, well, I tell ya, when we were on the picket line it was like twenty hours. Don't forget, we had picket lines at night because they always tried to get the dresses out. Up there in Pittston at Arthur Lori's shop, they [the trucks] came in. Min and I were in Sweet Valley at that time because there was that bad strike in Sweet Valley. We got a phone call to get back to Pittston because there was a riot going on up at Lori's. So we left immediately.

They [truckers] tried to take the dresses out of this factory in Pittston. You see, this work was all finished when the strike was called. They couldn't take it out because there was a picket line. We got up there and the Friedman's truck was there. The girls smashed that truck! They actually smashed that truck because they wouldn't let that fella in. It wasn't a union Teamster that was driving the truck. It was a fella that worked at Friedman's, in the office. I remember that very clearly because my husband worked at Friedman's [office]. And believe me it wasn't very pleasant for him. *(laughs)* I was later on the picket line. They blamed Min and me for everything and we weren't even there. We were in Sweet Valley when it happened. When we went up, we saw that truck and couldn't believe it. Windows smashed and everything. Unbelievable.

Q: Were there other instances of violence?

DN: That's the only truck I know that they smashed. There were fights on the picket line, like if the scabs were going into the factory and the union people were on the picket line, they would have words and then they would end up punching each other every now and then. We were always swearing warrants out. They swore warrants out against us and then we swore warrant out against them. Nothing ever happened because the magistrate would throw it out sooner or later. But that went on for a long time up at Dolly Falcone's [shop]. A lot of warrants sworn out up there. I don't remember too many in the unionized shops.

Q: Did you ever have anyone call your home or otherwise threaten you?

DN: Well, when we worked in Pittston, one night they followed my husband, that crowd up there followed my husband. The next day they told me where he went. He went bowling. He used to bowl on Wednesday night. The state police used to ride around our house at night. I lived in Kingston then. They used to ride around Min's house [also in Kingston]. The one state trooper, I knew him, and he [talked to me when] that was going on with the Bufalino crowd up there. They were set on sending Bufalino back where he came from [i.e., deporting him to Italy]. They didn't want him around here. He wound up in jail anyhow. They [the gangsters] used to, in their own sort of a way, threaten us, but I didn't take it seriously. But then at one point I did. I used to be afraid to get into the car. I thought maybe they would blow the car up on me because you read stories about this. They followed [my husband] and then the state trooper told me that the police patrolled our house and my mother's house and Min's house.

Q: Was anyone ever beaten up?

DN: I remember one fella who was beat up on this Dolly Falcone picket line, but why he got beat up I have no clue. There used to be a restaurant right next to their factory and we used to go in there for lunch and that poor guy came on the picket line and they really beat him up. He was bleeding all over the place. And he wasn't with anybody. He wasn't with us and he wasn't with them. He just came on the picket line.

They [the mobsters] were in that crowd that came in from New York. The Teamsters went in that restaurant. They said that they [the gangsters] had guns and bats and everything. I don't know whether they were going to use them on us. I don't think they would use them on women. . . . I was scared that day. It was the first time you could say that I was really scared, but we wouldn't leave the picket line. As scared as we were, we wouldn't leave the picket line. Then the one fella, he had a shop up the street, he used to come down and sit on the top of our car and play "Taps" in the morning. When we got to the picket line, he'd sit on the hood of the car and play "Taps" with his horn. He played in an orchestra. [Alleged gangster] Angelo Sciandra. Trying to scare us, I guess.

But they never did scare us off the picket line. Never. And they knew that. Because we were too stupid! As I said, we really didn't know this until they raided that place [i.e., Apalachin, New York] that they were so powerful. We knew so many of the people who were there. I don't think I would have been as brave if I knew about Three-Finger Brown and all those guys that they tried in New York. Bufalino, I knew he was a big guy but I didn't think he was that big. Much later on we knew, but I mean in the beginning we didn't know. We used to sit in the restaurant and have coffee just like anybody else did, you know. But when I found out that he was really head of the Mafia in this part of Pennsylvania. . . .

He never bothered us though. He'd come around every once in a while, stop the car on the picket line, but he never hung around. He had Murph and Blackie do that. Angelo Sciandra had a factory right up the street. Nick Alaimo was also in the dress business. Yeah. Poor Nick. Nick never made any money in the dress business. I think they [the local organized crime gang] used Nick more than anything else. At least he'd tell me that. He went to jail for them. He did serve time in jail. It was for the Knox Mine disaster. He may have been a big guy, I don't know, but I never thought he was big in the Mafia, because he was too poor, like a slob. I don't think he ever made any money. He never lived high. To me, he was always poor.[9]

Q: You seem to speak of Nick as though he were an old friend.

DN: Well, as bad as they were, like Angelo Sciandra and all them, we used to talk to them all the time. But don't forget that they were employers; we had to deal with them. Everybody called him "Nick" and everybody called him "Angelo." That's what we called them. We didn't particularly like them but we had to deal with them. If we didn't deal with them, then god knows what. They certainly would never live up to a union contract if we didn't watch them. They never paid willingly to anything. They weren't the best shops in Pittston. I mean, we had some good shops that when the contract was signed that was it. They lived up to it and that was it. But there were some we had to watch all the time. Every payroll we had to check them out. They paid nothing willingly.

Q: How many shops did Nick Alaimo own?

DN: He only had one or two. He had a small one on Main Street in Pittston, I remember.

Q: Sciandra had how many?

DN: Sciandra had a big shop on Main Street at one time.

Q: Who was the person with the most shops in Pittston?

DN: There were employers that owned quite a few shops but they were really not the Mafia. I mean they started in the business and they expanded, like Lori—he had quite a few shops. I don't think he was in the Mafia. I'm sure he wasn't. Lee Manufacturing, they had a big one and then he [Louis Gutstein] bought a couple more.[10]

Q: What can you tell us about the very large Leslie Fay Company?

DN: We organized Leslie Fay when they moved in here from New York. It wasn't hard because they were union in New York. They just moved out of New York.

Q: Do you recall that organizing campaign?

DN: Yeah, they were [in the union] the next year then. That was their first shop, then they opened up a lot of shops. But Leslie Fay, when they signed the contract, you really didn't have to watch them. They pretty much paid everything that was in it. That's one thing I had to do—I was the business agent to Leslie Fay's shops. I really didn't have a problem. I didn't have to go in there and check them out every week. They had good people in there working, good union people. They didn't get away with much but they really didn't try. I would say that they were a better employer but don't forget that they had work all the time. They had their own work, you know. Don't forget they were jobbers. They weren't contractors, they were jobbers. So they had work when nobody else had work sometime.

Q: By a jobber, what do you mean?

DN: Well, that's those that got the work from New York.

Q: And what's a contractor?

DN: The ones that own the [local] shops. The jobbers are the ones that send the work to the Valley, to the contractors. Leslie Fay really wasn't a contractor because Leslie Fay owns Leslie Fay in New York. That's why they have the work. They own the work and they send it out to their shops. And they also contract work out to other shops, too. But if there's work, they're going to give to their own factories before they contracted out.

Q: Were there any other big employers like Leslie Fay?

DN: Not really. That was the biggest because most all the others were small. They owned maybe two or three factories, but not on a big scale. Small shops. . . .

Q: Where was the ILGWU's local headquarters?

DN: The first one was on South Main Street in Wilkes-Barre and then we opened one on Washington Street where they are now, where the clinic was, the Health Center. I worked all over—Wilkes-Barre, Pittston, Nanticoke—but then they split Pittston and Wilkes-Barre. It used to be one and then they split it up [into different locals]. They split it up and I went to Pittston. I had [responsibility] from Wyoming up to Duryea. I was the business agent. And then Min went to New York to work [in 1963]. The district managers after Min left were Sam Bianco and Paul Strongin.

Q: How long did you stay as a business agent?

DN: I retired in 1980.

Q: Do you recall some of the meetings or strategy sessions with Min and the other unionized people?

DN: We used to have a District Council. It was made up of a chairlady and a secretary from each shop. We'd have a meeting once a month, or once every two months, with all of the officers of the unionized shops. We never had trouble getting the people out. They used to pack the hall because they just loved to hear Min talk. She could convince anybody. Whatever she believed in, they believed in. Even to this day. The fella at the head of the whole area [the Northeast Department], a couple times he was there at meetings [after Min left for New York] and I heard him speak. I didn't hear him say it, but it came back me: what happened to all the people that used to be at these meetings when Min was the manager? They didn't get as many as when she was here.

   She always packed the hall, even if we had it at the [Hotel] Reddington [in Wilkes-Barre]. No matter where we had it, that hall was packed. There would be at least two from every shop. At one time we had at least eighty shops [in Wilkes-Barre]. And then others came, too. The Executive Board would be there, the [business] agents.

   A lot of the time we had speakers that would come and talk on different things. The United Way. We were active in all those organizations. We were very active in politics when Min was here. Very active. Most of the time we backed the Democratic Party. I mean, presidents, governors, senators, and representatives. I don't ever remember backing any Republicans, although we were friends with most of them. But we mostly backed the Democrats. Maybe locally we might back a Republican, someone who we knew that was local and he was a good person.

Q: I recall Mrs. Matheson saying that Harry Truman came here.

DN: Yes. That's when [they took] that picture I'm talking about [referring to a photo shown before the interview began]. They had the stage set up on Public Square [in Wilkes-Barre]. He was going to speak from there. We were standing right behind him, and Min and I were in the picture. I remember the day. There was a big crowd. Of course, I liked Harry Truman. I thought he was one of the greatest. He made a nice speech. People enjoyed him and he was elected. Almost everybody thought he wouldn't be elected [in 1948].

   Everything Min did was outstanding in my view. I remember when she left here to go to New York and they had that huge party for her that filled the Wilkes College [now Wilkes University] gym. One thing, Min got people out when she had a meeting. Anything she did, people came out.

Q: What do you think was the secret to her success?

DN: I don't know. She was a very loyal person. She was loyal to the union but she was very, very loyal to the members. I mean, she worried about the members. She just had something about her. She once worked in a factory and she knew what it was to work, and she really catered to the members and they knew that. If they had any problem, they knew they could walk into her office and talk to her. You never had to make an appointment with Min. You just went over to see her, that's all. She was very loyal to her union members and a very, very loyal friend to me for over forty years. . . .

I know Min's whole life was wrapped around the union. She put many, many hours in that office, even at night. I stayed with her when that big strike in '58 was going on and everybody was out. They used to come from New York and hold meetings at the theater to talk to the workers. Every night we wound up over at the newspaper office to see if they heard anything, *The Times Leader*.

Q: Were the newspapers generally favorable towards the union?

DN: I might say that everybody was pretty good to us. Maybe in some little town we had these crummy cops who were in with the employers who would be nasty. Well, in the beginning the cops weren't nice. They were not nice when we first started organizing, but when the union started to mean something and we were respected in the Valley, they changed their tune and some were very nice.

Q: I gather that a lot of the powers that be were eventually on your side?

DN: When the union got strong, yes. I would say yes, because we were active in the United Way—anything in the community we were active in. If there was a drive going on for the United Way, we talked to the people in the shop and asked them to give. Anything that was good for the community was good for the union. I think that's why the people respected the union. At one time, the union was very powerful. We had a big membership. We were strong in politics. Everybody that ran [for office] came to the union, Republicans and Democrats. . . .

Q: Do you recall Bill Matheson?

DN: Oh yes, yes. Bill was a great guy, a highly intelligent person. He used to write songs. They put shows on here. He and Jim Corbett put the shows on. Billy Gable and Clem Lyons [chap. 8] used to work with them. They put some terrific shows on in Wilkes-Barre at the Irem Temple [auditorium]. They had a chorus for years. They still have it. Then every few years they would put on a big show, like a Broadway production. Bill wrote a lot of the songs for the shows and the skits and things. He worked with Jim Corbett. Every three years when they had the national ILGWU convention, they always went to the convention to perform. In fact, they recently sang when the [traveling] Vietnam Memorial Wall was up here on Wednesday night.

Q: Did the skits have a labor theme?

DN: Oh, definitely, yes. About the poor lady and the boss and all that. I recall one song, I don't remember the words now, but whenever they sang [it], the girls just loved it, about the boss and the poor lady. Clem Lyons retired but she still works for the chorus, she and Billy Gable. She was a business agent, same as I was, but she always helped out with the chorus because she could sing. She has a beautiful voice. . . .

DOROTHY "DOT" NEY

FIG. 5 | Violence flares at an Arthur Lori Company strike in Pittston, Pennsylvania, March 1958. Photo courtesy of Lukasik Studio.

Bill [Matheson] really stayed in the background more than anything else. When we were on the picket lines, we gave out leaflets. He used to write the leaflets for us. He did all that work, mostly behind the scenes. He never really got credit for what he did, although he used to be on the picket line, too. He always came to the picket line, but mostly he stayed in the background. He never wanted to take anything away from Min. He was a great guy. . . . Very kind. For such a brilliant man, I couldn't believe he wound up with Alzheimer's disease because he was such a brilliant person and a nice person. One of my best friends.

Q: How would you describe the relationship between Bill and Min?

DN: Oh, probably one of the best relationships I ever saw. They got along. I never heard them argue. As many years as I've known them, I've never heard them argue. They seemed to agree with each other. I know Bill worried about her when she was out on picket lines and the cops were rapping at the door and things like that. I know he worried. My husband worried, too. But Bill always went along with whatever Min wanted to do. . . .

Q: Were there many shops in Pittston before the union came in?

DN: I would say yes. We had no problem organizing the people up there. It was the employers holding out, not the workers. If conditions were that great, they wouldn't want to bother with the union. We really had no shops—outside of that one factory that Larry Sitzman had—that when we called a strike, the people wouldn't come out.

Q: Were guys like Russell Bufalino around in the forties?

DN: Oh yeah. They were around. We knew they were there. Bufalino, he was connected with this Dolly Falcone shop. In fact, he owned the shop, I'm sure of that. Dolly Falcone was his niece.[11] Years ago when I first got active in the union, I used to see him in the restaurant up there. They used to say, "You've heard of the Mafia," but we didn't think anything of that. The Mafia is Italian in Pittston. We just didn't pay any attention to it, just like they called us dirty Irish or this or that, you know. *(laughs)* We used to talk to everybody in Pittston whether it was Bufalino or no matter who it was because at that time we didn't have the problem. But once we started organizing, [we had the problems].

A lot of them [women garment workers] were Italian [in Pittston]. They weren't all Italian. They were hardworking women. There were a lot of Italians there. And at that time there was very little work around. I mean, to even to get these people to go on strike was something because the men had no jobs. There were few men working around there. They were out hanging around Main Street while the women worked. And the women worked hard. Early up, get their kids up and then get them off to school and get to work at seven in the morning. A good bunch of people up there.

DOROTHY "DOT" NEY

2

William "Bill" Cherkes
Garment Shop Owner and Garment
Association President

FIG. 6
William Cherkes, 1994.
Photo courtesy of the
Northeastern Pennsylvania
Oral and Life History
Collection, Pennsylvania
State University.

William "Bill" Cherkes, from
an audio-recorded interview
with Robert P. Wolensky
conducted at Mr. Cherkes's
home in Kingston, Penn-
sylvania, on July 20, 1994.
The interview is included
in the Wyoming Valley Oral
History Project, which is one
of eight projects within the
Northeastern Pennsylvania
Oral and Life History Collection housed in the Eberly
Family Special Collections
Library, Penn State University Libraries.

A native New Yorker and second-generation garment shop proprietor,
William Cherkes came to direct the family "runaway" shop, which his
father started in the Wyoming Valley in the 1940s. With a clear and
didactic narrative style, he recalls the move out of the Garment Center,
his years of commuting to and from New York, and his eventual decision to reside permanently in Kingston, Pennsylvania. He discusses
his strong working and personal relationships with employees, many
of whom remained with his Ann Will Garment factory for several
years. Despite his dislike of union "interference" in New York, as well
as some union-management conflicts in the Wyoming Valley, Mr.
Cherkes describes the generally favorable dealings with ILGWU leaders, including Min Matheson (chap. 3). As a shop owner and a dress
contractors' association official, he downplays the importance—even
the presence—of organized crime in the industry.

WC: I was born in Bronx, New York, October 4, 1924. I'll be seventy at
my next birthday. I was educated at the city schools in New York.
I went to [college in] Lowell, Massachusetts, and from there to
the Eighth Air Force and served three years. After that, my father
had built a building in Kingston, Pennsylvania, for me to go to

work and not bother collecting my twenty-four dollars a week [i.e., the standard unemployment compensation for veterans at the time]. I came here, it would have been '45.

Q: What did you see and what did you gather when you first arrived in the Wyoming Valley?

WC: You have to understand what happened, and I have to go into a whole dialogue about that. The jobber in New York was the one who supervised the entire operation from making to selling. The garment industry was controlled by four [union] locals in the city of New York. At that time, there were Jewish locals that only spoke Jewish, and Italian locals that only spoke Italian. And they had the pressers' local, which was half Italian, half Jewish. They had the operators' local that was half Italian, half Jewish. They had the hand sewers' local that was half Italian, half Jewish, and they had the cutters' local—half Italian, half Jewish.

The dress industry is an immigrant industry. You'll find it on the seacoast but you won't find it inland at that time; you'll find inland now. But at that time [the 1930s] it was primarily an Italian and Jewish industry controlled by the four locals in [New York]. The way they controlled it was you would bring them the garment and they would price the various preparations on the garment based on the selling price of that garment.[1]

What happened in the forties [*sic*; thirties], a lot of people decided that they could do better outside of New York City by not being controlled [by the ILGWU]. So they migrated to Connecticut, Pennsylvania, Massachusetts to open their plants and price their own products without interference from the four locals. They didn't mind being union, that wasn't the part of it. The part they didn't want [was] to be controlled. [They wanted to have] the garments priced by what they're gonna get in return, which would be price fixing at this point and time, but at that time, it wasn't price fixing. At that time it was called unionization. I have to answer you the long way around, but I have to answer you that way because that's how we wound up here. We were part of that industrial revolution at that time. . . .

Q: In other words, you had to do business with these four locals if you were going to operate in New York, but by coming here, to northeastern Pennsylvania where there was no union, you could work independently.

WC: Yes, primarily yes. Now the reason I wound up here was all these various contractors who came out to the Pennsylvania towns and areas decided they should be organized into an association [the Northeast Apparel Association] so they could exchange information or whatever. My father, who was active in the union at that time, left the union and had a lot of knowledge about organizational type things and running associations, and he was accepted by the union.[2] That was a very important fact to remember; I'll bring that up in a minute. You had to be [recognized] by the union to be able to negotiate for various contractors. And so he became head of the Pennsylvania contractors' association, which at that time

WILLIAM "BILL" CHERKES

had something like 650 plants employing about an average of sixty-five people each. That was some time in the early forties.[3]

You have to remember that the dress industry went from here all the way to Harrisburg, Shamokin, Pottsville, Shenandoah, Hazleton, Scranton, and Carbondale, and up the New York State border to Binghamton and throughout the state of New York. Why it happened to grow bigger here in this area was because when the textile industry left, there was a migration here of shirtmakers, and they had some talented sewers. So the people [i.e., the shop owners] who came into this area, the Wilkes-Barre area, would already have available labor. This area was making overalls for the miners, they were making and selling caps for the miners, and they already had some training of people. At that time it would run an average of maybe $300 a person to train 'em to be a sewer. So if you came to the Wilkes-Barre area, you'd have a pool of people familiar with the sewing machine because they sewed miners' overalls or they made men's shirts and so forth. So this happened to grow quicker than other areas in the state.

Q: Were those overall and cap-making companies out of New York?

WC: No, no, no. Locally based and locally owned.

Q: Can you think of an example of a local firm that made overalls?

WC: There was one, Woodbury Mills, which was [owned by] Mr. Kellner, who's now dead for many years. His son [also] ran it. They were making a lot of military uniforms and military shirts and jackets and so forth. But primarily, when they started, they were making miners-type garments—workmen's shirts and things like that. This was primarily a men's pants and slack outfit area. This was not primarily a dress area. We had a men's pants and tailor industry for many, many years back in the early twenties and thirties. And Grassos [men's clothing company] we had for many, many years. . . .[4]

Q: When did piecework become a popular way to make a dress?

WC: Piecework—let me try and give you the history on that. The movement of the New York individual who became a contractor in Pennsylvania was primarily an American history story—a Horatio Alger story—because he came from the sewing [occupation]. He was an operator himself. He sat by the machine and he sewed the entire dress and it nearly took him an hour, a half hour, whatever. He got paid by the dress. And then he bought a machine because he wanted the American dream and he became an employer in Pennsylvania.

He [the contractor] developed the piecework system, and the reason he did was because to teach a girl to do a whole garment was a humongous, expensive task. But to teach her to do a dart, or a collar, or a seam was a simple task. So the piecework system came into effect because it was simpler to break a girl in quickly by just teaching her one operation than to do a whole operation. It developed in Pennsylvania, Connecticut, Massachusetts. You couldn't do it in New York City. You were not allowed to do it in New York City. They [the ILGWU] wouldn't allow it because they would price the entire dress. When you gave a dress to a person to make, you gave them the entire bundle—bundle meaning all the parts combined. But when we did it in here, we didn't do it that way. [Here] all the darts went to one girl, all the collars went to one girl, all the sleeves went to one girl, and so forth and so on.[5]

Q: When you personally arrived in the Wyoming Valley, what was it like for dress manufacturing?

WC: A very interesting concept in our little area. I know about Kingston, I know about Wilkes-Barre, I know about Allentown, I know about Hazleton 'cause we were there. I never encountered anti-Semitism because everybody had an accent. If you didn't have an accent, you were suspect! My father had a heavy Jewish-Russian accent. All his buddies locally were all the Russians and Polish people, Slavic, because he spoke their language and he was part of them. I was suspect because I had no accent! So really this area respected religious beliefs because they were all first-generation Americans, you know, or immigrants. They understood that if you had an accent, you came from someplace and you were looking for the same thing they were looking for. So it was very interesting to understand, to know that.

So when I got here, I had a problem 'cause I had no accent. I had to develop one to become friendly with people. And what you found was that the owners were either of Italian descent or Jewish descent. The Jews who were scattered throughout the world come from all different places and could speak Polish, or Russian, or Slavish, or whatever language. The Italians also could speak different languages. And they got along very well. I know when I came into the industry as a young kid, to learn the industry you had to speak either Jewish or Italian. Then you had to speak all sorts of different languages. Now you have to speak Chinese. I gave up on that; can't speak Chinese! That's the way the industry was and that's what I found when I came into this area.

Q: So most of the women and men who worked for you were first- or second-generation Americans?

WC: I would say primarily they were first-generation Americans, coming from immigrant parents.

Q: Coal-mining families?

WC: Primarily coal mining 'cause this was a coal-mining area. They were very industrious, hardworking people, because at that time, they had to get ahead and do better. They knew that if they do a better job, you'd respect 'em and pay 'em more, and do better by 'em. Which is what we're losing in this country now.

Q: How would you compare the work ethic and productivity in the Wyoming Valley with New York in those years?

WC: Far superior, far superior [here]. I mentioned that only because the work element [in the Wyoming Valley] was younger in age than the worker in New York who was an immigrant coming from some European country. He or she was up in years and he was doing it to just earn bread and butter. Here the lady was doing it for a reason. She was doing it for family income because the men, the miners, had no jobs; there was no jobs for men. They were the providers, the women were the providers. They paid for the college bill, they paid for the mortgage payments, they paid for the six-pack of beer the guy would drink. They would do a lot better. And they weren't involved with making an entire garment. They were doing one garment [operation] so it was much simpler doing one thing repetitively rather than doing many things. You get much more production that way.

Q: Were there any changes in the work ethic over time?

WC: Let me answer it this way. The needle industry is primarily an immigrant industry because it's easy to learn, requires very little education, background, and study. It's one of the reasons that the world picked up on the industry. That first-generation American- and that second-generation American-[born] didn't want their child to be involved in factories anymore. They wanted something better. They wanted 'em to be a schoolteacher, a municipal employee, a self-employed person. They wanted that person to have a college education. And so the industry generally shrunk because the daughters and the sons of the workers became different things—not factory people anymore.

I remember I used to drive here [from New York] on weekends with a person called Old Man Brown who had a factory in Luzerne. His son came out here after he died and opened a plant on the Heights in Wilkes-Barre. His son was the first boy to graduate from Misericordia [University]; he became Dr. Brown, the skin doctor in Kingston. And that symbolizes the industry and the growth of the industry, of what happens to the people as generations go on. They want it better [for] their offspring.

Q: When did you close Ann Will Garment?

WC: About three years ago [1991].

Q: Was that worker in 1991 as productive and industrious as the worker you had in 1960?

WC: Oh no, couldn't be. Just by age alone, because she was the same person then who was with me. We had a twenty-five-year club and we must have had fifty people that were members of it. So that just by the age alone you couldn't be as productive. Then the younger girls wouldn't come to work because they wanted to be where men were. They wanted to be in department stores, they wanted to be around where men were working so they could get to meet boys. In our shop we mainly had women, but I happened to have ten men because I had a cutting department.

Q: How many employees did you have at your peak at Ann Will Garment?

WC: Going back to sometime around the end of the forties, early fifties, I would say somewhere around three hundred. When we finally closed, we had about thirty-five. . . .

Q: How many members did you have in your owners' association?

WC: Well, that's another story. It split off. We had two associations at one point. I had 350 in my group and there was 350 in the other group. That's a whole other story.

Q: Yours was called the Northeast Apparel Association. What was the other one called?[6]

WC: United Pennsylvania Dress Makers Association.

Q: Where was that based?

WC: It was based down in Bangor, Pennsylvania, in the "slate belt" area [near Easton].

Q: Is there still a dressmakers' association?

WC: It's a token. Maybe there might be fifteen members. I'm talking Lackawanna County, Luzerne County, Carbon County. It's virtually extinct. I think we had at one point had fourteen thousand people in Luzerne County employed as needleworkers.

Q: Now you're just down to a couple hundred.

WC: Yeah. We're going through an industrial revolution. We have to understand that. We have to understand that we are now Eli Whitney with the cotton gin. That's where we are. We gotta find a new way to live in the next ten years. America will survive but we're gonna have to find a new way. It will have to be through education primarily. And it's gonna have to be something that we do better than somebody else. The congressmen and senators better understand that, because the taxation programs and the burdens they're putting on industry is making it worse from what I hear. I'm out of it [but] from what I hear, you know, when an average office secretary spends three days doing government paperwork, something is wrong. Our young people better understand that they gotta produce. No more games. They're gonna have to find a way. They're gonna have to go back to find a way to build a better mousetrap, [be] more competitive, and do a job.

Q: How did you stay competitive over the years?

WC: With each labor [wage and benefit] increase, we increased the price of our garment, [but we also] went to a higher price range of garment. So we were able to absorb the increases by charging more for our product. It wasn't the same product; it was a better product that we made. But we got to the point where we couldn't make any more better products. The only way we could do it would be reverting back to a hand-sewn-type product, and there's no hand sewers left in America. We just got to the point where we couldn't go any further. There's only so much you can get for an item.

Q: Did you bring in new technology, machines, or did that stay about the same?

WC: The dress industry, needle industry, is basically 75 or 80 percent manual. There are new modern devices and equipment, but it's not enough to offset the manual aspect of the industry. See, like the Caliraya shirt I saw in the trade show—if you make an Arrow shirt, every Arrow shirt has a collar. So they have a machine that sews the collar on, turns the collar up, presses the collar. But that's making like thousands of collars a day. Well, the dress industry is a highly styled industry; every dress doesn't have a collar. So why involve a machine? Every dress doesn't have a pocket. The [ladies'] needle industry [is not] highly repetitive like a shirt or a pair of boxer underwear. [We have to] have manual input. We can't automate. So how do you skill them?

Q: I wonder if we can go down to ground level again and talk about being a shop owner. What was the day-to-day personnel situation like? Were you involved with family situations, problems?

WC: I revert back to the immigration period when the little dress operator came out here and became an owner of a plant. He was the personnel man, he was the bookkeeper, he was the equipment buyer, he was everything. One of the things that you become involved with when you're a plant owner, like myself, is that you're everything. We have no money for a personnel manager, or a purchasing agent, or a price controller. You're everything. When Susie wants to talk to you about getting beat up last night 'cause her husband got drunk, you have to listen to her. Or when Susie wants to talk to you about a kid not having good grades in school, you listen to it 'cause that's part of being personnel manager. Then when you go out to price a piece of equipment you have to know about all the different prices that they sell the thing for. So while it's a plant employing fifty or sixty people, there's no money for all these different individual jobs that become your job.

Q: How many hours a week would you put in?

WC: It's very difficult to answer that because you do many different jobs. I had a buddy [a fellow owner] of mine who was a dress cutter. A cutter is one who cuts through the fabric. We lay it [fabric] on the table. You would get from fifty to sixty-five dollars [a day] to cut [it]. Well, he would cut that himself so he could take the fifty or sixty-five dollars and put it in his pocket. He wouldn't have to pay anybody. When the girls would go home at three o'clock, he'd work until four or five o'clock cutting so he could put the money in his pocket.

I mentioned before about Mr. Brown, whose son eventually became a doctor in Kingston. He loved to work a blind stitch machine. That was the thing that does the bottom of the dress; it hems up the bottom of the dress. He loved that. He would sit until eight, nine o'clock at night putting bottoms on dresses. He would save maybe twenty dollars in labor that would be his. So when you say hours, it depends how many hours you want to [put in]. Like myself sorting. We used to have a bad weekend and I couldn't go back to New York, so I would go and sort a couple of lots. I'd be working Saturday and Sunday just to do something, and I'd save maybe fifteen dollars. Sorting means assembling the parts of a dress into various operations and putting them into bundles.

Q: It wasn't a forty-hour-a-week position.

WC: Oh no, no, no. Oh, sixty, maybe sixty. Oh, sure. We began after an eight-hour day. The employer would begin working after the eighth hour [because] he'd have to get ready for the next shift. He'd have to work at least ten hours a day. Then the union fought for a seven-hour day. We gave 'em a seven-hour day, so we'd have to work at least two hours after the seven hours to prepare for the next day. There was no particular time schedule. I'd work five days a week. No Saturday, Sunday. Saturday was overtime so you tried to avoid working Saturday unless you had to, and the eighth hour was overtime. You're trying to avoid that, too.

Q: Do you have any thought about why there's not more attention devoted to garment-making history in this area?

WC: I don't know if I'm going to answer you properly or not. The individual plant owners never accepted the areas they lived in as home. Their home base was wherever they came from. So they would work here all week and they would go back on the weekends, probably Friday morning or Friday afternoon early, and come back like maybe Sunday night late or Monday morning or Monday afternoon. They never really participated in the day-to-day activities of the various communities. They were busy in their plants during the day, and on the weekends they would go home. So they never became an integral part [of community life], just like [many of] the coal barons and the various owners of other industries that were here in the area.

The reason they [the garment shop owners] never settled [was] because they didn't know how long they'd be allowed to remain in these areas and how long the union in New York would allow them to live here. So they never would take roots and say, "I'll settle here." That's the way it was. I think of Old Man Brown who lived next door to me in New York City. All his life he came here every week. He lived over the plant. Do you know Connolly's property there [in Luzerne]? He lived upstairs over the plant. Lived there for I don't know how many years. During the week [he'd be here] and on the weekends he went home to New York. Maybe he was here fifteen or twenty years.

Q: But you established roots here.

WC: Yeah. I got tired of going back and forth to New York. It didn't make much sense to do it. If I was going to live here, I had to live here, educate my kids here, have my wife learn to live here, be part of the community.

Q: Was she from New York as well?

WC: Yes. We had a rank [here]. We were established. We owned a building. We had the property that I had acquired over the years so it didn't make sense [to commute] anymore. Had to live someplace if we don't want to live all over the place!

Q: What percentage of the members in your association came from New York?

WC: Well, when you say New York, New York is five boroughs so it's a big area. I would [say] 100 percent came from the various boroughs throughout New York City. I know there was a John D. Giovanni, whose son became a Supreme Court judge in New York City because he lived there, but he [the father] had a plant in Shamokin. His son grew up [in New York] and became a Supreme Court judge in New York. They would never live in Shamokin. Some did become owners in

WILLIAM "BILL" CHERKES

the late sixties and seventies because they saw that this was a pretty good thing and they wanted to get into the act. They were local boys who worked in the various plants and they decided to go off on their own. In the late sixties and seventies, they became local owners. That happened, but it didn't happen 'til after, because the industry was foreign to the area.

Q: Didn't have the skills or the know-how?

wc: You're right exactly. So it took until that long for the local people to catch on to what's happening. Another generation and they said, "OK, let's try, let's see what this is all about. . . ." We had in Wilkes-Barre, it's called Engle Dress. Joe Engle, a native of Wilkes-Barre, [was] very active. Roxanne bathing suits was born and created here in Wilkes-Barre [by Mr. Engle]. He found out that he was making bras and brassieres and Puerto Rico took over that industry, long back—early fifties. So he switched his plant to making ladies' clothing. He still has several plants here. He's gone but his family controls them. They do Roxanne bathing suits—any woman knows Roxanne bathing suits. That's a very popular brand name. The plants are owned by his brother, run by his brother, who's in New York. . . .[7]

Q: Let me ask you about New York versus Pennsylvania tensions. I mention this because Min Matheson, a mutual acquaintance of ours, talked about the fact that there were always tensions between the New York union and the Wyoming Valley District union. I wonder if there were tensions between local owners, subcontractors, and New York subcontractors or New York jobbers?

wc: Let me try and answer as a dress contractor, which we were in this area, maybe 99 percent [of us]. We were never [considered] primary employers. Our union agreements and contracts were written with the jobber or manufacturer in New York City. There became tension between New York [union headquarters] and the local [District] union because the local union realized that we were [actually] the primary employers and they would have to negotiate [day-to-day problems] with us. What happened was they [the union] would write a contract in New York City with the jobber [there] and say this girl is going to get X dollars and so many days off and so forth and so on. Well, the local [District] unit realized that that's not right. They had to negotiate with individual plants and they had to recognize our piecework systems and the way we lived.

We don't live like they live in New York. So it became a tremendous friction between the local unions and the New York thinking. Their thinking was complete solid control, that we were nothing but a foreman that owned the plant and that the main owner was the jobber in New York. The jobber couldn't care less because he never put two cents back into the plant [like] we did here. The [District] union realized that and that's where that friction came from.

Q: How would you describe your relationships with the ILGWU and its people?

wc: That's a very difficult question because there were a lot of political ramifications at the time. The local unions were asked to do various things by the New

FIG. 7 | Men pulling clothing racks, New York City Garment District, 1955. Photo: Al Ravenna. New York World-Telegram and the Sun Newspaper Photograph Collection, Library of Congress, Washington, D.C.

York union to make us unhappy and pick away at us. They would use all sorts of devices and there was a constant war going on all the time because the local people were carrying out orders that New York wanted and realizing that New York was not always right. That struggle . . . New York wanted to bring back the industry [to the city] as much as they could and they would put as many roadblocks in our way as they could. And we were unionized! [We were still] "controlled" by the local unions who we could live with, but they were directed by the New York union who we could not live with. That gives you an idea of the contest.

Q: What about Min Matheson, the Wyoming Valley District leader?

wc: She's a great lady. You have to be involved in a situation personally to be able to understand it. Like I could explain hunger to you but you can't feel hunger until you're hungry. Well, Min Matheson comes from a labor family who understood labor and felt labor. The people we have today read about labor and they read about the situation, and they think they know, but they don't know her. Min Matheson's family go back to [Samuel] Gompers; they go back to Chicago, where they organized the tobacco workers. She had a long history of labor, you know. Her brother was killed because he was a labor organizer. Willy [Lurye] was killed in New York City for trying to organize. They were born labor people. You can't learn labor from a book. You can't tell people how to be blind unless you're blind. You can empathize with them, but you can't understand it until it happens to you.

Q: Did she ever call a strike at your shop?

WC: Not at my plant [because] we had no problems. Never had a strike there.[8] But there were many strikes in various areas. Oh yeah, many.

Q: How did you manage to avoid a strike at your shop?

WC: Well, we talked things out, you know. I was president of the dress association [the Northeast Apparel Association] for many years, so I had to be a little bit better 'cause I was always being watched. All the new experiments, the new labor devices, and all new techniques I had to always put up and I had to set an example for the rest of the industry. So I always felt a little close to labor. I always felt a little bit of their problem. I could understand a give-and-take argument, you know. What we would settle on here would go for the [local] industry at that time. There's no other way I can answer that really.

In the late fifties [1958] there was a statewide strike. It was run through the New York [ILGWU] because New York wanted to have more to say in the local area as far as piecework was concerned. They were off eighteen weeks or something like that. But it wasn't our individual plant's arguments; it was an industry argument.

Q: Did you ever have to call Mrs. Matheson to negotiate something?

WC: Oh yeah, we met many times on different circumstances. One of the things that I helped her with was interesting. We enforced clean bathrooms in all the dress plants because the people [workers] wanted it. Let me mention something to you while we're talking about it. The state of Pennsylvania never gave two cents to those people who built the plants and employed the people in the various factories throughout the state. The garages and the storefronts and all the buildings and all the plants were paid for and built by the people [i.e., the owners]. Most of them were just beginning in business and most of them were working with very limited capital. And they did some stupid things. One of the things they did was to have dirty bathrooms. Minnie and I we made the campaign of it at that time. That you had to have a certain amount of bathroom stalls and certain amount of cleanliness in each bathroom or you couldn't belong to the dress association. That was one of the projects that we did. I mean it sounds silly but it's very important when you're working in a place all day, to have a clean room. . . .

Q: Organized crime was supposed to have been involved locally with the garment industry. What can you tell us about that?

WC: When the union wants to establish a point, they begin by mesmerizing you. One of the things they used was very successful. There was some people in the industry who were crime figures and they [the union] made it appear as though the whole industry was crime ridden. But I was never personally involved with that kind of a situation. I knew people and they did have records and backgrounds, but it was blown out of proportion to establish a point, a union point.

Q: To get public support or sympathy?

WC: Yeah, that kind of a thing. Yeah, yeah.

Q: I gather Pittston was a case in point? Mrs. Matheson talked about relevant strikes there, for example, at the Jenkins Sportswear plant. Russell Bufalino, a reputed mob leader, supposedly owned or backed it.

WC: Yes.

Q: Was organized crime pretty much based in Pittston or was it in other areas?

WC: I really don't know. I really don't know. Between Pittston to Hazleton there was three hundred plants.

Q: Three hundred plants and the great majority were not organized crime–related?

WC: No, there's no organized crime—not to my knowledge.

3

Minnie "Min" Matheson
Labor Leader, Social Activist, and
ILGWU District Manager

FIG. 8
Min Matheson, circa 1960. Photo courtesy of Lukasik Studio.

Minnie Hindy Lurye "Min" Matheson, from an audio-recorded interview with Robert P. Wolensky conducted at Mrs. Matheson's home in Kingston, Pennsylvania, on December 5, 1988. The interview is included in the Wyoming Valley Oral History Project, which is one of eight projects within the Northeastern Pennsylvania Oral and Life History Collection housed in the Eberly Family Special Collections Library, Penn State University Libraries.

As a champion of workers' rights and the charismatic manager of the ILGWU Wyoming Valley District, Min Matheson stood out as an immensely popular and effective union leader. Her dedication to organized labor derived from family and personal experiences in Chicago, Paterson, New York, and the Wyoming Valley—most of which she shared with her husband and union partner, William "Bill" Matheson. Her narrative reveals that "solidarity unionism," and its reliance on local control and community support, formed the basis of her organizing philosophy, an approach that often clashed with the centralizing propensities of the ILGWU's officers in New York. In building and maintaining the union movement, she reveals a belief in individual and community resources in facilitating strikes, walkouts, demonstrations, mass meetings, radio broadcasts, and political rallies. Her family's violent history at the hands of organized crime in Chicago and New York greatly influenced her commitment to labor as well as her union-building strategies in the Wyoming Valley.

MM: You see, in the Wilkes-Barre and Kingston [areas], the towns on this end of the Valley, [the garment shops] were beginning to be organized [in the late 1930s].[1] We had some measure of a union. We had about eight hundred members when I first came here [in 1944] and six shops. At the Pittston end of the Valley, it was as if every empty store, every empty space, was occupied by a dress shop. They were runaways from New York. There were jobbers providing work here to get away from the New York [ILGWU] agreement, because after the 1933 strike we had won a lot of concessions. . . .[2]

So we decided we'd try to organize Pittston. We'd go into Pittston and the police would put us back on the train [the Laurel Line] and tell us, "You're not wanted here." So we started coming in my car because they used to watch that little railway station to see if we were coming.[3] We picked a factory on 77 South Main Street. . . . You can imagine the sensation it created when I arrived with a bunch of women and we were going to organize the factory. Of course, the women who worked in the factory were scared out of their wits. But we had leaflets and we had a message and we stuck by it.

They [the owners] called the police, and the police were very mean and nasty. One day, one of the police officers grabbed me and put my arm behind my back. I said, "What are you trying to do, break my arm?" He wouldn't let go of my arm. It was very painful. There was one of our girls on the picket line, Carmella Salatino, she had gone to school with him. She said, "Frank, let her go, let her go." And he wouldn't.

Across the street came a man whom we didn't know and he said, "Let her go." The cop wouldn't do it. The next thing you know, he let my arm go and I turned around and this man, whom we didn't know, had a gun in the officer's back. That's why he let me go! Then in all the commotion and the noise, he [the gunman] just slipped away. Later he called and he was in touch with me and we talked. He said he was a coal miner and he admired what we were doing, and it's about time somebody gave that Mafia crowd a fight. The fact that we weren't afraid of them [impressed him]. We got to be very good friends. Of course, he had to hide out for a while because they were looking for him. But by the time all the commotion was over, I think they had decided that he was local, you know, he was known, so they didn't pursue it.

Q: Do you have his name?

MM: Well, Angelo. He had a pet name: Rusty, Rusty DePasquale [chap. 4]. Just telling you this because if you called him up, he might talk to you. He worked in the mines for some years. He worked closely with us. He'd turn up on picket lines and, believe me, always when we needed him. He was staunch and brave, you know, the kind of courage from being really convinced that a union was important. He was a great help to us. Now we got that kind of support from the population of Pittston, but he was outstanding. That's why I mentioned his name. He was a coal miner.[4]

If it wasn't for the support of these kind of people in the Valley and the support of the women—the women were so [important]. . . . It was as if they

MINNIE "MIN" MATHESON

were subjected to a kind of life where they had no say for so long that suddenly they were somebody. Some of their men would come and take them off the picket line, pull them by the arm, and try to make them get off the picket line, and they would fight back. Sometimes they had to give in and we'd all gang up and try to help them. But that's how tense the fight was to organize Pittston.

If you read the *Reader's Digest* story, it was during one of those fights [in 1958] that [alleged crime boss] Russ [Bufalino] had a bunch of tough guys on the other side of the street and it was as if there was an undeclared war.[5] They were on one side of the street, we were on the [other] side of the street where the factory was. Cars were going back and forth. That [road] was like no man's land. They didn't come across to our side and we didn't go across to their side. . . .

They were always catcalling and trying to intimidate us. There was a restaurant on their side of the street and we knew the guy who owned [it]. Sometime[s] some of our girls would, just for the hell of it, go across the street and walk into Twinny's, and Twinny would say, "They're all in the backroom—get out! I don't want you drinking coffee here. I'll give you coffee." And he'd get rid of our girls. To this day, one of them lives in Baltimore and, for years, she still calls up and keeps in touch: Alice Reca [chap. 6]. But it wasn't Reca then, she's married now.[6] We had the kind of support that was unbelievable.

Another girl that we got from one of the shops was Helen Barnosky [later Helen Weiss, chap. 9].[7] I think they were Lithuanian. Anyhow, [one day] she was driving the car and we were going down to a very early morning picket line and there on the corner were all these tough guys. She said, "I don't think we'd better stop 'cause they got us outnumbered." What were we, five women in the car? I said, "Helen, no matter what happens today, we have to stop, because if we don't turn up today, this may hurt our chances to really get this town organized. We have just got to put up a very brave front." And I said, "But we have to think of something spectacular to worry them like they think they're worrying us."

We were scared. I don't want to make you think that we were so brave. You know, we were scared but we couldn't figure and we didn't have much time to talk because they saw our car coming. Then she turned around and we were coming up on their side of the street in order to stop in front of the factory. It's as if we all had one mind, that if they were going to get tough and come across and beat us up or do something rotten, really rotten, then we wanted people to know about it. So the minute we stopped, as we got out of the car, we were all screaming. We didn't make it up [in advance] at all. Later on, we laughed like kids, you know.

I got out of the car and I said, "You rotten, dirty hoodlums! What are you doing in this town? You don't live here. We live here, this is our town, not yours! And you do one little thing to hurt these women . . ." Because I was the leader. In the meantime, the other girls were screaming at them. Screaming at them! Pretty soon the windows [of nearby residents] were opening and people were putting their heads out. This is early, early in the morning. I said, "There are witnesses to anything you think you're going to do."

Honestly, these men almost went crazy. It was like, "My god, how can you do anything with a bunch of crazy women like that?" They were walking around, waving their hands, putting their hands over their ears. And not a squeak out of them, nothing, you see? 'Cause when we first saw them they were making like in the movie pictures, real tough guys. They were going to knock our heads off, and we were not so sure that they didn't have guns. We didn't know what they were going to do because they were adamant that they wouldn't let the union into Pittston. So I always said, it was the women that defeated them.[8]

One of the men that Russ [Bufalino] had in his group across the street to sort of intimidate us was a great big guy they called [John] "Blackie" Salvo. Blackie Salvo's son, Andy, worked in one of our shops, and he was a perfectly nice young man. He had gone off to the military and he kept in touch with me. He wrote to me. As a matter of fact, he wrote a poem, and I wish I could find it to show it to you. He liked Bill [Matheson] and Bill liked him, but he was killed, and the last letter that Andy wrote we got.[9] Of course, his parents were devastated [by his death]. We had, as part of our membership, a $1,000 death benefit. It was part of the [labor-management] agreement and, imagine, here is Andy, dead, and his father [is] out on that stupid line with Russ trying to intimidate us not to organize. . . .

When Andy was killed [in 1953], they wanted his body brought back to this country. So, we had this $1,000 death benefit and there was quite a bit of discussion amongst our girls, 'cause who were we giving it to? Andy was gone, he wasn't married, so we had to give it to Blackie and his wife. The question was, were we going to do it? Now, legally, it was their money. He was insured. But we had all this discussion because of the fight that was going on in Pittston. When Andy's body came home, we turned up en masse [for the wake]. You know they weren't friends, but *he* was a friend. He was a member of our union. You can imagine when we walked into the house. Oh, listen, nobody said anything but they were astonished.

We came as an official committee from the union, and we gave the mother the $1,000 death benefit. She cried and she asked if I would give her the letter. It would be the last thing she would have of Andy's. I said, "Yes, we'll make a copy for ourselves but we will give you the original, in his writing." And we did. Didn't change anything on the picket line but it was a story, a real human interest story. They gained a lot of respect for us anyhow. And all this is never secret. It gets around and there's buzz, buzz in church and all over town, in the restaurants, that this we had done. So they'd get mad at us for being such rowdies, which we were, but at the same time, they had a lot of respect for the things we did and accomplished. . . .

Q: Was Bufalino typically there with his men?

MM: Yeah, Russ. He's serving time in jail somewhere now. He's my own age.

Q: Was he very visible during all of this?

MM: Oh, very, very visible. The leader of the pack. They wouldn't do anything without asking him. He was in charge of the Mafia forces in northeastern Pennsylvania and he still is. In those years, nobody would believe us, but what he said went.

Q: Who was the leader before him?

MM: Angelo Sciandra's father. I don't know what his first name was [John].

Q: What do you recall about Angelo Sciandra, who was also a garment shop owner?

MM: One morning when we got there [to the picket line], Sciandra's sitting on top of his car and he's blowing "Taps" for us. He was a musician [trumpet]. He was very young in those years. It wasn't a very happy thing because, first of all, the war was on [World War II] and, you know, "Taps." . . . The girls said, "They're going to kill us today, listen to this." They used to come out from the factory with pails full of dirty water and throw it on our legs and on our clothes. It was not a peaceful picket line, if you know what I mean. There was something going on all the time.

So Sciandra was sitting up there on the car blowing "Taps" for us. Oh, we used to fight and catcall and tell them off and, in a way, they sort of admired the girls, especially some of them that were pretty—all young and pretty as can be. This Alice [Reca] that I told you about, who lives in Baltimore and still keeps in touch after thirty years, she was a daredevil. She used to say things to him and he to her, back and forth.

So we organized the factory. I know what brought it to a head. One day we were on the line and a truck and a car pull up and out comes a man that I knew from New York in those [early] years, which was the early thirties. He was a member of our union but he had gone into business [as a jobber]. He knew Pittston from just like, you say, Hammond, Indiana. It's a name. He was sending work to this factory. I can't think of his name now. He looked at me and I at him. We used to like each other. We were friends. So he came running over to me. My maiden name was Lurye and he says, "Lurye, Lurye, what are you doing here? And what's going on?" I said, "You mean you give them work? We're on strike." Well, he was very embarrassed for me, you know, and for the old times. He talked to Falzone [the owner of the factory]. Of course, Falzone couldn't do anything that the tough guys wouldn't let him do. The shoulder pads [pieces] used to arrive [from the jobber] with a big union label on them to this factory.[10]

Q: From New York?

MM: Yes. We used to say to the owner every day, "You're not [going to be in business] for long because we're stopping all this. You're not going to get a thread out, you're not going to get shoulder pads. It's going to be union or else." So we had that help. He talked to Falzone and Falzone went to Russ and there was all this business back and forth. We were gonna put him out of business 'cause we were gonna stop all the trimmings. There are all kinds of ways you could fight these people. But it was a long fight.

Q: When did you start organizing Falzone's shop?

MM: Early in 1945.

Q: When did you have it organized?

MM: Oh, I'd say sometime during that year. . . .

Q: Going back to the tough guys, I'm surprised that Angelo Sciandra didn't become the crime family's boss after his father [John] died.

MM: Well, Angelo was not that kind of person. He was a playboy. He was brought up pampered and he was a big kid. He blew the horn and fooled around, and even after we started organizing, he opened a dress shop. He had a big dress shop, but given the kind of person he was, he never made a real success of it and he lost the shop.

Q: Did you say that Mrs. Sciandra gave you a glass vase one time?

MM: That's his mother [Josephine Sciandra]. Angelo married a girl from Plymouth. Her name is Helen but I can't remember her maiden name. Very, very nice girl. We'd fight [Angelo], but we'd meet. We knew each other. It was after this big fight where he blew "Taps" and all this went on that she [his mother] insisted on giving me a present 'cause her son didn't act very nice. She was apologetic.

Q: Did she send the vase with a note?

MM: No, she told the girls—she lived right on Main Street [in Pittston] like she does now, and I haven't seen her in years and years—she told them, "It's for Min." One time she did ask if I would come and see her, and I did. I went in [to her house] and talked with her. There was a sort of peace period and then we'd start [organizing] again, depending on the shop.

On towards the end, before I was transferred to New York [the Union Label Department], Russ had a niece, Dolly Falcone.[11] Their factory was at the north end of Main Street and this one wasn't going to be union at all. You see, I went on the theory that if you let one factory stay nonunion, it would soon contaminate the others. There'd be the end of an agreement, there might be a strike, there might be other problems. The next thing you know . . . [there would be nonunion shops]. The way the town was controlled, we couldn't take that chance. So anytime a new shop opened, we were there, whether we had the people [with us] or not, we were there. The union was there. They had to be union.

She [Emanuella "Dolly" Falcone] was absolutely determined that they were not. I guess Russ was telling her. We didn't have the people [i.e., employees], that's true. We did not have the people [with us]. They controlled them but we wouldn't give up. The fighting got so bad that the mayor of Pittston padlocked the factory for public safety.[12] She [Dolly] was furious but we were strong enough by that time to be able to force that kind of action. Which wasn't fair, I grant you that. But they also imported tough guys, which spoiled it for them because the TV cameras came down and got pictures of them. This was '59 and early 1960.

MINNIE "MIN" MATHESON

Q: What can you tell us about [alleged gangster and garment shop owner] Dominick [Nick] Alaimo?

MM: Well, that was early in our organizing campaign. It was a probably in the early fifties. He had a factory right on Main Street. It was a big factory and he got a guy to run it by the name of Larry Sitzman, a Jewish guy. Yeah, I knew Larry Sitzman, and I said to Larry, "The shop's got to be union." "No" [he replied], "never be union if Nick is in." Nick was like a top assistant to Russell Bufalino. It was Russ and Nick and Sciandra and this Ettore Agolino, who was their attorney. He's still in Pittston. He's a lawyer, a full-fledged lawyer. You'd see the four of them hatching up something on whatever was going on. They ran the show.

That's before the picket line where Angelo [Sciandra] blew "Taps" and where Blackie Salvo and Russ and them were on the other side of the street yelling at us, "Bring your men down." That's the time I walked across the street and said to him [Bufalino], "I don't have to bring the men down, Russ, because I'm twice the man you'll ever be!"[13]

But before we tackled that one, we tackled Nick's shop and, of course, he wasn't gonna be union. [He told me] I was just wasting my time. So we were in our union hall, and I had sent for him. I could get away with that, you know. Sometimes I think now, what nerve to just tell him, "I'm gonna be in the office and I want you there" and so on, and he'd come. I was worried about the *men* in the union 'cause they [the tough guys] never seemed to touch the women. They'd bluster and threaten but they never touched us physically. I had to get the boys out of the union office, 'cause with them there, you never could tell what would happen. He [Bufalino] always walked about with so-called bodyguards.

Q: This was at your office in Pittston?

MM: Yeah, and when Nick came into the office, I said to him, "The shop has got to be union. You're a committeeman for the United Mine Workers. That's an old labor union, and no union is going to allow a member of the union, especially a committeeman, to run a nonunion shop. So I'm not gonna waste any time. I'm gonna come in and speak to your people and we're gonna sign them up." No, he would not. So I said, "OK, you have it your way but I'll do what I have to do." He said, "Yeah, and what's that?" I picked up the phone and he said, "What are you doing?" I said, "I'm calling Tom Kennedy." Tom Kennedy was the United Mine Workers union representative for the whole region, the whole anthracite region. He was a very important man. He was a member of [UMWA president] John L. Lewis's executive board.

Nick put his hand over my hand to put the phone down. He said, "You can't do that," like, you know, "What are you crazy or something? You're gonna ruin me." I said, "Well, we either come to an agreement about the shop being union or you quit being committeeman for the United Mine Workers." And by the way, his was the mine where the 1959 [Knox Mine] disaster took place.

What did the committeemen do in the United Mine Workers? They were supposed to settle grievances. There was always fights about the weight of the coal. The men were being cheated. There was always questions of earnings. There was a question of keeping the mines properly propped up so there wouldn't be accidents. A committeeman was a very, very powerful person in the United Mine Workers. Very powerful. Really controlled lives.

So Nick said, "You can't do that." I said, "I know I can't do that, but I'm gonna do that because I'm not gonna let your shop work nonunion. And as a matter of fact, just as I explained to you, I can't afford to have any shop nonunion 'cause you guys are gonna get ideas and we're gonna go back to the olden days and we're not goin' back. The women don't want to go back to that. It's not me saying it, it's them. They work hard and they deserve to have protection on the job."

I always had my little speech about democracy, which I still have, about [how] having the right to vote doesn't make it democratic. You've got to have a say in your working conditions because that's where you spend most of your life. If you can't determine your own life in the sense that you have some say in what kind of conditions you work under, you don't have democracy. I'm a great believer in American democracy and I still say it, that if you don't have a labor union or you don't have an organization to represent you on the job, you're really being denied your rights, your democratic rights.

Q: What did Nick do?

MM: He was going away and [would] come back in an hour. I figured he's going to ask Russ. He was really worried because he knew that I would go through with talking to Tom Kennedy, even going to Washington [D.C.] and talk to John L. Lewis. Nothing fazed me, you know. He said he'd be back in an hour, and Bill [Matheson] and Dot [Dorothy Ney] saw him leave with his two bodyguards. They [Bill and Dot] come in: "What happened? What happened?" I told them, "He'll be back in an hour." They said, "He'll be back in an hour with ten more of those hoodlums and they'll kill you." I told them what I did. That he [Kennedy] will never stand for it. They didn't want to leave. I wanted them out of headquarters 'cause I was always worried about them. Well, he came back in an hour. He said, "OK [we'll unionize]!" So you had to use all kinds of strategies. . . .

See, interestingly, there were legitimate employers. There was a big company from New York called McKitterick-Williams. They had a shop in West Pittston but they were operating nonunion [in the 1940s]. While we were trying to organize Falzone's, we were also trying to organize them. We always bit off a little too much. But they [McKitterick-Williams] were in a totally different position. Their showroom and center was in New York in a union building and we had all kinds of ways to pressure them.

Finally, the owner of McKitterick's came in. He had a manager running the place who was a local guy. He was sympathetic to us. He was not against us. They

FIG. 9 | Min Matheson, speaking at a Jenkins Sportswear strike, Pittston, Pennsylvania, 1958. Photo courtesy of Lukasik Studio.

really ran a nice factory and made a very nice dress. The McKitterick-Williams dresses were a better line of dresses. Jimmy Boyle, that was his name. He lived here in Kingston. Jimmy didn't care if we came in but he couldn't do anything. He wasn't the owner, but he used to come out and talk to us sometimes and tell us [when] the guy, the owner, was gonna come in [from New York]. So we had pickets there in order to find a way to get the union in. The women [workers] were very friendly and sympathetic to us. We had some of the shop out on strike, some of the really good operators who joined the picket line. We were [also] working [i.e., organizing] on Main Street in Pittston, which was really my aim because Main Street in Pittston was controlled by the tough guys.

We would try legitimate shops, so to speak, like Pittston Apparel or McKitterick-Williams, and we'd keep at these [other] shops that the tough guys controlled. We knew the tough guys controlled them because the women knew everything. I told you that in those years the men would come and try to drag the women off the picket line. The atmosphere in the town was that everything was controlled and the women had no say at all. They did the cooking, and the cleaning, and the sewing, and taking care of the lunches, and getting the children out to school and the husbands out to work in the mines. They were active in their churches and always crocheting and knitting and making things, and this was their life. But now we came along and we gave them status. . . .[14]

Q: Tell us about your dealings with Pittston's politics.

MM: We started getting mixed up with the politics of the town which, of course, as I say, everything was controlled. I would talk to them [public officials] and they'd laugh. Then I talked to the women at shop meetings or we'd have union meetings. If I was going to support someone in the elections, or try to get rid of some of these people who were running Pittston and see if we couldn't get some decent people in, I'd say, "Well, if you women put your heads to it, we would find a way." The first thing is, "Are you registered to vote?" Yes, they're registered to vote, but they don't vote. "Why don't you vote? Do you go down and vote?" "Well, we do, we go down and we register but we can't cast our vote. Our man has to cast our vote for us." I said, "Why?" "Well, that's the system." That's the system that the Mafia had ordained. The Mafia had ordained it in order to control the elections.

The women would go and sign in as citizens, but then the man [i.e., the husband or another male] would go in the polling place and cast their vote. The women were never allowed to vote. The first time I heard that I said, "Well, we'll just see about it." I would tell Bill and right away he was so good at writing these speeches with a little humor, and he'd start out by saying "So you think it's a free country? So you think we have a right to do this or that, but you don't know anything if you don't know the town of Pittston. They have their own laws there." Then we would tell the stories that people at this end [Wilkes-Barre] of the Valley just couldn't believe. Attorneys and judges, a lot of them knew, but it was all covered up. They could have stopped it. It was illegal.

In that first election, we picked the polling place, which was the hotbed for the Bufalino crowd. We took women from down here [Wilkes-Barre] because the Pittston women were afraid. But we had to get a [Pittston] family that would be willing to stick their necks out—one woman to go into the polling place and when they told her she couldn't vote, that her husband would vote for her, she would refuse. And she wouldn't sign the roster unless they agreed that she would vote [for herself].

So that was our first big fight, and Carmella is still alive—Carmella Salatino [was the first woman who tried to vote]. Her husband's name was Nick. Of course, we had not only briefed Nick and Carmella and her mother but her uncles, the whole family, before you could do anything. We didn't want to get anyone killed, you know, or get them into real trouble. Maybe they had a job and they would lose their job or whatever, so we had to [be careful]. But there was Carmella Salatino and she had a good husband who was willing, but he was afraid. It wasn't just a question of his being afraid, but [so were] all the relatives in the family. We had our work cut out, talking to all of them. They, of course, admired what we were doing and agreed with what we were doing because wages were disgustingly low. It was like, "The Messiah had arrived." We were going to change all this. . . .

When we were going to make that fight at the ballot box, I went on the air [i.e., the radio] the night before. I said, "I hope everyone in Pittston is listening because this is what we're going to do." I spelled out exactly what we were gonna do. "We're gonna be at this and that polling place." At that time it was radio. Little Bill Phillips ran WQXR [*sic*; WKQV].[15] We used him all through the 1958 strike. Every single day we were on the air, and people listened, not just people in Pittston but [people in] the Valley listened. They'd get a bang out of "What are they up to now?," you know. It was like an ongoing soap opera. We told them what we were going to do and they [the mobsters] were waiting for us. We didn't give a darn because we had lined up this family [the Salatinos] and we knew they'd stand up.

What happened was that the infighting in the polling place went on for so long that poor Carmella practically fainted. She had just exhausted her strength in standing up to them. Nick was scared because they kept threatening him and he'd say [to them], "Well, what can I do? She won't listen." And so on. It was terrible.

They [tough guys] knew that if they lost, [if we] just made the one break, it was gonna break their hold. And the women were very independent. Once they got into that booth with the curtain, they would do what they wanted to do and they knew that I had enough persuasion that they would vote my way. They couldn't control the town or the elections the way they did in the past. So they were hell-bent on us not [voting]. Well, we didn't win that day because Carmella couldn't go through [with it]. In the end she was physically exhausted. But we made a start.

Q: She ended up not voting?

MM: It ended up that Nick voted for her and they came out and they were very apologetic. Carm was in tears but I told them, "Don't let it [bother you]." I knew if it had gone [forward] that day I would have been amazed. I didn't say that to them in advance but I had said to Bill, "We're taking a very, very big risk and I don't know what they're gonna do to the family when this is over."

But we had declared ourselves [for voting rights] and you would be surprised how the women immediately got ideas. This [voting] had become a daily argument within the family. [The women would say to their husbands], "You don't think you're gonna tell me [what to do]. I'm gonna do this and . . ." They gained a lot of strength and a lot of independence by being part of the union and part of everything that we were trying to do. That was extremely gratifying to me, as hard as we worked from early in the morning 'til all hours of the night. I never refused a telephone call. . . .

Q: What were the wages like in the early days?

MM: It's very hard to say. First of all, they would work the women and say, "I'm teaching you," and they'd pay them nothing for weeks. It was absolutely astounding 'cause those women could sew. But the employers [would say], "Well, when you learn [then we'll pay you]." The weeks would go by. There were laws in the land by that time about the hours. There was this twenty-five-cent minimum

[wage], which they paid. That's what they [supposedly] paid. A little later it was thirty-five cents and finally it was forty cents. You would be surprised how hard we had to work to get that forty cents, and it was the legal minimum of the country. This was some years later. It was always an uphill fight. When we demanded forty-five cents in union contracts, they [said], "We're all gonna go out of business."

It was also a free-for-all because the factories were in the neighborhoods where the people lived and you could go in, and you could go home to take the wash off the line if it's gonna rain, or you could see that Johnny gets his lunch, and go back [to work]. The same thing in the evening. So there was absolutely no control of hours, wages, and earnings. But the women were smart enough to know that they put in a very full day's work for which they were getting a pittance. So they were very much in our corner. I was the one who fought for them. You know, they were afraid to talk up because of all these problems in the background and they were afraid for their men, 'cause the Mafia wasn't exactly nonviolent.

I would come in and they all admired [what we were doing]. When I walked in, they knew something was gonna [happen] . . . drama . . . drama had arrived! To this day, we meet with some of the girls and they [say], "It was the greatest time of my life." I always used to worry because if I said, "Walk [strike]," they walked. [One time] I went into a factory with close to three hundred people and within five minutes I cleared the factory out. Stand at the door at the time clock and say, "Punch in, but go across the street." There were beer joints—you had to go somewhere, you know, to meet. The girls liked nothing better, even if they weren't mad about something or they were gonna lose that day's work. They loved the drama.[16]

We had some pretty tough employers. Sometimes it was really a question of showing these people that they couldn't run roughshod over the women. This factory that I told you I had cleaned it out in about five minutes, he had taken the doors off the washroom because the girls went into the washroom and stayed too long. Now I don't have to tell you, women, [especially] older women, have problems. And what? Even if they stayed too long, you can't take the doors off a washroom. Someone called my office and lucky they found me in, and said, "John St. George just took the doors off the washroom." I said, "You're kidding." They said, "Oh, no." That's what he did because Susie or whoever stayed there for a half hour and he's determined that they're not gonna smoke cigarettes and gossip in the washroom.

He thought the only way he's going to enforce it is by taking the doors off so they can't stay there. But the women have to go to the washroom and they were embarrassed. [The caller said], "What can we do about it?" I said, "You don't do anything. You just keep on working, but tell him Min's coming down and if he doesn't put the doors back while I'm there, we're gonna walk out. We're gonna go

MINNIE "MIN" MATHESON

across [the street]." This was in Wilkes-Barre, but don't worry, the whole Valley heard about it.

I went down and the minute I walked in, he was in a fury. He was about six foot two, and you know how big I am [five foot six]. I said, "John"—he didn't like my calling him by his first name; he wanted me to say, "Mr. St. George," which I would never give him the satisfaction of until the day he died—"John, I understand you took the doors off the ladies rooms? Well, put them back, now, while I'm here. If you don't, I'm gonna walk this factory right out across the street," to whatever that beer place was. There were two of them [taverns] and we took over both because it was a big shop. Oh, he raved and he fumed and [cited] all the grievances about how long they stay in there, and how dirty they [the bathrooms] were, and he cleans up the washroom, and they make it dirty, and all this nonsense that goes on in a shop and in everyday life. I said, "All that, OK, but put the doors back." So this went on for about an hour: "Put the doors back." Well, he wouldn't put the doors back. The girls were watching and they were really keyed up. You could see by their eyes and the way they weren't watching their needles, they were watching me and him.

Q: Were you in his office?

MM: No, right there [on the shop floor]. As I came through the door, he sort of met me and the big noise started. The factory was on Empire Street [in Wilkes-Barre] and, as a matter of fact, there's still factories in that building. It was called Kroger Dress. I had no intentions of moving off the floor 'cause I wanted the girls to hear and see. At any rate, he wouldn't resolve it. I walked over to the time clock, and I had told this woman who had called to tell me that the doors were off the washroom, "You pass the word that when they see me standing near the time clock you guys start coming to punch out." And he starts screaming, "Where you going? Where you going?" I said, "Put the doors back." All the time the girls were *ding*, punching out. "Put the doors back." *Ding, ding, ding, ding*, you know. Out the door they left and it was a picnic! What can I tell you? He put the doors back and the next day the girls went back to work. But the whole Valley was buzzing.

One time we were busy in Pittston organizing and along comes a car and Jimmy Boyle is in the car with a shop owner. He [Boyle] was the manager [of a shop]. He said, "I see you're busy, but you gotta come down and straighten something out in my shop. . . ." He said that I should get off the picket line and go with them to talk to the girls to straighten out whatever the hell, I don't remember what the issue was. This was a very legitimate shop.

Well, the girls were all keyed up about something. There was always problems with wages and piece rates. So I said to him, "I can't come now but I'll be in touch with you." [He said], "No, no. By the time you get in touch with me . . . [it will be too late]." He says, "Where do you think my girls [the workers] are now? [They are] out [at] Harveys Lake at my cottage!" He had a cottage at Harveys Lake.

"They said, 'We're not stayin' here [at work], we're goin' out to your [cottage].'" Everyone knows everything, you know. So they went out to Jimmy's cottage. He wasn't gonna chase them out of the shop because in a day or two they'd be back at work and you had to maintain relations. So they're at Jimmy's cottage swimming and having a ball and he has an empty factory because I didn't get down there in time to straighten out whatever had to be done.

It was a very interesting time and, as the union grew, I felt very badly about the people losing [work] time. The men weren't working. Times were very hard. [Representative] Dan Flood was promoting the Area Redevelopment Bill in Congress to get us help from the federal government.[17] Men were leaving town and going to Jersey and Maryland and other parts to get jobs. It was breaking up the fabric of the family because there were partings of the way after [a] while. The man is away from home, the women have the responsibility of the children and, actually, it was her income from the factory [that often kept the family going]. It bothered me very much that they should lose any [work] time, and there was always problems, always. When you have piecework and you make your living by the piece, the piece rates make a big difference.[18]

Q: Would the bosses try to cheat on the rates?

MM: Oh, how you set the piece rates, that's very tricky. You had very fast girls so they would set the piece rate [low] because, "See, she can do it." She's making what, three dollars a day, four dollars? But the slow ones [would suffer] so you couldn't set the piece rate by the fastest girls or the most skilled. You had to have an average. Naturally the employers would always have some girl to point to that she was making [a lot of money], and sure she was making it 'cause they all hustled and rushed. But, of course, you have differences in ability.

Then we had a lot of things in the [labor-management] agreement, like the Health Fund. It's like paying unemployment insurance to the government: they [employers] would wait and wait and wait until the government got after them and then they'd settle it for a fraction of what they should have paid. There were always tricks. We had the Health and Welfare [Fund]. Almost immediately we opened a Health Center for our people in Wilkes-Barre in 1948.[19] Our building is still there on Washington Street. Some local doctors were against it because they thought it was socialized medicine. We had the finest set of doctors and we tried in every way to help them [the members] maintain their health. All the important tests were done in the Health Center free to the members. I thought that if they [the employers] didn't pay into the Health Fund, the only way you could enforce it is by stopping the shop. It was always stopping the shop, stopping the shop.

In addition to making the work so rough for the handful [of business agents that] we had looking after things, the shops were spread out all over the Valley. I thought we'd have to find a way to keep everybody working while we settled the problems. On the piece-rate problem, there might be a temporary work stoppage right then and there on a particular problem, but on big issues like the Health Fund, that had to come from my office. [I might say], "Stop the shop; stop the shop."

Then there were problems in New York with the jobbers and the people who provided work. They [the New York ILGWU headquarters] would want us to stop our shops to enforce their part of the agreement and so on. So I thought, "Well, New York has an impartial chairman and we're not about to run to New York for every little grievance, even Health Fund grievances. We have to find an impartial chairman."

I talked to [Wilkes College president] Eugene Farley. We'd made friends at United Fund meetings and so on. He recommended to us Dr. Rosenberg, who was, I think, teaching economics [at Wilkes] and generally the kind of person that could function in that capacity. He agreed and he became our impartial chairman and we used to have cases three, four times a week before him. It helped a great deal to keep the shops on an even keel. He was accepted by the people [employees] and also by the employers. So he was a great help to us. . . .

Q: You held some twenty-four-hour strikes, didn't you?

MM: We had a twenty-four-hour picket line at Emkay. That shop had about three or four hundred workers in West Wyoming, on Eighth Street, the west end. Big factory. Clem [Lyons, chap. 9] worked in the Emkay.[20] There we had the kind of employer who . . . wanted to be loved by his people. He wanted them to feel that here was "The Great White Father" who was bringing them these marvelous chances to earn a living. He wanted to be acknowledged and accepted and catered to. The people weren't like that at all. Anyone who expects that kind of reaction in sewing factories is a little *fericked* because it's never that good.[21]

I don't care how good your agreement is and how much you earn, the work is hard. It's backbreaking, literally. In a sewing shop, when you sit hunched over a machine, or a pressing board, or a hand finisher, or whatever you do, it's hard work. Even when we reduced the hours from eight to seven, it's still hard work. So don't expect the employees to think you're the greatest because they never do. In many instances we had very fine employers, very fair, that tried very hard. It's also very hard to please a lot of people, you know.

Q: What was the big '58 strike about?

MM: The '58 strike was really New York–oriented. Now I can say it. The agreement expired and in New York they [the owners and the union] signed. They [the workers] went out and in a week they were back. But they [the union leaders] really didn't want to let us go back for all kinds of reasons, including the fact that we had gotten so big and we took a good chunk of their work.

Q: The wages were lower here, so was that part of the reason why you were getting more work?

MM: Yeah, well wages were lower but [we had] the good sewers and I was concerned for the people and the area because the mines were down. I told you the circumstances. I felt that we had paid our dues because we were no longer "NRA babies," you know, what they call NRA babies after the [National Recovery Administration] and the right to organize [in the mid-1930s]. After Roosevelt became president a lot of people joined unions.[22] But if you consider that we started [organizing in this region] in 1937 and by 1958 we had already been in the union for so many years, I felt we had as much right to it as anybody—to the work, to whatever.

But there's always within an organization people vying for power. Maybe they thought that I was trying to build up [power]. I never wanted anything and that's the truth. Like after the [1972 Tropical Storm Agnes] flood, people would say, "What's in it for you, Min?" I'd look at them because it was so abhorrent to me, the way I had been brought up, to think that anybody would use any situation for themselves. We had two children to bring up and we got very low pay from our union, we worked very hard, and we weren't in it to get anything for ourselves and we never did. We never would and it was the same with the [Agnes] flood [and the FVAC]. A lot of people did a lot of things, which to this day [bothers me]. We fought hard to get the people, to organize them, and to do the things that would call attention to our plight.

Q: How long were you on strike in 1958?

MM: We walked out on March 6, 1958. We were out about at least six weeks. As the weeks went on, it was rough. We had money. The money wasn't a problem. We paid some strike benefits. Of course, we couldn't compensate people for the wages they were losing but there was a lot involved. The way the union kept us out is because the employers' association [the Pennsylvania Garment Manufacturers Association (PGMA)] wouldn't sign. The employers' association here wouldn't sign the New York agreement. In the end, we had to organize a new employers' association under another name and get new officers, and they signed. But in the background was also the Mafia and the tough guys in New York who did not [want to sign], who wanted to give the union a fight. They wouldn't allow this association that they controlled here to sign. So the strike went on.

There was a lot going on in the background. We were going to try to break the hold that some of these tough guys had on this association, and I know of my own knowledge that they did. See, there's a lot of money in this industry and they [organized crime] put money in and they set up shops. I believe personally that they're still here. They had factories here. They were independent concerns. I don't even know if people like Bill [Cherkes, chap. 2] still [want] to talk about it.[23] You know what I mean? I've had people say to me, "Why are you always against so-and-so? He's the nicest man." Sure, they're nice. They can be very nice. They have the money and they're not uneducated.

We had a factory out in Sweet Valley that was owned by Three-Finger Brown [Thomas Lucchese], one of the top [Mafia] leaders in the country. He was called to testify before a U.S. Senate investigating committee [the McClellan Committee].[24]

We had a hard time organizing that shop because he had a son, Robert Brown. That was not his real name; that was an assumed name. He'd gone to West Point, I think. How the hell he [Lucchese] got him into West Point, I'll never know. But he [the son] came here and he went amongst the leaders of the area and he was eminently accepted. We were [not appreciated]: "Get out of here! Who needs these violent union people?" you know. As if *we* were the gangsters. Until we were so lucky that right in the middle of our fight, the Senate had this investigating committee and his father appeared before the committee and the people couldn't believe their ears. "How many people had been killed, how many people had been muscled, how many people had been bombed?" Do you know what I mean?

Q: Lucchese was from New York?[25]

MM: Yes, full regalia. There's the Gambino family [connection] and Three-Finger Brown was the key man [in the Lucchese family].[26]

Q: Did you ever unionize his shop?

MM: You're darn right we did [under a different owner]. It was one of our best shops. In 1958 they fought to the bitter end and we got rid of him. He had to leave. We used to think maybe he kept drugs or illicit money or whatever in the basement 'cause always that door was closed. You know, we used to invent a lot of stories.[27]

But the girls—the women were terrific. When they [the owners] tried to make deliveries, they [the workers] would be out there literally with pitchforks, brooms. They had made up signs themselves [saying] "The Black Hand," and they had a hand [imprint] on it. I had one of those signs; I kept it for years. They did it themselves. The Mafia was known as "The Black Hand," so they made up a sign with a black hand. "Go," you know, "leave."

But he [Lucchese] had a nice little thing in Sweet Valley. It's really a beautiful place. It's still there, in the heart of all that beauty, that restful country. With good workers he made money in that shop. Then in the '58 strike, he was one of those we got rid of. He sold. He finally sold the shop. Some closed up, you see? But none of these guys still to this day are willing to talk about what was really behind the strike. It was a try by the toughies to fight the union in a very secretive way, and we were the key. But we couldn't [tell the full story]. As much as I talked on radio every day, we never told the story.[28]

Q: Were you on radio just about every day during the strike?

MM: Every day during that strike. We were buying time. Little Bill Phillips welcomed us because we made the station very prominent. People would tune in on their automobiles going home. We took the time, between five and six [o'clock in the evening], and as some of the girls would say, "Everything stopped in our house." We took about a half hour. Sometimes I'd have a picket [line worker] as a guest.[29] Sometimes I'd have someone else. It depended on what we were up to. But it was a good period. Bill [Matheson] wrote all the speeches because I was busy out in the field, and by the time I'd get back to the office, he'd say, "Listen to this, Min." Then we'd go over it. I would fill him in [about] what happened here, what happened there. Or during the day [I'd] call in by telephone or we'd talk the night before on what we were going to pursue the next day. We were a good team, he and I. . . .

Q: Did the UMWA help you in your efforts? You mentioned that you were going to call Tom Kennedy.

MM: I don't know what Tom would have done. He was friendly to me. I was a woman and he was very polite. They were all very gallant, you know. But no, they didn't help us. I'll tell you who did help us: the Teamsters. At the time [ILGWU president David] Dubinsky was fighting with them. The Teamsters had withdrawn from the AFL-CIO. They were especially mad at Dubinsky for a speech he had made or something. Here [in the Wyoming Valley] we had Leo Namey, who was president of the Teamsters' local, and they would not deliver [materials]. Do you know what a difference it made to us in the strike? The Teamsters wouldn't deliver or would not pick up at all through our '58 strike. That wins your battle. In all these strikes down the line, he [Namey] said, "When Min's girls are on strike, nothing moves." That's what he said, and that's what they did. If it hadn't been for their help, I don't think we would have gotten as far as we did.[30]

Q: Why wasn't the UMWA more helpful?

MM: It's hard for me to explain. The leadership, of course. I finally met [District I president] August Lippi personally and talked with him. In my eyes, he was not a leader. Certainly not a Mother Jones.[31] Not a leader, even like I had known down southern Illinois, 'cause I lived in Chicago and I went down to southern Illinois during some of their labor troubles and I met a Freeman Thompson, George Voysey, [Glenn E.] Watts.[32] These were leaders. They were men out of the mines but they were with the people and they fought. Lippi was nothing. It wasn't the old years. There was no leadership. Kennedy was just a very nice, mild kind of a guy. Not a very inspiring speaker. It wasn't the Johnny Mitchell days—even within their own ranks.[33]

We went to get in [the viewing] line one day when one of the men had been killed in the [Knox] mine down there. His wife was a member of our Executive Board and this was out of respect, you know. We sent a wreath to the funeral and we went down, and when we came in we were surrounded by the miners and they said to me, "Why is your union so different? Do you see anybody here from our union [leadership]? Did they even call up and say anything to the widow? Do they even care?" These were the men talking to us. It was very painful and pathetic. I said, "Well maybe because we're mostly women that we act differently. A man was killed and he's an active member of our union; we wouldn't think of not coming down. . . ."[34]

Q: How did you relate to Wyoming Valley politicians?

MM: When we had our anniversary affairs, there was not a single important official in the county that didn't come, including the sheriff, the law enforcement officer in Sweet Valley. . . . But every judge came, every judge. Judge [Frank L.] Pinola was the head judge in the [Luzerne County] courthouse. He knew what we were doing in Pittston, and he was worried about our safety. He called. He came one time to my office personally to talk to me. Judge [J. Harold] Flannery [came]. Judge Lewis [came], who was Republican and we were Democrats. Everyone, I'm telling you, including the mayor [of Wilkes-Barre], everybody was for us. They admired what we were doing. We were very active in the community. We were active in the United Fund. We were active in the Red Cross donating blood. They could never have accomplished many of these things except that we took the leadership and told our people, "This we should do."

Q: Do you think they supported you in part because they knew you were organizing against gangsters in Pittston?

MM: No, I think they supported us because they thought it was good for the community, for the people to have an organization as good as ours that was so community-conscious and upped the earning of the people, which made it better for the community as far as income. They were *for* us.

Q: I believe that Luther Kniffen was the mayor of Wilkes-Barre at that time.

MM: Yeah. He was a friend of mine, and afterwards there was [Republican Party chairman Thomas A.] Evans.[35] Then there was [Mayor Frank] Slattery.[36] At our [ILGWU] twentieth- or twenty-fifth-anniversary affair, we had these big tables. Everybody was there. I don't think there was an important official [missing]. . . .

Q: Tell us about the ILGWU classes at Wilkes College.

MM: We had classes. I asked Dr. Rosenberg and Dean Farley if they would have classes for our people. They thought it was a great idea. I thought it was a great idea because to me college was something none of us could afford in our years. To be able to say that we're going to school at Wilkes College was a real feather in our cap. So they set up classes for us.

Q: Labor studies?

MM: Well, all sorts of things. And the women loved it. We kept that going for quite a long time. We got certificates [for them] and we had graduation and so on. We had our own little college education. . . .[37]

Q: What was your husband Bill's title within the union?

MM: He was the educational director for the state of Pennsylvania. He did a lot of traveling. He set up classes in different areas, he taught classes, he arranged for others to teach them. He got out these bulletins [newsletters] in different districts.

Q: How long did he serve in that position?

MM: From when he came [to Pennsylvania] in 1941. He was there [in Sayre] while I was still in New York. Marianne was born in '41, and we went to Sayre where Bill was working at the time. There was a big mill there, Blue Swan Mills, about six hundred people. He was the union representative. Later on in '44, they asked us whether we wouldn't go to Wilkes-Barre where there were so many shops unorganized, and then [they asked] later whether I wouldn't take time off from the children and just go back temporarily to help organize. I had been very active in New York, and I had been an officer of the union.[38] So there we were, leaving Sayre and moving to the Wilkes-Barre area in '44.

Q: Did he serve the entire state of Pennsylvania as educational director?

MM: He was on the road quite a bit. But he'd come back here [to Wilkes-Barre] since this was the home base. It was not so difficult, you know. You can go to Hazleton, Pottsville, Harrisburg, it's all within [reach]. Allentown, Easton, they're very close. You could go and come back the same day. He didn't have anything up Pittsburgh way. We had a local in Johnstown, finally, but not in the early years. So it was mostly here.

Q: Did you come here as a package?

MM: No. Bill was working on staff, and then one day, they [the union leaders] turned up at my house on Second Avenue [in Kingston] and they said [to me], "How's about getting someone to look out for the kids [and] go organizing for a while, temporary, 'til we clean up this mess down here." They knew there were a lot of [unorganized] shops, but they didn't know how bad it really was.[39]

We were lucky to get a housekeeper [when I went organizing], and she was good. That was our first one of many 'cause they never last. They always have boyfriends or other things. They come and they go. It was very difficult. There was no childcare at the time so we had a rough time of it. We hated to leave the children but organizing was in my blood.

Q: Do you recall your wage when you started?

MM: It was thirty-five dollars a week, which we were giving to a housekeeper. . . .

Q: Did you worry very much about your daughters?

MM: Oh yeah. It was very, very tough. If Bill wasn't the kind of person he was, I don't think we would have managed. I would have had to quit. Even then it was hard 'cause it's a long day and you're never free. Even when you're home, the telephone rings. If I went into town [i.e., downtown Wilkes-Barre], every two steps somebody stopped to talk—you know, Saturdays and Sundays. But they grew up very self-sufficient. When they were like six, they would call a taxi and go to town. They learned to do things on their own. They were really good kids. . . .

Q: You mentioned that at one time the ILGWU leaders in New York were somewhat afraid of you.[40]

MM: Well yes, I think they were afraid to rock the boat. I got a reputation for being unorthodox, if that's the word. If something needed to be done, I did it. There were still some shops that were nonunion from the time I was here, but they [the other ILGWU leaders] never went on organizing the way I did. I would never allow a shop to be nonunion. There was a group of shops, three shops owned by a man by the name of Rocky Schillaci. I know he was tied in with the mob in some fashion. I can't prove it but I'd say it to his face. His shops were nonunion and I'd like to know why. . . .[41]

Q: You mentioned that you had to relearn certain things when you first came to northeastern Pennsylvania.

MM: Well, you know, I was an extremist. I come out of Chicago. The Haymarket case was very fresh in everybody's minds.[42] We hated the courts. We hated the judges. We hated the police, especially we hated them. We had certain procedures for keeping ourselves pure trade unionists. We would not sit down and break bread with an employer. We would not participate with elected officials who were not pro-union. When I came here, it was a totally different thing because this is a small community. A woman who worked in the shops had brothers on the police force. People in the ranks had fought and worked hard to elect officials that were from their family. It wasn't a big city where a Capone mob controlled the Chicago courts and cops and tried to take over the unions.[43]

And so I had to start from scratch sort of, to accept the fact that the cop on the corner was related to a girl in a factory, that the Chamber of Commerce president was really concerned with the standards and livelihood of our workers, that the officials of [the] Red Cross were not just meeting with me because they were mercenary but because they really had some compassion and felt for the people. The community here was so different [from] anywhere I had ever lived. It was good in a sense that I came here and unlearned, or relearned, and added to my knowledge an acceptance of people on their own terms, not on a theory, you know, but on principle.

Q: After your retirement you tried to get back into the union as a part-time organizer.

MM: Well, Bill had prostate cancer diagnosed in 1980. He had a bad heart, he had Parkinson's. He had a lot of things physically but his mind was good. He had, you know, an exceptionally fine mind, a sort of photographic memory, he could remember so much. But then gradually his mind started going, and in the end when he died, he had Alzheimer's.

But I kept him home from 1980 and he died in '87. He only spent eight months in the nursing home. I couldn't take care of him anymore [so I had] to send him to the nursing home. I needed a lot of money, $2,400 a month. And I had used up all my savings—all of it. So the [Luzerne County] Bureau of Aging said, "Well it's all right, you go on welfare and we'll pay half and you pay half, if you have anything." But I had nothing. I didn't have a car. I didn't own a home. They would take that you know. But I didn't have anything for them to take.

And I had very little in the bank at the time. I was just barely able to meet my own living expenses. And to pay for Bill's nursing home . . . you know nursing homes, you buy them underwear and socks and things and the next time you come, it's gone. What can you do about it? Every week I was spending six, seven dollars. You may think it's a trifle, but you try spending that every week and still when they'd sometimes bring him by ambulance to the doctor who took care of his prostate condition, he'd have no shirt, no underpants, no socks, just

FIG. 10 | Min Matheson designed this label as director of the Union Label Department, circa 1965. It remained the union label until the ILGWU merged with the ATWU in 1995. Photo courtesy of the Kheel Center, Cornell University.

a rough pair of pants and an overshirt and it would infuriate me. Every week I was buying supplies. Well, they pay people in those nursing homes very little, the help, and I guess they just took it.

Q: Do you have a pension from the union?

MM: Yeah, I have a small pension from the union. It's not that great, no. I manage now. But I have to be very careful. I have to pay rent, I have to pay for heat and light and gas and insurance and food and clothes, you know. And bottled water, because you can't drink this contaminated water.[44] And my own medical expenses, so that I just about manage.

Q: So you talked to New York officials in 1982?

MM: I was told that I had to go on welfare and I didn't like the idea at all. After all, we had worked all our lives. We've never even collected unemployment insurance once. And now I'm gonna go on welfare? So I went to New York to see one of the top [ILGWU] officials and see if there wasn't some way we could work something out, and in spite of the fact that my own health was not that good I was willing to do part-time work for the union. Matter of fact, I had heard from people in this area [i.e., garment workers] who would call up from time to time to complain to me about conditions in the shops, which I didn't interfere with because there was no way I could do anything for them. But generally speaking, I thought it wouldn't hurt if they'd put me on part-time and paid fairly decently

MINNIE "MIN" MATHESON

so that then I could take care of Bill. There wasn't gonna be any extras for me, but I would just not have to go on welfare.

I thought it would serve a dual purpose. First, it would keep me off welfare: if Bill ever knew he was on welfare . . . He was a very proud Scotsman and he would never like that. But more than that, it would do something for the shops, because in our own way, we had established a certain relationship with the people and with the employers, and I felt it would do good.

Since the impact of the imports, it seems as if every complaint a girl makes . . . well, you know, is about the imports. Now that should not be used as an excuse not to enforce conditions and not to organize. I told our officials in New York that, and they listened and they were sympathetic, but then they wouldn't do it. I thought I was offering them a lot to at this age, to want to go back part-time on the staff and do what I could. I talked and talked with one of our top officials. He finally called me back and he told me they couldn't do it. They considered it.

Q: Why do you think they didn't want you to come back?[45]

MM: Well, I think they're sort of complacent and they're not looking for trouble, if you know what I mean. I feel just the opposite. I feel that a union has to constantly be on its toes and force conditions to see that the employers live up to their agreement, and the girls have pride in their organization. Otherwise the whole concept of unionism just withers and dies, and I wouldn't want to see that. . . .[46]

Q: Do you have a sense that conditions have gone downhill in the union?

MM: Oh yes, very much so, because people call me but I'm not able to help them. Oh, they're mad at some representative of the union or the manager of the union. They're mad at the boss and they're complaining, "These aren't the old days."[47]

4

Angelo "Rusty" "Bill" DePasquale

Mineworker and ILGWU Organizer and "Enforcer"

A "tough guy" in his own way, former coal miner Angelo DePasquale served as the ILGWU's enforcer and point man in several unionization drives. He was a defender of working-class rights without being actively ideological, and his presence and methods showed that the ILGWU realized the need for "muscle" to protect itself from organized crime and other untoward influences. His admonishment by union president David Dubinsky over a strike-related shooting incident pointed to the delicate relationship between the New York and Pennsylvania union offices and between organized criminals and ILGWU leaders. Although he was strongly committed to Min Matheson and organized labor, in the end he could not get over Dubinsky's chastisement. His plainspoken and forthright narrative reveals the importance of oral history in gathering information not usually included in the printed record.

AD: Angelo is my real name. Rusty is a nickname. I'll tell you another thing—they all know me by Bill. All the workers at the strikes we pulled, like even Minnie [Min Matheson, chap. 3], she knew me by Bill. . . .

Q: Tell us how you started working with the ILGWU.

FIG. 11

Angelo "Rusty" "Bill" DePasquale, 1993. Photo courtesy of the Northeastern Pennsylvania Oral and Life History Collection, Pennsylvania State University.

Angelo DePasquale, from an audio-recorded interview with Robert P. Wolensky conducted at Mr. DePasquale's home in Yatesville, Pennsylvania on July 23, 1993. The interview is is included in the Wyoming Valley Oral History Project, which is one of eight projects within the Northeastern Pennsylvania Oral and Life History Collection housed in the Eberly Family Special Collections Library, Penn State University Libraries.

AD: Well, how the hell did I get started? She came to me. I don't know if it was at a dance; it must have been at a union dance or somethin' because I used to go to all these dances and maybe one of the girls introduced me to Minnie. It happened somethin' like that.[1] She asked me about Pittston. Well, I was from there. Pittston is only a mile from here [his home in Yatesville]. She asked me if I would go along helpin' her to try to organize this [town]. [I said], "Well, if I could do somethin' . . . [I would]." What the hell did I know about union organizing or anything like that? Organizing, I didn't know. So she talked and, well, I did it—I went [to work for her]. I met her and we went to Pittston, and she showed me the shop [they were organizing at the time] and everything else. Then she sent me out organizing some of the girls that I knew who worked in that shop, to try to get them signed up.[2]

Q: What shop was it?

AD: Charlie Gretna's. So anyway, you went out there and you started organizing. I think she was doin' this right after the war [World War II]. We had a little trouble with the police in Pittston.

Q: What happened?

AD: Well, see, I was sort of a nutty bachelor. I wouldn't take no shit from nobody, you know. But anyhow, the girls are walkin' up and down with the [picket] signs and the cops were there. And there were a couple of wise guys [hoodlums] that was workin' there with this Needlepoint [Needle Workers' Association].[3] They came over and razzed the girls and all that shit. I said to the guys—they knew me from Yatesville—and I said, "Now look, let the girls alone because you are goin' to get it one of these days."

Two cops come over. I had a guy organizing with me by the name of Johnny Justin [chap. 7] who was from New York.[4] He was a Jewish kid, Jewish folk. Anyhow, two cops come over and they grab Minnie and they grabbed this guy [Justin] and threw them in the car. When I saw that, the way they mistreated Minnie, I ran over to the car and one guy—one cop who was Irish—I grabbed him and I pulled him out of the car and I even cursed at him—everything. I said, "You son of a bitch, you don't do that to a woman! I'll punch you right in the mouth." And then the other cop got out a club. Some of the girls got in between [us]. They took Minnie and Johnny Justin for a hearing. So we had a little trouble there. From there we went to Edwardsville [Anita Dress]—we pulled a strike there, and I had trouble with the scabs down there.[5]

Q: Tell us about that strike.

AD: Well, I get hit over the head with the club by one of the cops. There was a fight with a couple of the girls who were workin' there and their husbands come to pick them up. They [the husbands] started a squabble, ya know, they started arguin' and all. I start swingin'—whatever the hell happened. The cops were there, and they were watchin' me because they knew, they figured I was a troublemaker. Not that I was a troublemaker, but I was really fightin' for the union. One of the cops said to me, he said, "I'll get you one of these days." And he did. That was his opportunity to hit me over the head with a club.

Q: You were hit by the Edwardsville police?

AD: Yeah. So they locked me up. They brought me in [to the local jail] for a little while. Then Minnie come to see me. She was new here, you know, she didn't even know about lawyers or anything like that. She said to me, "Bill, where could I get a good lawyer?" I gave her the name of Dan Flood. At the time, he was a lawyer; he was a good lawyer, one of the best. So she got him and I'll never forget [what happened].

I'm locked up downstairs and Dan Flood come down with the chief of police. Flood asked me, "What's your name?" and all that, and I told him. He said, "What are you doin' here?" I said, "You ask *him* what I'm doin' here." I said, "You see, my ear is still bleeding. When he hit me, he cut my ear." I said, "They hit me over the head two weeks ago, too." "Yeah?" [he said]. I said, "Yeah, well, there it is." So he says to the cop, "What is he doing here?" The cop said, "I got him charged for startin' a riot." Dan Flood said, "Well, who do you have that he started the riot with?" The cop was all messed up, you know, the chief. He released me right there and then. . . .

He [Dan Flood] was number one. She [Min Matheson] called him up and he come down that night. Ten minutes, he wasn't there ten minutes! They let me out and they dropped all charges. He sent Minnie a bill for $200. At that time, $200 was big money, right? Minnie was just startin' [out] and she figured if she'd sent that bill to [ILGWU president David] Dubinsky she's gonna get hell or something, so she called me up. She said, "Bill, my god, you know what? That Mr. Flood sent me a bill for $200 for five minutes' work." She said, "Oh, my god, I don't know what's gonna happen with it." She was squawkin' about it. She was talkin' about what Dubinsky would say to her. "You asked me about a good lawyer so I got you the lawyer," I said. But that was what he charged. She paid it. That was big money, what the hell, for a couple minutes' work? Jesus Christ! But he was a number one man, Dan Flood. He was a smart boy. . . .

But before that, one night I got called up. It was about three o'clock in the morning. It was when we had that strike goin' on down there [Edwardsville]. I got called up by my two guys. I had two guys there watchin' that shop. This is about three o'clock in the morning they call me up and said, "Bill, come down. There is a truck here loadin' stuff." I said, "Well, stop them." They said, "Well, we're here." They were afraid, you know. So anyhow, I went down and when I'm goin' across the Market Street Bridge [from Wilkes-Barre toward Edwardsville], I see a truck comin' by, but I wasn't sure what truck it was. So I went to the strike headquarters [in Edwardsville] and I asked them what kind of truck it was. They described it. One of the guys was another Jewish fellow. He was workin' there, he was watchin' there.

Q: What was his name, do you remember?

AD: I remember his name because he had the same name as a ballplayer at the time—Bill Page, his name was Bill Page. I said, "Well, Bill, why didn't you [stop the truck]?" He was six foot six inches; he was a big, heavy, brawny-lookin' guy, right? "No," he said, "You can't fool around with guys like that. You don't know who they are and they might have guns." I said, "Get in the car. I want you to make sure that we have the right truck." So we went up to [Route] 115 towards the Effort Mountain [the road to New York City]. I followed the route and sure enough [we found the truck]. It was snowin' and all. I tried to pull the truck aside. I wanted to get that truck back to Edwardsville and unload it and burn the truck, whatever, you know, or distribute the clothes to the poor people. I was gonna do that but he kept pushin' me back over [off the road] so I couldn't [stop him]. He had a big truck, where was I gonna go?

We went as far as the Effort Mountain and we come back. So I said to this Bill Page, I said, "Bill, you son of a bitch. Don't you say anything to Minnie about this," because Minnie was of the notion that I was a little too rough sometime and that I took too many chances. So [he said], "No, no, no, Bill." He was afraid. "No, no, I won't say nothin'."

That morning about ten o'clock I get a call. [It was Minnie] and she said, "Bill, come down. You have to drive me to New York." I said, "Alright, I'll be right down." I get down [to the main office in Wilkes-Barre] and she said again we have to go to New York. She said, "Dave Dubinsky wants to talk to us." Dave Dubinsky—that was the president of the union. David Dubinsky!

So I said, "What's up?" She said, "Well, what did you do this morning?" I said, "That son of a bitch." She said, "What are you talkin' about." I said, "Bill [Page] must have [told you]." She said, "No, no, no, no. Well, what happened?" [So I said], "I went up and I tried to get the truck to come back. He ditched me. I couldn't get him back," and all that. She said, "But you were shootin' at the truck?!" I said, "Shootin' at the tires, tryin' to get him to come back. I was drivin'. I was tryin' to do that because he [Bill] wouldn't take the gun to shoot the tire." So anyhow, [I said], "I couldn't hit him [in the tires] because I was drivin' and he was pushin' me off to the side," and all that shit. "I had to turn around and come back."

Yeah. That's why we were called to New York. At the time, Frank Costello was a head in the Mafia. I believe he called Dubinsky up and said, "If your boys want to play that way there, we'll start playin' that way, too," you know.[6] So that's why I was called into Dubinsky's office. When we got into Dubinsky's office, he had guards. He was powerful, that son of a bitch. Got a big cigar—the cigar was that long. (gestures) I had to sit there [waiting]. Minnie went into his office, then two guards come out and they said to me, "Alright, you're wanted in."

They brought me in. He says, "So you're DePasquale?" I said, "Yes sir." [Before we went in] Minnie said to me, "Please, Bill." She knew I had a hot temper. She said, "Please, Bill, don't argue with him. Whatever [he says], it's just, 'yes,' and [go along with] whatever he says." So anyhow, I got in there and I was "yessing" him. He said, "Billy DePasquale?" I said, "Yes sir." He said, "Who am I?" Ya know, wise guy, ya know what I mean? "Who am I!?" I said. "You're David Dubinsky." [He said], "What am I?" just like that. "Well, you're the president of the ILGWU." "OK," he said. "Well, who gives the orders around here? Do I give orders or do you do what you want to do?"

Well, I was stuck there. He said, "Answer me." I could've choked the son of a bitch. "So," I said, lookin' [at him], "Minnie put me there, head of the strike headquarters." I said, "And when they were takin' the clothes out of there, I tried . . ." He interrupted me: "No," he said. "What were you doing? Why were you going after the truck? What did you do to the truck?" I said, "Well, I wanted to get the truck back to Edwardsville so I could distribute the clothes to the poor people that needed them." I said, "It was a scab truck and Minnie put me at the head of the strike and I thought I'd take it over." He said, "Any time that anything like that is done," he said, "I'll tell you what to do." I couldn't answer. What was I gonna say? He said, "You're dismissed."[7]

"OK," I thought, "You son of a bitch!" I went out and Minnie stayed in there for a little while. She come out and she was all smiles. She said, "He likes you. He said, 'Boy, he's gotta a lot of guts. Make sure you hold onto that man.'" In other words, he wanted me to know that he was the boss, and yeah, I had to take orders from him. Well, I went on for a couple months. I was workin' in the coal mines and [also] helpin' Minnie. I wasn't steady [full-time with the ILGWU]. I mean, she paid me.

Well, then I knew this vice president—his name was Bill Ross, a vice president of the ILG. Him and me were pretty close. We met different times, and they all liked me because I had lots of guts. This one morning Minnie calls me up. She said, "What are you doin', Bill?" I said, "Nothin,' why?" She said, "Come down. Somebody here to see you." So I went down [to the district's main office in Wilkes-Barre] at about eleven o'clock and who was there but this Bill Ross.

Well, he grabbed me. I said, "Bill, what the hell's up? What are you doin'?" He said, "You're in [good with Dubinsky]." [I said], "Nope," because I already knew from when Minnie told me [that Dubinsky liked me], and I said [to her then], "I'll get even with that son of a bitch Dubinsky." I said, "One of these days," you know. "Nah," she said. "Don't be like that. He likes you." I said, "Never mind. The way he talked to me? Nobody talks to me that way." I said, "I held my temper on account of you [Min Matheson]. If not, I'd have told him to go to hell right off." I told her [at that time], I said, "I'll get even with him."

So this time, this day here, when Bill Ross come down, he said to me, "You're in." I said, "No kidding. What do you mean?" He said, "Well, he [Dubinsky] wants you to go to Rochester [New York] because there are a lot of Italian people there and we can get them shops organized. We have a guy that looks like Sid

FIG. 12 | ILGWU president David Dubinsky (*right*) with UMWA president John L. Lewis (*left*), 1945. Photo courtesy of the Kheel Center, Cornell University.

Caesar—you look just like Sid Caesar—and he's a double [too]."[8] He said, "He's gonna organize with you and that's gonna be an honor." I said, "Oh yeah? Well, whose idea was it?" "Oh," he said, "Dave's." I said, "No kiddin'." I said, "Well, you know what? I hate to say this but will you tell Dave to shove it up his ass, because I'm not goin'." "Bill," he said, "don't talk that way about Mr. DD [David Dubinsky]."

Yeah, Minnie was goin' crazy. "Now Bill, wait a minute, wait a minute." I said, "No—didn't I tell you that I'd get even with him?" I said, "Well, now, I got even with him." [Bill Ross said], "Jeez, I can use ya." "You don't have to use me," I said. "You know I never wanted to be here. I was helpin' you [Min Matheson] out. I helped you out. I even went to jail for you. But nobody talks to me that way." I said, "I just don't worry about it."

FIG. 13 | Modesto "Murph" Loquasto. Anthracite Needle Workers' Association manager and alleged member of organized crime, circa 1958. Photo from U.S. Department of the Treasury, *Mafia: The Government's Secret File on Organized Crime* (New York: HarperCollins, 2007).

So anyhow, that was the end of it. That was the end of me workin' for the ILG. But, in fact, I drove Bill Ross around [that day]. He said, "Well, will you do me a favor, will you drive me to Hazleton? I have to go to Hazleton." "Yeah, I'll drive you up there, why not?" So he begged me on the way there to organize for him but I said, "Nah, I'm through, that's it." . . .

I was only with her a couple years. I wasn't steady because I worked in the mines, too. She called me different times [after that] to help her out. I said, "No, Minnie, I told you I quit and I'd forget about it." She asked me about some guy from Pittston, Murph [Modesto] Loquasto. He belonged to the Mafia, I guess. I don't know. He was a rough guy. Murph and I were pretty [close]. He's dead now, but anyhow, he wouldn't take no shit from nobody either and she asked me one time, I'll never forget it, she said, "Well, Bill, how about this Murph Loquasto?" She said, "He was down here after me to hire him, you know to organize." I said, "He's a good man. He's got a lot of guts. A guy like him, you know, the guts he's got." I said, "For him to do somethin' like that, go ahead and put him on." So she put him on. I don't know what the hell happened after that.

Q: Did Mrs. Matheson hire him as an organizer?

AD: Yeah, later on, for how long, that I don't know. She put him on for a while or whatever happened, I don't know.[9] That was it. What else could I tell you? . . .

Q: What about this other garment union?

ANGELO "RUSTY" "BILL" DEPASQUALE

AD: They went by the Needle Workers [i.e., the Anthracite Needle Workers' Association of Pennsylvania]. Nick Benfante was the manager.[10] They were startin' their own union and they wanted to take over because we [the ILGWU] had the girls organized. They thought they could step in because they knew this guy that ran the shop, Nick Alaimo.

Q: Was that union successful?

AD: Nah, nah, they never got many members, no. Tell you the truth, he [Nick Benfante] called me in while a strike was goin' on, and he thought he was a big shot—big Mafia—whatever the hell. He must have been under Russ Bufalino. But a guy come to me one time, a guy that was born and raised with me in this town. I knew him pretty good, you know. He come to me and he said, "Rusty, Nick [Benfante] wants to talk to you." I said, "Talk to me about what? What do I know?" He said, "He just asked me to [ask you]. He knows I know you good. He wants to just talk to you, so c'mon." We go up to Nick's office. He had his office right across from the [ILGWU] headquarters [in Pittston]. "C'mon," he said, so we went up.

Nick shook my hand and all that shit and he said, "Well, what are you doin' with that union [ILGWU]?" I said, "What do you mean, 'What am I doin' with that union?' I'm helpin' that union. Why, what's the matter with that union?" He said, "Well, I'm startin' the Needle Workers' Association. Why don't you go along with me?" He said, "Why don't you work with me? We could take that shop over." I said, "You're not doin' no such a thing. We're as far as we are and we're goin' to stay that far. We're gonna go further than that. Don't you bother me." That's the way it was. So I walked out on him. That was it with him.

Q: Mrs. Matheson was trying to organize all these shops in Pittston at that time, correct?

AD: Yeah, and she got them. She got them organized, yeah, sure.

Q: She got them, but who was usually against her? Was it these tough guys?

AD: Yeah, that's it.

Q: Do you have any other memories of working with her?

AD: Well, we pulled out a shop down in Plymouth one time. Minnie tells me that we had the shop goin' pretty good, and then she said to me one day, "You know, Bill, they sent a bunch of guys in from New York, a bunch of cutters and they're cuttin' the material for different shops." I knew where the shop was so I went down there and I knocked on the door. Somebody come to the door and when they saw me, they [tried to close it]. I put my foot in and said, "Wait a minute." I could see that they had machines down there where they were cuttin'. I said, "What are you doing? What are you doing?" [He said], "Well, we're sittin' in here." I said, "Be out of here before eight o'clock tonight or you're gonna get blown the hell out of here." That was it. I walked away. They were gone. I don't know if the Mafia sent them in or who sent them in, but the next day there was nobody around. They took the machines and everything out. I mean that was the action I had, you know.[11]

Q: Mrs. Matheson must have really relied on you for certain things.

AD: Oh Jesus, yeah, yeah. Another time, in Pittston there were a few people that was givin' us a lot of trouble, goin' to work [during a strike] and all that shit. So I got a couple of the boys and I told them, I said, "You know what? Give 'em a little scare." And so they followed their car one day and the people never came back to work anymore. You know, things like that happened. We had to get rough, too, at the time. Those girls were comin' to work, they were comin' in, and I had a couple of my boys [scare them]. They would do anything for me. [I said to them], "Lookit, just follow 'em, find out where they live, and just tell 'em to keep away from work or they're gonna get hurt." And they did, and the girls never showed up for work. That's why we won some of these strikes, you know. Had them put the pressure on some of 'em.

Q: So Min Matheson and the union could count on you to be tough sometimes?

AD: Yeah. Oh yeah. She'd give me hell. She'd say, "Now you're gettin' a little too rough." She did, but that's what she wanted. . . . Did you read the *Reader's Digest* story about Minnie? Now she calls me up that night. She said, "Bill, did you get the *Reader's Digest*?" I never bothered, shit, why? She said, "Well, come down, I want to talk to you." So I go down. I had a buddy with me and I said, "Come on, take a ride, I have to go down to Minnie's. I don't know what the hell she wants."

She gives me the magazine and said, "Read this." I read it. [She said], "Now is that right?" I said, "What do you mean, is it right?" "It is right?" [she said]. It was about her and the Mafia, that she fought the Mafia. "The Lady that Fought the Mafia," or something.[12] She said, "I feel hurt. They don't have your name. You're the one that fought the Mafia, not me!" She felt bad about it. She said, "You should have been in here, not me. Why me? You're the one that did all the work for me."

They [the organized criminals] knew it because they knew they were fightin' me, the whole goddamned gang. That's why she felt hurt. I'll never forget that time. "Did you read that, 'The Lady and the Mob [*sic*; Gangsters]'? The truth is that you fought them, not me," she said. "I was the backup person." But she sure had a lot of guts. Minnie had a lot of nerve. Nobody was backin' her up on nothin'. She was a fighter. She was a fighter. In fact, her brother got killed, you know. Yeah, in a telephone booth [in New York]. . . .[13]

Q: Were you ever threatened by the tough guys?

AD: No, well, not that it bothered me, you know. They might have. One guy came to me one time and he said, "You better get out of Pittston." I said, "Nobody is chasin' me out of Pittston." Nothin' was ever done. In fact, I had a couple guys that [would help me out]. One time, somebody come to me. He said, "There's a couple of strangers in Pittston from New York," while a strike was goin' on.

ANGELO "RUSTY" "BILL" DEPASQUALE

So I said to the boys, to my boys—who were always hangin' around Pittston, so they knew most of the Pittston gang—I said, "There's a couple of strangers in town. Get rid of the sons-a-bitches," and they did. A couple days after, they were gone, those strangers were gone.

Q: How did they get rid of them?

AD: Whatever happened, I don't know.

Q: Just threaten them?

AD: They must have. They [the strangers] must have either found out that we were after them, or something' like that, but they disappeared. They [my boys] come to me a couple a days after and said, "They're gone, Rusty." "OK," and that was it.

Q: Who were "your boys?"

AD: Some of my boys from Yatesville. Both of them are dead now.

Q: Buddies from way back?

AD: Yeah, yeah. They wouldn't take no shit from anybody either, you know.

Q: So it took that kind of toughness?

AD: Yeah, yeah. You had to, at the time. It was worse, I mean it. No matter where you went, they're fightin' you. All these shops, even in Wilkes-Barre one time, they were. This one big [union] shop in Wilkes-Barre, I even forget the name of it, but Minnie tells me they were sendin' this work into this scab shop in Pittston that we were organizing. So I went down to them [the Wilkes-Barre shop] and I told them who I was, and I told them what we were doin'. The owner said, "Yeah." I said, "You stop sendin' work up to them." He said, "No, no we're not." I said, "Don't give me that shit. Just stop and don't give them no more work," and that was it. And that was it! They didn't get any more work. You had to do things like that. I would do it, you know. It must have went a long ways because we got a lot of shops organized.

Q: How many shops were there in Pittston during this time?

AD: The Lee [Manufacturing Company], we organized. There were two, three, oh Christ, must have organized about four or five in that time, when she [Min Matheson] first come in.

Q: Did the tough guys own most of those shops?

AD: Yeah, that's all it was. There was all Mafia, the sons-a-bitches. Sure, they still run them. Yeah.[14]

Q: There's a guy named Dominick Alaimo. Did you know Nick?

AD: That's the guy [who wanted to bring] the Needle Workers [Association] to his shops. There were three brothers who owned the shops—Sammy, Willy, and Nick. [Nick] Benfante was the organizer [of the Needle Workers Association]. I worked for Sammy.[15] He was organized [under the ILGWU] at the time. Sure he was. Why not? . . .

Q: Why was the mob in the garment industry?

AD: Big money—that was big money for them. You know this Bufalino? I heard he used to get five dollars a dress [kickback] no matter where the shop was. That was his cut no matter who had the shop. In Pittston, maybe Scranton, Wilkes-Barre, maybe Luzerne County, I don't know. A dozen things you hear. I don't know how true it is. I really don't know.

Q: Do you think most of the shops were influenced by the mob?

AD: Yeah, shit, yeah.

Q: Even in Nanticoke and Kingston and Wilkes-Barre?

AD: No, no, no. I don't know about them down there. Just around this section [Pittston]. Even Edwardsville, I don't think Edwardsville was either.[16] You know, from Port Griffith down.[17]

Q: Why did you want to do these things for Min Matheson?

AD: Why did I want to help her? Like I said, Minnie asked me to help her. "Will you help me start Pittston?" [she said]. Because I was from Pittston, I went along with her. I said, "Alright, what do you want me to do?" She gave me an idea what to do, to organize and just sign the girls up and talk to them, and go talk to the people that work for the shops and stuff like that. That's how I got into it.

Q: Were you a strong union backer before then?

AD: Yeah, I was always in the union with the coal miners. Sure. I worked with labor unions most of my life. [I belonged to the] construction [union]. Even before Minnie, I was always union, since I was a kid. . . .

Q: Why were you carrying a gun that day with the truck incident?

AD: Oh, well, I always carried a gun in the car, Christ, you know. Not to kill anybody, that's for sure. Nah, nah. For protection because you don't know. It was tough them days, Christ yeah, especially when you're muckin' around with the Pittston gang.

Q: Did you ever use your gun with the ILGWU again?

AD: Nah, no, no. That was the only time. I happened to have it in the trunk of the car and I thought, "Well, you son of a bitch." Like I say, I wanted to get the truck back [to Edwardsville] but never knowin' that it was a Mafia truck. I wanted to give the gun to this Bill Page because he's sittin' on the [passenger] side. He had shoulders that were this wide on him, *(gestures)* and when I started shootin', he got under the dash. He was a big sucker. He was six foot six inches. He crawled in under the dash. I had a Packard [automobile], you know. "Please, Billy [stop]," he was goin' on. "You son of a bitch," I said, "get down."

I tried to give him the gun. I wanted to give him the gun. He says, "No, no, no, no, no." He was afraid to even look at the gun. So I had to shoot over his shoulders. And drivin'. The guy [in the truck] was pushin' me over and it was snowin', and the road was only a two-lane highway. I think it's still a two-lane. That's all it is, a two-lane goin' up [Route] 115 to Mount Effort [toward New York]. He pushed me over. So I had this son of a bitch of a gun. I couldn't do anything with it so then when I got to about Mount Effort, I turned around and come

ANGELO "RUSTY" "BILL" DEPASQUALE

back. That's when we got called in that morning, but I didn't know why. I didn't know it was a Mafia truck. . . .

Q: Did Mrs. Matheson miss you when you left?

AD: Well, yeah. She called me a few times to help her out.

Q: Who took your place as organizer?

AD: She had different women.

Q: Did any of them do the kinds of things you did?

AD: No, but they . . . I don't know. They kept organizing. They got their shops. Maybe I was too goddamned much? I don't know the hell of it. I really went all out for her, you know. Like she'd even be givin' me hell. One time she asked me to do something and I said, "Alright, I'll burn that son of a bitch's car." [She said], "Don't you dare, don't you!" I said, "I'll get rid of him and burn the goddamned car." She said, "No, no, please, please, please."

Q: Would you have done it?

AD: Well, not me. The boys, the boys [would have]. I'd have the boys do it, you know what I mean? Them boys. And all I'd do is buy them a meal once in a while. They never wanted any money. They were good buddies of mine. They were just two rough bastards, I'm tellin' you. They didn't give a goddamn for nobody. They were really rough guys.

Q: Were you raised with them?

AD: Yeah. They were two or three years younger than I was. I was like their leader. . . .

Q: What are your thoughts about Min Matheson and the union today?

AD: She was a good woman, she was. The way that she talked, the way she spoke to people, the way she treated me. She'd do anything for me, you know. She was a good woman, a good woman. Minnie would come to me. She would come up to the house. She'd have dinner with me—her and her sisters. Yeah, we were close. I went down to see her a few times but then when she died, I didn't know what the hell happened. I heard about it after [later]. I don't know what happened or where I was. I said, "Holy Jesus Christ, of all people." . . .

Once we got started maybe she must have thought, "Well, hey, this is the right man for me," you know. Whatever shops she wanted to pull [out on strike], I was there to pull them, and I was there to fight them. Even Edwardsville, [where] the cop said, "I'll get you." I said [to him], "Hey, you'll get yours." And [I added], "Another thing—I'm not from New York, I'm right from here in Luzerne County." I said, "You're not bullshittin' me." To the chief, this was. He said, "I'll get you for that remark," and he did, the son of a bitch. He waited for the chance. I got it good. One of the scabs' husbands, he give me a shove or somethin' and I nailed him one. I knocked him right on his ass. "You son of a bitch, [I said to him]." That's what the cop was waitin' for. Bang! I felt it right across the head, my ear. Not that he knocked me out or anything but he hit me on the head and swiped my ear. My ear was all cut up. Then they grabbed me, a couple cops grabbed me, and they said, "We got you now!"[18]

5

Anthony "Tony" D'Angelo
Garment Presser and Barber

Anthony D'Angelo delivers his narrative with humor, irony, and panache. A forthrightly honest storyteller, he does not mind shocking the interviewer (and the reader) with tales of double-dealing, arson, and police corruption—as well as his involvement with a criminally related person. His laudatory evaluations of one garment employer (William Cherkes, chap. 2) speak to the often harmonious relationships between labor and management that carried well beyond the shop floor. Like virtually all local apparel workers, he displays a wide knowledge of the industry, the ILGWU, and many of the associated individuals.

FIG. 14
Anthony "Tony" D'Angelo, 1988. Photo courtesy of the Northeastern Pennsylvania Oral and Life History Collection, Pennsylvania State University.

Anthony "Tony" D'Angelo, from audio-recorded interviews with Robert P. Wolensky conducted at Mr. D'Angelo's home in West Pittston, Pennsylvania, on December 18, 1988, and with Robert P. Wolensky and Kenneth C. Wolensky conducted at Mr. D'Angelo's home on February 17, 1994. These interviews are included in the Wyoming Valley Oral History Project, which is one of eight projects within the Northeastern Pennsylvania Oral and Life History Collection housed in the Eberly Special Collections Library, Penn State University Libraries.

AD: So Sam Alaimo had a dress factory in Pittston. His brother, Dominick, was working for him and [one day] Dominick says, "Sam, I want to start my own dress factory." Sam says, "You're crazy. You've got everything right here. You don't start your own dress factory." He says, "You don't have the women, you don't have the girls to start with, you don't have the contacts in New York. How are you gonna do that?" Dominick says, "Well, I want to start my own."[1]

They were brothers. So Sam said again, "You can't. Number one, 'they' won't allow you." "They"—the people in New York, in

[New] Jersey.[2] So the guy there says [to Sam], "He can't do that, your brother; he can't do that. Tell your brother he can't operate. He can't open." Well, his brother was what we call *capatosta*—he's hardheaded.[3] This brother is hardheaded and he goes and opens up a storefront [garment shop] anyway, like a gypsy.

Well, his store finally opens and he hires twenty girls. He pirates twelve from someplace [plus] special operators. They were important, special operators. They did the zippers, they did certain types of hemming, they did clamps, they did clasps, they did all special operation, not just regular sewing. They were hard to find so you had to go pirate them. [If] they were getting $1.15 an hour from "Johnny," then "Chucky" gave them $1.17 an hour to come and work for him. If "Chucky" is giving them $1.17 an hour, then "Johnny" would promise them $1.18 an hour. Then you give them Friday afternoon off at three o'clock so they can go to church. That's a big thing. You could tell them, "Give you time off to go to church," and they loved you.

So Dominick opened up his own dress factory. His first payroll—his brother hijacked his first payroll! Right down here on South Main Street in Pittston, right near the South Main Street Armory. Yeah. . . . They stop at a traffic light down on South Main Street and his brother's gang gets in the car and says, "Out—and go out empty-handed." So they got out of the car and left all the money in the car, the payroll in the car. It was goin' to the bank to have checks made to give to the girls. It was all cash. His own brother hijacked the car. Stole his own brother's money. His brother!

You might think it's like a big goddamn joke, don't you? His brother [Sam] hijacked his payroll, and then he says [to Dominick], "Go fish." He says, "You're nothing. You have no money to pay the girls." So [some of] the girls went to Sam and they say, "What are we gonna do?" Sam says, "I told you not to go work for him. You went to work for him and now you're stuck. You worked the whole week, you don't have any money. Now what are you gonna do? You gonna come back to work for me, or are you gonna go work for him who can't afford to pay you?" So they said, "OK, we'll go back to work for you." "So," he says, "OK, you come back to work for me."

The dress workers [that stayed with Sam] got their money, they got their money, and those that were working [for Dominick] they got *bananas*—they got nothing. For all the work he [Dominick] did that whole goddamn month, setting up contracts, they were sucking him in. They were letting him in. They [the jobbers from New York] were giving him the work and they didn't have to. They didn't have to give him that little bit of work. They gave him a little piece here, they gave him a little piece there, they gave him a couple belts to work on and a couple zippers to do and shit like that. Just to keep him happy. In the meantime, they knew what they were gonna do. They knew that they were gonna take that payroll away from him just to teach him a lesson because they weren't gonna let him get away with that. He didn't have the friends in there, like his brother did. . . .

So the girls quit and now Dominick comes back with his tail between his legs and he says, "Hey, Sam, I need a job." Sam says, "You dummy, what do you want from me? I told ya don't go into business yourself. Now, go scratch, go find a job somewhere [else]. I don't need ya." He threw his brother out. They became friends again later on, four or five years, six years later when one of the family died.

Q: You had to have the contacts.

AD: Oh, absolutely. Arthur Lori in Pittston, Charlie Turco in Pittston, Angelo Sciandra in Inkerman—back in those days [they had the contacts]. I worked for Angelo Sciandra and, I don't care if you put this on tape or not, but he burned his own factory down. I helped him burn his factory down. I didn't light the match. I didn't light his match, but I took all his material out of the factory before he torched it.

Q: What was that about?

AD: Well, he needed money. His chief mechanic was Lenny Blandina. Lenny Blandina was a sewing machine mechanic. . . . Lenny was up at the Apalachin hideout [organized crime summit] in 1958 [sic; 1957]. Lenny Blandina must have grown wings because he got out of that [i.e., escaped from the scene]. Nobody knows how Lenny got out but he got out.[4]

Q: Was he from Pittston?

AD: Yeah, Pittston. Lenny Blandina supplied all the sewing-machine heads for every dress factory for as long as you could breathe. As far as you can go and breathe, Lenny Blandina supplied the heads for the sewing machines. They [the owners] didn't care where you bought the tables but Lenny had the heads to go on the tables. You can get anybody to supply the tables but Lenny had the heads.

Q: He had a monopoly.

AD: Mm-hmm. You couldn't open up a factory without Lenny coming first. Lenny and Angelo Sciandra were good friends. They were raised together in Pittston. Well, I was born and raised there with Angelo myself. I was going to barber school, going to school at night, and working for Angelo [in the day]. He comes around every day, passing by all his operators, and he says, "Work tonight? Work tonight?" *Boom, boom, boom, boom,* hacking on us, hitting on our tables. "Work tonight? Work tonight?" I say, "Hey, I can't." "Well," he said, "OK, you're fired." "OK, so I'm fired."

I didn't show up for work the next day and the foreman called. He says, "Hey, where the f___ are ya?" I said, "I'm home, where am I?" He says, "You're supposed to be at work." I said, "Angelo fired me." [He said], "Ah, he don't know what the f___ he's doin'." I said, "Well, I'm not goin' to work—he fired me." "Ah, OK," he said. So I get a call the next day. It's Angelo. He says, "Hey, I didn't fire you." I said, "Well, you fired me because I wouldn't work overtime." He said, "That's not what I meant." I said, "I don't care what you meant." So he said, "Come in to work." So I come into work [the next day] and he says, "The next

DAILY ● NEWS
NEW YORK'S PICTURE NEWSPAPER®

FINAL ★★★★★

5¢

Vol. 39, No. 123 *Copr. 1957 News Syndicate Co. Inc.*   New York 17, N.Y., Friday, November 15, 1957●   WEATHER: Partly cloudy, mild.

SEIZE 62 MAFIA CHIEFTAINS IN UPSTATE RAID

Story on Page 2

FIG. 15 | Apalachin, New York, organized crime meeting headline. Photo from the *New York Daily News*, November 15, 1957.

time I tell ya you're fired, come in and work the next day." *(laughs)* He says, "Ya know, I blow up easy, I blow up easy."

Then he tells us, he says, "Now, you and Rocky and Charlie and Carmen, you're gonna work next Saturday." I said, "OK." So I'm not gonna come in [i.e., I have no choice but to go to work]? Now he had contract work for Sears, Roebuck. Contract work is [when] you do the same dress maybe in four or five different colors, but the same style dress until they tell you to stop. Which amounts to, I mean this, hundreds of thousands of dresses. Where Sears was gettin' rid of them, I don't know. We were workin' on that same style, I bet you, for two and a half years. Same style dress.

So we came in on Saturday, like he said. He says, "I want all them dresses off the hangers and I want them all in boxes." So we figured, Sears, this is the way they want them shipped. I said, "Well, where the hell are the girls? What happened?" There was nobody there except us guys. We take all the dresses off the hangers but no belts. He said, "I want the belts left on the hangers." I thought, well, this is odd. But I never worked for Angelo before like this so I don't know what he's like. I [originally] went to work there because a friend of the family said he's a good man to work for. So I went there.

Q: You were a presser, correct?

AD: Yeah, I was a presser. I was a presser and I was going to barber school at night.[5] So myself and Charlie and Carmen and Rocky we took every dress out of the factory that [Saturday] night. We took every dress out of that factory and left the belts on the hangers. Every dress we took out of that factory and took them up to the Yatesville [suburban Pittston] police station. Are you listening to me?! The Yatesville police station, in boxes! And we stored them on the second floor of the police station up in Yatesville. Thirty-five thousand dresses, maybe. And the belts from the dresses were left hung on the hangers and eight buttons were dropped at every belt, OK?

Then [we went back to the factory and] Lenny took every sewing machine head off most of the expensive machines. And Rocky, Carmen, myself, and Lenny took burnt machines, *burnt machines*, and put them in place. Machines that were already in a fire. These machines were charred, they were burnt. You could see they were in a fire. We put every one of those machines in place of the new machines and took the new machines up to the second floor of the Yatesville police station. And three days later, the factory was torched!

I didn't know what was happening. We were naïve, OK? Because we were young, we were young. He torched the factory and he got paid insurance for thirty-five thousand dresses and for the machines that were lost in the fire. And, all the while, they were up in the police station! . . . Unbeknownst to everybody else, those machines were used in another fire on South Main Street in Pittston later on.

Q: Same machines?

AD: Same machines were used in another fire.

Q: Do you think the police were in on the first fire?

AD: Sure they were. They were very cooperative with Angelo. Oh, certainly, they knew. They knew Angelo. Maybe they didn't know exactly what he was doing. They didn't know why he was doing it. But he had a friend, yeah, he had a friend somewhere, you know. . . .

Q: Did his shop never become unionized?[6]

AD: No. They burned it down before anything else. I think they burned it down because he couldn't get the business. Yeah, because, you know, New York was tough then. They started then to get business mostly from the union people, because of the pressure from the union.

Q: What other shops in the Valley joined the union?

AD: Oh yeah, there was a lot of 'em. Lot of 'em in Wilkes-Barre, they were union. Pittston was tough. Pittston and Old Forge, Duryea, they were tough. Duryea I think was the worst. They had sweatshops up there, boy, in Duryea. Oh, geez, I went up to work one time as a presser in an old bank building, and they took like the mezzanine of the bank and they put a [work] floor on it. They put machines upstairs, pressing machines, and there was barely enough room up there to stand. Honest to god, you should see that place.

ANTHONY "TONY" D'ANGELO

Q: Did Min Matheson ever try to organize that shop?

AD: Oh yeah, oh yeah, but they threw her out real fast. Yeah, I didn't stay up there. I didn't stay there. . . . I remember Min Matheson. I met her when I worked for Angelo Sciandra in Inkerman. I can't remember the name of the shop—Angelo's Fashions? Angelo Sciandra lived in Wyoming. He was having trouble with the union and she came to proclaim all the goodness of the union and try to get him in the fold and, of course, he was anti-union. I'm trying to think of the year. I got married in '45 and then, in '46, I was operated on and I couldn't do the work I was doing for the Pittston Gas Company, so a friend of mine suggested I get a job in a dress factory.

Q: So his dress factory was nonunion?

AD: Yeah, nonunion. It was the little schoolhouse down in Inkerman, which Angelo torched. *(laughs)* She came to try and organize it several times. Several times she was there and Angelo didn't wanna have no part of it. Apparently he was . . . I would say he was tougher than she was and that was why she backed out. Yeah, she backed off. It was quite a while before she came back. After several visits, we never saw her again and then she got involved in Lori Fashions.

Arthur Lori was the guy's [name]. That was in Pittston. He had opened up a chain, you might say, of factories. He had one in Plains, I think two in Pittston, one on North Main Street, and one down on South Main Street. He was a little guy, Arthur Lori, but they weren't union [at first]. I'm sure they weren't union. And then [later], even Arthur tried to get Angelo involved in it [unionization]. Why Angelo, I don't know, because, god, there was several, several dozen shops in Pittston at that time or in the outlying areas of Pittston Township.[7]

Q: Did they all eventually become a union?

AD: No, no, no, no, no. Charlie Turco up on Pine Street in Pittston, he never got in any union. Yeah, then the next time, let's see, after Angelo Sciandra, I bounced around a little bit and then I saw an ad in the paper for pressers down at Ann Will Garment, for pleats and corners.

Q: That was Bill Cherkes's shop, correct?

AD: Yeah, Bill Cherkes [chap. 2]. There was a strike looming. We were union. Ann Will Garment was a union shop. Yeah, she [Min Matheson] organized it before I got there. But a strike was comin' up. Trying to think of the date—1948, '49, '50, in that time period. It was a matter of cents, pennies, that the union was fighting for and she sent word to all the employees that there was no work tomorrow morning at that particular shop. She told Bill that pickets would be outside the shop at six thirty in the morning and she told Bill to prepare for it. And Bill, of course, he called up many of his employees and asked them not to honor the picket line, to come right past the picket line. Bill, he was a fair employer, he was. All of his employees liked him, and his father before him they adored.

So that morning the pickets were out there with signs and many of his employees went in, including me. Because at that time I thought the union, the

things they were asking for, were not stupid but irrelevant to why we were working. The pickets were in the back in the parking lot and that's where I parked.
We walked around the front and there were pickets out in front of the building,
too.

Q: Was Mrs. Matheson on the picket line?

AD: She was right there. Min Matheson was right there. Then Bill Cherkes came out
of the building and we all came out of the building. All the employees came out.
We were on the sidewalk. And her and Bill were jawin' back and forth. I mean,
they were nose to nose, nose to nose.

Q: Shouting at each other?

AD: No, no, they were just in a heavy conversation, you know.

Q: How many pickets were there, would you say?

AD: There was about six or seven. There were only three women [in the front] and
there were three men in the back. Why three in the back and three in the front,
I don't know. Probably the only volunteers they could get at that time. And so
they talked, and they talked, and they talked. It was a mild morning. It wasn't a
cold day. It was in March, I think, and he was out there in his short sleeves, and
then they walked up the street to the Top Hat Diner.

They walked to Top Hat Diner and they got to the doorway and were gonna
go in. They went up the steps and opened the door, and then they come back
down again, *(laughs)* and they walked down the street and went into Bill's office.
Before that, she wasn't in the shop. She didn't go into the shop all the while we
were there. We were outside hangin' around for at least an hour. She told us to
stay—stay out. So I asked her, "Should we go home?" She said, "No, don't go
home." There were mostly women there because the only men were myself and
maybe a mechanic—we [the men] were very much a minority. So sure enough
we hung around. We went up to the Top Hat for coffee and even the guys in
there were kiddin' us, ya know. One says, "I don't hear any gunshots, must be
pretty safe down there?" *(laughs)* It was resolved.

Q: Everybody went back to work?

AD: Yeah. I don't remember [the details]. . . . Did I tell you about when I left Bill
Cherkes to open up the barbershop [in Wilkes-Barre]? He sent his electrician
over and put brand new lights in the barbershop. Yeah, yup. He paid my phone
bill for the first two months 'til I got a pay phone put in the shop, a public phone.
He painted the shop, too. On South River Street [in Wilkes-Barre]. And what else
did he do? Oh, he gave me an air conditioner. Yeah. And he called every Friday.
He'd call me.

Jean was his secretary, and Jean and I went to school together. Every Friday,
she'd call the shop and say, "Tony, Bill's on the phone." And the first thing he said,
"Are you happy?" He must've called me for, I betcha, four or five years. He called
every Friday to see if I was happy, if I needed anything! You know, I was [located]
in a Jewish neighborhood in South Wilkes-Barre. It was a big apartment building

ANTHONY "TONY" D'ANGELO

down on the corner. I was downstairs, sure. I was there eighteen years, until the [Agnes] flood hit in '72. Then I went to the Brooks [barbershop], and that's when I met you! *(laughs)* . . . Well, I'll tell ya. It took me three years, untimely years, anyway it took me a long while to finally find a guy like Bill Cherkes.

Q: What do you mean?

AD: A conscientious employer. A guy that cared about his people.

Q: A lot of employers weren't like that?

AD: Oh no, no, no, nah. A lot of 'em couldn't care whether you lived or died. They don't care. Bill Cherkes I think went to every funeral of any person who died in his group. He still does it today, would send a card [to the family] when he finds out if one of us [died]. I remember a lady by the name of Maslow from Edwardsville who worked for him and she passed away, and he sent a card to the family. She was a younger girl at that time. Then he mentioned it to me when he came for a haircut. "Did you know Anna Maslow?" I says. "Yeah, I remember. I saw it in the paper that she passed away." So he's still [doing this] today. He's pretty conscientious.

Q: What were wages like back then? Did the union help you get better wages?

AD: Oh yeah, certainly, absolutely they did. Oh yeah. It was one of those deals where, in April, you got another half cent on this dress and come maybe in November you're gonna get another quarter cent on this dress, or maybe another half cent depending on who the contract was with. If it was Sears and Roebuck, ya only got a half a penny, but for some dress manufacturers who want a good dress, they'd give ya a cent more. The union, if you could get on the union wages, ya might've got fourteen cents for pressing a dress. And if ya could get 140 dresses, ya did pretty good for the day. It was all piecework. The only ones not on piecework—and they did later go on piecework—were the cleaners. After the garment was made, they'd come along and snip off all the threads. We called them cleaners. They were never on piecework. But I think they are now. Now they use clippers. . . .

Q: Let me ask you about organized crime's involvement in garment shops.

AD: Yeah, they say there was.

Q: How do think Min and Bill Matheson dealt with that?

AD: Well, [it was] one of the reasons she came here to begin with. I think it was after her brother [Will Lurye] got killed in New York.[8] I don't know if he was an organizer or not but he was killed as a direct result of the garment industry. When she came here, she was pretty, pretty staunch. I mean she was tough. She was a tough baby, I'll tell ya. I don't think she ever gave in to anyone. If anything, they met her halfway rather than get her dander up, ya know. 'Cause they know what she could do to them. She coulda wrecked 'em. She coulda put the whole Valley out [on strike]. Oh yeah, Min Matheson was a powerful woman. And ya didn't have to know her. Just being in the area you could tell that she was somebody. Oh yeah, oh yes. She used to have a column in the newsletter, too. She used to have a radio show. "News and Views," something like that. I know WARM [*sic*; WKXV] was a big of supporter of her. . . . But the Alaimo brothers in Pittston, they couldn't stand Min Matheson. They hated her guts because she was stronger than they were, that's why.

Q: Stronger in what way?

AD: Stronger will–minded, and every way around, and she had more power than them. She organized the Valley from Nanticoke up to Duryea.

Q: People weren't afraid to join?

AD: No, not as long as she was there. She was their guardian, ya know, she was their buffer. If you let her talk, she'd get to ya.

Q: Did you ever hear her give a speech?

AD: Oh yeah, many times. Many times. There was always ILG meetings, and she was always appearing in the Valley. She was quite prominent. She had a New York accent.[9] She was a good speaker. And she always talked about her brother. She talked about him constantly because she wanted to remind 'em [ILGers] that's what could happen, ya know.

Q: I wonder if she ever thought it could happen to her?

AD: I'm sure she did. Oh, I'm sure she did. They [certain shop owners] were against her. Any [owner] that was conscious and alive would've said, "If I could only get rid of her," ya know. *(laughs)* "She's a pain in the butt." But everybody was afraid of her. She was so put together in her mind, she knew what she wanted to do, and she went with it.

FIG. 16
Alice Reca, 1995.
Photo courtesy of the
Northeastern Pennsylvania
Oral and Life History
Collection, Pennsylvania
State University.

Alice Reca, from an
audio-recorded interview
with Robert P. Wolensky
conducted at Mrs. Reca's
home in Baltimore, Mary-
land, on July 26, 1995. The
interview is included in
the Wyoming Valley Oral
History Project, which is one
of eight projects within the
Northeastern Pennsylvania
Oral and Life History Collection housed in the Eberly
Family Special Collections
Library, Penn State University Libraries.

Alice Reca

Garment Worker, Union Organizer,
and Business Agent

Alice Reca's animated narrative begins with her first sewing position in a nonunion factory and proceeds through her experiences as
an ILGWU member, labor organizer, and business agent. Along the
way, she worked as an undercover agent for the union (organizing
shops from the inside), participated in strikes against allegedly mob-
owned factories, and accepted transfers to the Harrisburg and the
Baltimore union districts. Her coffee shop conflict with Pittston mob
owners and managers is noteworthy as a gendered confrontation, for
the antagonists sought to defeat her efforts by deriding her reputation
as a moral and honorable woman. She withstood the onslaught, but
not without some difficulty. She eventually resigned from the ILGWU
staff to raise a third child.

AR: I married a soldier when I was very young and, after the war,
we moved to Larksville, Pennsylvania [near Wilkes-Barre]. Things
were kind of difficult and we needed money like everyone. I had
friends that worked in a [garment] shop and I heard stories. I
thought, "Hey, that's for me," because they seem to be having
a lot of fun. The union was well organized when I went there.
You know, a lot of these shops were unionized and I wanted to

go into a union shop with my friends, but they didn't take learners. So I went into a nonunion shop [Clover Dress] to learn to run the industrial machines, and then, whoever spoke to [recruit] me, I went into Stella Dress.

Stella Dress was on Kingston Corners. Everyone knew Stella Dress and the Stella Dress workers. Mr. George, he ran the other shop, Clover Dress. He once said, "My god, what those girls won't do for a cup of coffee and a donut!" The first shop, it was small. But at Stella Dress, I would guess there were a hundred and some workers there. So that's how I got into the union shops.

Whenever there was a shop that the union was trying to organize, we'd go in the morning on the picket line and [then] come to work. Sometimes [we'd] cut out [from work] early and go [back to the striking shop] when they were getting out. I met Min [Matheson, chap. 3], naturally, through this. I was just so taken with this person, you know. I think I would've just followed her right off the Bay Bridge if that's where she was going. I would've gone right [off] because, I'm telling you, I just knew instinctively that it was the right thing to do, and I just had no questions asked.

Stella Dress was a good place to work. We worked on piecework and everybody wanted to make a buck. We would fight [the owner] for higher prices for our piecework and we would hide tickets, hold back tickets, until we got a better price. We'd try to slide them in so we could get more money. The ticket came on the bundle. Like the pocket setters took that ticket off, the zipper setters would take that ticket off, and someone has the [ticket for the] dots because that's what she did. They always did the dots.[1] You just put the tickets in your drawer at the end of the day.

Q: So you would hold some tickets back because tomorrow's prices might be higher?

AR: Yeah. Well, you'd tell your business agent and, if you had a sharp agent, he'd tell you right off, "Honey, that's a good price on that." But it didn't hurt to keep trying. . . .

Q: You mentioned an organizing strategy that took you into nonunion shops.

AR: Well, I would go and get a job in a nonunion shop and try to make the acquaintance of the coworkers, the people working around, as well as see where the work was coming from and where it was going to. I'd get as many names of the workers as I possibly could and hopefully addresses or phone numbers in order to visit with them. Sometimes you would be able to call a meeting [at night] and there would be a nucleus of people from the shop would come and from there you spread out. Sometimes you had successes and sometimes you didn't.

Q: Did Min Matheson ask you to go into those shops for that purpose?[2]

AR: Oh yeah, yeah, yeah. One that I'm remembering was in Kingston and think it was Laura's, the lingerie shop. They made very good lingerie. It was top line. We seemed to be making some successes there but the parent firm was in another city so we couldn't do anything with the parent firm. If you can't get the parent firm—whatever's district that was in—you sure, lord, are not going to get a subsidiary shop.[3]

ALICE RECA

FIG. 17 | ILGWU Local 295, Pittston, Pennsylvania, bowling league, 1963. Photo courtesy of Lukasik Studio.

I recall Min coming in and speaking to these girls. What I remember of that shop, as I tried to carry it [the experience] with me in other attempts to organize in different places, was what she said and told them about the union. She told them about the benefits that you could derive from the union. She said, "If you're not convinced that this is the way you should go, it's not your fault, it's my fault because I haven't explained it to you right. Once I do that, there's no doubt in my mind, nor will there be any doubt in your mind, that you want to sign a union card, bring the shop in, and follow the union." You know, something [like that], when the shop was not close to being organized. Min kind of startled me with that. [An organizer might think], "They didn't listen to me so they're dumb, they're stupid." But Min says, "It's not their fault, no." [She] taught me. I didn't call anybody dumb and stupid after that. Didn't do that.

Q: How many times did you go into a nonunion shop to see if you could start organizing from the inside?

AR: In the Wyoming Valley, there was only a couple of shops. Laura's was the one that I remember. I went there for a good while. As a matter of fact, they knew I worked for the union and they [the managers of the shop] wanted me to quit. They couldn't fire me so they put my machine in a corner. They put my machine

FIG. 18 | ILGWU strike scene near the Twin Restaurant, Main Street, Pittston, Pennsylvania, circa 1958. Photo courtesy of Lukasik Studio.

in a corner and it was like I stood in the corner all day. They knew that the wall was what I saw and if I got up to go to the ladies room, the floorlady went with me, or someone [else] who could report back, "She just went to the ladies room. Didn't have any time to do any tags," or whatever.

Q: How did they find out that you were with the union?

AR: They found out because I talked to people about the union and someone always tells. I was awfully glad when Min said, "You don't have to go back to Laura's because I think you've spent enough time there." I run my mouth a lot and it's terrible for someone with that kind of a habit to be isolated in a corner. You can't talk to anyone.

Q: How long were you in that shop?

AR: Maybe a month and a half, I don't know, but each day seemed like a month.

Q: Did they try to fire you?

AR: I don't know why they wouldn't fire me! They wanted me to quit and I don't know if there had been a law passed at that time that you couldn't be fired for union activity. But if it wasn't for Min, I would have quit in the first hour when my machine went in that corner. . . .

Q: Can you tell us about some of your other experiences as an organizer?

AR: Well, I don't know how to tell you about that experience. It was an experience that I've never forgotten. There were times [when I was afraid], but I think I

ALICE RECA

was more afraid *after* I left Pittston. After I left to go home [at night] it was kind of scary. I'd hear different odd sounds outside the house. A time or two I called somebody and said, "I think somebody's outside."

But it was scary in [the daytime in] Pittston as well. I was in a big fight up there. You have to ask Dot [Dorothy Ney, chap. 1] about that one. Some man came and I don't recall if he was one of our business agents or whatever. Anyway, it was like [they were on him] in the blink of an eyelash. He was this big, big guy. So we knew there were hazards there, that it was dangerous.

Q: Were you ever roughed up physically?

AR: No, no, not physically, no. But some of it was from that scum, who threw insulting remarks at you. You know what I'm saying? For instance, across the street from the [striking] shop was Twinny's Diner. Those guys hung out there. [Alleged crime boss] Russell Bufalino was there every day. [Alleged gangster] Angelo Sciandra, those guys all hung out there. We usually didn't have any problem with them when we went into Twinny's to get a soda or a bag of peanuts. [But if] you went down the street further . . . [there could be trouble]. A lot of people, not a lot but a few, would say, "Boy, you're taking a chance to go in there. They can get ahold of you, drag you in that back room and, man, nobody'd ever see you again. Do you know there are bottomless mines around here?" So, you know, that's kind of scary to think about. Didn't happen but it's kind of scary to think about.

Like one guy, I'm sure his name was Larry Sitzman. . . . He was the owner [*sic*; manager] of a shop.[4] . . . I always went up [to Pittston] with Dot and I mean it was early, we had to leave early before the girls went in to work. I stayed in Pittston all day. We had to stay there. I was in Twinny's just getting something and this Larry Sitzman walks in. "They told me that she spent the night with whoever," he said. "I don't believe that. Do you?" And [he continued], "They told me that she did this and that." Well, you know, real, real scum. "I don't believe that, do you?" Anyway, this went on and I asked him to shut up a couple times but he was just having a good time with me and I was getting furious.

I stood up and I grabbed this peanut jug that was screwed down to the counter. I grabbed this peanut jug because I was going to crack him with it, but it was screwed down. I was going to crack that sucker with it. Angelo Sciandra was behind the counter. They would wait on themselves. Well, he just jumped that counter and was right over there. Really agile, wouldn't you think? He grabbed me. But I think Russ Bufalino told him to get out and go get a bath and shave or something. Somebody told him and he left. I was furious. Now, when I get really angry, I'll cry, you know, really. I just needed to hit him so bad.

So I went outside and Dot saw me. She was in the car. I was in tears and she said, "What happened? What happened?" I was trying to tell her and she jumped out of that car, and she ran into Twinny's and said to them, "What did you do to Alice? What did you do to her?" Angelo Sciandra came over. He saw me and he put his head down [to the car window] and he says, "When you start a fight, you ought to have everybody on your side," or something to that effect. If I'd gotten that peanut jug up, I wouldn't have needed anyone on my side. I would have ended it right there. I felt like a fool, that's what. I was embarrassed. I was so embarrassed that it just kind of wiped me out. I don't think that they wanted any incidents takin' place in there, in the diner. It wasn't even a diner [and] I can't remember why they called [it] Twinny's Diner. They [the tough guys] didn't want any incident to take place with any of us around that Sitzman.

We had a union office there [in Pittston]. It was several blocks up the street and you had to go up these steps. Louise Platt was the business agent. [One time] I went up to the union hall with her and we had to go up this long flight, a high flight of stairs, and she went to open the door and it didn't go open. She grabbed me, she hollered something, and said, "Run, run!" And here's both of us tumbling down those steps to get out of there. She thought it was a body up against the door! But, you know, these were just our imaginations taking over. I thought, "Oh, well, they intimidated you all the time." But *we* did a little intimidating, too. Sciandra would bring his trumpet and he'd play "Taps" and I'd put on a babushka (a peasant head wrap) and stand beside him with a paper cup. I mean we did a little intimidating, too!

Q: You'd stand right next to him in the street?

AR: Absolutely, right beside him. People'd go by and I'd say, "Help this poor guy please, he needs it!"

Q: Was that your idea?

AR: Well, I'm sure it was my idea. If he's going to get up there . . . And don't people [musicians] on the [street] play for money or something? That's what happened.

Q: What else would they do to intimidate you?

AR: Well, they would talk about what they could have done to us. Nobody ever came up and told me that they were going to cut my legs off or any of that kind of stuff, but I swear they tried to run me off the road once. . . . [Another time], Dot had left her turn signal on and when she started the ignition—it tick, tick, ticked. "There's a bomb! Get out of here!" So, you know, it was these kinda things that, for a moment, you were very startled, kind of frightened. But then after she started the car, you'd laugh about it.

I remember that we sat down one time, Min and I, and it was Dot's birthday. We sent her a bonsai tree. They're rather expensive little things, you know. We sent her this bonsai tree, and she put it in the bathtub and filled the package with water. She thought maybe it might be a bomb! So there went the bonsai tree—that's true! Dot would get arrested. God bless [her]. I don't know why they [the police] were always picking on her. . . .

The truckers, Friedman's Express, respected our [picket] line. Dot's husband was a dispatcher for Friedman's, so the Friedman truckers and other truckers wouldn't stop, wouldn't bring in goods. They [the garment shop owners] got this nonunion truck to come in. They must have been bringing stuff in or taking

ALICE RECA

88

stuff out.[5] Anyway he [one driver] had like a brown paper bag on the floor of the truck. I forget who was with me, maybe Min, but anyway I started giving him the whole spiel: "This is a labor dispute going on here," and this and that and the other thing. He gave a few choice words and he pulled a gun [from that paper bag]. He pulled a gun and he stepped forward, and when he did, his foot went through the bottom of the truck!

Q: Lucky the gun didn't go off.

AR: Well, he just would have blown a hole out of the top of the truck, but it may not have been loaded.

Q: Was Sitzman's the same shop where they would throw water on your legs?

AR: Oh yeah, he'd turn the hose on. Throw water out there. He once said, "How [much] worse can it get? A bunch of mice have been turned loose out there." I said, "We didn't run from a rat like you; why you'd think we'd run from a mouse?" Then I called him a name. See, at that time, "Oh, you can't do that." You know, this one joker [police officer] that was supposed to be our protection [said], "[You] can't say that. You called him this, you can't do that, you can't do this."

I remember Min saying "I know you're afraid, Alice." I remember that. We had a meeting—I think it was Min, Dot, myself, and maybe someone else. She said, "Why don't you want to go back to Pittston?" Something to that effect. "Are you afraid?" I told her, "Yes." I said, "It's not that as much as I want someone there with me that I can trust. Someone that if something happens to me, [they] will get some help somewhere or try to." Because Dot was always in jail—not *always* in jail—but Dot was not there [with me] all the time. Min said, "Well, who, who? Who do you think?" I told her Ann Lieb. Well, she [Ann] was pregnant and said, "Thanks a lot." But Ann came up.[6]

Q: How long did the Sitzman strike go on?

AR: It seemed [like] forever. I can't remember, but it sure, god, seemed [like] forever. At the end of the strike I went back to work.

Q: Where were you working at that point?

AR: Stella [Dress]. And then, I don't know how long [afterward], but I went on the organizing staff. I was never in charge of organizing. I've organized under [some-one]. That meant that you go out and picket and visit and give a report. And when it seemed like you had better than just a nucleus of people, you had something to work with and they [other picketers] come in.

Q: Were you raised in a union family?

AR: God no. I did not [know anything about unions]. [When] they talked about a picket line, I thought it was a picket fence! I didn't know what a picket line was. God no. I went up there [Pittston] and they went on strike, and I had some friends who were involved in it. I couldn't understand. I'd talk to them. I didn't understand because they were on strike, and I'm doing this mental calculation of, well, you lost this much money. You're not getting this back. How many years will you have to work if you go to a fifty-cent-an-hour raise before you make that [back]?

SEWN IN COAL COUNTRY

It just didn't make sense to me until they sat me down and told me all about it, the struggle. So then you'd eat mush just to have the freedom of having a union behind you—to back you, give you some benefits, some rights, make you feel like a human being.

Q: Were you also part of the union's musical revues?

AR: Yeah, part of the chorus, but I didn't have any outstanding talent. I modeled, you know, we modeled the clothes that were made in Wyoming Valley.

Q: There seemed to be a strong social component to the union.

AR: Yeah, there was also a lot of cooperation between the various unions, too. We went out and picketed bakeries to help the bakery workers, and we picketed outdoor theaters for the projection workers at one adult theater. So, you know, it's one hand washing the other. There's a lot of pride in being a union member. If you scabbed, if you were a scab, three generations later, they'd say, "Well, her great-grandfather was a scab." I mean, nobody will have anything to do with her. Those miners had [a strong union] at one time in the Wyoming Valley. What industry was here [was union]. Min fought so hard to bring [other] industries into the Wyoming Valley and succeeded in several instances, for men—M-E-N. Because the only option was the coal mines, and the mine owners fought tooth and nail [along] with the Chamber of Commerce because they didn't want any industry in there.[7] Miners made good money. They did. But after a while, [the jobs disappeared].

Ann's father was killed in the mines. They brought her father home and threw him on the back porch and said, "Woman, here's your man." That was on Good Friday. Ann's mother was pregnant. She had six daughters [and] it was a lot for her mother. "Here's your man." No insurance, no nothing. Nothing, no one. . . .[8]

Q: Do you have any recollections of Bill Matheson?

AR: God, he was great. He was great. We had a testimonial dinner for Min, and he was called on to speak. Bill went on picket lines. Oh yeah, he went on picket lines and he was not [always] in the background. He worked on the Education Department of the union, and he was a brain, an absolute brain. A good-hearted person, dedicated person, a very interesting person just to be around. They were a pair. They were really a pair. She was very fiery, there's no question about that, but Bill was right there giving her all the support. All the support in the world. And those two girls, Betty and Marianne—Min and Bill loved them better than their next breath, you know. They were their pride and joy, and [they] still put themselves in a lot of danger. I think Min was in a lot of danger. You know, her brother was killed.

Have you ever heard of a Victor Riesel [*sic*; Lester Velie]? He wrote for *Reader's Digest*, and he wrote an article, "The Lady and the Gangsters," that was all about the Pittston story. It was about the strike we won, when she was walking [picketing] on the street and they were threatening her. Victor Riesel was blinded by these guys. They [the mobsters] threw acid in his eyes.[9]

ALICE RECA

Q: When did you leave Wilkes-Barre?

AR: I went on [ILGWU] staff and was sent to Harrisburg. I worked in Harrisburg for a while and then I wanted to go back home. I had a little boy, and I wanted to take him and go back home [to the Wyoming Valley]. But I didn't go home. I went further, further away [to Baltimore]. I think Min was instrumental in helping me to do that, because she called here [Baltimore] for Angela [Bambace] who ran the department.[10] The [Upper] South Department it was called. The [Upper] South was three entire states and parts of three others. . . .[11]

Q: You were in the Wyoming Valley for how many years?

AR: Oh, I don't know, five, six. And what was I here [Baltimore]? I don't know, maybe six or seven. Yeah, maybe that. I went off staff because I have three sons. I have four, a buried son in Wilkes-Barre, but I have three sons here and one is going to be forty-eight. One is thirty-eight and the other one is thirty-three. So it's like raising three families. But I left [the job] after my third son was born because I wanted, you know, I wanted to be with him.

John "Johnny" Justin

Garment Worker, Labor Organizer,
and ILGWU District Manager

A strong believer in working-class rights and collective bargaining, John Justin was a former Communist and Socialist who organized for the ILGWU in Harrisburg before World War II. Upon returning from the military, he helped start the Wyoming Valley District with Min Matheson. He later served as the district manager in Harrisburg and Pottsville, Pennsylvania. His vivid memory and detailed narrative style help bring frontline events, famous and infamous personages, and controversial dealings to life. His decision-making tug-of-war with the New York union office exhibits the disparity between his "solidarity unionist" perspective and the administrative-business unionism of the ILGWU's national leaders. Despite their occasional disagreements, Min Matheson called on him for on-the-scene assistance, and he joined her for a time at the Union Label Department in New York. Mr. Justin remained a strong advocate of the ILGWU's political and educational programs, as he also applauded members' involvement in the Democratic Party and encouraged their seeking school board and other local offices. Born in Massachusetts, raised in New York City, and adopted by Pennsylvania, in the early 1970s he retired to Wilkes-Barre, where he kept in touch with the Mathesons and other union members.

FIG. 19
John Justin, 1988. Photo courtesy of the Northeastern Pennsylvania Oral and Life History Collection, Pennsylvania State University.

John Justin, from an audio-recorded interview with Robert P. Wolensky conducted at Mr. Justin's apartment in Wilkes-Barre, Pennsylvania, on July 28, 1988. The interview is included in the Wyoming Valley Oral History Project, which is one of eight projects within the Northeastern Pennsylvania Oral and Life History Collection housed in the Eberly Family Special Collections Library, Penn State University Libraries.

JJ: When I worked in the Harrisburg area as an organizer for the garment workers, I considered Harrisburg my home. I enlisted in the [Army] Air Corps [during World War II] for four and a half years. When the war was over, I came out of the service and the Ladies' Garment Workers called the people back. Within ninety days you could get your old job back. Well, they were in contact with me continuously and wanted me to come back as an organizer. This was primarily what I did in Harrisburg, and before I knew it, they sent me to Scranton.

At the time [in 1945], Scranton was the [area's] home of the ILGWU, and it was being supervised by Israel Zimmerman, whose brother [Charles S. Zimmerman] was very influential in the union in New York. Mr. Zimmerman was in charge and wasn't even in the office when I came in. I had begun more or less researching the region. Being that I had no car, it was very difficult to function as an organizer. So I checked and we had the Laurel Line in those days that went all the way from Scranton to down here [Wilkes-Barre], stopping at every town. The unorganized shops were centered around Pittston. There were about forty of these shops in that area, and being that I had some connections in Harrisburg, I knew exactly how many shops were here, who [owned them], what they manufactured, and so forth. I had gotten some research from some friends in the state office and I decided to open up an office in Pittston.[1]

I was the very first one there. In the meantime, Zimmerman, as the head of the thing, he wants to know why I opened the office [in Pittston], but not in any questioning [way]. He was quite friendly to me, though at one time, several years before, I had antagonized "Zimmy" [over a] group that he was organizing, a political group who had a newspaper called the *Workers Age*.[2] I think back then and I said something to the effect that "I believe in democracy and therefore I don't believe I could belong to your group."

So here now I am, he's my boss five, six years after, and he's the head of the [Scranton-area] ILGWU. He knew who I was and, of course, I knew him as a former "Lovestonite." Jay Lovestone was the head of the Communist Party for many years until he was expelled. He was much disliked being that he was a "Commie," but when they [the ILGWU] made peace with the Commies, Dubinsky hired him, and he opened up a political committee. The ILG was very political, Dubinsky particularly was very, very political, and he made him [Lovestone] the head of this anti-Communist group. There's nothing more poisonous probably than a former Communist who is no longer charmed by their policies, and they become bitter enemies. Subsequently, Jay became the head of the AFL [American Federation of Labor] Political Department. . . .[3]

Well anyway, Zimmy is my boss. When I opened up the office, we had a big conference. We were changing the name at that time. We were known as the Cotton Garment and Miscellaneous Trades Department of the ILG and now we had grown to the Northeast [Department]. We took in the whole Northeast outside of New York City and Philadelphia. I opened up this office and the next thing I

FIG. 20 | *Workers Age* (a newspaper of the Communist Party USA), January 23, 1932.

know there is some situation where one Mr. Falzone come in and he wants to see "this goddamn Justin." So I said, "I'm he." He says, "You're interfering with my cathouses, goddamn you," and all this other stuff, and he got almost violent.

Q: Cathouses?[4]

JJ: I said, "I didn't know that you were a veterinarian!" Of course, that made him angrier because he said, "Oh, you're a smart guy." He had a little shop and he said that we were trying to organize it. Now frankly, I didn't even know it existed 'cause it was so small and insignificant. . . . The very first thing he says is "Why do you have a picket line?" I told him if he can't behave himself, he can get the heck out. . . .

When Falzone's employees came in and said, "We can't do it [work there anymore]," then we took them out on strike. There were only about fifteen or twenty people at the most. They were out one week or two weeks and we paid them strike benefits. It was authorized. I had a department fund at the time and we put them on the [picket line], and we gave them fifteen dollars a week, which was more than they made in the shop, I guess. Anyone that was married got fifteen dollars, and I think the majority had a family.

Anyway, here comes Falzone. He says, "What are you doing to my shop?" His people [workers] would say to us, "We aren't gonna join the union if you can't get Falzone [to go along]." This is a little shop. Min [Matheson, chap. 3] then comes into the picture and I said, "Look Min, we need Falzone like we need ten bullets in our head. Who gives a damn?" Now, we are concerned about the workers, we are concerned with every worker. But the [union] sign doesn't sit in Falzone's shop. We don't need it. We don't even want the damn thing. Why? He's got five members of the family working in the shop. As I told him, "I'm not gonna make it my life's work sitting in your shop trying to see that you pay five cents for a pocket, because your wife is going to do this and your mother and somebody else [is doing it]. Who needs you? Now either you behave yourself or you can get the hell out. We don't care if you join the union or not." But the Teamsters wouldn't deliver [his materials], so he comes back. He wants to sign [the union contract]. . . .

When Min Matheson comes into the picture, she was the business agent in Wilkes-Barre. I was the organizer, and I was in charge of whatever I thought an organizer does—frankly everything. We used to laugh and play it by ear. It's not that anybody came in and said, "This is the way you do things." I wrote the leaflets and we distributed them. We knew that we had to distribute them. [If] there's a [positive] response, then we moved in. Whatever shop gave us the response, that's where we moved in. . . .

In the meantime, Zimmerman got ill. Within months he was in the hospital for a week and then he died. This is 1946. So they needed to split the district. Mr. [David] Gingold was the director [of the Northeast Department]. During the war years, Mr. Weisberg, who was the director, had died. At that time, I think the department had no more than five thousand members, if it had that many. We were growing [i.e., the Northeast Department] into thirty thousand or forty thousand members, and he decided to split the [northeastern Pennsylvania] district [into] Wilkes-Barre and Scranton. They made me an acting manager [of Scranton]. Shortly thereafter [he said], "I want you to go back to Harrisburg," 'cause that's what I considered my home. . . .

Well, [when the district] was divided in two, Min is made manager of Wilkes-Barre [the Wyoming Valley District]. I go back to Harrisburg and, in Scranton, they eventually put in a good fellow who was the business agent, Enzo Grassi. Min then began to do the work [in the Wyoming Valley] and periodically she'd call me. I'd say, "Min, I can't come up because the bosses didn't say so." So [one time] Dave [Gingold] calls and said, "John, we got stuck up there, we need you to go back. I want to know what's going on because they have a strike that seems to be endless. Go there and we'll put a finish to it, there'll be a conclusion." . . .

[After the war], we made a list [of shops] that we needed to organize. I had written to New York and they sent in about eight or ten people [i.e., organizers]. When the war was over, they decided to organize this region, and one of the "chains" was the [Louis] Gutstein chain. Now, Gutstein had one plant called Lee Manufacturing, and Lee was in the old armory building [in Pittston]. It was sort of foreboding because most of our shops were just little holes in the wall, so here's an armory![5]

In the meantime, I found out that a few months before I opened up the office [in Pittston], they had sent in an organizer to the region, and this guy went into a little place in Dupont. It was a garment shop owned by Gutstein and it was run by the chief of police! They took this organizer, a big fellow, and beat the hell out of him, sent him to the hospital for six weeks, and the ILG then sent him to California. . . .

The Gutstein shop employed about 120 people. There was a very lovely woman there, very well liked, who was quite popular even with her boss. But for some reason, I don't know what she had said or done, but he told her to get the hell out and pushed her out—the boss pushed her out—and everybody [i.e., the workers] ran out in the street [i.e., walked out]. The next thing we know is that we have another strike. Min was in this region and Enzo was in Scranton. It was a Thursday [when] the fight took place between this boss and this particular girl, Angela—lovely, just an elegant, beautiful woman—Italian woman.

So Monday morning who comes in but Enzo Grassi. "We gotta put 'em back, Johnny, Johnny, Johnny," he says. I said, "What are you talking about?" He says, "We have to put these people back." I says, "How could you put them back? We don't even have our bearings first? And under what pretense? You don't go and tell people, 'You go back to work.' For what? We don't even know the boss." "Well," he says, "I won't be telling you this if I didn't get orders from home [the ILGWU New York office], from the director." I nod: "Did you ask him under what circumstances? Is he [the owner] taking Angela back? Is everybody going back? Is he actually talking to us?" I said, "This is nonsense." So he says, "OK, I have to call Gingold."

So he calls the boss and says, "Mr. Gingold, have you ever put . . ." I [immediately took the phone and] I says, "What's the situation?" [Gingold said], "Well, you know we can't go in and put the chief of police's shop on strike." I said, "I didn't pull it out. This is what happened. The people are out. What do we tell him [the chief]? Get in touch with you?" He says, "Of course." I says, "If he does, then he has to get in touch with me so I can tell the people that your boss is calling [you back to work], and under what circumstances." Anyway, to make the story short, finally, they [Gingold and the New York officers] thought, "We're gonna put them back." But I says, "We don't put people back like this, this is nonsense."

So he [the chief] comes in and he wants to talk to me. I says, "Well, come in. Now these are your people. Would *you* pull them out? To begin with, we knew that the big chance was that it could stifle the shop. We can't pull out one shop out of six or seven that is Gutstein-owned." He says to me, "Well, you know who I am?" I says, "I know, you're the chief of police, and I'm sure it's not your ability to make garments that won you this position. And the last shop that I would want to pull is yours. We want to have some settlement and we're not gonna have a settlement by coming here and strangulating you and getting you fired." I said, "What about the girl, this young lady?" I said to him, "If you take anybody back . . . [i.e., you have to take Angela back]. And you're forgetting [forgiving] them everything, [and will] you make some adjustments under loss of pay? And would you be talking to me at least unofficially when these people go back? The reason we're sending the people back is because we know that there is no particular point in pulling one shop out of seven [owned by Gutstein]."

At any rate, he says, "At least I respect your integrity," whatever that meant. I said, "Now look, there's lots of things I might tell you that you wouldn't like.

We could disagree but we don't have to be disagreeable. These people are yours, they work in your community, they go to your church, and I certainly don't want to come in and create a situation where these people would not be able to function." Well, they went back [to work] and after that I went back to Harrisburg.

I went back again to make sure that everything was smooth so he thinks we did well by him. The Gutsteins supposedly had a lot of influence with the union in New York for some reason, which is very difficult to describe. At one time the union talked to them when they moved to this region. They moved into small communities, getting free rent from the communities and no tax for a number of years. Why? Because the wages that they would bring, the tax they would [eventually] bring, and people would be taken off the relief rolls. That alone was an incentive to open up shops.

On the other hand, the New York ILG did not want these shops in existence [here] because they knew they [the New York garment workers and industry] were in tremendous competition [with Wyoming Valley shops], even if they [the latter] were organized. Why? Because the people of the International from New York in those days wanted to send them [runaway shops] back to the big cities. Well, who the heck is gonna give up a job, or join a union, just to lose a job? We had to find an approach, contrary to what the International said. We said, "Now, you want the shops [unionized]? This is the way it's gonna be done." But at least we were able to bring in the membership so that this region [Wyoming Valley] grew to fifteen thousand members whereas Scranton, that originally had seven thousand, was about nine thousand.

Q: Why was northeastern Pennsylvania a main destination for the New York shops?

JJ: They were going other places but this was closest to New York. Now there were a number of [New] Jersey districts, but for some reason the people in Jersey had reputations of fighting. There was a period in the late twenties when [the Socialist presidential candidate] Norman Thomas was arrested many times in Jersey City and on the Boardwalk [in Atlantic City] and all that, so that the employers [in New York] were not anxious to go across the river. Another thing is that the union from New York City could cross the river fast because it was near, so that they [the owners] also thought they [the New York City ILGWU] would bring in gangs of pickets. They [the owners] moved here because there was enough unemployment and, even though the miners had a reputation of being militant, many of the mines had been closed for one reason or the other and there was no pay whatever coming in, so the wives were brought into the shops.

Some of the people [i.e., shop owners] that came in were in the union at one time, and a few were even union officials who fell out of grace, whatever may have happened. They became employers that came here and they opened up a plant. When we [the ILGWU] came in we tried to unscramble who is this and who is that, you know, who's friendly? But as soon as you got to the door, the friendship disappeared. In other words, at one time they were in the union, or they were officials of the union, but they wanted this freedom.

Gutstein said the union told him they would not organize [his shops].[6] I don't know what deals were made but the important thing is this: that if the union made some kind of an arrangement, they didn't say [to the union's field staff], "If the workers come to us, you behave in such a manner." If the workers come to us, we certainly were not going to refuse them because this is the function of the union. And what would stop them from going to the Teamsters or District 69, the one district that was a catchall that the CIO [Congress of Industrial Organizations] had?[7] This was something that was a weapon we would use.

Say look, if people [employers] on some occasions had problems . . . [I worked with them]. When I was in Pottsville, this one employer would come across with some raises that were a necessary part of the agreement. He had a guy who, I remember, was a veteran that had been in jail. He hires him and I don't know what kind of money he paid him, very little, obviously, not even the standard. When I went in to talk to him [the owner] about it, he said, "Well, this guy's dumb." I said, "Well, I saw this crate that he lifts, which is at least three hundred pounds. I'm sure you're not paying him to be an adviser to you. But you're not paying him a decent wage, you're not even paying him a minimum wage, and you're taking advantage of this guy."

So Gingold—I don't know what influence he [the owner] had—calls me up and says, "What gives?" I said, "This man called you in New York over one individual?" I said, "Now look, the Teamsters came in and told me that some of the people [i.e., workers in the shop], they don't want our union. Certainly this guy [the owner] is not gonna come in and tell me he's a good friend of mine. I wouldn't care if we lost the shop, but not under these conditions. We're not gonna have a situation where we would be ashamed to walk down the street [and hear people say], 'You're selling our people down [the river; i.e., failing them].'"

So I says [to the owner], "You can have your shop." He called him [Gingold] back. I got the raise and I got everything else! Now let them prove that what I told Gingold was true or not. It certainly was true because the standards were absolutely outrageous. The point is you have to continuously be alert if you have the concern of the people, and we certainly did. At no time did they ever say—they maybe disagreed with me and my policies—but no one ever said that I did not stand up for our people.

I use the words "stand up" rather than "fight" because it's very loosely used, this fight business. We have to have decent standards, and when we went into the shop, we wanted a certain rate. . . . We knew that we had some understanding about how long it took [to make a garment] so in the Garment Workers' Union we had to really know rates—and know the difference between the cloths and what took longer to make, and the colors that have to be changed, the threads and all these various things. . . .

JOHN "JOHNNY" JUSTIN

In the trade union movement, we had a more solid arrangement, because once we got the contract, we were able to establish not just the dues, but in our union we had sick benefits. They [the workers] got paid holidays from the employer and they also got vacation pay from the union. We gave them 2 percent [of their pay] at that time in July and 2 [percent] in December. Subsequently, that alone was more than the [union] dues they paid. The dues have come up considerably, they increased it, but in those days, they knew [they had benefits]. Then came retirement, which we also established, and that we had to sweat because in many districts the International had talked about retirement but didn't all the time follow up.

We also had the Health Center here [in Wilkes-Barre], which *we* established—not because New York wanted it. Credit is due to Min Matheson because when she did it, they [the union leaders in New York] wanted to know what kind of feathers is she sprouting, or wings, or all this. These are some of the beautiful terms that were used to tell you, "Who the hell are you?" We said, "The union talked about health centers, they have it in New York, they have it in Philadelphia, why not here?" So we opened it. We had it in our office.

I [once] had the office in Pittston, but in recent times, they closed the office in Pittston, they closed the office in Hazelton, they will [soon] close the office in Scranton. We're shrinking so that they're moving backward and they're not organizing. In the days when we first organized, believe me, the union was very poor. I remember the time when the miners' union loaned the ILG $100,000. It was public, but the miners' union had shrank and went backward, and we became great big and powerful. In those days, we had a lot of spirit and no money. Subsequently, we got the sick benefits, which we established and remain, but we closed the health centers because they became too expensive.

Q: When did the Health Center in the Wyoming Valley close?

JJ: It's been about a year. They closed it in Allentown about a year ago. They closed it in Philadelphia recently. They closed it in Chicago about three years ago. There's none in San Francisco. But New York City still remains. When we first opened it [in the Wyoming Valley], our shops were scattered and we had what they called the mobile health unit that was like a bus with all the equipment. In those days it cost almost a quarter of a million dollars to organize it, get a bus like that, specially made, which meant that they took all kinds of tests, blood, urinalysis, X-ray, with a doctor and a nurse going into the shop, of course, with the knowledge and consent of the employer. So [we did] that instead of the workers coming in from some distance. All it took was ten minutes' time, fifteen minutes' time. We sort of did it in such a well-organized [way] that it'd be outside, connected to the shop. We had the list [of members] and there was only one waiting in line, and as soon as you come out, the next one goes; so that everyone in the shop that was willing was given a thorough examination. Nobody could be forced. We gave them all kinds of services in those days. . . .

The people who are in charge of the union today are certainly not the founders or the builders. When I speak of builders, I'm not thinking of the 1910 period because actually they were skeleton organizations. But in the thirties, the unions really took some root in the country. In the thirties they were built.

Q: Let me ask you about organized crime in the Wyoming Valley area. Can you shed any light on that topic?

JJ: Well, it's a very difficult thing to really pinpoint, but we know that the underworld had considerable influence. Now in my shops—when I say "my" I mean the shops that I serviced—I was in Pottsville [for a time], but I was in this region [the Wyoming Valley], too, and I managed in Harrisburg. At least I don't know that they were as visible [in Pottsville and Harrisburg], but in this region we had a number of shops that had connections, they said.

I do remember this particular shop [in Pottsville] where the employer didn't want to pay for the holiday, for example. He wanted to negotiate. He was friendly and at one time he was even in the Leftist movement. Some of them [like him] claimed that they knew and read Leftist publications, and they knew all about Marx—for whatever it was worth. I said, "Well, that has nothing to do with the ILG anyway. We're not interested in Karl Marx, Mr. Steel." They [former Leftist owners] were people who already had enough knowledge. They were not dummies and yet they had made certain stands. This particular guy just didn't want to pay. He wanted to negotiate. I said, "But we already negotiated this agreement and you accepted the New York contract. I can't negotiate on a contract that's already been accepted because, in the first place, you had already signed it, which means you accepted this agreement. And, secondly, you want to undo what everybody else has? It's not that you want to do something; you just don't want to pay. And if you don't pay, why should the other guy pay? So this is uniform, but [if] it's fair or unfair, this is what everybody has—the same standards [for everyone] who makes the same garment, same hours, same minimums. We'll give you a certain [amount of] time until you get acclimated, until your people become more proficient, but otherwise the standards are the same." He went [away angry] and he says he's gonna bring in his "friends."

He brought in this guy, Mike Pappadio. Pappadio was supposed to own a shop in New York City—pleating, embroidery. He says he's his partner and I'll have to meet with him. But everybody knew that Mike Pappadio had certain "connections," supposedly. He was with the Lucchese [crime] family, so they said. Well, he comes in and I says, "Now look, Mike, do you want certain things different than anybody else? Why? What am I supposed to tell your workers—not that I need your help or advice—but why are you different than anybody else? After all, there are sisters and uncles and aunts [that] work in the shops so they know each other, they know the standards, they know when a holiday pulls in. You know, we got certain special holidays." He says, "You're right!"[8]

JOHN "JOHNNY" JUSTIN

One time there was a stoppage. [Victor] Amuso was also supposed to be with the underworld.[9] Every shop was out, every shop that makes this garment by name. We said, "OK, we're not gonna work. We'll withhold our services." He calls up and he says, "John, what are you doing to my shop?" Oh, before that, he calls my business agent, Morris Schuman, and I see he's shaking. I says, "What is it, Morris?" He says, "Mike Pappadio and Amuso are on the telephone." I says, "What do they want?" So I get on the phone and I says, "Yes, what is it? I'm the manager here and do you have a problem?" "Why are you scaring my workers?" he said. "You got the people out [on strike]." I says, "Where are you calling from, Sol Greene's office or someplace in the International [office in New York]?" I says, "You know the agreement better than I do because you negotiated this agreement and we swallowed it. Now you come in and you ask what are we gonna do? Tell me this: you want your people back?" He said, "Yes." I said, "Well, suppose I put them back, what should I tell them? Why are you different than anybody else? Please tell me, so I [can] tell them. Are you different? Are you an employer, or aren't you an employer?"

There he was, a bit apologetic. I said, "After all, it's the people. They work for you, they don't work for me, and if I tell them you settled something, and the International would tell me you settled, then the people'd go back. So I should tell them you called me and I'm doing it different than anybody else?" I said, "I'm only asking you." I hear the other guy say, "The question answers itself." So he says, "OK, they go back whenever the rest of them do." I said, "*You* talk to them." Now some of this was directed to Morris Schuman. They told him, "I know you got a wife and child, and if you want them to be well, you better send my people back." That's when I got on the telephone.

Q: They threatened him?

JJ: That's it exactly.

Q: Were you ever threatened?

JJ: Not in this particular manner, but one day when I was in New York at the Current Restaurant and Mike Pappadio came in and says, "Hi." He greeted me very warmly, and he says, "John, I understand you're having a lot of problems with the union." I said, "Well, I don't know Mike, thank you for the information. I've only been with them for twenty-five years and you seem to know more than me." He says "John, believe me, I know what I'm talking about, and I can help you." He says, "I know you know my number but I'm going to give you my card, and all you have to do is call me and I will help you." He had a factory in New York. I never bothered [with it]. I knew that it existed but I never checked it. But he gave me the card.

Q: Did Pappadio have any branches in the Wyoming Valley?

JJ: No. He had that shop with this particular guy in Pottsville, but we still don't know [for certain]. He came in and out. When I "graduated," Mike Pappadio was in the office. I use the word "graduated" because gradually I was "promoted" out of the region. I was going to New York. I went here or there. Mike Pappadio became a very constant visitor [before I left]. I wasn't always there, but one morning he was [in the Pottsville office] and I called New York, and I said, "If this guy doesn't work out [i.e., cooperate with the ILGWU], there's gonna be a revolution here." He left the office. So I was able to do what I had to do. I was leaving the district at the time. The point is, they were there.

Q: Any others?

JJ: Another time [Victor] Amuso was in the region. One of the shops I had gone into—at the time Min was in charge of the [Wyoming Valley] District—and I went into some shop in Pittston or Duryea, I don't remember. The boss was not in. [There was a problem] involving something with the contract. As I was leaving, I see a car pull in. I was just getting into my car. The guy, he says, "Hey you, hey you," and I say, "Yes?" He said, "What are you doing here?" I said, "Well, I represent the union." He tells me that he's the boss and begins saying something pretty loud, I don't even remember exactly, but it wasn't complimentary. I said, "Well, I came in to see you, and I was told you were out."

The next thing I know, he said, "Come in to talk." And who was in the back? Amuso. So he says, "John, John, come in." I walked in that place, the office of this factory, and Amuso says, "You sit here," points to the desk. I said, "No, no, this is fine." He tells him [the shop boss], "I want you to know one thing: don't you dare ever talk to Mr. Justin in that manner 'cause I had many a disagreement with John Justin, but no one talks to him in that manner." I said, "This is not necessary." "No, no," he says, "John, I know we battled together." I said, "Well, I don't know that we did battle." "Anyway," he says, "you been pretty fair. Whatever you intended [to do] you told us, you mentioned the words, there was no roundabout double-talking, which this union is very well-known for."

Well, I didn't know who he [the shop boss] was, but there was a certain amount [of contact with mobsters]. I don't even know if he was putting on an act or whatever. They never actually physically touched me, even with Pappadio, or Falzone, or Amuso, or [alleged crime boss Russell] Bufalino. When his [Bufalino's] people had been at that shop [in Pittston], they were always very nice to me. For whatever reason, he stayed away. . . .

Q: You mentioned that the miners helped you. What about other union cooperation?

JJ: Well, when we had the problem in Pittston particularly, we didn't have any serious charges or arrests [against us] but they [the police] tried to take us in. I called [Thomas] Kennedy who was lieutenant governor [of Pennsylvania] and also treasurer of the [United Mine Workers] union, and I told him, "The mayor [of Pittston] told me that you're a friend of the union. I don't expect you go out of your way and do something that's improper, but we've been taken in [arrested] for what? Because we are acting from the sidewalk picketing?" There was some little fight, if that's the word. One of the pickets was pushed by a policeman and I think he pushed him back. We weren't even there at the time, but I got there while this thing was going on and Min was with me. Min told something to the policeman. The next thing I know, they were really wrestling on the floor, the policeman and [Angelo] DePasquale.

Q: Who was DePasquale [chap. 4]?

JJ: He was on our picket line. He was a local boy. As a matter of fact, his girlfriend was a chairlady of one of the union shops. I don't frankly even remember what his status was. He was a sympathizer [of the ILGWU].[10] But anyway, because of the fact that he was on the picket line, the policeman pushed him at that little shop Falzone [owned]. They were wrestling on the floor. I said something, Min said something, and the next thing you know the policeman says, "You're under arrest." So we went, we followed him. First Min. Min said that he was pulling her arm. I was in the other room and nothing really happened to me. He just took me in, didn't even book me, and the mayor comes in.

He greeted me warmly, and I said, "Now, here we are. We're under arrest and I don't even know why." He said, "You're not under arrest." I said, "But Min is in the next room." He calls her in and he says, "No, no, there's no charges against you." We were getting ready to go, and I said, "Just a minute. I have to tell you what really happened in the line. This fellow was wrestling with a policeman and I don't know, I think the policeman took his gun out and put it on the ground. I kicked it under the automobile because I didn't know what was gonna happen." I said, "Here they are, the policeman lost his gun as they were wrestling, so I just want you to know about it." He said, "Tell him not to be around, tell DePasquale to get the hell out of the thing."[11]

I mentioned to the mayor the fact that Lieutenant Governor Kennedy said that we are going to find friends in Pittston. [I said], "Not this situation where we are harassed on the picket line." I don't even know what started this argument because I just got in when they were already on the ground, the policeman and DePasquale. They were wrestling but we were taken in because we sort of interfered with the thing. If that could be called an incident, I don't know, but it was very mild. Still, Kennedy called him and said that the ILG is not going to create any incompatible situations within the community.

However, some of the local people, in particular one of the organizers who was a local man, said that some terrible incidents developed in Pittston long before I got there. Some of them [shops] were burned, they said.[12] I don't even know because it's not our responsibility to say it. But anyway, some shops never came to the union during the two, three years prior to my arrival [in 1946] and I asked [the New York leaders], "Why didn't you tell me this? Are you trying to discourage me?" Whatever I was going to do, I did. Of course, I knew one thing, which is very important: whoever went there [before me] never had an office. I opened up the office with the OK of the International. . . .

Q: How long were you in the Wyoming Valley District?

JJ: Well, on and off, I spent two years, then I came back again and they opened an office for me in Nanticoke and I managed that area. This is after 1962, I opened

FIG. 21 | ILGWU general strike rally, 1958. Photo courtesy of the Kheel Center, Cornell University.

up an office in Nanticoke. I had that area, [including] Sweet Valley and all that. Min had insisted I come down. Of course, nothing happens without the International but it wasn't exactly that I volunteered.

I wasn't too particularly interested on this occasion and other occasions because I had certain differences [with Mrs. Matheson]. I was very fond of Min, I still am. We're very good friends. And yet at the time, Min could be very militant and then be compelled, I suppose, to make changes in her procedure and policy without telling. I was the only one, frankly, that not only objected but just did what we originally stated. We can't arbitrarily just change our mind, because we're dealing with people and we can't change them. I can change my position, not my views, but I'm not gonna go in and tell the girls, "The jig is up," [i.e., what we had agreed on has changed] or something of this sort. We had some people come in and say, "Orders from the boss [i.e., Min]." "Well," I said, "tell our Napoleon [that] the queen of Jerusalem's crown has been sent and she can't give orders without wearing that crown. Now you can go and jump." And we went ahead and did what we had to do because in the long run we had to

JOHN "JOHNNY" JUSTIN

deliver the shop, and this was exactly even with New York. Many of these people [organizers] did what they were ordered and lost the shop. . . .

Q: Was this area tougher to organize than, say, Harrisburg?

JJ: There was a different element here. There was a different approach. Min was more militant. We didn't have to do some of the same things in Harrisburg. But in organizing the shops [in the Wyoming Valley], we used the pressure of getting as many people in the union as possible, maybe the whole shop, so that the employer had no choice but to sign. We used the method of getting the Teamsters not to deliver and that would sort of paralyze the employer. Eventually, we didn't even have to use those tactics because they knew that we would use everything possible, not anything violent, but everything possible to bring it to a conclusion.

So we never had any long drawn out affairs except the few, which I remembered. One [shop] in Edwardsville eventually came in [to the union] and he was also a part of what they called the Kaplan-Elias gang, whatever that meant. They were also part of this Lucchese gang. All these people that we talked about [organized crime] were really not visible. Were not visible. It was just certain ones who they're aligned with. We never saw them together. We knew that they could pull certain strings, that they could do certain things, but how?[13] Through telephones, through reaching certain people at a higher level [in the ILGWU], or whatever it was.[14] But actually to come in and stop us physically, they can't, with the exception of the few instances that I told you about. They never did anything harmful to me, anyways, but they were there.

Q: Was Harrisburg easier to organize for that reason?

JJ: I would think so, yeah, because we had to work harder [in the Wyoming Valley]. We had a radio program, for example, called *Mary Brown*, where we talked and recited. In those days there were no TVs. We talked about this girl [Mary Brown], why she joined the union, what she found out, how she earned so little money, and there was the question of holidays. We decided [to focus on] the experience of this girl, what happened to her after she joined the union, and how much she learned.[15]

The truth of the matter is that we had a very fine educational program. They [the members] became active in the Democratic Party. Some of us probably thought that we should go even further than that, but people who were not politically motivated became active because of what we did. We had active committees in the shops so they [the members] became community leaders in many instances and in some cases our girls ran for school boards or other things. To that degree, we succeeded in getting our people more alert.

Q: When you say Min was militant, do you think it was because she had to be militant in order to organize, or do you think it was a personality style?

JJ: No, yes, no! Well, her personality was [such that] she's a more aggressive individual even though her husband was a little more reserved and could change many of the plans. That was possibly the reason why Min would plan something and sometimes not carry it through. But the area was more aggressive. There was more resistance by the employers here and they had more "connections" [i.e., to organized crime or to high-ranking ILGWU leaders]. Again, these connections we couldn't put our finger on. And they [some owners] just wouldn't do certain things, even after they said they would. So what happened? Somebody got into the picture, somebody called so-and-so, somebody did this. The point is that the shop didn't [cooperate]. We were unable to enforce the contract. After all, she was only the manager. She had business agents but she couldn't explain [the connections].

These people [the workers] couldn't see those things because many of them were local. It didn't matter to them. They went to the shop and they asked for another dime. They knew something of piece rates, and the girls had to get to their business agent [if they had a problem]. They didn't go any further. Even some of the business agents wanted that kept to New York—they were immune to controversy. We, on the other hand, said that we invited it, that is, by our policies. In other words, we thought we had certain principles that we wanted to realize, and so did Min. We tried to go through [with it].

Q: Why didn't this type of thing happen as often in Harrisburg?

JJ: Because here [the Wyoming Valley], maybe the employers' association [PGMA] was more involved, they may have been closer to the situation. And the manufacturers and jobbers [in New York] that they got work from also had connections in New York. For example, there was the shop in Sweet Valley that was owned by [alleged mobster Thomas] Lucchese, that was Three-Finger Brown, whose son-in-law was a Gambino.[16] By the way, Sherwood Fashions in New York City was a shop owned by Lucchese and Gambino. I don't even know who runs it today. . . .

When Leslie Fay came into the picture, they [the ILGWU leaders in New York] didn't want them here. I don't know what the point was. They said that we were responsible for bringing them in but we didn't ask them. "They would come in just because we asked them?" I said. They didn't even mention the name of the person who was in charge at the time [owner Fred Pomerantz], but New York was furious. Eventually he was organized, but they wanted him in New York.

Q: Why?

JJ: Well, because the union was based in New York. They're not interested in building a union. Subsequently, when we resisted in the later years, we were told that Dubinsky was supposed to have said—I don't even know if it's so—that he "doesn't give a damn if you lose a shop because the same work will be done in another union shop in Oregon" for all he cares. So long as it was union, he didn't care if it was made in Oregon or in South Carolina. The truth of the matter is that it wasn't really so, because the New York union certainly didn't want the shops to slip out of hand. Their whole strength depended on that, and the more people they have, the stronger they are.

JOHN "JOHNNY" JUSTIN

But as the employers began to move out, that was the threat. They [the owners] will come to the workers [in New York] and tell them, "You see what happened to your sister's shop? They went out to New Jersey, or they went to Pennsylvania, and now if you gonna force me, I'm gonna close up my doors. The union is putting on too much pressure." If the union was not doing its job, then it's corrupt, and if the union was doing its job, then we were putting on too much pressure and they were gonna leave.

Don't forget, we're not dealing with steel and mining where they can't easily move the factory or a mine. They could move the whole damn shop overnight. [One time] we went in there [to a particular shop], we looked in the window—nobody in it. We saw it, but the machines were gone overnight, in a weekend. I remember this was in New Cumberland [Pennsylvania], honestly. It was a union shop. It just went. In New Cumberland, just across the river from Harrisburg. . . .

Q: New York was the largest region. Northeastern Pennsylvania was one of the larger garment localities outside of New York. In this region we had individuals like you, and Min and Bill Matheson, who were seen by the union leadership in New York as rebellious in a certain sense. Was that the case?

JJ: To some degree, we were independent.

Q: Was the New York union leadership disturbed by what had been happening in Pennsylvania?

JJ: Very unhappy, obviously, very unhappy. It seems that there was going to be a house cleaning of a lot of "independent" people. There must have been an awful lot of people because Oscar Newman, who was in Allentown on some pretense or another, was being removed and he had been appointed when Sol Greene, who was very popular at one time, got "promoted" to a New York setup, at a New York local. So he was being removed. . . .

The International, by the way, I told them that the underworld was trying to get a foothold in the union [in northeastern Pennsylvania]. Which probably I made a mistake [doing because] I'd written a letter to Dubinsky. It's foolish to write to your president to tell him [something] that he already no doubt knows, and if you tell him in writing he has to tell you what he will do. I mean, the fact that I'm in the International doesn't necessarily mean I couldn't have been an FBI agent, too. I don't know what was forcing the [issue], but certainly it [the letter] didn't work to our benefit.

When I eventually went in to see Dubinsky, he wanted to know if I signed it [the letter]. [I said], "My name is on it. I signed it. It's mine." He just started to scream. I said, "Now look, President Dubinsky, you're good enough to give me fifteen minutes of your very valuable time. I have fought for this union with courage and dignity, and if I can't defend myself, what value am I to this union? Now you told me you'll give me this time." I got up because he was screaming. I said, "If you continue screaming, you'll be spending the fifteen minutes. I won't have any time left and you'll have laryngitis." Then he called his secretary and

FIG. 22 | Sol "Chick" Chaiken, president of the ILGWU, speaking at a dinner, circa 1984. Photo courtesy of the Kheel Center, Cornell University.

says, "Call Chick [Sol Chaiken] down, call Chick down." He [Chaiken] became the assistant to Gingold. We misjudged Chaiken. Subsequently, Chick became the [Northeast Department assistant] director and later the [ILGWU] president. But we didn't think that this would happen. It didn't even matter. We were not on his [Dubinsky's] side, obviously, and he said something [to the effect] that I was entitled to six weeks' vacation. I said, "I ain't comin' to talk to you about a vacation and you know that." We just talked for a few more minutes and that was the end of the hearing.

The point is, I went in to talk to him about certain things that were going on. Jack Halpern, who was my friend and assistant to the director, came in [later] and said, "What happened?" I said, "All right, he screamed. I don't know if I won anything. I just stood there." This is some of the things that politically [went on]. They didn't like some of the things we did. . . .

Even though the Ladies' Garment Workers' Union was, I would say, 80 percent women, there was a very small percentage of women who really had the position of manager. They had one vice president of the twenty-one [members], Rose Pesotta. She wrote *Bread and Roses* [*sic; Bread upon the Waters*], but subsequently she resigned in disgust because she said that she was just there [had no real influence].[17] Pesotta had grown very critical of the ILGWU's predominately

JOHN "JOHNNY" JUSTIN

male hierarchy and their treatment of women. She was the only female vice president of the union. Subsequently, they always had one woman. They had Evelyn Dubrow as one of the vice presidents.[18] She was the lobbyist. Not an elected position, not a position where you have members [under you], and if you don't have members, you have nothing in any union. It's the members. If you're an assistant to the president, or educational director, or director of the union label, or something like that, it's meaningless. They're merely appointed jobs. You have no members under you. You could come in and make a beautiful speech, but it means nothing in the long run as far as influence and power in the union.[19]

Clementine "Clem" Lyons

Garment Worker, Business Agent, and
Chorus Performer and Director

One of the best-known individuals in the Wyoming Valley ILGWU, "Clem" Lyons occupied multiple union roles during her career: worker, organizer, business agent, show performer, playwright, chorus director, and confidante to Min Matheson (chap. 3). Her passionately told story reveals an immensely energetic and dedicated person who cultivated a vast store of personal and community resources. She describes her vigorous participation in organizing campaigns, including some against criminally affiliated shops in Pittston where she served as a business agent. She nonchalantly describes several intimidations and warnings about personal assaults, material threats to her home, as well as car and package bombs. Through it all, she remained steadfast in the drive to build and maintain the ILGWU. The chorus stands as one of her main contributions to building union and community solidarity.

Clementine "Clem" Lyons, from audio-recorded interviews with Robert P. Wolensky conducted at Ms. Lyons's home in Wyoming, Pennsylvania, on July 5, 1990, and with Robert P. Wolensky and Kenneth C. Wolensky conducted at Ms. Lyons's home on July 24, 1993. The interviews are included in the Wyoming Valley Oral History Project, which is one of eight projects within the Northeastern Pennsylvania Oral and Life History Collection housed in the Eberly Family Special Collections Library, Penn State University Libraries.

CL: I became a member of the ILGWU in April of 1947. That came about because on a Thursday afternoon a rumor spread through the factory that anyone who is over thirty-eight years old was gonna be laid off. The following Monday morning when we got back to work, there were people who had gray hair from the time I could remember knowin' them, but they heard the rumor and

FIG. 24 | Emkay Manufacturing Company, Wyoming, Pennsylvania, 1953. Photo courtesy of Lukasik Studio.

they went home over the weekend and the [hair-dye] bottles caught hell and some were red-haired and some were black-haired. Everybody wanted to hang on to their jobs. We were makin' forty-five cents an hour.

Q: What shop was it?

CL: The shop was here on West Sixth Street in Wyoming, and it was called the Emkay Manufacturing Company. It was owned by a man named Mac Kahn. He was one of the four richest men in New York City. But he was very adamant. He didn't want the union in the very beginning but all they had to do was keep playing on this rumor that anybody over thirty-eight years old was on their way out. . . .

He had got a lot of assistance from the Chamber of Commerce out of Pittston and the Committee of 100 in Wilkes-Barre [to promote economic development], where they let him have, I guess, ten years or somethin' like that before he had to pay any taxes. We had some women in the factory who had worked in union shops—dress factories—on Eighth Street in Wyoming and they were smart enough not to say anything, but on their lunch hour, they went up to the grocery store and called Mrs. Matheson. They explained the threats that were being made about "If you're thirty-eight, out you go," and some other nasty things that were said by some of their hatchet women they had as floorladies. I would say that day and the next day when we came out of work, it was an organizer's dream come true! Everybody was walkin' over to the telephone pole [across the street] and signin' the cards for the ILG. It took from maybe October 'til April to get it straightened out and we were made members of the ILG on April 1, 1947.

Q: Did Mrs. Matheson come right over?

FIG. 25 | Wyoming Valley ILGWU members' fashion show, circa 1965. Photo courtesy of Lukasik Studio.

CL: Oh yes. She was there when we came out of work that afternoon. She spoke to some of the people that she knew, and others of us were introduced to her at the time. I had been away for four and a half years, so I didn't know her, but I met her that day. From that day on, she and I became very good friends. I'll tell ya, she came to town sometime in the thirties [*sic*; forties] and she was the best thing that ever happened to this Valley because once King Coal went out, there was nothin' here. New York was fortunate to take over this Valley because [President Franklin D.] Roosevelt had all those sewing projects in the thirties. He had all his sewing projects where the women learned to sew. Right here. He trained the women and paid them eighty dollars a month. When the sewing projects stopped, there wasn't anything for these women to do and some of them even went back to high school.[1]

When Mac Kahn came in and saw how many high school class rings were being worn, he thought that he had a group of [educated] people. I guess, from the way his stool pigeons had talked to him, he was expecting to find a lot of illiterates who didn't know the score. [He found out that] they just weren't gonna sit still for it. These women were smart enough to know that if you had a union, it would make a difference. It was the best thing in the world, you know.

CLEMENTINE "CLEM" LYONS

Mrs. Matheson organized from Duryea to Nanticoke, and at one time, I think we had close to two hundred shops in the district. She had eleven people on her field staff. Now that's a lot of people, you know what I mean. . . . And the one shop fell into line and the next shop fell into line. Some of the bigger ones fell into line first, like McKitterick[-Williams] and Leslie Fay, and then the others began to trickle in, but it wasn't an easy battle. It was a constant battle.

Q: Do you recall any specific battles?

CL: Well, in '53, the dress manufacturers in Pittston caused a strike. I think it was August 10, if I remember correctly, and they were only out for a couple of days. [The] New York [union leadership] settled with the dress people this quick. (*snaps fingers*) We had gone out in sympathy with the dress people [in New York] because we knew our contract was comin' up shortly and Emkay wouldn't settle with us. So we were out from August 10 until October 3. They [the ILGWU] set up tents down on West Sixth Street [in Wyoming] across the street from the plant.

We had our picketers out twenty-four hours a day carryin' signs. Nothin' was in, nothin' was out, and Mrs. Matheson used to come every day to check on the activities and make sure that we wouldn't get into any trouble if there had been any altercation of any sort. She wanted to make sure that we didn't do anything that we shouldn't do.

Q: Did you ever run into the shop owner while you were on that picket line?

CL: Oh yes. We went to picket his place in New York City in bathing suits. We made the bathing suits here and then when he wouldn't sit down to negotiate with us, Mrs. Matheson came up with the idea that we should go to New York and show him that he'd better sit down because we weren't gonna sit still for the silliness he wanted to pull on us. He wanted to take our Christmas bonus off us, and the piecework rates weren't that great. As I said, we were makin' forty-five cents an hour [in 1947], so we might have been makin' sixty-five or seventy-five cents an hour by that time [1953].

Q: What was the outcome of your trip to New York?

CL: They took us in to see the judge, and his name was Murphy! (*laughs*)

Q: You were arrested on what charge?

CL: Oh, being more than three hundred yards away from the nearest swimming pool! We held up traffic on the corner of Twenty-Third [Street] and Fifth Avenue [in Manhattan] for an hour and half from twelve noon to one thirty in the afternoon. I think there were nine of us. John Cameron Swayze carried it on [NBC News] television and it was a big hullabaloo. It was a real Madison Avenue approach to a very bad situation, but it worked out in our favor. It was wonderful. There were people who stopped and claimed that we really weren't factory workers. They said that we were people [i.e., actors] in the musical revues in New York and that they [the union] had hired us professionally to come and do the picketing. Then we had to stand with the cameras and tell them where we were from and that we weren't professionals [actors], and that all we wanted was for Mac Kahn to sit down and negotiate with us.

Q: What did the judge say?

CL: Well, he had a hell of a time restraining himself [from laughing], but he was there in all his robes and all his glory. He said to us, "How do you plead?" Of course, the union had a lawyer there for us. I don't even remember what the plea was because I was so worried about being in court, in New York above all, ya know. At least around here, you know people, you could call somebody. In New York, it was a different story. But I guess the New York [union] had the right connections, too, because he gave us a suspended sentence of some sort and told us if we wanted to do any picketing from here on in, we should be back in Wyoming Valley in Pennsylvania to do it.

Q: Was Mrs. Matheson with you?

CL: I don't remember. Her husband [Bill] was with us, and there were several people from the New York office there. I had a "Gay Nineties" suit on, and somebody grabbed me by the hand [after the court case] and we ran through the streets like two nuts and got over to 1710 Broadway where the [union's] New York main office is. When we got off the elevator, you'd think that we had just come from heaven because we had pulled this thing off and got the attention that it needed. It was a real Madison Avenue approach. It was Mrs. Matheson's brainstorm. And then when we saw the cameras, we went to our places [on the picket line] and did a little dance for the news reporters and so forth and so on.

Q: Sounds like you had a successful trip.

CL: We did. We did until we got picked up, but the cops were very understanding. I thought they were very mean and miserable, and I said a few nasty things to them, but I was in the labor movement long enough that I realized that some of the cops who came to take us in probably were friends of unions. They were much nicer to us than some of our own when we came back here. That was '53.[2]

Then we got a contract and there were, oh, I'd say, maybe 350 people in that plant in Wyoming. In 1955 Art Cheston, who was one of Mrs. Matheson's business agents, had a heart problem—he had a little setback—and she was up to her ears in extra work. In the meantime, I had been doin' some work with the [union's] Education Department and she said to me, "Clem, do you think you can leave Emkay for a couple of months?" She said, "Come on staff and take Art Cheston's place until he feels better, and we'll see what happens from there." I said to her, "Well, you talk to him [the boss] at Emkay 'cause I have nine and a half years in." By that time, I had nine and half years of seniority there, and I was single and I didn't feel like I wanted to give up the years. I wanted to make sure that my job would be there for me if and when the three months were over.

Sure enough, Art Cheston came back to work on Christmas week, so I went to her. I said to Mrs. Matheson, "Mr. Cheston is back this morning and if you want me to sit and talk with him for a couple of minutes, I'll tell him what I've done while he was off and I'll go back to Emkay on Monday morning. She said to me, "You're not goin' back to Emkay on Monday morning." So . . . *(crying)*

Q: We'll wait a minute. *(interview temporarily ceased, then continued)* Then you went on permanent staff?

CL: In '55.

Q: What was your first assignment?

CL: Well, they sent me out with a business agent. Her name was Helen Barnosky [later Weiss, chap. 9].[3] She had a problem in a Leslie Fay shop. Of course, I wanted to make a very good impression, so I got all dressed up in a beautiful suit and the shoes to match and the gloves, carrying the gloves even though I didn't need them in October. I wanted to go in and out of shops lookin' like a part of the fashion world. You couldn't go in just any old way.

We got into the shop where there was a very, very bad problem. The man's name was Lumen, the manager of the shop. There were a couple of real tough union members there, I mean, from way back when we had first organized there in the forties. They said to Helen, "He won't move on that [piece rate] price," and they had stopped working. Some of them were sittin' on the sorting table and some of them were just standin' around in their own little cliques. "He won't move on the price and we're not gonna go back to work until he does." Helen said, "According to the law, he doesn't have to negotiate until you go back to work. You go back to work while we negotiate and then everything will be retroactive," which is, you know, favorable.

[It] wasn't favorable to them. They weren't gonna move until it got straightened out. The one girl in particular sat there—I'd say she was in her twenties—and she said, "Well, the only reason why he holds this job, it isn't because of his knowledge, but he's related to Mr. Pomerantz who owns Leslie Fay." With that, the one man who was the big representative for Leslie Fay, Zachary Buckhalter was his name, came out on the floor. He said, "That's it. I heard it. I'm putting the lock on the door today." All I could think of in all this chaos was "Did I leave Emkay to come to this?" Because by that time, Emkay was the place for people to find what was at that time a decent job, you know.

When I came home, my sister was still living—she was like my mother—and I said to her, "My god, Jenny, I don't know whether I did the right thing or not." I said, "I went into that shop this morning and the abuse that Helen Barnosky took, I could never begin to explain." I said, "The women seem so unreasonable and the boss was even worse. He tried to put a lock on the place." I told her that Helen had to call Mrs. Matheson.

Everybody just milled around until Mrs. Matheson got there. She straightened the situation out and got them back to work—and got them a little bit of an increase. But I said, "If that goes on every day and they have fifteen or sixteen or eighteen shops to take care of, I'll end up in the 'booby hatch'" [psychiatric hospital]. My sister said to me, "Don't you complain about it. You go back to work tomorrow and whatever they tell you to do, you do." And it just so happened that I did. No matter what they said to do, I did. If it was go on the picket line, I went on the picket line. If it was go and get dressed up to see somebody special, I did that. And if it was to go to New York, or to hell, to sit in on negotiations—no matter what they told me, I was there. I was there at any hour of the day and night. I never regretted a day of it because I was working with people. I like to help people. Some of them were impossible, but the majority of them were, my god, very, very grateful for anything that you could do for them.

I could remember when we started to talk about fifty dollars for maternity benefits. Oh my god, that seemed like such a big amount of money at the time. And when they first mentioned pensions for the regular workers, that was so far-fetched that it was referred to in the newspapers around here as "pie in the sky." You know, that kind of thing. Then we had the Health Center for many years where the Wilkes-Barre office is now, and Mrs. Matheson was instrumental in getting Dr. Feinberg to take it over and hire a staff of doctors. They did physical examinations free of charge. They didn't treat anybody, really. They'd send a report to your family doctor and then the family doctor would take it from there. So it was a good move because lots of people would have died of cancer long before their time if our doctors hadn't found it. It's just unfortunate that we lost the membership and had to do away with the local [office and, therefore, the Health Center].[4]

Q: What else did Mrs. Matheson say to you about not going back to Emkay?

CL: She told me she had other things in mind for me.

Q: Did she see leadership abilities in you?

CL: I suppose so.

Q: What happened after that first day?

CL: Well, the usual things where people would need a piece-rate adjustment or somebody would give you a health application. In addition to being on the road all day, I'd go back and open up the office in Pittston at three thirty in the afternoon and take dues, or if somebody was out sick and needed a ride to the Health Center, I'd take them. Things like that. Then we had our [chorus] rehearsals on Tuesday and Friday nights. It got to the point where there wasn't a thing goin' on in the community that the ILG wasn't in or invited to. If you mentioned "the union" when you came to town, all you had to do was say, "Where is the union office?" and the place they sent you was the ILG. We became part of the community. See, I had done a lot of work with several [community] groups up there in Pittston, so it was kinda easy for me to get in and talk to some of the women who were active in the organizations.

Q: For example?

CL: The Today's Club at St. Rocco's [Catholic] Church, and there was a group from Our Lady of Mount Carmel [Catholic Church] that was very active up at St. Alphonse's [Catholic] Retreat House. I had been in on several affairs with them.

I had entertained the Mother's Day affairs and things like that, sang for some of their kids' weddings, which made me kind of a native of Pittston. I spent more time in Pittston than I did anyplace else. I could walk into a shop of eighty people and if I didn't see a certain girl there I'd say, "Where's Alberta Carter today?" ya know.

Q: You came to know them very well.[5]

CL: Yeah. If they had somethin' goin' on where they needed a donation, I would sit and help them write a letter to the [ILGWU District] Executive Board to see if we could donate. Mrs. Matheson was really into public relations, which was very good for the union.

And every four years we would convene elections [to select convention delegates]. Each local was given so many delegates and the women would run for elections, and they'd really have campaigns to get to go to the convention. Now they convene every three years and we still have a nice delegation with those.

Q: How many people were usually elected?

CL: I think the time we went to Chicago there might have been eight or nine in our delegation. I think they gave you a delegate for each thousand members or something like that. So if we had 3,600 [members] up in Pittston, they'd have four delegates. Of course, the manager of the district would always go—Mrs. Matheson, who as I said was the best thing that ever happened to the Valley. . . .

Q: You had another big strike in '58.

CL: Yeah. I was on [the administrative] staff in '55 and that strike was in March of '58. Again, a rumor had started that the employers were not gonna give the increases that the union was demanding in their negotiations, and as a show of strength there was a strike called. I think it was for a Thursday morning. I suppose the union bigwigs felt that Thursday was close to the weekend and if the show of strength was there and our people were willing to stick together, they'd have all day Thursday, all day Friday, all day Saturday, and all day Sunday to negotiate with the powers that be. Some of the big ones [the owners in New York] sat down immediately and got straightened out and they went back to work maybe the following Tuesday or Wednesday morning. But there were several holdouts and most of them were the jobbers who had to work in our shops right here in this area. You see, it's a very complicated business. . . .

Q: What was the key to the 1958 strike?

CL: The key there was that most of the contractors who refused to pay were from a certain element that I don't want to even discuss [i.e., organized crime]. Everybody else had settled and we were left holding the bag with these few.

Q: Were these people mainly in Pittston?

CL: Pittston, Sweet Valley, some in Wilkes-Barre. There were others who called and said they wanted to settle but they were afraid. They were afraid to settle because, you know, you don't want to get your front porch blown off after you've worked twenty years to put it on there. And there were threats. All kinds of threats and telephone calls.

Q: Were you ever threatened personally?

CL: Oh yes. I never took the threats seriously. I used to laugh at them and I'd say, "Well, you'd better make the first punch count because an Irishman won't get a punch in the back. We'll always get a punch in the face. I'll come in. I'll lead with my chin!" I think the reason why New York felt they were better off with women business agents in Pittston was the fact that those guys [mob shop owners], as bad as some of them were, knew about a pair of high heel shoes and silk stockings—they wouldn't put their hands on the women. But they didn't think anything of picking the men up and throwin' them out of the shops. I had some of them open the door and tell me to get out or they'd call the cops and things like that. I'd say, "Well, call the cops. I'll be here when they get here." I had another one tell me he had twenty-seven guns at home and he was gonna go home and get two of them and come back and blow my brains out.

Q: What did you say?

CL: I said, "Well, you go ahead, Arthur. I'll be right here when you come back." He had a little leather couch inside the door and I went and sat down. The man across the street from that shop, who ran another dress factory but was of a different caliber and a different disposition—he had been an old coal miner at one time—he came over and he said to me, "Clem, he's serious. You'd better get out of here." I said, "Charlie, you're a friend of his and I'll say right now: he's my enemy. You go take a walk for yourself. I'm gonna show him that I'm not afraid of him." When he [the owner] came back through that door that day, he was like a little monkey on a string. He only weighed 130 pounds. If he had ever said anything to me, I would have given him a slap in the puss and walked away from him. But he didn't pull any guns on me.

Q: Did you finally resolve the dispute?

CL: Oh yeah. We got it straightened out. I called Mrs. Matheson, and we sat down, and we negotiated with him for about two and a half hours. I think it was only a 7 percent increase, or somethin' like that, that we were tryin' to enforce.

Q: How would Mrs. Matheson work in these situations? How was she able to settle things?

CL: She was a good negotiator and she had a way with people. I wouldn't say she could manipulate them, because some of those guys would look you right straight in the eye and tell you one thing, and the next day, when the business agent would go in, they'd have a different story completely and the fight would start all over again. But it seemed to be in Mrs. Matheson's blood and, boy, she could play up a situation like a fine-tuned fiddle. I got to the point where I was able to negotiate a little bit like that, too. Make them think it was their idea.

Q: So you learned from her?

CL: Oh, everything I ever knew about it. Well, all my family was union. My father was a coal miner. But everything that I learned about ILG, I learned from Mrs. Matheson. I found out that in other districts, they were always gonna do wonders, and when you'd follow them up on the situation, you'd find out that they didn't do near what Mrs. Matheson had done in our district. I don't say that because I worked in this district. I say it because I know it to be a fact. At that time, there were only two women [district] managers—well, I think maybe three women managers—in the whole country. We [the ILGWU] covered thirty-eight states, Puerto Rico, and parts of Canada.

Mrs. Matheson could be a very good negotiator. When she'd walk into a room, if I was in high gear, I'd calm down and the other side would calm down and she'd get center stage. This [other district] manager was the kind who would go in with blood and thunder. Sometimes you'd get more with sugar than you do with vinegar. You know it was one of these things where you really had to know how to deal with people. There were shops where they wouldn't let Dorothy [Ney, chap. 1] and me in.[6]

Q: Because of your organizing and administrative style?

CL: Yeah. And, as I said, it was nothin' for us business agents to get thrown out of the shop. Mrs. Matheson had an eye for being able to pick out people from the shops who had a little bit of savvy and she'd surround herself with them and put them into different positions. Sometimes the business agents who came from New York just didn't work out because, first of all, they didn't want to give it the time, and they were only using it for a stepping-stone to get into the bigger union [jobs] where bigger money was being paid. Our salaries weren't that great in the very beginning, but once Mr. [Sol "Chick"] Chaiken became the president [in 1975], he had a different outlook as far as what the staff people should earn, and he wanted them to be looked up to. Where[as] [former president David] Dubinsky always felt that if you need it, you earn it. But Dubinsky was a man—oh, what a man! . . .

Mrs. Matheson, when she left here, he put her as director of the Union Label Department in New York, and she had such good ideas that some of the top designers in the garment industry from Seventh Avenue and from all over the world wanted her to have something to say about their garments. She called me one time and told me that she needed a group in New York to put on a fashion show. Jim Corbett was supposed to be in charge of the fashion show, but Jim had some problems with sugar [diabetes] and he took sick the day of the show. Our girls had to fill in and they did a fantastic job at the Americana Hotel. The fashion show was put on for five thousand jobbers and their workers in the main ballroom there. And, of course, Mrs. Matheson got up and made a speech that day. She was workin' with Harry Belafonte's wife [Julie Robinson] and others. [It was] public relations for the fashion industry, and we had thirty-eight of our [Wyoming Valley District] people in the show.

But the district grew. I'd say after the '53 strike, the district began to grow in leaps and bounds, and no matter what went on throughout the state, all you had to do was mention Min Matheson and everybody knew her. If she ever got into the political arena, and things were the way they are today, she would have been a shoo-in [for elected office]. She was quite a personality.

Q: The union seemed to have gained a lot of political influence.

CL: Oh yes. We always took good care of them [i.e., politicians] and, if it was our candidate, we brought them to town and had our people meet them. We rented the American Theater [in Pittston] or maybe the [Paramount] theater [in Wilkes-Barre] where the Kirby [Center] is today.

Q: Whom did you bring to town?

CL: Teddy Kennedy on several occasions [in 1976]. John Kennedy stopped in Pittston when he went through the area [in 1960]. We had Dubinsky in town during the '58 strike along with [Luzerne County state senator] Marty Murray and [Rep.] Dan Flood. Dan Flood'll tell ya once he starts to talk about Min Matheson. He's gonna tell you that she came to him on Sunday morning and told him she couldn't get a lawyer to take a case against Pioneer [Manufacturing] in Wilkes-Barre. No lawyer would be bothered with the case. They made children's dresses at the plant down there, and I don't have too many of the details because this was back in '46. Finally, somebody told her to go and see Dan Flood and she explained the situation to him. Of course, he turned on the charm and he became the lawyer for the district for years.[7] We changed the lyrics to different songs to serenade him when he was runnin' [for office] even when he didn't have any opposition for all the years that he was in Congress. He'd say [kiddingly to the audience], "You know that I just wrote the words to those songs an hour before I came in here." Oh, the songs that we [used] to serenade him with . . . Min just had an "in" with everybody. . . .

Q: So she was well respected by local politicians.

CL: Oh yeah. She had a lot of respect. Senator Marty Murray, [Wilkes-Barre mayor Frank] Slattery, the lawyer. In fact, Slattery was a personal friend of mine and [one time] he said to me, "My god Clem, I haven't seen you in years." I said, "No, you haven't seen me since before World War II, and now I'm back here working in the labor field." He said, "I heard that," and then he said, "When I heard you were working for Mrs. Matheson, I wanted to see ya." She had brought [ILGWU president David] Dubinsky in to see him a couple of times. "She really knew how to do things with a flair that nobody else would have," he said. . . . We were *the* union. As in Pittston, if you went into Wilkes-Barre and you said, "Where's the union office here?" they'd send you to the ILG. . . . I think the only barrier that we didn't break was the one with the women at the Westmoreland Club [an exclusive men's club in Wilkes-Barre].[8] *(laughs)*

Q: Did you try to get in?

CL: I understand that before I went on staff, some of our people tried and it just didn't work out. But I was always active in Rotary [Club]. My brother was president of the Wyoming Rotary in 1941. As soon as I got in Pittston, the Rotary Club called and asked if I could make arrangements to have Mrs. Matheson come and address us. So they took us to lunch at the Fox Hill Country Club, and she explained how we started with next to nothing and grew to ten thousand or twelve thousand members in the area. Then she said she was willing to answer some questions, and the local eye doctor [Dr. Galletzi] took the floor. He praised the ILG to the highest because of our Antonini out of New York. Antonini his name was, Luigi Antonini. He wore a hat like the pope, you know the big round black hat. He was a real labor man. We had him in town when we found out that he was such a celebrity, and Galletzi had paid so much tribute to him.

The day that Mrs. Matheson was there, she said, "Clemie, we're gonna have to bring Antonini in." So we did. We brought him in during the '58 strike. [For that strike] we had theaters rented and places for people to congregate, but we still had twenty-four-hour picket lines and she visited those picket lines religiously, not at the same time every day because you could never do that. They were out for the first couple of days, and then when their jobbers straightened things out, [they] went back to work.

Q: You rented a theater and who came to see him?

CL: Oh, the whole community'd come out. When they'd hear that somebody was in town like that, everybody was there. We invited everybody. The Mine Workers [i.e., the UMWA] always tried to come along with whatever we had goin' on. Luigi Antonini was a very powerful man in the New York office because he had his own Italian Local [No. 89]. Otherwise, there would have been a language barrier. They even issued the [ILGWU] newspaper, *Justice*, in Italian, which was the union paper that all members received. They still issue it in Spanish and English. . . . Then, as we moved from [strikes in] '53 to '58, we run into January of '59—the Knox Mine disaster.

Q: Can you talk about that disaster and the ILGWU?

CL: Well, it was a Thursday night and I was on my way to Hazleton. I had the radio on and [heard that] the river had broken through and went into the Knox Coal Company [mine in Port Griffith near Pittston] where they were mining eighteen inches below the river. Eighteen inches! The men had been workin' in there for the previous four or five weeks in raincoats and hats with the river drippin' in on them. There were eleven [*sic*; twelve] people lost, never recovered, and the whole mines in this area were flooded, and that was the end of the coal mining here.

So, after that we were [among] the only ones to replace the jobs so that people could eat. The men stayed home and the women went to work. Jobs were at a premium because the women needed the work. In most cases they worked their fingers to the bone to educate their kids. Your mother probably did [that] herself because she didn't want to put you in that position.

And believe me, when I found out that they were gonna let women into the University of Scranton, I was one of the first ones to go up there to study industrial relations and business administration. I think it was 1956 when they allowed women in. We had thirty people in the class and twenty-six were men, and the other four were women. Three of us, I think, were from the ILG and there was one from IBEW [International Brotherhood of Electrical Workers] or something like that.

Q: Did the ILG pay your tuition?

CL: No, no. I paid for that myself but it was well worth it. Then I went up there later after I had myself established on the [ILG] staff. I went up there later and took special courses. . . .

Q: Going back to Pittston, you earlier alluded to some tough guys and their threats.

CL: Well, they did come to the house. We lived in an apartment—my brother who belonged to the Rotary Club and a sister of mine who worked with me at Emkay. She was like my mother and he was like my father because I was only seven months old when my father died and only five years old when my mother died. There were six of us. This sister and brother kept the family together. So we were in an apartment over on Seventh Street in Wyoming and some of the runners for the big boys [organized criminals] from Pittston came to Seventh Street.

They went into the local tavern and they told our landlord, who owned the place that we lived in, that there would be trouble if I went to the picket line the following morning. He was afraid that they'd do damage to his building, so he was waiting for me when I came home that night. Big Lithuanian guy. "Hey Calamity [nickname], I don't think you should go on those picket lines tomorrow and blah, blah, blah, blah, blah." I said, "Jake, my sister pays the rent on time. I have a job to do and as soon as those guys realize that, the better off I'm gonna be and the better off they're gonna be." I said, "If they were gonna do somethin' to me, they wouldn't threaten me. They'd do it and talk about it after." I said, "They're not gonna let people know that they had this in their mind." And I added, "You should use your head better." He said, "Well, I guess so. I guess so." It was little things like that.

Of course, they came there another night. Jake called my sister and said, "Jenny, those guys are back here again and they're talkin' about this picket line and about Clem's car," and all this goin' on. She said, "Send the bastards up. I'll chop their heads off with the coal shovel from the kitchen stove!" She said, "I'm not afraid of them." That was the last we heard of them because it was just harassment. They didn't mean anything by it. In fact, after things cooled down over the years, they didn't have the power that they did before 1958 [sic; 1957] and their big powwow up in Apalachin [New York].

Q: How did that organized crime meeting relate to the garment industry?

CL: Well, most of them were dress manufacturers. Once they lost their power then, they had to mellow a little bit. Once the FBI got on to them, they were on the downslide from there on. But they'd still pull some awful tricks, like the situation out there in Old Boston [suburban Pittston]. They took over an old one-room school building with the Roma Club underneath it. Yeah, a real Sicilian Club. There they made wedding gowns for Elegante, which was one of the best jobbers for wedding gowns at that time. They were movin' them out in garbage cans! Now, if you have a daughter and she pays eight hundred dollars for a wedding gown and she goes to walk down the aisle and she's a little warmer because it's a day like today—and she gets the smell of garbage! *(laughs)*

Q: They moved them out in garbage cans?

CL: To ship them because we had a picket line there. We wouldn't let anything go in and we wouldn't let anything go out. Friedman's trucks, the trucks that were union, driven by [Teamsters] union men, wouldn't pick the garments up, so they brought in their own trucks. Instead of carryin' them out—'cause we wouldn't let them take anything out of the shop—they'd make believe they were carryin' garbage out. What could you do? We knew it all the time. We couldn't do much about it.

There was one machine in the factory, and it was similar to what we used to put the "bones" in the front of the corsets. The guy was a real crook. He was just a stooge for the big shots, but he thought he was a big shot. He came out of the factory and he was cursin', and the girls [on the picket line] were hollerin', "What's the matter, Willy? Aren't you gonna make a shipment in the garbage cans today?" You know, givin' him the ol' [ribbing], and he says, "Yeah, the boning machine is broke down." I said, "Oh, I ran one of them at Emkay. I could fix that for ya." He fell for it. I went in. I "fixed" the machine, OK. I don't think it runs to this day!

Q: What did you do?

CL: Nothing in particular. It's very difficult to tell you because the machine was difficult to operate and I knew how to operate it. It was about a six-needle machine, a very intricate machine. See, instead of [the bride] wearing a girdle, they'd put the "bones" in the dress so the dress would lay flat from the bust line down under their bellies, and if some of them were pregnant, it would cover up a multitude of sins, you know. So I "fixed" his boning machine for him!

But everything cooled off and then *The Untouchables* came on television. Oh, you'd walk down the street and some of them [tough guys] would say, "Hey Calamity! Did you see *The Untouchables* last night? All the guys were Irish on that program last night." I would say, "Why do I have to watch television when I can come to work in the morning and see you here on the corner at nine o'clock?" We wouldn't get mad at one another, you know. It was terrible, some of the things we would say back and forth, but we just learned that we had to put up with one another.

Q: Why did they call you Calamity?

CL: Calamity Jane. My family always called me Calamity. I guess from the time I started to talk—I never stopped![9]

Q: Regarding these tough guys—so you would joke with each other?

CL: Well, [alleged mobster] Angelo Sciandra used to bring his trumpet to the picket line in the morning. He'd sit on the hood of a car and, when the Angelus was ringin' at St. Rocco's Church, he'd play "Taps" while they took their stooges to the picket line.

Q: I'm sure you recall alleged mobster Nick Alaimo.

CL: Well, Nick always wanted everybody to think that he was a top man [in organized crime], the head honcho, you know. But he was actually just a runner for them, I think. I don't believe he had the connections that he professed to have, although he had his two brothers in the business with him. They all ran shops in Pittston.

Q: How many shops did they have?

CL: Nick must've had three or four.

Q: Were they union shops?

CL: We made them union after 1953.

Q: Was it tough organizing them?

CL: Yeah, it was tough. That was tough. We'd get out of work at Emkay and a gang of us would get on the bus [in Wyoming]. In fact, sometimes we'd leave work fifteen minutes early so that we could get the three-thirty bus on the corner of Sixth Street. We'd go over to the picket line in Pittston where the Gramercy [Restaurant] is now. The shop was in the cellar and it was nothin' for a fight to break out when the scabs would come out and the floorlady would come out and throw scrub water on our girls—anything to aggravate us. The cops would be there, and some cops weren't too nice to us. Some were, some weren't. They had their lieutenants and we had our lieutenants, and it was interesting, to say the least.

Q: Was anybody hurt?

CL: Oh yeah. One time, a guy by the name of Joe McCall [joined us and] four or five ganged up on him and threw him down into that cellar where the Gramercy is, and they beat him unmercifully. There was concrete flyin' and everything.

Q: Were these Nick's [Alaimo] tough guys?

CL: I wouldn't say they were Nick's, but they were affiliated with that element. He [McCall] was in a bad way. Oh, terrible, and he was a nice guy. Joe McCall, I'll never forget. He was an innocent bystander and they wanted to make a spectacle.

Q: He wasn't a member of the union?

CL: No, he was just goin' through Pittston and he saw what was goin' on, because there was a skirmish when scabs come out of the dress factory where the Columbus statue [on Main Street] is now. He saw the skirmish and he pulled over to see what was goin' on. They just wanted to pick on somebody that they didn't know so that it would be a message to others.

[Some men] came and took their women off the picket line, you know. Some of the women would call when they'd get home [after work] and say they wanted to come to the union office [in Pittston], and the husbands wouldn't let them. It was a tough battle, it was. I was fortunate in that I was single. As I say, I had lots of friends in that town, and I had that union office open the biggest part of the day. I'd get there at eight in the morning, sometimes earlier, and be there still at ten or eleven o'clock at night.

Q: Were there any bombings?

CL: Yeah. [Attorney Arthur] Silverblatt had his front porch blown off one time. They got to him and told him that he shouldn't represent us.[10] I don't know what his response was to them, but his front porch was blown off and nobody could ever prove anything. And my car caught on fire while we were in the [Luzerne County] Courthouse having hearings on our counter-cases [with the criminal element] over the skirmishes that had happened. . . .

Q: What were those skirmishes?

CL: Back and forth. Sure. Dolly Bufalino [Falcone] was the lawyer for them, and I had four or five women [pickets] with me. The one woman that I had—her maiden last name was Mecadon—her brother had been involved [murdered] in a [dynamite] blast over a coal mine strike. You've probably heard the name. I think it was Dominick [sic; Charles] Mecadon. He got in the car and turned on the ignition and the car blew up.[11] So I had this Mecadon girl in the car and four other ladies, and I was drivin' a beautiful '58 Chevy. I parked at the courthouse [in Wilkes-Barre], and I always took good care of the cars that I drove because I never knew who would be in and out of them. When we came out, we got in the car and I went to take them up River Street [toward Pittston]. And when we got to the General Hospital, I thought I smelled smoke—but, you know, women smoking cigarettes and everything. I just turned the window [down] a little bit but it seemed that I could still smell smoke.

When we got to where the United Furniture used to be [about a half mile up the road], black smoke was comin' out from under the dashboard. So I pulled the car over to the side of the road, and the one lady was smart enough to know how to open the hood, which I didn't want her to do. But she said, "I'll open it up and see what's goin' on." Well, when she opened it the whole car was lit up like a toaster. Somebody had tinkered with the wires. It was just enough to scare us, you know. So I hailed down some car and it just so happened that it was a man from Exeter who worked in the courthouse that I knew, and I asked him to take the women home. I stayed with the car, and I waited and waited for the AAA [American Automobile Association] to come. So I thought, "Well, I'd better get this car over to the [Pennsylvania State Police] barracks [in Wyoming] before it gets too dark." I got in that car and drove it over to the barracks, which everybody said I was crazy to do, but I was afraid that they'd do more damage to it if I left it there.

Now, they couldn't prove anything. They, the state troopers, went over the car and dusted it and said, "What the hell kind of a car does that Calamity, that

FIG. 26 | ILGWU chorus musical
revue rehearsal, 1954; standing on
the right is Clementine Lyons. Photo
courtesy of Lukasik Studio.

Clem Lyons, drive? There must be six hundred sets of [finger] prints on it."
Well, you know, being on a picket line, being on Main Street in Pittston with
everybody goin' by, everybody leanin' up against the car. . . . So they marked it
up to the fact that maybe somebody, when they were changin' a headlight or
somethin' like that, crossed the wires. But for it to happen when we were in the
courthouse, no less—that [was] just an example.

Q: Mrs. Matheson brought her children to the picket line a couple times, didn't
she?

CL: She did. That picket line that I spoke about where that Joe McCall got hurt, the
men [tough guys] got very nasty and they used some very foul language. They
said to the women who were helping Mrs. Matheson, "You're nothin' but sluts,
whores," this kinda thing. They told Min, "You're not fit to lead the good women
of Pittston." She eyeballed them and told them, "Well, if you think that I'm not
good enough to lead your people, we'll get virgins in here to lead the people [i.e.,
workers]," and she called and had the kids dressed up in their best dresses. I
think they were three and four or five and six years old, and she put them at the
head of the picket line. The street was lined with the bad element. And it didn't
mean a thing [because] her kids went around just as though nothing [happened].
Newspapers [covered it]. Everybody was there to see the situation.

CLEMENTINE "CLEM" LYONS

Q: Were the kids ever in danger, do you think?

CL: No. They [the tough guys] knew better because some of them had records as long as your arm, and they knew that if they hit a woman, or they bothered those children, they'd really be in for trouble. It was a game of who was gonna be the smartest in the situation. There were so many creepy things that went on, you know, creepy people around up there in Pittston, like that Nick Benfante who tried to organize the Needle Workers' [Association], which was in opposition to the ILG.

Q: Tell us about that.

CL: He was a crackpot. He just wanted an easy way to make a living, and he wanted to organize these women instead of letting the ILG come in. I don't think he owned a shop. He had an affiliation with them [the organized criminals] and he wanted to be their representative. He was one of them and what kind of representation could he give the women there? Most of the women knew that he was a bad egg to begin with because most of the women are all related up there in Pittston. Then years later, as proof of why the women didn't want to be bothered with him, he went up to the Chrysler plant and tried some of his shenanigans [there] and, boy, the auto workers grabbed a hold of him and they beat the bejesus out of him. They ran him right out of Scranton.

Q: Did this rump [garment] union get anywhere?

CL: No. Never really got off the ground.

Q: Not even one shop?

CL: No. To my knowledge, he didn't have one shop. He claimed that he had a few, but he had no proof of anything.

Q: Was it all about breaking your union?[12]

CL: That was it. He wanted to break the ILG so that he could go and make believe he was the representative and get paid from two sides. Like you see on television!

Q: What was the Three-Finger Brown strike about?

CL: His name was Tom Lucchese, and he was one of the top gangsters out of New York. He came here and opened a shop in Sweet Valley. He didn't want to go back to work [i.e., settle the major strike] in 1958. He didn't want to negotiate. He wanted to operate nonunion. And, of course, that's Ku Kluxer territory out there. People raise hell with me even today for sayin' "Ku Kluxers," but that's the truth. Ku Kluxers were always active out there in the Back Mountain [i.e., rural Luzerne County].

I can remember when we lived in the [coal] company [housing] over there in Wyoming on Sharp Street. Saturday night was a big night. Warm like this, and you'd go out on the front porch and somebody'd bring out their Victrola—you know, that you crank up—and they'd play for a while, and some of the young fellas and girls who were keepin' company would come out and dance on the sidewalk. Around nine thirty at night, everything would stop, and everybody would sit on the porches to look up the mountain there, which they call "Nancy's

Crotch" [a crevice in the mountain] and watch them burnin' the crosses at the
Grange Hall. All through Kingston Township that organization is still strong.

A couple a weeks ago, there were [KKK] guys in town. It was on television that they were gonna come back and try to reactivate it. I said, "Reactivate it? It never died!" Some of those Ku Kluxers were out there in Sweet Valley, and the minister of their church the one night gave us a rough time. Finally, the guy who owned the taxi company in Wilkes-Barre—Harry Lieberman, I think his name was—he took over that dress shop. He bought Lucchese out, and then the union became very strong there. . . .

Q: How many shops did the mobster element have in this area?

CL: Everything except Leslie Fay and McKitterick's—and, of course, Emkay.

Q: Owned them or had influence on them, one way or another?

CL: That's what makes it difficult, because [for example] the American Auto [department store in Kingston], they have a great big plant and they've sunk a lot of money [into it], and they have to just stay there. With our guys [i.e., local garment owners], any nut with five machines can put them in the cellar and start a dress factory even today. That nut and screwball that slept for eight years in the White House [Ronald Reagan]—they went and repealed the law about homeworking, so now they say there's as much homework in New York as there is factory work being done again. They've turned the clock back.[13]

Q: Was there ever much homeworking in this Valley?

CL: I'd say goin' back fifteen years it started to crop up again. In the thirties and forties, there might have been [some] but it was cut out because we forbid it. And [later in the 1950s] we found girls who were doin' work at home [at nights] while they were workin' in the factory. You couldn't be subject to two masters.

Q: Of the two hundred or so shops in this district, did you say that the majority were under the influence of the tough-guy element?

CL: I would say in some way or another. There were some good people in the business. Mike Turco is a great guy. He has the Del-Mar [Sportswear Company] in Pittston. He was a graduate of Villanova University.

Q: There are far fewer shops today, but is that undesirable element still around?

CL: No. Most of them have gone. . . .

Q: There was piecework and straight time, and how was that determined?

CL: Yeah. Well, waist making—the top of the dress from the waist to the shoulders—that was supposed to be the cream of the crop. If you were a good operator, you could make [good straight time] money. Then, of course, the zipper setter was a premium-paying [piece-work] job when zippers first came out during World War II. During the war, they didn't have zippers, they had fly buttons, but as soon as zippers came on the market, they started puttin' them in the back of the dress, on the side of the dress, up the front of the dress. The women were afraid to work on them because if the needle hit the metal zipper there was a chance of the needle goin' in their eye 'cause needles would shatter. As a result, the zippers were overpriced and the zipper setters made fantastic money. Then they got a special foot pedal to put on the machine and a special gadget that would help to set the zippers, but they [the union] didn't let them [the owners] adjust the prices. And if you give something to somebody one day and go to take it off them the next day, they're gonna hand you your head. The zipper setters always made good money, and the pressers [too], but the pressers worked very, very hard. . . .

Q: What happened to the district after the Mathesons left?

CL: Sammy Bianco [eventually became the manager]. He was from up in Vandling, Pennsylvania. It's above Carbondale, almost into Forest City. Sammy was all right but he wasn't a Min Matheson. Her shoes were pretty hard to fill because she just had a way where she could sense what was goin' and [know how] she wanted things to go. She was very determined in what she needed and what should be done.

Oh yeah, when Sammy went to Wilkes-Barre, [the decline started]. Most of these guys who have passed on—you know the element that we spoke of in the beginning [i.e., the mobsters]—not too many of their kids wanted to be bothered with the business. So they didn't only close up because they couldn't get operators, but they closed because they had no leadership. And then the increasing health costs. In order for the union to stay solvent, to be able to keep the contracts as good as they always were, these guys [the new generation of owners] just tried to cut corners wherever they could. Now the big thing is that everything is back in New York.

I would say Min was at her best when there was a strike. She worked wonderful under stress. She was a taskmaster and she wanted a good job done, but when she got an audience, she could milk that audience like the best on Broadway. When she went to address Congress, I don't know what it was for, but the Dubinsky Center [sponsored an event that day] and this is what stands out most in my mind.[14] There must have been five thousand people there, and when she stood up to the microphone, all she said was, "How many of you remember Franklin Delano Roosevelt?" She had them in her hands like this. Of course, there was lots of people who were jealous of Mrs. Matheson's ability, and they didn't even want to hear about it, to rehash it, when she came home or when she went back to the New York office. However, her talk [in Congress] got national acclaim. I really think that she never got the recognition that was due her. My brother was at this meeting where she commanded it. He said he never heard anything like it. She was marvelous. . . .

In the meantime, Mrs. Matheson tried to build up a good political committee so that we took part in all of the activities in the community. We had a good educational program and she always had a heart as far as people [were concerned]. She could touch people and make them feel as though they were needed and wanted. She was just a great humanitarian. . . .

Q: Do you think that Dubinsky appreciated her?

CL: They never gave her the credit that she deserved. No. She was held in high esteem and they knew that she had this Valley tied up. They knew that she had it organized and, as I say, had it been another day and age, she might have been the top man on the [union] totem pole. . . .

Q: I know you were in charge of the district chorus for quite a long time.

CL: I still do it.

Q: How long have you been associated with the chorus?

CL: Well, in 1947, Mrs. Matheson called the chairlady at the Emkay, who was Mrs. Edith McDonald from West Pittston. She said [to her], "We found a gentlemen who is gonna put a show on at the Kingston Armory this coming Friday night. We want to model some clothes from every shop in the district. Do you think we can get some girls from your place to model bathing suits and girdles?" Mrs. McDonald was a beautiful Irish woman. She had been a telephone operator for many years before she got married. She was from over in the Parsons section of Wilkes-Barre and she said, "Well Mrs. Matheson, I'll try my best to find some people."

Well, first of all, quite a few from the town had been in shows years ago for my brother [at Rotary International] and then, as soon as the notice was put up on the bulletin board, they came to me to try and find people to go to the first meeting for the shows. So I got about eight or ten to go to the meeting and, sure enough, they put on the show down at the Kingston Armory. Jim Corbett [the chorus director] had me do [sing] a number and Min said, "Where's that girl from?" They told her, "That's Clem Lyons from up at the Emkay." She said, "I want to see more of that girl." So it was one of those things.

For three or four years, Corbett was the top man putting on the shows. Of course, I participated and I took girls with me from the Emkay and from Wyoming Garment. Then it got to the point where he was asked to go into other districts to help them put on musical revues. Jim was kind of happy-go-lucky. So Mrs. Matheson asked him, in 1953, to put on a kiddie show. She wanted to use children from three to thirteen years old. He didn't have time for that. So she asked me if I'd take it up. Millie Dotter, who worked at Emkay, and I took on the first kiddie show. We called it *The Lollypop Revue*. We packed Pittston High School for three nights.

In 1954, when it came time to go into rehearsals for the regular, annual musical, Mrs. Matheson asked Jim when he was gonna get the group together, and he said, "Oh, I'm gonna be busy in Easton, or in Harrisburg," or it might have been Reading. She said, "OK." She called me and she said, "Clem, do you think you want to do the show?" I said, "Well, we'll do the best we can." And by god, we loaded up the auditorium another three nights. Standing room only. We had an opening number and a closing number. It ran it into two acts. [We did] the one big yearly revue. Then we'd take excerpts to the [Wilkes-Barre] Veteran's

CLEMENTINE "CLEM" LYONS

FIG. 27 | *Up n' at 'Em*, a musical revue by the ILGWU Wyoming Valley chorus, March 25–26, 1960. Photo courtesy of the Kheel Center, Cornell University.

Hospital or to the firemen's gathering in Moosic, or wherever you got an invitation to go. Plus, we sang at our own affairs. We still have the chorus.

Q: How many years would that make it?

CL: From '53 to '90. In fact, the last three conventions that we've had in Hollywood, Florida, I've been the featured soloist. Our entire group [sings], too—thirty-eight people. . . .

Q: I'm sure it was good publicity for the union.[15]

CL: Well, this was it. . . . Then after *The Lollypop Revue* was so successful, Mrs. Matheson wanted to put on a big musical revue down at the Irem Temple in Wilkes-Barre. In fact, that was even before the guy that she had put [in charge of] a show in 1947, which was *The Spring Festival*. He didn't want to work with the kids. He just wanted to bring in a couple of professionals, what did they call them, like ringers. You know, he would use ILG women, but when it came time for the nice solos and things like that it was "Bring in a ringer." He didn't want to work with the kids, so that was why she had me do *The Lollypop Revue*.

So we got those shows going at first. We were, in fact, the first local to ever put on a musical revue—I should say in the Northeast Department. I don't want to be a real hog because they had *Pins and Needles* in New York before the war and that played on Broadway until 1942 [*sic;* 1940] until they lost their cast members to the war. Right after that, they got this crazy idea that the locals should start to have these shows [on a regular basis]. So when this guy got so busy that he couldn't give Mrs. Matheson the time that she wanted, she let me and Billy Gable do the shows. Yeah, he [Bill Gable] works in the Wilkes-Barre office now.

Q: How often would you have shows in the Wyoming Valley District?

CL: Every year. I helped with the revues from '54 to '77, but I had been in them from 1947. In fact, I'll tell you, not that I want to brag because I was only a part of the show, but the shows began to be a part of the social calendar around the area. People would stop and say, "When are you going to have another show?" Or "When are you going to have tickets for me?" Or "Is the gang from the ILG going to be there? We'll buy tickets." That kind of thing. And here from June 9 of 1993, I got this [showing a copy of the ILGWU's *Pittston Guide* newsletter from 1993]. How do you like that? Somebody had cut it out and had it all these years [and it was reprinted in the newsletter].

Q: *(reading a headline from the "Pittston Guide")* "'ILG Musical Revue Pleases Audience,' February 23, 1959." This was sent to you by the County Commission for Veterans Affairs. I see that Luigi Antonini, first vice president of the ILGWU, sent you $500 on behalf of his New York Local [No. 89] to help the miners' relief funds. This must have been a revue benefit for the Knox Mine disaster families.

CL: Sure, the Knox Mine disaster happened in January [1959] and this is February [1959].

Q: Another title here is "*Everything Goes* at Pittston High School for the Benefit of the Miners' Disaster Fund." So you had shows to benefit certain causes?

CL: Yeah. In fact, one year we sent $450 to St. Michael's [Orphanage] to buy athletic equipment for the kids up there. At that time that was a lot of money. I think we charged people fifty cents to get in. Then we sent the money.

Q: What would the shows actually involve?

CL: It was a full-scale musical revue, one and two acts. Since I retired, the New York [ILGWU office] has contacted me and I've sung at their conventions. There were six of us [in the production] and five of us sang.

Q: Were the performers all local people?

CL: Yeah, these were people from the [garment] shops. This [showing another clipping] was from the *Pittston Guide*. It seems each month the newsletter did a profile on a different shop. This was what I got together. I didn't like to do [i.e., submit items to] the ILG newspaper [*Justice*] because they censored [edited] it. By the time my ideas would get there, it didn't even sound like what I had written. And you don't do that to an Irishman! Why the hell don't you tell me before I go to print that it's not right or you don't like it? It wasn't that they didn't like it, but sometimes it would be just that it wasn't their idea and they'd save it for a couple months and then use it and put their own name on it.

Q: Did your local troupe perform at Unity House?

CL: Oh, many times, many times. When Reagan was giving us a rough time on the "notch years" [for Social Security], I wrote some nasty things to him and got some crazy letters back.[16] They were wordy but they didn't contain much information. So I wrote:

> Remember the kids in the city, remember the kids in the town,
> Remember the kids in the notch years: shame on you for letting them down.
> Remember the Seventh Commandment that tells us not to steal,
> But if many of your pensions were cut, you'd know just how we feel.
> Now that your birthday is dawning near, you and Nancy are painted and curled.
> It's time to say happy birthday from notch kids around the world.

And I sent it to him. . . . My family was always holding their breath because I did get in a lot of trouble. But as a general rule, it was straightened out.

Q: Here is a photo of the ILG singers and dancers, in 1954. Is that you right there?

CL: Yeah. Lead singer. We did shows at the University of Scranton when they first started taking women up there. I enrolled in the labor relations class, and I got friendly with two of the people that were in the class and they belonged to the Alumni Association. When they had their yearly affair, their spring get-together, they asked us to be part of it and put on a show.

Q: Would you sing union songs?

CL: Some. And some would be maybe [from] popular shows that were on Broadway at the time, but most of them would be union in flavor. Veteran's Hospital, we used to go to the Veteran's Hospital [in Wilkes-Barre] every Thursday night for years. We helped the American Italian Association with their show.

Q: By 1976, you were the [overall] director, correct?

CL: Yes, and Billy Gable was the musical director. We'd hire a dance instructor but we could only afford a dance instructor once a month so I'd teach them dancing, too.

Q: I see here that you had what was called a "Union Label Discussion." What would that be?

CL: That would be a skit. You might have somebody fight with the boss because of a rate or something like that, and you'd have maybe two girls involved. "I need one more cent or I need two more cents," and you'd put it to music. "Not enough . . . not enough." Then maybe the boss would get up and he wouldn't have any pants on or something like that. It was sometimes risqué, sometimes not.

Q: Did anybody ever record the revues?

CL: New York has recently, in the last six years or so, recorded some that we've put on at the convention center in Hollywood, Florida. But not locally because we didn't have the equipment. They did send the editors from *Justice* and they took pictures but they were mostly the eight-by-ten-inch glossies that could be used in that newspaper. Then they didn't care what happened to the ones that were published. . . . When we got the group together, I used them kind of as the mainstay, and then the other business agents got a couple of groups in each of their shops. Over the years, we had maybe forty-eight people in the group. I had thirty-two shops that I had affiliations with [as business agent] and [when I retired] they had twenty-nine parties for me! They had this big [retirement] party up at the Gramercy [Restaurant] for me.

Q: What was your official title when you retired?

CL: Well, I was business agent and educational director for the Pittston local.

Q: Was a big part of your job as educational director to work with the chorus and the revues?

CL: Yes, and on top of that if somebody had a problem at home or death in the family or something, and needed to go to some of the agencies, I'd take them to the agencies or the United Way to help them, get them whatever help we could. I used to help them file their income tax. You know when I think of it now—I think I was nuts! I worked eighteen hours a day, sixteen hours a day. I was just lucky that I had a sister who did my laundry and cooked. But I very seldom came home to eat. See [the programs] here? *(looking at a memorabilia file)* Each one of them signed. . . . We used to go into New York and bring curtains home right from the Great White Way [i.e., Broadway Theater District]. Oh, [photographer] Stevie Lukasik used to do a good job. Here's [the program for] *Darkness on the Delta*. We did a medley of that one time. . . . And here's [the program for] *Buttons and Bows* from 1954. . . .

In the meantime, they hired Jim Corbett, who was a local boy attending what was then St. Thomas College [later the University of Scranton]. He was quite a musician, quite a comic, and he had a flair, a very good flair for music. He wrote some lyrics, and he and Mike Johnson wrote the lyrics for a show that played along the eastern seacoast for many years. In fact, the one song was John Kennedy's favorite. Even though we don't have a piano, it went something like this: *(singing)*

So tell your friends and your neighbors, too, that every worker must go to bat,
Tell them all to get out and vote, if you don't then you're the goat.
If your senator or your congressman doesn't vote for the workingman,
If he doesn't prove that he's labor's friend, you both will get him in the end.
You gotta know the score. You gotta know the score. You gotta know the score.
So don't give in because you're bound to win when you know the score.

When you take yourself to a baseball game, you like to know every player's name.
You want to know how he hits the ball, if he's giving it his all.
When you cast your vote on Election Day, you like to know how the players play.
You look up his record, and there you'll see if he's on the ball for you and me.
You gotta know the score. You gotta know the score. You gotta know the score.
You gotta know the score. So don't give in 'cause you're bound to win,
When you know the score. . . .

Q: So the chorus became well-known at the ILGWU conventions?

CL: They'd wait for us. They'd say that it's the highlight of the convention. Just recently we came home from Pittsburgh. We opened a steel workers' convention there. It's a real musical revue with a union flavor.[17]

GALLERY

G1 | ILGWU headquarters, Broadway, New York, circa 1943. Photo courtesy of the Kheel Center, Cornell University.

G2 | Thomas "Three-Finger Brown" Lucchese, dress shop owner and alleged crime boss, testifying before U.S. Senate McClellan hearings, 1958. Photo: Bettmann / Getty Images.

G3 | Lori Dress strike rally, Pittston, Pennsylvania, March 18, 1958. Photo courtesy of Lukasik Studio.

G4 | Strike at Harvic Fashion, a garment shop owned by Thomas "Three-Finger Brown" Lucchese and Harry "Nig" Rosen. Photo courtesy of Lukasik Studio.

Our Union headquarters, 77 South Main Street, Pittston.

G5 | ILGWU headquarters, Pittston, Pennsylvania, circa 1955. Photo courtesy of Lukasik Studio.

G6 | Dominick Alaimo, garment shop owner and alleged organized crime member, circa 1950s. Photo: U.S. Department of the Treasury, *Mafia: The Government's Secret File on Organized Crime* (New York: HarperCollins, 2007).

G7 | Alaimo Dress strike, Pittston, Pennsylvania, circa 1953. Photo courtesy of Lukasik Studio.

G8 | Clover Dress Company strike, Wilkes-Barre, Pennsylvania, 1958. The strikers referred to the strike trailer area as "Picket Heaven." Photo courtesy of the ILGWU Wyoming Valley District Archives, Kheel Center.

G9 | Ann-Lee Frocks building, Pittston, Pennsylvania,once owned by alleged crime boss Russell Bufalino. Photo courtesy of the Northeastern Pennsylvania Oral and Life History Collection, Pennsylvania State University.

G10 | Russell Bufalino, Angelo Sciandra, and James Osticco (*left to right*) at their 1959 arraignment for charges stemming from the Apalachin, New York, organized crime meeting. Photo courtesy of *Citizens' Voice*.

GREATER PITTSTON
LOCAL 295

INTERNATIONAL LADIES'
GARMENT WORKERS UNION

thanks the people
of Pittston for
their help in the
dressmakers strike.

Carmella Salatino
President

Jennie Bialis
Vice President

Rose DeRosa
Secretary

Clem Lyons
Union Representative

Min Matheson
District Manager

G11 | ILGWU Pittston Local 295 "Thank-You," 1958. Photo courtesy of the Kheel Center, Cornell University.

G12 | Ribbon cutting, ILGWU–Democratic Party headquarters, Pittston, Pennsylvania, 1970. Photo courtesy of Lukasik Studio.

G13 | ILGWU members contributing to a Red Cross truck at the Knox Mine disaster, 1959. Photo courtesy of Lukasik Studio.

G14 | James Corbett and ILGWU members in rehearsal, circa 1960; on the right is Clementine Lyons. Photo courtesy of Lukasik Studio.

G15 | ILGWU parade float, featuring Clementine Lyons, (top center) circa 1960. Photo courtesy of Lukasik Studio.

G16 | Garment workers in a large shop, circa 1970. Photo courtesy of the Kheel Center, Cornell University.

G17 | Wyoming Valley District, Local Union Officers' Meeting, circa 1968. Photo courtesy of Lukasik Studio.

G18 | Unity House aerial view, circa 1948. Photo courtesy of the Kheel Center, Cornell University.

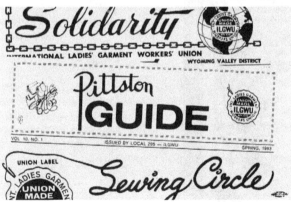

Mrs. Roosevelt Urges Every Woman to Look for Union Label in Dresses

G19 (*left top*) | Eleanor Roosevelt, David Dubinsky, and Harry Greenberg at Unity House, circa 1945. Photo courtesy of the Kheel Center, Cornell University.

G20 (*left bottom*) | *Pittston Guide*, newsletter of ILGWU Local No. 295, 1963. Photo courtesy of Min Matheson.

G21 (*above*) | Eleanor Roosevelt endorses ILGWU clothing, 1936. Photo courtesy of the Kheel Center, Cornell University.

G22 | Swearing in of union staff and chairladies, ILWGU Wyoming Valley District, circa 1970. Photo courtesy of Lukasik Studio.

G23 | Tenth anniversary of the Wyoming Valley District Health Center, 1958. Photo courtesy of the ILGWU Wyoming Valley District Archives, Kheel Center, Cornell University.

G24 | Garment cutter at the work table, circa 1960s. Photo courtesy of the Kheel Center, Cornell University.

G25 | Min Matheson addressing a union rally, circa 1955. Photo courtesy of the Kheel Center, Cornell University.

G26 | J. C. Penney–Leslie Fay protest, 1994. Photo courtesy of the Kheel Center, Cornell University.

G27 | Will Lurye's funeral procession, Broadway, New York, May 12, 1949. Photo courtesy of the Kheel Center, Cornell University.

G28 | Bill and Min Matheson, circa 1960. Photo courtesy of Lukasik Studio.

G29 | Michael Pilato, detail of mural depicting Min Matheson, with local sculptor Edgar Patience on the bottom left, Pittston, PA. Photo courtesy of the Center for the Small City, University of Wisconsin-Stevens Point. Robert P. Wolensky.

FIG. 28
Helen Weiss, 1997.
Photo courtesy of the
Northeastern Pennsylvania
Oral and Life History
Collection, Pennsylvania
State University.

Helen (Barnosky) Weiss,
from an audio-recorded
interview with Robert P.
Wolensky conducted at Mrs.
Weiss's home in Butler, New
Jersey, on June 20, 1997.
The interview is included
in the Wyoming Valley Oral
History Project, which is one
of eight projects within the
Northeastern Pennsylvania
Oral and Life History Collec-
tion housed in the Eberly
Family Special Collections
Library, Penn State Univer-
sity Libraries.

Helen Weiss

Garment Worker, Business Agent,
and Chorus Performer

After beginning in a nonunion garment shop, Helen Weiss changed
to a unionized company and became a member of the ILGWU. She
accepted an invitation to join the union staff as an organizer and business agent, with Min Matheson as her mentor. Unlike most ILGWU
members, she had little prior union experience but learned quickly
and became a champion of the cause in the Wyoming Valley and in
Easton, Pennsylvania, where she served as the district manager. One
of her accomplishments involved the creation of what she called the
"bible"—a ledger containing piecework prices across companies, the
goal being to standardize and equalize wages throughout the district.
She describes with real intensity her clashes with crime-affiliated shop
owners who generated some traumatizing memories. She acknowl-
edges gender as a resource in dealing with the "tough guys" who
usually would not harm picketing women because "they thought of
us like a mother."

HW: While I'm sewing at home one day—this is how I began to get
into the garment industry—a man, a Lithuanian man, comes to
visit my mother, and he walks through the house and he sees
me [at my] sewing machine in the living room. He says to my

mother, "What's your daughter doing in the living room sewing?" [She said], "Oh, my daughter likes to sew. She's sewing for the neighbor across the street." [He said], "Why should she sew for the neighbor across the street? My wife has a shop called the Rander factory on Main Street in Edwardsville and they make aprons. Let her go there. My wife's looking for workers. She'll hire her right away and she could be makin' money instead of dirtying up her own house." Which is exactly what I did. My mother said, "You'd better go there and see," and I did. That's how I started to work for Mrs. Rander making aprons. I think it had to be 1940 or '41. Sometime around when the war was on.

Q: Was it a union shop?

HW: Oh, this is what I'm going to tell you—now starts everything. Mrs. Rander owned the shop by herself when a man from New York comes around to see her. He wants her to go into business with him but he wants to make dresses. He didn't want to make aprons 'cause there was no money in aprons. He says to her, "You'll have to move your shop from Edwardsville to Kingston; we'll make dresses [there] and I'll get all the work you want." Which is exactly what he did.

So I started to work in there. Mrs. Rander didn't know anything about dresses so she was not able to teach us. She knew very little. The guy, her partner, got a floorlady to come in from New York to show us how to work on dresses. She didn't have to show me much because I made clothes at home, so I knew. What I didn't know is about the bundles [garment pieces]. Instead of making one dress at a time, they'd make twelve dresses at a time. Listen, this lady from New York came and showed us exactly what to do. So Mrs. Rander got a little PO'd [angry] because she was second fiddle by this time. . . . The guy that she was in business with kept her for a while but eventually she left and somebody else bought the shop. And that's when it became big doins'. He [the new owner] was from New York and he brought the work in from New York. . . . Then he got another floorlady from New York to teach us how to sew, how to work, how to do the bundles and all that.

I was workin' a few years already, workin' on the tops of dresses, and the floorlady, her name was Stella, asked me, "I need a floorlady to help me. I can't do it by myself 'cause we're hiring more people. Will you come and work for me, with me?" I said to her, "Stella, I'll tell ya, I can't. I can't because I can't be on the other side with the union." I said, "I just can't do it." So I never became the floorlady. I just sat and worked at the machine. By this time, when she asked me to do that, the union was already in our shop. Prior to that, my mother got very sick and got cancer, and I had to stay home and take care of my mother. Work was not important to me then. My mother was more important. When I came back to the shop, the union was in.

Q: What year was that?

HW: When I joined the union it was 1945.

Q: What was the name of the shop?

HW: Stella Dress. When I came back I had to sign the union card—the union was in. The girl sittin' next [to me] in the row was a foreign-born woman. I think she was Slovak. Stella began bringing work back to her to do over because it wasn't done good. There was one dress came back, two dresses came back, I don't know how many came back, and I said, "Hey Stella, why are you giving her all this work? How do you know it's *her* work?" [She said], "Well, that's the kind of work that she does. That's her work." I said, "No, it's not her work. I didn't see her workin' on anything like that."

Stella puckered up 'cause she didn't like that. She was the boss and why should I interfere with what she was trying to do with the worker? I said, "I feel sorry for her because it is not her work." Stella walked away. Prior to that, after she brought one or two bundles back to the lady to fix, the lady says to me, "Helen, they're not mine." That's why I knew I could say that. But Stella says, "What business is it of yours?" I said, "It's all my business." I said, "You're not gonna do [that to] people because she can't speak English good. You can't do that to her." I was what they called *pyskaty*. I was one that said anything I wanted to say! I never cared 'cause I didn't care about my job. I think that word is Polish. It means sassy. You know, answering back and you're sassy.

Anyway, that's how I started to work. Then the union began to organize in the different shops and they needed picketers. They used to call the chairlady of our shop, who was Dorothy Ney [chap. 1]. I was not even the assistant chairlady. I was the secretary [of the shop union], and there was Dorothy [Ney], and Mary Evans was the assistant chairlady. Mary Evans—remember that name because she's the one that went on a picket line with me, which I will tell you about.

While we were in the shop one day Dorothy or somebody comes up and they gave leaflets to Mary Evans at her house, and they said, "We want you to organize a shop in Edwardsville. You go and get Helen Barnosky [later Helen Weiss] to help you because you're both close by." I lived at the end of Zerby Avenue [in Edwardsville], and she lived on the other side on Kingston off Second Avenue or Third Avenue. We both met in Edwardsville on the Main Street to go to the shop to give them these leaflets and introduce ourselves. I don't remember what the leaflets said, something about "Join the union!" and all that. . . .

So *(laughs)* Mary Evans and I were givin' out the leaflets, passing out the leaflets as the people were goin' in. A lot of people wouldn't take the leaflet. They were afraid that the boss was inside lookin'. We moved a little away from the shop so the boss wouldn't see who was takin' the leaflet. Now that was the end of that picket line for me and Mary Evans because we were instigators—we gave out the leaflets!

Q: What year was that?

HW: Let's see, '46 or '47?[1] Dorothy could tell ya because she was on that picket line when there was a great big stink. My mother was so afraid of the unions on account of the, you know, the miners' strikes and the police come on horses and hit the people on the head with their sticks. On our very street was a miner—he was a scab. He crossed all the picket lines in Edwardsville to go into the mines to work. All the other men wouldn't go in but he was a scab and he went in. So everybody knew from then on what he did.

Q: How did your mother feel about your becoming an organizer?

HW: She didn't mind me being a union person, but she didn't want me to get hit on the head! She didn't want me to be on any picket line. She didn't know I was givin' these leaflets out because I got up early and I went there early and then I went back to Stella Dress to work. The next day after we gave out the leaflets, Min [Matheson, chap. 3] and them got together and they had a whole bunch of [unionized] people at that shop to hold the [nonunionized] people from goin' in to work, to keep them out 'til they'd join the union.

Mary Evans and me—no! She told Mary Evans and me not to go [back on the picket line] because we instigated it when we gave out the leaflets, and now they [the owners] are going to be mad at us so we're not gonna go. All the other people, Dorothy, Min, and everybody was there, and that was a very long strike. I never went back on that picket line. It was a terrible strike. They were throwing hot coffee on the picketers who were in front. Dorothy tells the story because she was there all the time and they had it [i.e., they were tired of the strike]. Even [the ILGWU lawyer] Dan Flood, I think, had to come there. They had a meeting with the mayor in his office to try to settle the strike. The union finally got in.

Q: Who owned the shop?

HW: I really don't know who owned it. He had to be a New York guy. It couldn't be a local guy; he'd join [cooperate with] the union. I know the local people would [go along]. Many came from New York to Pennsylvania to get cheap labor and they didn't want the union. But then they had no choice because they wouldn't get the work, ya see. They had to get the union in that shop if there was [jobber-provided] union work from New York. That's how they organized a lot of the shops because, for instance, our shop that I worked in became union because our dresses [i.e., dress pieces] that we were working on were union-made in New York. So they had no choice. They had to become union when they went to Pennsylvania.[2] But if you didn't catch them, if you didn't picket them, and if you didn't try to organize the people to join the union, they'd go without the union.

They [the dress pieces] would come to Pennsylvania in bundles. Our factory's [piecework] came cut 'cause we didn't have a cutting room. Our work would come in great big bins on wheels. I forget what they called them. Then they separated them and that's how we got our work. But some factories were big and they had cutting rooms, so they [the jobbers] sent only the bolts of material and they [the spreaders] spread the material out and laid the pattern and [the cutters] cut it out. That's how cutters became union, too.

Q: Did you go back to Stella Dress after that?

HW: Oh yeah, I stayed in Stella Dress. Then one time Ray Shore [of the ILGWU Northeast Department] came into Stella Dress. He was gonna organize some shops and he wanted to meet the girls who could picket. That would be Dorothy and me 'cause Dorothy would get me to go and Mary Evans and whoever else she wanted. There were others that went, too.

There was a time when I was working in Stella Dress, and on Kingston's Corners there was Ann Will Garment [see William Cherkes, chap. 2]. Somebody from the union—I don't remember who—called me at home and said that I should go in front of Ann Will Garment and not let those people in [the shop] to work. It was a union shop already but they told me that I should keep the people from working because there was some friction about the jobber in New York not paying the Health and Welfare [Fund] money to the union. So they had to stop working to show the people in New York that they'd have to pay that money to the Health and Welfare.[3]

It wasn't too far from where I lived. I knew the chairlady there. [The Wyoming Valley District office told me to] tell her not to [go in], and when she comes [to work] she'll help me. I thought there was gonna be other people coming to help me because I was alone. What do I know about it? I can't hold the people! I don't know all the people and I can't hold them from goin' in. But lucky for me, those that were coming, they didn't go in and I told them to go to Wilkes-Barre to the union office. When the chairlady of the shop came, she met me on the street and she [also] shipped them [to Wilkes-Barre]. They listened to her more [than me]. . . .

Q: How long did you stay at Stella Dress?

HW: I left Stella Dress on March 9 of 1953. So [I worked there] from '44 or '45 to '53. Now you have to hear this [story]—it's really funny. I said to her [the owner of Stella Dress], "I'm going to work with Min Matheson." They all knew her. "But I don't think I'm gonna like it and I don't want to lose my job here because I wanna come back if I don't like it or if they don't like me." I said, "I haven't got any kind of education to be goin' and doin' this." So they kept my machine. The Stella Dress [owner] married a guy, and he became her mechanic. He says, "OK, I'll keep your machine." He kept my machine! Nobody worked on it. [It was] sittin' and waitin' for me to come back. I said, "If I'm not good, I'll be back in six weeks," because I said to Min Matheson, "Either you're gonna like me or you're not gonna like me, but after six weeks, I'm gonna go back to Stella Dress or I'm gonna stay on, depends on whether you'll like me or I don't like it." And that's what I did.

It was already about three months that I was out of the factory when Stella's husband called me at home, and he said, "Helen, are you comin' back?" He said, "I'm savin' your machine for you to come back." I said, "I don't think so. I don't think I'm gonna come back." I was stayin' with the union and that's how it was. I thought it was pretty cute that he saved the machine and nobody worked on it 'til I was sure I was comin' back.

HELEN WEISS

Q: What was your first job with the union?

HW: I knew where all of the factories were because I helped organize most of them with Dorothy and all the others. Or if I didn't, I was there for the [Luzerne County] United Fund 'cause I used to raise money for them. I used to make speeches in the [garment] factories for the United Fund. We called it Red Feather at that time. When there was somebody [who] needed to go to any factory, they sent me to the shop to speak on the United Fund, or the Red Feather. So yes, Min came and asked me to work for the union [as a business agent], and I say, "God bless her," because she is the one that started me. I have my retirement today because she started me in it and I stayed in it. For twenty-one years I worked [with the union].

The day I started, Louise Platt—she was the business agent who came to ask me to join the union [staff] with Min Matheson—she said, "I'll show you and tell you what to do, and if you run into any kind of trouble, you come and talk to me." She took me to twenty-two shops in the Pittston area, the Avoca area, and all those little towns around there, and showed me the twenty-two shops that I was gonna service. That's how I started. One week [with Louise], and the next week I was on my own. I would go into the shop, see the chairlady, find out her problems, and then go home at the end of the day. I'd come to the [main] office and I would tell Min Matheson what problems I had or if I didn't have any, or who talked to me, or whatever. And she encouraged me.

After I was doin' that for maybe a month, I went to one shop on Slocum Street in Swoyersville—some factory they had there. I went in and the girl working at a machine—she was doin' an operation like putting zippers on the side [of a skirt]—and she says, "Helen, we can't make any money. It's not a good price on this zipper. We just can't make any money doin' it." She said, "You gotta do somethin' for us." Lucky for me that the boss of that factory was a beautiful, wonderful boss. I took him in the office and I said to him, "You see the zipper on this dress? How much are you paying for it?" He told me. I said, "You know it isn't enough, because when I look at that, they can't make any money on it. They need a couple pennies more." They got paid by the dozen. I said, "So you gotta give them a little bit more peanuts." "Well," he said, "How much do you think I should give them?" Because he also didn't know. I said, "Give 'em two or three cents [more] at least to start with and see what they're gonna make." He said, "OK, you got it."

I went back to the girl and I told her how much it's gonna be. "Oh," she says, "good." Two or three cents, listen to this! [I] came back to the office and I said, "Min, you gotta hear this." *(laughs)* And I told her the story. She says, "See, don't ya get some good feelings after you do something like that?" She said, "Well, ya have to know how to talk to the people." I never would leave a factory mad. No matter how much I would argue with the boss, no matter what I would say to him, I would always leave on good terms 'cause I knew that I'd have to come back another day.

Q: Why do you think Min Matheson asked you to join the staff?

HW: I'll tell ya' why, I think. Dorothy Ney should have been the first one to go, but she didn't ask Dorothy. The reason is because I was more levelheaded than Dorothy. She was like fire. The union was first, came first and foremost with her, and so it did with me. But I took it in stride, whereas she knew that that was the thing to do, that people should join the union. So when Min had to look for somebody who would be able to talk to people and talk to them quietly, she talked it over with Louise Platt, who said to her, "If you wanna know between Helen and Dorothy, I think you should ask Helen first. If she turns out good for you, then you can then ask Dorothy, but try Helen first."

New York only wanted her [Min Matheson] to get business agents from New York because New York was first on the totem pole. I was doin' the job for six weeks, and Min was payin' me from the local. It was fifty dollars a week plus ten dollars a week for my car. I had to travel back and forth with the car and I wanna tell you that I had a car that was ten years old and I just learned how to drive in 1952. So for six weeks she paid me, and then she went to New York, and they said, "Well, you're getting a lot of shops, don't you need maybe [more] business agents?" She says, "No, Helen Barnosky is my business agent. And they said, "Her?" You know, 'cause I was always the meek one. Dorothy was the one that talked. "Her?" And she said, "Yes, she's going to twenty-two shops now for six weeks and did you hear anything bad about her?" They said, "No."

She told me this later. Then the next pay, the next week when I got paid, it was from New York and I found out later that they retroacted [sic] my pay to her to put in the kitty of the local. My pay went up to fifty-five dollars plus five dollars more for my car. I was savin' my money and then when I was already [working] about six months, I had to get another car because the car that I had was ten years old and it had runnin' board fenders that were gettin' rusty! . . .

Q: Did you have that same area for very long, those twenty-two shops?

HW: Oh, maybe a year or two, but not too long because they liked [business agents] to change shops, and I'll give you the reason why. When you go to a place over and over, the boss gets familiar with you. He knows you good, the people know you good, and everybody knows you too good. And then you don't sweep as clean. When you get another group of shops, you gotta start all over again, and you gotta open your ears and listen. That's why I think they did it. I think it's a good idea, personally. I didn't like it 'cause I had to start learning names all over again and I have no memory for names—never had. But that's how it all started.

Q: Did you have many strikes in those early years?

HW: Yes. I was almost on every picket line in Pittston with the strikes. Min Matheson, along with my [future] husband [Jack Weiss], who was a business agent at that time, they decided they were gonna try to organize as many shops as they could in the Pittston area. This was before I became a business agent. When I became a business agent, most shops were already organized.

HELEN WEISS

Since it was a Pittston shop a lot of people who lived and worked in Pittston were well-known in our union. They would have friends working in those factories and they would have them look up and see who's work are they doing. So let's say they were doing "Tom Smith's" work from New York. Tom Smith in New York is organized. But in Pittston he [the shop doing his work] is not organized. All we had to do was go to see the boss and say, "Hey, you're not gonna get that work anymore unless you join the union because it has to be a union shop to do union work from New York." That's how it started. That's how one shop after another came on.

Q: Most of the shops in Pittston were organized by what date?

HW: When I started to work in '53, most of it was organized. Here and there, they were not organized. They'd start up a new shop then we'd have to find out through the people that worked in other shops who's working in there. You gotta talk to them and find out what kinda work they're doing. But the goons [organized criminals] were [there].

Now see, in 1958 there was that big strike, including New York. It was the first big strike for twenty years or twenty-five years or whatever it was. They settled the shops in New York within weeks, but some of the shops in the outlying areas, like in the Pittston and Wilkes-Barre areas, did not want to sign. So we had eight or however many shops that were still out on strike for a long time. It took a few months for us to get them organized. [There] was one [shop] that I sat in my car in front of so they wouldn't take the work out [i.e., transport it to New York City].

Q: Tell us that story.

HW: Well, there was the Jenkins [Sportswear] shop.[4] We were trying to organize that shop in Pittston on Main Street. In the daytime our girls were picketing and we didn't want the people [i.e., workers] to go in. But most of the people went in because they were *goombodies* [Italian slang for close friend or relative], they were neighbors, they're all in-laws, they were godfathers and godmothers and all that. It's rough [up there]. We were trying to organize that shop in the morning and in the daytime. I was working as a business agent at the other shops, so at night they [the union] had to have somebody watch the shop so they [the owners] wouldn't take the work out. They said to me, "You're in the Pittston area, so instead of comin' home, you stay there and you be in front of the shop and watch that they don't take the work out after the other pickets go home."

The other pickets would go home around six o'clock. So I'd have my supper when I got out of work, then I'd go to the picket line in my car, and my friend Carmella Salatino, who was my best friend, she came and she sat with me.[5] She said, "You're not gonna sit here by yourself and be in front of it." 'Cause all ya had to do was stay there either in the car or out of the car, so that you [can] see a truck comin' in to take out the piece goods. . . .

This Jenkins Sportswear [strike], that went on for weeks and weeks. I tell ya, I was so tired at the end of that time because I would work all day. I had to be in the office at nine o'clock in the morning, and I had to go to the shops right away—run from one shop to the other for my meetings—then I'd come [home to] have my supper, and then I'd go on that picket line. I'd get home at eleven o'clock at night. I'd leave Carmella off at her house. Carmella's brother-in-law was watching, taking good care of us. He was in the bar across the street lookin' out the window to see that nobody came and did any harm to us.

That was the funniest part of all. We didn't have to worry. We were not afraid. Why was I not afraid? I thought that they weren't gonna do anything to a little girl like me! I never was afraid. If it was a man, you can bet your bottom dollar he'd have a split head because that's the way they worked. The people that were against the union, they felt sorry for women. I think they kind of [thought of us] like a mother, ya know? I didn't have gray hair at that time, but I wasn't young. I was born in 1910.

Q: Who owned the Jenkins shop?

HW: It was one of them [organized crime people], yeah. Another shop that was [affiliated with reputed organize crime boss Russell] Bufalino was [Dominick] Alaimo's. Now I can tell you a little story about that. I was working in Easton at the time [1957], and there was a big [organized crime] meeting at Apalachin. The big stew was about the police comin' to Apalachin, New York. Well, [at] Apalachin was Alaimo from Pittston, you know what I'm sayin'? I think his shop was Ann-Lee.

One time, I was comin' into the shop and I wanted to see the chairlady and the boss. He [Alaimo] was goin' out and he said, "I only got a minute so come on with me. I gotta go to see somebody right by the river." I had a shop problem; I needed [piece rate] increases. I said, "No, I'll stay here and I'll wait." He said, "Come on, we can do the talkin' while you're in the car. You won't waste my time when you come back; you'll talk to me in the car." So innocently, I get into the car and I went with him to this place. He went in and I stayed out. I found out later that it was Russell Bufalino's office! He went in and he didn't stay long inside, maybe ten minutes, and he came out. He kept his word with me and he took me back to the Ann-Lee shop.

Q: Do you think Alaimo was a front man for Bufalino, or do you think he really owned that shop?

HW: Nah, none of them owned the shop by themselves. I think they were all with Bufalino, who I think had a piece of everything.

Q: Including Jenkins Sportswear?

HW: Oh yeah, I'm sure.[6] I never wanted to hear about those [guys]. The less I knew about their records, I tell you, the more guts I had. I could do a lot of hollerin' but I knew when to keep my mouth shut, too, because I knew if I had to come back, you better be careful. Now Russell Bufalino . . . oh, you know what it was? [Emanuella "Dolly"] Falcone [managed it]. That's the shop [Jenkins Sportswear].

HELEN WEISS

I'm sure that was strictly Bufalino's shop. When I got into that shop, I said, "I wanna see [i.e., talk to] the girls at the machines because I don't like to see them in the office." They let me go in, but they didn't let me go while they were working. They said, "You have to come to this shop at the noon hour while they're having lunch. Then you could go in the shop and you could talk to the people." Now wasn't that stupid of them? I coulda done a whole lot at the noon hour—a lot of trouble! If they would've let me come in while the girl was at the machine, I could make less trouble.

But I was not a troublemaker, see, so they [the workers] were not afraid. I would go in to see them at noon. I not only talked to the chairlady, but I talked to everybody that was there. But don't you worry, those people were godfathers and godmothers of each other. The whole shop, they knew each other. You couldn't say anything bad or mad because it would go to the next person, go to the boss, or go to everybody. Ya had to keep your mouth shut.

Q: When Dolly Falcone's shop reopened after the strike, was it union-affiliated?

HW: Oh yeah, it was not gonna open unless it was a union shop, and it was a union shop, and I was in it.[7]

Q: Was their New York jobber also union?

HW: Had to be. Sure. That was in 1960, because right after that I moved away to work in Easton. There was violence, like when they threw the coffee on the people. The mayor said, "You'll have no violence there," and he padlocked that shop after weeks of picketing. . . .

Q: What can you tell us about New York–Wyoming Valley union relationship?

HW: With regard to piece rates, we had what they called the "bible" and it contained piece rates that they paid in New York. They never wanted to show Pennsylvania what they were paying in New York because they didn't want us to learn. But, somehow, Min got hold of the piece-rate book from New York and she brought it home, brought it in, and then she says, "Let's make [the same] piece rates here in Pennsylvania." They [the owners] eventually had to pay New York prices. In Easton, Easton Dress [eventually] had to pay New York prices.

I was on the [Price Settlement] Committee to help make the prices. We couldn't make what they were paying in New York [at first], because we were in Pennsylvania and it would be less.[8] How did I get to know about it [piece rates]? When I was going from one factory to another, I would always say to the girls, "Gee, what is your boss paying you for joining these seams?" The girl would say ten cents or fifteen cents or five cents or whatever. I got my little book and I would write it in the book. I would write, "Ann Will is paying ten cents a dozen for putting the seams on skirts," and I would put the dates. I had a little book where I was collecting prices from everywhere. I never showed it to anybody, never even told anybody I had it, because that was me. So, when they come to make these prices, Min put me on the committee, and right at that time I went [was transferred] to work in Easton.

FIG. 29 | Garment workers on strike, Old Forge, Pennsylvania, 1958. Photo courtesy of the Kheel Center, Cornell University.

In Easton, they didn't know what I knew [regarding piece rates], and they didn't know what I could do. I got on the committee [and my husband] was furious with me because, [he'd say], "Helen, you're not pushing yourself to go and tell them." I said, "I don't wanna tell them." He said, "But Helen you need to; somebody has to know something about it in order to make these prices." So finally I agreed, and I went to some of the meetings [in Easton] and would open up my mouth. But I was not the head of that because they had a few other people. They got a girl from New York to head the . . . Price Settlement Committee, and I was there only on the sideline because I was a business agent and I had other factories to do.

Q: So there were higher rates in New York?

HW: Oh, much more in New York.

Q: And you eventually got prices adjusted upward in Wilkes-Barre and in Easton?

HW: We started to. [At first], we didn't have [standardized] piece rates in Wilkes-Barre; the boss paid what he wanted. That's when I went around and I said, "I need two cents more on that, or three cents more," and he gave it because he didn't know whether it was right or wrong. The only thing we could tell when people were making enough money was because we took payroll. See, every month I went to the factories—not at the beginning but later—and they would give us their payroll book and we'd see what everybody was makin' at the end of the week. And if it was low—let's say it was twenty dollars a week or thirty dollars

HELEN WEISS

a week—we knew that wasn't enough. It had to be a minimum wage, which would bring you up to somethin' higher than they would've gotten [without us].

Q: So New York had the bible with all their piece rates?

HW: Because they were New York. Don't forget they organized in 1900! Sure we ended up with a bible, but that was 1960–1967. Then I went to work in Easton and they had a guy that was heading that [Price Settlement] Committee. He was a troubleshooter, and he would go to a place. Let's say that Easton had a shop that didn't know what the piece rates should be. They would send for him, and he would come, and he would go over the prices. He'd say, "This is not good. Yeah, this is a good price here, but you put all of it on this part and you should've put it on that part." That I knew because I was doing it myself, see? He went to Pottsville, Pottstown, or wherever [because] he was a troubleshooter, but it was not only him. There was a girl from New York [who was also a troubleshooter], and she used to come here and go home to New York on weekends. What did I ever do with that "bible" I made?

Q: Were you surprised that there wasn't a such a piece-rate book in the Wyoming Valley or Easton before the 1960s?

HW: New York [union headquarters] didn't want us to have it. New York did not want to let the dresses come [here]! New York did not want this. I know it had to be [true]. New York did not really want them to send their material to be made outside of New York. But the cheaper they got it made [outside of New York], they [the jobbers] would go there. So they [the New York ILGWU] had to give in. They agreed and it was at the very beginning when Min started.

Q: Why exactly didn't New York want Wilkes-Barre to have a "bible"?

HW: To keep Wilkes-Barre in the dark. They didn't want to give Min any kind of a chance to get ahead of anywhere. They just didn't want her to know. . . . See, now, we were lucky in organizing Pittston because if the owner had a union [in his shop] in New York, he had to be union here. That was the biggest thing to organizing any shop in Pittston, and that's how we got the bulk of them. There were ones that we couldn't get, such as Jenkins Sportswear and that other one that [Dolly] Falcone had. They were standouts; they would not, did not want to join [negotiate with] the group. There were eight jobbers, if my memory serves me right, who did not want to join the union. They stood out. They took months after the 1958 strike before they came in, and that's why we had those strikes in Pittston. . . .[9]

When I went to work in Easton, from Wilkes-Barre, they were shocked at the [low] wages that I was making. When I came to Easton, my boss there used to tell New York, "Pay Helen more." She used to keep tellin' them. They wouldn't give me an increase right off the bat. I was so low on the totem pole that they gave me periodic increases until I could catch up.

Q: So Wilkes-Barre [i.e., the Wyoming Valley] had really low pay?

HW: Yeah. Wilkes-Barre was worse. Wilkes-Barre was awful. Oh yeah. When I went to work in Easton, she [the boss] had to look [at my pay] and she was shocked. I had to give her my pay envelope 'cause she wanted—everyone did—to see what everybody else was making in Easton. She wanted to keep us all on an even keel, and I was the bottom of the totem pole.

Q: Why would Easton pay so much more?

HW: Because Easton was closer to New York—to the metropolitan area. So the jobbers in Easton, I don't know exactly why, but they paid [more]. I had one big strike in Easton. We sort of followed [district manager] Grace Birkel and did what she said, because she had a mouth. We think Min had a mouth! Grace had a bigger mouth! When she went out [to the shops], the bosses didn't wanna hear her. Oh, did she holler! Maybe Grace Birkel was stronger, or I don't want to say the word stronger, maybe she was more . . . she never gave in. Min, if you would get Min in a corner and [the owner would say], "I can't afford it [higher piece rates]," she'd give in maybe a couple of pennies, so it held it [wages] down a little bit.

Q: Did you show Min Matheson the Easton "bible" so she could compare piece rates?

HW: She was dealing with the same [thing]. We all had to do that. But in Wilkes-Barre, we couldn't get the prices that we got in Easton. We had the "bible," yeah, but that's where we started to make [i.e., create] it—when I was in Wilkes-Barre. I even went to Scranton and met the people from Scranton, and [met] the people from Allentown, the key people like myself that knew somethin' about piece rates. We were makin' the bible. . . .

When I stopped workin' and retired, I gave them my book. I used to carry that around everywhere I went as a business agent. It was hard cover. It was all the piece rates that we were doin'. God, why was I so stupid? I shoulda taken it instead of givin' it to this guy that took my place. I was tryin' to teach him. See, men that I knew were not as precise in what they were doing. I'm talkin' about business agents. They're nice people, I wanna tell ya that. The women loved them. When a woman sees me comin', she might say, "What does she know?" But when they see a man—because he's wearing a long pair of pants—they think he knows everything. That's psychology for ya! So I gave everything to this man when I was teachin' him [about] how go into factories. Grace Birkel insisted that I retire in 1974. She was payin' me to take him to the shops because I was getting my money from New York, my retirement fund already, and I wasn't gonna turn that down. She paid me to go with him and teach him because she wanted him to learn from me. But he wouldn't learn. . . .

Q: You were going to talk about a strike [in 1958] in Easton.

HW: Yeah. This was cute. This dress shop was the Cangelosi's Dress Shop. Cangelosi was Italian—Charlie Cangelosi. He was makin' not the best dress; he was makin' the cheaper dress and the mediocre dress. But anyway, New York told us, or Grace [Birkel] told us, that we had to get an increase in piece rates on certain kinds of dresses. Easton followed a lot [of] what New York said; that's why our wages were better in Easton than in Wilkes-Barre. And then we had a strike. We had a strike at all the shops. The bosses of the shops that we were to strike agreed to [settle]. They were too close to New York. They agreed to go to work. "We're not gonna strike; we're gonna give you what you want. But you have to give us, like, a week or two to get it," or whatever. And we, the agents, had to go in and take payroll and see if they were payin' the prices that they were supposed to pay.

As time went on, this one shop that I had—Cangelosi's Dress Shop—did not pay the increase. I said, "I'm not gonna wait any longer with the payroll." I didn't have it and he didn't pay it. He was gonna pay it . . . he was gonna pay it . . . but he didn't. So one night I called the chairlady from the shop—and she happened to be a black girl—there's just a few black people in the factories in Easton. Called her at home and I said, "Now look, here's what you have to do for me." I said, "When you go to work tomorrow, when you see ten o'clock, stop all your people from working. Stop the whole shop; nobody works. You can tell them [in advance], but I don't want the boss to know this." They started to work at seven o'clock in the morning. When ten o'clock came, they all stopped working. I also said, "And tell them to go home for lunch and come back from lunch at one o'clock or whenever their lunch is over, and go back to their machines and not work. When it's three thirty in the afternoon, go home."

The next day they come in at seven o'clock. The boss, if he locks them out, it's gonna be a lockout. And, of course, that goes to the National Labor Relations Board. So that's what I did. They stopped, went home for lunch, they come back, and the boss said, "Oh, they're gonna go back to work now." They didn't start to work, and at three thirty in the afternoon, they went home and that was it. That night, I'm keeping in touch with the chairlady by telephone. [She said that] the boss is lookin' for me. He calls the office and he can't find me, 'cause I told the office, "Don't you tell him where I am. I don't want him to know because I gotta get this thing done."

The next day they come in the same way: they don't start to work, they don't do anything, they go home for lunch, they come back, and they don't work. The end of the day, the boss leaves me a message at our office: "Helen, when you come to work tomorrow, come to see me." I went up [the next day] and he gave us everything that I wanted, and the girls went to work. That was somethin'! Mind you, I didn't go into the shop. They were goons [i.e., organized crime]. They were goons from New York [who owned the shop]. Charlie [Cangelosi] was the one that [I met with]. His brother [John] had a [men's] pants factory downstairs and the dress factory was upstairs. It was the Amalgamated [men's apparel union] downstairs, with the [ILGWU] dress factory upstairs.

I would never ask anything outrageous. Piece rates—I got out my bible and I showed him what it was. I said, "Let me teach your office girl. If I teach your office girl how to do it [set piece rates], then I won't have to come and break down the dress and make the piece rates." 'Cause I used to have to go into Charlie Cangelosi's shop when they got a new style. I used to have to go up there [and

set] piece rates for the shoulders, piece rates for the neck and everything. Some set] piece rates for the shoulders, piece rates for the neck and everything. Some
necks had collars, some necks had French piping. I would have to make the prices on them. I said, "Charlie, why don't you let me teach your bookkeeper how to do it and you won't have to call me to do it." He said, "You got the bible, you do it." I said, "No, that's takin' up my time, let me teach her."

Well, I taught that girl and, I wanna tell ya, we got to be kind of buddies. I explained to her how to do it and she followed the bible. If she wasn't sure about anything she'd call the office and say, "Helen, we got one dress that I'm not quite sure if I'm paying right. Come up here and do it with me the first time if you could." And I would. He never stopped me. He trusted me because I never went above it [a fair piece rate]. Not that I want to brag about myself, but I had a bible. I didn't do it on my own. The Northeast Department [helped].

Q: Did the Northeast Department help the Wyoming Valley with wages?

HW: They did [later], but the Wilkes-Barre bosses wouldn't pay the [rates]. They wouldn't pay. Say it was supposed to be ten cents . . . they'd only pay eight. See, I had left Wilkes-Barre. I don't know, after a while, maybe they did pay it. They had a bible after we made it, yeah; they had it later.

Q: How long were you in Easton?

HW: From 1960 'til I retired in 1974, fourteen years.

Q: I gather that you used some of the organizing strategies that you learned from Min Matheson?

HW: Oh, all the time.

Q: For example?

HW: We didn't have very many strikes in Easton but, for instance, the strike that I told you about [at Cangelosi's shop]—I didn't learn that by myself, I learned that from Min.

Q: Have the workers show up but not actually work, and make the owner look for you?

HW: Sure, sure. Had to do it that way. But one thing about my boss in Easton, Grace Birkel: if I said, "That moon is green," she'd agree with me. She never contradicted me in front of any employer. If she would contradict me, she'd contradict me on the side about anything.

Q: Did Easton have as many tough guys or goons as Pittston?

HW: No! No! No! Pittston was the world's worst! Pittston was a hellhole. It was awful. Pittston was awful. Even Wilkes-Barre wasn't that bad. It was Pittston where they had all the goons. . . . Pittston, forget it! Pittston is a country of its own! Min, believe me when I tell ya, Min should have had a halo on her head and a crown on her head for organizing Pittston. The people that helped her organize, like Dorothy, should have two crowns. . . .

In Easton, the only goon was the one I told you about [Cangelosi] that had [forced] this strike. And when I went to the wake to see Charlie [when he died], his brother that had the Amalgamated shop, came over to me and said, "Helen, of all the people to come to see Charlie, I knew that you were a good person." But it wasn't that I was a good person, it's just that I developed them. I developed them because they did everything that I wanted. I certainly didn't bend back for them.

Q: Was it easier to work in Easton?

HW: Oh, much easier, much easier. Working in the Wilkes-Barre area to try to get a nickel in piece rates from anybody was torture! I got it, I don't say that I didn't, but it was hard to do. You have to know when you're goin' into a factory, you'd have to know how to speak to the boss. Well this boss, you have to build it around him, and that boss you gotta take it from the top. You gotta know, yeah. You had to know how to negotiate with them. Easton, they made much better [money] than in Wilkes-Barre, much better, but in Easton there were not that many dress shops. . . .

Q: Did you ever get to Unity House in the Pocono Mountains?

HW: Oh, that was beautiful. I can tell you a cute story about Unity House when Truman was president. After Roosevelt died then he became president. We used to have a weekend in Unity House from the Northeast Department where one or two girls from all the shops would go. When Truman was running for president, I was for Truman. I really liked him, and I wanted him to get in. So I would go from one building to another and I would stand on the table and I'd make my speech. I had it all prepared and I knew exactly what I was gonna say, from the heart. These were union people, business agents, some of them were workers from the factories, and then they'd go back and they tell their people. I wanted them to go back to the factory and tell the people to vote for Truman. I'd come to the buildings A, B, C, ya know, X, Y, Z, ya know, all those little bungalows.

When Roosevelt got in, and did what he did, it really brought me on my feet 'cause I got married, and things got a little better. So then Truman gets in, and I wanted them to be sure not to go back to the Depression days. I knew what I was sayin' because I was only tellin' things that I had lived through. Dorothy used to laugh and say, "Helen." And I guess I had one or two beers already, and I was ready to go 'cause I was not much of a drinker. I never wanted to drink too much 'cause I didn't want to forget what I was sayin'. I'd have enough to stimulate me to go, and that's how that started at Unity House. I would speak. When I got older, I went out West to see Truman's library, and I had to tell them that I worked so hard to get him elected. I said, "He's my best president in the whole world!"

Q: What else did you do at Unity House?

HW: [We went there] for a good time. Just for a good time. Your breakfast was served, your dinner was served, and your lunch. You went swimming or you played basketball or baseball. I was playing baseball, which I forgot that I did. I went swimming in the beautiful lake there. We always swam. Then sitting by the water. That was the typical day in the sun, getting a little tan. In the evening after dinner, there was a show in the new theater. The old theater was down by the lake, where they had shows come in, live shows from New York. No hoity-toity things, no junky stuff, but real nice good stuff. Singers, which I can't remember the name of the singers, but they were good opera singers. When they built the new theater in later years, they had Broadway shows. Not the whole show, but the people from the show, like the comedian and the headliner maybe. We would go free. It's all free. Once you got in up there, you didn't have to pay one penny.

Q: Do you recall the educational programs there?

HW: Oh, they always had educational programs at certain times, not every time we went up there. Certain weeks they had educational programs, which were only for different people who needed to be educated in politics or in sewing. . . .

Q: Were you involved with the chorus?

HW: When Jim Corbett was making these shows in New York and all, he was making one show and one of the songs was "So long, Jenny, we'll drink a toast to you, wish the most for you, when you're in clover." You know, like she's a retiree; she was retiring. Let her retire. Well, in one of the shows, I was Jenny and we went to Miami Beach. We also put on this show for the Northeast Department in Atlantic City. We put on [several] shows. This Jenny was [supposed to be] from Wilkes-Barre.

Then I was in another show in Easton and one in Miami. Jim Corbett was leading the show, and we went to Atlantic City and he made me sing in front all the time. In one of the skits, I was [again] Jenny: "So long, Jenny . . ." *(sings)* I had to pretend I was crying and I had the gifts they were giving me. I was dressed like an older lady ready to retire. After the show was over, you know how you mingle with everybody? In Atlantic City, a lot of the bosses came there because it was the union convention and there was a show on. So one of them came over to me, a president of the manufacturers' association. He came over to me and he says, "You were crying." I said, "I was not crying." "You sure looked like you were crying. You'd think you were retiring already. You were crying. . . ."

Q: You were in the chorus for how many years?

HW: From when he [Jim Corbett] first started until I went to Easton.

Q: Were most of the business agents in the chorus?

HW: If they didn't wanna be, they weren't.

Q: You were in it, Clem [Lyons, chap. 8] was in it, and the same with Dorothy [Ney]. You were all business agents.

HW: Yeah. . . .

Q: After you retired in '74, did you remain active in the union?

HW: Yeah, they had a union retiree's club. I was not heading that club but was more or less like a spokesperson for it. They had people from the shops that were there. I was never a leader, let me tell ya. I never wanted to lead it. I was a follower. The union wanted me to take hold of that retiree's club, but I couldn't do it because I didn't want to do it. I don't like that part, so let the other girls do it and I would only do what they needed. They would ask me and I would help them whatever they needed. . . .

Q: It seems like you have kept in touch with ILG people from Wilkes-Barre over the years.

HW: Oh yeah. This Carmella [Salatino] that I was telling ya about, she died. She was a vice president of a [union] local in Pittston. She opened a shop [later]. I used to go visit her, sure. Used to visit her all the time. In fact, I didn't go one year and I didn't know that she had died. I sent her a Christmas card and she never answered me. Min, I used to call her when I'd go to Wilkes-Barre 'cause I had cousins in Wilkes-Barre and my girlfriend was in Wilkes-Barre. I used to call Min and I would talk to her. I used to tear out a lot of things from the paper and I gave [i.e., sent] them to Min, little articles that I thought she would be interested in or she wanted for her children or grandchildren. She [may have] wanted them to know.

I saw her just before she died, about a year or less than that, and she was not feeling good. That's the sad part. I'll say this: she gave me the start of my livelihood by asking me to work with the union. I finished with the union. I retired from the union, and now I have a fairly nice retirement because of the union. That's what I can remember her for, for giving me the opportunity; coming to the house and asking me to do what hardly anybody would ask. I didn't have any kind of education. I only went to eighth grade! But she and whoever else sent me to school—I don't want to say "school," but to seminars—and I was learning and wanted to learn. That's how I picked up what I do know. I didn't have to know about being an attorney, because there were attorneys, but I had to know more psychology in how to deal with people.

Q: She had faith in you.

HW: I suppose she did because she asked me to do it. I was the first, and then there were other people, like Dorothy, that did the same kind of work. . . . And I tell you, I'm talkin' to my girlfriend on the phone last night, and she says, "Unions are not as strong. They're trying to organize the government workers. They already have a good pay." I said, "Hey, Jane, just a minute. If it wasn't for the unions from way back, to get what we did—the hourly and yearly increases, and the minimum wage," I said, "if it wasn't for us, those people working for the government wouldn't even get the money that they're getting today." But see, this Jane friend, she doesn't know anything because her father was a lawyer and she was raised with a silver spoon [in her mouth]. She had everything. She worked for a doctor before she retired. When I talk to her sometimes, it goes in one ear and out the other 'cause she's not interested in what I'm sayin'. She can't follow me because she didn't know anything about a union.

George and Lucy Zorgo
Union Printers and Labor Advocates

The unionized Zorgo Printing Company of Pittston provided essential services to the ILGWU Wyoming Valley District by producing newsletters, flyers, posters, pamphlets, and anniversary brochures—often on a day's notice. Owners George and Lucy Zorgo were strong labor advocates who assisted the union's efforts during strikes and at other times. Aware of the potential danger in performing work for the ILGWU, the couple endured threats on more than one occasion. They befriended Min and Bill Matheson and enjoyed social time with them. The Zorgos stand as an example of the type of community support that typified the district's solidary unionism approach to organizing and building a labor union.

GZ: When they [the ILGWU] first came into the Valley, they were looking for a printer, and because everyone [garment shop owners] was afraid of a union at that time, nobody [other printers] wanted to get involved. I had a Sunday school teacher that was a garment worker. Her name was Eleanor Leone. She started having people [workers] sign cards for the union. Of course, there was a lot of opposition to that in the area, and when they [the ILGWU] looked for a union printer, there weren't that many. I was a union printer,

FIG. 30
George Zorgo, 1993. (Lucy Zorgo chose not participate in the photograph associated with this interview.) Photo courtesy of the Northeastern Pennsylvania Oral and Life History Collection, Pennsylvania State University.

George Zorgo, from an audio-recorded interview with Robert P. Wolensky conducted at Mr. Zorgo's home in Pittston, Pennsylvania, on July 26, 1993. Lucy Zorgo participated in part of the interview. The interview is included in the Wyoming Valley Oral History Project, which is one of eight projects within the Northeastern Pennsylvania Oral and Life History Project housed in the Eberly Family Special Collections Library, Penn State University Libraries.

and they asked if I would do leaflet work for them and picket signs and strike posters and things of that sort. So I agreed.

LZ: No one would do it.

GZ: Others, they just steered clear because there was this known feeling that you may get involved in something that you couldn't handle. Johnny Justin [chap. 7] was one of the first people that got us working for them. Johnny somehow knew of my background, that I had been sympathetic to labor back in the early forties. In fact, I was chief steward in a plant of over one hundred people down in Philadelphia when I was twenty-one years old. Lucy worked in the office there, and I worked in a plant. With Johnny knowing about this, he approached me on doing work. At the time, the union was not nearly as strong as it is now. Johnny said, "You know, wherever we go, people ask for money up front." He said, "We don't have any [money now], but if you do our work, I'll see that you get paid." "Well," I said, "sure, I'll do your work and if I get paid, fine. If I don't, well, we both lose because you'll lose the opportunity to organize and I'll lose a few dollars invested." So this stimulated—how should I put it—*loyalty* towards us amongst the union people.

LZ: And then Min [Matheson] came into the shop and wanted to know who we were.

GZ: Her children were very small at the time. Betty and Marianne were just toddlers. David Dubinsky was the president of the International and, of course, Min and Bill were very good friends of Dubinsky. I'm leading up to *Needlepoint* now in a roundabout way. She had a "cut" [i.e., a photo] of David Dubinsky, and they were making mimeograph bulletins that they gave out to their membership, and she brought in this cut and asked if I would pull a proof of it so that they could get it on their publication. When I went to take the brayer and bray over the cut with ink, Marianne looked startled and she said, "What's he doin' to DD?" David Dubinsky was DD to them. "What's he doin' to DD?" I was sacrilegiously smearing ink all over his face. After a while, they were turning these things out in newsletters of eight or nine pages.

It was printed on the mimeograph, and the ink would go through and it would smudge so we couldn't print two sides of a sheet. We were printing about eight or nine pages and it meant a lot of paper because—how many members?—I don't know what they were at the time but it was already in the thousands. That was times eight [pages], and cutting all these stencils, and running the machine, and collating and stapling 'em, and giving 'em to their business agents to pass out . . . So I came up with an idea. I said, "Mrs. Matheson, I got an idea I'd like to talk to you about. Come down any time."

So Bill [Matheson] came out and greeted me as usual and I went over it with Bill. I said I had made up a chart showing what it cost them in paper alone plus cutting the stencils plus the labor that it took. I said we could print everything that you have on these eight pages on a small sheet of paper, two sides, and make a little folder out of it. Everything that you have ink on, we could add artwork

Number 63   Issued by Wilkes-Barre - Pittston - Nanticoke District Council   May, 1962

OUR MANAGER'S COLUMN

Our shops, generally, are busy in this post-Easter season which is a welcome change from the past.

NEW AGREEMENTS

New Agreements with blouse, sportswear and children's dress shops have been signed with minimums ranging from $1.35 to $1.43 and with percentage increases on piece rates.

DRESS

Four thousand operators employed in 86 contract dress shops were involved in a stoppage beginning March 5th in another effort to settle piece rates. Many attempts have been made in the past to reach a solution of this all-important question and I would like to quote a few words from one of many letters received dealing with this recent stoppage: "I want to thank you from the bottom of my heart for all your efforts in trying to get justice for each and every girl employed in the shops. Each try makes a big improvement towards our goal." I think that note expresses the situation very well. There may be no final answer to the question of proper piece rates but each effort that we have made has brought an improvement.

APPLYING THE INCREASE

The 10% increase resulting from the stoppage is being applied in all contract shops in an attempt to correct those operations where rates were low. Of course here are arguments and disputes but I believe we have made real headway and it is a pleasure to see so many members attending classes on piece rate settlements.

I would like to point out to our members that as new styles are brought into the shops constant vigilance is necessary to make sure that the gains we have made are not lost.

SPLENDID SPIRIT OF SOLIDARITY

I want to thank and congratulate our members on the splendid spirit of solidarity shown by their united action on March 5th. It was the beginning of a busy season after a period of slack times and yet the almost unanimous and immediate response to a call on short notice, "No work".

25th ANNIVERSARY

Many things have happened since our last issue of Needlepoint. We celebrated our 25th Anniversary and issued an Anniversary booklet that took the place of Needlepoint. If you haven't received your copy, ask for it.

ANNIVERSARY DINNERS

Our Anniversary dinners at the Fox

(continued on next page)

FIG. 31 | *Needlepoint*, the official Wyoming Valley ILGWU district newsletter, May 1962. Photo courtesy of Betty Greenberg.

[to], we could put in as many photographs as you want, and it would cost less than it's costing you now. And it would have a [Zorgo] union label. Well, this was great. As soon as Min was finished with whomever she [was talking to], she came in and said to Bill, "When can you get some material for George?" And so (*laughs*) that's the beginning of *Needlepoint*.

It was very well received. In fact, before the first issue was out, Bill asked me—as Min's representative, of course—would I be interested in doing this for other districts? I said, "Well, yes, if they would want me to do it I'd be glad to." By then I had given them some proofs of what we were going to do. He said, "Well, [district manager] Harry Schindler up in Scranton is interested and could we maybe use the two inside pages as uniform for both districts and just change the outside two pages, to localize it." Well, even before we had those two out, Easton came on the scene. This thing just grew, mushroomed.

Apparently, this was an effective tool for keeping their membership informed and for organizing events. No use blowing my own horn. So that's it. From there it went throughout the whole Northeast Department. Actually, every district with the exception of Johnstown became involved with a little publication of some sort that we did. Then the Northeast Department got into it. Of course, *Justice* has been published by the International [Ladies' Garment Workers] for many years but the Northeast Department decided they would put out a quarterly [newsletter].

GEORGE AND LUCY ZORGO

As far as Min and Bill goes, she would call me up at four, five o'clock in the afternoon and say, "George, we're gonna have pickets out tomorrow morning at seven o'clock. Could you do so and so for us?" If I had to work all night, it was done. [For one major convention] I think we had less than ten days to create the whole thing [i.e., the program], start to finish. We finished after they were already down there [at the convention], so we had to ship it down by airfreight.

Q: How many copies did you run?

GZ: Couple thousand. It was given to everybody that attended the ILGWU convention of the International representatives from all over the country.

LZ: What we should say is, through Min, we got friendly with the whole union. The people from New York were comin' in then to work with us.

GZ: They wanted to know who was the agency that prepared this. There's no agency involved. It was a little printer in a little town of Pittston that created the whole thing. They thought that it was a real expensive job. It wasn't. We did the whole job for less than an agency in New York would charge to even just come up with a concept.

LZ: Well, they were dealing with New York printers that charged them for everything. They thought we were a joke. You know, that nobody in Pittston could turn out a job [like this]. You had to be from New York!

Q: How many employees did you have at the time?

GZ: Three. Lucy, me, and my son. We did the whole thing. We'd get a part-time woman to help with some things.

LZ: To the Union Label Department [in New York] we were a joke.

Q: Why do you think Min and the ILGWU wanted to deal with you?

GZ: Because she was so honest and we were so honest that nobody could even question our dealings. If she dealt with us, they knew we were honest, and it holds true to this day. I will mention a name, Marty Burger, who is an organizer of the program that they call AIM, Affiliated ILG Members.[1] He started from scratch with nothing and he has built up a very nice membership in this organization. We were involved in a number of different things like the AIM newsletter. So here again, if New York asked him—he works out of the New York office—what do you get from these people? What [kind of a kickback] do you get from Zorgo? They can't conceive of somebody [like us]. So he said, "Oh, I do fine."

LZ: Well, when they shipped her to the Union Label Department in New York, she knew why they did it. They put her up in this office and they figured, "Well now, we're going to watch her," right? But she kept going. There was a man that was the big chief, and when she would see his bills comin' in for these different [printing] jobs, she couldn't believe it. She would scribble a note to us and say, "George, this is what they charged for so and so, and so and so," and she asked us to [provide a] quote on several jobs.

GZ: Yes, and some of them were substantial jobs, good size jobs. So I said, "I'll prepare a quote," and I did, and I sent it in to her. She called and said, "I have this on my desk. Are you sure? Can you check these figures?" I said, "Well, I'll check my figures; I'll go over them again." So I went over them again and got back to her. She then said, "Can you make your expenses on something like this?" I said, "Yes, and even a profit, not a generous profit, but I can make a profit on it." She said, "This is about one-third of what we paid last year!" This was common.

LZ: So we caused quite an uproar.

GZ: We caused a stir.

Q: Did you get that particular job?

GZ: We got it.

LZ: We got many jobs.

GZ: But as soon as she would be out of town, they would send the jobs to their connections [in New York].

LZ: She did a lot of battling for us because she liked working with us. She knew what she was getting. She enjoyed visiting us.

GZ: In fact, do you have one of the Christmas cards? The little Christmas cards?

LZ: Oh, that one with Lisa and Betty's [Greenberg, chap. 15] eldest daughter, Lori Jo, who was about the same age as our daughter Lisa. They would be about thirty-two now, I guess. When they were little kids, four or five years old, Min wanted to get out something for Christmas—a size thing so that you could put down the size of your wife, your mother, whatever, and dress it up. So I got my brother-in-law to put on a Santa Claus outfit for Lisa and Lori Jo. They sat on his lap and they were holding up the hems of their dresses showing the union label and reciting a cute little poem that Bill wrote. She got hundreds of thousands of these and passed them out. The only expense that we had was my brother-in-law, who I gave ten bucks for puttin' the suit on and posing. If you did that in a metropolitan area just the modeling fees alone would probably be thousands of dollars. So we did a lot of things that we enjoyed doing, not for the profit angle or anything else, but we enjoyed doing it.[2]

Q: It seems like the ILGWU received good value from you.

GZ: Excellent value, and Min made it known that she got excellent value. She passed us on to a number of people such as Sol Hoffman, who is now an International vice president and director of the Northeast Department.[3]

LZ: (showing the Christmas picture) Bill Matheson—this was his idea. This is our daughter here and this is Lori Jo. Santa Claus was my Uncle Jack. We had a Santa Claus suit. Mrs. Matheson tried to tell people to "Buy American." How many banners [did we print] that would say, "Buy American," "Buy American. The job you save [may be your own]"?

GZ: Buy union! We focused on this "Buy American" theme. (shows a poster)

Q: Very nice. And you ran thousands of these?

GZ: Hundreds of thousands.

LZ: That's another thing that made New York mad because they couldn't see [i.e., understand] that it was comin' from us. You know, she took a lot of flak for us.

Q: Were relations with New York often tense?

GZ: Very tense.

LZ: Without her in this area, there wouldn't have been any union. I don't care what anybody says.

Q: You mentioned the early forties. What was it like at that time?

GZ: Well, they [the ILGWU] were discouraged from organizing in Wyoming Valley. For what reason, who can say, even they wouldn't say, but they were discouraged from organizing in the Wyoming Valley. They wanted to organize up in the Lackawanna [County] area—Carbondale, Honesdale, and so forth. But there was a great influx of garment factories into the Wyoming Valley from around the mid-thirties. We have pictures in the twenty-fifth anniversary book when some of the bigger plants were organized. In fact, Bill brought in a whole slew of pictures when we were going to do the anniversary book. He said, "Look through these, George, and see what you would like to do." Well, we used practically all the pictures. What we did was we took '37, when this first large plant was organized, and put it on the front page and then we went from there through all the different forms of activities. We had politics, we had organizing, we had shows, we had so many different categories and pictures in each category. Then the last picture was '62—the most recent picture of a big plant and it said, "We're sticking to the union." That was the way the book closed. So by '37 they would already have some of the bigger plants in the area.

Q: There was an element in the area, let's call them "tough guys" because that's what others have called them. Were they here as early as 1937?

GZ: Yes, because they were [among] the ones who brought in what they called the runaway shops. New York [ILGWU headquarters] had the thing pretty well organized even in North Jersey. To get away from paying union wages and union benefits, these people brought the shops into the coal regions and to the Slate Belt down around Bangor [near Easton, Pennsylvania] where men were no longer the breadwinners because the mines were down. King Coal was dying and people had to get money into this area. Women went to work, wives and daughters went to work in the dress factories, and they worked very cheap. They didn't know about union benefits and union conditions. The runaway shops that came out of New York set up just wherever there was a storefront, wherever there was a vacant building. They put in a dress factory or a blouse factory or a belt factory or whatever might be related to the garment industry.

There was a new way of doing things here, too. In New York, at most of the places, a woman would make a whole garment. She would start from top and go to bottom. Here, they got into what I believe they called sectional work [piecework].[4] One woman did a waist, another would do a top, another would do collars, another belts, and then all of these things were assembled. The stuff came to them in bundles. All they did was take a bundle, do their own operation, and it would go on from there, which was a much cheaper way of doing it than in New York. And, of course, there were no benefit payments [here]. If you worked for seven bucks a week, that's all you got. If you got sick, tough luck. If there was a holiday or vacation, it was without pay. It was really exploiting the workers in this area and that's where the union came in.

We were at that time, in this area, the way it's now overseas—they look for cheap labor. Now here we're crying 'cause our jobs are goin' to Mexico and Puerto Rico. Well, not Puerto Rico as much, which is pretty well organized, but the Dominican Republic, for example, and all these other places. We say these are runaway jobs and they're stealing our jobs. Well, we stole the jobs out of New York originally, if we want to be honest about it.

Q: So the "tough guys" were part of the garment industry from an early time?

GZ: Oh yes, yes. Then it got to where even the trucking industry was controlled by them, and when they shipped a garment, it wasn't shipped by weight or anything, it was shipped by the [individual] garment. We'll say it might cost them fifteen cents to ship one garment, but the same size garment in a different price bracket would cost them thirty-five cents to ship. . . . The trucking industry charged them so much to ship from Pittston to New York, the distribution center. It was all based on that and it was controlled. Nobody moved trucks except the ones that they [the criminal element] wanted to move.[5]

Q: The "tough guys" were in Pittston, but what about in Wilkes-Barre or Nanticoke or other towns?

GZ: No, not down that way [but they were] even down into the Slate Belt area around Bangor, west of Easton. . . .

Q: I don't know if you have knowledge on this but I wonder what percentage of the shops in the Pittston area were owned by the "tough guys"? What percentage were controlled or influenced by them, and what percentage were sort of free of them?

GZ: That would be hard. You'd have to get that from the union office. I mean, I wouldn't have that kind of knowledge. I do know that there were a lot of straw owners—in other words, people who were named as owners but who weren't. . . .

Well, these "tough guys" were discouraging anybody from supporting the union or working with the union. Did you hear about Will Lurye [Min Matheson's brother]? Will Lurye was stabbed to death in a phone booth in New York. Soon afterwards, to show you the courage of this woman, she called me up and said, "George, I want to see you. Do you have some time this morning or this afternoon?" I said, "Sure. What's it about, Min?" She said, "Well, I don't want to talk over the phone. My phone may be tapped and it's possible your phone is tapped." So I said, "OK."

She came over and said that she wanted to "jack up" the International Union [because] they were not doin' enough about Will Lurye's murder. She said, "Would you prepare a leaflet for me on this?" She said, "But under no circumstances put your union label on it because they will know who printed it and they'll come

GEORGE AND LUCY ZORGO

FIG. 32 | A parade on Main Street, Pittston, Pennsylvania, circa 1958; on the right is Pittston Frocks garment shop. Photo courtesy of Lukasik Studio.

after you." She said, "I don't care if they come after me. If they come after me, then somebody will go after them." But she said, "I don't want them coming after you." I said, "I won't think of having you put out anything without a union label on it." She said, "No please, George, don't put the union label on it." So I proofed the thing up and showed it to her and then when she OK'd it, I put my union label on it. She then went on the corner where Will was murdered, assassinated, and she passed these leaflets out.[6]

Q: It reads, "Remember Will Lurye."

GZ: This was the sort of relationship that we had through our lifetime. I ran several thousand, and she stood on the corner, right on the corner, right next to the phone booth where he was killed, and she passed them out. Well, I think it probably jacked things up a little bit [in the ILGWU and in New York].

Q: Did you ever feel threatened by the "tough guys"?

GZ: Well, I don't remember just how it was, but the inference was there: "If you continue to print, you won't print." It was as much to say that if I continue to work with the union, and work against them, then I won't be printing for anybody. I think it was on the phone. They didn't like me.[7] Occasionally Min would be threatened. They called her a Communist because she was for the people. They would throw a can of open red paint on her porch and things like that. Never anything damaging to her. One time—it was probably kids—threw some eggs at the front of my place. When I didn't wash them off soon enough, it took some of the paint off of the siding. I don't blame anybody but maybe just kids, mischievous kids or somebody. Other than that there was never anything, no problem.

Q: Were you surprised there wasn't some rough stuff?

GZ: I thought that there would be, but surprisingly no. Now maybe it's because "Junior" Volpe was my next-door neighbor, I don't know.[8]

Q: That would make it look a little too obvious?

GZ: Too, too close. There was, in the block below our shop, a plant, and the owner was a niece of [alleged crime boss] Russ Bufalino. Her husband was an attorney. Actually, everybody knew that it was a Bufalino plant. There was a pretty vicious strike there for quite a while. Our shop is the second door up from this side of Mill Street and that shop was about the third door down on the other side of Mill Street, on Main Street. It was Jenkins Sportswear. The strike was prolonged.

The Bufalino family had a photographer up on the roof across the street taking pictures of everybody that was picketing. Sort of a subtle intimidation: "If you're gonna be picketing, we're gonna know who you are," and things of that sort. It ran into winter and it was pretty cold so we always had the coffee pot goin' in our shop, and the pickets would come in to use our telephone and help themselves to some coffee and try to warm up.

There was the time when Bill called me from [the ILGWU office in] Wilkes-Barre and said, "George, what's going on up there on Main Street?" I said, "What do you mean, Bill? Everything seems to be OK here." "No," he says, "on South Main." He said, "Some of the Teamster boys are comin' in here and they've been beat up. They're comin' in the Health Center and getting patched up." I said, "I didn't know anything about it." So he told me where on South Main Street.

I walked down because it wasn't that far, and sure enough, the street was almost impassable because there were so many people. Every once in a while a car would inch its way through and the crowd would separate. Dorothy Ney [chap. 1] was on the fringe of the crowd, and when I saw her, I said, "Dorothy, where's Min?" She said, "She's over there." Min was right in the midst of all this. I heard her saying, "Get that license number; why does he have the right to push through here?" You know, she was kind of a fiery person, Min was. I worked my way over to her, and she looked at me and was sort of surprised, and she said, "What are you doin' here?" I said, "Bill called me and asked what's going on? Do you need any help?" She said, "No, the Teamsters are keepin' things kinda quiet." I said, "Well, that's what Bill called about. Some of them are going to the Health Center." She said, "Yeah, they're sort of rough on the men but they're not touching the women, so get out of here." With that I left. I went back to the phone and I called Bill and I told him about the situation. "Oh," he said, "well, OK, she seems to have a handle on it." These are some of the incidents; there were a number of them. I really have no right to be sitting here talking to you!

Q: No right to be sitting here?

GZ: Because of the some of the stupid things that I did, the risks.

Q: What motivated you to take the risks?

GZ: I don't know. I've been pro-labor just about all of my life. Like I say, I was chief steward in a plant when I was only twenty-one years old. My feeling is that workers have been exploited. Sometimes, now, the shoe is on the other foot, and the workers are exploiting the employers. But for many years, it was exploitation of workers and I couldn't see that. They say, "It's not fair." These are the people that are making this country strong. These are the people that are producing the products that are making the country strong, and they should share in some of the profits. Eventually that's what unions did, but then sometimes they have overstepped and gone beyond that.

Q: How would you characterize Min Matheson's philosophy of life and labor?

GZ: Well, Socialist, naturally. Any dedicated labor leader is a Socialist. This is why she was given the Mother Jones Award. But Socialism is not Communism. It's not the "ism" that people are so afraid of. Without Socialism, or the philosophy of Socialism, we wouldn't have Social Security, we wouldn't have Workman's Compensation, we wouldn't have Unemployment Compensation. There's so many worthwhile things that we have today that we would not have if somebody didn't go and work for it. It's not that the government said, "Hey, I think you people should have this goodie." Somebody had to work and fight for it.

These are people that I respect. I don't respect the ones that capitalize on it. I do respect dedicated people who try to make living better for others. This was the way I saw Min. This is the way we felt when we would get to talkin' about different things. One time I said to her, "Is there ever hope of having an ideal factory with good communication between the employer and employee, owner and union? She said, "George, if you're thinkin' about it, don't." Now, she didn't say why, but it was evident that [from her point of view] there is no such way of ever doing something like that. It's sad.

Q: Would you say she was mainly an idealist or a realist?

GZ: She was very naïve.

Q: In what sense?

GZ: She couldn't believe that some of the people would do some of the things that they would do. Idealistic, yeah, I think in a way. I don't know that Min was much of a realist. Min's father was really labor-oriented. I forget whether he was in the cigar makers' union or what. Now he felt that women didn't have any place in a man's world, and unions were a man's world. He sort of looked down on Min because she accepted a salary as a union organizer, as a union representative. It was OK for Will Lurye to take money for it because he was a man and that was a man's world. So I guess maybe Min could have been the original NOW [National Organization for Women] member or something like that.[9] She was a visionary. She could see these things. But I don't think she was a realist. She thought that everybody was like her and she was disappointed when she found out that they weren't.

Talk about realism, I think she almost single-handedly got Dan Flood elected [to the U.S. House of Representatives]. I've gone to many union affairs and whatnot when Dan Flood was the speaker, and he always gave credit to Min and her girls. You're not supposed to say "girls" today because that's a no-no. But he credited Min Matheson—I think he always said Min Lurye Matheson—with putting him in Washington and keeping him there, Min and her "girls." So I guess, yes, she had a practical side.

She was friendly with presidents—the Kennedys, Bobby and Jack, she knew personally and she could go up and talk to them. There were some that she wasn't so keen on. Of course, Eleanor Roosevelt was her heroine. Republican president Abe Lincoln was her hero. She collected a lot of Lincoln things, which were lost in the [Agnes] flood [of 1972], incidentally. She would quote Lincoln.

Now Bill did more quoting of Lincoln than she did. But then he used to make a joke out of it, you know, that if he were to study all the things originating with Lincoln, he wouldn't have time to do anything else. He was a reader. Like myself, he didn't have much in a way of formal education, but he was a reader and he retained more than anybody I know. He could quote poetry that he learned in the lower grades. Bill was substantially older than I am. He would be well into his nineties now if he were alive. I don't remember how old Bill was [when he died]. But he could tell you about presidents, he could tell you about anybody in history, whether it be the Roman Empire or whether it be United States history. He would talk and tell us about all of these subjects. Bill was quite a guy. They were a good match.

Q: They complemented each other?

GZ: Min was the fiery type. She could get up and hold a group in the palm of her hands. Bill was the quiet type but he did a lot of research for Min. People didn't even know Bill; he was around sometimes. But Min, you always knew that she was around. Yet they made such a good combination. They rented a cottage up at Harveys Lake [suburban Wyoming Valley] many years ago, and I went up one day to spend some time with them, and Bill and I were sitting out on the porch. He said, "Would you like a beer, George?" Well, I'm not a drinker but once in a blue moon, so I said, "Geez, it's a warm day, I think I would." Over his shoulder he says, "Hey Maud, there's a couple of thirsty guys out here who want beers!" Now, Maud . . . this was the idol of so many thousands of garment workers, but to him, "Maud." That was not her name, of course; he just meant she was a maid, "Maud, the maid, come and serve these men!"[10]

They got along so well. She really missed Bill when he died. When he was well into his problem with Alzheimer's and he was in a nursing home, they were still permitted to put restraints on their patients—now it's illegal to restrain patients—but at that time he was sitting in his wheelchair and his hands were strapped to the arms of the wheelchair and he motioned to me like he wanted my hand. So I put my hand over there, and he turned it over, and in a lucid moment, he said, "Hard work." My hands: "Hard work." This is how he viewed me. I was a worker. I wasn't a plant owner, I wasn't a businessman, I was a worker. Which is what I've been all my life. We were very close to both of them. I miss them. It wasn't a case where we ran in and out of one another's house or anything, but if they needed something, which was very rarely, they knew they could ask for help. If I needed something, I only had to ask and they would help me.[11]

Philomena "Minnie" Caputo

Garment Worker, Union Activist,
Chairlady, and Floorlady

Philomena "Minnie" Caputo displayed a staunch determination in the
ILGWU's organizing campaign at the Jenkins Sportswear Company
in Pittston. As an employee, she learned about the shop's nonunion,
mob-affiliated operations, so she and her fellow workers cooperated
with the union and staged a strike that lasted nearly an entire year.
She explains her duties as strike captain and a stalwart member of
the picket line throughout the ordeal. Her enthusiastic storytelling
style takes the reader into a world of resolve and tenacity in the face
of confrontation and danger. She describes the post-Matheson era as
less than satisfactory, as the owners acquired greater control over the
workplace, the workers, and the union. Later in her career she took
positions as a chairlady in a shop, representing the union, and, somewhat surprisingly, as a floorlady in another shop where she represented
the company's interests. Ironically, she "felt sorry" for the workers
in the latter instance because, she said, without a strong union, they
were treated quite poorly. She is one of the few interview subjects who
reported physical violence against picketing women.

PC: I was born in Pittston and I worked in the garment industry. I was
young when I started, sixteen or seventeen. I'm seventy-five now.

FIG. 33
Philomena "Minnie"
Caputo, 1993. Photo
courtesy of the
Northeastern Pennsylvania
Oral and Life History
Collection, Pennsylvania
State University.

Philomena "Minnie"
Caputo, from an audio-
recorded interview with
Robert P. Wolensky
conducted at Mrs. Caputo's
home in Pittston, Penn-
sylvania, on July 22, 1993.
The interview is included
in the Wyoming Valley Oral
History Project, which is one
of eight projects within the
Northeastern Pennsylvania
Oral and Life History Collection housed in the Eberly
Family Special Collections
Library, Penn State University Libraries.

I worked for Lee Manufacturing, [owned by Louis] Gutstein [see Leo Gutstein, chap. 13]. He [Gutstein] had a factory over in West Pittston. That was the first dress factory around here and it was nonunion. I think I got ten cents an hour. I remember my first pay. Well, all I worked was twenty-four hours and I think I got two dollars and forty cents in pay at that time. That was a lot of money! That's the first wages I ever got. I worked there for a while, and then I went into New York because a girlfriend of mine went to New York and my sister was there as a nanny. I worked there for a while and met my husband.

We came back here and we were married, and then he went into the service. I worked in the garment industry from then on. Well, I didn't work while I had my children, but then I worked steady from 1954 until I retired at the age of sixty-nine, six years ago [1987]. . . .

Q: Did you have any benefits in the early days, before the ILGWU?

PC: Nothing. We didn't have nothin'. It was just ten or twenty cents an hour and that was it. They were really sweatshops. You couldn't complain. There were no piece rates. We got piece rates after the union got in there. Like for every operation, you got a certain amount of money. You set a sleeve, you got so much an hour, but before it was just ten cents and twenty cents, you know. Then [after the union negotiated the contract] we got a percentage. When the union got in there, of all the work we did—10 percent, 15 percent. That percentage went higher and higher. We made money that way. The other way all you did was work for ten or fifteen cents. After the union [got a foothold] then it went up to eighty-five cents and then one dollar.

But then we were all on piece rates. [With] the piece rates, we made money with the percentage. If you worked overtime, you never got time and a half [prior to the ILGWU contract]. Don't forget the union got us down to seven hours a day and any hours after that we got paid time and a half. Then [with the union representing us] we got our holidays, we got our vacation pay, we got our health and welfare. We got a lot of benefits . . .

Q: Tell us about those early union days.

PC: I met Mrs. Matheson [chap. 3]. We went to union meetings and we had a few strikes, general strikes here. Boy, that Mrs. Matheson was somethin', let me tell you, when she first organized. She fought, had all the girls behind her, fought for this union, very strong. They went with her 100 percent. I don't know how she fought them all—[alleged mobsters] Nick Alaimo, Angelo Sciandra, all these guys. In fact, when she was organizing, they would be on the roof with guns. I mean that. She really was amazing, strong. After the shops were organized, we got rid of the sweatshops and got better wages. Girls were always behind her 100 percent because they knew she was with them, with us. . . .

I started at Jenkins Sportswear. That was owned by Charlie Bufalino's daughter, [Emanuella] "Dolly" Bufalino [Falcone], and her husband. She was [alleged mob boss] Russell Bufalino's niece. I worked a while in there [under a

FIG. 34 | Jenkins Sportswear strike, at the shop operated by Emanuella "Dolly" Falcone, Pittston, Pennsylvania, 1958–59. Photo courtesy of Lukasik Studio.

previous unionized owner] and then [when Dolly Falcone took over], we were doin' nonunion work.[1]

Q: So that shop was once organized?

PC: Yeah, oh yeah. We were organized in there [before Falcone took over in 1957]. We were paying our union dues but then she put in nonunion work so we wouldn't get our holiday pay, we wouldn't get our health and welfare [benefits], we wouldn't get nothin', vacation pay. Well, we had a meeting and we were pulled out on strike. That was tough there picketing. The whole shop went out. After we were there awhile, the owner had guys comin' in.

Q: "Tough guys" [i.e., organized crime]?

PC: Yeah. When [they] passed us [in their car], we knew what they were there for. It was tough there and it was tough with Dolly, the owner, and her husband, and then these guys comin' in. There were a few girls goin' in [i.e., crossing the picket line]. The girls that I didn't—we didn't—know [were] very few. Mostly it was the guys [who gave us trouble]. We picketed for a long time. While we were picketing, there was a mine disaster. We had the Knox Coal Company flooded right around the time. Lot of our husbands were workin' in the mines.[2]

PHILOMENA "MINNIE" CAPUTO

Min Matheson walked right along with us on that picket line. Another woman was Dorothy Ney [chap. 1]. She was very good with the girls. Min Matheson stood behind us 100 percent. Believe me, [if] we brought a complaint, she made sure she took care of it. Every month she had shop meetings. All the chairladies from different shops would be at the meetings, and she would call on every one of us. If we had any complaints on how was the shop run . . . [she'd take care of it]. That was somethin' really great. The girls were not afraid to complain because they knew she would be behind them. It was a different ballgame when she was there. It was wonderful.

We had a lot of trouble. We were arrested I don't know how many times. I think I was in every alderman's [office] in West Pittston, Swoyersville, Pittston! Every day I went down to the picket line [at Jenkins Sportswear]. [One time] I got a summons. The guy—the alderman, the squire, or deputy—come up with a few other girls [in the car]. They arrested us [and said] that we beat them [other workers] up. I was about ninety pounds! They said I beat them up! They were tryin' to get us off the picket line but we stuck, every girl. I was there the longest—me and a few other girls—well over a year. . . . Over a year, rain or shine. Winter. Down there five thirty or a quarter to six every morning. Walked down, stayed there all day.

Q: Who were the women that crossed the picket line?

PC: We didn't even know [most of] them. I only knew one girl that would walk through the picket line, and I don't ever remember her workin' in a dress factory. But the other few that came, I think they were [relatives and friends of the owner]. I don't know where they came from. There was not that many, just a few and, like I told you, they took in a couple of the guys. I think two or three of them [tough guys] were from Pittston—Buscemi, Giambra, Bufalino. . . .

But I'm tellin' you, you know what kept us goin'? I'll tell you the truth. If we didn't have somebody like Min Matheson with us, I believe we would have given up because she was so strong and she was down there with us. We knew when we were in a shop how she fought for every girl and you weren't gonna give all that up. It would be foolish for us after she fought so hard.

I think she had it hard. You should have seen one time across the street from the post office [in Pittston] when they had that big riot. It was a field day there, and [garment shipping] trucks were there, and the women really got riled up. That was the general strike [of 1958] and the men come down, the husbands. They had guns on them, because if anybody touched their wives, they would've got shot. It wasn't easy, you know, this area. There were smashed windshields, smashed on trucks that were nonunion. They [the owners] were tryin' to break the union. Sure. And you couldn't let them. . . .

I remember I'd [say], "Well, gee, this is wonderful. We're gettin' ten cents, and twenty cents, and a quarter [piecework]." I said, "Boy, we are workin' hard." Everybody worked hard to get that percentage and make a couple dollars extra, and the union was behind you.[3] Now why would you want to give up anything like that? You got your holiday pay, you got your vacation pay, you got your health and welfare, you know. If you went to a nonunion dress shop, they wouldn't pay you all those things. Then besides, [when you were unionized], if you had a complaint it would have been taken care of. You knew that about Mrs. Matheson. I mean, she was really down to earth.

During the Jenkins Sportswear strike, I got very close to her, worked with her.[4] It was unbelievable. Well, every girl felt that way towards her, the way she was easy to talk to. She helped you whenever, in any shop. If you needed a business agent, you'd tell her, "I'm having a problem at the shop." She'd say, "Well, tomorrow morning, I'll send Dorothy out or Helen Weiss [chap. 9]," and they'd come in the morning and straighten out everything. . . .

After a while [during the Jenkins strike], Mrs. Matheson placed most of the girls [in other shops] and kept a few of us there to fight. It was over a year we were there. We fought. A few of us were arrested every time we turned around. [They said] we were beatin' somebody up. We didn't. The goons were after us. In fact, I think of us on St. Patty's Day [in 1959]. We were picketing, and I saw this truck parked in front of the factory. I saw a man get out of his car, and I recognized him as a WPTS [radio station] announcer down here in Pittston, and I thought, "Somethin' is goin' on." Then I seen channel 16 TV [and] channel 22 TV was there. Dorothy [Ney] was with me that day and [I said to her], "They're so busy today, Dorothy, somethin's goin' on."

Sure enough, one of the [tough] guys came down and started beatin' up on one of us girls. There were [television] tapes of it. The guys come near our car and put their hands in their jacket like they were gonna take out a gun. We had our windows down but as soon as we seen 'em comin', we rolled up our windows. It was scary picketing there but we stuck because, why not? We weren't gonna go back to the old days, because if they broke the union there, other shops will follow.

Q: Why were TV channels 22 and 16 and WPTS radio there?

PC: Well, they [the shop owners] called [them]. You see, they [the shop owners] were gonna start a commotion, like maybe touch one of us, which they did. And before you knew it, everybody went tryin' to get in there and save the girl, or [push off] the guys punching her. In fact, there were three of them had one girl against the car. She was on the picket line with us. The guy was there from the Pittston [radio] station and then TV channel 16 and TV channel 22. *We* didn't call them, *they* called them. When I seen all of this, I said to Dorothy, "Somethin' is goin' on today." It was on St. Patty's Day because that's a day I'll never forget. We were banged around. . . .[5]

Q: Were you hit or bruised?

PC: Sure. Then we left and went to the union office. . . . [Modesto] Murph Loquasto was supposed to be Russ Bufalino's bodyguard and he was there. They took the [TV] tape, and it was [Luzerne County] Judge Flannery [who] watched the tape because they were goin' into court and saying what we were out there doin'. I guess Mrs. Matheson called channel 16 and 22 and got whatever tapes they had of everything.

I wrote a letter to the judge before that, when I knew this [case] was gonna come up. I wrote to the judge and I took it down to Mrs. Matheson. She said, "Why did you [write it]?" I said, "I just wanted [him] to understand why we girls are out on strike. I explained to him, we weren't workin' for ten cents an hour like when these dress factories decided to come in. We didn't want to go back to that." I don't know all that I wrote, I wrote such a big letter. She said, "If you want to mail it, go ahead."

We had to go to court, and they were showing the tape of this big thing that went on that day. Dolly denied that Murph Loquasto was there. She denied all that was goin' on, so Flannery had to watch the tapes. [They showed] that it wasn't us [who were at fault]. Maybe that was the reason that we weren't [found guilty]. We were picketing peacefully. Tapes showed the way they beat us up, sure. They had this one girl up against a car. I don't know if there were two or three guys punching her.

Q: Then you went on the radio?

PC: Yeah. I was very nervous. We told them why we were out, what we were out for. Of course, you've got to realize that if she [Dolly] reopened the shop, she's gonna get nonunion work in here, right? We'd be dumb if we allowed nonunion work. If we lost that strike, we would have had them all down the line. . . .

Another time I was arrested when we were goin' down [to Jenkins Sportswear]. He [the policeman] was busy with three of us, three girls. Another time we went next door where the girls went to have a sandwich and in there was two fellas that she brought in to break the strike, Dolly. They start throwing bottles and two of the girls ran out the door. But before I got out, they start pushing me around and everything, and finally I got out and went next door to this alderman. We, three of us, got in there and we called the police.

The Pittston police came. This one [tough] guy told the police to leave. We couldn't go anyplace. We were stuck in there because they [the tough guys] came in and started beating up on the alderman. I finally called [the business agent] Clem Lyons [chap. 8]. I said, "We're stuck down here. We can't get out. There are guys out there waiting for us." She said, "Did you call the police?" I said, "Yeah, they were here but they were chased, they left." She called the State Police barracks and they, in turn, called the Pittston police. So they came down [again]. Everyone at the Pittston police, every one of them, came down. The alderman made sure we got home safe. That's what we had to do. . . .

Q: Were there any other happenings on the Jenkins Sportswear picket line?

PC: Yeah, one time he [William Falcone, Dolly Falcone's husband] came down [in his car] and we were standing at the curb. If we didn't move fast, he would have run us down. He was related to Bufalino also, I think. They're in Florida now. She was bad news, Dolly.

Dolly would come after us with a big, long stick. She was foxy [i.e., sneaky]. See, the entrance door was there, and then there was another entrance like that. *(indicates a right angle)* She'd make sure she didn't come way out and let anybody see her, you know, with that big stick, that big thing she had. One of the girls threw me up [i.e., exposed me as a union agent earlier] and that's why she didn't like me anyway. I saw the stick in her office. I said, "Boy, you should see what she has in that office." Sure enough, she came out with it. "Get out of here," [she said], but she made sure that she didn't come out far enough for anybody to see her. We'd say, "Boy, she's smart."

Another time, here was this girl [who] went in [i.e., crossed the picket line] and she said I pulled her hair, and she turns around and starts beating up on me, and I start beating up on her. They started little things so they would get us off the picket line. But I was gonna stay there—do or die—because I wasn't gonna walk away. Those other girls felt the same way because they said, "This [shop] will be nonunion [if we don't fight]. Then Arthur Lori's [shops] will start." You know, they were all in one big [effort], all these guys, breakin' the union.

Q: Were you being paid by the union during that strike?

PC: We were paid. Every one of us got paid. [Before the strike], we weren't makin' [much] because she [Dolly Falcone] cut prices. We were doin' nonunion work. We got paid when we went out picketing. Like I said, there was always so much activity around the picket line with the goons that came in. When they brought them guys in, well, there was only three of us left. I guess they figured, you know, maybe we'd all go. But we didn't go, we didn't leave until the end.

Q: What finally happened to that shop?

PC: The company agreed to go back [i.e., reopen], but none of us [on the picket line] went back. They [the other workers] went back then—[and they were] union. Then a short time after that, she closed up. But she agreed to go back. As long as they agreed to go back, then we were taken off the picket line. None of the girls [on the picket line] went back to work. Could you see us goin' in there? We might get killed, you never know! I would never go back because they had it in for *me* mostly. You know, the way they were carrying on. They wanted to take *me* out maybe because I opened my mouth.

Q: Did you ever get threatening calls to your house?

PC: Yes. "Don't you come in tomorrow. Don't you be on that picket line." I was afraid to go out. My husband had an old car—all we could afford. I was afraid to get in that car because I thought, you know, [it might blow up]. Then, another time, a guy came up. He used to hang around Club 82, which was Russell Bufalino's place down here [in Pittston]. I knew him, I knew him for ages, that man. He used to work there, go in and clean up. So one night, he came up and knocked

PHILOMENA "MINNIE" CAPUTO

on our door. It was summertime. I lived up the hill. He said, "Minnie, Russ Bufalino wants to see you." I said, "For what?"

My husband was home—I don't think he was workin'. I said, "I can't." It was nine o'clock or nine thirty in the morning. I says, "What do you mean, he wants to see me? What does he want to see me for?" He said, "I don't know, he just wants to talk to you." I said, "No, no way." My husband said, "Who the heck was that?" He said, "Don't go." I thought, well . . . So I reported it to Min. I told Min and I told Dorothy. Eddie Marchett, his name was. He was always at Club 82 down here, just the opposite side of the street on the corner. That was Russell Bufalino's place, Club 82 beer garden. I thought, "No way."

Other girls on the picket line would get threats: "Don't be on that picket line tomorrow morning." I used to walk down, all the way down, but I'd run up the hill. Then a few times, when my husband had that old car, I'd say, "Jesus, go out and start the car, Mike." I'd listen for the noise [i.e., explosion]. It was awful, it was spooky. Like that scene, the incident in Kitowski's [coffee shop], when we went in for a sandwich and them two guys were there. They were beating up on us. We called the Pittston police. They were in there grabbing the cop by the throat because they didn't like the idea that he would take our case [i.e., side]. They didn't like him because the [police] were there arresting *their* people when they did somethin' [wrong]. The Pittston cops left and we didn't know where to go. We didn't know; there was no back way. There was a high wall in the back. We were cornered. We were cornered in there. . . .

We were being followed home by cars and everything. They threw everything at us. Did Min Matheson tell you about the [black] crepe on the door [of the union office]? Yeah! They put the crepe on the door. We called the police. We got there and we saw this big crepe on the door, a regular crepe like for dead people. I wondered what the heck that crepe is doin' on, because I was there early every morning, me and Dorothy. The police came down and the cop said, "Who put that on?" I said, "It was there when we got here." You see, things like that, they tried to get us out of there, to give up, but we wouldn't.

Then they [the police] planted a cop there—that [Officer] Mantione. We would picket, and he would have his club out, and he was mean, I'll tell you. If we did anything, he'd come after us. He said, "You stay away from the door and don't come too close to the window," and all that. He kept waving that stick at us. He was a dog. He passed away, too, and nobody was sorry to see him go, no one in town.

She was bad news, Dolly. She was a witch. And then when people were around, she always had that smile on her face, you know, putting it on when she came out where people could see her. But boy, she would come out with that big, long club. It had a long string so she'd hang it on the wall and she'd wave it at us. I had a habit [during the strike] of the girls lifting me up and looking [into the shop]. She'd see me looking at the window. She'd run for the club like she was gonna throw it at me through the window.

Q: I gather everyone was happy when the strike ended?

PC: I was never home. I was never home. . . .[6] We didn't want to go back to [the old days of] ten cents an hour and behind us [a guy] with a stopwatch. "How much did you get out?" It was unbelievable, let me tell you. Yeah, he'd stand behind us and he'd say, "You and you, work together." Now maybe I was a little faster than her [but] we worked on the same bundle. He'd have the girls in pairs, you know. I couldn't say to him, "What do you [think you're doing]?" He'd say, "You only did eight." Well, I couldn't say to him, "I did six out of that eight, or five out of that eight." I should have asked, "Why are you letting us work [in pairs]? Let me do my own work and her do her own work. Why should I rush, and I put out a little more than her, and I'm gettin' blamed for her not putting [out]?" It was awful. He'd stay in there and he would time you. . . .

Then one of the girls came down one night when we were arrested near the Jenkins shop, and her husband came with her. Well, they beat up her husband, the goons that were there. See they were there, they were all milling [around] when we went in. There was this Murph Loquasto. He was Russell's bodyguard, they said. He'd be in there. We would wonder what the heck did they do [to earn a living], you know. They would be all around. Anytime there was a hearing, too, they were there. Min Matheson was on the picket line a lot when we were there. Dorothy Ney was always with us. They [the tough guys] would stand and they'd sit on the roof of Club 82. No one could look at us. Girls used to say, "Jesus, I wonder if they're gonna shoot us today."

Q: Were some these guys from out of town?

PC: Well, they were, I think they were. They were called to come in. One of [the local toughs] is serving in prison—Buscemi, Jimmy Buscemi. Yeah, then Albert Giambra, and there was a Bufalino there, Angelo Bufalino the photographer, one of the relatives of Russ Bufalino. Guys were goin' in and out of there, but we didn't budge. In fact, Jim Brown—he was our [ILGWU] lawyer—he had a guard to watch his house. We were threatened.

Q: It seems surprising that Mrs. Matheson wasn't seriously hurt.

PC: I'm surprised, too. I know what you mean, I am, too. . . . She told me a story once during the general strike [of 1958]. She said that Nick Alaimo called her into his shop for somethin' and he had her arm and was twisting it all the way back. She thought it was broken. They tried everything. I told you they went on the roof in those places in Pittston with guns and that didn't scare her off. In fact, a few times she had her children walkin' down Main Street with her. She had them all dressed up. We were organizing then, I'm sure it was, yeah. I'll tell you, she had those two little girls dressed up, and they marched with her down Main Street [on a picket line]. She had guts. She believed in it.

PHILOMENA "MINNIE" CAPUTO

She was also arrested, taken out of her home. Toni Pardini and her were [arrested and] dragged, and they were taken out of their houses at night. I'll tell you another thing. One morning I went down [to Jenkins Sportswear] a little later. I was always down there real early, but for some reason that morning I went down a little later. When I got down there, I saw Clem Lyons, who I hardly ever saw at the picket line. She was always with the chorus girls and whatever. I said, "Clem, what's the matter? Where's Mrs. Matheson and Dorothy?" She said, "Minnie, Agnes Sarti went up and started a fight with her, pushing Mrs. Matheson around. The Pittston police were called and they took Mrs. Matheson and Dorothy. They're down at city hall." I said, "Well, that doesn't make sense." When there's a couple of people fighting, usually they pull in the two. I said, "There is somethin' wrong, Clem, because too many things have been goin' against us, the pickets. The police aren't protecting us," do you understand? This was way before the incident with Kitowski's. She said, "Yeah, I think they're playing hopscotch [i.e., messing around with us]." I said, "I think they are, too."

So I went down to city hall and Mrs. Matheson came out of the office. I said, "Mrs. Matheson, how come [you were brought in]? What went on?" She said, "I was just talking to Agnes, and Agnes started to push me around." Well, I was mad, and I hollered in the police station. I said, "How come you were the one arrested, and why wasn't it Agnes, too?" Agnes was a little slow and they put her up to a lot of things at Bufalino's [i.e., Jenkins Sportswear]. [One day] she was the only one that stayed in there [working] when we were out [on strike].

If you saw Agnes, Agnes was unbelievably big and husky, her hair was . . . [not very nice]. When we went to court [on another occasion], I saw her on the witness stand and she accused me of beating her up. They had her dressed up so beautiful, the Bufalinos. I never saw her dressed up—you know, all her hair, nice outfit on her, and so quiet—and I said, "Brother, I couldn't believe it." I was tryin' to tell the truth and he wouldn't even let me say anything. I forget that guy's name [Ivo Giannini, the first assistant district attorney of Luzerne County]. I was gonna punch him in the nose after that when I saw him. But just browbeatin' on me, like I committed a murder. "What did you do, how far away from the curb were you picketing?" And it went on and on and on. . . .[7]

In this case, they believed everybody but me. I had a hung jury. See, for some reason they made an example of me—the other side made me out like the big mouth or whatever. They wanted to get me out of that picket line. They went on and said that I beat this one up, I beat that one up. We went to court in this case where this girl [Agnes], she would go in and out of there [Jenkins shop]. We were chummy with her, Agnes. She was the only one that stayed in the shop, was Agnes Sarti. She didn't come out [on strike] with us because her and Dolly were good friends. God, she was a big girl. They said I beat her up, so we went to court.[8] They questioned all the other ones that they arrested, and there was a few others who got on the stand. They had Clem Lyons on the stand. . . .

Q: Who else was picketing with you?

PC: Dolores Matt and Toni Pardini, she was from another shop but she was sent up there to stay with me. The rest of them, they had to be sent [by the union] to [other] work after six months, or three months. Mrs. Matheson placed them [in jobs elsewhere]. She thought, well, maybe we could handle it. Of course, I had Dorothy Ney down there every day, too. . . .

I couldn't understand why they had them girls in there [who crossed the picket line]. I don't know what work they were doin' at Jenkins, with nothin' [no garments] coming out. But they had these girls goin' in and doin' a couple little things. And these guys came to the shop every day like they were gonna scare us. They'd come by the car and put their hand under their jacket like they were gonna take out a gun while we were standing there. Cripes, they could have blown us to smithereens. We'd look for them.

I would aggravate them in a way because a few times [when they were inside] I hollered [to fictitious strikebreakers], "You can't go in there. This place is on strike." Boom! You'd see these guys runnin' out, lookin' around. They probably were holdin' the girls back who heard me. [Then I'd say to the girls inside], "Come out, don't stay in there, this place is on strike." I did that a couple of times, but I didn't do it anymore because I was afraid. The guys would come runnin' out, look up and down [the street] like, "Where's the girls, where's the girls that wanted to come in?" We would be laughin'. Jeez, they were ready to kill us.

Q: Did the miners' union help much?

PC: No.

Q: Any other unions help?

PC: Oh, the truckers [i.e., the Teamsters]. Look, any time we went on strike, we'd tell them, "Do not pick up work or drop work off." They went along with the strike, with the girls. In fact, I was in the shop and Helen Weiss said to me, this was way after Jenkins Sportswear: "Do me a favor. Could you get a couple girls to go up [to the Dixie Frocks shop] with you?" Well, I had to get a girl that owned a car because I couldn't drive up to Dixie Frocks. She said, "We are having a little problem there and I don't want anything goin' into that shop or out." I said, "Yeah."

So I set up this girl [with a car] and three of us went up. They stayed in the front, and I was in the back. I saw a truck pull up, Interstate [Trucking Company]. The driver went in, and I saw him comin' out with two samples, dresses, because you usually make a sample and send it to New York when you got a new line. He's a big guy. I said, "Sir, we're on strike here." I said, "You can't take anything out of here." He said, "OK." He went right back in and came out without the dresses. Helen Weiss was just comin' up. She parked the car and was comin' toward us. She said to me, "Minnie!" She was laughin'. She said, "A little girl like you [and] the guy went back in!" Well, they honored the ILG. If the girls were on strike, they would not take in anything or take out anything. They wouldn't go past a picket line.

PHILOMENA "MINNIE" CAPUTO

Q: Did Interstate have most of the trucking?[9]

PC: Yes, oh yes. They had all of it and they did honor a picket line. They would never cross a picket line to pick up a dress or anything as long as we were on strike.

Q: Do you remember Mrs. Matheson on the radio during these strikes?

PC: Yeah. I went on the radio, too, in Pittston, WPTS, when I was on the Jenkins [picket line]. I wanted to explain why we went on strike. It was me plus a couple of other girls. I just told them that we wanted the union in there. We should be allowed. I remember Mrs. Matheson calling me up after I was on the radio. . . .

Q: Was Min on the radio very often?

PC: Yeah, she was. She fought and she was like that about any union. There were some unions having a problem. People [were] having strikes. We picketed stores in Scranton when they were sending in nonunion dresses. [Following our protests], they had union labels on everything.

Q: So the ILGWU districts supported each other?

PC: They would. Everybody would support each other. All the girls would come in. Busloads would come in. Busloads would come in from Allentown or wherever, Hazleton, or Nanticoke, or Wyoming. The girls were all supporting the ILG. They'd be fools if they didn't.

Q: Did the Jenkins strike draw those out-of-town people, too?

PC: One time we had a big [union] rally there. The girls came by the busload from different places. That time they were really all out. They came for us. One thing about them, you could always depend on the girls. . . .

Today we don't have that many shops. We had a lot of shops around here. Leo Gutstein has survived. He's in partners with Lou Allison. Leslie Fay is open. Not many are here. Oh, Sally Dress up on Broad Street—that's part of Leslie Fay. The dressing industry is what kept this town goin'. You know, there was nothin' here for the men. There were just the mines and when that went, it was all just the women workin'. . . .

I think Mrs. Matheson must have mentioned Leo Gutstein. His father had a business, the Junction Dress. Then he moved on Main Street, the son did. I remember when Min was tryin' to organize the place. I think he was the only one [i.e., owner] that would let her in the shop when she was organizing. We [usually] just paraded up and down Main Street when she was tryin' to organize. But Leo Gutstein was the only that would allow her in the shop. The other guys wouldn't let her in.

Q: How did she talk to the girls if they wouldn't let her in the shop?

PC: When they all came out.

Q: So they were brave enough to listen to her?

PC: Why not? What do you mean? There was a crowd of us. Everybody went out who wanted a union.

Q: Weren't you afraid of being fired?

PC: No, not when they [everybody] walked out. We figured when the union gets in there, we'll all be back to work. There were so many factories here anyway. They'd be glad to get anybody to work. There was a lot of shops. You know what I'm sayin'? You left one shop, you could go on the next shop that'd hire you. Every block there was a couple shops. . . .

We had big shops that were like Angelo Sciandra's. I worked for him for a short time. He must have had a couple hundred girls, and then he had a big cutting room downstairs. Nick Alaimo's shop was smaller. Jenkins Sportswear, we had quite a few girls down there. When I say quite a few, there was maybe about fifty. Arthur Lori had a pretty big shop. Mike Turco's shop was [big]. I think Angelo had the biggest shop and the more modern shop. . . .

[After the Jenkins strike], I went to work [when] Mrs. Matheson placed me in a shop. It wasn't easy for me to get work anymore around the area because, you know, bosses seen you comin'—you were blackballed. But Mrs. Matheson put me in a shop. I can't say enough good things about Mrs. Matheson. It was a different ballgame when you went to work; you knew she was there. After that [i.e., after she left], I had no heart. After a while, I went to work for Willie Alaimo. Nick Alaimo was in prison at the time and his brother was takin' care of the shops. I worked for Willie. Willie was good. Willie was nice. I had worked for Willie years before that and he stopped me on the street and he said, "Where are you workin'?" I said, "I'm workin' over in Forty Fort." He said, "Why?" I said, "Well, you know, I was on the picket line at Pittston." He said, "Why are you workin' there? Come and work for me." He had a shop across from the union office a little further [down on Main Street]. He said, "Oh, come to work with me. I'll take you." So I said, "OK."

Well, I worked with him for a while and I get paid one Friday. This was after Min moved out of the area. Sam Bianco got in there [as ILGWU District manager]. So I happen to check in and I saw this business agent, Ann I think her name was. I don't even remember half of these business agents. The only one that stuck in my mind was Dorothy [Ney] because she was with us down here at Jenkins, and then I had her for a business agent in the shop. I said, "Ann, do you know what? I'm not gettin' the right price on that sleeve I'm settin'. I expected so much pay, and I don't know, he must have cut the price on it." That was on a Friday. She said, "I'll take it up with Sam."

I went in on a Monday and Willie called me in the office. He said, "Minnie, I want you to do me a favor. When you have a complaint, I don't want you to go to the union, I want you to come to me." He said, "Now, I'll tell ya, Sam Bianco called me this morning and told me you were complaining." Now, I know Willie. I worked for him before and I know he wasn't tellin' any lies because he said to me, "You could go across the street and ask him [to verify what I'm going to tell you]. Go up there and tell him I told you." He said that Sammy called and said, "Willie, Minnie's complaining about the prices. If she gives you a problem, fire her but don't do it right away. Wait a couple of weeks and get rid of her." And Willie said [to me], "I'll never [let you go]. I wouldn't do that. If you don't believe me," he said, "You can go up and tell him what I said, and he can't deny it because he told me." Willie kept me on then.

Q: Did he correct the price?

PC: Willie did, and he said to me, "Don't ever do that anymore." Willie was a great guy to work with. Sam was just a figurehead there. He didn't do anything. Another time, after I went to work for Rosemary's shop and I was chairlady there, the girls were complaining about prices and they were gettin' fed up. They didn't want to keep workin'. Usually when Min Matheson was there, if he didn't give you the [correct] price, the girls were allowed to stop workin' until the business agent got there and straightened it out. But Sammy [Bianco] didn't [do that]. So I called Sammy and I said, "Do you know what they're doin'?" He said, "Pull the girls out." It was on a Friday. He said, "I'll send the business agent up there on Monday and straighten things out, so don't go to work." So we didn't [work]. She [the owner] had a small shop. She might have had about twenty [workers] there, and nine or ten of us walked out. Well, Monday came along, I didn't hear nothin'. Tuesday came along and I didn't hear anything. So the girls were callin' me. They said Minnie, "When are you gonna straighten this out?" I said, "Well, I'll call Sammy." When we were leavin' [that day after picketing], Angelo, the boss, came up to me and he said we were complaining, and so he gave me a push and I almost fell over. I bumped the bin and everything.

So I called Sammy and I said, "Sammy, we're out." I said, "I thought you were gonna [fix things]." He said, "Out? What do you mean you're out?" I said, "Well, you told me to get the girls out of there and that you'd send a business agent up." He said, "Gee, I don't remember." Would you believe this? Huh? That was Sammy. It was a different. Gradually, things started changing with the union. Everything started goin' wrong. Girls couldn't complain. . . .

Later I took a job as a floorlady [at a company] because it got to the point where [I said to myself], "Gee, I'm going to work. I worked. I could do what the floorlady did. I'll play it by ear. I know enough about every [aspect of the shop]. Not that tough." So I took a job as a floorlady.

You'd go around, see, and you couldn't even let them tie their bundle. You grabbed it from them if they were on the last garment and you bring it to the next operator. Then you grabbed that one. It got so bad that I thought these girls are afraid to open their mouth. It's back to the sweatshop. Mrs. Matheson always said, "You tie up your bundle and put it in the bin." That worked. "When you're done, that work should be [yours]." We complained about it. When you tie up that bundle, then they should pick that work up. But it was like half a bundle, grab it off her, bring to the other one. It was a mad house. I was on the floor over fifteen years and, believe me, I felt sorry [for the workers].

They didn't let the girls make a dime. Maybe, the only operation that made money in a shop after a while was the zipper setter. I was on the floor, I seen a presser, they didn't pay those girls. This I know. I told the girls, "When I get out of this shop, when I retire, I'm gonna write a book!" There's so many stories I could say about this. . . .

Q: So the workers didn't have the union as much on their side anymore?

PC: No, no way. . . . If a girl was thrown out for any reason, Mrs. Matheson would send a business agent down to that shop and she'd say, "Stop the whole shop." You don't get rid of a girl because she complains, if she's legitimate in what she's saying. You don't get rid of a girl for complaining about a price or anything. It was terrible. It got terrible, and I watched these women work and I felt bad for them the way I had to push them. But that was my job. I had to get the work out and pull work from under them. The only thing I can do is pull it out from under their machines. I mean, it was terrible.

Q: Was there pressure on you to do this?

PC: It was pressure on me, absolutely, because he'd say, "I want this." He [the owner] was like a dog. He was like a dog, that guy, my boss. He was a creep and he didn't know anything about a dress. He was a cutter. Pete Lucchino had been my boss and he was a wonderful boss. Then they sent him out of town to work, Pete. I don't know where he went to work, for a factory that opened up someplace. Then they sent this dummy down and he was manager. He called me in the office. He was unbelievable. Girls couldn't pick up their heads. If they talked to the girl next door, next to them, and if he saw them, [he'd say], "What in the hell is goin' on there? What are they having, a birthday party out there?" Amazing! He'd give orders: "I want this out and when you come in, count this and this and this. This has to be out before eleven thirty in the morning. You'd better put two or three more girls on this." Then he'd say, "How come she's changed that?" I'd say, "Well, you told me, you needed a lot out. You wanted me to put different girls on so you could get it out before eleven thirty." So you had to do that but he didn't understand anything. He was unbelievable. . . .

Q: Mrs. Matheson mentioned that some of the gangsters really didn't know how to deal with women.

PC: They were no good. Verbally, they would abuse the women. These goons roughed us up, but who called them in? She [Dolly Falcone] did—and her husband was just as bad as them. Like I told you, he almost ran us over. But they were, you know, [with] their mouths. They weren't easy to work for. If we didn't get the union in there, they didn't care. They treated us like we were nothing. We couldn't complain. We had to do what they said. They wouldn't listen if you'd tried to explain anything to them. When we got the union, we didn't have to talk to them at all. We just talked to our floorlady and then she went to the union, and the union took care of them. Which is the way it should be. . . .

PHILOMENA "MINNIE" CAPUTO

FIG. 35 | ILGWU strike at an unknown garment shop in Pittston, Pennsylvania, circa 1950s. Photo courtesy of Lukasik Studio.

You know what I think? They just opened this Jenkins Sportswear [to break the union]. For a while there, I saw the floorlady and the manager [coming in and out]. After a while, I saw Dolly Bufalino [Falcone] and her husband comin' in and that made me wonder. In fact, I did ask the lady, the manager. I said, "Do you own this?" I forget her name. "No, I own this place, [said Dolly Falcone]." But right afterwards, Dolly knew there was a little problem comin' up because we found out it was nonunion work, and we had meetings. This lady quit, her manager, and the supervisor quit. I don't think they had anything to do with it [the nonunion operation of the shop]. And then we walked out, all of us. . . .[10]

Q: So you were kind of a "union plant" in the Jenkins factory?

PC: Yeah, I was. Then we got pulled [out on strike]. I told her what was goin' on. . . .

Q: Did Mrs. Matheson ask you to "go undercover" before you took a job there?

PC: No, after. . . .[11]

Q: Why do you think the ILGWU moved Min Matheson out of the area?

PC: I think that they [the New York ILGWU] forced her [out]. During the Jenkins Sportswear [strike], we heard rumors that she was gonna be moved, and we started calling. We didn't want her moved. After that, that was it. They were gonna have her moved no matter what we did. They didn't back her up. They said that they needed her [in New York] for the union label thing and all that. No. I think, believe me, that when she struck Jenkins Sportswear, that was a no-no.

Q: Stepping on too many toes?

PC: I believe so. That's me. I was long enough in the area and seen a lot that she fought and she just touched the wrong persons down there. . . . But I still say that I don't think she wanted to leave the area because she organized, she worked, fought hard to organize. None of the girls wanted her to leave. . . . "We need her in New York." A lot of bull, as far as I was concerned. There was a few of them with me felt the same way: "This is bull, they needed her in New York." They tried to take her while we were picketing [at another strike] not long after. We heard the rumor and we all started calling up and everything. "No, it was just a rumor," [they said]. But then after that, they took her out of this area. [Rep.] Dan Flood and her were very close. He was sorry to see her go. . . .

But she was a good person. She took a lot of abuse, and when you stop to think of it, who was it for? It was for me, and she made it better for everybody else. I really feel bad sometimes that we didn't keep in touch. I talked to her a few times but I wasn't socially close to her. Anytime there was anything wrong on the picket line, she'd come down. It was something I'll never forget. You don't forget a person like Mrs. Matheson, what she did for this area. She stuck to her guns. I can't forget her for that. I thought, "This lady is all out for us."

12

Dr. Albert Schiowitz

Physician and Director of the Wyoming Valley ILGWU Health Center

FIG. 36
Dr. Albert Schiowitz, 2001.
Photo courtesy of the
Northeastern Pennsylvania
Oral and Life History
Collection, Pennsylvania
State University.

Dr. Albert Schiowitz, from
an audio-recorded interview
with Robert P. Wolensky
conducted at Dr. Schiowitz's
office in Wilkes-Barre, Pennsylvania, on August 6, 2001.
The interview is included
in the Wyoming Valley Oral
History Project, which is one
of eight projects within the
Northeastern Pennsylvania
Oral and Life History Collection housed in the Eberly
Family Special Collections
Department, Penn State
University Libraries.

As part of its pioneering health program, the ILGWU established a Health Center in Wilkes-Barre in 1958. Dr. Albert Schiowitz served as associate director and then as director. He expresses pride in the Center's diagnostic and immunization program, the results of which were forwarded to each member's family physician. Through these free services—augmented by a mobile unit that traveled from shop to shop—the Center discovered colon, gastrointestinal, pulmonary and other problems, including cancers, that led to medical treatments and saved lives.

AS: I first became involved because of the late Dr. Albert Feinberg, who was the [first] director of the Health Center. He asked me to assist him in this project, which I did for a period of time. I don't remember the exact period of time. However, after his demise, I was appointed director of the Health Center. This was at the direction of one of the heads of the ILG in New York, Mr. [Sol "Chick"] Chaiken. The actual head of the ILG at that time was Mr. Dubinsky, David Dubinsky, and Chaiken was his immedi-ate associate. My association with the Health Center was for a period of years, of which I don't remember, but it terminated on

November 1, 1998, as a result of the diminution of the membership in the ILG as manifest in this letter I am showing you.

Q: You have a letter from Sol Hoffman, vice president and comanager, to you, dated November 13, 1998.[1] What were your duties at the Health Center?

AS: Well, actually, we periodically examined all the members. I was instrumental in instituting one thing that was very effective, and that was doing sigmoidoscopic examinations on all who acquiesced to have it. Some people did not wish to have it done. Sigmoidoscopy is an inspection of the sigmoid colon through a scope, which traversed some twenty-five centimeters. Now, since that time, colonoscopy has come into [greater] practice. When we found something positive in our examination, we referred them for a colonoscopy. As a result of this colonoscopic examination, we were able to find very early cancerous and precancerous conditions. I never documented the number of cases. They were in the thousands that we did [i.e., examined] over many years. We had a staff of doctors and nurses. This went on and on for many years up until the time that they [the union] elected to discontinue it.

Q: Did the members receive the services free of charge?

AS: Oh yes, this was free. There was no cost. Now, the results of the examinations were referred to their family doctors, and they carried on from there if there were any things needed to be done, surgical or medical. It was a very worthy project, the entire procedure.

Now we had approximately sixteen doctors and six nurses [at the peak]. It was started in '58, under the auspices of Mrs. Matheson [chap. 3]. She got Dr. Feinberg to start the directorship, and I succeeded him at his demise. We conducted the Health Center on 37 South Washington Street [in Wilkes-Barre]. As a matter of fact, there's something [a proposal about] making that a historical site or something like that. I don't know whether they're tearing it down now or not.[2] But in any case, that's where the examinations were conducted. It was preventive medicine that we were practicing in attempting to ferret out any unknown disease processes that could be treated.

Q: Did you have X-rays there as well?

AS: Oh yes, we had X-rays. We had a laboratory.

Q: Blood tests and things like that?

AS: Yes, we did all those down there.

Q: Would you do minor surgery?

AS: No. Didn't do any definitive surgery at all. The only thing I did from a surgical standpoint as director [was] I did all the sigmoidoscopies. That is something that I instituted even while Feinberg was still director. I did all the sigmoidoscopies.

Q: You say you examined thousands of members.

AS: Oh yes, they had a lot of members. I think it was a thirty-five-year [sic; forty-year] period [from when] the Center started in '58 and closed [in '98]. The clinic itself was closed on Washington Street. Thereafter we conducted all the examinations,

DR. ALBERT SCHIOWITZ

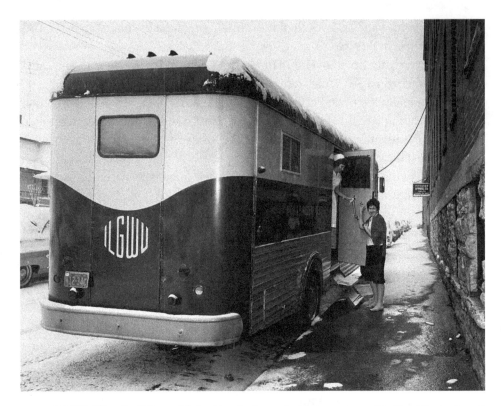

FIG. 37 | ILGWU Wyoming Valley mobile health unit, circa 1960. Photo courtesy of the Kheel Center, Cornell University.

at the General Hospital. In other words, the union paid the hospital for the use of the facility and personnel and so forth. I don't know what a range they had monetarily. That terminated in 2000.

Q: Why did you decide to get involved with the Health Center?

AS: Well, I was interested in preventive medicine, and Dr. Feinberg was a very close friend of mine, and he wanted a surgical [person]. I was a surgical consultant, too. I did all the surgical consultations there. He wanted a surgeon and he asked me to be the associate.

Q: Did you know Min Matheson very well?

AS: Oh yes, oh yeah, real good.

Q: Did her presence influence your decision to join the facility?

AS: I can't say that was the case. I think my presence was there because of Dr. Feinberg. I mean his association with Mrs. Matheson coincided with my association with her, and that's how I knew her.

Q: Was there any interest in unionism on your behalf?

AS: Oh, no. The union part had nothing to do with my [participating]. I had a high respect for their motivation. Their motivation was very, very significant in giving their members this opportunity. They had had other things—they had a recreation center called Unity House up near Tannersville [Pennsylvania]. As a matter of fact, we were invited to go up there in the summer if we wanted to. They did a lot of nice things for their members.

Q: I gather it was one of more than a few health centers of its type?

AS: The principle was motivated by the Mayo Health Center at the Mayo Clinic. Their diagnostic centers were like what we had. We did the things that they did—examined people routinely and referred them, although they did some of the definitive aftercare. We didn't. We did not do any definitive aftercare, unless, let's say, I found something on a patient who was mine. There was no reason why I wouldn't take care of it. In other words, I didn't do any surgery or anything insofar as my practice was concerned, but if my patient happened to be one of them, why I would filter her into my practice. But that was minimal. I mean that was nothing. . . .

Q: Were these women and men more susceptible to certain health problems, like cancers, than other populations?

AS: No, no, there was no industry predisposition, no.

Q: What was the public's response to the Health Center?

AS: Well, let me say this: the [Luzerne] County Medical Society, as I remember, approved of it. They were not against it, although, for the most part, they resented any other intrusion into their domain. But my recollection was that we had the approval of the [Luzerne] County Medical Society. I don't remember the specifics of it.

Dr. Feinberg was well thought of by the [Luzerne] County Medical Society, and there was no problem with them in [our] running this institution. The nice part about it was that it did not constitute infringement on the practice of medicine on the patients that were involved. This was a service afforded to them, the results of which went to their doctor. It wasn't used as in any proselytizing way by our doctors. Our doctors were there just for diagnosis. We made the diagnosis, we did the examination, and forwarded the reports. . . .

Q: Did you ever have any crises at the Center?

AS: No, there was no problem. The only problem there was the diminution of the number of ILG [members]. I might add that I also processed health benefits. They [the members] got health benefits. If they became ill, their doctor would submit a report and I would process it. That was one of my responsibilities, to process these things. They got X number of weeks' sick benefits at so much a week. I can't remember exactly what it was. I think it was thirteen weeks and they received monetary remuneration.

Q: From the union?

AS: From the union, yes. I'm trying to remember whether there were any actual surgical benefits. I think they were just sick benefits and such. But I processed those [forms]—both at the time we were in the Health Center down there and at the General Hospital. I got all the sick benefits [information], I made out a report, and I was remunerated for doing it.

WELCOME TO YOUR
UNION HEALTH CENTER

A MEMBER'S INFORMATION GUIDE
TRI-DISTRICT HEALTH CENTER
International Ladies' Garment Workers' Union, AFL-CIO

FIG. 38 | Workers entering the ILGWU Wyoming Valley Health Center, 1956. Photo courtesy of the ILGWU Wyoming Valley District Archives, Kheel Center, Cornell University.

Q: Were there certain kinds of illnesses that were more common than others?[3]

AS: No, no, if you are thinking of any predisposition by virtue of their work, there was no predisposition.

Q: Or by virtue of their residence in this area—for example, the garment dust or the coal dust as related [to] asthma?[4]

AS: No, no, I mean, the incidence of a disease was the same as the incidence in the general public.

Q: Were they a fairly healthy group of people, overall, would you say?

AS: They were like the average public. Some are super healthy; others have problems. If there were problems present then they were the same problems that were present in the general population.

Q: If you could have made one improvement, what would it have been?

AS: I made all the improvements that were necessary. I ran the organization according to my principles and any improvements that needed to be made, I made them as it went along. That was my prerogative. They gave me a free hand. If I wanted something, I got it. If I ever needed another piece of equipment, I got it. I ran the show, as did Dr. Feinberg.

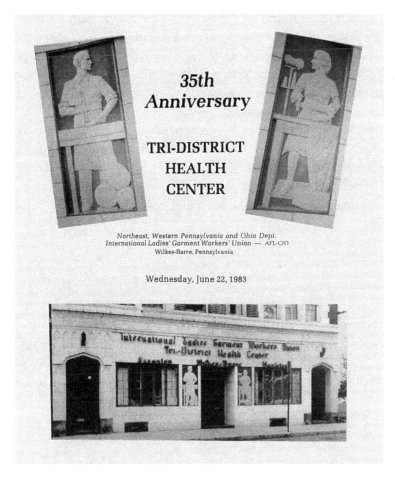

35th
Anniversary

TRI-DISTRICT
HEALTH
CENTER

Northeast, Western Pennsylvania and Ohio Dept.
International Ladies' Garment Workers' Union — AFL-CIO
Wilkes-Barre, Pennsylvania

Wednesday, June 22, 1983

FIG. 39 | The thirty-fifth anniversary of the ILGWU Wyoming Valley Health Center, 1983. Photo courtesy of the ILGWU Wyoming Valley District Archives, Kheel Center, Cornell University.

Q: Were there ever any problems over ordering equipment or other medically related matters?

AS: Oh, no, no, there was no problem with that. They were good employers, let me tell you. They didn't mix into anything medical. All they did was to provide the funds and the facilities. They were good people.

Q: There were similar operations in New York and elsewhere, weren't there?

AS: Yes, I think they did have an operation in New York.[5]

Q: Did you ever tour or see that facility?

AS: No, I never really [did]. . . .

Q: Did you get paid a fair fee?

AS: Yes, yes. It wasn't magnificent. I can't remember what it was. I don't remember how much they paid me but whatever they paid me, I was content. They established a fee and Dr. Lester Saidman became my associate director in the clinic.

DR. ALBERT SCHIOWITZ

He died just recently and he stayed with me until the demise of the clinic. I thought it was, in all modesty, a well-run organization because we rendered a service which was very utilitarian. The [family] doctors appreciated getting the reports, which were at no cost to the patient. The laboratory work was all done free of charge. . . .

Q: Did you ever catch any advanced cancers in the examinations?

AS: Oh sure. We found cancer in the rectum, or precancerous lesions, or cancers elsewhere. We found them. Routine examination of the chest—if we found a lesion on the chest we reported it. I mean these things happened, but it happened in all systems, whether it was the colon or gastrointestinal tract or pulmonary tract. In other words, any place we found it we reported it. We found a lot of cancers.

Leo Gutstein

Family Garment Shop Owner and
Garment Association President

The son of a "runaway" garment shop owner, Leo Gutstein was born in the Wyoming Valley but identified as a New Yorker because of his family roots. He commuted from the city to the Wyoming Valley for several years before settling in the area. After working alongside his father, Louis, at Lee Manufacturing in Pittston, he took over the business and displayed strong entrepreneurial abilities in opening additional Pennsylvania shops in Sayre, Carbondale, and Mayfield. As global competition mounted, he tried but failed at a venture in the Dominican Republic. His factually presented oral history delves into the up-and-down experiences of a business owner. He also discusses his generally favorable relationships with employees and union leaders, including Min Matheson. He addresses the issue of organized crime in the union and the industry by recognizing its presence locally though maintaining that it was controlled from New York.

LG: I was born in Exeter [near Pittston]. I lived there 'til I was two, but I was raised outside of New York in Nassau County, in a town called Great Neck. I came back here in the early sixties and have been back here since. I went through the Great Neck schools. I went to a military high school and attended Nichols College in

FIG. 40
Leo Gutstein, 1997.
Photo courtesy of the
Northeastern Pennsylvania
Oral and Life History
Collection, Pennsylvania
State University.

Leo Gutstein, from an
audio-recorded interview
with Robert P. Wolensky
conducted at the Lee
Manufacturing Company
office in Pittston, Pennsylvania, on June 26, 1997.
The interview is included
in the Wyoming Valley Oral
History Project, which is one
of eight projects within the
Northeastern Pennsylvania
Oral and Life History Collection housed in the Eberly
Family Special Collections
Department, Penn State
University Libraries.

Dudley, Massachusetts. In my second year of college, my father [Louis Gutstein] got ill and also had gone bankrupt. We had a [garment] showroom in New York and had a business based in New York, and he came back here to run the factory, but he got ill. So I came here and attended night schools at the University of Scranton, planning on being here temporarily, and that was thirty-five years ago! Most of my life has been here, although I still think of myself as a New Yorker. In fact, I think I lived all of eighteen or nineteen years in New York. I was born in 1943.

Q: Tell us about the family manufacturing business.

LG: Well, it started in the early thirties. My father first came to northeastern Pennsylvania around 1933 or '35. I'm not exactly sure when. I can really base that by when my sisters were born because two of them were born in New York and one of them was born here. Dad moved back into the New York region with showrooms in 1945. This facility that we're sitting in [the former Pittston Armory], we've been here since about 1941 when he acquired it. He was in a larger building in West Pittston. It had about 1,200 people working in it and that building was sold prior to them having the ability to buy this one. My father at that point split those 1,200 people up into four different locations, this being the largest one. He had about three hundred working here. Through the years, some of the factories were closed. This factory has always existed, and it existed as a fully operating sewing factory until two years ago [1995]. Just through import price pressures, we decided to close down most of the manufacturing.

In the last thirty years, I had expanded it [i.e., the business]. I was spread out all over the state. I had about 1,100 people working for me in various parts of Pennsylvania. I was probably a larger than the normal contractor in those years. I didn't design my own manufactured products. I manufactured on a contract basis for other people, such as Leslie Fay, Liz Claiborne—examples of the companies that I did business with. My operation was broken up into nine separate corporations, all similar to the one that we're sitting in. Lee Manufacturing was known to the trade as my primary company because I always dealt with all of my customers as Lee Manufacturing. Internally, I would subcontract to my own entities for work that was acquired by Lee Manufacturing. It was probably in the mid-to-late eighties that I was at my peak. In the late eighties, the business really started to get bad. Work was very difficult to come by, especially in a union environment. I have been a union environment for the last thirty-some-odd years.

I went and started to do government contracting. I was very successful at that for a number of years but that, too, started to slow down as procurements were lessened and budgets were tightened. It became an extremely competitive marketplace. Plus there were some internal problems—some people in the [military] agency were being indicted for various things, and I was very uncomfortable dealing in that marketplace. I just made a decision to discontinue.

FIG. 41 | Pittston Armory, headquarters of Lee Manufacturing Inc., circa 1960. Photo courtesy of Lukasik Studio.

At that point, when I started to do government work, I was probably employing about five hundred people and no more than that. I shut down about four factories. They were in Sayre, Pennsylvania, and I was also operating in Carbondale, Pennsylvania, and Mayfield, Pennsylvania.[1] Those were the four plants. This one here [in Pittston] was not involved in government contract work but the others were involved in that work. We made fragmentation vests for the marines, we made fatigue uniforms for the army, we made toxicological decontamination suits. We made some very intricate, interesting things.

I think my success and longevity in this industry is because I've always gone after what everybody else chose not to do, including work on the "distasteful." I found that I had much less competition that way. Anybody can do the easy product; most people try to stay away from the difficult. Again, the difficult ones don't give you as much competition so there was still some market doing that type of thing.

Q: Are you doing any difficult garments now?

LG: No, I actually do the easy now! I had worked [very long hours], personally. My day didn't end until seven, or eight, or nine at night, which was not the norm to this industry because the factories generally closed at two thirty in the afternoon. In the area that I live in, Kingston, there were four or five other contractors that lived on my block, and they were home by three o'clock in the afternoon.

LEO GUTSTEIN

My wife always complained that, "Ya know, how come they're home at three, and you're home by eight or nine at night?" I must have a girlfriend![2] *(laughs)* But they had individual factories with thirty or forty or fifty or sixty employees in one building. It was just that I had a different kind of a business. Now she complains that I should get a life because I'm home too early. *(laughs)* But my business has changed drastically.

Q: Why Pennsylvania? You had all of your shops in Pennsylvania. Why weren't you in New York or New Jersey?

LG: The reason I stayed in Pennsylvania was my expansions were based not so much on where a factory was available but where management was available. If I had somebody who was a strong manager, or didn't press me, and he was living somewhere in New York State, and if I took a ride up to the area and liked the area, I might have set a factory up somewhere in upper state New York. I wouldn't have gone to Manhattan [because] it's not an area that I personally would want to live in, or even travel to, on a daily basis. Even when I had all of the factories, I was out on the road two or three days a week just making a loop to all the factories.

The way I developed a factory was finding strong management. If I found strong management, then I would find a building. Machinery was easy to come by. I had enough [machinery] stored in this building through all those years to expand out of it. I had the luxury of having other factories so if I was missing certain expertise within one particular plant, within my others I could always do that portion of the garment until I developed the ability [to make it in the other plant]. So at some point in the life of any one of my factories, they all became freestanding, able to exist on their own, perform all of the functions necessary to produce products without having to share any resources from other factories.

Q: Why did you set up shop in Sayre?

LG: Sayre was an area that had a lot of employment in the needle industry at one time. There was one factory up there with over 1,100 people employed, and they went down to about 150. There were three or four other factories that closed up. Sayre was actually different than all of the other [shops that] I had developed. In Sayre I found a workforce first, and I found a building second, and I had to entice somebody locally to move up to Sayre to develop the factory. It wasn't that I found somebody from the Sayre area who came to me. In all the others, I found somebody from the area who had come to me.

Q: To manage the plant?

LG: With the purported skills. I would have them work in one of my other plants for a while, and if they proved themselves, then I would develop a factory around them. In most cases they would always have a percentage of equity ownership in the plant. So that, you know, they had an invested interest as much as I did. But Sayre was a little different. Sayre was a labor market that I chased in the seventies and early eighties when labor was very difficult to come by. Work was easier to come by. Customers existed but the production capacity [i.e., labor] was not [easily available].

In this area—the Wilkes-Barre, Scranton, Pittston area—it was really too competitive for labor. There were too many factories so I looked to going into rural areas and that's how I spread out all over the state. [It was a] combination of having strong management and finding an area with available labor, some nucleus of skilled labor. We also set up training facilities in each of the plants and we did train many of our own people. We would start with a less complicated product in the less adept shops until they became able to handle any product that we chose to handle. But again, as the industry changed, labor was no longer the problem. It was readily available. Finding customers that were willing to come out [i.e., send contract work] to this area became the problem. That's progressively why I had to reverse myself and get smaller.

Q: Were you always a union shop?

LG: It was not. I was always a union shop since I've been here [i.e., in Pittston]. The factory opened up in this building, as I said, in the early forties, and it wasn't union until the late fifties. I came here in the early sixties and by the time I came, it had already been a union shop.[3]

Q: What about the plants in these other areas?

LG: They were all union shops [eventually].

Q: You mentioned Pittston as a real garment-manufacturing center at one time. What can you tell us about that?

LG: Main Street in Pittston had close to forty factories. Today we're sitting in the only one that's still standing. The industry became an offshoot of my father mainly, who came out here in the mid-thirties. Many of the factories were offshoots of key personnel that had worked for him, that opened up their own factory, employing family and starting with six, eight, ten, or twelve operators. Most of the employees were related to each other. He was one of the first [to come here].

He came running away from the union that was organizing in New York City. He had a factory in New York, and he came to this area with my aunt and a woman who had run the floor for him for many years in the factory on Twenty-Third Street in Manhattan. They both worked for him for a few years here, and then they both went out and opened their own factories. That's how many of the factories evolved in Pittston. Many of the owners that were in Pittston [as recently as] three, four, and five years ago originally started in this factory—Lee Manufacturing.

Q: Why did your father come specifically to this area?

LG: I really don't know the answer to that. I don't know what brought him here initially. I think that there was, first of all, a large labor force. The labor force was used to working on production lines. There was a large woman labor force here that had been in the silk mills for many years. The silk industry had closed down a few years before that and there was a large employable women's population that had worked on production lines. And the mines were also struggling at that time so that there was cheap labor out here, and somewhat of a skilled labor force.

Q: What about the work ethic?

LG: The work ethic in those years was excellent. I don't think that it is quite today what it was. Even when I came here in the sixties [there] was an excellent work ethic. People were very reliable. Most of them were women at that point, women with second earnings, putting their kids through college on those earnings, while the husbands supported the household. They were very reliable, very industrious people. Family structure was different in the sixties than it is in the nineties.

What I find today is that there developed a stigma to the industry through the strikes involving the ILG. The strikes were always [about] "the sweatshops" and how terrible the sweatshops were to work in. Well, they did a good job in convincing the employable public that the sweatshops were terrible places to work. The reality is they really weren't sweatshops and they paid fairly good wages, but the stigma stayed with the industry and has always remained. It's difficult to get the type of employee that I used to get. Plus, the industry has also scared people because it has shrunk so drastically over the last few years. People don't look at it as a long-term investment in their future. For that reason, it's also tough to get good people.

Q: Looking back on Main Street, Pittston, could you tell us some of the shop names?

LG: Off the top of my head there was a Lori Dress, Del-Mar Sportswear, Pittston Frocks, Pittston Fashions, Green Fashions, Jenkins Sportswear, Anthony Fashions—these are just a few names that come to mind, and there were many, many more.

Q: Was there a particular ethnic pattern to ownership?

LG: I would say initially the industry had been predominately Jewish ownership. Today it is probably mostly Italian. Through the sixties and into the eighties it was probably half and half. I think originally the owners of the shops were tailors from eastern Europe that had immigrated to New York City and the Lower East Side of New York and grew up in the garment industry in the Lower East Side.[4] They [later] moved out to Northeast Pennsylvania, or to Pennsylvania in general. . . .

Most people operated and owned one factory. They were owner-operators and had their own floorpeople, their own management, their own sweeper, their jack-of-all-trades. I was different in that I grew up doing that *and* I could sit down and sew a product together. That's my background, my technical background. But probably for the last twenty years, I haven't sat at a sewing machine. I ran around and managed these factories all over the place.

Q: Can you tell us about your union relationships?

LG: I've never had a problem with unions. I believe that they perform a function. I think that owners without somebody looking over their shoulder would have a tendency to be abusive to the help. They would blame it on the fact that market conditions require them to do it. That, in some cases, may be true. But I think that currently unions are no longer an asset to the industry. When I first came into the industry, it was predominately union. I believe that the people that I had employed with me had a fairly high skill level and technical ability. Given a semi-even playing field, I think that we could compete with anybody. We existed in the sixties and seventies when the union was very strong, and the playing field was fairly even, and my competition had to exist under the same rules that I had to exist under. It was a very good business for me. We competed by ability and customer service in the eighties.

Now in the nineties, the union is an insignificant portion of the industry. The playing field is no longer level. I can have very strong relations with my customers and, as long as I might have been 3 or 4 or 5 percent more expensive than my competition to my customers, they would still do business with me because of reliability, comfort, quality. When I became 25 or 30 percent more than my competition, they could love me, they could be related to me, [but] they're not going to do business with me. It's just prudent business sense. I can be upset by it, but I can understand it.[5]

Q: Is your competition nonunion domestic labor, or is it foreign labor, or is it a combination?

LG: My competition is nonunion. My competition is foreign labor. My competition is union facilities that are uncontrollable by the union, or so the union reports. Even though the factories are [technically] union in the Lower East Side of New York—their [workers] are mostly Chinese, Hispanic, Korean—and they [the owners] say they have a language barrier. They [the ILGWU] can't control the fact that these people work sixty- and seventy-hour workweeks for below minimum-wage rates. They exist under the same contract that I exist under but they don't abide by the contract. We will always abide by the contract. For what is left of the union segment of the industry, it's a very uneven playing field.

Q: What percent of the industry is union, would you say?

LG: I'm not sure any longer, but the erosion in the industry [has been great]. Just to quote some articles that I've read recently, the industry peaked nationally at somewhere around 1.5 million employees. Not necessarily union, but in the needle trades industry. The current employment level, as I understand it, is under eight hundred thousand. It has been losing a few hundred thousand a year for the last few years. I mean, there's been drastic decline in the last three or four years. I think three or four years ago there was still well over a million employees.

The membership in the ILGWU, as I have been told at one point, was over half a million nationally. Today it is under one hundred thousand, including Puerto Rico and Canada. That's the ILGWU—which actually no longer exists. Now there is UNITE and it's a joint union with the Amalgamated Clothing

LEO GUTSTEIN

Workers union. I don't know what the membership is there, but I don't think the combined membership there equals what just the ILG had at some point. It's an industry that has become an international industry. When I started, it was a domestic industry, so my competition was all domestic.

Being an international industry, I've had the fortunate, or unfortunate, experience of going to the Orient and seeing what my competition does there. It had been very intimidating 'til I was actually there. After having spent some time in shops in Hong Kong and Korea and Taiwan, I realized they didn't really have a skill level that was anything better than my employees had. In fact, I believe that my employees were much more productive and had a better skill level. The difference was they received one-tenth the pay of my employees. If they used three or four times the amount of people that I required and slowed down the shop, they made a very nice product out of the Orient. They had to use four times the operators but, even using four times the operators, still they were only [paying] one quarter of my labor cost. So it became an insurmountable competition. I've also had the experience of spending time in the Caribbean and looking at factories there. The skill level is terrible, but the pay again is something that is very difficult to compete with.

Q: Are they doing all levels of production or just the lower levels?

LG: Today they're doing all levels. We can't even compete at the premium levels. They don't do the couturier, but neither do I, and neither did anybody else. Those are little tailor shops doing very small runs of items, but in the moderate-to-better market that I existed in . . . [I can't compete]. I don't know if I mentioned it to you but we've had a state trade association [the Northeast Apparel Association]. You said you had spoken to Bill Cherkes [chap. 2] a while ago. Bill was president of that association for many years. I forgot who was president after Bill. Then it was a gentleman by the name of Larry Hollander who was president for a number of years. I've been president of the trade association now for I guess upwards of ten years. When I took it over, we had two-hundred-some-odd members. I currently have seven. So you can see the erosion that has happened in the industry.

Q: What was the geographical area of the association?

LG: It was all over the state of Pennsylvania but predominately in northeastern Pennsylvania. I still have members in western Pennsylvania, but the industry itself was consolidated in the northeastern part of the state—Luzerne and Lackawanna Counties, and a little south of Hazleton, Allentown, Bethlehem, Pottsville, Reading, Harrisburg. That was the majority of the industry in the state of Pennsylvania. Pittsburgh has some, and there are still some members in the Johnstown area, but there were not as many as there were in this area.

The factories actually were larger in the western part of the state than they were here. Here they were little mom-and-pop shops: somebody who was a supervisor for somebody else and decided to go out on their own with their husband or wife, and roll up their sleeves, and work twelve- or fourteen-hour

FIG. 42 | Factory in the city of Villa Altagracia, Dominican Republic, 2013. Photo courtesy of John Landefeld and Katherine Burmaster.

days. They were very industrious people. The reality was that they probably could have made more money working for somebody else than they actually did owning their own business, but they still had that initiative. I give them credit for having the initiative to want to have their own business and get ahead in that manner.

Q: I noticed that you have a sales outlet in this factory. Is that something new?

LG: That's something that I just have the space for. I have [i.e., own] the building, I have it here, and I have another one up in Sayre, and another location where I have a factory. It's something that I opened up here about three years ago. It wasn't a matter of being competitive. It was just a matter of another business that I chose to go into and pursue.

Again, I have lived in the garment industry my whole life and it's all I've ever known. Even as a kid growing up in New York, I worked for my father in the summers, so it's the only thing I've ever known. I have a number of friends still in the industry, and I buy from them—products we don't manufacture, items that I purchase out in the marketplace, but I'm able to purchase them competitively and sell them at discount prices. So it's just another venture that I chose to go into since I'm sitting with space anyway.

Q: Have you thought about going nonunion, or moving to Puerto Rico or elsewhere?

LG: I was in the Dominican Republic with a factory for a while. It was my intent to spend some time initially getting it set up and operating, and it was a viable circumstance. I had a partner there who was supposed to be the one who was going stay there and run it. His wife was originally from the Dominican Republic. It was a bad business judgment on my part, so I took my losses and left.

LEO GUTSTEIN

I'm not old but I'm probably too old at this point in my life, too comfortable, to have to go out and start all over again. I would start all over again, but I'm not about to uproot myself and my family. I like living here. It took me a number of years [to get used to living in the area] when I first came here from New York. I was in my late teens or early twenties and my life was in New York. I was upset that I had to come out here, but I understood why I had to come. I would run back on weekends, and if I had to be at work [on Monday] at seven o'clock in the morning, I left from some friend's house in New York at five o'clock in the morning and just made it to work. Now I go in [to New York] on business a few times a month and I don't stay over. I still have family [there]. I have sisters that live in Manhattan. A lot of my relatives still live there and it's a nice place to visit. I prefer living out here.

Q: What are you manufacturing now?

LG: We still manufacture ladies' dresses. It's the line that I have always existed in. The industry has basically been a very segmented industry. There were factories that specifically made dresses and most of our members, in the association, were dress contractors. There were factories that specifically did bottoms. There were factories that did blouses and others did knit goods. It was the dress factories that were probably the most versatile because you had to have all the skills or disciplines in order to do a dress.

A dress encompasses everything that a blouse can have and many things that a skirt or a pant can have. In many cases, what has evolved to be a dress is a pants suit, a skirt set. There are still class-fighting dress departments. When I first started in this industry, a dress was a dress. A dress company made only dresses—be it housedresses or evening dresses, they made only dresses. There were companies that made, sold, and designed only suits. There were companies that only did bottoms and companies that only did tops. Those were smaller companies. Today the industry is dominated by some major companies that make all lines. . . .

One thing that has changed in the industry in the last ten or fifteen years is a term called "private label." Private label circumvented the traditional manufacturer-jobber [system]. It would [likely] be a retailer. Take Macy's—only because they come to mind. They and everybody else in the industry do the same thing. They'll take what they have decided is a good product for their stores, for their customers, and bypass the manufacturer even though he might have been the one who originally shipped them the first example of that product. They [the private labels] come to somebody like myself direct. I'm sewing for them only, sewing this label, which is their retail label, into the product. They have bypassed what they hope is the [cost] margin that the design house would have to necessarily put on top of my labor. So today, the retailer has also become a jobber. . . .[6]

But the dress shops were the most versatile. We were also the most expensive because, being the most versatile, we had the best skilled operating hands.

They were the best skilled operating hands, so they received, and rightly so, the highest pay in the industry. These people could make a collar, set a collar, do multiple operations. In most of the sportswear plants where they only made one specific product, an operator sat and set a left sleeve seven hours a day, five days a week, and that's all she knew from. My operators switched from operation to operation. I mean they did a predominately single classification of operation, but even that single classification of operation was a multiple of operations. So there was more flexibility.

Surprisingly, the lower-end sportswear separate market still exists. Not to the degree that it did. There is another trade association in the state. It's based out of Allentown, Pennsylvania. At one point, I think they had five hundred or six hundred members. I think they're down to about thirty or forty members. They were an association of people that did bottoms, tops, and blouses. I could not compete with them on a blouse, but they could not even begin to make a dress. I could make the blouse, but I couldn't compete with them on a price point.

Q: Has that area of the state been well-known for blouse manufacturing?

LG: Blouse manufacturing, yeah. The Allentown, Bethlehem, Reading, and Phillipsburg area.

Q: And you made mainly dresses up this way?

LG: Dresses up this way. Not that they weren't in the Allentown area also, but dresses were predominately in this area. And what's happened is that dresses have evolved, the dresses have moved into the Lower East Side of New York. That's the immigrant labor. . . .

Q: Were certain jobbers in the earlier days known to deal with nonunion shops while others dealt with union shops?

LG: Absolutely. Nonunion jobbers would deal with nonunion shops and union jobbers would deal with union shops. Union jobbers could only work in nonunion shops if there were no union shops available. [Then] the union gave them the right to work using a nonunion factory. Nonunion jobbers couldn't work in a union factory unless that factory could show the union that it couldn't get union work. There was a prohibition against that happening.[7] Today, all bets are off. I mean, you work for whomever you can get work from at this point.

Q: The so-called unsavory element in Pittston that owned or ran shops—men such as Russ Bufalino and Nick Alaimo—must have had a nonunion jobber, but many became union-affiliated after a big strike of 1958, correct?

LG: They all became union at that point. Nick spent some time away in jail. Having grown up in the community, you can't help but know these people. I just come into this office in Pittston for the past thirty-five years and you know what I'm doing for lunch! But Nick and the others that were also "unsavory" were [eventually] union. In the sixties, the right way to be was union, because if you were a jobber, there weren't enough nonunion sewing sources for you to contract with, so you were better off being union.

LEO GUTSTEIN

This is a very cyclical industry. We peak from January through May, and then there is the slow period of the year. In that four- or five-month [peak] period years ago, as much as anybody could produce, that's how much they could sell. As much as I could sew, that's how much work I could get [contracted to me] in those years. Since the majority of the industry was union, most everybody [i.e., the shop owners] opted to be union. They would complain about it, they would bitch about it—that they lost all control of their own business and they couldn't make their own decisions, and they had to get permission from somebody to do this or that. The fact is that the people [i.e., the owners] that did the best were union. When all of the controls disappeared—savory or unsavory—the correct way to be today is nonunion. If I were to start all over again, I would not start union only because it is no longer the predominant driving force in the industry. . . .

Q: The ILG built a very powerful operation in New York and in Wilkes-Barre. You dealt with the union over the years. How would you characterize the change in its operations into the eighties?

LG: Well, I believe in the original concept of the union, which is as a movement. And the intent of the movement is to defend and protect its members and have a bargaining agent, an individual who represents many people and, therefore, will have more strength dealing with any owner for new contracts or [wage] increases. It was made up of people who were idealists, who came into the movement because it was what they believed in, not because it was a good-paying job. I think today the ILGWU, or UNITE, in many cases is made up of people who came into it because it's a good-paying job and not because it was a movement that they believed in. When it was idealists that I dealt with, I respected them, I understood who they were, who they represented, what their job was, and would deal with them on that basis.

Today there are some older people still in the ILG, or UNITE, from the old school who were idealists, who I still have a lot of respect for. I understand when they're coming to me with complaints that my employees may have, that they're coming to me with real problems, and I will address them as real problems. But I believe they are a minority in that movement, [because most] are just very comfortable in their positions and are looking forward to their retirement and trying to make sure they have a very nice life for themselves. If by having a very nice life for themselves by accident they happened to help a member, OK, and if they don't, that's OK, too. So I don't have the same respect for the union that I did and that's all I can say about that.[8] *(laughs)*

Q: You must have known and dealt with Min Matheson [chap. 3] and the ILGWU.

LG: I knew Min Matheson. Min was an idealist. Min was a very strong personality. I knew her really as a kid growing up [because] she happened to have been a friend of my father's. She was a friend of my father before he was union, and she was a friend of my father after he became union. When I first came out here,

Min was the district manager of what was a very large district in northeastern Pennsylvania. From sort of hearsay, secondhand information from my dad, Min's area [eventually] became a threat to the New York office and the officers in New York. She wielded a lot of power, she had a large member base. This was an area that she had organized and had a lot of control over.

I think because of that [she had problems], and again you have to recognize that the union movement is no different than any other political organization. Somebody becomes president or vice president or any officer within that union by being nominated at a convention, having a constituency that would vote for him, and that's how the president of the ILG gets to become president of the ILG. Min had developed a very large membership base. She intimidated—I don't recall who was president or vice president in those years—those individuals, and they thought that she might make a run for being an officer in the International office of the ILGWU. They basically demoted her. They moved her, I think at that time, to New Jersey [*sic*; New York City] and kept her there for many years so that her political base eroded over the years. It was not unique to her.

Many years later there was another individual that was elected president of the ILGWU, and he was elected president because he was the vice president and his region [that he controlled was] then called the Northeast region, which encompassed Pennsylvania, Ohio, New Jersey, and I think parts of New England. It didn't encompass anything in upstate New York, and it didn't encompass anything in New York City. In that region, northeastern Pennsylvania was the largest constituency base, it was the largest local [i.e., district] within the ILGWU. So he became president. Now to ensure that whoever was now going to be a vice president—and then head of that same region—could not garner that same constituency base, the Northeast region was divided into the Upper South region, the Northeast Department (which was Pennsylvania), the New England region, and the New Jersey region, so that there was no political base to challenge him.

I think the first case [of reorganization] was done worrying about Min. The second one was just another example of how the union functions. I mean, the current president of the ILGWU [Jay Mazur] came [into office] because now the largest local in the International is in the Lower East Side of New York. He was the vice president and director of what was the Lower East Side of New York. So he had again the largest constituency base and was able to become president after the president before him retired. He will be president for, I believe, another four years, six at most. I think the agreement between the ILGWU and the Amalgamated [in UNITE!] states that he can only run for two terms and then the next president has to be somebody out of the Amalgamated.

Q: Did you ever tangle with Min on a labor dispute?

LG: No, no. She was sort of gone when I was on my own.

Q: Your father was her friend. It seems kind of unique in that one was an owner and the other was a union leader, and yet they were friends.

LEO GUTSTEIN

LG: My father was her friend. It was just a personal thing. I think they had both come out of similar backgrounds. I don't know where the friendship developed from, but they were friends. . . . Lois Hartel is the current district manager. Pittston was [for some years] its own local, but, because of the erosion in the area, the ILG consolidated and Scranton, Pittston, Hazleton, Tamaqua, the area south of Hazleton all are under one. They may still be classified as separate locals but there's one district manager. There's one office now. Where Pittston had its office three blocks down the road, and Scranton had an office, and Hazleton had an office—each one had its own manager, [but now] there's only one district manager encompassing basically all of the northeastern Pennsylvania.

Q: Where are the women working in this area now that the garment industry has declined?

LG: That's a good question because I have spoken to some shop owners who still exist, and they have a difficult time getting help. It shouldn't be [that way] because a year and a half ago Leslie Fay closed a facility that had six hundred or seven hundred employees. Now it may have been that those employees were going through some training programs that the federal government provided for them, and the state government, and they had extended unemployment benefits, so I imagine that, for at least a year, they weren't actively out looking for new jobs. Maybe now that all of those benefits provided to them [are gone]—because the Trade Adjustment Act has expired—they may be out [looking] again.

But the industry is an older industry. Even when I closed my factory, this factory, the average [employee age] had to be in the mid-fifties. You asked me at one point why I chose [to open a factory in] Sayre. When I went up to Sayre, that was a young labor force and my average age in that factory was in its mid-to-late thirties. So that factory was twenty or thirty years ahead of here. Whereas here in this area, most of the factories had an average age in the mid-to-late fifties. . . .

Because I have this outlet, a few days a week I work [in this building] at the outlet. Some of my former employees come in here and [ask], Have I changed my mind? Do I want to reopen? They would love to come back. Even though it was a hard job, it was a fairly good-paying job for a productive person. Even though it was a hard job, people liked it. They might have complained about it while they were doing it, but they really miss it.

Q: Was there a kind of camaraderie in the shop?

LG: Yes, even on the side of the owner. I had one of my [trade association] members who had gone out of business. He had been beaten up the last few years financially. He hadn't gone bust, but he was hurting by the time he finally closed his business. Then he was floating around for two or three years in other industries, and he came to me one day and he said, "Leo," he said, "Are there any factories available for sale?" I had him in this office. His name was Joe, and I said, "Joe, you know, probably every factory is for sale. Everybody I know would like to get out of the industry, get out of the business." I said, "You just came off of a couple

of bad years. What's making you think about going back into this industry?"
"You know why," he sighed. He said [after] having worked his whole life in this industry, everything else was boring to him.

I said that I could relate to him. It's a very demanding, hardworking industry. It's a tough industry. It's not that you're making cookie cutters. I mean, it's not that simple to sew any product. Fabrics give you problems. Weather gives you problems. There's a number of things that affect what you're doing in any given day. It was a very challenging business. You could sit down and make your plan for tomorrow, and at seven the following morning, your plan is out the window because four people didn't show up on the production line and you got to reschedule everything. You still have to satisfy the customer. When you went home, you literally ran out at the end of the day exhausted.

What he was saying is that whatever he was doing, he would go home with energy. *(laughs)* I could relate to it because what I currently do is simple to me—having run all these factories and spent the hours that I spent, and coming home physically exhausted, yet I liked it. I liked it because it provided me an adequate living. I liked it because there was a lot of creativity to it. It's a demanding business. But I don't like it any longer. I don't like the sewing portion of it any longer. It didn't provide me an adequate living [lately], which probably is the reward or the accolades for what you do. What I currently do is insufficiently challenging. It's just too easy. So I can relate to what he said, though I think I convinced him not to go back into the industry.

Q: Will there be a Lee Manufacturing in five years?

LG: I hope so. I plan on staying, yes, yes.

Q: Do you want to get new factories going?

LG: I'm looking at some other things for the future.

Q: Do you need to diversify, for example?

LG: Well, the last few years I was in business, it cost me money. If I had shut my doors ten years ago I probably could have retired but I chose to try and continue and survive in an industry that just wasn't allowing me to survive. Plus, I had people working here since the day I came [to] this area. I still had people that have been with me for the thirty-five years. Oh yeah, I had quite a few. I just felt that I had an obligation to them. They had been very, very industrious employees and provided me with more than an adequate living for very many years of my life. I sent my children through college. I felt I had an obligation, until it just became too much of a financial burden to absorb that obligation.

I went through a period of extreme depression when I closed up this factory—this being the first one [we opened]. It took me probably six months to get over the fact. When I finally made the decision, within a month I had divested myself of every piece of equipment that I had. I didn't want to change my mind. I didn't want to see them [i.e., the machines] sitting in there. Now I don't miss it that much. But I think that if a circumstance came along that looked like it could be

LEO GUTSTEIN

profitable, I would entertain going back into it because I've never shied away from work. In fact, I thrive on it.

Q: Going back to the earlier days, Pittston had a reputation not only in garment manufacturing but also for having an unsavory element that controlled a lot of the industry.

LG: It's a fact of the industry, but I don't think that Pittston was the area that was [controlling]. I think the controls came out of New York. This area was just an extension of New York City as far as the garment industry went. This industry was very controlled for very many years.[9] The trucking portion the union will profess to having never been controlled, but the union was very controlled.[10] This has changed since the RICO [Racketeer Influenced and Corrupt Organization] laws and some other methods of indicting unsavory individuals [have been enacted]. I don't know that it is totally gone from the industry, but it's not now the driving factor.

Q: Is it one driving factor, for example, behind the immigrant labor we now see on the Lower East Side now?

LG: It is. It was and is controlled; it's what developed. Yes, but [in the early days] it was controlled through the trucking industry. When I was growing up in this industry, you could not choose the truck [company] when you did business. Somewhere there were three or four people that sat in a room and said, "OK, this is *his* truck man, this is *his* truck man, and this is *his* truck man," and never should you change unless you get the approval from somebody. I remember as a kid we had a trucking company that had serviced us for many years. We once got a call saying that they will not appear at your door ever again, and they never did. Another company appeared at the door the following day, and they were our trucking company until they went out of business. The stories about the control in the industry—it did exist.

My father grew up in Lower East Side of New York. Came out of a very tough neighborhood and one piece of advice he had given me as a kid was, "If you ever get asked a favor by somebody who is an unsavory individual, to the best of your ability do it as long as you're not putting yourself in jeopardy or doing something illegal. But never *ask* a favor. Once you've asked a favor, you're obligated." That's the way I've lived my life. . . .

Q: It seems to me that New York sort of won the labor battles with Pennsylvania in a sense.

LG: New York won. Manufacturing is back there and it's with immigrant labor. When the industry developed here, it became mostly union, and the contract that this area operated under was at a lower rate than the same segments of the industry in Manhattan operated under. Then [the] Lower East Side and Chinatown started to develop as very good, difficult competition to us in the sixties. It just came about all of a sudden, but their skill levels developed doing unskilled products. Through years and years of production, their skill levels have come up so that they now are very skilled [and they make] very detailed items. The dress portion of the industry didn't feel the impact of it because, again, we had the higher skill level necessary to make the products that we made.

But the union segment of the industry in New York used to complain that we [in northeastern Pennsylvania] operated under a lower-rate union contract than they operated under. Of course, we had higher trucking rates. There were some things that did cost us more. But the union became a realist and said, "OK, if we're going to go after all these factories in Pennsylvania to organize them and make them pay the same rates that they're paying in New York, they're not going to stay in business because why would anybody in New York bring the work out here when it's actually going to end up being more expensive?" They'll stay with those they were working with. And so we got a lower-rate union contract.

Through the years, the level of our contract came up and basically our contract today and for a number of years has been the same rates they pay in New York—except *we* pay them! In New York it doesn't make a difference what the contract says any longer—*they* pay what they pay [i.e., lower than scale]. So the work has gone back into New York and, yes, we have lost.

But in all fairness, a good portion of the work has gone offshore. Remember, even in the sixties there really was not an international industry. It was still a national, domestic industry so that all of your competition was just labor competition within various areas. The South developed as a very strong manufacturing area, predominately nonunion. For whatever reason, the union was never able to organize the factories in the South, but [it was] mostly an unskilled type of product—a T-shirt, an inexpensive blouse, an inexpensive pant. Large runs of simple products rather than the small runs of the detail products that we made up here. It's still nonunion, most of the South is still nonunion. They're feeling the same impact because so much of the product now is made offshore.

Pearl Novak

Garment Worker, Union Organizer, and Social Activist

FIG. 43
Pearl Novak, 1997.
Photo courtesy of the
Northeastern Pennsylvania
Oral and Life History
Collection, Pennsylvania
State University.

Pearl Novak, from an
audio-recorded interview
with Robert P. Wolensky
conducted at Mrs. Novak's
home in Bear Creek, Penn-
sylvania, on June 19, 1997.
The interview is included
in the Wyoming Valley Oral
History Project, which is one
of eight projects within the
Northeastern Pennsylvania
Oral and Life History Collection housed in the Eberly
Family Special Collections
Department, Penn State
University Libraries.

Pearl Novak admits that she is still a committed "tiger" on behalf of the ILGWU—its people, purposes, and causes. Beginning as a garment worker in her teens, she remained a dedicated union member for nearly five decades. Her final challenge was to serve as strike captain for a union-authorized shutdown at the Leslie Fay Corporation's factory in an effort to save, or at least postpone, the closure of the Wyoming Valley's last major garment employer. The campaign took her beyond the picket line to meetings, rallies, and demonstrations in New York, Guatemala, Texas, and beyond. An indefatigable activist, she concludes with some thoughtful observations about the future of the American garment industry and the working class.

Q: Tell us how you began in the garment industry.

PN: Well, my mother already worked there. When they [the women workers] were all laid off [from war industry], my mother went into the garment industry in 1946. She worked there until 1968 at her death. She worked for Pioneer Manufacturing [in Wilkes-Barre] for twenty-two years. I entered at age fifteen in 1948. She got me the job. [Back then], you went to work. You didn't have a choice in the matter. You just went to work. So I went there at fifteen, and I wasn't sixteen until four or five days later. I soon went with Min Matheson and [later] started organizing. I [first] went with my mother and I was caught in with her [during a strike] 'cause they were gonna take Min to jail and a few others that they said were troublemakers.

Q: Strikers?

PN: Yeah, or troublemakers, or whatever they would call them. I was caught in it. Well, now, I wasn't old enough to be in that [strike] and Min Matheson said to me, "Pearl, cry." So I cried like you wouldn't believe! She told the cops that I was just a child with her and with my mother, so they let me go. Fifteen. Yes, I had just started.

Q: Who taught you how to sew?

PN: Well, they taught you there [in the shop], and my mother helped. I mean, she showed me. At first I didn't start as a sewer. I started at what they called trimming. Trimming is where they would start you, and if you showed any interest . . . [they would promote you]. Then I got to be quite a sewer. I was put in with my mother. I was in the same department with my mother.

Q: Did you want to go to high school or did you want to go work?

PN: I wanted to go to high school, definitely.[1]

Q: What did you tell your mother?

PN: Well, at that time, my father was out of a job, my mother had to work, and that went on for a couple of years before he could find anything. We were on relief. We got eight dollars a week. So there was no way for her to help me. She only made, I think she started as a waitress at first, and she only made like eight dollars a week. So, it was tough and she didn't want to be on relief because at that time it was not the biggest thing, you know. After that she went into the garment industry.

Q: You didn't protest having to work?

PN: No. At that time you did what you were told. I knew we had it tough. If there was going to be food on the table, then I would have to help, which I did until I was twenty-one. I always gave my mother my pay. They did what little they could on the house to make it better. My dad finally did get a job as an auto mechanic, but there was not very much money. Even with my help, it was tough—those days were tough. This was in the fifties, we're talkin' about. He was laid off [from the coal mines'] in the forties. It was not good. In the fifties it really went down. They [the coal companies] became greedy. That's what it is—just like in the garment industry—they had become greedy. The same thing with the coal mines. They undermined everything. They [the garment shop owners] weren't paying [good wages] until the union went in, and then they got a little better wages. But the people from the beginning did not get paid a lot of money. They worked practically for nothing, and they worked hard. And they were young, they were young when they went in, a lot of them.

Q: Were there many young women at Pioneer Manufacturing?

PN: Oh yes, oh yes. Pioneer was a big, big factory. It was in Wilkes-Barre, and I would say at one time it certainly employed at least six hundred people. It was

PEARL NOVAK

very big. I became involved in the "110 walkout"—110 people walked outta there to protest the firing of, I think he was a mechanic. He was very good and it was an unfair [firing]. So 110 people walked out.

Min Matheson took us all back [in]. She said, "Everybody else go back but that 110." We were paid on the street! *(laughs)* Paid on the sidewalk; they wouldn't even let us in the factory. They locked us out. Everybody struck. She was a very smart woman. She took us back [in] and then they locked us out. So right there she had them because then we struck *everything*. She not only struck Pioneer, she went out with about eight thousand [union members]. She struck everybody in the Valley. We were "Prim and Pretty"—that was the label we worked under. Oh, there were so many factories here. I can't even tell ya how many there were at that time, but there was a lot of factories. Factories sprung up all over, and they were in the homes and basements and all over. Like in Pittston alone, there was forty-five shops, stuck in corners, anyplace they could stick them. It became really tremendous, the number of people that were [working]. Thousands of workers.

When Min came in, she only had six hundred [unionized members]. Six hundred members here, and when she left she had eleven thousand and maybe more. So they really followed her. She had charisma. She had that fight. She had that "Go get this" [attitude]. People would follow her like the Pied Piper. I mean, she could talk to women and men. There was a lot of men in the factories, too. There was no other jobs so there was a lot of men in factories. That's how it deteriorated after [mining faded].

Q: What year was that lockout and strike?

PN: I would say it was '50 or '51, something like that. Because we were on Waller Street in Lee Park after they moved from Wilkes-Barre to Lee Park. We picketed day and night. I can't remember how long it went on, but I know I was out of work after a lot of them went back when they settled. I was 'round the clock [on the picket line]. I'd say it was at least a month or a month and a half, maybe more. They [the owners] really fought to hold on, but she did win. Big time. They took everybody back but it took a while for some of us. My mother went back immediately because she was in the ruffle department and she did a lot, she knew a lot.

Q: Do you know who owned Pioneer Manufacturing?

PN: Harris, I think it was Harris.

Q: Was he a local guy or did he come from someplace else?

PN: I have no idea where he came from, but I know he owned it. Jim Harris I think it was, and somebody else. The only one I remember is Harris, but there were more involved than him. I worked there for five years until I got married in 1953. Then I got jobs in West Pittston and Pittston, and everywhere I could go. The [one] strike they had in Pittston—at that time I was pregnant. Min, she was organizing Pittston, which was the tough one. I was at the strike but I was pregnant, so she told me to go home. I had done my thing, as much as I could do. I had twins in 1954. . . . [When] I got married and moved to Pittston, I went to work for Star Garment in West Pittston. I worked there for thirty-three years and they went out. I worked from 1953 to 1985 or '86—for thirty-three years.

Q: Do you recall who owned Star?

PN: Hertzberg, his name was [Stanley] Hertzberg. When he passed away, it went to his wife, and then John Lanunziata took over. He was just a kid, 'cause he's younger than me. I don't think he would have known Min. I think he took over at around the time Lois [Hartel] came in [as district manager]. He knew Sam Bianco and Lois Hartel.[2]

Q: What was it like working at Star?

PN: Star was a union job. We did have a strike there. I would say in maybe '57, something like that, '56 or '57. It had to be around that time because the company was being moved to Exeter, from West Pittston to Exeter. That building was [built] in 1956. It still has the corner stone on it, so I know it was that year. Hertzberg was still there—I mean, he owned it. He didn't last long though. He went along [with union demands] and it was over, but then we went back to work [at another shop] part-time and we couldn't get into the union. From '53 to '65 we could not get into the union because we didn't work enough hours. The union at that time did not allow you in until you had [so many hours]. We fought for that. In 1965 we got it and part-time workers were allowed to join. That was a hard bargain [for part-timers] because you were not part of the union, but yet you were fightin' for this union.

I was still in it, still doin' [work], you know. While I was workin' there, I went to other factories and we found out what was goin' on in other factories. Because [when] we were laid off, we would have to do something [to keep busy]. When you were part-time, you couldn't get that much for unemployment [compensation]. So we would go work in other shops. I worked in a lot of other shops and that was a basis of finding out, you know, how things were. In most of the shops, things were terrible.

Q: Would Min ever come to you and say, "Pearl, do me a favor and go work in this or that shop."

PN: It was mostly that we had to find out what was happening, how the people would react: What do they think? Would they want a union? Are they gonna go along with it? This was something you found out in the shops that were actually terrible, really, really terrible. They weren't fit to work in, to tell you the truth. I would go in many of these shops. These were [run by] the families that owned them and mostly it was relations—cousins, the whole rigmarole, you know. So you'd go in there, maybe it'd last two or three days, and then you'd be out. But in that two and three days you found out what was going on. They were all nonunion shops.

Q: So Min asked you to go into a specific shop?

PN: Well, I would know what was happening in them, and, you know, we wanted to help them. We just didn't want them to go on like that.

Q: Would you find them receptive to the union in most cases?

PN: Yeah. Min would rally them so they were ready to go into the union. It was a tough battle for her. I was in five strikes and the latest was Leslie Fay. . . . Don't forget [that at first] we only made forty cents an hour—sixteen dollars a week. And if you didn't have the union, I mean they'd never give you a raise. So you had to have the union. Most of these people were workin' for forty cents an hour and they were workin' hard. A lot of these places that I went into they had home-working. They would take machines, put them in homes, and those women would work at home. They would punch their time clocks—their families would punch their time clocks.

Q: So there were some real sweatshop conditions here.

PN: Yes, there was, at that time, yes. Min really went in and cleaned house. She didn't have it easy but she was a strong woman. . . .

Q: What were the typical reasons for the strikes?

PN: Wages, health—we wanted to get well. Higher wages and we got clinics. We got the shorter day, seven-hour day; we fought for that. We fought for health clinics, which we got. Health and welfare. A lot that we got we ended up givin' back in the end. But we held it up pretty well until 1994. ILG protected their people, and when we went out on strike, they took care of us. They stayed with us. . . .

Q: Why were there so many factories around here?

PN: Because it was big business. Garments were in demand. We did not have overseas production, and everything was made in the USA. So everything worked. The garment industries became really big. The shoe industry, all kinds of industries were in the USA where they were all booming. Garments sprung up all over the USA, not just here. Canada, everywhere they sprung up because it was a big business. It became bigger until 1994. Only 20 percent was left in the United States; 80 percent [of the manufacturing] was being shipped overseas. And now I don't even know if there's that much.

The ILG is down and they merged [with the Amalgamated Clothing Workers Union to form UNITE!]. They didn't have enough members so they could no longer survive unless the unions merged. I think our biggest mistake was letting all that go overseas. The government should've stopped some of this. They were warned in 1984. Even our union knew in 1984 that we would be going down. We went down a little bit before that, [starting] in '74. I think we had shops that started to close and then they would perk up again. Then in '78, it was a good year because we were making a lot, and then in 1984 it started to go down. But I think it started more so in '78, '79, or even earlier. It was underneath. We actually thought it was slow, but I think from the time I started at Leslie Fay, I'd say in 1986, I was amazed at how much was being done overseas. . . .[3]

LESLIE FAY:

Stay in the USA!

LESLIE FAY is one of the largest apparel manufacturers in the world, its success built on the labor and skill of hard-working Americans.

Now it has decided to throw 2,000 workers on to the unemployment lines in Northeastern Pennsylvania and shift all of its production overseas to places like Guatemala, where workers are paid starvation wages and fired—or worse—when they protest or try to join unions.

Leslie Fay says it must move all its production overseas in order to keep up with the competition and solve its serious financial problems. But the company's difficulties have nothing to do with domestic production. They are the result of financial scandal and high-level mismanagement by executives who now expect the workers to pay for their mistakes.

FIG. 44 | Leslie Fay "Stay in the USA" poster, distributed by the ILGWU, 1994. Photo courtesy of the Kheel Center, Cornell University.

Q: You were in the last Leslie Fay strike. Can you give us some background on that shutdown?[4]

PN: Actually, Leslie Fay was a good place to work. I worked there nine years. But it was a good place to work and the wages were good. The only reason the strike was on was because when we went for negotiations to renew our contract on June 1, [1994], they told us that they were gonna not have any more domestic production here. Well, at that time there was a lot of older workers at Leslie Fay. There was a lot younger ones, too, but there was also people who maybe had a year or two to retire. You know, that they could go out with a little dignity. This was mostly about respect and dignity. We worked hard, and we did everything we could for them so that they became a company that was in the [*Fortune*] 500. They had [a] high stock [price]. Some of our people even owned stock in Leslie Fay—some of the workers there, like Jack [Granahan], he worked there for thirty-eight years.[5] Like I said, it was a good place to work.

But it was not about wages that we went out. It was because they wanted to close down. We still had a year on our contract, but they didn't want to give us that year. They wanted to go out. So we struck on June 1 of '94. We started at midnight. One minute after midnight we were there. We put up our stands at the Leslie Fay entrance and we stayed there continuously around the clock for twenty-four hours. The factory was up in Laflin [near Pittston] and, actually, nobody sees Laflin. We started out with trying to get them to negotiate but they wouldn't. Finally, negotiations fell apart and that's how we came to strike. They wanted to leave, they just wanted to leave. They wanted to go out in '94. We kept them for another year, until '95. That became the big thing, to keep them for that year, which helped a lot. Some people, not all—it helped some. Our union stood by us.

We stopped them everywhere they turned. We had people on the road. We had people at the docks in the yard. We had people in South Carolina. We had people in Texas. We went to Texas and New York. We had people day and night [at their

PEARL NOVAK

facilities]. Trucks with license plate numbers taken so that we knew exactly where they were headed and where they were going. We had like a base, you know. And finally, we got them to a point where they were at a standstill. They did bring in some people [i.e., strikebreakers] at Laflin. They went across the picket lines. They brought in [workers] from New York or wherever, New Jersey. But not that many, not enough to keep the factory going. We were there about eight weeks, day and night. Then [ILGWU/UNITE! president] Jay Mazur got together with them. They had a meeting and they resolved it and we went back to work.

Q: How many went out on strike?

PN: They had [factories in] Throop [near Scranton] and Laflin [near Pittston]. Altogether I think it was about two thousand [employees]. They did manage to close Throop but it was not the main place. That [the main plant] was where we struck—on [U.S. Route] 315 [in Laflin]. That was the main shop. That was the shop they were getting rid of. They paid that [Michael J.] Babcock [Leslie Fay's president and chief operating officer] $2 million and then they were in bankruptcy. Babcock took over for—I forget his name, John [Pomerantz]—the son of the man that started the business here in the first place.[6]

Q: What was your role in the strike?

PN: I was the strike captain. We got the people picketing at all hours and we had schedules. The strike captain kept everyone [organized] so that there was always somebody there, that it was always a good showing. And we got a lot of support. We got support from the Catholic Church. In fact, they donated $10,000 to help out the people that needed it. It was called Hardship Committee. I was on that.

Then we went to New York. I went [with] a whole busload of us and I spoke in New York to about two thousand people from Ohio, and New York, and Jersey, and I guess some from Oklahoma, Florida, South Carolina. There was people from all over who came in and backed us. Directly from that speech, I went to see the [New York Catholic] cardinal [John O'Connor] and asked his help. He agreed to help us, to stand by us.[7]

Then from the cardinal, I went to the *New York Times* and gave them a story on what was happening—the ripple that it caused, it wasn't just two thousand workers. That's only in that factory or the factories that were involved. But how about the people [i.e., workers], where they go to buy food and other stores? It involves a lot more people. In Pennsylvania a lot of the shops were disappearing, they were gone. In fact, they're still closing at this time, now. Roxanne's just closed, the bathing suit place. I mean, there's nothing left here.

Most everything is gone, and this is why we tried to keep this place here even though they had difficulty—like somebody stole money from them in their own organization.[8] Now they should have been able to find out before he stole all this money and put Leslie Fay in jeopardy. After all this, they are picking up and coming back [i.e., restructuring the company]. They still have Laflin here and Andy Fashions. They still have those small shops. They don't do a lot.[9]

A lot of our [union] people went to Guatemala during this. We found the people working there and brought them back here. We spoke at those committees because they [the Guatemalan workers] were making skirts that we were making right here for maybe thirty-five cents an hour and selling them for a dollar more than we were selling them in the United States. My picture is in one of the papers holding up that skirt at the time. I went to Guatemala, and when I came back I went on channel 28 TV [in Wilkes-Barre]. I went up to Forty Fort [near Wilkes-Barre] and they had a debate on it. And I went to Texas, too.

Q: What was the Texas trip about?

PN: J. C. Penney. It was in the paper that J. C. Penney signed a contract with Leslie Fay to sell their products. So we went to Texas to let the board members and the stockholders know that Leslie Fay was making clothes overseas. I mean, people were working on them for thirty cents an hour or thirty-five cents an hour. They [J. C. Penney] had a code of conduct, so that's what we wanted to get in there. I asked them, "If they have a code of conduct, then why would they sell clothes at high prices that were made for very low prices?" The CEO said they would look into it, and I think that sort of broke the camel's back after a while because that was their [Leslie Fay's] big thing, to get J. C. Penney's to sell. We also went into stores [like] Saks in New York, we went to Bloomingdale's, and we would talk to managers. They [Leslie Fay] didn't like it, but we did it.

Q: Did you go with pickets?

PN: No, there was a committee of four or five. Jack and I and a couple more. Jack Granahan. He testified, too. He's from right here in Plains. He worked there for thirty-eight years, at Leslie Fay. Yeah, he was an ole-timer. Not really an ole-timer, but he just retired and he still workin' [part-time].

Q: Did you own stock or have some other way of speaking in Texas?

PN: Yeah, a stock certificate that we owned, so many shares in J. C. Penney.

Q: Did you get that from the union?

PN: Well, it was donated to us by "unknown."

Q: I see. And you spoke at this meeting?

PN: Yes, and [so did] Tim Wagner, who told them all about what was goin' on in Guatemala and what the working conditions were [like]—that they were pitiful. They have pictures of that. Then I got up and spoke on what they were doin' in Pennsylvania and other parts where they owned factories. J. C. Penney had a code of conduct, and we wanted to find out how they could make a contract with Leslie Fay when that was against their code of conduct. They did not believe in that and it sort of helped. Maybe it didn't stop it, but it did give the CEO thoughts about it.

We were going into the stores, and we were boycotting right at their headquarters. We had people come from Oklahoma, from AIM [Associate ILGWU Members], to make a big thing outside of this place. So you had some influence there. I think it was a help because after that they [the Leslie Fay executives] did agree to sit down, which they had not done before. . . . We were quite happy with how it turned out. We got a lot of media, a lot of press, you know. . . . And, of course, we had a lot of support. We had all the unions. The truckers' union, they would blow when they went by. We had people blowing at us as they went up and down [the highway] to show their [support], because we had signs [that read], "If you're with us, blow." And they would blow and there was a lot of activity. We had a lot of support.

They started to meet after that. We kept on with it. We had them pretty well bottled up here and there and all over, because New York knew, New Jersey knew, I mean they couldn't do too much without us knowin' it. After that trip, we went to New York, and then some of us went to Connecticut and Babcock's home, which he did not appreciate. They were getting a lot of pressure from the papers, especially our papers here. The news media and our TV stations were quite active, [such as] channel 28—28 is a union station, which followed a lot of things that we did. [Channel] 28 was a big help, WBRE-TV. The *Times Leader* gave us press, but they're nonunion. The *Citizens' Voice* is [pro-]union, so you'll see most of the articles there, but the *Times Leader* did have some spreads recently too, about when we went to Peerless in Canada. We were picketing outside [their store] to let them know [about Leslie Fay]. We were giving out shopping bags at Christmas to let the people know that they were selling suits, men's suits. They [Leslie Fay] made men's suits. And then we were there for Amanda Smith clothing sweatshops, as of right now, as of today. We wanted to let people know. . . .

Q: As I recall, Leslie Fay was the last big manufacturer in this area.

PN: Yes, Leslie Fay was the last big one. That's why they were so important because they employed a lot of people and they were very important. It hurt. I think after Leslie Fay left then other shops started to go, too, because they just couldn't compete. Everything was opened up, everything. Don't forget, when we started, everything was made in the USA and sold in the USA. Now you've come to the point where there's nothing made in the USA. They call it progress and they say, "Oh, we have to do this to stay competitive," and all that. I don't see how they're staying competitive when they're weakening the United States. . . .

Q: So you are still active in picketing, distributing information, and generally supporting the union?

PN: Oh yeah. In fact, we have an AIM chapter now, chapter 30. I am president of chapter 30.

Q: What is AIM?

PN: Associate ILGWU Member, which is now changed because there is no longer an ILG. It will become the Senior Citizens' Service Program later on. Now there's only about three [chapters] left. At one time it was like over four thousand members in the AIM. The ILG was active in all ways, you know. When you were old enough to retire, Marty Berger came up with AIM and he had over four thousand members. Marty Berger has been with the union for forty or fifty years. He's from Jersey. He worked out of New York and he worked out of Pennsylvania here. He's now state coordinator for the AIM, for the retirees.[10]

Q: What did you negotiate with Leslie Fay?

PN: We ended up getting an extra year that we weren't going to get. And then we did get our severance pay, thanks to the union. That was another help because a lot of them [i.e., garment companies] didn't [give it]. In fact, I don't think many did. So with the union, right to the end, we did get everything that we could. Then we got TRA [i.e., the Trade Relief Agreement; see app. 2] and help from that. . . .

Q: Was the New York union office helpful in this strike?

PN: Oh yeah. They held down the fort in New York where Leslie Fay had shops, too. That's where they [Leslie Fay] came here from. Sassco [Fashions] in Jersey, they were on strike. We went down to help them. In fact, we went down to help the Coca-Cola workers when they were on strike after our strike was over. We went to help the Teamsters when the truckers were on strike. [We had] fifty cars with their headlights on. I mean, we never stopped even though we went back to work for a year. [We helped with a strike at] the Coca-Cola plant right down here in Plains Township. . . .

Q: When you were striking at Leslie Fay, did you use any of the tactics and strategies from the old days with Min Matheson?

PN: We used quite a bit of what we learned from then, sure. Stopping their trucks, jumping on their trucks. Linda Whitaker jumped on a truck and about scared the guy to death. There was a lot that we used. We went in there wrapped in chains. We were gonna chain ourselves to the machines like they did in the old days. That's what you did in case the cops came in [to remove you from the factory].

Q: Did you chain yourself to machines?

PN: No. We had them concealed under our clothes. I don't think anybody ever knew we had [chains]. We were chained to each other, chained to ourselves. . . . Lois Hartel was very supportive in the Leslie Fay strike. She did everything for us, everything. She had everything down, everything done for us. And Linda Whitaker carried it off. She brought all those people together in the end when she started with a few, started with altogether eleven people.

Q: Did you ever think about Mrs. Matheson while you were on the picket lines?

PN: Oh, I always thought about Min because, like I said, Linda reminded me of her. We were very close. Marion Malachi, she was another business agent; she's an organizer now. Malachi, and Linda Whitaker, and Nancy Ziegler out of Philadelphia. Linda was from New York and Marion was [from] right here. Gee, I always thought of them as our tigers.

Q: The union still has tigers?

PN: Oh definitely. Yes they do. In fact, Linda was organizing in Reading and she was doing very well and, Marion, too, and Nancy. They're three very terrific women.

Q: And you're still a tiger?!

PEARL NOVAK

PN: Oh yeah. I'd be out there in a minute, in a heartbeat. I'd be out there with them and they know it. So, if they need us, we will be there and they know that. If Lois needs us, she only has to call. She knows we'll be there. . . .

Q: Were you ever arrested?

PN: No, I always kept out of it. There was just the one time that I was saved by Min. But no, I was never arrested.

Q: Were there any arrests during the last strike at Leslie Fay?

PN: I think there was one with Tom Matthews and one of the girls who overstepped into some situation. They were arrested but they were let go. They didn't spend any time [in jail] or anything. It was just that they crossed over on somebody's property, which they said was a mistake. This was not that kind of a strike.

Q: What keeps you so motivated after forty-eight years?

PN: Well, I guess I just love it. I loved the union, and I loved what they did for the people. They not only helped people when they needed it. You could go to the union and if you had a tough time of it, they would try to help you. They would try to get you a job. In Min's time, I mean, it was like thirty cents an hour. People were working for peanuts and they were working so hard. It was an eight-hour day, and it wasn't like we had it at Leslie Fay [where] nobody bothered you—you worked, you were on piecework, you worked hard but you worked for yourself under the union-negotiated contract. The money you made was [based on] how fast you worked and everything was for you. But in days [before the union] you worked hard and they were on ya, you know. The union took care of that. We had people on the shop committee that took care of each section, and if something went wrong, they went and fought for us. So in later years, we didn't have to fight that much because we had good people, a lot of good union people. That's why I stuck with it. And I still do, I still speak on it. In fact, I was just in the paper, in February, I think.

Q: For what?

PN: At Kaufman's [Department Store in the Wyoming Valley Mall].[11] We want them to take responsibility for what they do. Oh yeah, I'm still involved. Everybody says it's the beginning of the end. I think it will be an end of a beginning. There's already sweatshops. Everything that was there years ago is being done now in every state in the union, and they're getting away with it. I mean there's home shops, there's [garments] being made in the prisons, which would not have ever happened if there was a union. Seem there's things going on today that I think are even worse because we know what to do about it. But today they don't care as much. They don't care about the neighbor or the people that are hurt. They don't care as much. People never move until they're burned and then you see how fast they get up and get together and they'll fight. They'll have to fight 'cause there's nothing left here.

Then, how long do you think overseas is gonna [continue like it is]? You think they're not gonna start a fire there? How long do you think they're gonna live in poverty while these overseers—and that's what they are, overseers—are there with guns and everything in the factory. They proved that. How long do you think those people are gonna take it? There'll be uprisings over there.

These Americans, they forgot that this country was fought hard for, and to undermine it like they're doing, I mean they should all be ashamed. It's corporations. It's corporations that did this without any thought of the people or what was gonna happen to them or anything like that because everybody's not gonna be a computer expert, let me tell ya. People forty and forty-five [years old] who I know have been to school and they can't even get jobs. Your biggest problem is those part-timers now because senior citizens, or your retirees, can't live on what they're getting. They have to go out and get part-time jobs. So they started that part-time work. Now, everybody's on part-time. Very few people are working on full-time with benefits. This is another thing: you have fewer full-time workers, but you'll have all these people who will come in from nine o'clock to twelve noon or four in the afternoon to eight in the evening, and work four hours—four hours here, four hours there. Right?

Q: The union—which is now called UNITE! after a merger with the Amalgamated—do you think it's doing what it should be to meet current problems?

PN: They're trying. They're trying. They are going to colleges and talking—there is a summer union thing where the young people are learning about unions. They started that. They certainly are trying, if a little bit late. But if you don't try, you don't succeed. We're still in it trying to help out even though we're retired. We're still involved in the union and what they do. . . .

Q: Where are people working locally nowadays after the garment jobs have gone?

PN: I guess some of them [i.e., former garment workers] went to school. A lot don't even have jobs. A lot are lookin'. A lot can't find [work]. Now with the welfare [i.e., the ILGWU Health and Welfare fund] shuttin' down, I don't know what they're gonna do. I have no idea. I think it will result in possibly more crime, which is already shown. I think people, if they are desperate enough, there will be robbing. They won't be safe. They'll have to bring out more police. I mean, you won't be safe in your own home because when people have to feed a family, they're gonna do it. They're gonna do it before they'll see them starve, right? Everything's rosy and everything's good, if you believe statistics. But that can't always be believed. . . .

What they don't foresee is the future. I know [President] Clinton says he wants us to cross that bridge into the twenty-first century. I think he better realize that, unless we're all together, half are gonna be back there and the other half are gonna go [forward]. You have to have everything together. The only way you're gonna win anything here in the United States is by sticking together. The people have to have the say.

Clinton was not everybody's choice. A lot of people didn't really want him. The people still have the power. The people have the power, if they only knew

PEARL NOVAK

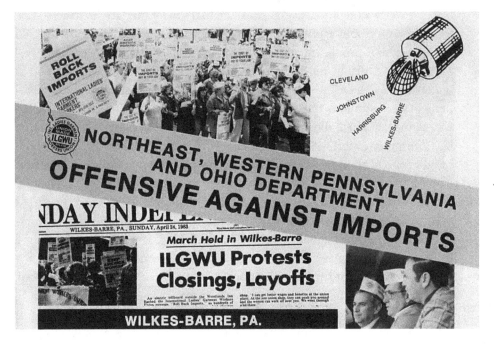

FIG. 45 | Anti-import campaign flyer distributed by the ILGWU on April 24, 1983. Photo courtesy of the Kheel Center, Cornell University.

it. The only way they'll ever win is to stick together, when they all stand up, like they did in the old days and fought. I know that was the past and this is the future. A lot of things are going back to the past and that's where we should've learned; that's where the United States should have learned. They opened the United States [market] to everybody [i.e., other countries' garments]—that's fine. You make some, we'll make some. But don't ever leave us with 10 percent and 90 percent from you. We're weakening our own country. This is the country we fought for. That we have pride in—we still have pride in. That's what the younger people have to know. And that's where unions will make it a lot better.

Q: Are you optimistic about the future?

PN: [We need to] have these older people let them [i.e., the younger people] know what happened in those days, let them know how bad we had it. People do not know. People do not bother to read anymore. People don't care. "It's goin' good, the stock market's up." What's that mean? Stock market could be down in no time. Unions were up. They fought. They got on top. Did they forget what they learned? I'd say they did. But they can go back [up], they're gonna go back [up], and they're gonna rebuild. Then everybody's gonna rebuild. You know, forty years ago they laughed when, in the funny papers and in these comic books, they'd have a man on the moon. We did. We laughed years ago, but we did it! . . .

Q: What's your favorite memory of Min Matheson?

PN: My favorite, I guess, would be that she cared. She cared for the people and she did her utmost to stand by them, no matter what. Whether she was getting flak from whoever at the time, she would stand by her people. I think the most [important] thing about her is that I *learned*. I learned an awful lot. She taught me. She taught me a lot of things that in later life I used, as in Leslie Fay. We used a lot [from her] because she taught us all the way to '63, and after that we still had good people here that could continue her work, until things started to get really bad.

There wasn't anything she couldn't do, and there wasn't anything she wouldn't do, for the union. Her heart was for the union, which was proved when her brother [Will Lurye] was stabbed in New York. I was with her that time. She got a telephone call when she was addressing a meeting, and she went to the phone. That's when they told her. She was a brave lady. She came back out and finished and then left for New York. She was a great lady.[12]

She is the foundation of this union, especially in this Valley. There was nobody like her, you know. Everything that she did, it still comes out today because of the people she taught. A lot of them were still in the factories in 1994 when we had the strike at Leslie Fay.[13] There were still a lot of people that had been in the union and who knew [what to do]. Besides, there were people that came from New York, like Linda Whitaker. To me, she was a second Min Matheson. She had charisma. She got people to follow her on that [Leslie Fay] strike.

Q: Some people have said that Min Matheson was fearless.

PN: Yes, she was. Yes, she was. She had guts you wouldn't believe. She would go out and do things that nobody [would do]. Everybody was afraid, but she would [go].

Q: Mobsters?

PN: They did not faze her. No, she would ride through the city, Pittston, on a truck with her kids. Somebody called Min Matheson a "slut" once and she drove through Pittston with her kids. She took her kids on a truck. She drove through, right through Pittston. She was fearless, fearless![14]

15

Betty Greenberg
Mother, Spouse, Activist, and the Mathesons' Daughter

FIG. 46
Betty Greenberg, 1995.
Photo courtesy of the
Northeastern Pennsylvania
Oral and Life History
Collection, Pennsylvania
State University.

Betty (Matheson) Greenberg,
from an audio-recorded
interview with Robert P.
Wolensky conducted at
Mrs. Greenberg's home in
Kingston, Pennsylvania,
on January 11, 1995. The
interview is included in
the Wyoming Valley Oral
History Project, which is one
of eight projects within the
Northeastern Pennsylvania
Oral and Life History Collec-
tion housed in the Eberly
Family Special Collections
Department, Penn State
University Libraries.

Betty Greenberg recalls in vivid detail numerous aspects of her life as the child of two well-known ILGWU and community leaders. She also provides important insights into her parents' public, union, and personal trials. In telling the stories, she benefits not only from a strong memory, but also from participation in regular family discussions and events as she was growing up. She recalls exciting times on picket lines, as well as difficult times when her parents underwent federal investigations as Communists in the 1950s. She paints a remarkable picture of her father's intellectualism and progressivism, as well as her mother's dedication to "her girls" and her constant battles with organized crime and certain New York union leaders.

BG: My mother and my father were quite good at their jobs because they believed in it. They believed very much in the fact that human beings should not allow themselves to be put in a position where they have nothing to say about what they earn, and nothing to say about how they work. We should not allow locked shops and sweatshops and children working. I mean, that was all very much a part of their thought, and so they organized.

Many, many times my mother would be called to do various things in other places for the same reason. They [the ILGWU union officials] would never give her proper due, but they knew her ability. So they would just milk it. They never wanted to say, "Min did this." They would then step in and say they did it.

Whatever it was, like one time when she was pregnant with my sister, they called her to come to work because they had a really tough time organizing a factory out on Long Island. They called her to come out [from Sayre, Pennsylvania] to talk to the girls. It was in one of these theaters, a huge movie theater, and she walked in pregnant.

She just said one sentence to them and it would have to do with, "I'm one of you," [that] was the way she started. "Let me tell you, if you don't join," something about "If you don't join the union, you're always going to be where you are now." Something like that, but it was much more clever and she had them immediately. Everybody else that had gotten up and tried to talk to these girls, [they got] "Boo! Boo!" Wouldn't even let them talk. Don't ask me how she did it. She had them and she was so pregnant at the time. And, of course, they [the other ILGWU officials] took credit for it, but they never forgot it.

They were always amazed at whatever she did all through her years. She knew how to organize, and that's all I can say. She always believed in not leaving things to chance. If you're having a meeting and you want people to come, you don't say, "We're having a meeting. We hope you come." You've got to do a little work. You've got to tell the people why you want them to come and why it's important for them to come, because people have things to do. . . .

Q: When your mother and father began organizing, they took on the runaway shops, as the term was used, out of New York City.

BG: The union hated it [the runaway shop drive], resented it, and fought her tooth and nail. One of the biggest ones that went out of New York was Leslie Fay. My mother was definitely instrumental in getting them here.

Q: How so?

BG: The union said, "No way will they be allowed to open a factory here." She went into New York, she begged and fought, and finally she said, "Look, we need it. The people here have no work, they have no money. We need it." They [the New York union leaders] said, "Oh, we don't care." So she went around to back doors and she made a lot of enemies. She said, "Let them come. So one hundred girls will get work. How much work would you lose?"

Of course, Leslie Fay became a very, very big problem to New York because, after all, this was Leslie Fay. [Eventually] this area [the Wyoming Valley] *was* Leslie Fay. There were, I think, several shops here that were Leslie Fay's—plus a big factory that had thousands of people working in it. [Their factories were] all over the place. So, in the end, I guess they [the New York union] had to worry. They were right, but the fact is that she knew the people needed jobs here.

My mother had to worry about the people she represented. Most of the people that worked for the union listened to what the union officials told them to do.

BETTY GREENBERG

FIG. 47 | Twentieth-anniversary banquet for the ILGWU Wyoming Valley District, 1957. Photo courtesy of the ILGWU Wyoming Valley District Archives, Kheel Center, Cornell University.

My mother represented the people that she represented, if you can follow that. She represented the people from here; this is what they needed. She can't be worried about what New York needs. . . .

They [her mother and father] were courageous and the people felt they were with them. When there was a fight, they could count on them. All those things went into it. . . . And then when there were picket lines and there were some serious times, it was important for my mother to show that she wasn't afraid—that she had a lot of belief in what the girls were doing. She would take my sister and me to the picket line. One time my father was going to "shoot" [severely criticize] her because he was furious with her. And then later she realized he was right. The *owner* of the factory came and stuck us [kids] in his car and took us away.

Q: Was that picket line in Pittston?

BG: Yes. That's when we were very little. But there were many other times. One time I asked to go [on the picket line] when a factory was having a very bad fight and they'd been on strike for a long time. It was coming near Christmas. [The picket line was at] Emkay [in Wyoming, Pennsylvania]. They made bras and girdles, and the girls had a tent in the front. I went with her. That was something to see. When she got there, it meant everything to them, everything. It was about six thirty in the morning and it was cold; it was November. She had said to my father, "Bill, wake me." He said, "But, Min, you're so tired." She said, "Wake me, Bill, it's important. I've got to go out there." It was dark and I wanted to go, so we went. "Min's here!" they said, "Min's here! Put the coffee on!" One of the things about my mother, she could be dragging and she'd get that adrenaline going, and then, "Let's sing a song, girls!"

Then afterwards, coming back home, now my mother didn't drive. Today it would be unheard of but it was much different then. So my father was driving us, and she said, "Oh, poor girls [i.e., the strikers]." My mother said, "Oh, Bill, I feel so badly. So badly. They [the strikers] are not going even be able to buy their kids presents for Christmas." They both, really, genuinely felt badly, not "made up" badly, but really badly. "Shoot, we have to do something. We've got to do something."

And they did do some things. They went out and bought some things and brought them to the girls to give to their kids. Many, many years later, we were shopping and my mother was retired a long time. We met some of the girls from the Emkay. "Didn't we have fun? The best time in my life was that horrible strike." I can't tell you what it did for my mother. It was like somebody lifted this huge guilt for all the strikes because it was a burden to her.

Q: How old were you during the Emkay strike?

BG: Oh, god . . . eleven.

Q: You had school that day?

BG: Oh sure.

Q: And you were back in time?

BG: Yeah, we went there [to the strike] early in the morning.

Q: Why did you want to go?

BG: Oh, I loved it. I loved to be with my parents. At the time, we were at that age when my parents had more or less stopped protecting us completely, although they were still very protective. We never knew when there were really hard times. They never told us. I don't know why. When my Uncle Will [Lurye] was killed [1949], we had to be picked up and taken to school every day for well over a year, about sixteen months. We knew there was a reason. My father [would say], "Don't get in anybody's car; don't go with anybody." "OK." You know I was little, I was five when my Uncle Will was killed. Yeah. What did it mean to us? Nothing. "Oh, goody, we don't have to walk." That's all it meant.

We didn't know my mother would go on the air [i.e., radio]. Somebody would say something at school [like] "Your mother with her big mouth." We didn't even know she was on the radio. I think I heard my mother on the radio once. She would be on the radio when we were still in school; school was 'til 3:30 p.m. She would go on Little Bill Phillips's program at 3:00 p.m., or 2:30 p.m., somewhere around there, and we never heard her. I didn't know what people [were talking about]. This was how sheltered we were. We never knew what in the hell was going on.

BETTY GREENBERG

One time she was having a terrible strike. One of the people [owners] she was having a strike with, we were friends with his children. And there was a bomb scare [at our house]. [The owner said to my mother], "You send them over to our house." So we went to their house, which was really weird if you think about it.

Q: He was the shop owner?

BG: Of one of the [striking] factories. We were friends with his daughters. My mother called us and said, "You've gotta get out of the house, kids—there could be problems." We said, "Could we go to Sue's?" And she said, "Sure." Never told us they were fighting with Jerry. Never. Never said anything. We never knew. My mother called him to thank him. He said, "Are you crazy, Min? Ridiculous. One thing has nothing to do with the other."

Sometimes we would know the kids and the guy that we were fighting with, and he would make some snide remark to us when we were at their house. Happened to me once, and I still remember because my mother could never get along with him. See, he brought it to his personal life. Most people didn't. Kids were kids. That's how my parents pretty much brought us up. We were to have a nice, normal childhood. Not be hurt, but so many people in school would hold it against us and we didn't even know it. We didn't know what they [our parents] were doing. . . .

That's another thing: a lot of our friends didn't understand why we were so political—politically interested in all things—because they didn't care about politics. That was sort of another really nice thing. They [our parents] included us in their conversations. We didn't always understand what they were saying, but they included us. When the McCarthy hearings were going on [in the 1950s], we were like ready to jump ship. That was day and night, that they had the [U.S. Senate] McCarthy hearings on, and that was a scary time for my parents, but we didn't know, they never told us.

Q: Why was it scary for them?

BG: They were going to come after them. Westbrook Pegler had written an article, nationally syndicated article, stating that my mother was a Communist.[1] He said they should come and look for her here, and then ensued a discussion about whether they [the ILGWU] should take her out of the Valley. Would her ability to organize and lead the people be accepted under the circumstances?

Q: Was the New York office considering that?

BG: Right. And, oh god, my mother was involved with the Chamber of Commerce and they were involved with Wilkes College. Other people [supported them]. Rev. Dr. Jule Ayres, Dr. Albert Feinberg, and the guy that headed the Chamber of Commerce, Bill Sword. He went to New York and said, "What the hell are you thinking about? Take Min out of here? Don't be foolish. The girls know exactly who she is and what she is, and they know she's not a Communist."

Q: Why would Westbrook Pegler write that?

BG: Oh, he was out to ruin her. I guess there's a lot of reasons. Someone put him up to it.

Q: I wonder who would put him up to it?

BG: Mafia, *the* Mafia. Maybe he didn't know they were mafioso, but definitely [they were]. You know, J. Edgar Hoover hated her. I'd like to send for that [FBI dossier]. I should do that. She knows that it's huge. Somebody told her. A friend of theirs told her that she has a huge file. And my father does, too. They were always trying to find things against them.

I told you what Charlie Adams said when he investigated my father. He was the FBI investigator and he went all over the country, including Wisconsin and Illinois, all over that area, because that's where my father started out. He was trying to find somebody that would know him, to see what they had to say about him. He interviewed people in the neighborhood [in Kingston, Pennsylvania] and everywhere. He said, "I've never gone out and interviewed hundreds of people and not had at least one of them say something against the person that I'm investigating." He added, "Not one bad thing was ever said about him. Just the opposite."

My father was the kind of a person that would pitch in if he stayed in someone's house and they were gonna be late coming home. He'd make the meal. If the floor needed to be washed, he'd wash the floor. Most women never saw a man do that kind of thing. I mean, that's a long time ago. If somebody needed help, he gave them help. He always took menial jobs in those days, because he believed very strongly in the workingman. People would say, "Bill, Bill with your ability you can write. Why are you doing this? Such a waste." He'd say, "Hard work is never a waste. That's what we should all be doing. We're all equals, there should be no separation." 'Cause that's what he believed and he really lived, both of them lived, their life like they were never anything [better than anyone else]. They were all workers trying to survive.

Q: Going back to the McCarthy hearings, it was indeed the case that your parents belonged to the Communist Party at one time, correct?

BG: Right. Well, my mother was a member of the Young Communist League, and my father was an actual [member]—because he was thirteen years older than my mother—of the Communist Party. He was a Canadian, and there were [coal] mines in his area of Nova Scotia—and not much better conditions than there were around here during the heyday of the mines. There was that strata of the wealthy owners and the company store, same thing. He was very, very strong, very interested in getting that changed.

During that time, they asked him if he wanted to run for Parliament. He didn't believe in that kind of thing. He felt that, "We're workingmen, we don't put ourselves above." People tried to tell him at the time that they needed someone to represent them. He said, "No. I'm afraid I can't do that," because he had that feeling of wanting to be part of change rather than in charge of what was there. I don't know why.

My sister tested my father when she went to graduate school and was taking psychology. He tested well over 186 in his IQ. He could do just about any job, and he took many jobs. I mean he worked as a lumberjack, he worked as a plumber, he worked as a window washer, and always they would say, "Why are you doing this? Why don't you [do something better]? You wrote pamphlets, why don't you just write pamphlets?" Or "You make such a good speech, why don't you go around making speeches?" "No, no I've gotta do this," [he'd say].

For many years he was like that. People would always find him to have that kind of mind and they would always push him to make the speeches. He made a lot of social security speeches [before the Social Security Act was passed in 1935] and got arrested lots of times, which came out around the time of the McCarthy hearings when they were looking for Communists. That was a disgusting time. They tried to get people. They went to my parents' friends, tried to get them to say they were Communists, to get them in trouble.

Q: Here in the Wyoming Valley?

BG: Yes, everywhere. People would laugh [and say], "Communists? They're not Communists, they're Democrats." And, oh, [charged the government], "They're Communists?" My father was going to be deported! They had a trial. The only reason Marianne [i.e., her sister] and I knew about the trial was because they were told by their lawyer that they should bring the kids, so they would see he's a family man. You know how that looks? It's important. It's horrible, but it's important.

Q: What year was that?

BG: I think I was nine, so about 1954, '55 maybe.

Q: Was he tried here?

BG: No, in Philadelphia, by a federal court.

Q: What was the charge?

BG: I guess treason—not treason, un-American activities. All those speeches. Well, by then, Social Security was in [the law], and when the judge looked down, he said, "Arrests? Mostly these arrests were because you were speaking on behalf of Social Security." The judge looked up [and said], "People got arrested for speaking on Social Security?" Because, once it was passed [in 1935], everybody acted like it was always there. So I don't understand why he [my dad] was given such a hard time.

Q: I gather your dad gave those speeches in the twenties and thirties?

BG: Yeah. In the twenties and the thirties. All over the place. Never went back to Canada. He was not a citizen here—he was in this country illegally. That was one of the other charges: he was in the country illegally!

Q: Did he ever become a citizen?

BG: After that. It was quite a thing for him. . . . Never until I was much older did I realize that it really was a good possibility—they thought he was going to be deported. They could not believe that he wasn't. One of the big reasons, Charlie Adams later told them, was because there wasn't one person who said a bad thing about him. When they went around the neighborhood [checking on him], people said my mother was "an old battle-ax!" Two different people said the same thing. "But Mr. Matheson is a fine man"—that's what they said.

Q: Was your mother ever arrested?

BG: Oh god, yeah. But she never stayed in jail. She always got out. But he was actually put in jail [in Canada].

Q: Why was your mother arrested?

BG: Striking—once in the Valley and a few times in Chicago in the earlier years. You know her father was from the cigar makers' union and, I mean, that was his whole life. He would go to work for a week in a cigar factory and the next thing they were on strike. I think one time he made it for three weeks, but mostly he was on strike. Which meant nothing [i.e., no money], 'cause there were no benefits in those days, there was nothing. That meant no money, which is why my grandmother went to work. Oh, my poor grandmother. Well, my mother never told us much about her mother, 'cause my mother was much more of a strong advocate of her father, which was pretty sad 'cause I really think that my mother got her brains from my grandmother. . . .

Q: Where did your mother work in the early years?

BG: Well, when she first left school, she worked for [Communist Party leader] Jay Lovestone, as a secretary.

Q: That was in the ninth grade?

BG: Yes.

Q: She was that good?

BG: She was not good in typing, although she could type, and she wasn't that good at shorthand, although she could take shorthand, 'cause that was one of the things she had been taught. When you graduated from the ninth grade, it was really a big deal. Very few people went to high school in those years. It was almost like going to college. So they had these huge graduations from the ninth grade; that was a big deal.

By then, I guess she had a fairly decent education and she was smart. She knew a lot of things that other people did not know. Let's face it, [it was] because of her background with her father and labor. They hid out people from the Palmer Raids [of 1920] in their house. God almighty, it's a wonder they didn't all get put in prison. I guess she just had the lingo, and the ability, and whatever else.

So she went to work for him [Lovestone] and she worked for him for quite a while [in New York]. Then she was part of the Young Communist group. She said one of the worst things that ever happened to her was when she turned eighteen, somebody said, "Some of these people don't belong in it [i.e., the Young Communist League USA], because they're so old." She realized they were talking about her. All her life she never thought of herself as old. Even when she was old, she didn't think of herself as old. So she was surprised. That was the one time age bothered her. She knew she had to leave. But it was right around the time when things had changed.

It was during that period of time when she met my father. She said he was so clean, and tall, and he was handsome. My father was almost six foot and in

BETTY GREENBERG

that day that was very tall. He was thirty years old when she first met him. She was eighteen and she'd follow him around. And he would be like, "That little girl is following me around again." He wasn't in the least bit interested in her. She would try everything she could think of to get him interested in her. Then one day, he heard her speak, she made a speech, and my mother could speak, she could speak well. She knew how to put words together so well to get her point across. She never bored people. She never went on like a river. My father was a good speaker, but he was also a very factual speaker, and if he wrote a speech, he stuck to the speech. My mother always ad-libbed. She knew when she was losing the people, where he would continue with the speech as written.

When she went to speak before the U.S. Senate and Congress [in the 1950s], on how bad the Valley was doing economically, she saw that they were bored by the statistics [of earlier speakers]. They'd heard a million statistics. You know how you go to a thing on economics and one person after another gets up and says 10 percent of the population is working, 33 percent of the population is . . . and after a while you're like . . . [bored]. She thought, "They're not even listening." She noticed some of the people were asleep. When she got up, she didn't give any statistics. She said, "You've already heard the statistics so I don't have to go into them. But I'm going to tell you . . ." And she told stories. Now my father had written her speech and he was not happy that she didn't read the speech as it was written. But she said, "I would've lost them, Bill. They were already sick of it, sick to the teeth of hearing [a read speech]."

Q: Was that in the fifties?

BG: In the late fifties. I think it was '58.

Q: That was before Senator Jack Kennedy's committee?[2]

BG: Yeah. I wish we had seen that. She was shaking, she said, but they gave her a standing ovation. That grip, see? Whatever it was. For everybody else, it was a little polite applause when they sat down. But not her, because she always had the touch. *(crying)* I'm not crying 'cause my mother's dead. I always cry when I tell that story 'cause I'm very proud of her. . . .

Q: Did they leave Chicago and go to New York together?

BG: Yeah. My mother went to work in a dress shop for the money. It didn't take long for her to be recognized and asked to be an official of the union.

Q: Why did they go to New York?

BG: To do work for the Party, period. What they were told to do, and what they did there—I have to be honest—I only know some stories. I don't know actually why they went to New York or how they went to New York. I just know the Party sent them. And my father was away a lot. My mother has lots of letters from my father. My mother figured my father was dumping her because he was away for a very long time. She was heartbroken, absolutely heartbroken. He was off on the road, going all over the place, all over the country.

Q: Speaking?

BG: Yes. . . .

Q: You said your mother was very naïve about a lot of things.

BG: Oh, very. Men made passes at my mother and my mother would always dismiss it. When we got older, we would notice. I would anyway. Marianne was a little bit like my mother. She just didn't see things, but I always saw things like that. I would say, "So-and-so made a pass at you." "Oh no he didn't." I shouldn't even tell this, but one time she was going up the steps and [name] pinched her behind. My mother was heavy at the time, and, of course, when we women are chubby we don't think anybody thinks of us in that way. We only think that men would be interested in us if we looked nice. She was so shocked. I had told her that I thought he liked her. So the two together sort of scared her. She passed it off and said, "Oh him. Aren't you getting carried away?" She was propositioned once by someone and that just about ruined their relationship. She said, "I'm very complimented, but you know how much I love Bill."

Q: Was it a person in the union?

BG: Yes. [A union official] called her in her room at a convention, and he told her in no uncertain terms to be in his room. She said to him, "That will *never* happen." After that he made her life miserable, miserable.

Q: Was that sort of thing expected in the ILG? Was it common?

BG: Well, I think that men thought my mother had a lot of fire, and they thought the fires burned sexually. Little did they know her. Wow! Because that was the last thing [on her mind].

Q: How did the union official make life difficult for her?

BG: Oh, he made it hell for her. One of the things was Leslie Fay. He was one of the people instrumental in not wanting Leslie Fay to leave [New York]. He was going to definitely [keep the company there], and he was not going to allow [it]. He was not allowing her that. The funny thing is, we loved [name]. I mean, we thought he was a friend. And this is another thing: my parents never told us that this man made trouble for her. They never told us anybody ever made trouble for them until many years later.

Q: As I recall, your mother's friend, Jennie Silverman, said in her interview that this person gave her some trouble.[3]

BG: Oh god, yeah. He went after everybody and my mother said to him the thing about my father, but she also said, "I could *never* do that to [his spouse's name]." The funny thing is, she got the blame whether she played the [game or not]. Because [spouse's name] hated her, always thought she had an affair with her husband. Now, whether he said something to her, my mother never knew. After that for years, for years [spouse's name] hated her. We didn't know this, and we would say hello to them and kiss them and hug them when we saw them.

Q: Did your mother's naïveté ever come up with Dubinsky?

BG: Always. They all thought she wanted something. They all thought she wanted to be on the [International] Executive Board. Some people thought she wanted to be president of the union. If you'd ask the girls here, they all thought she was! . . .

BETTY GREENBERG

But they always thought she was after something. One time Dubinsky called her into New York and asked her what she was after. She knew somebody had been putting a bug in his ear. She said, "I'd like a few more factories for the girls." He said, "No, no, no. What do *you* want?" She said, "What do *I* want?" She laughed and said, "Well, I hope my little girls grow up and things go well for them." "No, no, no, no, no," he said to her. "Don't play a game." She absolutely did not know what he was talking about.

Finally it dawned on her, and she said, "I don't *want* anything. I'm perfectly happy where I am." He said, "I don't think so. That's not what I hear. That's not what I hear." She said, "Well, whoever's telling you that is not telling you the truth." But it didn't matter because they always believed it.

There were people around here that were told my mother was going to run for [political] office, and they believed it. That was also what [they assumed] she was going to get out of [her FVAC leadership during] the flood [of 1972], because there always had to be a reason for killing yourself. I mean, my mother used to work eighteen-hour days. Why would she do that? Six days a week. Why would she be doing that if she wasn't "ambitious"? Well, *they* were all ambitious, but she wasn't. She was trying to do something for people and, really, I think that's what made [local union] people accept and believe in her. She never spoke down to people. She never got up and lorded over them. Never. . . .

Q: Can you tell us about the union pay and salary situation of your parents?

BG: Well, with my parents there's two things. My mother was always paid less than anybody that worked in New York. It didn't matter that her membership was larger than almost every other local in the country, other than some [in] New York. She was paid less than everyone. And my mother and father were paid as if they were one person.

Q: They received one paycheck?

BG: Well, they each got a paycheck but it was divided. My mother would make thirty-five dollars and my father would make twenty-five dollars. My mother made more money than my father because she was the manager. Then there came a point when my father was head of the Northeast Educational Department. He made, at that point, I think he made seventy-five dollars and my mother made seventy-five dollars. I don't know if they made that much ever, 'cause when my mother went to New York and my father was retired, they promised her that she would made $200 a week, and before she retired she still hadn't gotten that much money.[4] Unlike most people that worked for unions, there were no freebies. The only freebies my mother ever got was discounts at factories, if she went there to get her clothing. At Christmastime, a million people would send her gifts, which was a standing joke because my mother would give them back. Two different times she gave a gift to somebody who had given her that gift the previous year. She was never interested in that kind of thing.

Q: So they received two paychecks, split in half. What was the logic there?

FIG. 48 | ILGWU General Executive Board, 1940–42; Rose Pesotta (*front row, second on left*) is the lone woman member. Photo courtesy of the Kheel Center, Cornell University.

BG: Well, they said that there was a rule that husbands and wives couldn't work for the union at the same time. My parents never wanted to make a stink about it. That's what they said. Then the other thing was, my parents felt it was that old thing about taking money for what you were [supposed to be] doing. That ideology my parents believed in pretty strongly. They never felt they should ask for more than what they needed. When Marianne and I were both in college at the same time that was a real hardship for them. They went to New York and asked for more money and they got a fifteen-dollars-a-week raise. That was the only time they ever asked for more money.

Q: Of course, New York was fully aware of their pay situation.

BG: Oh yeah, absolutely. My mother [told Dubinsky] that "It's sort of hard when you send people in to work underneath me that earn more money than I do." Dubinsky was embarrassed but then he said that they [other union officials] had to feed a family in New York and the cost of living was higher. Rose Brader was the head of the United Fund in town, the Community Chest. She and my mother were meeting for lunch one time and my mother said, "Oh, dear, I'm not going to have time to get to the bank," because the banks closed at three o'clock. Rose said, "Well, how much is the check for?" My mother, I think she was getting

BETTY GREENBERG

forty-five [dollars]. Rose said, "What is that, your expense account, Min?" My mother said, "No, I don't have an expense account; that's my paycheck." . . .

Q: Why do you think she was transferred to New York in 1963.

BG: That was to get rid of her. They wanted her out of here because of the Mafia business. I mean, she knew that. They [the ILGWU officials] were making deals. They made deals with the Mafia for many years.

Q: Who did?

BG: The union [in New York]. And she was not making deals. She didn't know they were making deals at the time. She didn't find that out until long after she retired that they had made deals.

Q: What kind of deals?

BG: Well, let's say we'll look the other way at your factories that are in blah, blah, blah [towns]. We won't bother [to unionize] you. Those kinda deals. One of them was Three-Finger Brown's [i.e., Thomas Lucchese's] factory in Sweet Valley. She fought him tooth and nail. They [the ILGWU leaders in New York] called her in over and over again: why is she fighting like this for this little factory? She very naïvely but honestly said, "If we let this one go, we're gonna lose all of them," and she wasn't gonna let it go. They would have had to say to her, "We're making deals, and this is part of the deal." Well, in the end they finally said to her, "You've gotta let this one [i.e., some specific shop] go." She got the message. But they wanted her out of here.[5]

Q: Was Dubinsky still in office when she was transferred?

BG: Dubinsky was still there. Stolberg was the vice president. Dubinsky, after she retired, called her into New York and asked her to organize the South. My mother started to laugh [and said], "Not me, I'm too old. I'm sick. I'm not going to go organizing the South. What are you talking about?" That was the first time that he ever said to her that she had any ability. Well, it wasn't just a compliment. He admitted to her that she, he actually said, word for word, "Well, you always could get the people and we need someone like you." She said to him, because by then she was very angry about a lot of things, "It's too bad that you didn't recognize that all I ever wanted was that." She had no reason to be afraid anymore. Not that she was afraid. I can't say that she was afraid because one time she quit, and he had to come to her.

Q: What was that about?

BG: He wanted her to put the girls out on strike. It was really a New York maneuver because it wasn't necessary for the Valley. She said, "I'm not going to do it. I'm not gonna do it. You just raised the girls' dues fifty cents. That fifty cents is a lot of money to them. A lot of money. And you're not gonna do this. They can't afford it. They don't need it, and you're not gonna do it." They had a very bad argument and she said, "I'll walk out and I will tell every single member of the press why I'm doing it." He thought she'd back down, and she didn't because she really felt it was a wrong thing to do. See, these were the reasons she was never very popular and they were so afraid of her.

I'll tell you one thing, [attorney and later federal circuit judge] Max Rosenn said of her, "Well, you're looking for headlines," but that was not the way he put it. It was very derogatory the way he put it. He said, "You're just a headline-seeker." In any case, he never [really] knew my mother. I said to her, "Why do we always have to have the press?" She said, "Betty, what the hell good is it if we have a big meeting and nobody knows about it? What are we going to get done? What good it going to be? People have to know that three hundred people are meeting and saying, 'We don't like what's being done.' What's the point of it? It would be just three hundred people having a secret meeting and going home?" She said, "We've got to have the press there. They have to hear the people, how angry they are." And she was right. Even if it was one person saying it to the press, it would mean something rather than have three hundred people meet secretly and nobody knows about it. But Max never wanted to see it that way. . . .[6]

Q: Was your mother hurt by the transfer to New York?

BG: Well, [when she was here] she saw ahead nothing but fight after fight with New York, and fights with the people [i.e., union members] because they didn't want the strike [of 1959].[7] If the people you're representing say to you, "I don't want a strike. We don't need the money," is it right to make them go on strike? To give up their money? Is it fair to do that to them? [Is it fair] if four hundred people vote that they don't want to strike and you make them strike because New York said to strike? She was absolutely right. They ruined themselves, a lot of them.

She knew who they were fighting. They were fighting people like my husband who have a small business—some years [the business is] not so bad, and other years terrible—not people that were wealthy manufacturers.[8] I mean, yes, there were the Leslie Fays, but there were mostly little guys that owned little factories that were making a living. That is, they weren't millionaires. They couldn't afford to pay whatever the union was asking for. One after another factories went out of business here. I know there's good and there's bad, and sometimes the union has to step back and say, "Look, these people need their jobs."

Q: When you were speaking about New York calling the Wyoming Valley District out on strike, what was the upshot of the strike?

BG: My mother wouldn't take the girls out. That was really . . . that was one of the straws. This is how she ended up. They [the New York union officials] couldn't very well get her out [because] the people loved her here. They couldn't very well remove [i.e., fire] her. Between the business of fighting the Mafia, and not bending, and not listening to what she was told to do, they constantly tried to get her out of here. Constantly. All through the years. Made her life miserable. A few people that she trained backstabbed her all the time, all the time. They all thought she wanted something. . . .

Q: Did New York reprimand her for not going on strike?

BG: Oh god, they wanted to fire her. Times were changing and the wind was blowing the way it is now [i.e., in an unsettling direction]. The people loved her. That wasn't the first time they tried to get rid of her. They tried many times. But the people loved her.

Q: Did she know they were trying to get her? Or was her naïveté at work here, too?

BG: That time she knew. One of the reasons she went to New York was because she knew they weren't going to rest. They were always gonna make her life miserable and she thought she'd take the Union Label job. I'll tell you something else they did to her with the Union Label job. My mother gets to New York and the first thing she did, she sat down one day and drew a [new] union label. That's the union label they use now! Never got any credit for it. Never got mentioned for it, never got any claim for it, whatsoever. But she designed the union label that's used now.

When she got to New York, whoever was in there before her was getting kickbacks. When they heard—you know, my mother and father—what they were gonna charge her to have these union labels made, she went back to Wilkes-Barre and talked to people here and had them made here for one-sixteenth of the money! Never thought anything of it.

Then whenever she'd had leaflets made or anything [printed], she'd have them made here. So somebody told somebody who told somebody [in New York], "She must be getting kickbacks." Yeah, to make trouble for her. Didn't look down at the books. Just imagine how stupid they were not to have looked at the books first. Here's a book that says $60,000 for so many union labels. Min's having them made for $3,000? We're not talking a $100 or fifty cents. What's going to be the kickback? What kind of kickback do you think they're gonna be giving for their making the same union labels? How much could they give her? They didn't even look at the books, they just heard what she was doing and they called her in. It was a friend, a close friend that she was giving the [leaflet] business to [see George and Lucy Zorgo, chap. 10].

So, of course, they made it even worse for her. She didn't know what the hell they were talking about. She said, "What are you talking about, kickbacks?" She said, "Do you know what they [the previous director's office] were paying for those labels?" It was gross. It was $50,000 more than what she was paying for them. It was huge. "Well, how could you make them so cheap where you're going?" She said, "That's what they charged [in Wilkes-Barre]." "Well, what are you getting out of it?" "I'm not getting anything out of it."

Now, if they were only charging $3,000, how could they pay her anything? I mean, there was not much profit involved. They were making a little bit of money. They were making whatever they were making, and the guy was such a decent guy to her. It's pathetic. So, they took it all away from her. They wouldn't let her send it [i.e., any more orders] to Wilkes-Barre. It had to be done in New York.

Q: Was Dubinsky involved in this particular instance?

BG: Oh yeah, they all were. They never looked at the numbers; they just called her in. Of course, once they saw the numbers, I mean, what could she be getting? How could they possibly give her anything with such a big difference? And you know George Zorgo, to this day, he appreciated her so much that she thought about giving him work [printing jobs from the Union Label Department]. He is the most honest, decent [person]. They [the New York union officials] tried to ruin him, too, because he used to print their [ILGWU District] leaflets. He was in Pittston, on Main Street. They tried to ruin him many times. Believe me it was more trouble being her friend than it was what she did for him. But it happened that she gave him work when he needed work. . . .

Q: Can you talk about the time she went to New York surreptitiously to negotiate with mobsters?

BG: Oh, she went to tell them off, was really what she did. He [Abe Chait] called her in and she was furious that he had this nerve to do it. But she went into New York. She was in the midst of a huge fight [i.e., strike]—the Three-Finger Brown fight, I think it was. The word was sent that if she wanted to settle it, she had to go see this guy. It was Abe Chait. I thought this guy was a real creep. They got to be friends. There were thugs with guns [at the meeting]. There were thugs with guns to protect him. She told him off and she said, "I won't stay here, you insulting [thing], you piece of garbage, with men with guns. I won't put up with this."

When he said, "You're not leaving here," she turned around and she marched out and she went down about a block away. She went into this drug store and she was shaking like a leaf when she sat down. Little do you know, New York is really small town, it's not big town. Everybody knows everybody in their little areas. God only knows how this guy knew this [i.e., where she had gone], but, of course, the phone rings in the drug store and she knew that it was them the minute she heard the phone ring. "Please come back," they said to her. He [Chait] sent the men away with the guns. So she went back.[9]

They got to be friends, she never talked about that, but he [Chait] was a friend. Probably saved her life on a few occasions. He used to send Marianne and me presents when we were little. She told him one time, "You should have been a judge, but why are you doing this?" He said, "Oh Min, you're so naïve." He said, "I was brought up on the streets. I wanted to get out and this was my way out." She said, "You took the easy way out and you wasted a good mind." That's what she said to him. Instead of being insulted, he was very complimented.

Q: Did he call her to New York more than once?

BG: No, but he sent us kids presents for years. . . .

Q: I recall that Dubinsky didn't know she was in New York talking to Chait?

BG: It had to be. They told her, "Strict [secrecy]." If she wants to settle that strike, she had better come and meet with him. . . .

Q: Do you recall the Jenkins Sportswear–Dolly Falcone strike in Pittston?

BG: Oh, that was a beauty. That was when our house was bombed with a red paint bomb and we went to my girlfriend's [home]. That was during that period of time when she was fighting their factory on Main Street in Pittston. It's a small area, it's like they're all close. This was around the time [1958] when a big strike was going on, which was bad because the girls weren't particularly in love with being on strike. Although years later they said that was the best time of their lives. My mother made them fun! That I can tell you. I wish you could have seen her in action, I'm telling you. . . .

Q: Getting back to Dolly Falcone . . .

BG: Oh yes, that was a terrible strike. She hated my mother. They really gave my mother a fight and a half. My mother got into trouble with the law during that strike. They [the striking union members] always did crazy things. You know, my mother got blamed for things and she didn't do them. She took it on the chin because they [the police] felt that she instigated it. She'd tell them [the members] that you can't do this and you can't do that. But they would say, "What you don't know won't hurt you, Min." But it wasn't true and she didn't want them to go to jail. There were a few things that happened during that period that were bad for her, really bad for her.

Q: Do you mean incidents of violence?

BG: Well, somebody [i.e., a union member] pushed a girl that was pregnant and she got hurt. They [the police] brought charges against the girl who did it. My mother was an accessory because they said it [the strike] was her idea, which it wasn't. A judge called my mother and said, "I'm not supposed to do this. You're in really big trouble. This is a bad offense." I think it was a federal offense because if you're doing something as a union activity, and someone gets hurt, it becomes a federal offense. It's not a local offense. It's not like the cop around the corner's gonna come and arrest you; the federal officials are. They had a trial, and as my father said, she was damn lucky that the judges knew her and respected her. She told me she had nothing to do with it. Absolutely nothing. They [the workers] did it [called the strike] on their own. She would never have said they should do such a thing.

Q: What happened in her personal trial?

BG: The way they brought it up, she was guilty as hell. Now she could have said she knew nothing about it, but what she said was, "They're my girls, they're acting for the union. We cannot separate the two." My father said, "Min, Min, Min, the girls [i.e., our daughters], what are we gonna do? You'll go to jail." This is ten years or something you could get. My mother said she couldn't let the girls [i.e., the union members] down. In any case, the judge [dismissed the case]. My mother always felt she was very lucky.

Then another time, with Dorothy Ney [chap. 1], they were having this fight [with a shop] and they came to arrest my mother. They were having a strike and—I think—part of it was in Edwardsville. I don't remember whose factory that was. Dorothy was on the phone to my mother, and my mother said, "As we speak, they're coming to get me." Dorothy said, "They're not coming for you without me." She jumps in her car and drives over to our house to sit and wait for the police to come. They took both to jail! Only my mother and Dorothy could be this nuts. They said, "Aren't you gonna put cuffs on us? No?" They wanted the cuffs on them. I think my mother notified the press [before] they went. They were arraigned, or whatever they do to ya. They were arraigning them at the sheriff's office. My mother said, "Take a picture. Take a picture, they're putting women in jail for fighting for their rights." And this poor local sheriff said, "Min, Min I'm not putting you in jail. Don't take pictures!" *(laughs)* 'Cause how would he be elected again? *(laughs)*

Q: Well, she was well-known.

BG: I know. And in Edwardsville, holy gods, are you kidding? That was all part of a very big fight. That was very, very organized on the Mafia's side to ruin her.

Q: Whose shop was that in Edwardsville, again?

BG: Marie Law, I think owned it with someone at the time. They got to be good friends years later.[10]

Q: Was it a mob-controlled shop?

BG: I think that's [true of] all the shops that weren't union.

Q: How many shops were nonunion?

BG: In the beginning there were a lot. Almost everybody. I don't think any of them were union. My mother would always have these conversations with my father: "We can't allow it. We can't allow it." They would sometimes talk: "They're paying them well. The girls do not want to join the union." See this was a very important thing to them, how the girls were being paid, if they were being underpaid. You know: "Are we getting them to join the union so we can get their dues, or are we getting them to join the union because they're not being treated properly." This was a very big thing with my parents. But then the final thing is: "We can't allow it. It would be ruinous for us because no sooner would that be acceptable, then next guy, and the next guy would drop out [of the union], too." . . .[11]

Q: Was Dolly Falcone one of those nonunion shops?

BG: Oh, she was flagrant and she hated my mother. She hated her for all the fights from the past. All her family [the Bufalinos], all of those people were related. . . . [On one occasion this guy] came on the picket line and was going to beat the women up. One time when I was collecting [for a charity] in Laflin I went to his house. I didn't know it was Murph Loquasto's house. Got to [the door and] rang the doorbell and then I saw his name on the side. He opened the door and he was drunk. He wouldn't know me anyway, but my heart started pounding. I thought, "He wanted to kill my mother and I'm asking him for money. What am I nuts? But he gave money. He didn't know who I was, thank god. But I told my mother and she said, "Don't ever go there again." I know my mother must have known that this guy was related to Dolly. All the people that were in the Mafia were either cousins or sisters or brothers.

She [Dolly] was tough. She was a lawyer, I think. An educated woman my mother wasn't used to fighting. Most of the people that owned factories, they weren't well educated. They were like she was, came up the hard way, struggled, you know, so you could reach them on that level. But Dolly was a new breed. She was educated. And she didn't go for the schmaltz. She didn't give two damns about it. Didn't care about the girls, didn't care about any of those things, and what it would do. She was a very smart woman and she knew how to fight tough. My mother was in big trouble from both ends of the wheel, which was terrible. I never understood the union for that [i.e., making special deals], nor do I forgive them for it. I don't know why they made deals, and later they made even bigger deals.

Q: Was there a deal made with Dolly Falcone?

BG: Oh yeah, there was. She was let go [allowed to stay nonunion].[12] Allowed to be let go. She [Dolly Falcone] was related to Russ Bufalino, but that's not the name [of the guy who hit the girl on strike at Jenkins Sportswear]. This guy was a thug and he hit one of the girls and my mother made a big deal out of that. She hurt him very badly, humiliated the hell out of him. He was a big guy. I can't think of his name. He ended up being a drunk. He was big. You don't hit a woman when you're big because it makes you look this little. (*gestures with fingers*) And that's what my mother did. "You put a hand on a woman?" And real loud, and in Pittston in a little street, they could all hear her. Humiliated him, totally made him feel like an absolute jerk. She wasn't afraid. "I'm not afraid of you, you no-good thug, you. There's a word for a man that beats a woman—that you would hit a woman who can't fight back. Well, you'll see fighting back. We're strong 'cause we're together."

And, of course, all the girls rallied: "You're not going to hurt Min!" Maybe he could take one [person] on but he wasn't going to take the whole group on. I think they jumped on him, if I'm not mistaken. Two of the girls jumped on him. Humiliated him totally. They threw a red paint bomb at our house [during this strike] and they certainly could have killed her. Could have been a real bomb. We were in the house asleep. Paint all over the house. We didn't even hear it. Outside, they threw it outside. It was the whole idea. It was expensive—we had to get someone to take all this crap off our house. You know what I mean? It's true we could've been killed, but I'm saying that it was also an expense. It went on the neighbor's house, too. You should've heard *them*. They started a petition that we should be moved out of the neighborhood. Yeah.

Q: Were most of the shops run by organized crime?

BG: No. In Pittston, a lot of them were. If they weren't run by the mob, they had mob connections to get the work—which makes it pretty much the same.

Q: Mob connections in New York?

BG: Yeah, yeah. The mob was controlling the work coming in so they [they local owners] were beholden to the mob. Even now the few factories that are left, a lot of them are like that. I'm not saying that it's an innocent business because I'm sure they knew who their big bosses were in New York, what they had to do to get the work from them. . . .

Q: What percentage of the shops, would you say, in the whole district, were mob-owned? Are we talking 5 percent?

BG: More than that, I'm sure.

Q: [Maybe] 10 percent?

BG: Yeah, and they were always the toughest ones to organize 'cause they had goons. Listen, with that kind of money, they don't lose anything if you go on strike. They don't give a damn. That's a big difference than some little guy that's making a living. He's gonna knuckle under. Can't afford not to be making a living. Can't afford a day, let alone weeks [on strike], but they could. It's like the Teamsters. Can we afford [to go] without trucks? I mean, that's their clout, let's face it. They call a nationwide strike and the whole nation goes into a funk. You know, that's too much power for anybody. A couple of times she supported the Teamsters in their [strike] fights here. Lot of bad things happened. One of the things that was good, though, was that if she had a fight [i.e., strike], the Teamsters would support her.

Q: Which is interesting because she might have been on the wrong side of the fence with some Teamsters.

BG: Yeah. Oh god, I'm sure it cost them a world of troubles, 'cause the Teamsters were so connected to the mob.

Q: Even here in the Valley?

BG: I don't know. I just know that some of the truckers . . . sometimes when she had problems with the trucks coming in to get the stuff, she would go to the Teamsters, and they'd say, "We won't do anything about that [i.e., they wouldn't transport dresses], Min." So there had to be something. . . .

Yet another time she was accused of stealing from a political fund, which was another trumped-up thing to get her out. That was when they tried to get her out during a big fight [i.e., strike]. They didn't know what they were talking about. Boy, did they make a mistake on that because my mother had nothing to do with it. See, my mother believed in the people. She had the people running it, not herself; she didn't know anything about it. She was so naïve about that, she never knew what they were talking about. She'd say, "Well, I'll have to ask Dottie." They said, "Who's Dottie?" "Oh, well, she's in charge of our political fund." "Well, aren't you in charge of it?" My mother would say, "Oh no, I, I don't have anything to do with it at all." Well, they didn't believe her, of course. They had the feds [federal government investigators] there.

Q: The New York office was behind it?

BG: And they got it [the records]. Those girls had everything written down, 'cause that's the way my mother always did everything—by the book.

Q: She must've frustrated the officials in New York.

BG: Oh god, I'm sure. My father, too. They were always looking to catch them both on something. Not only couldn't they catch them [but they would falsely accuse them]. My father and mother were so old-fashioned, they bought a house on Reynolds Street [in Kingston] and they paid $13,500 for it. Anyway, somebody

OUR MANAGER'S COLUMN

There are words that are hard to say and one of the hardest is "farewell" and yet that word has been said many times by us all. Sometimes it was said in deep sorrow over death. Sometimes sorrow is linked with hope as one leaves loved friends to take up some new task. That last is how it is with me today.

ALMOST TWENTY YEARS

I have worked and fought in this Valley too long, learned to love its people too well, to leave without deep regret. I am sure our members and friends know that. Those who know me best know that the needs, the troubles, the sorrows, the hopes of every segment of this Valley have been shared by me for almost twenty years.

given.

ANSWERING A CALL

We have members and officers of our Union in this Valley who never failed to answer when I called on them for any Union task. "When do you want me, Min?" was their answer. I am sure that they knew in their hearts that when I was called on, my answer would be as theirs, "When do you want me?"

I HESITATED

But when the President of our Union asked me to take on this new assignment, I hesitated. I was not sure that I was qualified. I was not sure that I could tear up roots so imbedded in the life of this Valley. It was a hard decision to make. My heart said, "no" but my union training said, "yes".

TWO DISTRICTS

Our Union in this Valley will now comprise two districts, Greater Pittston

tion. Contractors contending for work, manufacturers contending for markets, strive to secure any advantage possible. That is why the ILGWU must be alert and vigorous in defending the wages and conditions of its members, many of whom are mothers, and breadwinners for their homes at the same time. In that task our Union needs the understanding and sympathy of the community. I think we have that here today. We will need it in the future as well.

HOW YOU CAN HELP

There is one simple way in which that sympathy and support can be expressed throughout the year. It is to make sure that all the women's or children's garments you buy bear the symbol of decency, fair labor standards and the American way of life, the ILGWU Label.

AND NOW, FAREWELL

And now I must say farewell to those I will not see again before I go. I want

FIG. 49 | Min Matheson's farewell column in *Needlepoint*, February 1963. Photo courtesy of the ILGWU Wyoming Valley District Archives, Kheel Center, Cornell University.

said, "Min paid cash for the house. She bought herself a big mansion and she paid cash for it. Where'd she get the money?" So Dubinsky, without looking up anything, calls my mother to New York. What happened that my mother and father bought the house?

Of course, probably on their lousy salaries with four deductions, they probably had nothing to deduct anyway, after that they probably were getting money back from Uncle Sam every year. They had very little savings. When my father would get enough for a car, he'd buy the car. He never paid interest. They couldn't stand the idea of paying interest. They didn't realize that if you pay interest, you can deduct it. Never understood any of that. They went around and asked people that they knew if they could borrow money from them [for the house]. They lived so frugally and paid back the money within a few years. That's how they did it.

But anyway, back to the "big mansion." Dubinsky comes in and he goes, "I hear you bought a house." "Oh yes, we did. How did you hear about it?" "I hear it's a very nice house." She said, "Oh, it's a beautiful home. We're very happy with it. We had some problems with the electrical and we had to fix the roof, and then the furnace wasn't that good, we had to fix that. So, we had some bumps, but now it's very [nice]. We're very happy with it." *(in an accent)* "Vell, vhat did you pay for it?" My mother said, "What did we pay for it? We paid $13,500." He said, "You can buy a house for $13,500?" Now, [you can't compare] New York to Wilkes-Barre. He probably paid $50,000 for his apartment. She said, "Yes." He said, "You can buy a big house for dat?" She said, "Well, it's not that big." "It's not that small. It has three bedrooms," he said. "Three bedrooms—that's big?" she said. "Is it in a nice neighborhood?" "Oh yeah, it's a lovely neighborhood." She didn't catch on . . . right over her head.

Then after the fiftieth question or so, she realized, "Why would he call her in for this?" She said, "Is this why you called me to New York?" Then he had to tell her. How did she pay for it? She told him about everybody that she borrowed money [from]. She borrowed money from people that worked for her—whatever she could. I think they had $5,000 [saved], and they just borrowed all the rest of the money, and they paid it back in two years. He said, "But didn't you have to pay them interest?" She said, "Yes," she said, "but it wasn't the kind of interest that we were gonna have to pay to the bank."

And she did. She paid it back. George Zorgo, in fact, was talking to me one day. George was one of the people she borrowed $1,500 from, which was a lot of money at that time. He said, "She paid me back every penny, with interest. I said to her, 'It's not necessary.' She said, 'No, George, no, it would be no good.'" So they [New York union representatives] contacted all these people, and of course they all said the same thing.

Q: New York contacted them?

BG: *Somebody* contacted them to check it out. Then he [Dubinsky] had egg on his face. He thought that she bought some $50,000 home, handed somebody $50,000, and that she must have gotten it under the table. It was just another way to make her life miserable.

But, see, this they found time to do because they were always afraid of her. I don't give a damn who they were, or how good they were, they could never do what she did. They could organize factories, they did, but they never had the feelings that she had here. After she left, the girls did much better because the people [the workers and their union representatives] went strictly by the book. No one was harassing them anymore. She said that if she ever realized it, she would never have stayed here. A lot of the problems she had were manufactured problems to cause her trouble, to get rid of her. As opposed to the bosses or the owners of the factories—*they* were after her from the other side. Not fair. She never played anything but straight down the middle—very fair.

Listen, I don't want to whitewash her because they did some crazy things during the strikes. She would not say, "Go steal that truck." She never said that, but the people [i.e., the workers] did it. She would fire people up. She had that ability to make people nuts and want to do things, want to get the job done for her. Sometimes because of it they got carried away. The time that they took that truck—they took a whole truck filled with dresses and hid it for a month!

Q: Was that out at Three-Finger Brown's shop in Sweet Valley?

BG: Yeah. For a month they hid it! Think how the goods [would be] if they were hidden out somewhere. God, did she get into trouble for that one, too. See,

BETTY GREENBERG

these were offenses. That's stealing. But my mother never walked away from her people. [That was] another reason they liked her, but that was the way she was. She backed them no matter what, 100 percent. Never walked away from anybody. Now if they came to her and said they were gonna do it [i.e., steal a truck], she would say, "*No*, we can't." . . .

The girls in the factories, they not only did their factory work, most of them, all of them, did their housework and they took care of their kids and they made the meals. Their husbands didn't do anything to help them. Most of them [the husbands] were out of work. They went and stood at bars all day. That's why the [garment] factories grew here, because the men were out of work in the mines and there was no money. If the women didn't go to work, there would be no paychecks. The men would stand outside the factories and take the girls' paychecks when they came out on Friday. And when the girls voted, the men went and they voted for the girls.

I mean it was a very, very chauvinistic society and very accepted like that. It was difficult to change because it was almost like trying to emasculate the men. They already didn't have jobs and had no prospect of getting any, 'cause most of them weren't educated past the third grade. The only thing they had to feel lord and master over was their wives and kids. Now you're going to take that away from them, too? It's hard for me because I thought it was so wrong, but I could understand now, looking back, why they must have felt so threatened.

Also the girls would be begging—because a lot of the men drank the money up—"Just let me have enough for the rent. Just let me have enough for the rent." Some of the men that were "the good ones," as the girls called them, would let their wives have the money for the rent and little for food. The rest of them, a lot of the men, would say, "I'll let you have what I want to let you have." And that was it. It was their money. . . .

That's one of the things that's so hard [to understand] about groups or organizations. You can go to one community and the Democrats can be the worst dregs of society, and you can go to another community and they're all upstanding people. Then you can go two blocks down and they're the dregs again. It's the same thing with unions. You can go to a small community and they [the unions] are very well liked, and in this community [the Wyoming Valley], they're very big on unions. The people are very big on unions—maybe not the upper [class] people, but the majority of the people are. This is a union area because of the [anthracite] miners.[13]

Labor, Working-Class, Gender, and Oral History

Q: Of the two hundred or so shops in this district, did you say that the majority were under the influence of the tough-guy element?

CL: I would say in some way or another.

—CLEMENTINE LYONS, GARMENT WORKER AND UNION OFFICIAL

There was no big labor problem here. We had a shithouse operation, about sixty to seventy girls at its peak.

—DOMINICK ALAIMO, DRESS-SHOP OWNER AND
ALLEGED ORGANIZED CRIMINAL

No, there's no organized crime—not to my knowledge.

—WILLIAM CHERKES, DRESS-SHOP PROPRIETOR
AND OWNERS' ASSOCIATION OFFICIAL

In his oral history classic *The Voice of the Past*, sociologist Paul R. Thompson contended that "all history ultimately depends upon its social purpose."[1] The social purpose of the present volume has been primarily historiographical—that is, to help everyday people

FIG. 50 | Jay Lovestone with David Dubinsky in the background, circa 1930s. Jay Lovestone Papers, Envelope A, Hoover Institution Archives, Stanford University.

as well as scholars, journalists, and others understand how individuals lived, coped, and even thrived in their working lives. Oral history has been used as the method to pursue three interrelated goals: to capture the memories of workers, owners, and other actors in the epic story of garment industrialization and deindustrialization in a hinterland area; to describe the expansion of the ladies' garment-making businesses while organized labor used a solidarity approach to build an effective organization; and to understand the interview subjects' perspective on maintaining their positions against powerful forces, including ILGWU officials at the main office in New York, local and distant organized crime, and a globalizing garment trade.

The first task of this chapter is to scrutinize the oral history accounts for their broader implications on four substantive areas of historiographical inquiry: labor, working-class, gender, and oral history. The second task will be to delve further into the narratives for what they can reveal about three other, related topics: the nuanced relationships between workers and organized crime, a new phase in the deindustrialization of the Wyoming Valley, and the public memory of the garment industry.

Labor History

Staughton Lynd and Elizabeth Faue have been among the labor historians who have studied the 1920s and early 1930s, the period immediately preceding the Wagner Act in 1935 and the subsequent transfer of decision making from the local to the national union office.[2] They found that the most effective unions relied on a locally oriented, community-based organizing philosophy and strategy they referred to as "solidarity unionism." The ILGWU had advocated the approach during the early twentieth century in part because many, if not most, garment workers endorsed a grassroots, crusading radicalism that lent itself to the method.[3] As determined participants in the radical-activist currents of the 1920s, Min and Bill Matheson vigorously supported the idea. As evidence of her radicalism, the fifteen-year-old Minnie Hindy Lurye (her full maiden name) served as the personal secretary to ILGWU member and CPUSA chief, Jay Lovestone (fig. 50).

As a young couple, the Mathesons participated in the fracturing that took place between the CPUSA and the ILGWU.[4] They were among those who joined with Lovestone and left the Party during the 1930s to advocate for President Franklin D. Roosevelt's New Deal. They especially endorsed the National Labor Relations Act (1935), which legalized an employee's right to unionize but which, ironically, facilitated the centralization and bureaucratization of union power. As Elizabeth Faue put it, the result was that "by routinizing how unions interacted with employers, national labor unions slowly exchanged community-based unionism for workplace contractualism."[5]

The situation became even more difficult during the last quarter of the twentieth century in the face of worldwide capital flight. As Doreen Masscy observed, "The spatial mobility of capital is pitted against the geographical solidarity of labor. Capital can make positive use, in a way labor cannot, of distance and differentiation."[6] The trifecta of globalizing businesses, corporate union busting, and government anti-union policies functioned to labor's punishing disadvantage.

Yet many garment workers did not abandon the solidarity approach and its social unionism and moral economy corollaries.[7] Although David Dubinsky, Charles "Chick" Chaiken, Julius Hochman, and other New York officers had been grassroots activists early in their careers, their turn toward authoritarian business unionism occasioned regular clashes with community-oriented managers such as Min Matheson (chap. 3) in the Wyoming Valley and John Justin (chap. 7) in Harrisburg and Pottsville, and with field organizers such as Angelo DePasquale (chap. 4) in Pittston.[8]

Despite national-local union skirmishes, the Matheson, as "organic intellectuals," nevertheless continued to foster solidarity unionism for over twenty years within the Wyoming Valley.[9] Mrs. Matheson spoke to the policy: "I think they [the community] supported us because they thought it was good for the community, for the people to have an organization as good as ours that was so community-conscious and upped the earning of the people, which made it better for the community as far as income. They were *for* us." Indeed, the unionization drives that began in the mid-1940s widened into a social, political, and economic movement by the 1950s.[10] Leaders and workers marshaled support on the shop floor and also created alliances with community members, civic leaders, public officials, and business owners. The crusade led to multifaceted relationships that encompassed civic involvement, political participation, economic development, and public betterment. As Clementine Lyons (chap. 8) expounded, "It got to the point where there wasn't a thing goin' on in the community that the ILG wasn't in or invited to. If you mentioned 'the union' when you came to town, all you had to do was say, 'Where is the union office?' and the place they sent you was the ILG. We became part of the community."

Along with the community, the second pillar of the solidarity approach involved the union members themselves: their sense of identity, mutuality, and loyalty. The ILGWU's success in the Wyoming Valley, therefore, flourished on both the broader community's endorsement and validation and the members' shared bonds and commitments. It should come as no surprise, therefore, that the garment worker-storytellers in this volume discussed the informal side of work, family, and social obligation, which, in turn, had a direct bearing on their concerted social and political actions. For beyond the picket lines, members cultivated a penetrating sense of common cause through picnics and dinners, choruses and revues, birthday and holiday parties. Historian Jennifer Guglielmo found a similar pattern among earlier garment workers in New York City: "The knowledge and experience that women gleaned from these everyday activities would inform their more organized, formal struggles for widespread, collective change." Likewise, Annelise Orleck reported that biographical accounts such as these "help us to unravel the tangled interaction between the personal relationships activists build and the political strategies they pursue."[11]

To sustain the members' loyalties and the community's backing, the union offered an array of services, benefits, and protections, supplemented by a generous menu of rallies, radio broadcasts, newspaper stories, newsletters, chorus performances, political forums and excursions, and educational and recreational programs. The ILGWU was always in people's lives and in the news. Accordingly, the organization was not simply *in* the Wyoming Valley but *of* the Wyoming Valley, and the participants were not merely union members—they *were* the union.

The solidarity dimension was on sharp display at the wake of former garment worker Andy Salvo (son of alleged gangster and anti-unionist John "Blackie" Salvo), who had perished in an overseas military accident. The members' entrance into the funeral home en masse drew the mourners' immediate attention. After paying respects to the deceased, Mrs. Matheson greeted the parents and handed Mrs. Salvo a check for a $1,000 union death benefit. She promised to give her the original copy of her son's last letter, which he had recently sent to the district office in Wilkes-Barre. Those present took notice of the bold yet sympathetic encounter. The union's reputation grew because it was apparent that Mr. Salvo's violent reputation did not prevent this demonstration of genuine kindness.

On the business side, by the mid-1950s the majority of shop owners realized that the Wyoming Valley District union offered a chance for fair-minded cooperation. They came to understand their ILGWU dealings as "win-win" because revenues and profits rose for them as wages and benefits accrued to their employees. Proprietors William Cherkes (chap. 2) and Leo Gutstein (chap. 13) accentuated their willingness to collaborate with the union, as they also stressed the skill and faithfulness of their employees.[12]

The union's immersion in civic affairs through the United Way, the Community Chest, the Chamber of Commerce, the Committee of 100 (for economic development), and other local groups was integral to the solidarity focus.[13] In the political realm, for example, elected officials such as Rep. Daniel J. Flood regularly declared his electoral debt to "Min and her girls." Wilkes-Barre city councilman Joseph Williams showed his high regard for Mrs. Matheson when he said, "There should be a statue of Min on Public Square [in Wilkes-Barre] for all that she's done for this Valley."[14] A statue was never erected, but the Pennsylvania Historical and Museum Commission did install a historical marker on Public Square in 1999, recognizing the Mathesons' contributions (fig. 55).[15] The union came to be held in such high esteem that the leaders and members grew confident enough to speak about various social issues, such as the environmental implications of federal and state open-pit mining laws.[16]

The case of the ILGWU in the Wyoming Valley, therefore, reinforces the arguments made by the Lynds, Faue, and other researchers concerning the effectiveness solidarity unionism.[17] The strategy benefitted from the coal region's labor and working-class activism, even as it modified and strengthened it.

Working-Class History

As discussed in the introduction, anthracite once employed thousands of people in mining, processing, managing, and transporting hard coal. Like virtually every other extractive enterprise, it left a trail of exploitation, conflict, and environmental degradation. The unionization drives among the mineworkers between the 1840s and the 1930s witnessed some of the most violent labor-management battles in American labor history.

The struggle called on the men and their unions to cultivate an infrastructure of mutualistic norms and values, which by the turn of the century resonated with the communalistic mores of over two dozen immigrant groups. Ethnic cultures meshed with labor unionism in providing decades of successful labor actions.[18] In his analysis of Slavic (Polish, Ukrainian, Slovak, Russian, etc.) immigrant mineworkers, historian Victor Greene discovered that labor's success lay in what amounted to a form of solidarity unionism: a reliance on "sociological" resources and motivations that included family, church, and community.[19]

Much to its fortune, the Wyoming Valley's garment workers drew from this deep well of ethnic and working-class union fervor. Alice Reca (chap. 6) recalled a relevant memory from her youth: "There's a lot of pride in being a union member. If you scabbed, if you were a scab, three generations later, they'd say, 'Well, her great-grandfather was a scab.' I mean, nobody will have anything to do with her." Betty Greenberg (chap. 15) acknowledged the legacy: "In this community [the Wyoming Valley], they're very big on unions. The people are very big on unions—maybe not the upper [class] people, but the majority of the people are. This is a union area because of the [anthracite] miners." And Dorothy Ney (chap. 1) confirmed the proposition: "Don't forget this was a 'union valley.'"

By the 1920s, the region had become a stronghold for numerous branches of organized labor. While mineworkers in West Virginia, Kentucky, and other Appalachian coal districts regularly exhibited a sense of powerlessness in the face of the coal companies' hegemonic control, such was not the case in the anthracite fields during the late nineteenth century and first third of the twentieth century.[20] The powerful "countervailing forces" of organized labor within the coal, silk, lace, textile, railroad, garment, and other industries meant that the workers continually challenged owners and managers, and thereby established one of the stouter examples of working-class empowerment in the United States.[21] It was clear that the ILGWU benefited greatly from the region's union tradition while also adding significantly to it.[22]

Gender

Gender served as a vital asset in the garment movement. For example, Pittston's ILGers took full advantage of their opponents' generally hands-off approach to women, "especially some of them that were pretty—all young and pretty as can be," as Min Matheson expressed. Clementine Lyons agreed: "I think the reason why New York [union officials] felt they were better off with women business agents in Pittston was the fact that those guys [mob shop owners], as bad as some of them were, knew about a pair of high heel shoes and silk stockings—they wouldn't put their hands on the women. But they didn't think anything of picking the men up and throwin' them out of the shops." On the same topic, Dorothy Ney recalled a tough guy saying, "We won't harm the girls but don't bring any men up here, don't bring any men up here."

Min Matheson and her colleagues took advantage of women's roles on one occasion when handful of strikers confronted a group of thugs with screams and shouts:

> Honestly, these men almost went crazy. It was like, "My god, how can you do anything with a bunch of crazy women like that?" They were walking around, waving their hands, putting their hands over their ears. And not a squeak out of them, nothing, you see? 'Cause when we first saw them they were making like in the movie pictures, real tough guys. They were going to knock our heads off, and we were not so sure that they didn't have guns. We didn't know what they were going to do because they were adamant that they wouldn't let the union into Pittston. So I always said, it was the women that defeated them.

Betty Greenberg remembered one scene where a hoodlum went after a striking woman:

This guy was a thug and he hit one of the girls and my mother made a big deal out of that. She hurt him very badly, humiliated the hell out of him. He was a big guy. I can't think of his name. He ended up being a drunk. He was big. You don't hit a woman when you're big because it makes you look this little. (*gestures with fingers*) And that's what my mother did. "You put a hand on a woman?" And real loud, and in Pittston in a little street, they could all hear her. Humiliated him, totally made him feel like an absolute jerk. She wasn't afraid. "I'm not afraid of you, you no-good thug, you. There's a word for a man that beats a woman—that you would hit a woman who can't fight back. Well, you'll see fighting back. We're strong 'cause we're together."

Despite gender's advantages, the issue actually cut both ways. That is, the thugs could use more than fists and guns to intimidate an enemy, as Alice Reca recalled. During one particular strike, a group of toughs verbally assaulted her with sexual innuendoes after she entered Twinny's Diner. The barrage of slurs and epithets caused her to cry and flee the scene. "I was embarrassed," she recalled. "I was so embarrassed that it just kind of wiped me out."

There were other instances of paternalistic intimidation in the community and the union. For example, there was a historic pattern of male dominance within the ILGWU hierarchy, despite most rank and file members being women. Betty Greenberg believed that many of her mother's tribulations stemmed from the inability of the union's male leaders to work with a strong-minded and intelligent female.[23] Mrs. Matheson apparently enflamed many anxieties because the Wyoming Valley District had experienced such remarkable growth and influence. Leading union figures in New York worried that Matheson's local stature could translate into national office, despite her having emphasized to Dubinsky and other officials that she held no such ambitions.[24] Moreover, she likely antagonized her bosses by refusing to permit certain mob-affiliated or other nonunion shops to operate, seemingly in opposition to "special deals" that some high-ranking union officials had apparently brokered with certain mobsters.[25] Hers was a familiar position within the ILGWU, however, for "the woman problem" had also dogged Rose Pesotta (who, out of frustration, resigned in 1946 as the union's only female vice president and Executive Board member), as well as other union stalwarts such as Pauline Newman, Rose Schneiderman, Fannia Cohn, and Clara Lemlich Shavelson.[26]

There was also the Wyoming Valley's traditionalistic society, which placed significant constraints on women's public roles and occupational positions. Throughout the twentieth century, the area's working-class population consisted largely of the second-generation descendants of southern and eastern European mining families who were steeped in a parochial way of life.[27] For most women, the task was to accommodate to a highly stratified, limiting, and patriarchal culture.[28]

The pattern confirmed Roger Waldinger's observations on New York City garment workers during the first third of the twentieth century: "Tendencies toward female activism were also limited by familial responsibilities and constraints (as in the case of Italian immigrants), or undercut (as with young Jewish unionists influenced by cultural norms emphasizing marriage and home)."[29] The problems for female labor activists were even more difficult, as Alice Kessler-Harris observed: "The wage-earning women who undertook the difficult task of organizing their coworkers also face another problem: they had to reconcile active involvement in labor unionism with community traditions that often discouraged worldly roles."[30] As a result, women's acclimation to the social and cultural landscape necessitated an obsequiousness not unlike that endured by minority populations in oppressive colonial societies.[31]

But the ILGWU changed the pattern in the Wyoming Valley, especially in Pittston. Although women held the lowest rank within the stratification system, the union offered status, influence, and a new voice, as Min Matheson heralded:

> The atmosphere in the town was that everything was controlled and the women had no say at all. They did the cooking, and the cleaning, and the sewing, and taking care of the lunches, and getting the children out to school and the husbands out to work in the mines. They were active in their churches and always crocheting and knitting and making things, and this was their life. But now we came along and we gave them status.
>
> Actually, you think, this was the forties and women weren't very prominent, weren't expected to know anything except house and children. As we got to know different families, particularly the men couldn't understand how I could know these things or speak on these subjects. The backwardness toward women was unbelievable. Eventually the women were really coming into their own, so to speak. I'd say they were excellent and very capable. Of course, I'm prejudiced. In my eyes most of them were far and above the men they were married to. They had a habit of referring to the good ones: "*He's a good one, Min.*" Some miner was killed in the mines and they'd say, "It's too bad, because he was one of the good ones, Min." The bad ones were the men who drank up their wages, beat the women, who dominated and had tempers like fiends. The women worked and carried on and kept the house together. It was [often] a poor kind of marriage relationship.

Voting rights offered a case in point. Through the union's staunch public protests and repeated electoral attempts, officials eventually allowed women to vote in Pittston (where the problem was most prevalent) during the mid-1950s, decades after the franchise had been extended nationwide. And once in the voting booth, women insisted on their own choices. A public voice had emerged where none had existed, and women were now breadwinners *and* citizens. The movement encouraged union members as well as women in other segments of the working class to realize what sociologist Doug McAdam called "a new sense of efficacy."[32] The status of such heretofore marginalized persons had been transformed to a point where "the boundaries between home and work, community and polity were not formidable obstacles to action in the public sphere."[33]

Gender was also a factor in the training and selecting of district leaders. Mrs. Matheson had a sharp eye for organizational and managerial potential. Some of those chosen were men, but most were women. After careful consideration, she selected a core group of organizers, business agents, shop stewards, and floorladies to whom she taught her version of solidarity unionism. They, in turn, advanced the rank and file, nourished community connections, and promulgated the ILGWU's agenda. The narratives by Dorothy Ney, Clementine Lyons, Pearl Novak (chap. 14), and Helen Weiss (chap. 9) acknowledge their debt in this regard. Moreover, the fact that the great majority of operatives were from working-class, ethnic backgrounds suggested a degree of "female bonding" within the union staff.[34] It further seems likely that such firsthand relationships enhanced the sense of commonality and empathy between and among the staff members.

The Mathesons themselves must be considered as subjects for gender analysis on at least two fronts. First, as Betty Greenberg pointed out, her mother faced sexual harassment situations more than a few times at the hands of ILGWU officials: "Well, I think that men thought my mother had a lot of fire, and they thought the fires burned sexually. Little did they know her. Wow! Because that was the last thing [on her mind]." In her naïveté, Mrs. Matheson seemed to have not recognized the sexual advances, according to her daughter. However, that didn't stop one of the harassers from making life difficult because of the refusals: "Oh, he made it hell for her," said Mrs. Greenberg.

Second, in a reversal of traditional gender roles, Bill Matheson toiled in a low-key manner behind the scenes, while Min was out in front. He devised strategies, edited the newsletter, wrote speeches, handled press releases, and composed song lyrics, while she delivered the speeches, organized workers, supervised picket lines, addressed the press, appeared on radio programs, negotiated with shop owners, and participated in community development projects. Those interviewed for this project were in virtual unanimous agreement that he was a keen, empathetic, and reserved gentleman who provided the perfect complement to his outspoken and dynamic spouse.

Although many workers and shop owners believed that Mrs. Matheson was "born to organize," her sometimes contentious, abrasive style could prove off-putting: a response almost certainly rooted in, or triggered by, her avid devotion to organized labor.[35] As an "industrial feminist," she had no problem battling the prejudiced view that women should not engage in assertive or aggressive behavior.[36] This is to say that she could often rankle even her close colleagues. Fellow union manager John Justin recalled telling a union messenger that he was not willing to obey one of her more truculent directives ("Well, tell our Napoleon [that] the queen of Jerusalem's crown has been sent and she can't give orders without wearing that crown. Now you can go and jump"). Former ILGWU and UNITE! president Jay Mazur characterized Min

Matheson's energetic bearing thusly: "She had a big pair of balls! She was tough. You know, her brother Bernie [sic; Will] Lurye was killed in the Garment Center. She had strong feelings about it. She came out of Pennsylvania. She was in the union then, which was dominated by males. She was one of the few women. She was strong."[37]

Mrs. Matheson's steely determination was on display during a well-known confrontation with alleged gang leader Russell Bufalino during the Jenkins Sportswear shutdown in 1958. As the gangsters grew frustrated by their inability to break the strike, picketers and toughs exchanged a volley of hostile remarks across the street separating them. One hoodlum bellowed that Mrs. Matheson should bring her husband to the picket line and see how long he'd last. Incensed by the affront, she steamed across the no-man's land, singled out Mr. Bufalino, pointed her finger in his face, and exclaimed, "I don't need to bring Bill up here, Russ, because I'm twice the man you'll ever be!" The show of intrepid tenacity was not lost on the pickets and citizens back across the street and, indeed, Bufalino's surrounding lieutenants reacted with a mix of surprise and amusement. Yet it seems probable that her status as a woman not only emboldened her actions but, as discussed above, also provided a type of protection from harm.

Along another gender dimension, women's work and union immersion enriched what sociologist Pierre Bourdieu referred to as a people's "embodied cultural capital." The Wyoming Valley's garment setting broadened members' lived experiences, personal knowledge, and sense of worth. Even as the association relied on the community as a main resource, it simultaneously (and purposely) challenged its provincial values and customs. Many union members were further able to enhance what Bourdieu referred to as their "linguistic cultural capital" by improving their language, articulation, and general communication skills.[38] Betty Greenberg recalled that her father helped several women, including his own wife, improve their public speaking abilities:

> He took my mother and he tried to tell her in a nice way that she needed to speak properly. She didn't say her Rs and couldn't say Ds. She said "dese and dose." He explained to her what it would mean to her when she was making a speech, if she could speak properly. Still she said "don't" a lot when she was older. As such little brats, we would say [to our mother], "You said, 'She don't, he don't.'" It wasn't meant meanly, but my father was a stickler. We had to speak properly. He always felt that if you didn't speak properly, people wouldn't listen to you.

She goes to recall that one member named Mary benefited greatly from the tutelage: "There was a girl that worked in one of the factories here, her name was Mary, and she was a lovely looking young girl. My father said to her one day, 'Mary, you're a very smart girl.' He said, 'There's only one thing, and I hope you understand what I'm saying. The way you speak, it makes you sound stupid. You don't want people to think you're stupid.' He said, 'I don't mean that to be insulting, but you must learn to speak properly.'" Mary's language capabilities were significantly enriched, and she offered a gracious thank-you to her "teacher" years later.[39]

With regard to gender, therefore, the ILGWU movement acted as a revolutionary force in at least four ways: (1) by challenging the status quo of women's nonunion garment work; (2) by relying on women to confront and overcome the organized criminal element; (3) by helping transform the restrains on women's social and political roles; and (4) by enhancing women's social, educational, and linguistic capital. The ILGWU and its methods demonstrated that labor activism "unfolds at a variety of levels—in the workplace, on the labor market, in the community, and in national and international politics."[40]

Oral History

After noting that women constituted up to a third of the British workforce in the twentieth century, Paul R. Thompson, in the 1978 edition of his book *The Voice of the Past*, criticized their marginalization in labor research: "Industrial sociology, labor history, and the history and sociology of class consciousness, so long as they exclude women from equal consideration in the scope of their analysis, will be bound to generate misinterpretation of the past and false predictions of the future."[41] Since Thompson's words were written, researchers have conducted a great number of studies on women and work, and many have relied on oral history. Therefore, it comes as no surprise that Thompson made no such admonition in the fourth edition of *The Voice of the Past*, published in 2017. Instead, he attributed "the feminist revival" with the expansion of oral and labor history studies.[42] Through a variety of approaches, including first-person accounts, recent scholarship has allowed for a deeper appreciation of women's experiences as laborers, union members, organizers, and leaders.[43]

Of course, the process of "doing oral history" involves much more than recording, transcribing, and relating spoken memoirs. A good deal has been written about the procedural and theoretical issues facing oral history as a research tool (see app. 1). One conclusion has been that subjects, as well as interrogators, bring biographically and culturally shaped dispositions to the interview setting. The type of questions asked, the nature of the answers given, the tone of the dialogue, and other communicative factors will invariably influence the proceedings.

Another insight has been that the topics omitted from an interview account—what interviewees don't say, or what they imply—are often as important as what they say. In this regard, Alessandro Portelli found that "most oral narrators, folk storytellers, and working-class historians have a tendency to couch their ideas in narrative form, thus leaving their discourse open to the possibilities of the untold, the symbolic, the implicit, and the ambiguous."[44] This is to say that oral memoirs typically contain obscurities, overemphases, and even false but presumably "factual" statements that require the historian to search for the communicative keys that can unlock the how and why of particular meanings. At this point, one might ask: What were the interpretive keys that can reveal the meanings within the ILGWU narratives?

Moreover, as Luisa Passerini has argued, oral narratives contain embedded subtexts derived from values, ideologies, conflicts, traumas, and various social conditions. As such, they can reflect personal, historical, or cultural occurrences.[45] It again seems important to ask: What were the social and cultural underpinnings that can help interpret and understand these oral histories?[46]

In analyzing these Wyoming Valley narratives, it seems clear that factual errors, informational omissions, or obscurities and opacities do not offer the main interpretative insights. Rather, the primary indicator points to the thematic emphasis (indeed, the overemphasis) on organized crime. For, without fuller knowledge of local the ownership patterns, these narrative accounts can give the impression that gangsters owned or controlled the great majority of the district's 168 garment shops.

Clementine Lyons typified the outlook:

Q: Of the two hundred or so shops in this district, did you say that the majority were under the influence of the tough-guy element?

CL: I would say in some way or another.

Mrs. Matheson stated that her top priority was to organize Pittston's Main Street because the storefront shops were dominated by the underworld: "We were [also] working [i.e., organizing] on Main Street in Pittston, which was really my aim because Main Street in Pittston was controlled by the tough guys." Betty Greenberg spoke of a large number of unorganized factories, which she saw as, by definition, mob-coordinated: "In Pittston, a lot of them were [mob-influenced]. If they weren't run by the mob, they had mob connections to get the work—which makes it pretty much the same." George Zorgo (chap. 10) was not certain about the tough guys' ownership patterns, but he believed that numerous "straw owners," or "front men," were part of an effective conspiracy of possession and command. Angelo DePasquale saw it the same way:

Q: Did the tough guys own most of those shops [in Pittston]?

AD: Yeah, that's all it was. There was all Mafia, the sons-a-bitches. Sure, they still run them. Yeah.

On the owners' side, William Cherkes downplayed the involvement by organized crime and instead blamed ILGWU propaganda for the intrigue:

WC: When the union wants to establish a point, they begin by mesmerizing you. One of the things they used was very successful. There was some people in the industry who were crime figures and they [the union] made it appear as though the whole industry was crime ridden. But I was never personally involved with that kind of a situation. I knew people and they did have records and backgrounds, but it was blown out of proportion to establish a point, a union point.

Q: To get public support or sympathy?

WC: Yeah, that kind of a thing. Yeah, yeah. . . .

Q: Was organized crime pretty much based in Pittston or was it in other areas?

wc: I really don't know. I really don't know. Between Pittston to Hazleton there was three hundred plants.

q: Three hundred plants and the great majority were not organized crime–related?

wc: No, there's no organized crime—not to my knowledge.

Alternatively, owner Leo Gutstein acknowledged the criminal faction's proprietorship and power, but envisioned a larger scheme whereby "unsavory individuals," not from the Wyoming Valley but from New York, directed most local operations. In so doing, he added another aspect to the overemphasis theme:

> It [organized crime] is a fact of the industry, but I don't think that Pittston was the area that was controlled. I think the controls came out of New York. This area was just an extension of New York City as far as the garment industry went. This industry was very controlled for very many years. The trucking portion the union will profess to having never been controlled, but the union was very controlled. This has changed since the RICO [Racketeer Influenced and Corrupt Organization] laws and some other methods of indicting unsavory individuals [have been enacted]. I don't know that it is totally gone from the industry, but it's not now the driving factor.[47]

According to period FBI undercover investigations, about half of the fifty shops in Pittston were owned by runaway proprietors who hailed from New York City, while local entrepreneurs held the other half. Many of the latter, according to the FBI, had been "infiltrated" by "known racketeers."[48] Therefore, as accurately as can be determined, organized criminals owned, fronted, or influenced up to twenty of the fifty shops in Pittston. For example, Russell Bufalino reputedly owned or had interests in a number of shops including Ann-Lee Frocks, Alaimo Dress, Dixie Frocks, and Jenkins Sportswear (as well as Bonnie Steward Inc., Claudia Frocks, and other firms in New York). Angelo Sciandra held a similar number, as did Dominick Alaimo and the Alaimo brothers. Unnamed FBI informants stated that many local owners (as opposed to runaway owners) had to rely on Mr. Bufalino and his organization to secure work from jobbers; in return, he was said to have received a certain percentage or "commission" on finished dress sent to the city.[49]

At the same time, however, the "unsavory element" wielded little influence over the other thirty shops in Pittston and the 148 shops in the other sections of the Wyoming Valley District. Again, as best as can be determined, alleged mobsters owned only two factories outside of Pittston: Anita Dress in Edwardsville (the Kaplan-Elias gang, affiliated with Thomas "Three-Finger Brown" Lucchese's interests), and Harvic Fashion in Sweet Valley (owned by Lucchese and Harry "Nig" Rosen). Nonetheless, for many garment workers, the mobsters and their operations loomed extremely large and, according to one owner (Gutstein), gang members controlled much of the local trade from afar.[50]

In explaining the overemphasis among union members, it seems apparent that the Mathesons' mob-related family crises, coupled with the members' own organizing traumas, impelled the preoccupation with criminality. With regard to the latter, there were many distressing threats and intimidations, such as Angelo Sciandra's playing "Taps" at a strike site. When, by 1955, the ILGWU had organized over sixty new shops in the area, alleged organized criminals began sending Mrs. Matheson funeral-sized floral arrangements for each new shop brought into the fold.[51] In a similar incident, Philomena Caputo (chap. 11) recalled that the union's main office door in Pittston was covered in black crepe one morning and the police were called in.

Perhaps even more prominent, it was widely known that, in 1927, Al Capone's gang shot and nearly killed Min Matheson's father, Max Lurye, in Chicago; in 1949, criminal assassins murdered her brother, Will Lurye, an ILGWU organizer in New York;[52] and her father suffered a fatal heart attack within days of Will's death, resulting in their side-by-side burial, with their joint tombstone reading "With Devotion and Courage They Lived and Died for the Cause of Labor."[53] Of course, many members feared for Mrs. Matheson's life and were relieved that she was never seriously injured.[54]

Through innumerable interactions and communications, the social knowledge of such appalling occurrences became embedded both within the members' minds and within the the the union's Wyoming Valley culture, as ILGWU official Sol Hoffman realized:

> You know her brother was killed, so she had a personal stake in doing this. She had that personal stake to really go after them [organized criminals]. . . . During the '58 strike, I was organizing director at that time. And she got up on that truck, with that picture [of her brother], and with the guns [nearby], you know. They had the protection—I don't know if it was the National Guard out there—but they called in special police with guns on the rooftops, 'cause Pittston was known as a mob area. She was organizing, and she pointed to all of them—that Bufalino and the rest of them [and said], "I don't care if they kill me or what." She makes this speech and everybody's roaring, and I realize, "My god, what a woman!" I mean, she needed protection to go into Pittston for the meeting.[55]

Anthony D'Angelo (chap. 5) fortified the idea: "She was quite prominent. She had a New York accent. She was a good speaker. And she always talked about her brother. She talked about him constantly because she wanted to remind 'em [ILGers] that's what could happen, ya know."

For the members and staff, organizing gang-run businesses such as Jenkins Sportswear, Anita Dress, and Harvic Dress presented arduous undertakings that created substantial anxiety. The heartfelt sympathies for the Mathesons' distresses only exacerbated the apprehensions at the job site. And the dramatic arrests during and after the Apalachin, New York, criminal "summit" on November 14, 1957—which included garment owners Bufalino, Sciandra, Alaimo, and others from the Wyoming Valley—confirmed the alarm and pushed it to greater heights. Consequently, the interviews indicated that, for most subjects, organized crime served as one of the main representations of the garment-making past. As anthropologist Elizabeth Tonkin argued regarding culture and memory, "In order to think about the past, one must represent aspects of it to oneself, or to others. . . . Because history-as-recorded is a representation, it must be understood as such."[56]

On the other hand, the Mathesons' family story, as striking as it was in its own right, also resonated with the violent personal histories of many garment workers. The prevalence of violence in the Wyoming Valley can be traced back to the coal companies and the decades-long, internecine battle between capital and labor and even between labor and labor. Mining remained a dominant occupation for about a century, between 1850 and 1950, and, beginning in the 1910s the Pennsylvania Coal Company, with several collieries in and around Pittston, began subcontracting and leasing mineral rights to organized criminals. The company's goal was to boost output and profits, knowing that the mobsters would pillage the coal, "discipline" the workforce, break or limit the UMWA, and set up a high-output schedule for all lessee firms. The effort presented a clear instance of the upperworld's cooperation with the underworld.[57]

Widespread mining-related ferocity continued through the 1930s—from intimidations, to beatings, to assassinations—in a series of anthracite labor wars, where competing unions fought.[58] The Pittston area witnessed over thirty officially counted homicides during the 1920s, the large majority directly related to organized crime's role in mining and processing coal.[59] As residents of the Wyoming Valley, the garment narrators in these pages could not help but be aware of, and affected by, this brutal and intimidating history. In an important sense, therefore, the Mathesons' family story merged with many ordinary workers' stories and, indeed, much of Pittston's history.[60]

Such interpersonal and historical dynamics helped create what sociologist Maurice Halbwachs referred to as a social framework for the formation and articulation of collective memories: "It is in the sense that there exists a collective memory and social frameworks for memory; it is to the degree that our individual thought places itself in these frameworks and participates in this memory that it is capable of the act of recollection." In a similar vein, Elizabeth Tonkin wrote about "the social construction of oral history" and, therefore, of social memory.[61]

One methodological consequence was that the ILGWU interview subjects provided far fewer details about organizing experiences in the legitimate shops of Pittston and other towns where, in fact, the great majority of factories were found. It seemed evident that the battles against the criminal faction symbolized and represented a much larger fight for workers' empowerment. The prominence given to the hoodlums' enterprises, therefore, "lead[s] us through and beyond facts to their meanings,"[62] and the essential meanings for the ILGers derived from their pursuit of rights and benefits, not against the owners per se, but against the extremes of abusive power, exploitation, and injustice epitomized by organized crime.

LABOR, WORKING-CLASS, GENDER, AND ORAL HISTORY

274

FIG. 51 | The burial of murder victim
Will Lurye at Workmen's Cemetery
in Brooklyn, New York, on May 12,
1949. Photo: New York Daily News
Archive / Getty Images.

The salience of gang encounters in the community and on the job meant that the subjects' oral history "trees" had their "roots" among racketeers in Chicago, New York City, and Apalachin, and their "branches" among their counterparts in Pittston, Edwardsville, and Sweet Valley. If, as some have argued, oral history requires an agreement between an interviewee and an interviewer, it also necessitates a decision by an interviewee regarding "the relationship between self and history."[63] In this regard, it seems clear that many of the garment workers made two judgments. The first was rooted in their unwavering dedication to the union movement, while the second grew from a conceptualization of organized crime as the quintessential enemy of labor. Thus, frequent traumatizing work experiences had, in a fundamental way, shaped the workers' memories of their entire garment experience.[64]

On the owners' side, two interpretative frameworks can help unravel the Cherkes and Gutstein narratives. The first relates to the cognitive dissonance that most former New Yorkers experienced with the Wyoming Valley as a garment destination: on the one hand, it was a promised land of commercial opportunity. Along with lower labor and land costs, another advantage stemmed from an alteration in the organization of work. In New York, tradition demanded that a seamstress sew an entire dress, blouse, suit, or other raiment from start to finish. However, due to the higher outlays for the single-garment process, virtually all runaway businesses implemented a piecework system, as Mr. Cherkes described:

He [the contractor] developed the piecework system, and the reason he did was because to teach a girl to do a whole garment was a humongous, expensive task. But to teach her to do a dart, or a collar, or a seam was a simple task. So the piecework system came into effect because it was simpler to break a girl in quickly by just teaching her one operation than to do a whole operation. It developed in Pennsylvania, Connecticut, Massachusetts. You couldn't do it in New York City. You were not allowed to do it in New York City. They [the ILGWU] wouldn't allow it because they would price the entire dress. When you gave a dress to a person to make, you gave them the entire bundle—bundle meaning all the parts combined. But when we did it in here, we didn't do it that way. [Here] all the darts went to one girl, all the collars went to one girl, all the sleeves went to one girl, and so forth and so on.

Piecework introduced a nascent form of mass production that turned the highly accomplished occupation of "seamstress" into the lower-paid, unskilled or semi-skilled job of "sewer." With labor constituting the greatest share of operating costs, the runaways realized greater productivity and higher returns.

On the other hand, the proprietors had to face the realities of regional underdevelopment and remoteness. Both businessmen related similar accounts: as young adults they hesitantly joined their fathers' concerns in the Wyoming Valley "backwater." They saw themselves, first and foremost, as New Yorkers and wanted to maintain close ties with the city. While assisting with his family's Lee Manufacturing plants in the 1950s and 1960s, Gutstein commuted on weekends to Great Neck in Nassau County, New York. Cherkes made similar round trips to Brooklyn.

However, they eventually made the transition to permanent residency. According to Cherkes, "I got tired of going back and forth to New York. It didn't make much sense to do it. If I was going to live here, I had to live here, educate my kids here, have my wife learn to live here, be part of the community." Both men later assumed ownership and directorship of their respective businesses.[65]

Importantly, the shop owners were not categorically anti-union (except, of course, those affiliated with organized crime). Mr. Cherkes did not oppose unionism in principle, but rather the type of control that he believed inhibited trade:

But at that time [the 1930s] it was primarily an Italian and Jewish industry controlled by the four locals in [New York]. The way they controlled it was you would bring them the garment and they would price the various preparations on the garment based on the selling price of that garment. What happened in the forties [sic; thirties], a lot of people decided that they could do better outside of New York City by not being controlled [by the ILGWU]. So they migrated to Connecticut, Pennsylvania, Massachusetts to open their plants and price their own products without interference from the four locals. They didn't mind being union, that wasn't the part of it. The part they didn't want [was] to be controlled.

Ultimately, the great majority of runaway New York owners, as well as their local counterparts, accepted collective bargaining, in part because of the union's effective organizing campaigns, but also because they had no choice due to the Garment Industry Proviso in Section 8(e) of the National Labor Relations Act (1935). The Proviso required that a contractor (which all runaways were) operate a unionized shop if the jobber providing the work was unionized (which most were). In addition, the Landrum-Griffin Act of 1959 reinforced the policy by allowing a fine to be levied against unionized jobbers and manufacturers who worked with nonunion contractors.

By the mid-1950s, the ILGWU had become an established force in the Wyoming Valley and worked reasonably constructively with the owners through a series of formal agreements. Gutstein and Cherkes recalled their largely favorable dealings with the district union, including their common battle against globalization in the 1980s and 1990s.[66] They further pronounced that routine as well as major labor tensions did not prevent them from developing a genuine, if somewhat paternalistic, regard for their employees. Mr. Gutstein applauded the skill level and loyalty of his operatives and felt obliged to them: "I had people working here since the day I came [to] this area. I still had people that have been with me for the thirty-five years. Oh yeah, I had quite a few. I just felt that I had an obligation to them. They had been very, very industrious employees and provided me with more than an adequate living for very many years of my life. I sent my children through college. I felt I had an obligation, until it just became too much of a financial burden to absorb that obligation."

Cherkes similarly esteemed his employees' work ethic and sense of family responsibility. Both owners maintained contact with previous employees through the years, as Anthony D'Angelo exclaimed:

TD: Well, I'll tell ya. It took me three years, untimely years, anyway it took me a long while to finally find a guy like Bill Cherkes.

Q: What do you mean?

TD: A conscientious employer. A guy that cared about his people. . . . Bill Cherkes I think went to every funeral of any person who died in his group. He still does it today, would send a card [to the family] when he finds out if one of us [died].

Both Cherkes and Gutstein remained cordial to the union's leadership, as Cherkes remarked of Mrs. Matheson: "She's a great lady. . . . Min Matheson comes from a labor family who understood labor and felt labor. . . . Min Matheson's family go back to [Samuel] Gompers; they go back to Chicago, where they organized the tobacco workers. She had a long history of labor, you know. . . . They were born labor people." Mr. Gutstein echoed the sentiment: "Min was an idealist. Min was a very strong personality. I knew her really as a kid growing up [because] she happened to have been a friend of my father's. She was a friend of my father before he was union, and she was a friend of my father after he became union." Without overstating the case, both owners expressed favorable sentiments toward the union's pursuit of what historian E. P. Thompson referred to as "the moral economy," where fairness and mutuality are priority values.[67]

Equally, like Anthony D'Angelo, most workers spoke positively about their employers. Dorothy Ney, who began at the Stella Dress Company in the early 1940s, thought that it was "one of the best union shops in the Valley. I think the owner's name was Mr. Levine. He was from New York. Later on, he sold it to Mr. Carter. Mr. Levine was one of the best employers in this Valley." Clementine Lyons praised one of her bosses: "There were some good people in the business. Mike Turco is a great guy. He has the Del-Mar [Sportswear Company] in Pittston." Pearl Novak believed that "Leslie Fay was a good place to work." Ann Cajka, a thirty-five-year sewing veteran in Swoyersville and Luzerne (whose interview was not included here), spoke in superlatives about her bosses, Mrs. and Mr. Brown:

> I loved them both. They were Jews and I loved to work for them. They are both in heaven. Mr. Brown lived in New York and he'd go home every other weekend or so. He used to ask, "Who wants to go to the movies tonight?" So we'd meet at the Luzerne Theater on Main Street and he'd pay for as many girls that came to see the movie. He'd also say, "Now listen, if any of you need to borrow some money, don't go to a bank. Come and see me and we'll let you have the money and then take a little out of your pay each week." He never charged interest. We'd have birthday recognitions for the workers and everything.[68]

If, as sociologist William Gamson argued, one measures of a social movement's success can be found in the extent to which its main goals were attained, and the degree to which its opponents adopted some or most of its priorities, by this calculus it seems clear that the Wyoming Valley ILGWU achieved its aims on both counts.[69]

The Garment Worker, the Shop Owner, and the Organized Criminal

This study also provides insights into the nuanced relationships between workers and organized criminals. The narrative accounts challenge the Hollywood trope of the atavistically murderous mobster. For, in fact, when a strike occurred both sides had to manage the situation, construct and maintain certain boundaries and, in so doing, negotiate a set of informal norms. Dorothy Ney described the process: "Their job was to scare us. Scare us. But they never really scared us because we used to talk to them like I'm talking to you. They used to threaten us and we talked just like I'm talking to you. Not quite as nice but I mean we'd say hello, or if we passed them, we'd make some kind of remark or they'd make a remark, but they were doing what they were told to do."

Clementine Lyons referred to this dynamic in connection with a popular organized crime television program called *The Untouchables*. When a tough guy asked if she had seen last night's show, she replied, "'Why do I have to watch television when I can come to work in the morning and see you here on the corner at nine o'clock?' We wouldn't get mad at one another, you know. It was terrible, some of the things we would say back and forth, but we just learned that we had to put up with one another."

On another picket line, Alice Reca jokingly covered her head with a babushka, held out an empty cup, and sidled up to owner and alleged mobster, Angelo Sciandra, while he played "Taps." "I mean we did a little intimidating, too!" she confessed. "Absolutely, right beside him. People'd go by and I'd say, 'Help this poor guy please, he needs it!'" Sciandra obviously tolerated the antics. In a more respectful way, Min Matheson accepted a vase, as well as a note, from Josephine Sciandra in apology for her son Angelo's threatening behavior on the picket line. Mrs. Matheson later accepted an invitation to visit Mrs. Sciandra at her home, where they exchanged cordialities.

Philomena Caputo took satisfaction in taunting the tough guys protecting Jenkins Sportswear and the scabs working inside:

> I would aggravate them in a way because a few times [when they were inside] I hollered [to fictitious strikebreakers], "You can't go in there. This place is on strike." Boom! You'd see these guys runnin' out, lookin' around. They probably were holdin' the girls back who heard me. [Then I'd say to the girls inside], "Come out, don't stay in there, this place is on strike." I did that a couple of times, but I didn't do it anymore because I was afraid. The guys would come runnin' out, look up and down [the street] like, "Where's the girls, where's the girls that wanted to come in?" We would be laughin'. Jeez, they were ready to kill us.

Dorothy Ney expressed a common sentiment in this regard: "Well, as bad as they were, like Angelo Sciandra and all them, we used to talk to them all the time. But don't forget that they were employers; we had to deal with them. Everybody called him 'Nick' and everybody called him 'Angelo.' That's what we called them. We didn't particularly like them but we had to deal with them. If we didn't deal with them, then god knows what." There was also an occasion when John Justin resolutely, but fairly, negotiated with alleged hoodlums John Dioguardi and Victor Amuso, and thereby gained their respect and trust. In a similar though more dramatic encounter, Clementine Lyons told about her fight with one proprietor who threatened to return to his home where he kept twenty-seven guns, "get two of them and come back and blow my brains out." She defiantly replied to his warning, "Well, you go ahead, Arthur. I'll be right here when you get back." After one of his friends cautioned, "Clem, he's serious. You'd better get out of here," she rejoined, "'Charlie, you're a friend of his and I'll say right now: he's my enemy. You go take a walk for yourself. I'm gonna show him that I'm not afraid of him.' When he [the owner] came back through that door that day, he was like a little monkey on a string. He only weighed 130 pounds. If he had ever said anything to me, I would have given him a slap in the puss and walked away from him. But he didn't pull any guns on me." In this particular case, Ms. Lyons held firm, and the owner returned "like a little monkey on a string" showing that she had won the day by not backing down. Indeed, in their own unique ways, "not backing down" characterized each of the encounters mentioned above.

Certainly one of the most interesting examples of the nuanced relationship between the union and the mob involved Min Matheson and Abe Chait:

> I had an extraordinary, most interesting relationship [with him]. I said to him one day, "You know, Mr. Chait, you have a judicial mind and you wasted your life." He said, "What did you say? Repeat that." And I repeated it and he was as pleased as punch. Then he wants to know why I said it. I said, "You're always able to see through a problem." And he said, "Sure, you think I have a judicial mind because I rule in your favor." [I replied,] "Because, you know I was always right." *(laughs)*
>
> They [organized criminals] employed people that were horrors. I asked him once, "Why do you hire people like that?" Because they were so rotten, you know. Then I'd get the girls out on strike.
>
> I [once] walked into a factory of the Clover Dress [Company]. He had a manager who stood about six foot, four inches, an Italian with a violent temper. And right in front of his nose I walked out several hundred workers. I didn't run. I stayed there. I said, "You put me out." And he went for me.[70]

Finally, there was the case of Angelo "Rusty" DePasquale. As the official ILGWU "tough guy," he was not afraid to use thug-like tactics in support of the union's agenda. Yet his regular and forthright confrontations with alleged organized criminals resulted in no apparent harm. For example, when he was told by one mobster to "leave town or else," he refused ("Nobody is chasin' me out of Pittston"), and nothing followed. In another encounter, a gangster asked him to "switch sides" and become an organizer for the dual union, the Anthracite Needle Workers, and he forcefully declined ("That's the way it was"), with no untoward outcomes. Although there is no firm evidence to support the idea, his "immunity" likely resulted from a combination of his having been raised as a Sicilian American in Pittston with many of the tough guys, who knew him well, along with the fact that they did not want to incur the negative publicity that could result from violence.

On the owners' side, despite William Cherkes's downplaying the criminal involvement in local garment making, he had no choice but to develop strategies for accommodation. Projecting "the organized crime problem" on to the ILGWU could have been part of a denial-based coping strategy; however, the great majority of owners—legitimate and illegitimate—belonged to the PGMA and the NAA (including Cherkes, who served as president) and therefore would have known about and dealt with alleged mobsters a fairly regular basis.

For Leo Gutstein, on the other hand, whose main facility was in Pittston where criminal ownership was most prevalent, the "denial" strategy could not work. For this reason, he followed the advice that his father, Louis, gave him soon after he entered the trade: "If you ever get asked a favor by somebody who is an unsavory individual, to the best of your ability do it as long as you're not putting yourself in jeopardy or doing something illegal. But never *ask* a favor. Once you've asked a favor, you're obligated." Leo accepted his father's wisdom: "That's the way I've lived my life."

Mr. Gutstein acknowledged that a strategy of denying the presence of "unsavory individuals" was not possible. Exchanges with fellow garment owners—in either business dealings or community activities—could not be avoided. He had to appear collegial, respectful, and civic-minded—but the serious transactions had to be one-way.[71]

The Latest Deindustrialized Sector in the Anthracite Region

In a territory that had seen the decline or demise of the silk, lace, coal, mining equipment, railroad, iron, and knit goods industries, the arrival of a new manufacturing sector during the Great Depression offered a welcomed prospect. However, as the last quarter of the twentieth century began, ladies' apparel began to follow a familiar pattern. For among the thousands of plant closures nationwide after 1975 were those that fabricated ladies' garments in the Wyoming Valley. At the same time, imports soared and new sweatshops (some purportedly unionized) opened in New York, Los Angeles, and many other cities.

Throughout the 1980s and 1990s, workers, unions, owners, and trade associations mounted vigorous public relations and political lobbying campaigns against imported clothing—with none to lasting effect, despite the fact that, in 1997, the fiber, textile, and apparel industries employed 10 percent of the domestic labor force and stood as the largest manufacturing sector in the country with just under two million employees.[72] Indeed, the overall battle had been lost even before the January 1994 implementation of the North American Free Trade Agreement (NAFTA).[73] Yet, despite the flood of internationally made clothing, many of the job-exporting companies have maintained their headquarters in the United States and have sold their products under familiar labels such as Leslie Fay, Liz Claiborne, and Chorus Line.

Leo Gutstein visited garment-making operations in China and the Caribbean and reflected on the situation: "They [Chinese factories] had to use four times the operators but, even using four times the operators, still they were only [paying] one quarter of my labor cost. So it became an insurmountable competition. I've also had the experience of spending time in the Caribbean and looking at factories there. The skill level is terrible, but the pay again is something that is very difficult to compete with."[74]

His company could not compete with the new domestic industry either: "Even though the factories are [technically] union in the Lower East Side of New York—their [workers] are mostly Chinese, Hispanic, Korean—and they [the owners] say they have a language barrier. They [the ILGWU] can't control the fact that these people

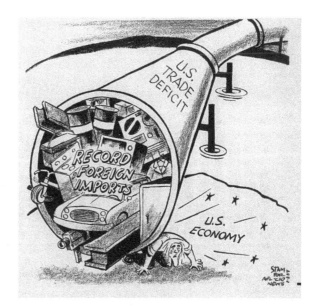

FIG. 52 | Newspaper cartoon critical of imported manufactured goods, circa 1985. Photo courtesy of the Kheel Center, Cornell University.

work sixty- and seventy-hour workweeks for below minimum-wage rates. They exist under the same contract that I exist under but they don't abide by the contract. We will always abide by the contract. For what is left of the union segment of the industry, it's a very uneven playing field."[75]

The American garment sector was overwhelmed by the same economic processes that led the runaways out of New York during the 1930—namely, capital flight to lower-cost production centers. Lazare Teper, director of the ILGWU's research department, saw the trend in the 1960s when he protested that it amounted to "a 'runaway shop' situation on an international scale."[76] Andrew Ross agreed: "The runaway shops are no longer in Trenton, New Jersey, or Scranton, Pennsylvania, or in anti-union states in the South, they're in the maquiladoras in the Caribbean basin, a species of labor organization that, at its worst, ranks just below the plantation on the scale of dehumanization."[77]

The results for the domestic garment making were catastrophic: in Pennsylvania, the number of apparel and textile workers peaked at 181,000 in 1965, fell to 102,000 in 1984, and slipped further to about 50,000 by 1995. The estimated number in 2016 was 7,200.[78] Pennsylvania was not alone. Virtually every other state and region experienced a deterioration. Whereas in the early 1980s, garments and textiles constituted the largest manufacturing sectors in the country with nearly two million employees (down from a high of 2.4 million in 1973), or 10 percent of all manufacturing workers,[79] by the mid-1980s sixty-two out of every hundred types of apparel sold in the United States were made overseas. The comparable number in the early 1960s was four out of every hundred.[80] The figure is much higher today, as imports make up the vast majority of garments sales. In looking at total purchases, in 1962 externally made garments amounted to $301 million of all clothing bought; by 1970 the amount had risen to $1.1 billion; ten years later it was $5.5 billion; in 1990

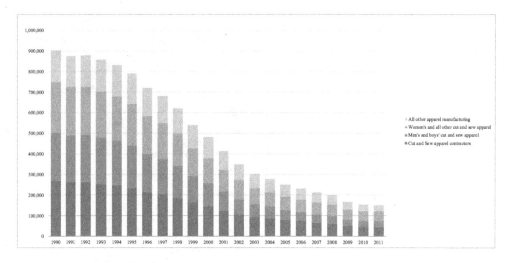

FIG. 53 | U.S. garment employment, 1990–2011. Source: U.S. Bureau of Labor Statistics.

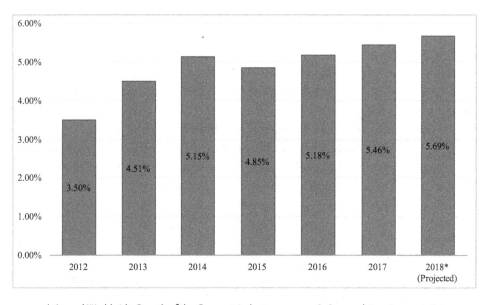

FIG. 54 | Annual Worldwide Growth of the Garment Industry 2012–2018. Source: https://www.statista.com /statistics/727541/apparel-market-growth-global/.

it had climbed to $21.9 billion; and by 1999 the total stood at $50 billion.[81] During these years, garments became "the most globalized industry of all, and the United States became the world's foremost clothing importer."[82]

All this meant that only 6.5 percent of American garment and textile employees belonged to a labor union in 2003.[83] The efforts by some firms to reenergize domestic production without sweatshop labor has not slowed the employment shrinkage (see figs. 53 and 54).[84] Reflecting the trend, the ILGWU's membership fell from a high of 457,00 in 1967, to 300,000 by 1981, to 130,473 in 1992.[85] The effects of the drift could be seen in the fact that, by 1999, the Wyoming Valley had only six unionized dress plants—the same number when the Mathesons arrived in 1944.

Yet lower overseas costs were not the only factor behind the transformation. During the 1980s, the logic of lower-cost production had been augmented by neoliberal corporate policies as well as globalist geopolitical strategies. This is to say that garments (as well the textiles) were, in the final analysis, sacrificed at the altar of free trade and foreign policy. The government not only failed to protect workers and owners from an "uneven playing field," but it yielded to globally focused corporate and political interests and thereby facilitated the process. One clear result has been the growing list of winners and losers.[86] The Wyoming Valley's apparel employees found themselves in the latter category.

The Public Memory of the Garment Industry

Many individuals and organizations have striven to document, interpret, and preserve the public memory of garment making and thereby reclaim an essential part of the coal region's industrial past. Panel discussions, documentaries, oral histories, plays, news stories, books, murals, and historical markers are among the many manifestations of these efforts. The most visible public tributes have been a massive mural painted on the side of a Main Street building in Pittston (displaying a large color painting of Min Matheson see p. 150) and two historical markers erected by the Pennsylvania Historical and Museum Commission (PHMC). The PHMC placed the first marker— dedicated to Min and Bill Matheson—on Wilkes-Barre's Public Square in 1999. In 2006, the PHMC installed a second marker on Main Street, Pittston, in recognition of garment workers in the greater Pittston area (see figs. 55 and 56).

Two lesser-known, but highly regarded, works of art—cobalt blue-and-white terracotta panels representing a female and a male garment worker—stand as additional physical monuments to the industry. Crafted by unknown artists in 1948, they were originally ensconced on the facade of the ILGWU District office and Health Center on Washington Street, near Public Square in downtown Wilkes-Barre. The city's Redevelopment Authority decided to demolish the building in the late 1990s; however, before doing so, it had to address Section 106 of the National Historic Preservation Act regarding the possible loss of significant historical materials. The PHMC contracted with a local historian to conduct an "historical impact assessment" that resulted in the preservation of the artworks (see the frontispiece).[87]

The Pennsylvania Department of Labor and Industry eventually purchased the property and erected a new administration building, which opened in 2005.[88] After removing the panels from the original structure, they were restored and set in a similar position on the facade of the new edifice.[89]

As a supplement to the physical reminders, several artistic advocates have contributed representations of the area's garment history. Playwright Maureen McGuigan wrote and produced the documentary *A Shop on Every Corner: Memories of the Garment*

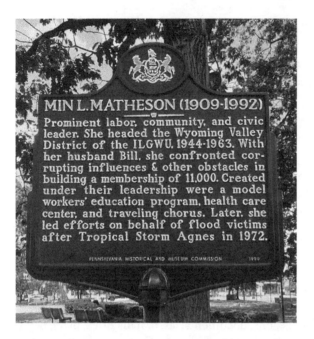

FIG. 55 | Pennsylvania Historical and Museum Commission marker, Wilkes-Barre, Pennsylvania, dedicated to Min Matheson in September 1999. Photo courtesy of the Northeastern Pennsylvania Oral and Life History Collection, Pennsylvania State University.

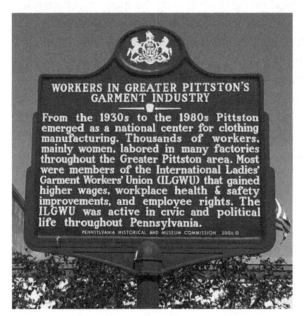

FIG. 56 | Pennsylvania Historical and Museum Commission marker, Pittston, Pennsylvania, dedicated to workers in greater Pittston's garment industry in June 2006. Photo courtesy of the Northeastern Pennsylvania Oral and Life History Collection, Pennsylvania State University.

Industry. In addition, she also wrote and produced a fictionalized drama called *Six Women in Labor* that focused on nursing, trucking, and garment making (Min Matheson is one of the six women).[90] Dramatist Michael Dowd wrote and produced a play about Mrs. Matheson titled *MIN: A Play for Radio.*[91] Erika Funke, host and producer of *ArtScene* at WVIA public radio, wrote and narrated an award-winning documentary about Mrs. Matheson that used clips from the Northeastern Pennsylvania Oral and

FIG. 57 | Labor-management cooperation plaque given to the ILGWU, 1994–95. Photo courtesy of the ILGWU Wyoming Valley District Archives, Kheel Center, Cornell University.

Life History Collection interviews used here. Historical markers, plays, fictionalized accounts, murals, and books thus stand as the main reminders of a once thriving, unionized, civically minded, politically connected, and well-paying industry.

Postscript: A Final Word

The arrival of the ladies' garment industry in the Wyoming Valley expansively transformed the lives of laboring, business, and community people, especially women. Through their oral history memoirs, the sixteen subjects in this volume revealed in common language the essence of Herbert Gutman's enduring project—namely, to document and understand how working persons experience, make choices about, and otherwise deal with changes and opportunities in their occupational and personal lives.[92] The interview subjects have used first-person voices to articulate their adaptations to an array of often bewildering currents that took them through a meteoric rise followed by a steep decline. They have humanized and historicized their multifaceted involvements and revealed their fears and triumphs. They have provided a glimpse into a world of violent threats and remote economic actors. In so doing, they have offered a ground-level, look at the human response to one of the most significant episodes in the industrial history of the region, state, and nation.[93]

Despite national, international, corporate, and governmental machinations over the fate of the industry, one aspect of ladies' garment making in the Wyoming Valley seems plain: the voices presented here belong to individuals who exercised personal and collective agency as best they could to influence everyday workplace decisions as well as the broader aspects of their daily lives, even though, in the final analysis, their efforts led to a seeming blind alley. Yet, for over half a century, they made significant differences in their own lives, the lives of their families, and the lives of the people of the Wyoming Valley. The alley might have turned blind, but the participants proceeded, often skillfully and artfully, with eyes wide open.

According to Patrick Collinson, in order to explain why "competent historians [can] come to radically different conclusions on the basis of the same evidence," we need to remember that "ninety-nine percent of the evidence, above all, *unrecorded speech*, is not available to us." Consequently, "in the place of *recorded speech*, historians have used documents such as letters, and this more formal deployment of language has been accepted as indicative of everyday speech, inevitably giving a misleading impression."[1]

Of course, the present volume directly addresses Collinson's critique by relying on the spoken words of individuals who had firsthand experiences within the ladies' garment industry between the mid-1940s and the mid-1990s. Yet, while eyewitness oral data can hopefully lead to greater verisimilitude, there are two other issues to consider. The first relates to the fact that the interviews contained herein (as with all oral histories) have been "edited down" from the original transcripts, which, in this case, averaged over one hundred double-spaced pages each (more on that aspect below). The second question is: Who were the interview subjects; and how and why were they selected for the larger project and for inclusion in this volume?

The Interview Subjects and Their Selection

To gain insights on as many aspects of the industry as possible, I originally interviewed three categories of people: (1) those representing various garment-making occupations (e.g., sewers, pressers, cutters, finishers); (2) those representing different ILGWU leadership categories (e.g., district managers, business agents, floorladies); and (3) garment business owners and managers. I made sure the subjects came from throughout the Wyoming Valley and, in the case of union members, from the three ILGWU local unions—in Wilkes-Barre, Pittston, and Nanticoke. The interviews were conducted between 1982 and 2017 as part of the Wyoming Valley Oral and Life History Project, which is one of eight projects within the Northeastern Pennsylvania Oral and Life History Collection, housed in the Eberly Family Special Collections Library at Pennsylvania State University–University Park.[2] All interviews were transcribed and digitized by student interns in the Center for the Small City at the University of Wisconsin–Stevens Point working under my supervision (see below).

The sixteen narrators in this volume were chosen from among the final list of sixty-three interview subjects who together contributed a total of eighty-four interviews. I conducted forty-two of the interviews, Kenneth C. Wolensky conducted twenty-one, and we did twenty-one together. I undertook all the interviews included in this volume, and Kenneth C. Wolensky participated with me in the second interviews with Anthony D'Angelo and Clementine Lyons, parts of which are included here.[3]

The sixteen subjects' demographic and occupational profiles show nine women (Caputo, Greenberg, Lyons, Matheson, Ney, Novak, Reca, Weiss, and Lucy Zorgo) and seven men (D'Angelo, Cherkes, DePasquale, Gutstein, Justin, Schiowitz, and George Zorgo). Nine were employed as garment workers at some time in their lives, most for over twenty years (Caputo, D'Angelo, Justin, Lyons, Matheson, Ney, Novak, Reca, and Weiss). In addition to garment work, two also served as ILGWU District managers (Justin and Matheson), and five held the position of business agent at one time or another (Justin, Lyons, Ney, Reca, and Weiss). One person also acted as an "enforcer" (DePasquale). Two operated a family-owned, unionized print shop that serviced the ILGWU (George and Lucy Zorgo). One did not work in the garment industry but had an intimate knowledge of it because she was Min and Bill Matheson's daughter (Greenberg). And, finally, a physician who directed the union's Health Center rounded out the list (Schiowitz).[4]

Securing the Oral History Interviews

A successful oral history interview requires collaboration between a researcher and a subject based on mutual interest and interpersonal confidence. The researcher must convince the subject that his or her story is important, and the subject needs to know that he or she can trust the researcher. The subject further needs to know that he or she can make a real contribution to the project and be assured that the researcher will conduct and process the interview in a professionally careful and ethically appropriate manner.

As such, a hypothetical subject would have every right to ask questions such as "Why did you choose me for your study?" (a question exacerbated by the fact that, as the literature has shown, many working-class subjects believe they have little or no story to tell); "How will you use what I tell you?" (a question involving trust); and "What will happen to my story after the project is completed?" (a question related to trust and legacy).

In securing the interviews, I began with Min Matheson, who, after our first recorded session and in periodic meetings thereafter, was asked to recommend potential subjects (Bill Matheson was incapacitated for all but one of these sessions). At the end of each subject's interview, I asked for additional nominations. Other potential interviewees came to my attention through discussions with family and friends who had worked in or otherwise had knowledge of the industry

I (or Ken Wolensky) first communicated with each subject by telephone. The initial contact involved a number of informational matters: a personal introduction, an overview of the project, a statement (where appropriate) that a subject had been recommended by someone whom they knew, the probable length of the interview (up to two hours), the audio recording of the interview, the required release form, the interview's future use for academic and other educational purposes, and the long-term intention to place the interview in a publicly accessible repository.[5]

I made a determined effort to build trust and confidence during the introductory phase. Every person that I contacted accepted the request, generally welcomed me with open arms, felt comfortable telling their story, and signed the release form. A few other factors facilitated the respondents' cooperation. I had the advantage of being a Wyoming Valley native with numerous relatives (including my mother, grandmother, and godmother) and friends who had been employed in the garment industry. Moreover, I had labored as a spreader in a Wilkes-Barre garment factory in 1968 for a short time during a college break. Finally, given the fact that the research was conducted in my hometown area, I could not help but remain sensitive to the phonology, inflection, morphology, and syntax of the local dialect. I believe that my having spoken "the local language" facilitated not only interpersonal communications but also entrée, trust, and legitimacy.[6]

Once in a subject's presence (usually at that person's home), I again treated her or him with full regard and encouragement. After a short greeting period, I proceeded to set up the equipment at the designated space. Before the interview commenced, I made clear that I could temporarily turn off the recorder should the person have a particular question in mind or want to go off record. This very rarely happened. I kept full eye contact during the interview and used nonverbal communications to reinforce the storytelling. And, to prevent the session from turning into a question-and-answer interview, I told the subjects up front that I was very interested in *stories*. As such, when there was some "dead air" during an interview, I remained silent for as long as possible in order to "inform" the subject that he or she would have to carry the ball.

Processing the Oral History Interviews

Transcriptions

While a researcher and a subject must establish a mutually fortifying relationship, a similarly trusting connection is required of a book's author and its readers. For example, a reader would have a perfect right to ask: "What were the procedures used to edit the interviews?" "Why were these sixteen persons selected from the larger group?" or "Wouldn't sixteen other subjects from the same collection—edited by a different researcher—produce a wholly or partly different outcome?"

With regard to transcriptions, carefully chosen and trained undergraduate interns transcribed the recordings. After one student had completed a transcription, another listened to the interview while reading a printed transcript draft to check and correct for accuracy. I then listened to each interview and made the appropriate edits as final safeguard. My students and I paid special attention to dialectical inflections, geographical place names, individual first and last names, and slang terms. To enhance precision, we created a dictionary that expanded to forty-two double-column pages and that included persons' names, place names, garment terms, slang terms, historical events, and colloquial phrases.

Selecting Persons for This Volume

After the transcriptions were completed, I read and scrutinized each one for possible inclusion in this volume. I based the final decision on four main criteria (not in any particular order): (1) a subject's recollection of events (did the person's memory seem clear, was there some depth to the recall of events?); (2) a subject's communication abilities (did the oral memoir flow, were its contents accurate, was the language understandable?); (3) a subject's positional experience (aiming for a diversity of workers, staff, organizers, business agents, shop owners, etc.); and (4) the need to include both women and men. Most of the interviews were not considered because many covered topics in a less satisfactory (i.e., less detailed, clear, or coherent) manner, or because a story was redundant or less accurately told compared to others. Space limitations also shaped the final decision, as certainly more than sixteen persons were "qualified."

Editing the Interviews

After I had "boiled" an interview down to an acceptable and readable length, the student interns and I read and reread the edited manuscript and compared it to the original version with an eye to answering the question: Does the edited version remain true to the subject's essential meanings and emphases? Needless to say, difficult decisions had to be made. A good deal of material had to be cut because of redundancies, tangential discussions, and unclear passages. Space limitations again figured into the picture.

I took certain editorial steps to facilitate flow and readability. Most of the interview questions were eliminated from the final transcripts, and I rearranged some paragraphs to maintain the logical flow of the discussion: ellipses of four successive periods indicate where this has been done (ellipses of three successive periods were used to indicate where the subject hesitated or stopped the dialogue for one reason or another). In making such changes, I again endeavored—checked, double-checked, and triple-checked—to remain faithful to the narrator's aims and intentions.

I left untouched local language patterns, such as the often-used verb-subject disagreement (e.g., "he come down") and the pattern of turning "ing" into "'in'" at the end of a word (e.g., "runnin'," "arguin'," "fightin',"). Also, when a subject cited a factually inaccurate statement, I added a correction in brackets. I left untouched colloquial phrases as well as technical garment terms, but with the latter I provided definitions in the glossary (app. 2).

The above arguments notwithstanding, I acknowledge the postmodern criticism that historical research—including oral history—must take into account the author's role in "constructing" the story. Consequently, while I believe that the interviews included in this volume are as reliable and valid as possible, I also acknowledge that they are, to a large extent, my creation, for I not only conducted (or co-conducted) the interviews but I edited them into a readable format. Certainly, it is not enough to say, "Such is the problem with all humanities and social science research," for in the final analysis, as Clifford Geertz pointed out, as the researcher interprets the "data" he or she necessarily "weaves" the story.[7]

On the other hand, each narrative was willingly contributed. And, furthermore, I believe that a professionally conscientious transcript editing cannot bend or twist an oral memoir terribly far. For example, I did not create the organized crime focus so evident in the interviews—even in the subjects not selected for inclusion. Indeed, virtually all of the interview subjects knew about the involvement of "the mob" within the garment industry. Even though I asked questions about numerous other matters, it was the subjects themselves who kept coming back to the criminal aspect. For example, Anthony D'Angelo, who was not nominated by Min Matheson, spent much of his interview recalling his pressing job at a mob-owned shop where he participated indirectly in an act of arson. He recalled the incident because it was one of the most impactful experiences of his working life.

If the study has one weakness, it may be that most of the interview subjects had a strong connection to Pittston, the seat of organized crime in northeastern Pennsylvania. Most either lived, worked, or otherwise spent time in the city. John Justin, for example, was employed for about a year there in helping establish the Wyoming Valley District and he visited the area many more times. Helen Weiss, Dorothy Ney, Alice Reca, and Clem Lyons did not live in the city, but they all worked in Pittston at one time or another. While the Mathesons resided in Kingston, they spent countless hours fighting for the union in Pittston. Consequently, the city's organized criminal activity emerged as a central theme in the interviews despite the gang-owned or -fronted shops constituting a small minority of the district's total number.

It should come as no surprise, therefore, as argued in chapter 16, that the subjects' focus on organized crime reflected how and why they remembered large parts of their working lives. Memory is a social, cultural, and personal construct, and it is often influenced by striking occurrences. Indeed, the violence and potential for violence that so many experienced no doubt had a traumatizing effect—and we know that trauma can have a filtering impact on memory creation and recall.[8]

APPENDIX 2: GLOSSARY OF SELECTED TERMS

A term in SMALL CAPS is itself defined within the glossary. A biographical sketch of a name in SMALL CAPS can be found in appendix 3.

Associate ILGWU Members (AIM) A voluntary association for retired ILGWU members.

Alaimo Dress Company Located in Pittston, Pennsylvania, the shop was owned by alleged ORGANIZED CRIMINAL DOMINICK "NICK" ALAIMO, in partnership with his brothers, SAMUEL and WILLIAM ALAIMO, and possibly RUSSELL BUFALINO, and others.

Amalgamated Clothing Workers of America (ACWA) Founded in 1914, and led by SIDNEY HILLMAN between 1919 and 1946, this New York–based union was known for SOCIAL UNIONISM and progressive politics. It dominated the men's garment industry and joined with other major unions in creating the CIO in 1935. It merged with the ILGWU in 1995 to form UNITE!

American Federation of Labor (AFL) Founded in Columbus, Ohio, in 1886, it united various craft unions to become the largest labor organization in the United States. During the mid-1930s, UMWA president JOHN L. LEWIS, ACWA president SIDNEY HILLMAN, ILGWU president DAVID DUBINSKY, and other union leaders became dissatisfied with the AFL's support of only skilled workers and, in 1935, established the CIO for the unskilled or semiskilled and their unions. The AFL and CIO worked together for two years before splitting. They reunited in 1955 to form the current AFL-CIO.

Andy Fashions It was one of six area garment shops owned and operated by the LESLIE FAY COMPANY. The ILGWU organized the workers in the early 1950s.

Anita Dress Company Located in Edwardsville, Pennsylvania, it was purportedly owned by alleged gangster ABE CHAIT, along with THOMAS "THREE-FINGER BROWN" LUCCHESE's allies, the KAPLAN AND ELIAS GARMENT COMPANY. The shop was the scene of a bitter strike in 1958.

Ann-Lee Frocks It was a Pittston, Pennsylvania, dressmaker owned and operated by alleged gangster ANGELO SCIANDRA in possible partnership with DOMINICK "NICK" ALAIMO, and WILLIAM ALBA.

Ann Will Garment Owned and operated by WILLIAM "BILL" CHERKES (chap. 2), it was located at Kingston Corners in Kingston, Pennsylvania.

anthracite Geologists have classified coal into three general categories: lignite, bituminous, and anthracite (with grades in between). As the highest grade, anthracite (also known as HARD COAL) is almost pure carbon, burns most efficiently, is nearly smokeless, and is quite rare. The ten-county area of northeastern Pennsylvania once contained 95 percent of the Western Hemisphere's reserves. Bituminous, or soft coal, generates far more smoke and is less efficient, but is much more plentiful as it can be found in thirty-five American states and in numerous countries around the world. All types of coal produce harmful climate crisis gases when burned.

Anthracite Needle Workers' Association of Pennsylvania Established in 1946 by criminally linked shop owners, its DUAL UNION purpose was to rival and replace the ILGWU. Two alleged crime figures directed its operations: NICK BENFANTE, manager; and MODESTO "MURPH" LOQUASTO, organizer. Its main office was located directly across the street from the ILGWU's Pittston headquarters. Despite calling for a major strike in the Pittston area in 1953, which was intended to break the ILGWU, the effort failed and the group eventually faded.

Apalachin, New York, organized crime summit of 1957   Held at the upstate New York mansion of former alleged Pittston mob boss JOSEPH BARBARA, the gathering brought together alleged ORGANIZED CRIMINALS from throughout the country. The garment business was the most common occupation listed among the sixty-five attendees, fifty-eight of whom were arrested in a police raid during the meeting (the others escaped from the scene by car and on foot). Among the Pittstonians attending were RUSSELL BUFALINO, JAMES DAVID OSTICCO, ANGELO SCIANDRA, and DOMINICK "NICK" ALAIMO, along with Anthony Argo, Vincenzo Sticco, and William D'Elia. DOMINICK "NICK" ALAIMO escaped arrest but was later apprehended. Two other garment industry CONTRATORS, WILLIAM ALAIMO and LENNY BLANDINA, were also alleged to have fled, as did alleged gang members JOHN "BLACKIE" SALVO and ROCKY SCHILLACI. Twenty-seven attendees were eventually indicted for conspiracy to commit perjury and obstruct justice, with twenty later convicted in court. However, the convictions were overturned on appeal. Twenty-two of the attendees were employed by labor unions or in labor-related positions.

Area Redevelopment Act   Also known as the FLOOD-DOUGLAS ACT OF 1961, the ILGWU WYOMING VALLEY DISTRICT lobbied on behalf of the federal measure, which was twice vetoed by President Dwight D. Eisenhower but signed into law by President John F. Kennedy in 1961. Under the law, the U.S. Commerce Department established the Area Redevelopment Administration (ARA) to administer millions of federal dollars of aid that went into "depressed" and "underdeveloped" regions. Wilkes-Barre became the ARA headquarters for the eastern United States. In 1965, the Appalachian Regional Commission assumed the administrative responsibilities of the ARA, and all of Pennsylvania's coal counties were defined as part of Appalachia. Wyoming Valley congressman DANIEL J. FLOOD was one of the bill's main sponsors. Flood also sponsored the Coal Mine Health and Safety

Act of 1969, which provided over $500 million in compensation to the twenty-five thousand mineworkers with black lung (or anthracosilicosis) living in his congressional district. The ILGWU WYOMING VALLEY DISTRICT, including MIN MATHESON, lobbied and spoke on behalf of these laws.

Arthur Lori Shops   A group of garment factories in the Pittston, Pennsylvania, area that were owned and operated by local native ARTHUR LORI and his family. The ILGWU organized the shops during the 1950s.

bible   Slang term for a large book created by HELEN WEISS (chap. 9) to log the PIECEWORK prices paid by the many different shops in the Wyoming Valley. Its purpose was to standardize the PIECE RATES and, therefore, the wages across companies. The New York union originated such a log for workers in the city, but Pennsylvania districts developed their own "bibles" much later.

big squeeze-out   JOHN "JOHNNY" JUSTIN (chap. 7) used this term in reference to the relocation of several "rebellious" ILGWU district managers during the late 1950s and early 1960s. Initiated by the New York office, it was intended to reinforce union discipline and centralized decision making.

bones   Instead of wearing a girdle, women bought dresses having "bones" (or plastic ribs) sewn inside, which allowed the dress to lie flat from the bust line to the waist. Factories dedicated a special machine to "boning" and some workers were particularly skilled at the practice, including CLEMENTINE LYONS (chap. 8). See SPECIAL OPERATORS.

brayer   A small, hand-held roller used to spread ink evenly across a plate in the printing process.

Budget Dress Company   A factory in Brooklyn, New York, owned by THOMAS "THREE-FINGER BROWN" LUCCHESE.

bundles   The term for packages of ready-cut garment pieces. The pieces were often prepared by CUTTERS in New York, especially during the 1930s–1950s, and then shipped to the Wyoming Valley and other locations for assembly. Larger local factories such as the LESLIE FAY COMPANY hired their own CUTTERS, but the final product was still bundled for local distribution to the pieceworkers.

business agent A union administrator within a specific local who dealt with grievances, the treatment of workers, the owners' compliance with the labor-management contract, and other matters.

business unionism A union philosophy emphasizing wages and benefits as well as cooperation and compromise with management on behalf of "labor peace." It also prioritizes centralized control and decision making by national union officials. It contrasts with SOLIDARITY UNIONISM.

bust out A type of bankruptcy whereby a corrupt group of businessmen create a company and make an investment through a large loan. The firm then sets up operations using the loan plus other investments. The main building is then set on fire by an arsonist in order to collect the insurance money. The firm declares bankruptcy and the original "investors" get most of the remaining assets before the secondary creditors can get a share. Alleged gangster MICHAEL PAPPADIO and his colleagues orchestrated such a scam through the Fashion Age Company in New York during the 1970s.

Canjelosi's Dress Shop A garment shop owned by JOHN CANJELOSI and his brothers in Easton, Pennsylvania.

capital flight Within capitalist economies, it is the movement of money or other assets out of one region, state, or country into another due to crisis, opportunity, or some other business climate factor. Corporations enjoy greater mobility than do laborers, resulting in unemployment and economic downturn in those places experiencing capital flight. On the other hand, those locales experiencing capital inflow can usually expect economic growth.

chairlady Analogous to a shop steward, it is a person elected by the workers to represent them and the union's interests in a garment factory. See FLOORLADY.

cleaners The occupational name given to workers who cut the extra threads and slips of cloth from a garment after all of its parts have been sewn together.

Committee of 100 An economic development organization established and directed by business and union leaders in the Wilkes-Barre / Luzerne County area in the 1950s, its goal was to diversify the local economy in pursuit of a post-ANTHRACITE industrial and commercial base.

Communist Party of the United States of America (CPUSA) Founded in 1919 after a split within the Socialist Party of America, it became one of the country's most influential left-wing political organizations. Membership peaked at eighty-five thousand in 1942, shortly after the United States entered World War II. ILGWU leader JAY LOVESTONE served as the Party's leader during the 1920s, and the organization counted numerous ILGWU members among its ranks, including MIN and BILL MATHESON. MIN MATHESON (chap. 3) served as LOVESTONE's secretary for a period of time. The Party experienced a series of internal conflicts during the 1920s, causing many, including Lovestone and the Mathesons, to leave.

Congress of Industrial Organizations (CIO) In 1935, UMWA president JOHN L. LEWIS and other union leaders protested the AMERICAN FEDERATION OF LABOR's inclusion of only skilled workers within its ranks, and decided to establish the CIO for unskilled workers and their unions. After a brief period of cooperation, the AFL and the CIO split and remained separate until 1955, when they rejoined to form current AFL-CIO.

contractor or subcontractor A term referring to the owners of small shops situated at the bottom of the MANUFACTURER-JOBBER-CONTRACTOR SYSTEM, their employees undertake garment assembly after they (the owners) obtain the work from a JOBBER who originally secured the order typically from a MANUFACTURER.

couturier A designer who makes and sells high fashion (haute couture), consisting of bespoke creations for specific clients.

cutter A skilled garment worker who operated a band saw to cut through a thick layer of fabric (with a paper pattern placed over it) that an unskilled SPREADER had set on a table containing thin, fourteen-inch steel spikes set at twelve-inch intervals.

dart   A fold or tuck coming to a point, and sewn into fabric to provide shape to a garment. Darts are used in all types of clothing to tailor a raiment to a wearer's body, or to incorporate an innovative shape.

decline of the ILGWU Wyoming Valley garment industry   During the 1960s, the area's garment industry worked to remain solvent in the face of growing competition from factories in the American South and Japan. To facilitate domestic industrial development, the state government created the Pennsylvania Industrial Development Authority in 1956, the federal government passed the AREA REDEVELOPMENT ACT in 1961, and the federal government also formed the Appalachian Regional Commission in 1965. All three programs promoted economic development in the ANTHRACITE region, including in the garment sector. In 1968, garment making reached peak employment. Yet, imported clothing from Asia, Central America, Mexico, and other places continued to capture larger market shares and the industry continued to decline. As ILWGU membership fell locally and nationally, the union shut down the Wilkes-Barre Health Center in 1986 and transferred care to the Wilkes-Barre General Hospital. The Wyoming Valley District merged with the Hazleton District in 1986.

Dixie Frocks Inc.   Alleged gang leader RUSSELL BUFALINO purportedly owned this Wyoming, Pennsylvania, factory.

dual union   A labor organization founded to draw members away from, and eventually destroy, an established union. See ANTHRACITE NEEDLE WORKERS' ASSOCIATION OF PENNSYLVANIA.

Emkay Manufacturing Company   Located in Wyoming, Pennsylvania, and owned by businessman MAC KAHN, it was one of the area's larger garment factories with some three to four hundred employees who made girdles and bathing suits.

Exeter Fashions   Sited in Exeter, Pennsylvania, this LESLIE FAY COMPANY outpost was one of the firm's six area garment factories. The ILGWU organized the shop in the early 1950s.

Flood-Douglas Act of 1961   See AREA REDEVELOPMENT ACT.

floorlady   A shop supervisor appointed by the management to oversee the workers and protect the company's interests on the shop floor. See CHAIRLADY.

Friedman's Express Trucking Company   A Wilkes Barre–based garment-trucking firm that, because its drivers were unionized under the INTERNATIONAL BROTHERHOOD OF TEAMSTERS, and because its director was an ally of the Mathesons, acted in accordance with the GARMENT INDUSTRY PROVISO and respected the ILGWU's picket lines by refusing to deliver unfinished materials or pick up completed garments. Alleged gangster ABE CHAIT was reported to have held an economic interest in the firm. See INTERSTATE DRESS CARRIERS INC.

Garment Center   Situated in Manhattan, it was also known as the Garment District, the Fashion District, and the Fashion Center. Bolstered by a largely immigrant workforce beginning in the mid-nineteenth century, it emerged as the nation's, and for a time the world's, fashion industry hub. Although it comprised an area of less than one square mile, it was (and still is) the home of hundreds of businesses covering all aspects of the industry from design and production, to showrooms and wholesaling, to training and trucking.

Garment Industry Proviso   Section 8(e) of the WAGNER ACT of 1935 stated that unions were allowed to implement a secondary boycott against apparel MANUFACTURERS and JOBBERS when they worked with CONTRACTORS that used nonunion labor. Moreover, the LANDRUM-GRIFFIN ACT of 1959 reinforced the policy by allowing the government to levy a fine against any manufacturers or jobbers who worked with a nonunion contracting shop. See LIQUIDATED DAMAGES.

garment industry pyramid   A depiction of the garment industry's hierarchal structure with a small group of corporate owners and manufacturers at the top, a larger group of jobbers and managers in the middle, and the majority of workers at the bottom. The pyramid also reflected each group's relative power, although for much of the twentieth century the workers had gained consider power and influence through the ILGWU (see fig. 2).

garment strike of 1958   As the ILGWU made inroads into Wyoming Valley shops and achieved higher wages and benefits during the late 1940s and 1950s, the owners became more resistant and demanded greater "flexibility" in running their businesses without union "interference." Under the PGMA, the CONTRACTORS had locked out workers for three days in October 1957 over a contract dispute. The ILGWU called an industry-wide strike on March 5, 1958 (the first general strike since 1933), which involved more than 140 factories and six thousand workers in the Wyoming Valley. Three mob-connected shops tried to reopen and break the strike, but picketers kept them shut. After a group of strikers had damaged a nonunion factory, workers in twenty-five of Pittston's unorganized shops joined the walkout. The New York union signed a three-year contract with manufacturers on March 11, but PGMA members would not go along. Prominent among the holdouts were the shops owned or operated by alleged gangsters. The strike continued for several weeks and some violence occurred. By late April, many local contractors had left the PGMA and signed individual agreements with the ILGWU WYOMING VALLEY DISTRICT. In the final analysis, the workers gained a thirty-five-hour workweek and increased wages, but still earned lower piece rates than their counterparts in New York City because, it was argued, Pennsylvania dressmaking incurred greater transportation costs. The contractors that stayed with the PGMA included several that were owned or controlled by alleged gangsters. As part of the strike, Pittston witnessed a yearlong shutdown at JENKINS SPORTSWEAR INC., run by RUSSELL BUFALINO's relative, EMANUELLA "DOLLY" FALCONE, in association with her husband, WILLIAM FALCONE, JR.

Greater Wilkes-Barre Labor Council   An organization that included the great majority of labor unions in the Wilkes-Barre area, including the ILGWU.

greenhorns   A pejorative term applied to newcomers, usually immigrants, to the ANTHRACITE coalfields and other places in the United States.

hard coal   See ANTHRACITE.

Harvic Fashions Company   A nonunion factory in Sweet Valley, Pennsylvania, owned by alleged gangsters THOMAS "THREE-FINGER BROWN" LUCCHESE and HARRY "NIG" ROSEN in the 1950s. It became the scene of a protracted ILGWU strike in 1958 as the workers attempted to unionize. Rather than agree to collective bargaining, the partners sold the business to HARRY LIEBERMAN and JOE SNARSKI, who renamed the shop JAY FASHIONS and reopened with an ILGWU agreement. See SWEET VALLEY GARMENT FACTORIES.

ILGWU District Councils   Union-sponsored bodies that consisted of a CHAIRLADY and a secretary from each shop, they met once a month to discuss union-related matters, including political and educational activities.

ILGWU Dressmakers' Local 22   With some thirty-two thousand members in 1940, this New York local was the largest in the union. MIN MATHESON (chap. 3) served as the elected CHAIRLADY from the early 1930s until 1941. CHARLES "SASHA" ZIMMERMAN was the long-standing president who also played an influential role in the national union between 1923 and 1958. See ILGWU NEW YORK DRESS JOINT BOARD.

ILGWU Education Department   It began in New York in 1918 when the members of ILGWU LOCAL 25 convinced the International office to initiate a series of ongoing educational programs. Once developed, it offered courses on union leadership, labor history, and labor law, as well as other classes on citizenship, the English language, and garment making. Union districts throughout the country offered educational programs as part of the ILGWU's commitment to SOCIAL UNIONISM. The union bought and built the UNITY HOUSE resort in the Pocono Mountains of Pennsylvania for educational and recreational purposes.

ILGWU General Executive Board   The highest governing authority in the ILGWU, it consisted of the president, the general secretary-treasurer, and a number of vice presidents and executive vice presidents. Meetings were held at least semiannually. For many years, ROSE PESOTTA sat as the only female member, a situation that frustratingly contributed to her resignation in 1944.

ILGWU Health Centers The union established the first health center in 1913 in New York's GARMENT CENTER. Other health facilities were started in Wilkes-Barre, Philadelphia, Chicago, Cleveland, St. Louis, Boston, Kansas City, Los Angeles, Newark, Montreal, Fall River, and Allentown. The union also operated mobile care units in Wilkes-Barre, Puerto Rico, the Southeast, the Midwest, and certain New England states. The effort was part of the ILGWU's commitment to SOCIAL UNIONISM. See ILGWU WYOMING VALLEY HEALTH CENTER.

ILGWU Local 25 See ILGWU NEW YORK DRESS JOINT BOARD.

ILGWU New York Dress Joint Board In 1920, ILGWU LOCAL 25 was the only organization in New York that covered the SHIRTWAIST and dress industry. With over twenty thousand members, management and service proved difficult. At the 1920 union convention, the ILGWU GENERAL EXECUTIVE BOARD enacted a resolution creating a joint board within ILGWU Local 25 and issued separate charters for dressmakers' and waist makers' locals. By 1921, the joint board comprised ILGWU Dressmakers Local 22, Local 25 Waist Makers, Local 58 Waist Buttonhole Makers, Local 60 Waist and Dress Pressers, Local 66 Bonnaz Embroidery Workers, Local 89 Italian Waist and Dressmakers, and the waist and dress branch of Cutters' Local 10. The joint board went on to become the union's main contract negotiator with employers, with the resulting contracts covering all members nationwide.

ILGWU Northeast Department The union created the Cotton Garment and Miscellaneous Trades Department in 1935 and renamed it the Northeast Department in 1946. It was responsible for ILGWU districts in Pennsylvania (outside Philadelphia), Massachusetts (outside Boston), New York (north of Albany), Delaware, Rhode Island, New Hampshire, Vermont, Maine, and parts of New Jersey. The department was reorganized as the Northeast, Western Pennsylvania, and Ohio Department in 1978.

ILGWU Union Label Department It was established in 1958 to create a new label design, a label control system, and a national promotional program. To enhance the ILGWU's status and quality, the union had established committees to design and foster the union label over the years, but the Union Label Department was the largest effort to date. JULIUS HOCHMAN became the first director. Union Label commercials, including the "LOOK FOR THE UNION LABEL" SONG AND PROMOTIONAL CAMPAIGN, ran for several years on television and radio. MIN MATHESON (chap. 3) became the director in 1963 and redesigned the label.

ILGWU Wyoming Valley chorus Led by director WILLIAM GABLE, and supplemented by talented union members such as CLEMENTINE LYONS (chap. 8) and HELEN WEISS (chap 9), the chorus's performances became well-known throughout northeastern Pennsylvania, and in the larger ILGWU, where the group often performed at national conventions. Continuing into the mid-2000s with retirees, the chorus became an integral part of the ILGWU's commitment to SOCIAL and SOLIDARITY UNIONISM.

ILGWU Wyoming Valley District The New York City headquarters of the union established the Wyoming Valley District in 1944 in response to the RUNAWAY SHOPS sprouting in the Wilkes-Barre/Pittston/Nanticoke areas. Scranton had been the union's regional office beginning in 1937, as the runaways started to enter the coal region. BILL MATHESON was appointed the first Wyoming Valley manager in 1944, JOHN "JOHNNY" JUSTIN (chap. 7) served as the first ORGANIZER in 1945, and MIN MATHESON (chap. 3) became the full-time manger in 1945. The district merged with the Hazleton District in 1986 due to declining membership numbers. See ILGWU WYOMING VALLEY CHORUS; ILGWU WYOMING VALLEY DISTRICT HEADQUARTERS; ILGWU WYOMING VALLEY DISTRICT LOCALS 249, 295, AND 327; and ILGWU WYOMING VALLEY HEALTH CENTER.

ILGWU Wyoming Valley District headquarters It was located in a building on South Washington Street in downtown Wilkes-Barre, with the Health Center situated across the street. Eventually, the Health Center relocated to the headquarters building. The district also had local offices in Pittston and Nanticoke.

ILGWU Wyoming Valley District Health Center Opened in 1948 to provide health services to union members, at its peak the Center employed a staff of sixteen doctors and six nurses. It provided services free of charge, including periodic physical examinations, sigmoidoscopy, X-rays, blood work, and various laboratory tests. The staff forwarded all results to the members' family physicians. DR. ALBERT FEINBERG was the first director. DR. ALBERT SCHIOWITZ (chap. 12), who during Feinberg's tenure was the associate director, became the second director. The clinic operated until 1998, whereupon services moved to the Wilkes-Barre General Hospital. In addition to the Wilkes-Barre Center, the ILGWU WYOMING VALLEY DISTRICT operated a mobile unit that traveled out to the shops. The union terminated that program in 2000. The effort was part of the ILGWU's commitment to SOCIAL UNIONISM.

ILGWU Wyoming Valley District Locals 249, 295, and 327   As the number of shops expanded into the 1950s, the ILGWU created three separate locals: 249 in Wilkes-Barre, 295 in Pittston, and 327 in Nanticoke. Local 249 covered Wilkes-Barre and neighboring towns such as Swoyersville, Edwardsville, Plymouth, Luzerne, and Kingston; Local 295 took in Pittston and surrounding towns such as Duryea, West Pittston, Wyoming, and West Wyoming; and Local 327 encompassed Nanticoke, West Nanticoke, Hanover Township, Shickshinny, and Sweet Valley. Every town in the Wyoming Valley area was covered by one of the locals. Each local had elected officers and maintained various social groups, such as bowling, baseball, or other recreational clubs. The ILGWU WYOMING VALLEY CHORUS drew participants from all three locals.

International Brotherhood of Teamsters   A labor union in the United States and Canada formed in 1903 by the merger of the Team Drivers International Union and the Teamsters National Union, its members transported raw materials and finished garments into and out of the Wyoming Valley. Certain national union officials were known to have had dealings with ORGANIZED CRIMINALS. In accordance with the GARMENT INDUSTRY PROVISO, the Wyoming Valley's branch of the Teamsters typically refused to cross the ILGWU's picket lines during strikes, thus helping insure a strike's success.

International Ladies' Garment Workers' Union (ILGWU)   Seven garment unions joined to form the ILGWU on June 3, 1900, in New York City. As one of the nation's largest labor unions between the 1930s and 1960s, it was the first to have a majority of female members, although the leadership remained overwhelmingly male. It was an early proponent of SOLIDARITY UNIONISM, a position it abandoned in favor of BUSINESS UNIONISM during the 1930s. As a strong proponent of SOCIAL UNIONISM, the organization fostered progressive workplace policies such as ILGWU HEALTH CARE CENTERS, pension plans, educational programs, improved working conditions, and the right to bargain collectively. In 1935, under President DAVID DUBINSKY, the ILGWU followed other major unions out of the AFL to form the CIO. The union also worked on behalf of progressive national social policies such as Social Security, Medicare, Medicaid, the minimum wage, and civil rights.

Interstate Dress Carriers Inc.   It was one of the firms that transported raw materials from New York City to the Wyoming Valley, and finished products back to the GARMENT DISTRICT for sales and distribution. Its drivers were members of the INTERNATIONAL BROTHERHOOD OF TEAMSTERS, which, in accordance with the GARMENT INDUSTRY PROVISO, typically honored garment workers' picket lines during strikes by not delivering or picking up. The drivers did this despite the company allegedly having ORGANIZED CRIME attachments through ABE CHAIT and HARRY "LEFTY" STRASSER. See FRIEDMAN'S EXPRESS TRUCKING COMPANY.

Jane Hogan Dress Company   A small shop located in Pittston, it was operated by alleged ORGANIZED CRIME associate DOMINICK "NICK" ALAIMO in likely partnership with others, including his brothers SAMUEL and WILLIAM ALAIMO as well as RUSSELL BUFALINO.

Jay Fashions   One of the SWEET VALLEY GARMENT FACTORIES, it formed when THOMAS "THREE-FINGER BROWN" LUCCHESE and HARRY "NIG" ROSEN sold their HARVIC FASHIONS COMPANY to HARRY LIEBERMAN and JOE SNARSKI, who renamed it Jay Fashions.

Jenkins Sportswear Inc.   Operating as a nonunion shop on Main Street in Pittston, Pennsylvania, it was owned or "fronted" by EMANUELLA "DOLLY" FALCONE, with assistance from her husband, WILLIAM FALCONE, JR., and in likely partnership with her relative, alleged mob boss RUSSELL BUFALINO. It became the scene of a prolonged strike in 1958–59 involving clashes between Bufalino's TOUGH GUYS and picketing garment workers. The ILGWU eventually organized the shop in 1960 after Falcone had sold it. See JENKINS SPORTSWEAR STRIKE OF 1958–59.

Jenkins Sportswear strike of 1958–59   Part of the general strike in 1958, this work stoppage lasted for over a year, continuing into 1959. The workers demanded union representation, better wages, holiday pay, and health and welfare benefits. See JENKINS SPORTSWEAR INC.

jobber   As the middleman in the GARMENT INDUSTRY PYRAMID, the jobber functioned between the MANUFACTURER and the CONTRACTOR in the MANUFACTURER-JOBBER-CONTRACTOR SYSTEM.

Kaplan and Elias Garment Company   This New York–based firm owned the ANITA DRESS COMPANY in Edwardsville, Pennsylvania, which refused to recognize the ILGWU in the 1950s. Aligned with alleged mobsters ABE CHAIT and THOMAS "THREE-FINGER BROWN" LUCCHESE, the shop experienced a bitter strike during which local police assaulted, arrested, and jailed ORGANIZER ANGELO "RUSTY" "BILL" DEPASQUALE (chap. 4). At another point during the strike, Mr. DePasquale chased and fired gunshots at a nonunion (and likely mob-owned) truck in a failed attempt to stop it from taking finished garments to New York City. The shop was later sold to another owner and unionized.

Karen Sportswear / Karen Manufacturing   One of the later unionized SWEET VALLEY GARMENT FACTORIES, it was owned by CHARLES CEFALO and managed JOHN LEVANDOWSKI.

Kitowski's Coffee Shop   An eatery in Pittston, Pennsylvania, located on Main Street near several garment shops, it was often the scene of conflict between striking garment workers and strikebreaking TOUGH GUYS.

Knox Coal Company   An infamous ANTHRACITE company, it was owned by persons connected with ORGANIZED CRIME, including alleged mob

boss JOHN SCIANDRA. The firm mined illegally under the Susquehanna River, causing the KNOX MINE DISASTER of January 22, 1959, when water broke into the coal workings. The catastrophe took twelve lives, ended deep mining in the Pittston area, and facilitated the demise of the Wyoming Valley's coal industry. Garment shop owner and alleged ORGANIZED CRIMINAL DOMINICK "NICK" ALAIMO was a committeeman (an officer) in the UMWA local at the company; he served jail time for accepting "labor peace" bribes from Knox officials. Garment workers provided food, donations, and other assistance during the search and rescue periods, particularly since many ILGWU members had mineworkers in their families, and one disaster victim was the father of a garment worker.

Knox Mine disaster   See KNOX COAL COMPANY.

Kroger Dress Company   A unionized garment shop with some three hundred employees located on Empire Street in Wilkes-Barre, it was owned by JOHN ST. GEORGE. MIN MATHESON (chap. 3) called a strike at the factory because the owner took the doors off the ladies' washroom (he said the workers were spending too much time there).

Landrum-Griffin Act of 1959   Among other provisions, it permitted a fine to be levied against manufacturers who used jobbers that worked with nonunion CONTRACTORS. It enjoyed broad congressional support with Jacob Javitz (R-N.Y.) and Barry Goldwater (R-Ariz.) among its co-sponsors.

Laura Fashions   A lingerie maker in Kingston, Pennsylvania, it was one of a small number of shops that were never unionized by the ILGWU WYOMING VALLEY DISTRICT.

Lee Manufacturing Company   A garment concern established by LOUIS GUTSTEIN as a RUNAWAY SHOP in the 1940s, its main factory was located in the Armory Building on Main Street, Pittston, Pennsylvania. LEO GUTSTEIN (chap. 13), Louis's son, took over from his father and became the company's president and chief operating officer.

Leslie Fay Company   It was the largest garment employer in the Wyoming Valley, with over two thousand employees. FRED P. POMERANTZ of Manhattan established the firm in the Wyoming Valley in 1947. The company operated ten shops in the area at its peak, and six facilities during the later years: MANDY FASHIONS, PITTSTON APPAREL, PITTSTON FASHION, SALLY DRESS, EXETER FASHIONS, and ANDY FASHIONS. After a supposed ILGWU-sanctioned period of nonunion operation, the company's shops were organized in the late 1940s and early 1950s. It built a new main plant in Laflin, Pennsylvania, near Pittston, during the mid-1950s that employed over one thousand workers. As one of the nation's more popular brands, the company sold apparel under various labels in some thirteen thousand retail stores. Management filed for bankruptcy in 1993, a situation caused by crooked internal financial maneuvers. Meanwhile, the officers refused to abide by the contract they had signed with the ILGWU and moved to shutter the Wyoming Valley factories in March 1994, an action that led to the LESLIE FAY STRIKE OF 1994. The company finally left the Wyoming Valley in 1995 and opened plants overseas.

Leslie Fay strike of 1994   Following the LESLIE FAY COMPANY's bankruptcy in 1993, management moved to close the firm's Wyoming Valley factories and shift production to other countries. In June 1994, the ILGWU staged a five-week walkout, with PEARL NOVAK (chap. 14) as the strike captain. The union augmented the action by initiating a nationwide protest movement that gained the support of numerous prominent persons and institutions. As a result, the corporation promised to keep its area shops open for one more year. Leslie Fay emerged from Chapter 11 bankruptcy in January 1995 and within months terminated its Wyoming Valley operations. Following an overseas reinvestment strategy, the firm rebounded with profits of more than $197 million in 1999. See LOIS HARTEL, MARION MALACHI, LINDA WHITAKER, and NANCY ZIEGLER.

liquidated damages   Beginning in the 1920s, the ILGWU negotiated a contract with the owners that contained a clause stating that any MANUFACTURER working with a nonunion JOBBER or CONTRACTOR would have to pay the union damages of 30 percent in compensation. The purpose was to provide an incentive to manufacturers to avoid nonunion labor. In the mid-1970s, as the flow of imported clothing increased, the union bargained for even higher damage costs for international contracting. By the

1990s, the union's income from this mechanism equaled the total dues payments from a declining membership. The ILGWU leadership used the funds for political lobbying and advertising campaigns against imported clothing and in favor of union-made domestic products. For example, some of the funds paid for a national "LOOK FOR THE UNION LABEL" SONG AND PROMOTIONAL CAMPAIGN.

"Look for the Union Label" song and promotional campaign   It was a jingle as well as a broad advertising effort that became the ILGWU anthem during the 1970s. The song was sung by garment workers in union-sponsored commercials on radio and television throughout the nation. The tune came from a union-sponsored contest among members designed to promote union-made clothing. It included the following lyrics:

Look for the union label
When you are buying a coat, dress, or blouse
Remember somewhere our union's sewing
Our wages going to feed the kids and run the house
We work hard, but who's complaining?
Thanks to the ILG, we're paying our way
So always look for the union label
It says we're able to make it in the USA!

The melody originated with the "Look for the Silver Lining" song featured in the 1919 Broadway musical *Zip Goes a Million*, by Jerome Kern and B. G. DeSylva. (The ILGWU track can be heard at http://unionsong.com/u103.html.)

Lovestonites   The nickname given to followers of JAY LOVESTONE, an ILGWU member and also the leader of the CPUSA during the 1920s. MIN MATHESON (chap. 3) served as his secretary in the 1920s until she joined several other members, including Lovestone, in breaking away from the Party in the 1920s.

Madison Dress Company   Located in Hazleton, Pennsylvania, it was owned by alleged gangster HARRY "LEFTY" STRASSER in partnership with another alleged gangster, ALBERT ANASTASIA.

Madison Wearing Apparel Company   A garment shop in Wilkes-Barre, Pennsylvania, in which alleged gangster ABE CHAIT was said to have had a financial interest.

Mafia   See ORGANIZED CRIME.

magistrate   A magistrate is an elected county official who heads a Magisterial District Court that is part of the judicial system of Pennsylvania. Magisterial district courts deal with relatively small local matters such as violations of municipal ordinances, landlord-tenant matters, public disputes, and small claims.

Mandy Fashions   One of six area garment factories owned and operated by the LESLIE FAY COMPANY. The ILGWU organized its workers in the late 1940s.

manufacturer   A larger corporate business situated at the top of the GARMENT INDUSTRY PYRAMID that usually conducted its own "inside" garment making, but often engaged in "outside" garment making with JOBBERS who, in turn, worked with CONTRACTORS, whose workers actually made the garments. Some manufacturers in recent years have functioned directly with contractors in a PRIVATE LABEL arrangement. See MANUFACTURER-JOBBER-CONTRACTOR SYSTEM and GARMENT INDUSTRY PYRAMID.

manufacturer-jobber-contractor system   A tiered system within the garment industry having origins in the mid-nineteenth century when MANUFACTURERS made agreements with small operators called CONTRACTORS (OR SUBCONTRACTORS) to produce a specific amount or type of work. The system expanded to include middlemen called JOBBERS, from who secured orders from manufacturers for their own shops and often found contractors whose employees performed a portion of the work, often in small, nonunion shops. Most of the RUNAWAY SHOPS in the Wyoming Valley were owned by contractors working with New York jobbers. The GARMENT INDUSTRY PROVISO in Section 8(e) of the WAGNER ACT of 1935 facilitated unionization of runaways because it required that any contractor doing work for a unionized jobber or manufacturer must also run a unionized shop. See GARMENT INDUSTRY PROVISO and GARMENT INDUSTRY PYRAMID.

Mary Brown   The title of a musical revue written, produced, and performed by the ILGWU WYOMING VALLEY CHORUS. The show featured a garment worker named Mary Brown who had to confront everyday dreams and problems. The chorus offered short dramatizations of the revue on local radio in support of the ILGWU HEALTH CARE CENTER.

McClellan Committee hearings   Formally called the SENATE SELECT COMMITTEE ON IMPROPER ACTIVITIES IN THE LABOR OR MANAGEMENT FIELD, it convened in 1958 to examine ORGANIZED CRIME'S involvement within organized labor. It focused exclusively on labor unions, rather than on the role of corporate management. The committee called several garment-affiliated persons with a northeastern Pennsylvania connection to testify, including RUSSELL BUFALINO, ANGELO SCIANDRA, DOMINICK "NICK" ALAIMO, THOMAS "THREE-FINGER BROWN" LUCCHESE, MICHAEL PAPPADIO, and ABE CHAIT.

McKitterick-Williams Inc.   A garment MANUFACTURER from New York City in the "better dress" (i.e., more expensive) category, the firm opened a factory in West Pittston, Pennsylvania, that employed upward of three hundred persons. THE ILGWU unionized the factory in the late 1940s.

Men from Montedoro   A colloquial term referring to ORGANIZED CRIME in northeastern Pennsylvania, which was based in Pittston, Pennsylvania. The criminal gang's origins date to the 1880s with a group of émigrés from Montedoro, Sicily, who formed a "Black Hand" cadre in the early twentieth century that engaged in protection rackets and later expanded into gambling, prostitution, alcohol bootlegging, and labor RACKETEERING. They laundered illegal gains into legitimate businesses such as coal companies, garment shops, and heavy equipment sales. SANTO VOLPE and STEVEN LATORRE were the alleged founders. JOHN SCIANDRA was allegedly the leader in the 1930s and 1940s, followed by JOSEPH BARBARA into the mid-1950s, and RUSSELL BUFALINO into the mid-1990s. In addition to Bufalino, the garment shop owners among them included ANGELO SCIANDRA, DOMINICK "NICK" ALAIMO, and others.

Monday Fashions   One of the SWEET VALLEY GARMENT FACTORIES, it was owned by CHARLES CEFALO and managed by JOHN LEVANDOWSKI.

moral economy   A term introduced by twentieth-century British labor historian E. P. Thompson.

It was based on the idea that worker protests against capitalist economic practices during the eighteenth and nineteenth centuries stemmed from a traditional moralistic view among workers that economic processes should primarily serve justice, fairness, and the common good, rather than simply profits and growth.

Mother Jones Award   An award given annually by the Pennsylvania Labor History Association. MIN MATHESON (chap. 3) received the honor in 1980.

narrative   As used in this volume, it is an oral history told by a subject to an interviewer based on a series of questions that focus on the subject's life as related to the garment industry in the Wyoming Valley of northeastern Pennsylvania.

National Labor Relations Act (NLRA)   See WAGNER ACT.

National Recovery Administration (NRA)   President Franklin D. Roosevelt created the organization by executive order following the enactment of the National Industrial Recovery Act in June 1933. In an effort to stabilize numerous industries, the NRA was empowered to create voluntary agreements called "industrial codes" negotiated between companies and employees (and their unions) regarding hours, pay rates, and prices. Until March 1934, the agency engaged chiefly in efforts to draw up codes for all industries. More than five hundred codes of fair practice were adopted (the ANTHRACITE industry never set up a code). Patriotic appeals were made as firms were asked to display the government's "blue eagle" seal of approval on behalf of an agreed-upon code and NRA participation. The agency's only enforcement power was to remove the blue eagle code of approval from a business when violations occurred.

Needlepoint   It was the monthly newsletter of the ILGWU WYOMING VALLEY DISTRICT. BILL MATHESON served as the editor and GEORGE and LUCY ZORGO (chap. 10), of Zorgo Printing Inc., handled the layout, production, and printing. The idea for the newsletter originated with the Zorgos.

North American Free Trade Agreement (NAFTA)   A trilateral trade arrangement between the national governments of Canada, Mexico, and the United States that commenced in 1994. Its purpose was to eliminate tariff, investment, and other trade barriers among the countries so as to encourage economic development. The policy has yielded winners as well as losers, with the garment industry falling in the latter category. It was renegotiated in 2018.

Northeast Apparel Association (NAA)   It was formed by a large group of garment CONTRACTORS who split from the PGMA following the GARMENT STRIKE OF 1958. The body's main task was to advocate the shop owners' interests, including during contract negotiations with the ILGWU. WILLIAM CHERKES (chap. 2) was a member of the board of directors during the 1980s, and also served as the group's publicity chairman. The officers in the 1980s were LAWRENCE HOLLANDER (president), MURRAY SCHOENHOLTZ (chairman of the board), SAMUEL BIANCO (first vice president), VINCENT MADAFFARI (second vice president), MICHAEL TURCO (secretary), and LEO GUTSTEIN (chap. 13; treasurer). The professional staff members were BEN GLADSTONE (executive director) and JOHN FERRARO (field manager). The Board of Directors included Cherkes, WILLIAM CARTER, KENNETH DORKOSKI, RALPH G. GAMBINI, SETH KATZMAN, TOM KELLY, JOSEPH PAPALIA, ANGELO SERINO, MARK WILLENSKY, and CARLOS ZUKOWSKI.

organized crime, organized criminals, criminal gangs   A term applied to persons and organizations that systematically violate the law in pursuit of profit, power, or some other advantage; and that use threats and/or violence to attain their goals. From colonial times to the westward expansion in the United States, criminal gangs were led by persons of British (including Irish) heritage. By the late nineteenth and early twentieth centuries, the dominant actors were of Irish, Sicilian, and Jewish ethnicities. Terms such as the "Black Hand" (late nineteenth and early twentieth centuries), "the syndicate" (late 1920s and 1930s), and "MAFIA" and "Cosa Nostra" (especially after 1950) have referred to national criminal groups comprising mainly second-generation Sicilians and other Italians, who often worked with persons from Irish, Jewish, African American, Hispanic, and other groups. In recent decades, the term has become a general moniker for gangs controlled by persons from these ethnicities, and also those from Chinese, Russian, Colombian, Puerto Rican, Mexican, and other groups. These so-called UNDERWORLD bodies almost invariably work with persons and institutions from the UPPERWORLD in order to attain their ends.

organized crime in the garment industry   New York gangsters such as ARNOLD ROTHSTEIN, JACOB "LITTLE AUGIE" ORGEN, and JACK "LEGS" DIAMOND became involved in the garment industry during the 1920s when both the shop owners and the ILGWU hired them to protect their interests: businesses to thwart unionization, and the union to foster it. The criminal element thereafter participated in both sides of the trade. Some became the visible or invisible owners of nonunion shops, some continued as RACKETEERS providing protection or preventing unionization for a price, and still others gained control of union locals while maintaining ties with high-level union leaders. Many of America's most notorious gangsters had garment-industry interests and dealings, including THOMAS "THREE-FINGER BROWN" LUCCHESE, ABE CHAIT, and RUSSELL BUFALINO.

organized crime in northeastern Pennsylvania   See the MEN FROM MONTEDORO.

organizer   An organizer is a staff person who engages in any number of activities to build and maintain a labor union. Organizers can bring new members into the union through conversations, rallies, promotions, and home visits. They can also mobilize members and use various resources to prevent a union from being "broken" or decertified by a company. Organizers can also participate as leaders and picketers during strikes.

Pennsylvania Garment Manufacturers Association (PGMA)   An organization for garment shop owners, to include legitimate proprietors as well as those affiliated with ORGANIZED CRIME, the association was said to have been highly influenced by alleged gangster ABE CHAIT. It was noted for locking out workers for three days in October 1957 and announcing plans to pull out of the labor-management pacts that had tied the owners to the New York–negotiated agreements. In 1958, the PGMA resisted signing a new compact with the ILGWU, resulting in the GARMENT STRIKE OF 1958. Those shops controlled by Mr. Chait and other alleged gangsters continued to resist the

agreement, but most legitimate shop owners settled the strike by signing individual agreements with the union.

percentage payment   As part of the negotiated contract with owners, the ILGWU secured a percentage payment system whereby a worker received additional wage increment based on the total value of their production beyond the expected PIECE RATE. It amounted to a type of productivity bonus.

piece rate   It is the wage paid to a worker per individual item produced. See PIECEWORK.

piecework   A manufacturing and wage system whereby a worker sewed only one part of a garment (e.g., a sleeve, a collar, a zipper) rather than the entire garment, and received wages (the PIECE RATE) according to the number of individual items, or pieces, produced. RUNAWAY SHOPS used this method of assembly because it required less training and was, therefore, more cost-effective, whereas the whole-garment production method used by most factories in the GARMENT CENTER of New York entailed higher production costs.

Pins and Needles   A successful musical show sponsored by the ILGWU EDUCATIONAL DEPARTMENT, it played with an amateur cast of garment workers and ran on Broadway from 1937 to 1940 and enjoyed later revivals.

Pioneer Manufacturing Inc.   A Wilkes-Barre firm with some six hundred employees, it was owned and operated by JAMES HARRIS. The company became known for "110 walkout" in the early 1950s, when a WILDCAT STRIKE of 110 workers continued for over a week until a mechanic, whom the ILGWU said had been unjustly fired, was rehired. The author worked for a short time as a SPREADER for the company in 1968.

Pittston Apparel   One of the LESLIE FAY COMPANY'S six area garment factories, this Pittston, Pennsylvania, shop made girdles and bras. The ILGWU organized its workers in 1949.

Pittston Fashions   One of six area garment shops owned and operated by the LESLIE FAY COMPANY, the ILGWU unionized its workers in the late 1940s.

presser   A semiskilled occupation requiring a worker to use a large, heated, clamp-like iron to press wrinkles out of a garment after it had been made.

private label   A practice developed in the 1980s that saw big-box clothing stores bypass the MANUFACTURER-JOBBER-CONTRACTOR SYSTEM and sign agreements directly with contractors for designing, producing, labeling, and delivering apparel products.

racketeering, racketeers   Associated with ORGANIZED CRIME, it is the act of offering a dishonest service (a racket) to solve a problem that would not otherwise exist without the service being offered. For example, a protection racket is one where a person offers "protection" to an individual or a business for a fee in order to prevent harm that said person, or one of his associates, would inflict if the fee were not paid. The RACKETEER INFLUENCED AND CORRUPT ORGANIZATION ACT included a list of thirty-five RACKETEERING crimes, each one carrying an a prison sentence of up to twenty years and a $25,000 fine.

Racketeer Influenced and Corrupt Organization Act (RICO)   The RICO law took effect in 1970 with the purpose of imposing criminal penalties and a civil course of action against individuals for illegal dealings within a criminal organization. Focused specifically on RACKETEERING, it allowed the leaders of a syndicate to be tried for the crimes they ordered others to commit. The act closed a loophole in the law that exempted criminal action against a person who instructed others to engage in a crime but did not commit the offence themselves.

Rosemary Garment Shop   It was one of the many dress shops in Pittston, Pennsylvania. PHILOMENA CAPUTO (chap. 11) served as the CHAIRLADY for a period of time in the 1970s.

runaway shop   A moniker for garment CONTRACTORS that departed New York City for distant locales outside the GARMENT CENTER beginning in the 1930s and continuing into the 1950s. They became a vital element in the MANUFACTURER-JOBBER-CONTRACTOR SYSTEM. Most runaway shop owners sought a nonunion environment with greater workplace control

and larger profits. Because Pennsylvania's ANTHRACITE mining towns were experiencing high unemployment due to the fading coal industry, they generally welcomed the new jobs. To counteract the often-exploitative pay and working conditions in the runaway shops, and to protect the unionized workers in New York, the ILGWU came to the area and eventually organized the great majority of the workers.

Sally Dress   A factory located on Broad Street in Pittston, Pennsylvania, it was owned and operated by the LESLIE FAY COMPANY as one of the firm's six area garment shops. The ILGWU organized the plant in the late 1940s.

Sassco Fashions   A garment company owned by the LESLIE FAY COMPANY until 1995, when it was sold in a bankruptcy reorganization. Sassco contributed about half of Leslie Fay's $535 million in revenues in 1994.

scab   A slang term for a person who crosses a picket line to work during a strike.

Senate Select Committee on Improper Activities in the Labor or Management Field   See MCCLELLAN COMMITTEE HEARINGS.

sewer   A seamstress who held what was considered the main skilled occupation in a garment factory.

shirtwaist   It was a tailored blouse often containing details from a men's shirt, worn mainly by working-class women in the early twentieth century.

social movement   It is a collective voluntary body in which leaders and members employ various tactics and strategies to promote or resist some social, political, economic, cultural, or other policy or process. SOCIAL MOVEMENT ORGANIZATIONS refer to the subgroups that constitute the larger movement.

social movement organizations   See SOCIAL MOVEMENT.

social unionism   A term referring to labor union–sponsored programs related to health care, education, training, recreation, and other areas, with the idea being to provide programs to improve workers' lives while also enhancing the life of the community. See SOLIDARITY UNIONISM.

solidarity unionism   A grassroots, community-based approach to organizing and sustaining a labor union, it is grounded in a social justice, local control, and a MORAL ECONOMY philosophy. It stands in contrast to the BUSINESS UNIONISM approach held by most American labor unions since the mid-1930s. The ILGWU WYOMING VALLEY DISTRICT used solidarity unionism, in conjunction with SOCIAL UNIONISM, to build and maintain the organization.

special operators   A general industry term for highly skilled employees who worked on zippers, hems, clamps, BONES, clasps, and other specialized tasks.

spreader   An unskilled worker who spreads, or lays out, several layers of cloth on a long table containing fourteen-inch steel spikes set at twelve-inch intervals. The work is done in preparation for the CUTTER, who places a paper pattern on top of the stacked cloth and cuts the fabric into the PIECEWORK items that SEWERS stitch together.

Star Garment   A shop located in West Pittston, Pennsylvania, it experienced a strike in 1957 when part-time workers walked out because the labor-management contract did not permit them join the ILGWU. The situation changed in 1965 when the new contract allowed part-timers to gain union membership.

Stella Dress Company   Located on Market Street, in Kingston, Pennsylvania, it was owned by MR. LEBEAN during the 1940s, during which time the shop employed about one hundred workers.

Sweet Valley Garment Factories   With the decline of ANTHRACITE following World War II, local investors in rural Sweet Valley, Luzerne County, Pennsylvania, formed the Sweet Valley Improvement Company to establish a dress factory and bolster employment. When the building opened in 1949, the HARVIC FASHIONS COMPANY, owned by Morris Ember, became the first tenant. After a few years, alleged gangster, THOMAS "THREE-FINGER BROWN" LUCCHESE, and his partner, alleged gangster HARRY "NIG" ROSEN, bought the facility. They kept the name, accepted work from nonunion JOBBERS

and trucking companies, and employed nonunion labor. In 1958, in conjunction with the general industry shutdown, the workers walked out into what became a nine-month strike. Rather than join the ILGWU, the owners sold the facility to HARRY LIEBERMAN and JOE SNARSKI, who reopened it as JAY FASHIONS and accepted the union. In the early 1960s, CHARLES CEFALO from West Pittston bought the building and reopened it as MONDAY FASHIONS, with JOHN LEVANDOWSKI as the manager. Cefalo sold the building to WILLIAM CARTER, who operated initially as KAREN SPORTSWEAR and later as KAREN MANUFACTURING. His son NEIL CARTER ran the business between 1981 and 1994. During its forty-five-year run, the factory employed anywhere from seventy-five to one hundred workers at any given time.

"Taps"   This is a military bugle or a trumpet call played at dusk, during flag ceremonies, and at funerals.

tough guys   This is a colloquial term used by garment workers to describe the reputed thugs who threatened and intimidated picketers during organizing campaigns and strikes.

Trade Adjustment Act of 1974 (TAA)   Intended to reduce the harmful effects of clothing and other imports on workers, companies, farmers, and communities, it was part of the trade act passed by the federal government in 1974. Each cabinet department assumed responsibility for a relevant aspect of the TAA program. The protections and compensations for workers, administered by the U.S. Department of Labor, had the largest single dollar outlay.

Trade Relief Agreement Act (TRA)   A federal program rarely used until 1974, when it was expanded as part of the TRADE ADJUSTMENT ACT OF 1974, it offered an amount of income in addition to a laid-off worker's unemployment compensation. The original program had no training or reemployment component, but the TAA contained a required training program. In 1981, the Reagan administration convinced Congress to sharply reduce the benefits. The Trade Adjustment Assistance Reform Act of 2002 expanded the program and was combined with the trade adjustment program provided under the NORTH AMERICAN FREE TRADE AGREEMENT (NAFTA).

trimmer Part of a garment finishing team, the unskilled trimmer used scissors to hand-clip loose threads, unravelings, or extra materials from a garment.

Twin Restaurant (aka Twinny's) A neighborhood coffee shop and eatery on Main Street in Pittston, Pennsylvania, owned by Michael "Twinny" and Nora DePrimo Sperazza, it was frequented by TOUGH GUYS and garment workers alike, and was often the scene of tensions and confrontations during strikes.

underworld A term referring to ORGANIZED CRIME and criminally associated persons, it has connotations of immoral and "foreign" actors who function "below" and against the established institutional and normative order. However, researchers have regularly found close cooperation between the UNDERWORLD and the UPPERWORLD of established institutions and seemingly "morally upstanding" organizations and leaders. Indeed, the prevailing view among criminologists is that the UNDERWORLD could not exist as it does without cooperation from, and collusion with, elements from the UPPERWORLD.

Unemployed Leagues or Councils Created in a number of large and small cities by the CPUSA during the 1930s, the bodies organized rallies, marches, and demonstrations on behalf of unemployed and poor persons suffering the effects of the Great Depression. Their ultimate purpose was to rally the masses on behalf of CPUSA goals.

UNITE! As the U.S. garment industry declined into the 1990s, the ILGWU and the ACWA merged to form this labor organization in 1995.

UNITE HERE! In 2004, UNITE! merged with the Hotel Employees and Restaurant Employees (HERE), inaugurating this new labor union to secure greater strength in numbers.

United Mine Workers of America (UMWA) Established by bituminous workers in 1890, it came to the ANTHRACITE fields in the mid-1890s and led successful strikes in 1900 and 1902, and other major strikes in 1922 and 1925–26. It has endured to the present as the most successful miners' union in North America, although corruption and infighting plagued the organization between the 1930s and the 1960s. The controversial JOHN L. LEWIS served as the president between 1919 and 1960. Garment shop owner and alleged ORGANIZED CRIMINAL DOMINICK "NICK" ALAIMO was as a UMWA local official in Pittston, Pennsylvania, and served jail time for accepting bribes from KNOX COAL COMPANY officials to insure labor peace during the 1950s. From a peak membership of about five hundred thousand in 1920 and in 1946, the UMWA's numbers had fallen to two hundred thousand in the 1990s, and under eighty thousand in 2017. Many members today are employed in health care, trucking, manufacturing, and public services in the United States and Canada.

Unity House An ILGWU-owned and -operated resort and educational retreat in the Pocono Mountains of Pennsylvania, the land was first purchased by New York ILGWU Local 22 and LOCAL 25 in 1919. Ownership passed to the International union in 1929. The facility consisted of a lake, 750 acres of land, and several buildings. It was open to union members and their families for relaxation and/or educational purposes. The ILGWU WYOMING VALLEY DISTRICT arranged numerous programs for members over the years. Unity House underwent a series of expansions and improvements until, due to declining union membership, it was closed and sold in 1989 for use as a performing arts center (which has since gone bankrupt). It now functions as a community center.

upperworld A term referring to the established institutional and normative order and its purportedly upstanding organizations and leaders, it includes corporations, banks and other financial concerns, small business, political institutions, the judiciary, law enforcement, government agencies, labor unions, universities and colleges, schools, religious bodies, and professional associations. Researchers have regularly found close cooperation between UPPERWORLD actors and the UNDERWORLD of ORGANIZED CRIME. Indeed, the prevailing view among criminologists is that the UNDERWORLD could not exist as it does without cooperation from, and collusion with, elements from the UPPERWORLD.

Wagner Act Formally titled the NATIONAL LABOR RELATIONS ACT, President Franklin D. Roosevelt signed the measure into law in 1935. One of its main provisions established the legal right of employees (excepting agricultural and domestic workers) to organize and join labor unions and bargain collectively with their employers.

wildcat strike An unsanctioned walkout or work suspension called by workers, often in violation of a collectively bargained agreement and/or a state statute.

Young Communist League USA Founded in New York in 1922, it was intended to direct young people into the CPUSA (with which it was affiliated). It fostered a belief in Marxism-Leninism and an active involvement in American working-class struggles. MIN MATHESON (chap. 3) was a member in her youth.

zipper setter This is a skilled garment occupation tasked with sewing zippers on dresses, skirts, coats, and other garments. See SPECIAL OPERATORS.

APPENDIX 3: BIOGRAPHICAL SKETCHES

An asterisk (*) in front of a person's name indicates that they are one of the sixteen oral history subjects included in this volume. A name in ALL CAPS indicates that the person's biographical sketch is included in this appendix, whereas a term in ALL CAPS indicates its inclusion in appendix 2.

Agolino, Ettore An attorney from Pittston, Pennsylvania, he was reputed to have had RUSSELL BUFALINO, ANGELO SCIANDRA, DOMINICK "NICK" ALAIMO, and other alleged ORGANIZED CRIMINALS among his clients.

Alaimo, Dominick "Nick" Born in Montedoro, Sicily, he was an alleged member of the Pittston crime organization, referred to as the MEN FROM MONTEDORO. He attended the APALACHIN, NEW YORK, ORGANIZED CRIME SUMMIT OF 1957, and escaped from the scene, but was later apprehended by police. He worked as a coal miner, a UMWA official at the KNOX COAL COMPANY, and a garment shop owner. As the proprietor of the ALAIMO DRESS COMPANY and the JANE HOGAN DRESS COMPANY (in likely partnership with other gangsters), he resisted unionization until MIN MATHESON (chap. 3) threatened to call UMWA vice president THOMAS KENNEDY and report that he was operating a nonunion shop. He attempted to have his shops organized by the short-lived DUAL UNION, the ANTHRACITE NEEDLE WORKERS' ASSOCIATION OF PENNSYLVANIA. In 1960, he was tried, convicted, and sentenced to a short prison sentence for labor law violations and bribery—both in conjunction with the infamous KNOX COAL COMPANY and the KNOX MINE DISASTER of 1959.

Alaimo, Samuel Brother of DOMINICK "NICK" and WILLIAM ALAIMO, he owned and operated nonunion garment shops in Pittston, Pennsylvania, which were later organized under the ANTHRACITE NEEDLE WORKERS' ASSOCIATION OF PENNSYLVANIA.

Alaimo, William Brother of DOMINICK "NICK" and SAMUEL ALAIMO, he owned and operated nonunion garment shops in Pittston, Pennsylvania, which were later organized under the ANTHRACITE NEEDLE WORKERS' ASSOCIATION OF PENNSYLVANIA. He purportedly attended and escaped from the APALACHIN, NEW YORK, ORGANIZED CRIME SUMMIT OF 1957.

Alba, William Co-owner of Ann-Lee Frocks, in Pittston, Pennsylvania, with ANGELO SCIANDRA, DOMINICK "NICK" ALAIMO, and others.

Amuso, Victor Allegedly in charge of THOMAS "THREE-FINGER BROWN" LUCCHESE's garment operations in New York, he became head of the gang between 1987 and 2012, following Lucchese's death. He was a regular visitor to northeastern Pennsylvania, where he attended to his garment business and other concerns. He gained the moniker of the "Deadly Don," as one of the nation's most violent ORGANIZED CRIMINALS. He became a fugitive when the federal government charged him with murder and RACKETEERING. Arrested by the FBI in 1991 in Scranton, Pennsylvania, he was tried, found guilty, and sentenced to life in prison. He is still serving the sentence.

Anastasia, Albert The boss of the Anastasia crime organization, he owned the MADISON DRESS COMPANY in Hazleton, Pennsylvania, in partnership with alleged gangster, HARRY "LEFTY" STRASSER.

Antonini, Luigi A powerful and charismatic ILGWU figure, he was the manager of Local 89 in New York, which was known as the Italian American Local. He was invited to the Wyoming Valley on numerous occasions to attend rallies and deliver speeches, particularly during strikes.

Azar, Jane   An ILGWU ORGANIZER from New York, she was assigned to the Wyoming Valley to assist workers with the LESLIE FAY STRIKE OF 1994.

Babcock, Michael J.   He was selected as the LESLIE FAY COMPANY's president in 1993 following a scandal that led to the company's bankruptcy. He served until 1995.

Bambace, Angela   Born in Brazil to Italian immigrant parents who immigrated to New York City in 1901, she followed her mother into the garment trade as a SEWER. After joining the union and becoming radicalized, she actively participated in union activities between 1917 and 1972 as an ORGANIZER, staff member, and officer. She began organizing shops in Baltimore during the 1930s and served as the first manager of the ILGWU's Maryland-Virginia District. She headed the Upper South Department until her retirement in 1972.

Barbara, Joseph   The reputed head of ORGANIZED CRIME IN NORTHEASTERN PENNSYLVANIA during the early 1950s, he moved to Apalachin, New York to continue with his "businesses." The APALACHIN, NEW YORK, ORGANIZED CRIME SUMMIT OF 1957 was held at his mansion.

Benfante, Nick   An alleged affiliate of ORGANIZED CRIME IN NORTHEASTERN PENNSYLVANIA, he became the general manager of the Pittston-based ANTHRACITE NEEDLE WORKERS' ASSOCIATION OF PENNSYLVANIA, a DUAL UNION and an anti-ILGWU labor organization that unsuccessfully tried to organize garment workers in the Pittston area.

Berger, Martin   A long-term ILGWU member from New Jersey, he held positions in New York and Pennsylvania. Toward the end of his career, he became the state coordinator for AIM, the union's retirees' association.

Bianco, Samuel   In 1962, he was appointed as assistant manager of the ILGWU's local office in Pittston, Pennsylvania, and later became the manager. He also served as first vice president of the NORTHEAST APPAREL ASSOCIATION and the

president of the Northeastern Pennsylvania Labor-Management Council. A disciple of MIN MATHESON (chap. 3), he became the manager of the ILGWU WYOMING VALLEY DISTRICT in 1978.

Blandina, Lenny   A sewing machine supplier and mechanic in the Pittston area with ORGANIZED CRIME ties, he was alleged to have attended and escaped from the APALACHIN, NEW YORK, ORGANIZED CRIME SUMMIT OF 1957. As described by ANTHONY "TONY" D'ANGELO (chap. 5), he allegedly participated (perhaps unknowingly and indirectly) in setting fire to a dress factory in Inkerman, Pennsylvania, owned by ANGELO SCIANDRA so that he (Sciandra) could collect the insurance money, perhaps as part of a BUST OUT.

Boyle, James   He was the general manager of the MCKITTERICK-WILLIAMS INC. in West Pittston, Pennsylvania, during the 1940s. A resident of Kingston, Pennsylvania, he resisted unionization during the 1940s on directions from the plant's owners. The ILGWU eventually organized the shop.

Brader, Rose   As a union member, she worked for thirty-one years to direct organized labor's contributions to the United Way of Wyoming Valley.

Brickel, Grace   Born in Italy as Grace Sardegna, she became the first general manager of the ILGWU's Easton District in 1936 and served in that capacity until her retirement in 1978.

Brown, James   A law partner with DANIEL J. FLOOD, he was the ILGWU WYOMING VALLEY DISTRICT's lawyer during the JENKINS SPORTSWEAR STRIKE OF 1958–59.

Buckhalter, Zachary   He was an administrative employee at the LESLIE FAY COMPANY's main plant in Laflin, Jenkins Township.

Bufalino, Russell   Born in Montedoro, Sicily, he immigrated to the United States as a young adult and began working as a laborer and then as a mechanical repairman for the Pennsylvania Coal Company in Pittston. A long-standing ORGANIZED CRIMINAL in northeastern Pennsylvania, he allegedly emerged as the gang's head in 1959 and held the position until his death in 1994. During his tenure, he served a fourteen-year prison sentence under two separate convictions. He was apprehended at the APALACHIN, NEW YORK, ORGANIZED CRIME SUMMIT OF 1957 and convicted of conspiracy and perjury, but the convictions were overturned on appeal. According to FBI reports, he owned seven dress factories in the Pittston area and a few others in New York. His garment-related holdings included Penn Drape and Curtain, Pittston; ABS Contracting, Pittston; Bonnie Steward Inc., New York (DOMINICK "NICK" ALAIMO and JAMES PULMERI allegedly had financial interests in this company); Claudia Frocks, New York (ANGELO SCIANDRA allegedly held an interest in this company); and Fair Frox Inc. (Sciandra was said to have had an interest in this firm as well). He was said to have fronted the JENKINS SPORTSWEAR COMPANY in Pittston, managed by his relative, EMANUELLA "DOLLY" FALCONE, with the support of her husband, alleged mob affiliate WILLIAM FALCONE, JR. The dress shop became the scene of the bitter JENKINS SPORTSWEAR STRIKE OF 1958–59. According to some sources, he was involved in the disappearance and death of INTERNATIONAL BROTHERHOOD OF TEAMSTERS president James R. Hoffa in 1975.

Buscemi, John   An alleged TOUGH GUY in ORGANIZED CRIME IN NORTHEASTERN PENNSYLVANIA, he intimidated and threatened ILGWU strikers in Pittston, Pennsylvania.

Canjelosi, Charles   He was the co-owner of the CANJELOSI DRESS SHOP in Easton, Pennsylvania, with his brother JOHN CANJELOSI.

Canjelosi, John   He was the co-owner of the CANJELOSI DRESS SHOP in Easton, Pennsylvania, with his brother CHARLES CANJELOSI.

*Caputo, Philomena "Minnie"   A garment worker from Pittston, she participated in several strikes as a member of the ILGWU. She sometimes went undercover for MIN MATHESON (chap. 3) by working in a shop to assess its problems and its potential for unionization. She worked in that capacity at the JENKINS SPORTSWEAR COMPANY and helped precipitate the conflict-ridden JENKINS SPORTSWEAR STRIKE OF 1958–59, of which she was one of the most ardent supporters. In later years, she worked as a FLOORLADY on behalf of a garment company. Her oral history interview is included in this volume (chap. 11).

Carter, Neil   The son of WILLIAM CARTER, he assumed control of the family garment business and ran KAREN MANUFACTURING between 1981 and 1994, which was among the SWEET VALLEY GARMENT FACTORIES.

Carter, William   A former resident of New York City, he moved to the Wyoming Valley and opened a number of garment factories. Following a strike, he purchased the Pittston shop that LARRY SITZMAN had managed on behalf of alleged ORGANIZED CRIMINAL DOMINICK "NICK" ALAIMO and soon accepted his employees' affiliation with the ILGWU. He also owned and operated KAREN SPORTSWEAR and, with his son, NEIL CARTER, KAREN MANUFACTURING, both of which were among the SWEET VALLEY GARMENT FACTORIES. He served on the Board of Directors of the NORTHEAST APPAREL ASSOCIATION. He was an admirer of MIN MATHESON (chap 3) and worked cooperatively with her.

Cefalo, Charles   The owner of Sunday Fashions in Plains Township, Pennsylvania, and MONDAY FASHIONS, in Sweet Valley, Pennsylvania.

Chaiken, Sol "Chick"   After serving as assistant director of the ILGWU's NORTHEAST DEPARTMENT and assistant to the director, DAVID GINGOLD, he went on to become president of the ILGWU between 1975 and 1986.

Chait, Abe   Allegedly one of the leading UNDERWORLD figures in the garment industry, he operated Champion Trucking in the New York garment district and was said to have held interests in FRIEDMAN'S EXPRESS TRUCKING COMPANY and possibly INTERSTATE DRESS CARRIERS INC. He was known to have controlled ILWGU Local 102, the Cloak and Dress Drivers' and Helpers' Union in New York. He contacted MIN MATHESON (chap. 3) during the bitter strike of 1958 and requested a secret meeting at his New York office, which she reluctantly attended in an effort to end the strike. The two developed a "special relationship" that included other such meetings. He was alleged to have made deals with ILGWU leaders in New York allowing him and other UNDERWORLD figures to own a certain number of nonunion shops in northeastern Pennsylvania and elsewhere, in return for relative labor peace.

Cherkes, William "Bill"   Originally from Brooklyn, New York, his father established a RUNAWAY GARMENT SHOP in the Wyoming Valley during the 1940s. Like all such shops, the company secured ladies' clothing orders through a JOBBER on a contract basis. He commuted to and from the city for many years before eventually settling in Kingston, Pennsylvania, with his family. He became the owner of the business, called ANN WILL GARMENT, located in Kingston, Pennsylvania. He and his father worked cooperatively with the ILGWU and enjoyed good relationships with their employees and with MIN MATHESON (chap. 3). He also served as president and board member of the NORTHEAST APPAREL ASSOCIATION. His oral history interview is included in this volume (chap. 2).

Cheston, Art   He was a BUSINESS AGENT in the ILGWU WYOMING VALLEY DISTRICT.

Cohn, Fannia   In 1916, she became the first female vice president of the ILGWU. She served as the secretary of the ILGWU EDUCATION DEPARTMENT at its launch in 1918. A champion of educational programming for members, she organized and encouraged courses and training for over fifty years in her capacity as director of the department. She believed that union-sponsored programs should have two goals: to educate individual members so they might achieve meaningful lives and a social consciousness, and also to develop future union leaders. She argued that social functions should be an integral part of the union's programming, to include dancing, singing, informal discussions, sports, and other gatherings.

Corbett, James   An ILGWU member who began by writing and directing freshly written revues and plays, he was later hired as the director of the ILGWU WYOMING VALLEY CHORUS, and worked with CLEMENTINE LYONS (chap. 8), WILLIAM GABLE, and many others.

☆D'Angelo, Anthony "Tony"   He was employed as a PRESSER in the Wyoming Valley garment industry, including stints at shops owned by ANGELO SCIANDRA and WILLIAM "BILL" CHERKES (chap. 2). While working for Sciandra, he was (unknowingly) recruited to participate in what became a fire in Sciandra's garment factory in Inkerman, Pennsylvania, so that he (Sciandra) could collect

the insurance money. He was a professional barber for many years following his garment employment. His oral history interview is included in this volume (chap. 5).

☆DePasquale, Angelo "Rusty" "Bill"   An ANTHRACITE mineworker who was also employed as an ORGANIZER for the Wyoming Valley district, he stayed with the union out of loyalty and friendship to MIN MATHESON (chap. 3), but also possibly because his girlfriend worked as a CHAIRLADY in a Pittston shop. As a native of Pittston he knew the major players in ORGANIZED CRIME IN NORTHEASTERN PENNSYLVANIA and showed no fear of them. As such, he and his "boys" often provided "muscle" on behalf of the union during organizing campaigns. In one instance, he allegedly held a gun to a police officer who was harassing Mrs. Matheson on a picket line. In another episode, he tried to shoot the tires out of a strikebreaking truck that crossed a picket line in Edwardsville, Pennsylvania, and began transporting finished goods to New York. The latter confrontation caused a major row with ILGWU president DAVID DUBINSKY, who summoned him to union headquarters and chastised him for the action. The berating eventually led to his resignation from the ILGWU. His oral history interview is included in this volume (chap. 4).

Diamond, Jack "Legs"   An alleged ORGANIZED CRIMINAL, he was hired by certain New York employers during the 1920s to keep workers from joining the ILGWU. See JACOB "LITTLE AUGIE" ORGEN and ARNOLD ROTHSTEIN.

Dioguardi, John   Also known as "Johnny Dio," he engaged in protection RACKETEERING in the New York GARMENT CENTER in the 1920s and was also convicted of extorting money from garment truckers in 1937 (for which he served a three-year term in New York's Sing Sing Correctional Facility). Following his release, he moved to Allentown, Pennsylvania, where he operated nonunion dress factories while also working to keep out the ILGWU. Following another jail sentence, he was called to testify at the MCCLELLAN COMMITTEE HEARINGS in 1958, where he invoked the Fifth Amendment several times. In 1956, authorities indicted him in an acid attack that blinded newspaper columnist

VICTOR RIESEL. Two co-conspirators were also indicted and later convicted, but Dioguardi escaped culpability when his colleagues recanted their testimony against him.

Dorkoski, Kenneth As a garment shop owner, he was a member of the Board of Directors of the NORTHEAST APPAREL ASSOCIATION.

Dotter, Mildred "Millie" An employee at the EMKAY MANUFACTURING COMPANY in Wyoming, Pennsylvania, she assisted CLEMENTINE LYONS (chap. 8) and others with the ILGWU WYOMING VALLEY DISTRICT CHORUS, including its first kiddie show, *The Lollypop Revue.*

Dubinsky, David An immigrant from Russia, he labored in the garment industry before rising through the ILGWU's ranks to become union president in 1933, an office he held until his retirement in 1966. Known to his colleagues as "DD," he was a strong proponent of SOCIAL UNIONISM and was the first American union president to "open the books" for the federal government's inspection. He realized the danger posed by out-of-town, RUNAWAY GARMENT SHOPS such as those migrating to the Wyoming Valley during the 1930s. He frequently visited northeastern Pennsylvania for union activities, although he mistrusted MIN MATHESON (chap. 3) to some degree for the (imagined) leadership competition she might have posed.

Dubrow, Evelyn She worked as lobbyist and vice president of the ILGWU from the 1950s until her death in 2006. President Bill Clinton awarded her the Presidential Medal of Freedom in 1999.

Evans, Mary She held the position of assistant CHAIRLADY at the STELLA DRESS COMPANY in the late 1940s.

Falcone, Emanuella "Dolly" She was alleged mob boss RUSSELL BUFALINO's first cousin (or niece by some accounts) and the wife of alleged mob affiliate WILLIAM FALCONE, JR., who supported his wife's operation of JENKINS SPORTSWEAR INC. in Pittston, Pennsylvania. The couple likely served as the "front" owners for Bufalino and, as such, vigorously resisted unionization. The shop became the scene of a prolonged and violent strike in

1958–59. It was eventually sold to another owner who accepted the ILGWU.

Falcone, William, Jr. An alleged ORGANIZED CRIME associate from Pittston, Pennsylvania, he supported his wife, EMANUELLA "DOLLY" FALCONE, in the operation of JENKINS SPORTSWEAR INC. in Pittston, Pennsylvania. He reportedly attended the APALACHIN, NEW YORK, ORGANIZED CRIME SUMMIT OF 1957.

Falzone, Mr. (first name unknown) One of the first runaway shop owners in Pittston, Pennsylvania, he resisted the ILGWU.

Farley, Eugene As the president of Wilkes College (now University) in Wilkes-Barre, Pennsylvania, from 1948 to 1970, he cooperated with MIN MATHESON in establishing a leadership program at the institution exclusively intended for ILGWU members. Taught by college faculty, the program, which lasted for several years, awarded successful students with an official Wilkes graduation certificate.

Feinberg, Dr. Albert A medical doctor who served as the first director of the ILGWU WYOMING VALLEY HEALTH CENTER. He planned and carried out the Health Center's operations while also providing many services to the workers.

Ferraro, John He was the field manager for the NORTHEAST APPAREL ASSOCIATION.

Flannery, J. Harold, Sr. As a Democrat and native of Pittston, Pennsylvania, he was an ally of organized labor and the ILGWU. After two terms in U.S. House of Representatives, he was elected to a ten-year term as a judge of the Luzerne County Court of Common Pleas, where he sat with THOMAS M. LEWIS and FRANK L. PINOLA. He regularly attended the ILGWU's testimonial dinners, anniversary banquets, and other functions, in part because he benefited from the members' support during elections.

Flood, Daniel J. He was the lawyer for the ILGWU Wyoming Valley District during the 1940s, and his former law firm continued in that capacity after he was elected to the U.S. House of Representatives in 1944. He lost the election of 1946, was elected again in 1948, lost the seat in 1952, returned to office in 1954, and went on to serve eleven more terms with little opposition. He often stated that he owed his electoral victories to "Min and her girls," who provided their endorsement and assiduously worked to bring out the vote during elections. He was the co-sponsor of the AREA REDEVELOPMENT ACT of 1961, which brought $394 million into economically depressed areas such as the Wyoming Valley, and the Coal Mine Health and Safety Act of 1969, which provided over $500 million in compensation to the twenty-five thousand ANTHRACITE mineworkers who contracted black lung (anthracosilicosis) disease. He was censured by Congress for bribery in 1979 and resigned from the House in 1980.

Gable, William   He was the musical director of the ILGWU WYOMING VALLEY DISTRICT CHORUS and director of its Broadway-type shows. See JIM CORBETT and CLEMENTINE "CLEM" LYONS (chap. 8).

Gambini, Ralph G.   A garment shop owner, he served on the Board of Directors for the NORTHEAST APPAREL ASSOCIATION.

Gambino, Thomas   The son of New York's alleged crime boss Carlo Gambino, he married THOMAS "THREE-FINGER BROWN" LUCCHESE's daughter, Frances, in 1962. He was the manager of the HARVIC FASHIONS COMPANY, one of the SWEET VALLEY GARMENT SHOPS, which experienced a nine-month strike beginning in 1958.

Giambra, Albert   An alleged TOUGH GUY affiliated with ORGANIZED CRIME IN NORTHEASTERN PENNSYLVANIA, he intimidated and threatened ILGWU strikers in Pittston, Pennsylvania.

Giannini, Ivo   The first assistant district attorney of Luzerne County, he grilled PHILOMENA "MINNIE" CAPUTO (chap. 11) and other ILGWU strikers in a court case that dealt with their alleged behavior on a picket line during the JENKINS SPORTSWEAR STRIKE OF 1958–59.

Gingold, David   Following a series of local union positions in New York, he became the director of the ILGWU's NORTHEAST DEPARTMENT in 1943 and held the post until his retirement in 1977. He also sat for many years on the ILGWU's GENERAL EXECUTIVE BOARD.

Gladstone, Benjamin   He was the executive director of the NORTHEAST APPAREL ASSOCIATION during the 1980s.

Grasso brothers (Joseph, Frank, and Samuel)   The brothers founded the United Pants Company in 1929 and relocated the factory from Old River Road in Wilkes-Barre to the former Luvan Silk Mill on Shoemaker and Simpson Streets in Swoyersville, Pennsylvania. They employed 650 operators in 1935 and 500 in 1940 (one of whom was the author's mother, ROSALIE SIRACUSE WOLENSKY). They secured government contracts for military uniforms and also manufactured civilian uniforms, coats, pants, trousers, and jackets. The business closed in March 1987.

*Greenburg, Betty (Matheson)   Born in Sayre and raised in Kingston, Pennsylvania, she is the second child of MIN and BILL MATHESON and the spouse of LARRY GREENBERG. She shared in her parents' many challenges and successes with her sister, MARIANNE KAUFMAN. She possesses a great deal of knowledge regarding her parents' union activities and daily lives, including their participation in the Flood Victims' Action Council, which she co-founded with them following the 1972 Tropical Storm Agnes flood. Her oral history interview is included in this volume (chap. 15).

Greenberg, Harry   He served as the manager-secretary of ILGWU Local 91 beginning in the 1920s before going on to serve as vice president of the union in the 1940s and 1950s. Described as a pragmatist rather than an ideologue, he was a strong supporter of SOCIAL UNIONISM.

Greenberg, Larry   The spouse of BETTY GREENBERG and son-in-law of MIN and BILL MATHESON, he owned a locksmith business and participated in the Flood Victims Action Council following the Tropical Storm Agnes disaster of 1972.

Greene, Sol   He held the manager's position in the ILGWU's Allentown District and went on to higher administrative and leadership positions with the union. As the director of organizing, he became the top ILGWU official in Pennsylvania and later served as assistant director of the union's Northeast Department and assistant general manager of the NEW YORK DRESS JOINT BOARD. In February 1959, he was severely beaten by three anti-union thugs in New York.

Grossi, Enzo   He was the manager of the ILGWU Scranton District during the 1940s and 1950s.

Guisto, John   In 1950, he was charged with the murder of WILLIAM "WILL" LURYE and subsequently went into hiding as a fugitive. His murdered body was found a short while later.

*Gutstein, Leo   Born in the Wyoming Valley town of Exeter, Pennsylvania, he eventually assumed ownership of the LEE MANUFACTURING COMPANY in Pittston, a firm that his father, LOUIS GUTSTEIN, had established as a RUNAWAY SHOP in the late 1930s. The company made ladies' clothing on a contract basis at its main location in the old Armory Building on Main Street in Pittston. The contracts came from JOBBERS and included work from firms such as the LESLIE FAY COMPANY and Liz Claiborne. He also operated shops in Sayre, Carbondale, and Mayfield, Pennsylvania, and, for a brief time, in the Dominican Republic. At first, he commuted weekly from Great Neck, New York, but he eventually moved to the Wyoming Valley with his family. He served as treasurer and later as president of the NORTHEAST APPAREL ASSOCIATION. He and his father worked cooperatively with the ILGWU and enjoyed good relationships with their employees and with MIN MATHESON (chap. 3). He recognized the presence of ORGANIZED CRIME in the local industry but said that much of the control came from gangsters in New York. He skillfully managed to avoid untoward encounters with the "unsavory element." His oral history interview is included in this volume (chap. 13).

Gutstein, Louis   A native New Yorker, he established one of the first RUNAWAY SHOPS in the Wyoming Valley in the late 1930s, the LEE MANUFACTURING COMPANY of Pittston, Pennsylvania. Perhaps through a special arrangement with New York leaders, his company did not unionize for the first years; however, he eventually joined the ILGWU under MIN MATHESON, with whom he worked cooperatively and respectfully.

Halperin, Jack   He served as field supervisor and assistant to the director of ILGWU NORTHEAST DEPARTMENT.

Harris, James   He was the owner and operator of PIONEER MANUFACTURING INC. in Wilkes-Barre, Pennsylvania, one of the larger garment operations in the Wyoming Valley.

Hartel, Lois   She served as the last manager of the ILGWU WYOMING VALLEY DISTRICT before it merged with the Hazleton District due to membership decline. In addition, she participated in the strike and the larger campaign to keep the LESLIE FAY COMPANY factories from closing in 1994. See MARION MALACHI, PEARL NOVAK (chap. 14), LINDA WHITAKER, and NANCY ZIEGLER.

Heit, David   He was the manager of PITTSTON APPAREL, which was owned by the LESLIE FAY COMPANY.

Hertzberg, Mrs. Stanley (first name unknown)   Upon the death of her husband, STANLEY HERTZBERG, she assumed ownership of the STAR GARMENT COMPANY of West Pittston, Pennsylvania, in partnership with JOHN LANUNZIATA.

Hertzberg, Stanley   Owner and operator of the STAR GARMENT COMPANY in West Pittston, Pennsylvania, which was a unionized firm. See MRS. STANLEY HERTZBERG.

Hillman, Sidney   He was president of the ACWA from 1914 to 1946 and, like his counterpart, DAVID DUBINSKY of the ILGWU, promoted SOCIAL UNIONISM. Hillman joined with Dubinsky, JOHN L. LEWIS of the UMWA, and other union leaders in establishing the CIO in 1935.

Hochman, Julius   He served as the BUSINESS AGENT of ILGWU LOCAL 25 in New York, general manager of the NEW YORK DRESS JOINT BOARD, first director of the ILGWU UNION LABEL DEPARTMENT, and vice president of the International union. He authored a report on the relationship between the ILGWU and ORGANIZED CRIME, which examined the history of a special deal between union leaders and alleged organized criminals that permitted certain mobsters to retain several nonunion shops in exchange for their less aggressive anti-union policy.

The arrangement brought a period of labor peace that apparently broke down during the strike of 1958. He clashed with MIN MATHESON (chap. 3) and other district mangers over the issue of centralized versus decentralized decision making.

Hoffa, James R. President of the INTERNATIONAL BROTHERHOOD OF TEAMSTERS, whose members transported unfinished goods and material from New York to the Wyoming Valley and took finished garment back to the city, he was alleged to have had ORGANIZED CRIME connections and dealings. See LEO NAMEY and RUSSELL BUFALINO.

Hoffman, Sol As director of the ILGWU NORTHEAST DEPARTMENT and vice president of the International union, he made routine visits to the ILGWU WYOMING VALLEY DISTRICT and had regular communications with local union leaders.

Hollander, Lawrence A garment shop owner from Kingston, Pennsylvania, he served as president of the NORTHEAST APPAREL ASSOCIATION in the 1960s.

*Justin, John "Johnny" Born in Massachusetts, he moved to Harlem, New York, with his mother and six siblings following the death of his father in the 1920s. He left school at age fifteen and, with assistance from an uncle, found work in a pajama and straw-hat factory. He later secured a position at Western Union to help with the family's finances while simultaneously attending night school to obtain a high school diploma. An enthusiastic community organizer, he was particularly adept at staging marches, rallies, and protest campaigns. As a young adult in the 1930s, he organized for the CPUSA and helped establish UNEMPLOYED LEAGUES in Harrisburg, Pennsylvania. He became an ILGWU ORGANIZER in Harrisburg shortly before leaving for military service during World War II. After the war, he returned as an ILGWU organizer in the Wilkes-Barre area and later served as district manager in Harrisburg and Pottsville. Later in his career he worked as an organizer and troubleshooter for the union in Wilmington, Delaware, Trenton, New Jersey, Chicago, Illinois, and in Maryland and Wisconsin. He eventually joined MIN MATHESON (chap. 3) as an assistant when she assumed leadership of the UNION LABEL DEPARTMENT in New York. He had several encounters with alleged organized criminals, including MICHAEL PAPPADIO

and VICTOR AMUSO. He remained a good friend and ally of MIN and BILL MATHESON, including during his retirement, which began in the 1970s when he settled in Wilkes-Barre. His oral history interview is included in this volume (chap. 7).

Kahn, Mac Reputedly one of the four richest men in New York City, he owned the EMKAY MANUFACTURING COMPANY in Wyoming, Pennsylvania, which employed up to two hundred workers who made girdles and bathing suits. After meeting early resistance, the ILGWU organized his shop in the late 1940s.

Katzman, Seth A former New Yorker, he was a garment shop owner and member of the Board of Directors of the NORTHEAST APPAREL ASSOCIATION.

Kaufman, Marianne (Matheson) The elder of MIN and BILL MATHESON's two children, she was born in New York City and raised in Kingston, Pennsylvania. She shared in her parents' many challenges and successes with her sister, BETTY GREENBERG (chap. 15).

Kelly, Thomas He was a garment shop owner who served on the Board of Directors of the NORTHEAST APPAREL ASSOCIATION.

Kennedy, Joseph The son of Robert F. Kennedy, he visited and spoke at several Wyoming Valley garment shops as part of his father's presidential campaign in 1967–68.

Kennedy, Thomas Born in 1887 in Lansford, Pennsylvania, he began working in the coal mines at age twelve. He joined the UMWA in 1900, and at age sixteen he was elected secretary of Local 1738. Despite his not having a formal education, he climbed the union ladder and was chosen as secretary-treasurer in 1925, vice president in 1947, and president between 1960 and 1962. He was elected lieutenant governor of Pennsylvania in 1934 and served for one term.

Kniffen, Luther A funeral director by profession, he was elected the Republican mayor of Wilkes-Barre in January 1948 and held the office until January 1960. He supported the ILGWU and its leaders, and regularly attended the union's programs and social gatherings.

LaTorre, Steven An immigrant from Montedoro, Sicily, he was the alleged cofounder, with SANTO VOLPE, of ORGANIZED CRIME IN NORTHEASTERN PENNSYLVANIA during the early twentieth century. He originally worked as a coal miner and a mining subcontractor. He had no recognized interests in the garment industry. See the MEN FROM MONTEDORO.

Lanunziata, John He was an owner of the STAR GARMENT COMPANY in West Pittston, Pennsylvania, in partnership with MRS. STANLEY HERTZBERG.

Lebean, Mr. (first name unknown) Originally from New York, he was the owner of the STELLA DRESS COMPANY in Kingston, Pennsylvania.

Lehahan, James DANIEL J. FLOOD'S law partner who represented the ILGWU WYOMING VALLEY DISTRICT when Flood was elected to the U.S. House of Representatives.

Levandowski, John Originally a garment worker from Wilkes-Barre, Pennsylvania, he was a well-respected shop manager and went on to serve in several managerial capacities, including the leadership role at MONDAY FASHIONS.

Lewis, John L. A native of Iowa, he served as president of the UMWA between 1920 and 1960.

Lewis, Thomas M. As a Republican, he sat on the Luzerne County Court of Common Pleas with FRANK L. PINOLA and J. HAROLD FLANNERY. He regularly attended the ILGWU's testimonial dinners, anniversary banquets, and other functions, in part because he enjoyed the members' support during elections.

Lieberman, Harry The proprietor of a taxi company in Wilkes-Barre, he joined with JOE SNARSKI to purchase the shop owned by THOMAS "THREE-FINGER BROWN" LUCCHESE and HARRY "NIG" ROSEN in Sweet Valley. The new owners renamed the shop JAY FASHIONS and the employees soon joined the ILGWU.

Lippi, August J. A coal miner and later a UMWA official, he served jail time for criminal conspiracy, income tax evasion, and bank fraud resulting from his secret and illegal ownership of the KNOX COAL COMPANY while he was also serving as president of UMWA District 1. Known to have had close dealings with ORGANIZED CRIME IN NORTHEASTERN PENNSYLVANIA, he escaped manslaughter and conspiracy charges (on appeal) in connection with the KNOX MINE DISASTER of 1959.

Loquasto, Modesto "Murph" As a TOUGH GUY, he was an alleged member of ORGANIZED CRIME IN NORTHEASTERN PENNSYLVANIA. He was supposed to have worked as RUSSELL BUFALINO'S bodyguard during the 1950s and 1960s. He also held the position as an ORGANIZER within the mob-initiated dual union, the ANTHRACITE NEEDLE WORKERS' ASSOCIATION OF PENNSYLVANIA.

Lori, Arthur After a period of nonunion operation, he went on to own and operate a group of unionized dress factories in Pittston, Pennsylvania, and in other towns, including one in Plains Township. As a member of the PGMA, he reluctantly signed the labor-management agreement following the bitter strike of 1958.

Lovestone, Jay An immigrant from latter-day Lithuania, he was the leader of the CPUSA during the 1920s in New York. MIN MATHESON (chap. 3) served as his secretary at age fifteen, as she entered the inner circle of the CPUSA. After a series of sharp disagreements over strategy and philosophy, CPUSA leaders purged Lovestone and other members, many of whom also belonged to the ILGWU. After their expulsions from the Party, DAVID DUBINSKY welcomed Lovestone, Min Matheson, and others into the union fold. Lovestone became the ILGWU's international representative and worked closely with the U.S. State Department and other groups in pursuit of anti-Communist policies and programs. He was eventually elected head of AFL's Political Department. See LOVESTONITES.

Lucchese, Thomas "Three-Finger Brown" Known as by his nickname because he had lost a thumb and index finger in a machining accident during his youth, he was the alleged leader of a New York criminal gang that counted garment RACKETEERING among its many "businesses." During the early 1950s, he and HARRY "NIG" ROSEN opened the nonunion HARVIC FASHIONS COMPANY as one of the SWEET VALLEY GARMENT SHOPS. The partners were among those owners who refused to negotiate with the ILGWU during the strike of 1958. As the head of a New York crime syndicate, he attended and fled from the APALACHIN, NEW YORK, ORGANIZED CRIME SUMMIT OF 1957. He was called to testify at the MCCLELLAN COMMITTEE HEARINGS in 1958, where he was referred to as "a dress contractor." In addition to the Sweet Valley operation, he had ownership interests in dozens of other garment factories in New York and Pennsylvania, including Kaska Sportswear in Kaska, Pennsylvania, as well as the Bal-Fran Blouse Company, BUDGET DRESS COMPANY, and Ann-Lyn Sportswear in New York. He also invested in the garment trucking business.

Lurye, Max   He was a Russian Jewish immigrant and the father of MIN MATHESON (chap. 3). As a cigar maker and radical labor activist, he helped found the Chicago Cigar Makers' Union. Largely through his influence, his daughter became fully immersed in a world of Jewish socialist culture, union struggles, and uncompromising dedication to labor's cause. Because of his labor involvements, Mr. Lurye was shot and wounded by Chicago's Capone gang in 1927. He endured the attack but did not survive the death of his son, WILLIAM "WILL" LURYE, who was murdered in New York City in 1949. Within days of the tragedy, Max Lurye died of a heart attack. Father and son were buried side by side in the Workmen's Circle Cemetery in Brooklyn.

Lurye, William "Will"   A thirty-five-year-old father of four, the son of MAX LURYE, and the brother of MIN MATHESON (chap. 3), he was murdered in the Manhattan GARMENT DISTRICT on May 4, 1949. BENEDICTO MACRI and JOHN GUISTO were charged with the death in June 1950. A jury acquitted Macri in 1951, while Guisto remained a fugitive until he was later found dead from foul play. Macri remained free until the spring of 1954, when he was knifed to death on a Lower East Side street. No one was ever convicted of Will Lurye's demise. A homicide patterned after his death figured prominently in the film *Garment Jungle* (1957), based on the writings of journalist LESTER VELIE.

*Lyons, Clementine "Clem"   A garment worker from Wyoming, Pennsylvania, she became a member of ILGWU in April 1947 and retired from the industry in 1984. She worked for many years as an ORGANIZER and BUSINESS AGENT in the Pittston area. Known for a fiery disposition, she

enthusiastically participated in strikes, rallies, and other forms of union action. She was recruited to the union cause by MIN MATHESON (chap. 3) and remained a staunch supporter of Mathesons and the ILGWU throughout her adult life. She also became well-known as a talented singer, performer, and director in the ILGWU WYOMING VALLEY DISTRICT CHORUS, where she operated alongside WILLIAM GABLE and JAMES CORBETT in bringing performances to the stage. Her oral history interview is included in this volume (chap. 8).

Macri, Benedicto   Charged with the death of WILLIAM "WILL" LURYE in 1950, he was tried and found not guilty. In 1954, he died of knife wounds on a Lower East Side Street, the victim of apparent foul play.

Madaffari, Vincent   As a garment shop owner, he served as the second vice president of the NORTHEAST APPAREL ASSOCIATION.

Malachi, Marion   An ILGWU ORGANIZER and BUSINESS AGENT from the Wyoming Valley, she assisted with the 1994 strike and the larger campaign to keep the LESLIE FAY COMPANY factories open. See LOIS HARTEL, PEARL NOVAK (chap.14), LINDA WHITAKER, and NANCY ZIEGLER.

Maloney, Hugh   A native of Scranton, Pennsylvania, he worked as an ORGANIZER for the ILGWU WYOMING VALLEY DISTRICT during the 1950s.

*Matheson, Minnie Hindy Lurye "Min"   Born in Chicago in 1909 to impoverished Russian Jewish immigrants, as a young girl she developed a deep commitment to the working class and its labor struggles thanks to her cigar-making, union activist father, MAX LURYE. Immersed in a world of radical Jewish Socialist labor, she regularly joined her father at rallies and meetings. She met BILL MATHESON at the Sunday meetings of the Chicago Federation of Labor. The couple later fell in love and established a household. With Bill's encouragement, she left Chicago to help striking textile workers in Paterson, New Jersey. The strike failed, whereupon she relocated to New York City, secured a job in a garment factory, and became a member (and in 1937 the CHAIRLADY) of ILGWU LOCAL 22 and its thirty-two thousand members. She joined the so-called LOVESTONITES while still in her teens and served as JAY LOVESTONE's secretary; at the same time, she became a member of the CPUSA's inner circle along with her friend JENNIE SILVERMAN. She left the CPUSA with Lovestone, Silverman, and many other ILGWU members to participate in the Socialist movement.

She was joined by Bill Matheson in New York and, by the 1930s, they both had embarked on careers in the ILGWU. In 1941, Bill accepted an organizing position in Sayre, Pennsylvania, while she continued in New York until they decided to get married and begin a family. She joined Bill in Sayre, and their first daughter, Marianne, was born in 1941. A second child, Betty, was born shortly thereafter.

The family moved to the Wyoming Valley in 1944 when Bill accepted a position with the Scranton regional office of the ILGWU, which covered the Wyoming Valley. Min returned to union work in 1945 to become the manager of the new ILWGU WYOMING VALLEY DISTRICT. An enthusiastic community organizer, she was particularly adept at staging marches, rallies, and protest campaigns, and convincing workers to join the union. Because of intraunion conflicts, in 1963, she was assigned to head the ILGWU UNION LABEL DEPARTMENT in New York. The Mathesons retired from the ILGWU in 1971 and returned to the Wyoming Valley. In 1973, the Northeastern Pennsylvania Public Employees AFSCME District Council 87 presented her with a Humanitarian Award, and, in 1980, she received the MOTHER JONES AWARD from the Pennsylvania Labor History Society. She was also a founder and first chairperson of the Flood Victims Action Council following the Tropical Storm Agnes flood of 1972. Her oral history interview is included in this volume (chap. 3).

Matheson, Wilfred "Bill"   He was MIN MATHESON's husband and well as her chief consultant and strategist. A working-class intellectual, he was born in Canada and became a committed Socialist and Communist in his early years. Along with his wife, he left the CPUSA in the 1920s and later supported New Deal labor policies such as the WAGNER ACT of 1935. In the early 1940s, he managed the district and organized shops in Sayre, Pennsylvania, before accepting a position in the Northeastern Pennsylvania in 1944. While in the

Wyoming Valley, he served as the statewide director of the ILGWU Pennsylvania Education Department. He enjoyed composing lyrics for the ILGWU WYOMING VALLEY CHORUS and writing speeches and press releases for his wife and the union. He started the district union's newsletter—called NEEDLEPOINT—and went on to initiate newsletters for other Pennsylvania districts. He set up classes for garment workers, taught some of the classes, and arranged for others to teach.

Matt, Delores   She was an ILGWU member who participated in picketing during strikes in Pittston.

Matthews, Tom   An ILGWU member, he was arrested during the LESLIE FAY STRIKE OF 1994.

Mazur, Jay   He sat as the last president of the ILGWU from 1986 to 1995 and became the first president of the new union, UNITE!, where he served from 1995 to 2001.

McCall, Joseph   He was an innocent bystander who was badly beaten by the TOUGH GUYS during a Pittston, Pennsylvania, strike at an allegedly ORGANIZED CRIME–affiliated garment shop.

McDonald, Edith   A resident of West Pittston, she worked as the CHAIRLADY at the EMKAY MANUFACTURING COMPANY in Wyoming, Pennsylvania.

Mock, Joseph   The sheriff of Sweet Valley, Pennsylvania, he was highly critical of garment workers during the strike of 1958. However, he later reconciled with the union and its leaders after one of the owners of the shop, THOMAS "THREE-FINGER BROWN" LUCCHESE, was found to have attended, and been arrested for, the APALACHIN, NEW YORK, ORGANIZED CRIME SUMMIT OF 1957.

Murray, Martin L.   He was elected to the Pennsylvania House of Representatives from a Luzerne County District and served from 1945 to 1948. He was later elected to the Pennsylvania State Senate in 1957 to represent the Fourteenth District, which included the Wyoming Valley. As a Democrat, he remained a strong supporter of the ILGWU and attended many of its rallies, dinners, parties, and testimonials. He enjoyed strong support from the union and its members during elections.

Namey, Leo   He was the longtime BUSINESS AGENT of the INTERNATIONAL BROTHERHOOD OF TEAMSTERS in the Wyoming Valley. Namey and his truck drivers were very supportive of the ILGWU during strikes when, with his approval and in conjunction with the GARMENT INDUSTRY PROVISO, the drivers refused to cross picket lines to drop off PIECEWORK or pick up finished apparel. He served with MIN MATHESON (chap. 3) on community and economic development committees as well as the GREATER WILKES-BARRE LABOR COUNCIL.

*****Ney, Dorothy "Dot"**   Born in Plains, Pennsylvania, she resided in Luzerne, Kingston, and Wilkes-Barre. She graduated from Luzerne High School in 1933. Her father was a coal miner who perished in a mining accident when he was sixty-two years old. She began working in the garment industry in 1943, joined the ILGWU staff in 1958 as an ORGANIZER and BUSINESS AGENT, and continued with the union until she retired in 1980. A disciple of MIN MATHESON, she was one of the first women chosen to train as a BUSINESS AGENT. She participated in many of the Wyoming Valley area strikes—including Pittston—during the 1940s and 1950s. She remained a steadfast supporter and friend of the Mathesons, and became well-known locally as an ILGWU leader. Her oral history interview is included in this volume (chap. 1).

*****Novak, Pearl**   Raised in a coal-mining family, she began her garment career at PIONEER MANUFACTURING INC. at age fifteen, working alongside her mother. She held a sewing position at STAR GARMENT for thirty-three years and later secured a similar job at the LESLIE FAY COMPANY, where she stayed for nine years, until the firm left the area. She served as the strike captain during the LESLIE FAY STRIKE OF 1994. In 1995, she retired, though she remained active in AIM, the union's retirees' association. Her oral history interview is included in this volume (chap. 14).

O'Connor, John J.   New York City's Catholic cardinal between 1984 and 2000, he had served as the bishop of the Diocese of Scranton in 1983–84, during which time several striking garment workers had met and consulted with him. He supported the workers in their strike against the LESLIE FAY COMPANY in 1994.

Orgen, Jacob "Little Augie"   He was a New York City mobster hired by the ILGWU in the 1920s to intimidate employers and counteract the TOUGH GUYS that shop owners had hired to keep the union out. See JACK "LEGS" DIAMOND and ARNOLD ROTHSTEIN.

Osticco, James David   A reputed member of ORGANIZED CRIME IN NORTHEASTERN PENNSYLVANIA, he was apprehended at the APALACHIN, NEW YORK, ORGANIZED CRIME SUMMIT OF 1957.

Pagarelski, Rosanne Siracuse   An office employee at the LESLIE FAY COMPANY's main plant in Laflin, Pennsylvania, she was the author's cousin and godmother.

Page, Bill   An ILGWU WYOMING VALLEY DISTRICT staff member, he was stationed on a picket line at the allegedly mob-owned ANITA DRESS COMPANY in 1958 and was responsible for keeping strikebreaking workers and truckers away. He and ANGELO "RUSTY" "BILL" DEPASQUALE (chap. 4) became involved in an intense car chase to stop a strikebreaking garment truck (purportedly owned by a mob-affiliated company) from taking finished products from the factory to the GARMENT CENTER in New York.

Papalia, Joseph   A garment shop owner, he served on the Board of Directors for the NORTHEAST APPAREL ASSOCIATION.

Pappadio, Michael   He was in charge of the THOMAS "THREE-FINGER BROWN" LUCCHESE's "rag trade" (garment business) in New York, which included shop ownership, garment trucking, protection rackets, and other undertakings in the GARMENT DISTRICT. After Lucchese's demise, the gang's new leader, VICTOR AMUSO, discovered that Pappadio had been skimming funds, which resulted in his murder in 1989. One of the methods he used to bilk funds from shop owners was to deny trucking services to those who refused to pay a regular extra amount that went into his pocket. He also used the BUST OUT tactic to make money.

Pardini, Toni   A picketing ILGWU member in Pittston, she was allegedly "dragged out of her home" by police and arrested in the middle of the night on a strike-related charge.

Pegler, Westbrook   A populist and conservative newspaper columnist between the 1930s and the 1960s, he was a critic of numerous "liberal" institutions, programs, and persons. He envisioned a world of criminal, Communist, and union conspiracies, often facilitated by the federal government. During the Communist scare of the 1950s, he accused MIN MATHESON (chap. 3) and BILL MATHESON of being Communists, which, in fact, they had been during the 1920s; by 1930, however, they had renounced the CPUSA and supported the New Deal and other liberal programs. He was also critical of WILL LURYE.

Pesotta, Rose   She was an ardent supporter of education, health, and other aspects of SOCIAL UNIONISM within the ILGWU. She participated in the Bryn Mawr Summer School for Women Workers, the Brookwood Labor College, and the Wisconsin Summer School. She began as a garment worker and ILGWU ORGANIZER, and went on to hold the position of vice president of the union board. However, conflicts and other tensions "in the field" prompted her to resign as an ORGANIZER in 1942 and return to her original sewing position in New York. Difficulties with the ILGWU GENERAL EXECUTIVE BOARD and with President DAVID DUBINSKY led to her resignation in 1944 as the board's vice president.

Phillips, William "Little Bill"   A host on radio station WPTS in Pittston, Pennsylvania, he facilitated MIN MATHESON's use of airtime to report on strikes, voter registration drives, and other union activities.

Pinola, Frank L.   As a Republican, he served as the president judge of the Luzerne County Court of Common Pleas, where he sat on the bench with THOMAS M. LEWIS and J. HAROLD FLANNERY. He befriended the Mathesons and other garment workers and regularly attended the ILGWU's testimonial dinners, banquets, and other functions, in part because he enjoyed the members' support during elections.

Policare, Charles   He was a worker at ANGELO SCIANDRA's garment factory in Inkerman, Pennsylvania.

Pomerantz, Fred P.   He was the founder and chairman of the LESLIE FAY COMPANY. Beginning in the Manhattan garment business at age eleven, he established Leslie Fay in 1947, naming it after his only daughter. He retired in 1982, whereupon he sold the company for $58 million to a group of investors headed by his son, JOHN J. POMERANTZ of New York, who served as president. Another investment group bought the firm in 1984 for $158 million, and John J. Pomerantz continued as president. The company experienced grave corruption and financial problems and was forced into bankruptcy prior to Fred Pomerantz's retirement in 1982. In a show of appreciation, his Wyoming Valley employees joined with other workers in contributing to the purchase of a purple Rolls-Royce automobile for his birthday in 1958. By the time he died in 1996, Leslie Fay had rebounded from bankruptcy to amass over $500 million in sales.

Pomerantz, John J.   The son of FRED D. POMERANTZ, he served as the president and chief operating officer of the LESLIE FAY COMPANY until MICHAEL J. BABCOCK assumed the role in 1992.

Pulmeri, James   He and alleged mobster DOMINICK "NICK" ALAIMO held financial interests in the Bonnie Steward garment company in New York.

Rander, Mrs. (first name unknown)   She was the owner of an apron factory in Edwardsville, Pennsylvania, at which HELEN WEISS (chap. 9) began her garment career.

*Reca, Alice   The former Alice Yudichak, she was recruited by MIN MATHESON (chap. 3) to join the ILGWU's administrative staff as an ORGANIZER and later as a BUSINESS AGENT. She participated in many of the Pittston, Pennsylvania, strikes in the 1950s, during which she was intimidated by, but also made efforts to herself intimidate, the TOUGH GUYS who harassed the strikers. She was one of the first individuals brought on the union staff by Mrs. Matheson and, with her mentor's encouragement, she later became a BUSINESS AGENT in the Baltimore area, where she worked under district manager ANGELA BAMBACE. Her oral history interview is included in this volume (chap. 6).

Riesel, Victor   A journalist and syndicated columnist for the *New York Mirror*, he wrote numerous articles about labor relations, labor unions, and ORGANIZED CRIME beginning in 1937. In 1956, an alleged mobster tossed sulfuric acid into his face on a New York City street, permanently blinding him. Authorities indicted JOHN DIOGUARDI, a garment shop owner, and two of his lieutenants for the assault. Dioguardi escaped conviction, although his lieutenants were indicted and convicted. Riesel often criticized organized labor, which he saw as infested with Communists and ORGANIZED CRIMINALS.

Rosen, Harry "Nig"   The assumed name of the person born as Hyman Stromberg. He was an alleged ORGANIZED CRIMINAL from Philadelphia who owned numerous garment shops, including one of the SWEET VALLEY GARMENT FACTORIES, HARVIC FASHIONS COMPANY, in partnership with THOMAS "THREE-FINGER BROWN" LUCCHESE. The duo established the nonunion business in the early 1950s. ILGWU picketers closed the plant during the 1958 strike because the partners refused to accept the union and negotiate. Shortly afterward, they sold the plant to HARRY LIEBERMAN and JOSEPH SNARSKI, who accepted the union and renamed the firm JAY FASHIONS.

Rosenberg, Samuel A.   Professor of economics at Wilkes College (now Wilkes University), he served as the impartial referee in settling labor-management disputes in the Wyoming Valley garment industry.

Ross, William   An official in the New York ILGWU office, he was a friend of ANGELO "RUSTY" "BILL" DEPASQUALE (chap. 4), who traveled to Wilkes-Barre and tried to convince the former ORGANIZER to return to the ILGWU with a new assignment in Rochester, New York. DePasquale declined the offer because of a conflict he had had with DAVID DUBINSKY over an ANITA DRESS COMPANY incident.

Rothstein, Arnold   He was the top New York gangster during the 1920s. The ILGWU enlisted him to call off the anti-union TOUGH GUYS that were operating under the direction of JACK "LEGS" DIAMOND, who had been hired by garment employers to attack picketing strikers and keep the union out of their shops. Rothstein reportedly took

care of the matter with a phone call to Diamond. ILGWU leaders then had a problem: how to remove the thugs they had hired, under the direction of mobster JACOB "LITTLE AUGIE" ORGEN, to intimidate the employers and counteract Diamond's thugs? Rothstein proceeded to call Orgen and took care of that matter as well, demonstrating his strong influence within ORGANIZED CRIME circles. According to labor journalist LESTER VELIE, the ILGWU's use of gangsters and their minions in this and other instances opened the gates to the mob's long-term involvement within the industry and the union.

Sacks, Barry   He was chairman of Chorus Line Inc., a major Los Angeles garment maker, who, in 1995, said he was planning to move about 25 percent of his firm's production offshore in order to compete with international competition.

Salatino, Carmella   During the early 1950s, she was selected by MIN MATHESON (chap. 3) and the ILGWU WYOMING VALLEY DISTRICT to become the first Pittston, Pennsylvania, woman to cast her own ballot in an election. She agreed to a strategy whereby she would enter the polling place and, when officials told her she could not vote—that her husband had to vote for her—she would refuse to cooperate. She would not sign the roster unless she could cast her own ballot. Her husband, DOMINICK SALATINO, also agreed to the plan even though threats were made against him. Because of the pressure and upheaval at the polling station, however, Mrs. Salatino did not cast her own ballot in this particular election, but she and the union believed the effort to do so was a start. She went on to serve as vice president and president of ILGWU LOCAL 295 in Pittston, and later opened her own garment shop. She eventually voted on her own behalf.

Salatino, Dominick   Husband of CARMELLA SALATINO, he, despite threats, supported his wife's failed effort to become the first woman in Pittston, Pennsylvania, to cast her own ballot in an election.

Salvo, Andrew   The son of alleged mobster JOHN "BLACKIE" SALVO, he worked in one of Pittston's unionized garment shops and was described by MIN MATHESON (chap. 3) as "a perfectly nice young man." He joined the U.S. Army and wrote letters to Mrs. Matheson during his service time. In 1953, she received a letter from him shortly before his death in an accident while stationed in Germany. A group of ILGWU members attended his wake, at which time Mrs. Matheson handed Mrs. Salvo a $1,000 check for Andrew's death benefit as part of his union membership. She also mentioned his last letter and promised to it pass it on to Mrs. Salvo, though she did retain a copy for the union's records.

Salvo, John "Blackie" A reputed member of ORGANIZED CRIME IN NORTHEASTERN PENNSYLVANIA, he threatened ILGWU strikers in Pittston, Pennsylvania. His son, ANDREW SALVO, was a garment worker and ILGWU member who perished in an accident while stationed with the U.S. military in Germany. Along with dress shop owner WILLIE ALAIMO and others, he was said to have attended and escaped from the APALACHIN, NEW YORK, ORGANIZED CRIME SUMMIT OF 1957.

Schillaci, Rocky He was the co-owner of ANN-LEE FROCKS in Pittston, Pennsylvania, with ANGELO SCIANDRA, RUSSELL BUFALINO, and others. He also held stakes in as many as three other garment factories in Pennsylvania and New York. An alleged member of ORGANIZED CRIME IN NORTHEASTERN PENNSYLVANIA, he was said to have escaped from the APALACHIN, NEW YORK, ORGANIZED CRIME SUMMIT OF 1957.

Schindler, Harry He was manager of the ILGWU Harrisburg District in the 1930s and 1940s, and manager of the union's Scranton District in the 1940s and 1950s.

*Schiowitz, Dr. Albert A physician who served as the second director of the ILGWU WYOMING VALLEY HEALTH CENTER, he began as the associate director and assumed the top position upon the demise of his predecessor, DR. ALBERT FEINBERG. During his tenure, he oversaw an expansion of diagnostic testing services for union members. His oral history interview is included in this volume (chap. 12).

Schoenholtz, Murray A garment shop owner in the Wyoming Valley, for a time he was chairman of the Board of Directors of the NORTHEAST APPAREL ASSOCIATION.

Schuman, Morris He served as the BUSINESS AGENT in the Pottsville, Pennsylvania, ILGWU District, when JOHN "JOHNNY" JUSTIN was the manager.

Sciandra, Angelo The son of alleged northeastern Pennsylvania ORGANIZED CRIME boss JOHN SCIANDRA, he was said to have been a ranking member in the organization. He co-owned ANN-LEE FROCKS in Pittston as well as other garment factories in Pennsylvania and New York, often in partnership with RUSSELL BUFALINO, ROCKY SCHILLACI, and others. He attended, and was captured at, the APALACHIN, NEW YORK, ORGANIZED CRIME SUMMIT OF 1957. Garment workers knew him for playing "TAPS" on his trumpet to intimidate strikers in Pittston. He was alleged to have set fire to his own dress factory, including the sewing machines, so that he could collect the insurance money, perhaps as part of a BUST OUT. See ANTHONY "TONY" D'ANGELO (chap. 5) and LENNY BLANDINA.

Sciandra, John The reputed head of Pittston, Pennsylvania, ORGANIZED CRIME between 1933 and his death from natural causes in 1949, he was also a coal miner and one of the original owners of the KNOX COAL COMPANY. He was married to JOSEPHINE SCIANDRA, and his son, ANGELO SCIANDRA, was a garment shop owner. See the MEN FROM MONTEDORO.

Sciandra, Josephine The wife of alleged crime boss JOHN SCIANDRA and the mother of ANGELO SCIANDRA, she gave MIN MATHESON (chap. 3) a vase as a peace offering for the poor treatment her son had inflicted on striking garment workers in Pittston, Pennsylvania. She was indicted in the aftermath of the KNOX MINE DISASTER because she had inherited her husband's shares in the KNOX COAL COMPANY. She was convicted of income tax evasion but was given a suspended sentence. See AUGUST J. LIPPI and DOMINICK 'NICK' ALAIMO.

Serino, Angelo A garment shop owner, he served on the Board of Directors of the NORTHEAST APPAREL ASSOCIATION.

Shore, Ray Associate director of the ILGWU NORTHEAST DEPARTMENT, he also served as the Pennsylvania state supervisor for the union.

Silverblatt, Arthur   He held the position of first assistant district attorney of Luzerne County between 1955 and 1959 and helped prosecute the corruption cases following the KNOX MINE DISASTER. During the investigations into the calamity, unknown assailants used dynamite to blow off the front porch of his home in Kingston, Pennsylvania. The sabotage occurred around the time that the ILGWU had been organizing shops in Pittston. When not in public office, he was a partner in Silverblatt and Townend law offices in Wilkes-Barre.

Silverman, Jennie   She was a good friend of MIN MATHESON (chap. 3), who taught her how to sew. Both were followers of ILGWU member and CPUSA leader JAY LOVESTONE. She joined Mrs. Matheson and others in abandoning the CPUSA in the late 1920s to continue as a garment worker and ILGWU activist.

Sitzman, Larry   He was the manager of a garment shop in Pittston, Pennsylvania, owned or fronted by alleged organized criminal DOMINICK "NICK" ALAIMO. Sitzman was known for harassing picket line workers during strikes.

Slattery, Frank   He was elected as the Democratic mayor of Wilkes-Barre and served between 1960 and 1968. As a friend of many ILGWU members and a supporter of the organization, he regularly attended union functions.

Snarski, Joseph   He became a partner with HARRY LIEBERMAN in JAY FASHIONS, one of the SWEET VALLEY GARMENT FACTORIES that accepted the ILGWU.

St. George, John   The owner of the KROGER DRESS COMPANY in Wilkes-Barre, Pennsylvania, in one incident he removed the doors from the washroom because, he said, the workers (all women) were spending too much time inside. MIN MATHESON (chap. 3) called a strike over the matter, which was quickly settled after the workers walked out.

Strasser, Harry "Lefty"   An alleged gangster, he owned dress companies in northeastern Pennsylvania, including MADISON DRESS in Hazleton, in partnership with alleged gangster ALBERT ANASTASIA. He also had financial interests in INTERSTATE DRESS CARRIERS INC.

Strongin, Paul   He immediately succeeded MIN MATHESON (chap. 3) as director of the ILGWU WYOMING VALLEY DISTRICT in 1963.

Stulberg, Louis   Born in Poland in 1904, he followed DAVID DUBINSKY as president of the ILGWU and remained in office between 1966 and 1975.

Teper, Lazare   He founded the ILGWU Research Department in 1937 and worked in that capacity until his retirement in 1980. Born in Odessa, Russia, he joined the union as a researcher in 1935.

Thompson, Freeman   He was a Communist member of the UMWA who was expelled from the union by JOHN L. LEWIS in the early 1920s.

Turco, Charles   A garment shop owner from Pittston, Pennsylvania, and brother of MICHAEL TURCO, he served as the secretary of the NORTHEAST APPAREL ASSOCIATION.

Turco, Michael   A garment shop owner from Pittston, Pennsylvania, and brother of CHARLES TURCO, he served as the secretary of the NORTHEAST APPAREL ASSOCIATION.

Velie, Lester   He was a New York journalist who devoted considerable attention to ORGANIZED CRIME's involvement in the garment industry. He wrote about MIN MATHESON (chap. 3) in a *Reader's Digest* article titled "The Lady and the Gangsters." His writings were used as the basis for the screenplay for *The Garment Jungle*, a movie released in 1957.

Volpe, "Junior"   He was the nephew of alleged ORGANIZED CRIME boss SANTO VOLPE.

Volpe, Santo   Born in Montedoro, Sicily, he was the alleged cofounder, with Steven LaTorre, and the first head of ORGANIZED CRIME IN NORTHEASTERN PENNSYLVANIA, a position he reportedly held from 1908 to 1933. He began work as a coal miner and went on to own one of the larger anthracite businesses in the area. He had no recognized interests in the garment industry. See the MEN FROM MONTEDORO.

*Weiss, Helen (Barnosky)   Born in 1910 in Edwardsville, Pennsylvania, she was the daughter of a Lithuanian-born father and an American-born mother of Lithuanian and Polish descent.

She joined the ILGWU in 1945 and married Jack Weiss (an ILGWU business agent) in 1957. Under MIN MATHESON's tutelage, she joined the union staff and became a BUSINESS AGENT in the ILGWU WYOMING VALLEY DISTRICT and, later, in the Easton District. She participated in many of the Wyoming Valley area strikes and organizing campaigns during the 1950s and 1960s, including those in Pittston. She was employed in the industry for twenty-one years until her retirement in 1994. Her oral history interview is included in this volume (chap. 9).

Whitaker, Linda She was an ILGWU ORGANIZER sent in by the New York union office to assist with the LESLIE FAY STRIKE OF 1994 and the larger campaign to keep the LESLIE FAY COMPANY's factories open in the Wyoming Valley. See LOIS HARTEL, MARION MALACHI, PEARL NOVAK (chap. 14), and NANCY ZIEGLER.

Willensky, Mark He was a garment shop owner who served on the Board of Directors of the NORTHEAST APPAREL ASSOCIATION.

Wolensky, Rosalie Siracuse The author's mother, she worked for a number of years in her youth at the GRASSO BROTHERS' men's pants factory in Swoyersville, Pennsylvania.

Wolinsky, Josephine She was an employee at the GRASSO BROTHERS' men's pants factory in Swoyersville, Pennsylvania, and at the Browns' garment shop in Luzerne.

Younger, Maud She was an early twentieth-century suffragist, feminist, and labor activist who supported garment workers during the strike of 1913.

Ziegler, Nancy An ILGWU ORGANIZER from Philadelphia, she assisted with the LESLIE FAY STRIKE OF 1994 and the larger campaign to keep the LESLIE FAY COMPANY factories open in the Wyoming Valley. See LOIS HARTEL, MARION MALACHI, PEARL NOVAK (chap. 14), and LINDA WHITAKER.

Zimmerman, Charles "Sasha" An immigrant from Russian Ukraine, he worked in a New York garment factory and went on to help form ILGWU LOCAL 25. As a follower of CPUSA leader JAY LOVESTONE, he was expelled from the union in 1925. Along with Lovestone, MIN MATHESON (chap. 3), JENNIE SILVERMAN, and many others, he renounced the CPUSA following the 1926 strike and rejoined the ILGWU. He continued as an active member of ILGWU DRESSMAKERS LOCAL 22 (where he was a colleague of Min Matheson and Jennie Silverman) and was elected as its manager in 1933, a position he held for the next forty years. He also served as the general manager of the ILGWU DRESS JOINT BOARD and the Dressmakers' Joint Council. He was the brother of ISRAEL ZIMMERMAN.

Zimmerman, Israel The holder of various positions within the ILGWU, he was the director of the Scranton District from the late 1930s to the mid-1940s. A former disciple of JAY LOVESTONE and a member of the CPUSA, he followed his brother CHARLES "SASHA" ZIMMERMAN out of the Party and back into the ILGWU.

*Zorgo, George George and LUCY ZORGO owned and operated a union print shop in Pittston, Pennsylvania, which became the official printer for the ILGWU WYOMING VALLEY DISTRICT. The couple became close friends with MIN and BILL MATHESON and strong supporters of the ILGWU's organizing campaigns. His oral history is included in this volume (chap. 10) as part of a joint interview with LUCY ZORGO.

*Zorgo, Lucy Lucy and GEORGE ZORGO owned and operated a union print shop in Pittston, Pennsylvania, which became the official printer for the ILGWU WYOMING VALLEY DISTRICT. The couple became close friends of MIN and BILL MATHESON and strong supporters of the ILGWU's organizing campaign. Her oral history is included in this volume (chap. 10) as part of a joint interview with George Zorgo.

Zukowski, Carlos He was a garment shop owner and member of the Board of Directors of the NORTHEAST APPAREL ASSOCIATION during the 1980s.

PREFACE

1. Stegner, "Sense of Place," 202. Northeastern Pennsylvania's place-ness has long been established, from the Native Americans who first settled the area, to the agrarian Connecticut Yankees who came in during the eighteenth century and laid the British cultural foundations, to the nineteenth- and twentieth-century capitalists who arrived mainly from New York and Philadelphia to exploit the anthracite coal. The fuel generated vast fortunes for landowners and investors, as it also provided opportunities for tens of thousands of European immigrants and helped spawn a distinct cultural and economic way of life that has been captured and preserved in numerous media. Julia Wolfe's Pulitzer Prize–winning oratorio, *Anthracite Fields*, described in the award citation as "a powerful oratorio for chorus and sextet evoking Pennsylvania coal-mining life around the turn of the 20th Century," represents a recent tribute ("*Anthracite Fields*, by Julia Wolfe [Red Poppy Music/G. Schirmer, Inc.]," Pulitzer Prizes, 2015, http://www.pulitzer.org/winners/julia-wolfe). See also, e.g., Shackel, "Meaning of Place."

2. On landscape research, see Meinig, *Interpretation of Ordinary Landscapes*; Lefebvre, *Production of Space*; Hayden, *Power of Place*; Harvey, *Spaces of Capital*, esp. chap. 9; Alanen and Melnick, *Preserving Cultural Landscapes*; Cannavò, *Working Landscape*; Roe and Taylor, *New Cultural Landscapes*; and Duineveld, Assche, and Beunen, "Re-conceptualising Political Landscapes."

3. The control exercised by New York capital interests over the Wyoming Valley's anthracite industry resonates with the core-periphery concept within dependency theory. While the approach has generally focused on advanced countries or empires and their hegemony over external colonies and states, another component has examined "internal colonies," or exploited regions within developed countries.

The case with anthracite is that the core areas of New York and Philadelphia and their railroad and banking corporations gained economic control over Pennsylvania's hard coal industries, institutions, and populations. Internal colonies typically face detrimental outcomes, including the exploitation of human capital, the physical environment, and natural resources. A corollary has been that core dominance typically leads to oppressive and corrupt political cultures. On the core-periphery concept, see, e.g., Appalachian Land Ownership Task Force, *Who Owns Appalachia?*; Wallerstein, *World-Systems Analysis*; Ferraro, "Dependency Theory"; and Abhijeet, "Dependency Theory." On the application of the concept to the anthracite region, see Miller and Sharpless, *Kingdom of Coal*, 74–75, and Couch, "Coal and Iron Police."

4. In this regard, the study stands at the crossroads of labor, regional, and economic history. See Batch, "Labored Mid-Atlantic Region."

5. On the first Tropical Storm Agnes project, see R. Wolensky, "Toward a Broader Conceptualization"; R. Wolensky and Miller, "Everyday versus the Disaster"; R. Wolensky, "Power Structure"; and R. Wolensky, *Better Than Ever!*

6. On the second Tropical Storm Agnes study, see R. Wolensky, *Power, Policy, and Disaster*; R. Wolensky, "POWER"; and R. Wolensky and K. Wolensky, "Local Government's Problem."

7. On the FVAC and Tropical Storm Agnes, see R. Wolensky and Miller, "Everyday versus the Disaster"; R. Wolensky, *Better Than Ever!*

8. I was also drawn to the garment industry for biographical reasons. My mother, Rosalie Siracuse Wolensky, worked in a men's pants factory in Swoyersville, Pennsylvania, during the 1940s, and my paternal grandmother, Catherine Wolensky, labored in various Wyoming Valley garment shops during the 1950s. Several

aunts, cousins, friends, and neighbors (male and female) were employed in the garment sector into the 1990s. In addition, for about one month during a college semester break in 1968, I worked full-time as a spreader (see appendix 2 for definitions of "spreader" and other terms) at the Pioneer Manufacturing Company in Wilkes-Barre. As a temporary worker, I was not expected to join the ILGWU.

9. Some examples from the vast ILGWU historiography could include Levine, *Women's Garment*; Laslett and Tyler, *ILGWU in Los Angeles*; Tyler, *Look for the Union Label*; and Witwer, "Dress Strike at Three-Finger Brown's."

10. Greenwald, review of *Fighting for the Union Label*, 277–78.

11. Bao, review of *Fighting for the Union Label*, 1593–94.

12. For a definition of narrative, see appendix 2.

13. Mills, *Sociological Imagination*.

14. Berger and Quinney, *Storytelling Sociology*. On this topic, see also Ochs and Capps, *Living Narrative*; Page and Thomas, *New Narratives*; and Bochner and Ellis, *Evocative Autoethnography*.

15. Bourdieu, "Forms of Capital."

16. Gutman, "Work, Culture, and Society." Zinn expressed the same view in *People's History*.

17. Thompson, *Making of the English Working Class*, 12.

18. E. P. Thompson, "History from Below," *Times Literary Supplement*, April 7, 1966. See also Lynd, *Doing History*.

19. Lynd and Lynd, *Rank and File*, and Lynd, *Solidarity Unionism*. See also Lynd, *"We Are All Leaders,"* and Lynd, *Doing History*.

20. Faue, *Community of Suffering*, 4, and Faue, "Paths of Unionization."

21. Portelli, *Death of Luigi Trastulli*; Portelli, *Battle of Valle*; Portelli, *Order Has Been Carried Out*; and Portelli, *They Say in Harlan County*.

22. Denzin, *Interpretive Biography*; Lawrence-Lightfoot and Davis, *Art and Science*; and Clandinin and Connelly, *Narrative Inquiry*.

23. Zieger, *John L. Lewis*; Zieger, *CIO*; and Zieger, *For Jobs and Freedom*.

INTRODUCTION

1. On the pivotal role of anthracite in the American industrial revolution, see Chandler, "Anthracite Coal."

2. Columbia, Dauphin, and Wyoming Counties also held small deposits of anthracite, while Sullivan County contained some measures of a lower grade called semi-anthracite.

3. For comprehensive histories of the anthracite regions, see Miller and Sharpless, *Kingdom of Coal*, and Dublin and Licht, *Face of Decline*.

4. The high profits and rates of return among the anthracite companies during the late nineteenth and early twentieth centuries were discussed in Jones, *Anthracite Coal*, 123; Nearing, *Anthracite*; and Bogen, *Anthracite Railroads*.

5. Warne, *Slav Invasion*, and Bodnar, *Ethnic Experience*.

6. Wallace (*St. Clair*, chap. 7) used the term "a state called anthracite" in reference to the hegemonic control the coal companies held over local institutions and residents. See also Shackel, "Immigration Heritage," and Shackel, *Remembering Lattimer*.

7. Aurand, *From the Molly Maguires*; R. Wolensky and Hastie, *Anthracite Labor Wars*.

8. According to the U.S. Census Bureau, the ten anthracite counties supported a population of 1.25 million in 2010. The figure for the five largest coal-producing counties was 762,427 in 2010, down from a peak of 996,192 in 1930 (Carolyn Stewart, "Census of Population and Housing," United States Census Bureau, August 19, 2011, http://www.census.gov/prod /www/decennial.html).

9. Glenn, *Daughters of the Shtetl*, chap. 6. See also Kessler-Harris, *Women Have Always Worked*, esp. chap. 3, and Stepenoff, *Their Fathers' Daughters*. For an early twentieth-century statement on the subject, see Cooley, *New Womanhood*.

10. Stepenoff, "Child Labor," 104; Stepenoff, *Their Fathers' Daughters*; and Howard, "Radicals Not Wanted." See also "The Silk Industry in Scranton: An Illustrated Description of the Sauquoit, Harvey's, and Meadow-Brook Silk Mills," *Scranton Republican*, December 8, 1891. In Luzerne County, the American Silk Mills Corporation and the Atwater Company were still in business in 2016.

11. On the Paterson strike of 1913 see Zieger, "Robin Hood"; Tripp, *IWW and the Paterson Silk Strike*; and Golin, *Fragile Bridge*.

12. Hutchins, *Labor and Silk*, 42–43. Aronsohn lived at the Plaza Hotel in New York,

where, Hutchins wrote, his room and board probably "cost more for one day than a young girl in his Scranton throwing mill can earn in a week."

13. Harvey and Smith, *History of Wilkes-Barre*, 86.

14. Stepenoff, "Child Labor," 108–9.

15. Howard, "Radicals Not Wanted." On the 1933 Paterson strike, see Ballam, *70,000 Silk Workers*. Another silk strike occurred the following year in Hazleton, Pennsylvania, as discussed by Sterba in "Family, Work, and Nation."

16. Kozura, "We Stood Our Ground"; Howard, *Anthracite Reds*; and R. Wolensky and Hastie, *Anthracite Labor Wars*.

17. Bureau of Statistics and Information, *Fourth Industrial Directory*, 488–96. The Duplan Silk Corporation, based in France, commenced operations in the late nineteenth century and went on to build ten plants in Pennsylvania, including those in Wilkes-Barre, Nanticoke, Kingston, and Hazleton. The company closed its doors in the late 1950s. For a brief history, see "Duplan Silk Mill Was Area's Second Biggest Employer," *Hazleton Standard-Speaker*, January 16, 2016.

18. Rupert, *Pennsylvania*, 50. On the lace mill workers, see Walter Arnold, "Scranton Lace Company" and "Nine Hundred Lace Mill Employees Receive Bonuses Totaling $43,000," both in *Wilkes-Barre Record Almanac*, December 16, 1938, 16. The lace mills included the Scranton Lace Company (where members of Hillary Rodham Clinton's family worked), the Wyoming Valley Lace Mills, and the Wilkes-Barre Lace Manufacturing Company.

19. Commonwealth of Pennsylvania, *Annual Report*, 57.

20. Palmer, *Labor Relations*, chap. 3.

21. Ibid., chap. 3, p. 50.

22. Well over one hundred years ago, John R. Commons discussed the link between the contractor (or subcontractor) and the sweatshop in his report "The Sweating System." Sweatshops are still evident today in U.S. garment centers, especially in New York and Los Angeles, as shown by Bonacich and Appelbaum, *Behind the Label*; Louie, *Sweatshop Warriors*; and Bao, "Sweatshops in Sunset Park."

23. On the history of contracting, subcontracting, and putting out, see also Hobsbawm, *Industry and Empire*, 15–16; Montgomery,

Workers' Control, 14–15; McCreesh, *Women in the Campaign*, 9–10; Guglielmo, *Living the Revolution*; and Willett, *Employment of Women*, 51. In 1902, Willett referred to the "evil in the contract system" (ibid.). She went on to characterize it as the introduction of "an irresponsible middleman between the manufacturer and the workman. The manufacturer disclaims all responsibility for the conditions surrounding the workers, since they are not in his employ. The contractor says that the price paid him by the manufacturer renders it impossible for him to pay higher wages, that he himself is helpless. The trade unions have found it impossible to enforce agreements made with contractors because of their lack of property. Under such conditions it is not strange that the abolition of the contract system is one of the chief objects of the trade unions in the clothing industry" (ibid., 51–52).

24. Bonacich and Appelbaum, *Behind the Label*, 136–40.

25. In analyzing today's global garment industry, Louie (*Sweatshop Warriors*, 4–7, 12–13, 248–50) wrote about the "sweatshop pyramid of exploitation" and its structural form, "subcontracting," as well as its relationship to "the feminization of labor."

26. Tyler, *Look for the Union Label*.

27. Membership figures are drawn from the Kheel Center, "Timeline," Cornell University, 2015, https://ilgwu.ilr.cornell.edu/timeline/.

28. Social and solidarity unionism are defined in appendix 2. On the ILGWU's commitment to social unionism, see Munts and Munts, "Welfare History," and Barbash, "I.L.G.W.U."

29. David Dubinsky referred to the Garment Center as New York City's "industrial heartland" in his autobiography (with Raskin), *David Dubinsky*, 12.

30. A brief history of Local 22 can be found in ILGWU, Local 22 Records, No. 5780/015, Kheel Center. See also Katz, *All Together Different*, 171–80.

31. For a striking eyewitness account of the oppressive working and living conditions in northeastern Pennsylvania at this time, see the oral history volume by Nelson, Barrett, and Ruck, *Steve Nelson*.

32. John Mitchell quoted in Klein and Hoogenboom, *History of Pennsylvania*, 331.

33. Susan Glenn (*Daughters of the Shtetl*, 118, 125, 126) discussed the exploitation involved in garment training programs among Jewish men and women. On Italian American garment workers in this regard, see Zappia, "Unionism and the Italian American," and Guglielmo, *Living the Revolution*.

34. Min Matheson, audio-recorded interview, November 30, 1982, NPOLHC.

35. The Pennsylvania Historical and Museum Commission described the criminal element's involvement in the Pittston garment industry:

In Pittston, however, organized crime, which had a long history in the valley, hindered their [the Mathesons'] efforts to organize the garment workers. A group of struggling Sicilian miners who had arrived in the 1880s had cultivated criminal links. Known as the "Men of Montedoro," they had gained control over a number of mines and infiltrated locals of the United Mine Workers [union], using "sweetheart" payments to prevent labor disruptions and investing their profits in bootlegging [alcohol], gambling, loan sharking, and eventually, the runaway garment business. In time, they owned as many as fifteen to twenty of the forty to fifty shops in Pittston, intimidated a number of others, and made in-roads into the associated trucking industry. They also [initially] cultivated close ties with the local police and in 1946 helped start the Anthracite Needle Workers' Association of Pennsylvania to oppose the ILGWU. As manager of ILGWU's Wyoming District, Min Matheson worked to organize Pittston, starting with shops lacking known criminal ties. (Explore Pennsylvania History, "Workers in Greater Pittston's Garment Industry Historical Marker," Historical Markers, 2011, http://explorepahistory.com/hmarker.php?markerId=1-A-362)

36. In addition to Pittston, which is often mentioned in this volume, a number of other eastern Pennsylvania cities witnessed criminal involvement in the garment trade. In Edwardsville, Luzerne County, alleged mobster Abe Chait formed a partnership with the Lucchese-connected Kaplan and Elias group at the Anita Dress Company (examined by several narrators in this volume). According to criminologist Gary W. Potter (*Criminal Organizations*, 53), by the early 1950s, alleged gangsters Harry Strasser, Carlo Gambino, Thomas Lucchese, and Albert Anastasia had entered into partnerships with a Scranton associate, Thomas Sesso, Sr., who was cited in the Pennsylvania Crime Commission's *Report on Organized Crime*. The U.S. Senate's McClellan Committee hearings on organized crime's influence in labor unions reported that Thomas Lucchese owned a dress factory in the suburban Scranton town of Peckville. In a study of organized crime in Philadelphia, Gary W. Potter and Philip Jenkins (*City and the Syndicate*) found that one of the city's leading crime figures, Harry "Nig" Rosen (aka Hyman Stromberg [birth name], Harry Rosen, and Joseph Bloom), operated a dress factory in Scranton. Potter and Jenkins further reported that Philadelphia's garment business came under the influence of alleged racketeers Louis Stromberg and others.

The Pennsylvania Crime Commission in 1984 indicated that Jack "The Dandy" Parisi, a former triggerman for New York's "Murder, Inc.," ran the Irene Dress Company in Hazleton in partnership with that organized crime group's founder, Albert Anastasia. Journalist Lester Velie (*Labor USA Today*, 92) stated that alleged gangster Johnny Dioguardi (aka Johnny Dio) owned a nonunion dress factory in Allentown. As indicated by ILGWU organizer and manager John Justin (chap. 7), alleged gangsters Mike Pappadio and Victor Amuso, also of the Lucchese ring, operated a dress factory in Pottsville. Paul Williams, the U.S. Attorney for New York during the 1950s and 1960s, stated that an estimated two hundred firms in the city—truckers, manufacturers, jobbers, and contractors—were participating in garment-related racketeering during the early 1960s and that many of them dealt with Pennsylvania counterparts (cited in Velie, *Labor USA Today*, 95). On organized crime in the Scranton vicinity, see also Ralph Blumenthal, "When the Mob Delivered the Goods," *New York Times*, July 26, 1992. On the McClellan Committee hearings, see *Hearings before the Select Committee on Improper Activities in the Labor or Management Field*, 85th Cong. (1957–58), 86th Cong. (1959).

37. Thomas Dublin authored an important book, *When the Mines Closed*, consisting of oral history interviews with garment workers in the Southern anthracite coal field. The volume made no mention of organized crime in that region.

38. "Impressive Tribute to Min L. Matheson," *Pittston Dispatch*, January 27, 1964; see also "Min Matheson, Key Figure in Area," *Wilkes-Barre Times Leader*, February 4, 1963.

39. The "Look for the Union Label" tune became the ILGWU's anthem during the 1970s. See appendix 2 for more information about the song, including its lyrics.

40. On the American deindustrialization that began in the latter part of the twentieth century, see Bluestone and Harrison, *De-industrialization of America*; Staudohar, *Deindustrialization*; Cowie and Heathcott, *Beyond the Ruins*; Greenhouse, *Big Squeeze*; McKee, *Problem of Jobs*; Rhodes, "Youngstown's 'Ghost'?"; and Grigor and Katchi, "Debris of What-Would-Have-Been." Minchin (*Empty Mills*, 2–3, 305–6) presented some reasons why the deindustrialization literature has paid more attention to heavy manufacturing than to lighter industries such as apparel and textiles.

41. Minchin (*Empty Mills*, chap. 5) argued that the "sellout" of the U.S. garment and textile industries to international producers derived from a combination of U.S. foreign policy and corporate influence, a topic further examined in chapter 16.

42. The UMWA District 1 office experienced widespread corruption in the Wilkes-Barre and Scranton areas between the late 1930s and the early 1960s. Organized criminals (including some with both coal and garment investments) infiltrated the highest union ranks and, in cooperation with major coal producers, such as the Pennsylvania Coal Company, established a culture of corruption that included bribery, "sweetheart" contracts, illegal mining, wage cheating, safety violations, and tax fraud. Illegal mining and other instances of malfeasance at the criminally affiliated Knox Coal Company precipitated the end of the coal industry in the Wyoming Valley with the Knox Mine disaster in 1959 (R. Wolensky, K. Wolensky, and N. Wolensky, *Knox Mine Disaster*, and R. Wolensky, K. Wolensky, and N. Wolensky, *Voices of the Knox Mine Disaster*).

43. Another irony faced by some garment workers was that the loss of their relatively well-paying, unionized manufacturing jobs led to their taking low-paying, nonunionized jobs in local big-box stores that sold cheap imported clothing.

1. Helen Weiss (chap. 9) also discusses her employment at the Stella Dress Company.

2. For additional commentary on the Anita Dress company strike in Edwardsville, Pennsylvania, see Angelo DePasquale (chap. 4), John Justin (chap. 7), and Betty Greenberg (chap. 15).

3. See Angelo DePasquale (chap. 4) and Clementine Lyons (chap. 8) for other views on how Daniel J. Flood became the lawyer for the ILGWU Wyoming Valley District. On Flood's biography, see Spear, *Daniel J. Flood*, and Kashatus, *Dapper Dan Flood*.

4. Lucchese owned the shop in partnership with alleged gangster Harry "Nig" Rosen of Philadelphia. One local commentary regarding the nine-month Sweet Valley shutdown stated that five of the plant's ILGWU strikers traveled to a Lucchese-owned garment factory in New York and set up picket lines there: "Even in the face of threats by 'Three Fingers [sic] Brown,' they persisted in sitting on the sidewalk, blocking access to scab workers, and were arrested for it. Meanwhile, back in Sweet Valley, the strikers strung some dead crows on a line across the plant's driveway as effigies to their bosses" (Neva Edwards Johns and Ron Hontz, "History of Sweet Valley Luzerne County, PA," Lower Luzerne County, 2005, http://web .archive.org/web/20071218201644/http://www .lowerluzernecounty.com/articles/historyof sweetvalley.htm).

5. Dorothy Ney's commentary at this point contradicts what other narrators have said about Teamster union truckers, who typically did not transport products in or out of an on-strike shop. Lucchese owned other dress shops such as the Bal-Fran Blouse Company and Ann-Lyn Sportswear, both in New York.

6. For an account of the strike at the Harvic Dress shop, see also Witwer, "Dress Strike at Three-Finger Brown's," 166–67.

7. Lucchese and Stromberg sold the shop to Harry Liberman and Joe Snarski, who renamed it Jay Fashions. Charles Cefalo of Pittston then bought the enterprise and called it Monday Fashions, in line with his other shop, Sunday Fashions, located in Plains Township, Pennsylvania, near Wilkes-Barre. William Carter of Kingston then bought the business. The ILGWU organized each of the businesses following Lucchese's departure. See Johns and Hontz, "History of Sweet Valley Luzerne

County, PA"; see also John Levandowski, audio-recorded interview, May 18, 2017.

8. By refusing to drop off and pick up when the Wyoming Valley ILGWU went on strike, the Teamsters essentially held a secondary boycott, which was legal according to the Garment Industry Proviso. However, it was surprising that the alleged organized criminals who had influence over certain Teamsters locals and trucking firms did not intervene more forcefully on behalf of the shop owners. Alleged organized crime leader Abe Chait of New York wielded considerable influence over garment trucking, including his investment interests in the Friedman's Express Trucking firm. For more on Mr. Chait, see Min Matheson (chap. 3), chapter 16, and appendix 2.

9. Min Matheson (chap. 3) discusses some of her dealings with Mr. Alaimo, as do Anthony D'Angelo (chap. 5) and Helen Weiss (chap. 9).

10. Leo Gutstein (chap. 13) followed his father, Louis, as the head of the Lee Manufacturing firm.

11. Others have stated that Mrs. Falcone was Russell Bufalino's cousin.

CHAPTER 2

1. See Helen Weiss (chap. 9) on the mechanics involved in the complicated task of pricing piecework items. She describes her efforts to create a "bible" to standardize prices and therefore allow for more consistent and fairer wages across the Wyoming Valley District.

2. Mr. Cherkes points to the fact that many runaway garment shop owners had worked in some capacity—sewing, cutting, pressing, et cetera—in the industry before becoming owners.

3. It therefore seems clear that the earlier garment work of Mr. Cherkes, Sr., in New York not only influenced his decision to open his own factory in Pennsylvania but also facilitated his efforts as leader of the owners' association when he participated in contract negotiations with the union.

4. On the Grasso brothers and their United Pants Company, see Mary Beth Siracuse, ed., "The History and Our Memories of Swoyersville Borough," Pennsylvania GenWeb, 1998, http://www.pagenweb.org/~luzerne/patk/swoy2.htm. The author's mother and several relatives and family friends were employed at the Grassos' men's pants factory in Swoyersville.

5. Mabel Herd Willett documented a piecework system among Jewish coat makers in New York that operated between 1876 and 1882. Termed the "task system," it divided labor into "teams" or "sets" of three persons, where "[one] does the basting, another the machine work or 'operating,' and the third the 'edge-basting' or finishing." She added that the plan "[was] found in no other American city." See Willet, *Employment of Women*, 36–38. On the task system, see also McCreesh, *Women in the Campaign*, 9.

6. Mr. Cherkes served on the board of directors of the Northeast Apparel Association (NAA) in the 1980s, where he also served as the group's publicity chairman. See William A. Cherkes to Senator John H. Heinz III, March 28, 1985, Carnegie Mellon University Archives.

7. The Roxanne Swimsuit firm closed its local plant in 1997. For an account of its demise, see Renita Fennick, "An Era Comes to a Close," *Times Leader*, May 9, 1997. However, the brand is still being made overseas and sold at outlets such as Macy's and Amazon.

8. Anthony D'Angelo, in chapter 5, recalls a heated dispute between Mrs. Matheson and Mr. Cherkes while he was an employee of the Ann Will Garment shop.

CHAPTER 3

1. John Justin (chap. 7) stated that he opened an ILGWU office in Pittston, Pennsylvania, in 1945, as he worked under the direction of the union's regional headquarters in Scranton. Because Bill and Min Matheson came to the area around this time, Mr. Justin and the Mathesons likely overlapped for a short period. Justin departed to direct the Harrisburg District in 1946. Meanwhile, Mrs. Matheson became the director of the Wyoming Valley office, which included Pittston, while Scranton remained a separate district.

2. Both garment shop owners William Cherkes (chap. 2) and Leo Gutstein (chap. 13) verified that their fathers left New York in order to get away from constraints imposed by the ILGWU and the union environment.

3. Pittston was a main stop on the Lackawanna and Wyoming Valley Railroad, also known as the Laurel Line, which provided commuter

service between Scranton and Wilkes-Barre between 1903 and 1952.

4. See Angelo DePasquale (chap. 4).

5. In a letter to William Blatt, Jr., Pennsylvania secretary of labor, on April 10, 1959, Mrs. Matheson listed the names of the "tough guys" at the scene: "Modesto Loquasto, Albert Giambra, John Buscemi, Ralph Mathewson, Mal Sciandra, Angelo Bufalino, and others" (Min L. Matheson to William Blatt, Jr., Box 296, File 4a, No. 5780, David Dubinsky Papers, Kheel Center). On Russell Bufalino, see memorandum by Special Agent in Charge of Philadelphia to the Director of the FBI, February 11, 1954, General Investigative Intelligence File (Top Hoodlum Coverage), FBI Philadelphia Office; Pennsylvania Crime Commission, *Report on Organized Crime*; Brandt, *I Heard You Paint Houses*; Sifakis, *Mafia Encyclopedia*; Birkbeck, *Quiet Don*; and appendixes 1 and 2.

6. See Alice Reca (chap. 6).

7. See Helen Weiss (chap. 9).

8. Min Matheson considered herself a feminist because of her life's work on behalf of garment employees (most of whom were women), as well as her general support of women in the professional, home, political, and economic realms. She was proud of her early membership in the National Organization for Women when it formed in 1966, although she later resigned over policy differences.

9. Andrew Salvo died an accidental death in 1953 during U.S. military service in Germany. On John "Blackie" Salvo's involvement with the region's organized crime group, see Libonati and Edelhertz, *Study of Property Ownership and Devolution*.

10. Mrs. Matheson is referring to the Garment Industry Proviso of the Wagner Act of 1935. See appendix 2.

11. The name Falcone should not be confused with Falzone, mentioned earlier in the interview.

12. "Mayor Closed Plant to Preserve Peace as Owner Plans Protest," *Pittston Gazette*, April 21, 1959.

13. Velie quoted this well-known line in "Lady and the Gangsters," *Readers' Digest*, January 1957. During Mr. Bufalino's sentencing hearing on January 13, 1960, federal judge Irving R. Kaufman of New York described him as "a man devoid of conscience. One who poses as a legitimate business man. Everything in his record indicates that society would be better off if he is segregated [imprisoned]. Five years in prison and a $10,000 fine" (Tyler, *Organized Crime*, 244; see also Newton, *Mafia at Apalachin*, 159).

14. The Mathesons' dedication to improving union members' personal and family circumstances likely derived from their earlier commitment to Socialist values and later support of New Deal principles. A large number of early ILGWU leaders and members had been dedicated Socialists. As Carolyn Daniel McCreesh (*Women in the Campaign*, 77) noted, "The ILGWU's adoption of Socialism added a note of moral fervor and ethical mission which was often absent in other unions." See also Katz, *All Together Different*. An examination of their biographies reveals that the Mathesons witnessed the virtual demise of three historic social and political movements: (1) the Jewish radical movement of her parents' immigrant generation and her generation; (2) the Communist movement in the United States; and (3) the Socialist movement in the United States, the latter two receiving their full support during their Chicago years, her Paterson, New Jersey, days, and their early ILGWU times in New York. They also regretted the decline of two other favored movements: (1) New Deal Liberalism, to which they had turned after abandoning Communism and Socialism, and (2) the American labor movement, which became the focus of their lives.

15. WKQV in Pittston was licensed to broadcast in the Wilkes-Barre and Scranton areas. As ownership changed, its future call letters were WARD and WPTS.

16. Min Matheson was speaking to her and her husband, Bill's, labor organizing approach, namely, solidarity unionism. She was, in effect, saying that she and Bill developed a type of "social infrastructure" that allowed the district union to command loyalty and dedication from the membership and the larger community in instances such as this walkout. See the discussion in the preface and chapter 16 regarding solidarity unionism; see also appendix 2.

17. Mrs. Matheson testified in favor of the Flood-Douglas Area Redevelopment Act before the U.S. Senate's Labor and Public Welfare Committee. President Dwight D. Eisenhower twice vetoed the measure, but it was finally signed into law in 1961 by President John

332

F. Kennedy. The Act brought considerable economic, transportation, and other development aid to the "depressed" regions of the country. On Mrs. Matheson's testimony, see Rep. Daniel J. Flood to David Dubinsky, Box 319, Folder 12b, No. 5780, David Dubinsky Papers, Kheel Center.

18. Economists have long recognized the incentivizing effects of piecework. It has been used in various industries, including anthracite mining, where many workers were paid by the number of loaded cars sent to the surface each day. Some economists have argued that piecework could cause some employees to overproduce and thereby injure themselves. For example, according to the classic liberal economist Adam Smith (*Inquiry into the Nature and Causes of the Wealth of Nations*, bk. 1, chap. 8, p. 44), writing in the late eighteenth century, "Workmen . . . when they are liberally paid by the piece, are very apt to overwork themselves, and to ruin their health and constitution in a few years."

19. See Dr. Albert Schiowitz (chap. 12), who served as the second director of the ILGWU Health Center in Wilkes-Barre. The International Union opened its first health center in New York in 1913.

20. See Clementine Lyons (chap. 8).

21. Mrs. Matheson was likely referring to the Yiddish phrase *doubis fericked*, which translates as "crazy" or "insane."

22. Jennifer Guglielmo (*Living the Revolution*, 267) researched women activists during the 1930s and found a pattern of political transformation similar to Mrs. Matheson's, from Communist, to Socialist, to New Dealer: "The majority of those active in Depression-era movements were the daughters of immigrant women who either migrated as children or were the first generation born in the United States. Their coming of age in the 1910s and 1920s occurred amidst aggressive antiradicalism, coercive nationalisms, and pervasive xenophobia. This forced a profound change in the focus of their activisms, as they increasingly turned away from revolutionary strategies toward more reformist and accommodationist visions of change."

23. In fact, Mr. Cherkes (chap. 2) believed that there was little or no organized crime influence over the Wyoming Valley garment industry and added that stories about the mob's control were overblown by the ILGWU in order to garner public support and sympathy. See also the discussion about this matter in chapter 16.

24. The committee, headed by Senator John L. McClellan, was formally known as the Select Committee on Improper Activities in the Labor or Management Field.

25. Thomas Lucchese testified before the Senate Select Committee on Improper Activities in the Labor or Management Field, chaired by Senator John McClellan (*Hearings before the Select Committee on Improper Activities in the Labor or Management Field*, 85th Cong. 12472–85 [1958]). David Witwer ("Dress Strike at Three-Finger Brown's") researched the recently released McClellan Committee documents and discovered heretofore unseen notes from a lengthy interview with Matheson conducted by one of the Committee's investigators who wanted to query her about garments and mobsters in northeastern Pennsylvania. According to the notes, Mrs. Matheson certainly opposed garment racketeering and provided useful information; however, she hedged her cooperation for three reasons. First, she saw the Committee as having some anti-union biases; second, she described past government investigations as generally futile; and third, she feared that her cooperation could make her vulnerable. It was unclear whether her disposition in this interview figured into her not being called to testify before the McClellan Committee.

26. Mrs. Matheson is referring to the marriage in 1962 between Frances Lucchese, daughter of Thomas Lucchese, and Thomas Gambino, son of New York's alleged top mob boss, Carlo Gambino. The Gambino and the Lucchese crime organizations had formed an alliance in the 1950s that enhanced their influence over several criminal "markets," including the garment trade.

27. Prominent among the holdout firms during the 1958 strike were those owned or operated by Thomas Lucchese, Harry "Nig" Rosen, Abe Chait, Angelo Sciandra, Harry "Lefty" Strasser, and Russell Bufalino—all of whom were alleged organized criminals. See notes 24 and 25 above, which refers to McClellan Committee testimony in 1959 dealing with the role of organized crime in prolonging the strike. See chapter 16 for further information regarding Min Matheson's statement that "we used to invent a lot of stories."

28. At one point during the garment strike of 1958, Min Matheson took the bold step of meeting secretly with Abe Chait, allegedly a leading underworld figure in the garment industry, and one who, according to Robert F. Kennedy, attorney for the 1958 McClellan Committee hearings, had ties to Russell Bufalino, Johnny Dioguardi, and other garment-industry mob characters. Chait was also said to have financial interests in garment trucking firms such as J. B. Express, Burton Transportation, Faultless Trucking Co., and Friedman's Express, and in several garment shops, including the Madison Wearing Apparel Company of Wilkes-Barre and the Anita Dress Company of Edwardsville. Chait took full advantage of the Fifth Amendment and provided no answers to Kennedy's questioning during the hearings. One line of inquiry related to the strike of 1958. According to Mrs. Matheson, during that shutdown, Chait contacted her and requested a meeting at his New York office. She reluctantly accepted the invitation despite having grave misgivings for any benefit it might bring and also for the harmful effect it would have on her relationship with David Dubinsky, should he find out about the gathering:

"So we traveled to New York and went to a building at Thirty-Sixth Street and Seventh Avenue, like I was told. When I walked in, who did I find? Not just Abe Chait, but Russell Bufalino, Dominick Alaimo, and Angelo Sciandra! Three shop owners and Mafia. We had been fighting with them in Pittston, and I came all the way to New York to fight with them here? There they were, waiting for me, sitting with Chait and a few other guys. I couldn't believe it. I was so angry I said to Chait, 'If I had known that you were going to have these rotten people here, these people from the sewers, I wouldn't have come. They are worse than from the sewers, and I won't have anything to do with them.' I thought that these secret talks would be between me and him, and that we might be able to negotiate something to settle the strike. So I stormed out of the building, and I walked across the street to a coffee shop. I was shaking I was so mad and bothered to find them here. He never told me.

"Well, I ordered a cup of coffee and as I was about to drink it, somebody grabbed my arm. 'You better come back in, Mrs. Matheson,' he said. It was one of Chait's lieutenants. I told him that I wasn't going to speak to the very people who were causing all the trouble back in Pittston. But he insisted and said that I better come back and that maybe something could be worked out. So I reluctantly went back with him. They knew I didn't like it but we talked for a while and reached no solution on anything. When it was all said and done, we never organized their shops. I knew all about the dangers of such a private, unauthorized negotiation.

I knew those gangsters had murdered my brother, Will, and could easily do the same to me. But I also realized that if DD [David Dubinsky] ever knew that I went to New York for such a meeting, he would have killed me. There were lots of tensions between New York and Pennsylvania [ILGWU offices], that's for sure." (Min Matheson, unrecorded discussion with the author, November 30, 1988)

See also the interview with Betty Greenberg (chap. 15). Elsewhere in her oral history interviews, Mrs. Matheson stated that the alleged mobsters' shops were eventually organized but under legitimate owners after they had been sold. Will Lurye's murder is again discussed in chapter 16. Mrs. Matheson had other meetings with Mr. Chait (accompanied by ILGWU officials) concerning strikes and other conflicts in the Wyoming Valley District; see chapter 16.

29. Minnie Caputo (chap. 11) stated that she participated as a guest on one of Mrs. Matheson's radio broadcasts to report on the Jenkins Sportswear strike in 1958.

30. In accordance with the Garment Industry Proviso (see appendix 2), the Wyoming Valley Local of the Brotherhood of Teamsters initiated a secondary boycott in support of the ILGWU's strike. The Teamsters' president, Leo Namey, was a strong union advocate and a close associate of Mrs. Matheson through their joint work in community associations. On the Teamsters union, see Witwer, *Corruption and Reform.*

31. The Pennsylvania Labor History Society bestowed its annual Mother Jones Award on Min Matheson in 1980. August J. Lippi served jail time after his conviction of income tax evasion and conspiracy in connection with his illegal ownership of the Knox Coal Company while he was also president of District 1 of the UMWA. He escaped manslaughter and mining law convictions in connection with the disaster.

32. UMWA president John L. Lewis expelled the Communist Freeman Thompson from the union in the 1920s. George Voysey was also

a Communist member of the UMWA in the 1920s. Glenn E. Watts served as president of the Communications Workers of America.

33. On John Mitchell and the strike of 1902, see Glück, *John Mitchell, Miner*, and Phelan, *Divided Loyalties*.

34. Officials from the UMWA did not attend the wake most likely because the District union president, August J. Lippi, was later indicted as a secret and illegal partner in the Knox Coal Company.

35. See the oral history interview with Thomas A. Evans's wife, Joan Evans, October 19, 1988, Northeastern Pennsylvania Oral and Life History Collection, Pennsylvania Historical and Museum Commission (hereafter cited as NPOLHC).

36. Attorney Frank Slattery served as the Democratic mayor of Wilkes-Barre between 1960 and 1968. See his audio-recorded oral history interview, May 28, 1983, NPOLHC.

37. The Mathesons strongly supported the values and philosophy underlying the ILGWU's educational commitment, as highlighted by the union's most ardent proponent of didactic programming, Fannia Cohn, who wrote, "The Labor Movement stands consciously or unconsciously for the reconstruction of society. It strives toward a new life. It dreams of a world where economic and social justice will prevail, where the welfare of mankind will be the aim of all activity, where society will be organized as a Cooperative Commonwealth and where love, friendship, and fellowship will replace selfishness" (Cohn, "What Workers' Education Really Is," 231; see also McCreesh, *Women in the Campaign*, 228). Similarly, union leader Rose Pesotta wrote to President Dubinsky in 1944 to emphasize the importance of learning endeavors: "With labor's gains in the economic field, mental discipline and knowledge of history and economics become indispensable for unionists living and working in a democracy" (Pesotta, *Bread upon the Waters*, 15). For these purposes, the union established the Educational Department in 1918, whose mission was to organize and supervise lectures and courses often held at the Unity House resort in the Pocono Mountains of Pennsylvania. Rose Pesotta and other ILGWUers also participated in institutes such as the ILGWU's Workers University at the Washington Irving High School in New York City in 1917, the Bryn Mawr Summer School

for Women Workers, the Brookwood Labor College, and the Wisconsin Summer School beginning in the 1920s (on Bryn Mawr, see McGuire, "Maintaining the Vitality of a Social Movement"). During the 1920s, Mrs. Matheson (then Minnie Hindy Lurye) attended the Wisconsin Summer School in Madison. In 1957, the union began providing scholarships for members' postsecondary education. The School for Workers within the University of Wisconsin–Extension has continued, to the present, to offer courses and training for employees and has maintained the Midwest School for Women Workers held each summer (see School for Workers, "Upcoming Classes," University of Wisconsin–Extension, 2019, http://schoolfor workers.uwex.edu/).

38. Until early 1941, Mrs. Matheson had served as the elected chairlady of Local 22 in New York City, which had some thirty-two thousand members, making it one of the largest locals in the nation. Later that year, she resigned in anticipation of her daughter Marianne's birth and soon moved to Sayre, Pennsylvania, to live with her husband, who had accepted a position organizing runaway shops in that city.

39. According to John Justin (chap. 7) in an unrecorded interview (May 30, 2000), Mrs. Matheson had been very close to Charles "Sasha" Zimmerman in the 1930s and 1940s, through their joint leadership positions in Local 22 in New York. Justin believed that Zimmerman encouraged her to leave the city because she was a charismatic and effective speaker, just the person to organize the runaway shops in Pennsylvania. Zimmerman may have recommended Mrs. Matheson to President Dubinsky.

40. One incident clearly demonstrated the tensions between Mrs. Matheson and the ILGWU leaders in New York, especially President David Dubinsky. It involved a strike payment to the workers:
"Right after the '58 strike, they pulled us out again. They told us to strike again. It was only to suit New York's purposes and to disrupt our situation here. But if I failed to carry out the order, which was the decision of the general executive board . . . You know there's discipline in the union. I was furious. I called Dubinsky. We had the people [workers] out for a few days.

"So, although I was of New York and from New York and the New York leaders were first my friends, if you know what I mean, I used to get pretty fed up with their nonsense. Right after these few days of striking, I knew the pay envelopes would be depleted, and I was very, very unhappy about the whole action. Although the girls stayed out, I was just hoping they would say to me, "The hell with you," and work. That's how mad I was.

"It was a Thursday in the evening and we were just closing up shop [at the main office] and this guy, my superior, called me up and he was in a rage. He must have just come out of a meeting where he likely had a big fight with the New York guys. And he said, 'If he [Dubinsky] wants a strike, let them pay for it.' That was the leader of the New York board! 'Let 'em pay for it,' he said. 'I want you to pay twenty dollars to every striker for strike benefits, and I'll make him pay it back to you.' I said, 'We have a lot of people out.' [He said,] 'Pay it. I want you to do it right away so they can't stop you.' It's Thursday, like four, five o'clock in the afternoon and there were a couple of girls in the office who heard this conversation because he was screaming so loud they could hear it.

"So I called the bank presidents and I said I need $50,000; we have to cover our shops. The girls were out and we've got to give them twenty dollars so they'll have it to buy groceries. The banks cooperated. We had accounts in a couple of banks and we got the money and Friday we passed it out. The girls were very surprised, you know. And when they started writing letters, the little devils, to Dubinsky, thanking him for the strike benefit, we were surprised! He called me up and he said he was surprised! And, 'What right did I have to pay this strike benefit without authorization?' Right away I knew there was big trouble. I could've answered and said [name] told me to do it but I didn't 'cause I realized instantly that he would be in deep, dark trouble.

"I don't know why I did it. I can't even explain to you to this day. I never told Dubinsky the truth. You know when it bothered me? When DD [Dubinsky] died. That day I couldn't rest. Why didn't I ever sit down with DD and tell him the truth? But I knew that this guy [who authorized the money], I don't know what would've happened [to him] and it couldn't be good for the department, and it couldn't be good for the politics of the union.

"I went into New York, and he [Dubinsky] was walking around talking in Jewish, Russian, and English and screaming '$50,000, $50,000

you gave away without permission. What made you do it?' He couldn't believe it. I said [to myself], that's the end of the strikes in Pennsylvania. . . . They came in and took my treasury away. They told all the bank presidents that they were not to honor my signature or my checks. The girls who were in the office and knew why I did it wanted me to tell the truth, the hell with [name]. I said, 'No, kids, it's gonna be worse. We can live with this. We'll keep right on doing what we're doing. They want to sign the checks, good. It's a pleasure. I don't have to waste my time signing checks. . . . Let the bastards sign it. Who cares?' So they took away our treasury." (Min Matheson, audio-recorded interview, November 30, 1988, NPOLHC)

41. Anthony D'Angelo (chap. 5) discussed Rocky Schillaci in connection with an arson incident at one of Angelo Sciandra's dress factories near Pittston. Mrs. Matheson's perplexity regarding Schillaci's shops remaining nonunion is likely a reference to the fact that, because of special "deals," certain shops were considered off-limits by the ILGWU's New York leadership. John Justin (chap. 7) refers to the "special deals" that were cut between union officials and particular shop owners. Although they had no firsthand knowledge of the plans, Mrs. Matheson and Mr. Justin could not explain the exceptions in any other way, and they remained deeply resentful of the situation. The special deals did, in fact, exist according to Witwer, "Dress Strike at Three-Finger Brown's."

42. The Haymarket episode stands as one of the most important and tragic of American labor crises. See Green, *Death in the Haymarket*, and Messer-Kruse, *Trial of the Haymarket Anarchists.*

43. Mrs. Matheson led her first strike as a twelve-year-old pupil in 1921, when she took fellow students out of their classes onto a picket line to protest the "harsh abuse" tendered by teachers: "They hit us with heavy rulers, pushed us around, and I decided that we should protest." It was one of the earliest strikes in the Chicago school system. See Libby Brennan, "A Salute to Women in Labor Force," *Sunday Independent*, September 6, 1987.

44. The entire Wyoming Valley area experienced a giardiasis-related water emergency that contaminated the drinking supply in the late 1980s. The crisis was originally caused by the economic development and waste disposal

policies of the Pennsylvania Gas and Water Company. On the water crisis and the citizen movement that formed to fight it, see R. Wolensky, "POWER."

45. For most of their ILGWU careers, Min and Bill Matheson received one paycheck between them, which meant that each actually worked for half pay. They did not complain about the arrangement because, they argued, their standard of living was adequate and, just as important, they viewed union work primarily as a moral undertaking, not as a pay-for-work job. Their disposition likely had roots in their earlier commitments to Communism and Socialism, their vocational commitment to the working class, and also the attitude expressed by Mrs. Matheson's father, Max Lurye, a devoted Socialist and unionist who once chastised his daughter for accepting *any* payment for union work with the ILGWU (see also chap 16).

46. Min Matheson became dismayed about the inability of the American labor movement and the Democratic Party to champion working-class interests during the 1970s and 1980s. The continuing growth of imported garments symbolized the problem, she opined.

47. In another oral history interview, Min Matheson spoke about the decline of grassroots union democracy and the rise of bureaucratic control:

MM: We're considered one of the most democratic unions in the world and I say it's a fake. So that actually if I could, I should have done it long ago and I should have made a fight. Which I suppose they [ILGWU officials in New York] would have found a way just to ease me out and shut me up, I don't know. But I tried in many ways, you know. While I was in there [as Wyoming Valley District manager], I took a lot of people out of the shop and put 'em on the staff. It was in constant disagreement with New York. They were always, "Can you trust her?" And it was always [with] women; not always, occasionally a man. . . . They would keep sending me guys from New York and I'd keep getting rid [of] 'em, and some of 'em were very nice guys but I didn't [want them]. [I'd say to them], "Go 'head, practice your law or do your accounting, but you don't belong on my staff. I've got girls that know piece rates who'll make a damn sight better business agent." I kept taking 'em [local

ILGWU members] out of the shops and putting 'em on [staff]. So that this area had people [on staff] who worked in the shops. But that's not true on the national level. And that's what they [the national union officials] use—accountants, because they can count the money, I guess, and look after the big bucks—and lawyers. That's what runs the Garment Workers' Union. It's not my kind of union.

Q: Do you feel that labor generally has lost its perspective in this regard?

MM: Oh, definitely, definitely. . . . It's disheartening, yes. And, of course, with the trade union movement, it has become fat and rich and has walked away from a lot of the old principles and ideals and I miss that. Now it's true that they say you get old and you try to hang on to the old even when it's useless, but I don't think that's very useless.

(Min [and Bill] Matheson, audio-recorded interview, November 30, 1982, NPOLHC)

CHAPTER 4

1. Min Matheson (chap. 3) discusses her first meeting with Mr. DePasquale on a Pittston picket, where he stuck a gun in an officer's back in order to rescue her from a police assault.

2. Another possible reason for Mr. DePasquale's willingness to assist the ILGWU related to his having a girlfriend who was the chairlady at one of the unionized shops in Pittston. John Justin (chap. 7) offered this observation.

3. The criminal element competed not only with the ILGWU but also with the legitimate dressmaking shops. There were many instances in both realms when the mob used illegal and threatening tactics to gain advantage. For example, according to an informant for the Federal Bureau of Investigation, about two hundred sewing machines in a dress factory owned by the legitimately run Arthur Lori Company were purposely damaged in a fire so that Bufalino-associated shops could poach Lori's workers (see memorandum by Special Agent in Charge of Philadelphia to the Director of the FBI, July 26,1956, General Investigative Intelligence File [Top Hoodlum Coverage], FBI Philadelphia Office).

4. See the interview with John Justin (chap. 7).

5. On the Edwardsville strike, see the interviews with John Justin (chap. 7), Dorothy Ney (chap. 1), Clementine Lyons (chap. 8), and Helen Weiss (chap. 9). Mr. Justin said that the Edwardsville garment shop (Anita Dress) was affiliated with the Kaplan and Elias company, which, in turn, had ties with alleged mobsters Abe Chait and Thomas Lucchese. Betty Greenberg (chap. 15) believed that the shop was managed by "Marie Law," about whom little is known. On the ties between Kaplan and Elias and organized crime, see Witwer, "Dress Strike at Three-Finger Brown's," 172–73.

6. Mr. DePasquale's encounter with David Dubinsky resonates with other characterizations of the union president. For example, Lester Velie (*Labor USA Today*, 82) wrote that, in addition to a stooped-over posture, which made him appear shorter than his five-feet-five frame, Dubinsky "has the round face of a Herbert Hoover or a Winston Churchill, but there all similarity ends. As incandescent as an electric bulb, the face lights up at the flick of the slightest emotion. And the emotion can range from childlike glee accompanied by joyful chuckles to purple rage. So animated by perpetual emotion, his face has an unlined, youthful look. The air of youthful vigor is deepened by Dubinsky's constitutional inability to sit still. An uninitiated visitor, new to Dubinsky's ways, watches with amazement as Dubinsky levitates about the room, his great head bobbing on his round body, and his voice raised to a shout. For Dubinsky doesn't talk, he yells—his voice rising to a falsetto shriek when he really warms to his conversational task. The volcano flow of words is peppered with earthly SOB's—pronounced 'sonsapitches'—and, whoever the visitor may be, with earthy Yiddishisms which Dubinsky doesn't pause to explain."

7. As it had done in the past, the Brotherhood of Teamsters held a secondary boycott in the Wyoming Valley when the ILGWU went on strike—in accordance with the Garment Industry Proviso (see appendix 2). However, the strike in Edwardsville represented an instance where a trucking company did cross a picket line. Therefore, it seems highly likely that the transgressing firm was nonunion. This possibility was further supported by David Dubinsky's severe chastisement of Mr. DePasquale, suggesting that he had offended a nonunion company. Moreover, given the ownership of the factory, it seems further likely that the trucking firm had organized crime connections.

8. Sid Caesar was a popular comedian, television star, and movie personality active in show business between 1946 and 2006.

9. Mrs. Matheson's consideration of Modesto "Murph" Loquasto as an ILGWU organizer is doubtful. An alleged member of the Bufalino crime organization, Loquasto also served as the manager of the Anthracite Needle Workers' Association, which, as Mr. DePasquale indicated, was formed in 1946 by criminally affiliated shop owners as an alternative to the ILGWU. Mr. DePasquale clearly understood the relationship between Loquasto (whom he knew from Pittston) and the Needle Workers' Association because the principal officer of the Needle Workers, Nick Benfante, had tried unsuccessfully to hire DePasquale away from the ILGWU. If Mr. Loquasto had been hired by the ILGWU, he could easily have served as a "double agent" on behalf of the mob. His role in the gang would certainly have come to the attention to Min Matheson, so it is very unlikely that she would have brought him into the union. See the interviews with Dorothy Ney (chap. 1) and Philomena Caputo (chap. 11) regarding Mr. Loquasto's status as one of Pittston's "tough guys." His photo and a police profile appeared, along with those of dozens of other alleged organized criminals, in the U.S. Department of Treasury book *Mafia*, 710.

10. Mr. Benfante's photo and profile, too, appeared along with those of dozens of other alleged organized criminals in the U.S. Treasury Department book *Mafia*, 702. According to an FBI undercover report issued on July 20, 1956, organized crime forces in Pittston established the Anthracite Needle Workers' Association in 1946 "in opposition to the ILGWU." See memorandum by Special Agent in Charge of Philadelphia to the Director of the FBI, February 11, 1954, General Investigative Intelligence File (Top Hoodlum Coverage), FBI Philadelphia Office.

11. It is clear that Mr. DePasquale took risks through his various run-ins with organized criminals and their garment operations, yet he suffered no apparent harmful consequences. His own Sicilian ancestry, along with his having "grown up" with members of the local gang, likely helped provide his apparent immunity.

12. Lester Velie, "Lady and the Gangsters," *Readers' Digest*, January 1957.

13. More than a few narrators in this volume referenced the murder of Min Matheson's brother and ILGWU organizer, Will Lurye, at the hands of alleged mobsters in New York. His death is discussed in chapter 16.

14. In reality, the criminally affiliated firms either owned, managed, or fronted between twelve and twenty shops in the Wyoming Valley, with the great majority located in Pittston, one in Edwardsville, and another in Sweet Valley. And while the alleged mobsters' *influence* might have extended to 20 to 25 percent of Pittston's forty to fifty factories, few of the more than one hundred other plants in the area fell under their sway. The Lee Manu-facturing Company, begun by Louis Gutstein and later owned by his son, Leo Gutstein, was decidedly not crime-affiliated (see Leo Gutstein, chap. 13, and Dorothy Ney, chap. 1). The discrepancy between the perceived and the actual number of mob-controlled garment shops is examined further in chapter 16.

15. Mr. DePasquale did not indicate the capacity in which he worked for Sam Alaimo.

16. As mentioned by John Justin (chap. 7), as well as other sources, the Kaplan and Elias Company from New York, an organized crime–affiliated firm, owned the Edwardsville shop named Anita Dress.

17. For reasons that remain puzzling, toward the end of the interview Mr. DePasquale offered a favorable opinion of the region's criminal gang members who also owned garment shops. After referring to them as "sons of bitches" and regretting their control of several garment shops earlier in the interview, he later changed his opinion: "Well, I tell you, Angelo [Sciandra] was well liked by all the women and all. He treated them good; he treated them people good. Angelo was a good boy, a good man as far as I know. He was a good fellow. Even Russ Bufalino was a good man. Still is, ya know, was always a good man. They call him the head of the Mafia; I think they're full of shit. He did good by the people, as far as I know. No, he was a good boy." One possible explanation is that, because many of the alleged organized crime members were still quite influential in the area at the time of the interview, he wanted to "hedge his bets" by ending the interview on a favorable note and

thereby minimizing possible negative repercus-sions from his earlier assessments.

18. Mr. DePasquale's employment as an organizer in the Wyoming Valley District recalled the ILGWU's use of much tougher characters during the organizing battles of the 1920s in New York. For example, according to Lester Velie (*Labor USA Today*, 91, 120–22), the union was said to have recruited the era's top gangster, Arnold Rothstein, to call off the anti-union "gorillas" under the direction of the infamous Jack "Legs" Diamond, who had been hired by the employers to inflict harm on pick-eting strikers. Rothstein did so with a phone call to Diamond. ILGWU leaders then had another problem: how to remove the thugs they had hired, under the direction of mobster Jacob "Little Augie" Orgen, to intimidate the employ-ers and counteract Diamond's gang? Rothstein proceeded to contact Orgen and took care of that matter as well, showing that he controlled, or at least had considerable influence over, both Diamond and Orgen. Velie argued that the ILGWU's use of gangsters and their minions in these and other instances helped open the gates to the mob's long-term involvement within the industry and the union.

CHAPTER 5

1. Because Dominick Alaimo was a purported member of the Pittston organized crime gang, this incident with his brother would have been extremely demeaning and embarrassing to him. However, Sam (Salvatore) Alaimo was also alleged to have been a member, as was a third brother, Willie Alaimo, who alleg-edly attended, and escaped from, the Apalachin organized crime summit in 1957 (see note 4 below). Dominick Alaimo eventually returned to the garment business and established the Alaimo Dress Company and the Jane Hogan Dress Company, probably in collaboration with other gang members. On Mr. Alaimo's connec-tions with organized crime, see Min Matheson (chap. 3); William A. Hastie, Sr., audio-recorded interview, July 1, 1989, NPOLHC; and Pennsyl-vania Crime Commission, *Report on Organized Crime*, 7–18. See also the notes from an unrecorded interview with Dominick Alaimo, August 8, 1989, NPOLHC.

2. "They" in Mr. D'Angelo's reenacted conversation between the brothers were the

nonunion jobbers in either New York or New Jersey who supplied garments to nonunion contracting shops, such as those of the Alaimos. David Witwer ("Dress Strike at Three-Finger Brown's," 177) noted that the alleged gangster Abe Chait and his operatives were known to have fulfilled this role. They also provided truck transportation to and from Pittston and New York.

3. *Capatosta* is a Neapolitan slang word meaning "stubborn" or, as stated, "hardheaded."

4. On the Apalachin crime meeting, see *United States v. Bufalino*, 285 F. 2d 408 (2d Cir. 1960), and appendix 2. The garment business was the most common trade listed among the sixty-five Apalachin attendees, fifty-eight of whom were arrested (see Bernstein, *Greatest Menace*, and Roth, *Global Organized Crime*, 102).

5. During the early years of the garment industry, pressers, sewers, cutters, and machine technicians belonged to separate unions. The ILGWU subsequently brought them into one organization, although they usually kept separate locals.

6. The remainder of the chapter is taken from a second interview with Mr. D'Angelo conducted by Robert P. Wolensky and Kenneth C. Wolensky, February 17, 1994, NPOLHC.

7. After an initial start-up period of nonunion operation, Arthur Lori ran unionized, legitimate shops. His motivation to move Mr. Sciandra to unionization remains unclear—perhaps he was acting as an intermediary in the hope of avoiding continuing conflicts and strikes in Pittston?

8. On Will Lurye's murder in 1949, see Min Matheson (chap. 3), Angelo DePasquale (chap. 4), and chapter 16; see also K. Wolensky, N. Wolensky, and R. Wolensky, *Fighting for the Union Label*, 82–88, chapter 16, and appendix 2.

9. Although Mrs. Matheson may have had a New York accent when she arrived in the Wyoming Valley in 1944, she had no such detectable inflection during her NPOLHC oral history interviews four and five decades later.

CHAPTER 6

1. One garment working job involved sewing dots, or colored circles, onto garments.

2. Philomena Caputo (chap. 11) also worked as an "undercover agent" for the ILGWU in a campaign to organize a nonunion shop.

3. Betty Greenberg (chap. 15) stated that Laura Fashions in Kingston (near the Mathesons' home) was one of the few Wyoming Valley shops that remained unorganized. The ILGWU tried but failed several times, and it was a vexing problem for her parents. However, Mrs. Greenberg acknowledged that Laura's three hundred employees were well treated and this was partly why they did not show a strong interest in unionization. On the other hand, Mrs. Matheson's (chap. 3) comment to Dominick Alaimo that "I can't afford to have any shop nonunion 'cause you guys are gonna get ideas and we're gonna go back to the olden days and we're not goin' back" obviously did not apply to Laura's case. Perhaps the owner had one of the alleged "special deals" with the New York ILGWU office to remain nonunion, to which Min Matheson (chap. 3) and John Justin (chap. 7) referred.

4. According to Dorothy Ney (chap. 1) and Min Matheson (chap. 3), Mr. Sitzman did not own the shop but managed it for alleged gangster Dominick Alaimo.

5. The trucking firm could have been one of those affiliated with alleged gangster Abe Chait.

6. See Anna Lieb, audio-recorded interview, June 30, 1997, NPOLHC.

7. Mrs. Reca is referring to a commonly held view among the region's working class that the coal companies—the area's major employers by far—did not encourage industrial expansion because new businesses would present employment and wage competition. For support of this idea, see the oral history with Richard Cronin (May 24, 1983, NPOLHC), who, for many years, was the executive director of the Greater Wilkes-Barre Chamber of Commerce.

8. Depositing the body of a dead mineworker on the family's front porch has been a verified and commonly told story across the anthracite region. It has invariably been used by the descendants of miners as the quintessential example of the heartless cruelty and exploitation exhibited by the coal companies and their owners, the so-called coal barons.

9. Mrs. Reca mistakenly referred to Victor Riesel, instead of Lester Velie, as the author of the *Reader's Digest* article. In 1956, New York authorities indicted John Dioguardi (aka Johnny Dio) in the acid attack that blinded Mr. Riesel,

who had been writing highly critical stories about organized crime, including its relationship to labor unions. Two other conspirators were indicted and later convicted, but Dioguardi escaped culpability when these two recanted their testimony against him. On the Riesel attack, see Max Frankel, "Johnny Dio and 4 Others Held as Masterminds in Riesel Attack," *New York Times*, August 29, 1956; "Freed in Riesel Case," *New York Times*, December 14, 1957; and Abadinsky, *Organized Crime*, 256. See Witwer's critical analysis of Riesel's writings in "Pattern for Partnership."

10. Mrs. Reca is saying that Min Matheson called Angela Bambace to recommend her for the position in Baltimore. On Angela Bambace, see Scarpaci, "Angela Bambace," 16, 58, 121, and Guglielmo, *Living the Revolution*, 84, 207.

11. On the Upper South Department's history, see ILGWU, Upper South Department Records, Kheel Center, and appendix 1.

CHAPTER 7

1. In another audio-recorded interview with Robert P. Wolensky on June 25, 1997, conducted at Mr. Justin's Wilkes-Barre apartment, he said that soon after opening the Pittston office, he made contact with a union-friendly printing company owned and operated by George and Lucy Zorgo of Pittston, who went on to become the ILGWU's printer over the next four decades. See the interview with the Zorgos (chap. 10).

2. Jay Lovestone led a group called the Labor League of America, which published a newspaper called the *Workers Age*. Israel Zimmerman was a member of the Labor League, as was his brother, Charles "Shasha" Zimmerman, who also sat on the editorial board of the newspaper, along with Lovestone and others (see Marxists' Internet Archive, "Organ of Jay Lovestone's Independent Labor League of America," MIA: History: USA: Publications: Workers Age, 1932–1941, 2013, http://www.marxists.org/history/usa/pubs/workers-age/1939).

3. The Lovestonites were named for the leader of the Communist Party of the USA (CPUSA), Jay Lovestone, of New York. Israel Zimmerman, brother of Charles "Sasha" Zimmerman, became a member of the group, as did Min Lurye (Matheson), who, at age fifteen, worked as Lovestone's secretary and

became a member of the CPUSA's inner circle along with her friend and fellow garment maker Jennie Silverman (see Jennie Silverman, audio-recorded interview, July 16, 1993, NPOLHC). Amid a series of sharp disagreements over strategy and philosophy during the 1930s, CPUSA leaders purged "uncooperative" persons such as Lovestone, the Zimmermans, and Min Lurye. The mainstream elements also disagreed strongly with ILGWU president David Dubinsky. After their expulsions, Dubinsky welcomed the "reformed" Lovestone, Zimmermans, and Lurye back to the union fold. Fashioning themselves as Progressives and then New Dealers, they were joined by many other prominent labor unionists who had abandoned the CPUSA at this time. On Jay Lovestone, see Alexander, *Right Opposition*; Morgan, *Covert Life*; and Le Blanc and Davenport, *"American Exceptionalism" of Jay Lovestone*.

4. "Cathouse," a term associated with prostitution, was apparently being used by this owner as a sexist slang term for a garment shop.

5. See the interview with Louis Gutstein's son, Leo Gutstein (chap. 13).

6. Louis Gutstein of Lee Manufacturing (a legitimate company) was alleged to have had an informal agreement with certain ILGWU leaders in New York that allowed his shops to remain nonunion until the operation was established in the Wyoming Valley. Witwer ("Dress Strike at Three-Finger Brown's," 179–80) provides evidence that informal agreements were indeed made between the ILGWU and nonunion runaway shops, with many of the deals involving organized criminals (see chap. 16).

7. On the Congress of Industrial Organizations, see Zieger, *CIO*.

8. State senator Franz Leichter, in a report on criminal activity to the New York State Legislature, described another form of corruption employed by Mr. Pappadio, such as the "bust out" or bankruptcy fraud (see Jacobs, Friel, and Raddick, *Gotham Unbound*, 28). See also appendix 2.

9. Victor Amuso emerged as the leader of the Lucchese crime organization following the death of Thomas "Three-Finger Brown" Lucchese in 1967 (see Jacobs, Friel, and Raddick, *Gotham Unbound*, 28, and Raab, *Five Families*, 477, 710).

10. See Angelo DePasquale (chap. 4) for another discussion of this Pittston strike. In his

interview, Mr. DePasquale did not mention his girlfriend, who was the chairlady of a unionized shop. Her involvement with ILGWU certainly could also have motivated Mr. DePasquale's decision to organize on behalf of the union.

11. The gun may not have belonged to the policeman but rather to Angelo DePasquale, who, according to Min Matheson (chap. 3), stuck a firearm into the back of a policeman who was hurting her during an arrest. In his interview, Mr. DePasquale (chap. 4) admits to keeping a gun in his car "for protection."

12. Anthony D'Angelo (chap. 5) relates his experiences in removing dresses and sewing machines from a shop owned by Angelo Sciandra just before it was set on fire in an act of arson.

13. Julius Hochman, manager of the ILGWU Joint Board Dress and Waistmakers' Union, authored a report in 1957 that outlined the history of the ILGWU's "special deals" with criminally affiliated jobbers, contractors, and trucking firms. In the report, he mentioned the rather large Kaplan and Elias Company of New York, which, following 1936 dress strike settlement, resisted the new agreement. The union set up picket lines to thwart the firm's operations in the city, whereupon Kaplan and Elias sought the assistance of alleged mobster Abe Chait, who supposedly controlled ILGWU Local 102, the Cloak and Dress Drivers' and Helpers' Union. The local was known for its mob connections, with President Dubinsky referring to it as "the problem child of the union" (Benin, *New Labor Radicalism*, 123). Historian David Witwer ("Dress Strike at Three-Finger Brown's," 172) wrote that Chait "arranged trucking services for firms that wanted to avoid the union's restrictions by having the garment pieces sewn together at nonunion shops located outside the city, often in the small towns of Northeastern Pennsylvania. Because of Chait's control over Local 102, the ILGWU's national leadership found itself helpless to stop him."

14. Selwyn Raab explained how organized crime gained influence in both the women's and the men's garment unions. The relationships began in the 1920s when both management and labor hired mobsters to protect their interests: managers to prevent unionization drives, and organized labor to foster them. Raab wrote that "when the confrontations ended, the gangsters who had worked illegally for

both sides stayed on, gaining influence in the unions and in management associations." Some became visible and invisible garment shop owners or financiers. He added that when the New York district attorney Thomas E. Dewey began his crusade against the city's gangs, he questioned both Sidney Hillman, president of the Amalgamated Clothing and Textile Workers Union (the men's clothing union), and David Dubinsky of the ILGWU, who insisted that they had no knowledge of mob involvement with their respective organizations. In his autobiography, however, Dewey expressed the opinion that "they both dealt with these gangsters and knew all about them. But they wouldn't give me the slightest bit of help of any kind" (quoted in Raab, *Five Families*, 71).

15. On *Mary Brown*, see William Gable, audio-recorded interview, December 3, 1999, NPOLHC.

16. The Harvic Dress shop in Sweet Valley, Pennsylvania, a rural area about fifteen miles from Wilkes-Barre, was owned by suspected gangsters Thomas "Three-Finger Brown" Lucchese and Harry "Nig" Rosen. It was managed by Thomas Gambino, son of New York's alleged top crime boss, Carlo Gambino, who married Thomas Lucchese's daughter, Frances, in 1962. On the connection between the Gambino and Lucchese criminal organizations, see Raab, *Five Families*. On the Sweet Valley shop, see Witwer, "Dress Strike at Three-Finger Brown's."

17. Rose Pesotta's memoir is titled *Bread upon the Waters*. On Pesotta, see also Jensen, "Inside and Outside the Unions," and Leeder, *Gentle General*.

18. A review of Evelyn Dubrow's life in the garment movement can be found in her obituary by Steven Greenhouse, "Labor Lobbyist, Dies at 95," *New York Times*, June 22, 2006.

19. In an unrecorded interview on May 30, 2000, Mr. Justin provided additional information about the workings of the ILGWU, including what he called "the big squeeze-out" during the late 1950s and early 1960s. It involved the relocation of several "rebellious" district managers within the Northeast Department. Among them were (1) Min Matheson, who was transferred from serving as manager of the Wyoming Valley District to director of the Union Label office in New York; (2) Murray Levin ("One of the most powerful men in

the union outside of New York," says Justin), who was moved from being manager of a Boston district to a managerial position in an unnamed location; (3) Oscar Newman, who was "promoted" from working as district manager in Mt. Carmel, Pennsylvania, to manager of the Fall River, Massachusetts, District; (4) Sol Greene, who was sent from his manager's position in Allentown, Pennsylvania, to become the manager of a New York City local; and (5) Mr. Justin, who was transferred from serving as manager of the Pottsville, Pennsylvania, District to work as a troubleshooter for the Union Label Department in New York, Chicago, Wisconsin, and other places. Min Matheson likely exerted some influence on Justin's transfer to the Union Label Department because it occurred the year after she became director in 1963, suggesting that she wanted him to assist with her efforts to revive and expand the office. Mr. Justin also briefly discussed his move to Union Label in a recorded interview on May 30, 1996, NPOLHC.

Justin argued that these transfers occurred because the "rebels" did not fit with the plans of Louis Rona, district manager of the Sham-okin, Pennsylvania, office (Justin said he was alleged to have ties to organized crime), and Ray Shore, Pennsylvania state supervisor for the union, both of whom "were very close to Chick Chaiken." He added that they were working with Chaiken to, in effect, purge uncooperative people who were too "independent" and would not toe the company line, as Chaiken defined it. Justin also believed that David Gingold (director of the Northeast Department) agreed with the transfers. Justin thought that Chaiken also had ties to organized crime: "He made no bones about it. And when he retired from the ILGWU, after eight years he became the director of the Javits Arena [in New York City], which was a payoff for his work with the mob." Justin highlighted Mr. Chaiken's connections to Rona, who, he added, was either a mobster or had dealings with criminally aligned persons.

Justin further indicated that the old guard of Progressive-minded ILGers, many of whom came out of the earlier Communist and Social-ist traditions, clashed with former Progressives such as Chaiken (Gingold's assistant and later the union president) and Gingold (later a vice president), as both became bureaucratically conservative and authoritarian in their manage-rial styles. The duo fostered centralized control

of decision making with "their own people" in the key decision posts. Dubinsky encouraged the trend because he was also a controlling person with a strong personality, said Justin, but he was not as centralizing as Chaiken. Justin added that Dubinsky would send out commands once in a while "about thus and so," but Chaiken "was doing it all the time."

Mr. Justin, therefore, presented an argu-ment for "the new ILGWU." On one occasion, when Chaiken had moved house to Long Island and held an elaborate housewarming party, the union bought flowers and plants for the affair, and later sent Justin, Min Matheson, and other district leaders a bill for about seventy-five dollars each as part of their share. "We didn't pay them," Justin insisted. "We never paid them." He and Matheson were not going along with such policies because he believed they amounted to a type of corruption. Justin also remarked that he and Mrs. Matheson did not attend certain union meetings as a mild protest against New York administrators and the manner in which they ran the union. These actions occurred in 1958, around the time of both the major strike and when the New York office took away Mrs. Mathe-son's checkbook following a strike where she distributed "grocery money" for strikers without permission from superiors (see Min Matheson, chap. 3).

In the late 1950s, union headquarters also wanted to transfer Bill Matheson to Allentown, Pennsylvania (sixty miles from the Wyoming Valley), where he would continue his educa-tional work. Although he would still edit the Wyoming Valley's *Needlepoint* newsletter, he did not go along with the idea. The Mathesons argued that there were other husband-and-wife teams who were allowed to work in the same city. Justin believed that the union higher-ups wanted to separate the couple in order to weaken Mrs. Matheson. Again, he saw Chaiken as the person behind the arrangement.

Finally, Mr. Justin once had the opportunity to confront Chaiken over his leadership in the union. According to Justin, he and Chaiken were among those attending an ILGWU meet-ing in Camden, New Jersey, when it started to snow. As they were leaving the gathering together, they began chatting and Chaiken commented on the strength of the storm. Justin could not restrain himself and quipped, "Chick, you have caused the biggest storms in the

ILGWU that I have ever seen." Chaiken could only reply, "Well, that's Johnny Justin for you." For a biographical perspective on Chaiken, see his book *Labor Viewpoint*.

CHAPTER 8

1. Bonnie Stepenoff ("Child Labor in Pennsylvania's Silk Mills") found that women silk workers in the early twentieth century regularly sought educational opportunities when they could. William Cherkes (chap. 2) commented on the existence of skilled sewers in the Wyoming Valley dating back to the men's garment industry earlier in the twentieth century, when a relatively small, largely female workforce made miners' work clothing.

2. On the 1953 Emkay strike, see Box 319, Folder 12c, No. 5780, Dubinsky Papers, Kheel Center.

3. See Helen Weiss (chap. 9).

4. See Dr. Albert Schiowitz (chap. 12).

5. As discussed in the preface and in chapter 16, the ILGWU's cooperation with, and cultivation of, the citizenry and community institutions composed an essential part of the Mathesons' solidarity unionism approach. The mention of Catholic churches in the previous paragraph reflected not only the fact that Clementine Lyons was a Catholic and, therefore, had numerous contacts within those communities but also that, by the 1920s, most of the area's working class—including garment workers—were Roman or Eastern Catholic.

6. See Dorothy Ney (chap. 1).

7. For other versions of how Rep. Daniel J. Flood became the attorney for the ILGWU's Wyoming Valley District, see the interviews with Dorothy Ney (chap. 1) and Angelo DePasquale (chap. 4).

8. As the ILGWU grew in numbers, gained broad legitimacy, and accrued numerous resources, the union expanded its agenda to included issues related to community development and betterment. For example, chapter 16 mentions the union's concerns and actions regarding strip (open pit) mining, including worker safety and the effects of the practice on the natural environment. In another challenge to the established order, the union worked to secure entry for women into the all-male Westmoreland Club, which finally occurred in 1990 ("Harris Remains Firm Despite Daughter's Westmoreland Entry," *Sunday Independent*, September 23, 1990). In a reference to Pennsylvania governor Gifford Pinchot's conservative economic philosophy during the 1930s, journalist Paul Beers (*Pennsylvania Politics*, 88) wrote, "Pinchot's economic conservatism appealed even to the dinosaurs at the Union League [Philadelphia], the Duquesne Club [Pittsburgh], and the Westmoreland Club [Wilkes-Barre]."

9. Martha Jane Canary (1852–1903) was one of the most famous women of the Old West, known by her nickname Calamity Jane. She entered popular culture with the Buffalo Bill Wild West Show and as a character in movies, television programs, and two plays with her name in the title.

10. There is no evidence that attorney Arthur Silverblatt served as a legal representative of the ILGWU. In an oral history interview (June 27, 1990, NPOLHC), he discussed the bombing of his front porch in 1960 but associated it with his position as the assistant district attorney of Luzerne County and his office's prosecution of Knox Mine disaster–related court cases in 1959 and 1960. Ms. Lyons's association of the bombing with the ILGWU strikes (at least one shop owner [Dominick Alaimo] also worked at the Knox Coal Company) reinforces Alessandro Portelli's research on human memory and the tendency to reinterpret historical events to reinforce preexisting salient dispositions, a matter discussed further in chapter 16. See also Portelli's *Death of Luigi Trastulli*.

11. On the Mecadon murder, see *Wilkes-Barre Record Almanac*, 1952, 58, and "Unsolved Murder of Union Head Recalled by Knox Disaster Probe," *Sunday Independent*, March 22, 1959.

12. The Anthracite Needle Workers' Association was created by alleged organized crime–affiliated garment shop owners in 1946 as an alternative to the ILGWU. On the organization's failed effort to unionize local garment workers, see *in re* Pocono Apparel Mfg. Co., Employer, and Anthracite Needle Workers' Association, Petitioner, No. 4-R-2373 (Scranton, Pa., May 6, 1947), http://labor-relations-board .vlex.com/vid/pocono-apparel-mfg-anthracite -needle-39982179, and appendix 2.

13. The Reagan administration lifted the forty-five-year-old ban on garment homeworking in November 1988 (see, e.g., Kenneth B. Noble, "U.S. Will End Ban on Work in Home," *New York Times*, November 11, 1988).

14. In the early 1960s, Mrs. Matheson testified before the U.S. Senate's Labor and Public Welfare Committee in support of the Area Redevelopment Act, signed into law by President John F. Kennedy in 1961. See also appendix 2.

15. The remainder of the chapter is from a second oral history interview with Clementine Lyons conducted by Robert P. Wolensky and Kenneth C. Wolensky on July 24, 1993, NPOLHC, which focused mainly on her activities in the ILGWU Wyoming Valley District chorus.

16. Born between 1917 and 1921, "notch year" Social Security recipients argued that they had received less than a fair share of benefits because of the changes Congress made to the system in 1977.

17. On the vital role of the chorus within the ILGWU Wyoming Valley District, see K. Wolensky, "We're Singin' for the Union."

CHAPTER 9

1. See the interviews with Angelo DePasquale (chap. 4), John Justin (chap. 7), Clementine Lyons (chap. 8), and Betty Greenberg (chap. 15) regarding the Edwardsville strike. John Justin said the shop was owned by Kaplan and Ellis, a firm connected to the Lucchese crime organization. Betty Greenberg thought that one "Marie Law" was one of the owners, or perhaps the manager, of the plant.

2. Mrs. Weiss was referring to the Garment Industry Proviso (see appendix 2).

3. Anthony D'Angelo (chap. 5) discusses another work stoppage at the Ann Will factory.

4. For other perspectives on the Jenkins Sportswear strike, see the interviews with Dorothy Ney (chap. 1), Min Matheson (chap. 3), and Philomena Caputo (chap. 11).

5. On Carmella Salatino's efforts to challenge the corrupt, male-dominated election system in Pittston, see the interview with Min Matheson (chap. 3).

6. Other sources indicated that Angelo Sciandra was an owner of the Ann-Lee Company, but Dominick Alaimo may also have held a partnership position in the firm. On Dominick Alaimo's garment business, see also the interviews with Min Matheson (chap. 3) and Anthony D'Angelo (chap. 5).

7. Other narrators have stated that Mrs. Falcone never unionized the shop, and instead sold it soon after the strike, whereupon the new owner accepted the ILGWU.

8. However, as Leigh David Benin (*New Labor Radicalism*, 78) pointed out, the ILGWU tried to help employers meet the competition to at least some extent: "To avoid being trampled by a stampede of runaway shops, the ILGWU committed itself to a strategy of keeping wages down in New York City to dissuade garment manufacturers from relocating to low-wage areas outside the city."

9. On the 1958 strike, see also Dorothy Ney (chap. 1), Min Matheson (chap. 3), and Clementine Lyons (chap. 8); K. Wolensky, N. Wolensky, and R. Wolensky, *Fighting for the Union Label* (chap. 6); and Witwer, "Dress Strike at Three-Finger Brown's."

CHAPTER 10

1. See the oral history interview with Martin Burger, December 16, 1997, NPOLHC.

2. Although not mentioned by Mr. and Mrs. Zorgo, Steven Lukasik of Lukasik Studio in Dupont, Pennsylvania, was the photographer for the Christmas card. He served as the ILGWU's official photographer from the early 1950s to the late 1970s. Several of his images appear in this volume courtesy of William Lukasik, Jr. and Sr., and Stephen Lukasik of Lukasik Studio. See also Steven Lukasik's oral history interview, June 21, 1999, NPOLHC.

3. See the oral history interview with Sol Hoffman and Ralph Reuter, March 6, 1998, NPOLHC.

4. On section work, or piecework, as compared to whole garment manufacturing, see William Cherkes (chap. 2).

5. Mr. Zorgo's suggestion that the criminal element controlled all aspects of garment trucking does not resonate with other narrators' statements that the local trucking firms, the local Teamsters union, as well as the unionized drivers supported garment strikers and would not take unsewn pieces into local factories or move finished goods to market.

6. On the protracted effort to find Will Lurye's murderers, see "Garment Unionists Visit Lurye Grave; 1,500 on Anniversary of Killing of Organizer Hear Leaders Pledge Solving of Crime," *New York Times*, May 8, 1950.

7. Betty Matheson Greenberg (chap. 15) commented on the threats and other difficulties the Zorgos endured because they were the ILGWU's printing house.

8. Junior Volpe was the nephew of the area's first alleged mob boss, Santo Volpe.

9. Min Matheson was among the early members of the National Organization for Women.

10. Bill Matheson's calling his wife "Maud" could possibly have been a reference to Maud Younger (1870–1936), an early twentieth-century suffragist, feminist, and labor activist who supported the garment workers and participated in the strike of 1913 (see Cott, *Grounding of Modern Feminism*, 34). This possibility is supported by Mr. Matheson's wide knowledge of American labor history and activism.

11. As an indication of the Zorgos' close relationship with the Mathesons, Mr. Zorgo discussed an occasion (not included in his narrative here) when, after making the appropriate contacts, Mrs. Matheson secured a summer job for his son at the ILGWU's Unity House resort in the Pocono Mountains.

CHAPTER 11

1. In addition to being alleged mob boss Russell Bufalino's niece or first cousin (see appendix 2), Emanuella "Dolly" Falcone married attorney William Falcone, who was alleged to have had ties to organized crime. Falcone was said to have attended the Apalachin, New York, organized crime meeting in 1957. On Falcone's mob connections, see George H. Martin's testimony in the *Hearings before the Select Committee on Improper Activities in the Labor or Management Field*, 85th Cong. 12472–85 (1958).

2. On the Knox Mine disaster, see also the interviews with Min Matheson (chap. 3) and Clementine Lyons (chap. 8).

3. For a definition of percentage, see appendix 1.

4. Min Matheson asked Mrs. Caputo to become the strike captain of the Jenkins Sportswear picket line, from where she provided regular reports on the shutdown and related goings-on.

5. Mrs. Caputo's descriptions of violence against women picketers contradict statements made by Clementine Lyons, Min Matheson,

and others to the effect that the "tough guys" were reluctant to physically harm women. She devotes more attention to this topic later in the interview.

6. Mrs. Caputo's husband, Mr. Michael Caputo, interjected at this point, "I was approached once in the beer garden across the street, Bufalino's beer garden—Club 82. 'Why don't I let my wife stay home and this and that,' you know. I told them, 'She's workin' for the union.' They never bothered me. They never bothered me." This sort of "tolerance" illustrated the nuanced relationships that developed between strikers and mobsters, as discussed in chapter 16.

7. For documentation on the court case about which Mrs. Caputo speaks, see Box 319, Folder 12a, No. 5780, David Dubinsky Papers, Kheel Center.

8. According to her daughter, Rose Linko, Agnes Sarti was so staunchly anti-union that she refused to work in any unionized factory. Indeed, she would quit working at a shop if the ILGWU organized it. She especially detested union dues because, her daughter quoted her as saying, "Those dues are taking the food out of my children's mouths." The mother of ten children, Mrs. Sarti lived in Swoyersville and often awoke to find ILGWU members picketing her home. According to Mrs. Linko (who was the eldest of the ten children), "We felt like we couldn't go out the front door because the pickets were there. We felt like they would come after us. We felt threatened. We thought that they might hurt the kids" (Rose Linko, personal communication, July 17, 2018).

9. Alleged gangster Abe Chait was reported to have had an ownership stake in the Interstate Trucking Company, so it is likely that drivers honored the picket line either because—as more than a few subjects indicated—their local Teamsters' office supported the ILGWU, and possibly because of the "special relationship" between Mr. Chait and Mrs. Matheson. See her interview (chap 3, note 28) for a detailed account of a meeting between Mrs. Matheson and Mr. Chait. See also chapter 16 on their relationship.

10. Emanuella "Dolly" Falcone sent a telegram to David Dubinsky on May 24, 1959, questioning his statement to reporters that the Jenkins Sportswear owners had encouraged violence against picketers. "I wish to stand

on record as opposing any form of violence," she said, "and I join you in your request that a complete and thorough investigation of these events be made." She ended by writing the following: "Threats and violence will never offer an intelligent solution of labor management disputes" (telegram, Emanuella Falcone to David Dubinsky, May 24, 1950, Box 227, Folder 4a, No. 5780, David Dubinsky Papers, Kheel Center). Pennsylvania's secretary of labor, William Batt, Jr., volunteered to mediate the confrontation, but Falcone turned down the offer. Min Matheson was kept informed about these communications and wrote to Batt criticizing Falcone's henchmen: "Today this group attacked our women pickets, injuring several of them and also viciously beat up a man, a passer-by, who attempted to intervene" (Min L. Matheson to William Batt, Jr., April 10, 1959, Box 227, Folder 4a, No. 5780, David Dubinsky Papers, Kheel Center).

11. Min Matheson confirmed Mrs. Caputo's undercover role at Jenkins Sportswear in an unrecorded interview on November 30, 1988, NPOLHC.

CHAPTER 12

1. Solomon Hoffman and Ralph Reuter contributed a joint oral history on June 6, 1998, NPOLHC.

2. The original ILGWU Health Center building on South Washington Street in downtown Wilkes-Barre was torn down in the early 1970s and the land purchased by the Genetti Hotel for a parking lot. The Center then moved to the union headquarters across the street from the original site. City officials later demolished the headquarters building as part of a redevelopment project, which, after some controversy, became the location of a new state of Pennsylvania office building. The two original garment worker friezes, in cobalt blue, were preserved and later placed on the front of the new office building. See the frontispiece of this book.

3. The questioning on workers' possible health problems was motivated by the case of Roseto, Pennsylvania, a small town with a large Italian immigrant population located in the Slate Belt region of Northampton County, less than one hundred miles south of the research site. Roseto had developed a thriving garment industry during the middle years of the twentieth century. When studied by health epidemiologists in the early 1960s, the community became known for the "Roseto Effect" due to the residents' low rates of cardiovascular disease despite their having fairly unhealthy diets, high rates of cigarette smoking, and considerable levels of alcohol consumption. Researchers linked the favorable health outcomes to the town's Italian-based culture and lifestyle characterized by close social networks and low stress levels. However, follow-up inquires found that, as the second and third generations became more "Americanized," heart disease and other maladies rose to rates similar to those of the general population. See Valletta, "Settlement of Roseto"; Egolf et al., "Roseto Effect"; and Ron Grossman and Charles Leroux, "A New 'Roseto Effect': People Are Nourished by Other People," *Chicago Tribune*, October 11, 1996.

4. The asthma question was motivated by the high levels of particulate matter within garment factories and the high levels of coal dust in the air of communities that hosted anthracite mine workings. Even after coal mining had declined, coal dust still presented a problem because of the huge culm banks or coal waste mountains that dotted the region. See, for example, Derickson, *Black Lung*, and Friis, *Occupational Health and Safety*.

5. The ILGWU established its first health center in New York in 1913. Along with New York and Wilkes-Barre, the union built centers in Philadelphia, Chicago, Cleveland, St. Louis, Boston, Kansas City, Los Angeles, Newark, Montreal, Fall River, and Allentown. Others operated under special arrangements with local clinics in Baltimore, Dallas, Houston, Laredo, San Francisco, Minneapolis, and San Antonio. In addition to Wilkes-Barre's mobile unit, there were similar units in Puerto Rico, the Southeast, the Midwest, and New England. At its peak, the health centers treated 95,086 individual patients and provided 1.056 million services annually. See Health and Safety, Box 1, Folder 7, No. 5780, ILGWU Papers, Kheel Center, and Tyler, *Look for the Union Label*.

CHAPTER 13

1. Sayre is located about eighty-five miles away from Wilkes-Barre in Bradford County,

and Carbondale and Mayfield are located near Scranton, in Lackawanna County.

2. See the interview of garment shop owner William Cherkes (chap. 2), who lived in Kingston and also commented on his long workday.

3. John Justin (chap. 7) discussed the inexplicable delay in unionizing Lee Manufacturing, and surmised that it was the result of one of the "special deals" made between union leaders and certain shop owners. See chapter 16 on this subject.

4. On the eastern European, particularly Jewish, immigration to New York City and its relationship to the garment industry, see Katz, *All Together Different.*

5. Mr. Gutstein's sentiments were echoed by Barry Sacks, chairman of Chorus Line Inc., a Los Angeles garment company, who, in 1995, said that he expected to move about 25 percent of his production offshore: "If we remained in the United States we would have no growth pattern. We wouldn't be competitive any more. The retailers are vicious." Although Chorus Line faced greater pressure from retailers such as Walmart than did Gutstein, both Sacks and Gutstein held that "market forces" prompted them to make difficult investment decisions, or as Sacks put it, "Because of tough price competition, the company had no choice [but to move numerous operations overseas]" (quoted in Bonacich and Appelbaum, *Behind the Label,* 6). See also Stuart Silverstein and George White, "Garment Maker Vows to Halt Salary Abuses: Chorus Line Corp.," *Los Angeles Times,* November 4, 1994. By 2000, Chorus Line had shifted 70 percent of its production to Mexico and kept the rest in the Los Angeles area.

6. Bonacich and Appelbaum (*Behind the Label,* 99–101) discussed private-label manufacturing: "A significant trend in retailing is the expansion of sales of private-label merchandise. Retailers selling goods under their own store label can bypass the manufacturer altogether." L. L. Bean, Gap, Walmart, Target, Sears, and J. C. Penney are among the firms using private labels.

7. Mr. Gutstein is referring to the Garment Industry Proviso of the Wagner Act of 1935. See appendix 2.

8. Jay Mazur, the last ILGWU and the first UNITE! president, stated that he began his union career at a lower managerial level with the encouragement of his father, an international union official. The union provided him with a job and an opportunity; as he moved up the ladder, he performed not as an ideologue but rather as a manager focused on organizational matters. In other words, he adopted a "business unionism" approach. See his oral history interview, March 6, 1998, NPOLHC.

9. For an insightful and provocative analysis of the controls put on the garment industry by organized crime, often in cooperation with ILGWU officials, see Witwer, "Dress Strike at Three-Finger Brown's," whose research is also cited in chapter 16.

10. In 1959 and 1960, a federal grand jury in New York investigated the relationship between the Wyoming Valley garment industry and the trucking business, as discussed in "Garment Industry Ties to Trucking Industry Being Investigated," *Wilkes-Barre Record,* January 14, 1960. On organized crime's influence over the garment trucking business (in this case, the Gambino and Genovese crime organizations), see Benjamin Weiser, "Reputed Crime Family Head Indicted in Extortion Case," *New York Times,* April 29, 1998. See also Witwer, "Dress Strike at Three-Finger Brown's," 172–73, and the Friedman's Express Trucking Company and the Interstate Dress Carriers entries in appendix 2.

CHAPTER 14

1. Numerous garment workers expressed similar views about educational attainment. Min Matheson (chap. 3) discussed the members' certificate program conducted by Wilkes College (now University). Clementine Lyons (chap. 8) spoke with pride about her enrollment at the University of Scranton during the 1950s while she was on the ILGWU District staff. Unity House regularly scheduled education and training programs for members. The pattern was much like what Stepenoff (*Their Fathers' Daughters,* 113) found in the northeastern Pennsylvania silk industry during the early twentieth century, where women employees regularly sought educational opportunities.

2. In 1963, Paul Strongin followed Min Matheson as manager of the ILGWU Wyoming Valley District, and he, in turn, was followed in 1977 by Sam Bianco, who had previously served as the assistant manager and manager of the Pittston Local 295. Lois Hartel succeeded Mr. Bianco as assistant manager in Pittston and

then became Wyoming Valley District manager in 1986. By that point, the Wyoming Valley District had merged with the Hazleton District. See the interviews with Samuel Bianco, March 11, 1996, and Lois Hartel, June 17, 1993, and March 15, 1996, NPOLHC.

3. Minchin (*Empty Mills*) provided an extensive description and analysis of the globalizing garment and textile industries, as well as the associated domestic and international policy conflicts.

4. On the Leslie Fay strike, see also the oral history interviews with Lois Hartel, June 17, 1993, and March 16, 1996, NPOLHC.

5. See the oral history interview with Jack Granahan, June 26, 1997, NPOLHC.

6. Fred Pomerantz of New York started the Leslie Fay Company in 1947.

7. Before becoming the archbishop and then cardinal of the Diocese of New York, O'Connor had been the bishop of the Diocese of Scranton, where several garment workers had met him and garnered his support during the Leslie Fay strike. For a study of the cardinal, see Hentoff, *John Cardinal O'Connor*.

8. On the Leslie Fay corruption scandal, see Stephanie Strom, "Accounting Scandal at Leslie Fay," *New York Times*, February 2, 1993, and Anand, Ashforth, and Joshi, "Business as Usual." On the firm's bankruptcy, see Stephanie Strom, "Leslie Fay Files for Chapter 11," *New York Times*, April 6, 1993, and "Leslie Fay Shareholders Sue Accounting Firm," *New York Times*, April 6, 1995. See also Leslie Fay's entry in appendix 2.

9. On the Leslie Fay strike, see also Leslie Fay Inc., David Dubinsky Papers, Kheel Center.

10. See the oral history interview with Martin Berger, December 16, 1997, NPOLHC.

11. The Wyoming Valley Mall housed a branch of the Kaufman's Department Store, an upscale chain that originated in Pittsburgh but has been owned by Macy's since 2006.

12. Mrs. Novak was referring to the murder of Mrs. Matheson's brother, Will Lurye, who was an organizer for the ILGWU in New York. See also Min Matheson (chap. 3) and appendix 3.

13. Claire Schechter, "Garment Workers Set Strike If Leslie Fay Co. Doesn't Submit a Negotiable Offer by May 31," *Times Leader*, May 26, 1994.

14. Mrs. Novak was referring to an incident during a strike in Pittston when Min Matheson,

in response to a thug who called her a "slut," proceeded to have her two young daughters dressed in finery and brought to the picket line, where they paraded with the strikers. The children were also driven through the city on a back of a flatbed truck, from which their mother addressed the striking workers.

CHAPTER 15

1. Right-wing syndicated columnist Westbrook Pegler's writings about the Mathesons' Communist and radical ties (as well as those of William Lurye, Mrs. Matheson's murdered brother) helped precipitate a federal investigation of the couple during the Communist scare of the 1950s (which Betty Greenberg refers to later in the interview). Pegler also accused ILGWU president David Dubinsky of being a Communist (see Parmet, *Master of Seventh Avenue*, 247, and Witwer, "Westbrook Pegler"). Although he used it as clear evidence of a fundamentally criminal personality, Pegler correctly pointed out that Will Lurye had been convicted of petty theft at age eighteen in 1928 and served a six-month sentence in an Illinois state prison. Mr. Lurye was again arrested for an unstated crime less than one year later and served over two years for that offense, gaining parole on May 20, 1931. He was arrested four other times thereafter, but none of the charges held and some may have been labor-related (see "Will Lurye Public Record," Box 319, Folder 12b, No. 5780, David Dubinsky Papers, Kheel Center). Will Lurye was one of at least three ILGers murdered around this time: Sol Moss of the Dressmakers' Union was shot by unknown assailants near Times Square on July 11, 1946, and Anthony Durante of the ILGWU was shot as he left his car on Bath Beach Street in New York on June 6, 1947 (see Charles S. Zimmerman to Members of Dressmakers' Union Local 22, "Lurye, the Latest of a Bloody Series," n.d., Box 319, Folder 12b, No. 5780, David Dubinsky Papers, Kheel Center).

2. The reference is to a U.S. Senate committee's hearings on the Area Redevelopment Act.

3. Jennie Silverman, audio-recorded interview, June 16, 1993, NPOLHC.

4. On the subject of pay, Mrs. Greenberg stated in an unrecorded interview (January 9, 1995):

"There were people brought into this district from New York as business agents, and my mother would make out their pay and see that they were making two or three times what she was making. One time she asked Dubinsky about the disparity in pay. All he could say was, 'Vell, they're from New York,' and that was that. I guess the idea was that they had to have more pay in New York. My parents were never in the union for anything material and they would rarely if ever say anything. My father was worse than my mother. He'd say, 'Look Min, it would look really bad if we made something of this.' It was also because she was a woman. She was a woman in a woman's union and she was always underpaid. People think that we inherited all her wealth, but she had no wealth because she was so low paid."

5. The Lucchese shop, called Harvic Sportswear, was later sold and unionized under a different owner.

6. As Min Matheson was directing the activities of the Flood Victims' Action Council following the Tropical Storm Agnes flood of 1972, her neighbor and a political adversary, federal judge Max Rosenn, served as the chairperson of the Flood Recovery Task Force (FRTF), created by local banking and business interests. With her emphasis on "ordinary" flood victims, and his concern for bankers and businessmen, the groups held a tenuous relationship. Indeed, the associations between Matheson and Rosenn had been tense since the 1950s, when he and his law firm represented garment owners in labor-management contract negotiations, while she, of course, spoke for the workers. (On the FVAC and FRTF dealings following the flood, see R. Wolensky, *Better Than Ever!*, 41–42, 130–31.)

7. This shutdown occurred shortly after the major strike of 1958. The workers did not want to walk off their jobs and the Mathesons did not want to take them out. See Min Matheson (chap. 3) regarding this conflict, which resulted in the New York headquarters taking away the Wyoming Valley District's treasury and checkbook because Mrs. Matheson issued unauthorized fifty-dollar "grocery money" checks to the strikers. Another New York–Wyoming Valley disagreement occurred in January 1956 when the New York office forced a general strike on the Wyoming Valley because a shop in Williamsport, called Terry Lee, would not accept the union (see Min Lurye Matheson to Louis Stulberg, January 24, 1956, Box 319, Folder 12b, No. 5780, David Dubinsky Papers, Kheel Center).

8. Betty Greenberg's husband, Larry, who was a locksmith, owned a small company in downtown Wilkes-Barre, which is still in the Greenberg family as Acme Locks Inc.

9. Mrs. Matheson told a slightly different story about her secret encounter with Mr. Chait. See note 28 of her interview (chap. 3).

10. In his interview, John Justin (chap. 7) states that the Kaplan-Elias firm of New York, which was associated with Thomas "Three-Finger Brown" Lucchese, owned or co-owned this Edwardsville shop.

11. In one segment of her audio-recorded interview (not included in the main text), Mrs. Greenberg mentioned Laura Fashions in Kingston, Pennsylvania, a maker of lingerie. The firm's workers never voted to join the union: "That was a thorn in her side. Three hundred people worked there and they were nonunion from the day she came 'til the day she left. It was a very prominent place but, unlike a lot of the other factories, the man that owned the factory treated the girls decently and paid them nicely. So, if it was like the difference of one or two cents, they would have had to pay union dues and the rest of it, and, of course, no one likes to pay dues. She was never able to organize them and they were right down the street from where we lived, too! It was very embarrassing. . . . She didn't push it. They had a very modern place, very clean, and clean bathrooms—better than most of the factories that she organized because they were not always very well-to-do people [i.e., the owners] and they couldn't afford to revamp the whole place and keep it up. I think Laura was one of the first factories in the area that was innovative and modern, and had a decent guy running it. It's that simple." Mrs. Greenberg did not know if the owner came out of New York. See also Alice Reca (chap. 6) on the effort to unionize the Laura shop. On American workers' long-standing resistance to unionization, see Richards, *Union-Free America*.

12. Mrs. Falcone did not permit the Jenkins Sportswear shop to unionize; however, she later sold the company to another operator, at which time the new owner's employees joined the ILGWU.

13. During one interview exchange from January 11, 1995 (not included in the main text), Betty Greenberg recalled a particular consequence of her family's commitment to organized labor. In the 1950s, some teachers in Kingston's public grade schools required students stand up and state their religion. Mrs. Greenberg's answer repeated what she had learned at home:

"I don't understand why to this day [we had to state our religion], but I remember in the first grade I said that I was 'half union and half Jewish.' And everybody laughed. I was sort of like shocked; like, why is everyone [laughing]? I said, 'Well, I am.' And everyone laughed some more. So I went home and told my parents, and [my sister] Marianne said, 'I said that, too.' And my father went like this: he looked over at my sister and he said, 'I'll be damned,' and he laughed. He thought it was the greatest joke. So my mother said, 'Well, they're not wrong, Bill.'"

CHAPTER 16

1. Thompson and Bornat, *Voice of the Past*, 1.

2. Lynd, *Solidarity Unionism*; Lynd, *"We Are All Leaders"*; Faue, *Community of Suffering*, 4; and Faue, "Paths of Unionization."

3. The ILGWU's dedication to solidarity unionism during the first third of the twentieth century drew on the cultural capital that members had gained from their eastern and southern European immigrant-ethnic origins. Jewish workers in New York, many of whom were from Russia or the children of Russian émigrés, were particularly disposed toward Socialism and Communism, which blended with their Yiddish communal values and history of resistance to oppression and persecution. Many Italian workers held strong Anarchist and Socialist dispositions, resulting from that country's repressive and exploitative politics and economics, especially during the second half of the nineteenth century. See, e.g., Katz, *All Together Different*, and Guglielmo, *Living the Revolution*. On the history of social unionism in the ILGWU, see Kheel Center, "History of the ILGWU: Social Unionism," Cornell University, 2015, https://ilgwu.ilr.cornell.edu/history/social-Unionism.html.

4. See Tyler (*Look for the Union Label*, chap. 11) on the Communist-Socialist rift within the ILGWU during the 1920s.

5. Faue, *Rethinking the American Labor Movement*, 79. Faue also pointed out that the Taft-Hartley Act of 1947 further weakened solidarity unionism because the employers' "'right to manage' took precedence over waning calls for shop floor democracy" (153). Taft-Hartley also contained anti-Communist provisions that "undermined progressive unionism and reinforced the power of union bureaucracy" (127).

6. Massey, *Spatial Divisions of Labor*, 57. See also Faue, *Rethinking the American Labor Movement*, 205–6, and Rosenfeld (*What Unions No Longer Do*), who argued that minority women workers have suffered especially deep wage and benefit losses because of de-unionization.

7. Thompson, "Moral Economy," 76–136. See also Götz, "Moral Economy," 147–62.

8. An example of the conflict over New York's centralizing tendencies can be seen in the volley of exchanges between Min Matheson, David Dubinsky, and Julius Hochman contained in Julius Hochman to David Dubinsky, February 21, 1952; Min Matheson to David Dubinsky, April 23, 1952; and Julius Hochman to David Dubinsky, June 11, 1952, Box 296, Folder 4a, No. 5780, David Dubinsky Papers, Kheel Center.

9. Antonio Gramsci (*Selections from the Prison Notebooks*, 10) described an organic intellectual, as distinguished from a traditional intellectual, as one having an empathetic understanding of the hegemonic contexts in which the working class lives on a daily basis, while also displaying an ability to work effectively in the pursuit of structural change to alleviate the oppression. He viewed traditional intellectuals as more prone to aloofness and co-optation. On the potential for co-optation among social movement leaders, see Gamson, *Strategy of Social Protest*.

10. See appendix 2 for a definition of "social movement." In many ways, the Wyoming Valley ILGWU District employed what sociologist Charles Tilly referred to as the "resource mobilization" strategy of collective action, whereby a movement and its members muster crucial resources and employ formidable tactics to attain their goals. The union also displayed characteristics of what sociologist Doug McAdam termed the "political process" approach, wherein a movement takes advantage of political opportunities and changing social environments to garner new resources

and employ new strategies, and members simultaneously undergo a social psychological transformation—a "cognitive liberation" that facilitates a "new sense of efficacy" (see Tilly, *From Mobilization to Revolution*; McAdam and Paulsen, "Specifying the Relationship"; and McAdam, *Political Process*).

11. Guglielmo, *Living the Revolution*, 113, and Orleck, *Common Sense*, 7.

12. Along with Bill Cherkes and Leo Gutstein, other shop owners or managers told of their favorable relationships with the workers and the union's leaders. For example, William Carter and his partner (and son), Neil, who were not interviewed for this study, expressed favorable opinions of Mrs. Matheson. "Min was a peach of a lady," said Neil Carter. "At one point when the union called a minor strike, my father told our people, 'This will all blow over soon. Go ahead and walk out so as to not defy your union'" (Neva Edwards Johns and Ron Hontz, "History of Sweet Valley Luzerne County, PA," Lower Luzerne County, 2005, http://web.archive .org/web/20071218201644/http://www.lower luzernecounty.com/articles/historyofsweet valley.htm). As another indicator of the ties between the union and the owners, Betty Greenberg recalled that "she [my mother] was having a terrible strike. One of the people [owners] she was having a strike with, we were friends with his children. And there was a bomb scare [at our house]. [The owner said to my mother], "You send them over to our house." On another occasion, when Mrs. Matheson brought her children to the picket line and violence flared, "the owner of the factory came and stuck us in his car and took us away [to safety]" (Betty Greenberg, audio-recorded interview, January 11, 1995, NPOLHC).

13. Mrs. Matheson described her anxiety during the initial meeting with local economic leaders:
"I remember the first time I had to sit down [at a meeting] in the Sterling Hotel [in downtown Wilkes-Barre]. One of our employers who headed the Employers' Association asked me if I would come to this luncheon, and I was very hesitant because I had been brought up strictly where labor doesn't mix with capital and you don't betray your workers and sit with them [owners] and eat with them, you know. I had all these very definite concepts. So I went with great trepidation to the Sterling and I met Jack

Sword, who was then head of the Chamber of Commerce and this head of our Employers' Association, and Frank Anderson of the Miners Bank. My first reaction was, "What am I doing here? What if somebody gets a picture of me and sends it to New York? They'll throw me out of the union!" You know, I had been brought up in such a rigid framework. But it was an interesting conversation. What they were trying to do was get our organized union shops to take part in the Community Chest. That did us a lot of good, which I didn't realize at the moment because once we got into that phase we were sort of accepted by the elite. . . . Not that I wasn't walking on eggshells at first. But they were very supportive of us." (Min Matheson, audio-recorded interview, November 30, 1982, NPOLHC)

14. Joseph Williams, audio-recorded interview, August 13, 1984, NPOLHC. A number of other community leaders shared Williams's sentiments. See, for example, the audio-recorded interviews with media manager and news editorialist Thomas Bigler, July 26, 1994; college administrator and businessman Andrew J. Shaw, December 7, 1988; Rep. Daniel J. Flood, July 5, 1990; and newspaper columnist Richard Cosgrove, May 13, 2003, NPOLHC.

15. The Pennsylvania Labor History Society presented Min Matheson with the Mother Jones Award in 1980.

16. "ILGWU Backs Drive for Better Mine Strip Laws," *Times Leader Evening News*, May 20, 1963.

17. The cultural conduciveness of the solidarity approach was reflected in historian John Bodnar's observation that northeastern Pennsylvanians survived the harsh economic and social realities of the coal industry by creating a "system of family groupings and communities, incorporating values and behavior patterns shaped by that industry's economy and dependent upon its good health and continued existence" (*Anthracite People*, 1). Michael Kozura ("We Stood Our Ground") wrote about the effectiveness of solidarity unionism among anthracite mineworkers during the 1930s, as did R. Wolensky and Hastie (*Anthracite Labor Wars*, chaps. 3–6).

18. During the late nineteenth and early twentieth centuries, the American coal industry (anthracite and bituminous together) experienced more strike action than any other sector

of the economy. Between 1881 and 1905, while about seventy-four workers per thousand in all industries went on strike, the number for coal mining was 196 per thousand. The tobacco industry had the next-highest strike frequency at one hundred per thousand (see Tilly and Tilly, *Work under Capitalism*, 50).

19. Greene, *Slavic Community*, 173. See also Bodnar, "Socialization and Adaptation," and Bodnar, "Immigration and Modernization."

20. The classic study on fear and intimidation in the southern Appalachian coal fields was conducted by Gaventa (*Power and Powerlessness*). The research dissected the "hidden face" of coal company political power and cultural influence that shaped decision making and public psychology in the mining towns and rural areas of Kentucky and Tennessee.

21. Reich (*Saving Capitalism*, chap. 18) discussed the vital, but declining, role of labor unions as an important "countervailing force" within American democracy, an argument articulated previously by Galbraith in *American Capitalism*.

22. Other works that examine the region's militant labor traditions include Aurand, *From the Molly Maguires*; Miller and Sharpless, *Kingdom of Coal*; Howard, *Anthracite Reds*; Dublin and Licht, *Face of Decline*; and R. Wolensky and Hastie, *Anthracite Labor Wars*.

23. From its founding days, the American labor movement in general, and the ILGWU in particular, adopted a masculine cultural ethic as well as a males-preferred leadership disposition (see, e.g., Gompers, *Seventy Years*, and Faue, *Rethinking the American Labor Movement*, chaps. 1 and 5).

24. Betty Greenberg presented an example of Dubinsky's deep suspicions toward her mother: "One time Dubinsky asked her what she wanted. 'You vant to be vice president [of the ILGWU]?' She said all she wanted was a good life for the girls. 'You mean your daughters?' She laughed. 'Well, them too,' she said. 'I mean the girls in the union,' she told him. He couldn't understand her only wanting this. They all thought she wanted money and power, but she only wanted something for her girls. Lots of people didn't understand her or my father on this" (Betty Greenberg, unrecorded interview, January 9, 1995).

25. Min Matheson undoubtedly worried David Dubinsky in smaller ways. For example,

on one occasion she requested his advice on whether to accept an invitation from *Life* magazine to participate in a coast-to-coast broadcast on NBC Radio, set for May 17, 1953. She wrote to him describing "a program which they say will deal with the garment industry and our union." Dubinsky's reply could not be found, but the likely question in his mind could have been: Why did NBC not invite *him*, as union president, to participate in the telecast instead of a district manager in a faraway area? (see Min Lurye Matheson to David Dubinsky, May 7, 1953, Box 319, Folder 12d, No. 5780, David Dubinsky Papers, Kheel Center). Mrs. Matheson assuredly gained Dubinsky's enmity by joining her family in pressuring him to use his office to pursue the killers of her brother, Will Lurye. George Zorgo (chap. 10) mentions the "Remember the Murder of Will Lurye" flyers that he printed for this purpose, and Mrs. Matheson's sister wrote an angry letter to Dubinsky demanding his action (see Maxine Tilly Lurye to David Dubinsky, March 18, 1952, Box 319, Folder 12b, No. 5780, David Dubinsky Papers, Kheel Center).

26. Rose Pesotta resigned from the Executive Board after several years, saying, "A lone woman vice president could not adequately represent the women who now make up 85 percent of the International's membership" (qtd. in Foner, *Women and the American Labor Movement*, 370). For biographies of Pauline Newman, Rose Schneiderman, Fannia Cohn, and Clara Lemlich Shavelson, see Orleck, *Common Sense*.

27. Bodnar, *Anthracite People*; Aurand, *Coalcracker Culture*; and MacGaffey, *Coal Dust*.

28. The situation for Wyoming Valley women was somewhat eased by their location within the local occupational system. Unlike women in other communities who had assumed a great number of war-related manufacturing jobs, Wyoming Valley women did not do so because the coal region had few military production facilities. The area's main war-related industry was anthracite, a vital fuel. Consequently, coal output spiked between 1940 and 1945 but fell precipitously afterward. Therefore, again unlike many other areas, the Wyoming Valley's postwar economic downturn occurred not mainly because of a military to civilian conversion, or because the returning GIs needed work (which they did); rather, it resulted from the precipitous decline in

demand for hard coal coupled with corruption and conflict within the anthracite industry itself. As civilian garment demand expanded during the postwar years, however, employment in women's dressmaking filled the income needs of many families.

29. Waldinger, "Another Look."

30. Kessler-Harris, *Gendering Labor History*, 38.

31. The coal region was examined as an "internal colony" in the preface.

32. McAdam, *Political Process*, 50.

33. Faue, *Community of Suffering*, 16.

34. See Kessler-Harris (*Gendering Labor History*, 91) on "female bonding" and "female friendship networks" in work and labor.

35. K. Wolensky and R. Wolensky, "Born to Organize."

36. Moore ("History of the Women's Trade Union League," 54–74) coined the term "industrial feminist" in 1915 in her writings on the Women's Trade Union League.

37. Jay Mazur, audio-recorded interview, March 6, 1998, NPOLHC.

38. Bourdieu, "Forms of Capital."

39. Mrs. Greenberg continued the story: "[Much later on] she [Mary] asked my father to meet her at Howard Johnson's [restaurant]. My father wasn't driving at the time, so I drove him to Howard Johnson's. She repeated the story, which my father had told us many times. One of the reasons he told us was because [he believed that] it was important what you said, and the way you said it. She said, 'You know, Bill, the most important thing in my life, you did for me.' He said, 'What was that, Mary?' She repeated the story. At that point, my father cried pretty easily, 'cause up until then he didn't cry very easily. He got tears in his eyes and said, 'I'm so glad, Mary, because I thought that you were insulted. I didn't want to do that to you.' She said, 'No way, Bill!' She had the utmost respect for my father when he told her she was smart. She didn't hear the insult, she only heard the good part and she learned to speak properly. She wanted him to know that. That she did. She was from the 'Heyna's.' That's what we call [local] people that say 'heyna' [local slang for 'ain't it' or 'isn't it'] around here. She would say 'heyna.' And he'd say, 'What does that mean?'" (Betty Greenberg, audio-recorded interview, January 11, 1995, from a section not included in chap. 15)

40. Silver and Karatasli, "Historical Dynamics."

41. Thompson, "Life Histories," 297.

42. Thompson and Bornat, *Voice of the Past*, 17.

43. A sampling of recent scholarship on woman's labor and working class history would include Greenwald, "Women and Pennsylvania"; Bender and Greenwald, *Sweatshop USA*; Cobble, *Other Women's Movement*; Milkman, *Women, Work and Protest*; Milkman, *On Gender*; Silver and Karatasli, "Historical Dynamics"; Turk, *Equality*; Porta, *Social Movements*; Fonow and Franzway, "Women's Activism"; and Faue, *Rethinking the American Movement*, 157–62.

44. Portelli, *Death of Luigi Trastulli*.

45. Passerini, *Fascism in Popular Memory*.

46. On theoretical approaches to narrative research, see Maines, "Narrative's Moment"; Maines, "Narrative Accounts"; Ochs and Capps, *Living Narrative*; Denzin and Lincoln, *Landscape*; R. Wolensky, "Working-Class Heroes"; Kim, *Understanding Narrative Inquiry*; and Beard, "Re-thinking Oral History."

47. In the late 1950s, Mayor Robert F. Wagner, Jr., of New York recognized the problems created by organized crime's infiltration of the garment industry, the city's largest manufacturing employer. He offered the police department's assistance in confronting the threat following the beating of Sol Greene, the assistant general manager of the ILGWU Dress Joint Council, by three thugs in February 1959 (see "Mayor Vows Aid to ILGWU in Its Fight on 'Evil Influences,'" *New York Times*, February 24, 1959).

48. The FBI information was obtained from an unnamed undercover informant working for the agency between 1954 and 1965 who focused on alleged criminal kingpin Russell Bufalino. The shop ownership numbers are from one of the entries in the Philadelphia General Investigative Intelligence File (Top Hoodlum Coverage), FBI Philadelphia Office.

49. Philadelphia General Investigative Intelligence File (Top Hoodlum Coverage), FBI Philadelphia Office. The Pennsylvania Historical and Museum Commission's website stated that about twenty of Pittston's garment shops were mob-influenced (see Explore Pennsylvania History, "Workers in Greater Pittston's Garment Industry Historical Marker," Historical Markers, 2011, http://explorepahistory.com/hmarker

.php?markerId=1-A-362). A Wyoming Valley District census of unionized factories in the three district union areas reported that Wilkes-Barre (Local 249) had ninety-three shops in 1962; Nanticoke (Local 327) had sixteen shops in 1962; and Pittston (Local 295) had fifty-one shops in 1962 (and seventy-one shops by 1968) (Membership Census, ILGWU Wyoming Valley District Archives, Kheel Center). No census evidence could be found regarding the number of unorganized shops in the Valley, but oral history evidence suggested that the number was quite small.

50. For obvious reasons, it was difficult to determine the exact number or percentage of shops owned, fronted, or in some way influenced by alleged criminals. Their estimated ownership of or influence over up to twenty shops seemed in line with the numbers provided by former U.S. attorney Paul Williams of New York, who stated that, of the thousands of garment-related businesses in New York, only two hundred firms—truckers, contractors, jobbers—were involved in garment racketeering (see Bonacich and Appelbaum, *Behind the Label*, 95). Betty Greenberg (chap. 15) estimated that around 10 percent of the district's shops were mob-owned or -influenced.

51. Birkbeck, *Quiet Don*, 5.

52. On Will Lurye's murder see People v. Benedict Macri, Legal transcripts and Scrapbook, No. 5780/170, Kheel Center; and "$25,000 Reward up for Lurye Killers—65,000 Will March in Funeral Procession Today in Protest against ILGWU Murder," *New York Times*, May 12, 1949.

53. John McKeon eulogized Will Lurye in *Catholic Worker*, June 1949.

54. "She was so innocent about everything," recalled daughter Betty Greenberg of her mother (unrecorded interview, January 9, 1995). "She didn't know when a guy was making a pass at her. She couldn't recognize it! We [the Matheson sisters] used to tell her things when we were a little bigger, and we were amazed about her naïveté. But she was naïve in other areas, like working against the gangsters. They could have killed her, but what did she know? She said we have to do what's right and best for the girls. She didn't know or care about danger. One time she said that the union had to stand and fight because if they beat us this time, we might lose everything."

55. Sol Hoffman, audio-recorded interview (joint with Ralph Reuter), March 6, 1998, NPOLHC.

56. Tonkin, *Narrating Our Pasts*, 2.

57. See appendix 2 for definitions of "upperworld" and "underworld."

58. R. Wolensky and Hastie, *Anthracite Labor Wars*.

59. The *Philadelphia Inquirer* reported that twenty-seven murders had occurred in Pittston between 1914 and 1920 ("27th Murder Stirs Pittston Residents," *Philadelphia Inquirer*, July 26, 1920). The *Wilkes-Barre Record* published a story referring to the "epidemic of murders" plaguing Luzerne County during the 1920s ("Murder Plains Main in Brutal Manner," July 20, 1920) and blamed "the foreign element" for the crisis. The same newspaper reported on thirteen homicides in the county in 1920 ("Murder a Month with One to Spare Is 1920 Record in County," December 1, 1920). Selekman ("Miners and Murder," 151) reported that Pittston witnessed thirty murders between 1919 and 1928, many of them associated with coal mining. The labor-related homicides continued into the late 1920s and 1930s.

60. I am grateful to Megan Hastie for this insight.

61. Halbwachs, *Collective Memory*, 38. See also Erll, *Memory in Culture*, 14; Tonkin, *Narrating Our Pasts*, chap. 1; and Assmann and Czaplicka, "Collective Memory and Cultural Identity."

62. Portelli, *Death of Luigi Trastulli*, 2.

63. Smith, "Popular Memory," 105. Smith interviewed Luisa Passerini about her work and followed with an extended review of her book, *Fascism in Popular Memory*.

64. Cave and Sloan (*Listening on the Edge*, 1–14) examined oral history as related to crises and other traumatizing situations. It can be argued that a secondary key to understanding the workers' oral histories lay in the control by, and clashes with, the New York office of the ILGWU. Such an assessment would be augmented by the Wyoming Valley's historic role as a peripheral place, an internal colony confronted with an external locus of control. Such was the case with the region's mining, railroad, silk, and other industries, where ownership and decision making resided in distant, core metropolitan centers. Such core-periphery dynamics often result not only in

exploitation at the periphery, but strong resentments and even rebellions by citizens against core persons and institutions.

65. The movement of thousands of garment shops out of New York City into peripheral areas alludes to the significant influence large metropolitan areas have historically had over the economic and social development of exurban cities, towns, and villages. The topic has been a perennial concern among researchers in urban sociology, urban geography, and urban politics (see, e.g., Lin and Mele, *Urban Sociology*; Jonas, McCann, and Thomas, *Urban Geography*; and Levine, *Urban Politics*).

66. However, William Cherkes, in another section of his interview not included in chapter 2, cynically decried what he saw as the New York ILGWU's role in taking advantage of globalization through the mechanism of liquidated damages: "Liquidated damages means—and it's very important you should understand—that if you have a union contract and you work in a nonunion place, you pay a penalty, 30 percent—30 percent goes in your [the union's] pocket. If you work in a nonunion place, the 30 percent has to be paid to the union and help in welfare benefits, and vacations, and retirements, and so forth." As might be expected, ILGWU officials had a different view of liquid damages. They saw them as a source of legitimate funds to stave off internationalization through political lobbying, ad campaigns, organizing drives, and membership investments. As Dana Frank (*Buy American*, 146–49) pointed out, beginning in the 1920s, the union negotiated the labor-management contract to include a liquid damages clause as an incentive for manufacturers to avoid nonunion contractors. As imported clothing increased in the mid-1970s, the union bargained for even higher liquidated damages for overseas contracting. However, the cost advantage to the manufacturers was often so significant that many found it cheaper to pay the damage "fines." As a result, during the 1970s, hundreds of thousands of dollars flowed into the union's coffers. The sum grew to $4.4 million in 1981 and climbed to over $10 million by 1988. The union's leadership decided to invest $2 million from the funds per year in the national "Look for the Union Label" advertisement program (see appendix 2). As the globalization trend continued and membership declined, "by the early 1990s, the

ILGWU'S income from liquidated damages came almost to match its income from members' dues" (Frank, *Buy American*, 148).

67. Thompson, "Moral Economy," 76–136.

68. Ann Cajka, unrecorded interview, July 24, 1994, NPOLHC. Josephine Wolinsky (unrecorded interview, June 9, 1998) worked for the Browns at the same shop and also spoke very highly of their treatment of employees, specifically their kindness, the good working conditions they provided, and their accurate wage payments. William Cherkes mentions Mr. Brown in his interview in chapter 2.

69. Gamson, "Defining Movement Success."

70. Min Matheson, interview by Alice Hoffman, September 21, 1983, Alice Hoffman Papers, Eberly Family Special Collections Library, Pennsylvania State University. Interestingly, David Witwer ("Dress Strike at Three-Finger Brown's," 179) argued that Mrs. Matheson may have been unwittingly involved in promoting Mr. Chait's criminal control over certain aspects of the garment industry. After reviewing a group of little-known documents associated with the ILGWU's cooperation with the mob between the late 1930s and the 1950s, Witwer observed:
"These accounts also depict the key ILGWU organizer in the Pennsylvania region, Min Matheson, actively engaged in [unknowingly] bolstering Chait's influence with local contractors. Referring to the Pennsylvania Garment Manufacturers' Association [PGMA], which Chait dominated, an informant asserted, 'The men in charge of the organization are able to put the squeeze on various manufacturers through the union local which is headed by a sister of William Lurye [i.e., Min Matheson].' By making a demand for higher wages or raising some other grievance, the informant explained, Matheson could force the contractor to turn to the PGMA, and by extension to Chait, for assistance."

71. Witwer ("Dress Strike at Three-Finger Brown's") also argued for a nuanced understanding of the relationship between the garment industry and organized crime but in a quite different way. Using a special report on the relationship between runaway shops and organized crime, written in 1947 by union official Julius Hochman for the Dress Joint Board, Witwer found that special arrangements had indeed been made between certain union

officials and organized criminals following the 1936 dress strike, when the runaway shop trend expanded. According to Witwer (172), "In 1939 one of the biggest firms, Kaplan and Elias, led the way in this effort and the union responded by imposing a picket line of the firm [possibly the Anita Dress shop in Edwardsville, Pennsylvania; see appendix 2]. [Quoting from the report:] 'But then, in stepped Mr. Abe Chait, who was the chief representative of gangsterism at the time, and he assumed responsibility for supplying nonunion contractors to Kaplan and Elias.'" Because of his control over ILGWU Local 102, which transported raw materials and finished garments to and from the Garment District, Chait was able to provide trucking services for nonunion jobbers and contractors, "often in the small towns of Northeast Pennsylvania."

In a clear example of the upperworld's cooperation with the underworld, Witwer (178) further reported that some union leaders decided to work with Chait and allow him and his associates to own or front a limited numbers of nonunion shops—exactly thirty-three by one account. Recall that Min Matheson (chaps. 3 and 16) spoke of her two meetings with Mr. Chait, and Witwer discovered at least two others—April 3, 1950, and September 15, 1950—where union officials David Gingold, Charles "Shasha" Zimmerman, and Jack Halpern also attended. These meetings were concerned with settling the recurring strikes and other difficulties in the Wyoming Valley District.

72. Ross, *No Sweat*, 30–31.

73. See Minchin, *Empty Mills*, 9–10, chapters 4 and 5. Minchin stated that the industry's battle against imported garments and textiles essentially failed in the mid-1980s when the Textile and Apparel Trade Enforcement Act of 1985 could not muster congressional approval, even though "no state had more sponsors than Pennsylvania, where a wave of plant closing had convinced thirteen congressmen to support the bill" (98). Another setback occurred when the Textile, Apparel, and Footwear Trade Act twice fell to President Ronald Reagan's veto pen, notwithstanding a major lobby campaign by the ILGWU, other unions, and many companies (145–50). It had become clear that the garment and textile sectors had, in large part, become the victims of bipartisan foreign and free trade policies (151). Along another dimension, ILGWU

historian Gus Tyler (*Look for the Union Label*, 270) maintained that a large number of elected officials "believed that America was really not a fit place for textile and apparel manufacture. They maintained that workers dispossessed in the textile and apparel trades would find better-paying jobs [elsewhere]."

74. Mr. Gutstein's assessments concurred with those of Barry Sacks, chairman of the Chorus Line company of California: "If we remained in the United States we would have no growth pattern. We wouldn't be competitive any more. The retailers are vicious. . . . Because of tough price competition, the company had no choice" (quoted in Bonacich and Appelbaum, *Behind the Label*, 61).

75. On this topic see Portes, Castells, and Benton (*Informal Economy*, 66–67) and Bao ("Sweatshops in Sunset Park"), who have researched informally organized, so-called underground sweatshops.

76. Ross, *No Sweat*, 15.

77. Quoted in Benin, *New Labor Radicalism*, 78.

78. The specific categories of remaining garment workers include sewing machine operators (4,920); hand sewers (260); tailors, dressmakers, custom sewers (1,670); and those working with textile, apparel, and furnishings (350). Pennsylvania Department of Labor and Industry, *Pennsylvania Occupational Employment*.

79. Bureau of Labor Statistics, *Employment Hours and Earnings, U.S., 1990–1994*.

80. "Ailing Garment Workers Union Faces More Problems," *New York Times*, November 29, 1981.

81. Bonacich and Appelbaum, *Behind the Label*, 9.

82. Ibid., 6.

83. Minchin, *Empty Mills*, 285.

84. Stephanie Clifford, "That 'Made in U.S.A.' Premium," *New York Times*, November 30, 2013; Heesun Wee, "'Made in USA' Fuels New Manufacturing Hubs in Apparel," CNBC, September 23, 2013, https://www.cnbc.com/2013/09/23/inside-made-in-the-usa-showcasing-skilled-garment-workers.html.

85. Kheel Center, "Timeline," Cornell University, 2015, https://ilgwu.ilr.cornell.edu/timeline/.

86. A sampling of sources from the vast globalization literature could include Ross and

Trachte, *Global Capitalism*; Moody, *Workers in a Lean World*; Rosen, *Making Sweatshops*; Collins, *Threads*; Ritzer, *Blackwell Companion*; Gills, *Globalization in Crisis*; and Stiglitz, *Globalization and Its Discontents*.

87. Melissa M. Janoski, "Building's Panels Should Be Removed, Historian Says," *Times Leader*, September 1, 2000.

88. "Development Building Conformed for Hole," *Times Leader*, June 26, 2004.

89. "State Must Relax Rules to Protect Historic Panels," *Times Leader*, September 4, 2000.

90. McGuigan, *Shop on Every Corner*, and McGuigan, *Six Women in Labor*.

91. Dowd, *MIN*.

92. Gutman, *Power and Culture*.

93. Kitch, *Pennsylvania in Public Memory*, and Batch, "Labored Mid-Atlantic Region."

APPENDIX 1

1. Patrick Collinson, "Not Biographable," *London Review of Books*, November 29, 2007, 33–34; italics added.

2. As mentioned in the preface, I gifted the more than seven hundred interviews in the Northeastern Pennsylvania Oral and Life History Collection to the Eberly Family Special Collections Library, Pennsylvania State University, in July 2018.

3. Because my interviews with Mr. D'Angelo and Ms. Lyons covered different topics than the interviews conducted by Kenneth C. Wolensky and myself, it was necessary to add the relevant sections from the joint interviews into the respective texts of my interviews. The exact point where the additions begin are indicated by endnotes.

4. Of course, it would have been helpful to collect interviews from shop owners who were also alleged organized criminals. Other than the fact that most had passed away or were in jail by the time I undertook the project, the "word on the street" was that none would have agreed to an interview and, if any did, they "wouldn't say anything anyway." However, I decided to try and secure at least one such meeting in August 1989. After refusing to accept my invitation "to get together and talk" (negotiated by a third party), I decided to pay an uninvited visit to Dominick "Nick" Alaimo at his high-rise retirement apartment in downtown Pittston. Upon knocking on the partially open door, a short, bald, cigarette-smoking senior citizen appeared with some hesitation. After offering my name and my hand, we shook and he gave me a very careful look-over and asked what I wanted. I quickly tried to establish my credibility: We both knew the party who had just called; I was born and raised in the Wyoming Valley; my father was a coal miner and my mother a garment worker; I have Italian heritage on my mother's side. He nodded and expressed some nonverbal interest. I added that I was currently a professor from Wisconsin and I was doing studies on the coal-mining industry and the garment industry. I wanted to talk to him because he had worked in both. He reluctantly invited me in. As we sat down, he lit a cigarette and he insisted on no recording and no note taking. We talked for about thirty minutes. The street advice was correct: he provided virtually no information about his garment days, and he denied any participation or wrongdoing in connection with the Knox Mine disaster (for which a bribery conviction sent him to jail). He agreed that he had known Min Matheson but offered no further details. We parted amicably.

5. There are a number of other garment and ILGWU-related oral history collections that focus on the northeastern United States and New York City in particular. A sampling would include "The New York City Immigrant Labor History Project," Robert Wagner Archives, Tamiment Library, New York University; "The World of Our Mothers Project," Henry A. Murray Research Center, Radcliffe College; "The Italian Immigrant Women in New York City's Garment Industry Project, Sophia Smith Collection, Smith College; and the many ILGWU oral histories at the Kheel Center, Cornell University. A sampling of other oral history collections containing some garment-related interviews would include Harvard University's "Black Women Oral History Project Interviews, 1976–1981"; the Library of Congress's "Working in Paterson (New Jersey) Project Collection," American Folklife Center; "Ground One: Voices from Post-9/11 Chinatown," Museum of Chinese Americans' Oral History Project (in partnership with the Columbia University Oral History Research Office); the Oral History Interviews Portal, Columbia University Center for Oral History; the Alice Hoffman Papers, Eberly Family

Special Collections Library, Pennsylvania State University; Temple University's Special Collections Oral History Repository; the Jewish Museum of Maryland's Oral History Collection; Norsie Breuler and Rosemary Wesson, ILGWU interviews, Eberly Family Special Collections Department, Pennsylvania State University, 1983; and the collections associated with two published books: Cox and Martinelli, *Garment Workers of South Jersey*, and Dublin, *When the Mines Closed*. On oral history research in other regions of the United States see, e.g., Hall et al., *Like a Family*; Haberland, *Striking Beauties*; and Tager, "Women in the Global Clothing and Textile Industry."

6. On the anthracite region's speech dialect, see, e.g., De Camp, "Scranton Pronunciation"; Herold, "Mechanisms of Merger"; and Coal Region Enterprises, "CoalSpeak: The Official CoalRegion Dictionary," Coal Region, 1995, http://www.coalregion.com/speak/speaka.php.

7. See, e.g., Evans, *In Defense of History*; see also the listing of thirty-two reviews of Evans's book, along with his response to the critics, in Institute of Historical Research. "Author's Response to His Critics," History in Focus, November 1999, https://www.history.ac.uk/ihr/Focus/Whatishistory/evans.html; Geertz, *Interpretation of Cultures*; and Maines, "Narrative's Moment."

8. On trauma, crisis, and oral history, see Cave and Sloan, *Listening on the Edge*, 1–14.

BIBLIOGRAPHY

ARCHIVES AND LIBRARIES

Carnegie Mellon University Archives
Citizens' Voice Newspaper Archives
D. Leonard Corgan Library, King's College
Eberly Family Special Collections Library, Penn
    State University Libraries
Eugene S. Farley Library, Wilkes University
FBI Philadelphia Office
Greater Pittston Historical Society
Harvey Andruss Library, Bloomsburg University
Hoover Institution Library and Archives
Kheel Center for Labor-Management
    Documentation and Archives, Cornell
    University Library
Lackawanna Historical Society
Library of Congress
Lukasik Studio Archive
Luzerne County Historical Society
Northeastern Pennsylvania Oral and Life
    History Collection, Pennsylvania State
    University
Osterhout Free Library of Wilkes-Barre
Penn State University Libraries
Times Leader Newspaper Archives
University of Exeter Forum Library
University of Wisconsin–Madison Memorial
    Library
University of Wisconsin–Stevens Point Library

ORAL HISTORY INTERVIEWS

Alaimo, Dominick. August 8, 1989 (unrecorded
    interview).
Berger, Martin. December 16, 1997 (conducted
    by Kenneth C. Wolensky).
Bianco, Sam. March 11, 1996 (conducted by
    Robert P. Wolensky and Kenneth C.
    Wolensky).
Bigler, Thomas. July 26, 1994.
Cajka, Ann. July 24, 1994 (unrecorded
    interview).

Calvey, Audrey. June 17, 1992.
*Caputo, Philomena "Minnie." July 22, 1993.
*Cherkes, William "Bill." July 20, 1994.
Cosgrove, Richard. May 13, 2003.
Cronin, Richard. May 24, 1983.
*D'Angelo, Anthony "Tony." December 18,
    1988; February 17, 1994 (conducted
    by Robert P. Wolensky and Kenneth C.
    Wolensky).
*DePasquale, Angelo "Bill," "Rusty." July 23,
    1993.
Dructor, Betty. March 12, 1996.
Evans, Joan. October 19, 1988.
Flood, Daniel J. July 5, 1990.
Gable, William. December 3, 1999.
Grabosky, Shirley. July 20, 2004 (recorded
    roundtable discussion among ILGWU
    retirees); July 27, 2004.
Granahan, Jack. June 26, 1997.
Greenberg, Betty (Matheson). October 7, 1999
    (conducted by Kenneth C. Wolensky);
    and the following unrecorded interviews:
    June 26, 1992 (joint interview with Min
    Matheson); June 8, 2015; January 9,
    1995; January 21, 2016.
Greenberg, Betty (Matheson), and Lawrence
    Greenberg. January 11, 1995.
*Greenberg, Betty (Matheson), and Lawrence
    Greenberg. October 7, 1999 (conducted
    by Kenneth C. Wolensky).
Grilz, Wayne. July 20, 2004 (recorded
    roundtable discussion among ILGWU
    retirees).
*Gutstein, Leo. June 26, 1997.
Hartel, Lois. June 17, 1993 (conducted by Robert
    P. Wolensky and Kenneth C. Wolensky);
    March 16, 1996 (conducted by Kenneth
    C. Wolensky); July 20, 2004 (recorded
    roundtable discussion among ILGWU
    retirees).

Jarrow, Evelyn. July 20, 2004 (recorded roundtable discussion among ILGWU retirees).

*Justin, John "Johnny." July 28, 1988; May 30, 1996; June 25, 1997; May 30, 2000 (unrecorded interview).

Levandowski, John. May 18, 2017.

Levin, Edith, Marilyn, and Ted. October 23, 1998 (conducted by Kenneth C. Wolensky).

Lieb, Anna. June 30, 1997.

Lori, Arthur. July 20, 2004 (recorded roundtable discussion among ILGWU retirees).

Lori, Rosemary. July 20, 2004 (recorded roundtable discussion among ILGWU retirees).

Lukasik, Steven. June 21, 1999.

*Lyons, Clementine "Clem." July 5, 1990 (conducted by Robert P. Wolensky); July 24, 1993 (conducted by Robert P. Wolensky and Kenneth C. Wolensky); July 20, 2004 (recorded roundtable discussion among ILGWU retirees).

Matheson, Bill. November 30, 1982 (joint interview with Min Matheson).

*Matheson, Min. November 30, 1982 (joint interview with Bill Matheson); September 21, 1983 (conducted by Alice Hoffman, No. 1881, Alice Hoffman Papers, Eberly Family Special Collections Library, Paterno Library, Pennsylvania State University); November 30, 1988 (unrecorded interview); December 5, 1988; June 28, 1990; June 26, 1992 (unrecorded joint interview with Betty Greenberg).

Matthews, Tom, and Bob Hostetter. July 1, 1993 (conducted by Kenneth C. Wolensky).

Mazur, Jay. March 6, 1998 (conducted by Kenneth C. Wolensky).

McHugh, May. July 20, 2004 (recorded roundtable discussion among ILGWU retirees).

Morand, Martin. December 4, 1997 (conducted by Kenneth C. Wolensky).

*Ney, Dorothy "Dot." July 3, 1990.

*Novak, Pearl. June 19, 1997; July 20, 2004 (recorded roundtable discussion among ILGWU retirees).

Potsko, Thomas. July 20, 2004 (recorded roundtable discussion among ILGWU retirees).

Prandy, Thelma. July 20, 2004 (recorded roundtable discussion among ILGWU retirees).

*Reca, Alice. July 26, 1995.

Sampiero, Helen. March 22, 1995.

Schfrendo, Mary. July 20, 2004 (recorded roundtable discussion among ILGWU retirees).

Schifano, Rose. July 20, 2004 (recorded roundtable discussion among ILGWU retirees).

*Schiowitz, Dr. Albert. August 6, 2001.

Shaw, Andrew J. December 7, 1988.

Silverman, Jennie. July 16, 1993 (conducted by Robert P. Wolensky and Kenneth C. Wolensky).

Slattery, Frank. May 27–28, 1983.

Solomon, Irwin, and Max Zimny. March 5, 1998 (conducted by Kenneth C. Wolensky).

[Unknown last name], Chester. July 20, 2004 (recorded roundtable discussion among ILGWU retirees).

[Unknown last name], Maria. July 20, 2004 (recorded roundtable discussion among ILGWU retirees).

*Weiss, Helen. June 20, 1997.

Whittaker, Celina and Nelson. April 19, 1999 (conducted by Kenneth C. Wolensky).

Williams, Joseph. August 13, 1984.

Wolensky, Rosalie Siracuse. August 22, 1985; June 4, 2000.

Wolinsky, Josephine Piazza. June 9, 1998 (unrecorded interview).

Zarnecki, Roxanne. July 20, 2004 (recorded roundtable discussion among ILGWU retirees).

Zobel, Sonia. May 5, 1998 (conducted by Kenneth C. Wolensky).

*Zorgo, George (joint interview with Lucy Zorgo). July 26, 1993.

*Zorgo, Lucy (joint interview with George Zorgo). July 26, 1993.

PRIMARY AND SECONDARY SOURCES

Abadinsky, Howard. *Organized Crime*. Boston: Cengage, 2017.

Abhijeet, Paul. "Dependency Theory." In *The Encyclopedia of Empire*, edited by John MacKenzie, 1–2. Malden, Mass.: Oxford Wiley Blackwell, 2015.

Alanen, Arnold R., and Robert Z. Melnick, eds. *Preserving Cultural Landscapes in America.*

Baltimore: Johns Hopkins University Press, 2000.

Alexander, Robert J. *The Right Opposition: The Lovestoneites and the International Communist Opposition of the 1930s.* Westport, Conn.: Greenwood Press, 1981.

Anand, Vikas, Blake E. Ashforth, and Mahendra Joshi. "Business as Usual: The Acceptance Perpetuation of Corruption in Organizations." *Academy of Management Perspectives* 18 (May 2004): 39–53.

Appalachian Land Ownership Task Force. *Who Owns Appalachia? Land Ownership and Its Impact.* Lexington: University Press of Kentucky, 1983.

Arnold, Jack, dir. *With These Hands.* Film, 1950. Internet Archive. https://archive.org /details/with-these-hands-1950.

Assmann, Jan, and John Czaplicka. "Collective Memory and Cultural Identity." *New German Critique* 65 (Spring–Summer 1995): 125–33.

Aurand, Harold. *Coalcracker Culture: Work and Values in Pennsylvania Anthracite, 1835–1935.* Selinsgrove: Susquehanna University Press, 2003.

———. *From the Molly Maguires to the United Mine Workers: The Social Ecology of an Industrial Union, 1869–1897.* Philadelphia: Temple University Press, 1971.

Ballam, John J. *70,000 Silk Workers Strike for Bread and Unity.* New York: Labor Unity, 1934.

Bao, Xiaolan. Review of *Fighting for the Union Label*, by Kenneth C. Wolensky, Nicole H. Wolensky, and Robert P. Wolensky. *American Historical Review* 107 (December 2002): 1593–94.

———. "Sweatshops in Sunset Park: A Variation of the Late 20th Century Chinese Garment Shops in New York City." *International Labor and Working-Class History* 61 (April 2002): 69–90.

Barbash, Jack. "The I.L.G.W.U. as an Organization in the Age of Dubinsky." Supplement, *Labor History* 9 (Spring 1968): 98–115.

Baron, Ava. "Gender and Labor History: Learning from the Past, Looking to the Future." In *Work Engendered: Toward a New History of American Labor*, edited by Ava Baron, 1–46. Ithaca: Cornell University Press, 1992.

Batch, Rachel. "A *Labored* Mid-Atlantic Region Defined, Not Discovered: Suggestions on the Intersections of Labor and Regional History." *Pennsylvania History* 82 (Summer 2015): 329–42.

Beard, Martha Rose. "Re-thinking Oral History: A Study of Narrative Performance." *Rethinking History: The Journal of Theory and Practice* 21, no. 4 (2017): 529–48.

Beers, Paul B. *Pennsylvania Politics Today and Yesterday: The Tolerable Accommodation.* University Park: Pennsylvania State University Press, 1980.

Bender, Daniel E., and Richard A. Greenwald. *Sweatshop USA: The American Sweatshop in Historical and Global Perspective.* New York: Taylor and Francis, 2003.

Benin, Leigh David. *The New Labor Radicalism and New York City's Garment Industry: Progressive Labor Insurgents in the 1960s.* New York: Garland, 2000.

Berger, Ronald J., and Richard Quinney. *Storytelling Sociology: Narrative as Social Inquiry.* Boulder, Colo.: Lynne Rienner, 2005.

Bernstein, Lee. *The Greatest Menace: Organized Crime in Cold War America; Culture, Politics, and the Cold War.* Amherst: University of Massachusetts Press, 2009.

Bertaux, Daniel, ed. *Biography and Society: The Life History Approach in the Social Sciences.* Beverly Hills, Calif.: Sage, 1981.

Birkbeck, Matt. *The Quiet Don.* New York: Berkley Books, 2013.

Bliven, Bruce. "*Murder on Thirty-Fifth Street.*" *New Republic* 20 (June 1949): 11–12.

Bluestone, Barry, and Bennett Harrison. *The De-industrialization of America: Plant Closings, Community Abandonment, and the Dismantling of Basic Industry.* New York: Basic Books, 1982.

Bochner, Arthur P., and Carolyn Ellis. *Evocative Autoethnography: Writing Lives and Telling Stories.* New York: Routledge, 2016.

Bodnar, John, ed. *Anthracite People: Families, Unions, and Work, 1900–1940.* Harrisburg: Pennsylvania Historical and Museum Commission, 1983.

———. *The Ethnic Experience in Pennsylvania.* Lewisburg: Bucknell University Press, 1973.

362

———. "The Family Economy and Labor Protest in Industrial America: Hard Coal Miners in the 1930s." In *Hard Times: Ethnicity and Labor in the Anthracite Region*, edited by David Salay, 79–83. Scranton, Pa.: Anthracite Museum Press, 1984.

———. "Immigration and Modernization: The Case of Slavic Peasants in Industrial America." *Journal of Social History* 10 (Autumn 1976): 44–71.

———. "Socialization and Adaptation: Immigrant Families in Scranton, 1880–1890." *Pennsylvania History* 43 (April 1976): 147–62.

Bogen, Jules I. *The Anthracite Railroads*. New York: Ronald Press, 1927.

Bonacich, Edna, and Richard P. Appelbaum. *Behind the Label: Inequality in the Los Angeles Apparel Industry*. Berkeley: University of California Press, 2000.

Bourdieu, Pierre. "The Forms of Capital." In *Handbook of Theory and Research for the Sociology of Education*, edited by John C. Richardson, 241–58. New York: Greenwood Press, 1986.

Brandt, Charles. *I Heard You Paint Houses: Frank "The Irishman" Sheeran and Closing the Case on Jimmy Hoffa*. Hanover, N.H.: Steerforth Press, 2005.

Bull, Anna Cento. *Social Identities and Political Cultures in Italy: Catholic, Communist, and "Leghist" Communities Between Civicness and Localism*. New York: Berghahn, 2001.

Bureau of Labor Statistics. *Employment Hours and Earnings, 1990–1994*. Washington, D.C.: U.S. Department of Labor, 1995.

Bureau of Statistics and Information. *Fourth Industrial Directory of the Commonwealth of Pennsylvania*. Harrisburg: Pennsylvania Department of Internal Affairs, 1922.

Cannavò, Peter F. *The Working Landscape: Founding, Preservation, and the Politics of Place*. Cambridge, Mass.: MIT Press, 2007.

Cave, Mark, and Stephen M. Sloan, eds. *Listening on the Edge: Oral History in the Aftermath of Crisis*. New York: Oxford University Press, 2014.

Chaiken, Sol. C. *A Labor Viewpoint: Another Opinion*. New York: Library Research Associates, 1980.

Chandler, Alfred D. "Anthracite Coal and the Beginnings of the Industrial Revolution in the United States." *Business History Review* 46 (1972): 141–81.

Clandinin, D. Jean, and F. Michael Connelly. *Narrative Inquiry: Experience and Story in Qualitative Research*. San Francisco: Josey-Bass, 2000.

Cobble, Dorothy Sue. *The Other Women's Movement: Workplace Justice and Social Rights in Modern America*. Princeton: Princeton University Press, 2004.

Cohn, Fannia M. "What Workers' Education Really Is." *Life and Labor* 11 (October 1921): 230–34.

Collins, Jane L. *Threads: Gender, Labor, and Power in the Global Apparel Industry*. Chicago: University of Chicago Press, 2003.

Commons, John R. "The Sweating System." *Report of the Industrial Commission* 15 (1901): 319–24.

Commonwealth of Pennsylvania. *Annual Report of the Secretary of Internal Affairs*. Harrisburg, Pa., 1899.

Cooley, Winnifred Harper. *The New Womanhood*. New York: Broadway, 1904. http://archive.org/details/cu3192401385 1435.

Corbin, David A. *Life, Work, and Rebellion in the Coal Fields: The Southern West Virginia Miners, 1880–1922*. Champaign: University of Illinois Press, 1981.

Cott, Nancy F. *The Grounding of Modern Feminism*. New Haven: Yale University Press, 1987.

Couch, Stephen R. "The Coal and Iron Police in Anthracite Country." In *Hard Coal, Hard Times: Ethnicity and Labor in the Anthracite Region*, edited by David L. Salay, 100–119. Scranton, Pa.: Anthracite Museum Press, 1984.

Couch, Stephen R., and Steven Kroll-Smith, eds. *Communities at Risk: Collective Responses to Technological Hazards*. New York: Peter Lang, 1991.

Coutin, Susan Bibler. *Nation of Emigrants: Shifting Boundaries of Citizenship in El Salvador and the United States*. Ithaca: Cornell University Press, 2007.

Cowie, Jefferson, and Joseph Heathcott, eds. *Beyond the Ruins: The Meanings of*

Deindustrialization. Ithaca: Cornell University Press, 2003.

Cox, Lisa, and Patricia A. Martinelli, eds. *Garment Workers of South Jersey: Nine Oral Histories*. Galloway, N.J.: South Jersey Culture and History Center, 2016.

Darrow, Clarence. *Attorney for the Damned*. Edited by Arthur Weinberg. New York: Simon & Schuster, 1957.

Davies, Edward, J. *The Anthracite Aristocracy: Leadership and Social Change in the Hard Coal Regions of Northeastern Pennsylvania, 1800–1930*. DeKalb: Northern Illinois University Press, 1985.

De Camp, L. Sprague. "Scranton Pronunciation." *American Speech* 15 (1940): 368–72.

Denzin, Norman K. *Interpretive Biography*. Thousand Oaks, Calif.: Sage, 1989.

Denzin, Norman K., and Yvonna S. Lincoln, eds. *The Landscape of Qualitative Research: Theories and Issues*. Newbury Park, Calif.: Sage, 2003.

Derickson, Alan. *Black Lung: Anatomy of a Public Health Disaster*. Ithaca: Cornell University Press, 1998.

Dodds, Malcom, arr. "Look for the Union Label." Song, 1975. Lyrics by Paula Green. UNITE. http://unionsong.com/u103 .html.

Dowd, Michael, writer and producer. *MIN: A Play for Radio*. Radio play, 2006.

Dowd, Jacquelyn H., James L. Leloudis, Robert R. Korstad, and Mary Murphy. *Like a Family: The Making of a Southern Cotton Mill World*. Chapel Hill: University of North Carolina Press, 1987.

Dubinsky, David, and A. H. Raskin. *David Dubinsky: A Life with Labor*. New York: Simon & Schuster, 1977.

Dublin, Thomas. *When the Mines Closed: Stories of Struggles in Hard Times*. Ithaca: Cornell University Press, 1998.

Dublin, Thomas, and Walter Licht. *The Face of Decline: The Pennsylvania Anthracite Region in the Twentieth Century*. Ithaca: Cornell University Press, 2005.

Dubofsky, Melvyn, and Warren Van Tine. *John L. Lewis: A Biography*. New York: Quadrangle / New York Times, 1977.

Duineveld, Martijn, Kristof Van Assche, and Raoul Beunen. "Re-conceptualising Political Landscapes After the Material Turn: A Typology of Material Events." *Landscape Research* 42 (2017): 375–84.

Early, Steve. *The Civil Wars in U.S. Labor: Birth of a New Workers' Movement or Death Throes of the Old?* Chicago: Haymarket Books, 2011.

Ecenbarger, William. *Kids for Cash: Two Judges, Thousands of Children, and a $2.8 Million Kickback Scheme*. New York: New Press, 2014.

Egolf, B., J. Lasker, S. Wolf, and L. Potvin. "The Roseto Effect: A 50-Year Comparison of Mortality Rates." *American Journal of Public Health* 82 (1992): 1089–92.

Egolf, Jennifer, Ken Fones-Wolf, and Louis C. Martin, eds. *Culture, Class, and Politics in Modern Appalachia: Essays in Honor of Ronald L. Lewis*. Morgantown: West Virginia University Press, 2009.

Erll, Astrid. *Memory in Culture*. New York: Palgrave Macmillan, 2011.

Evans, Richard J. *In Defense of History*. New York: W. W. Norton, 2000.

Faue, Elizabeth. *Community of Suffering and Struggle: Women, Men, and the Labor Movement in Minneapolis, 1915–1945*. Chapel Hill: University of North Carolina Press, 1991.

———. "Paths of Unionization: Community, Bureaucracy and Gender in the Minneapolis Labor Movement of the 1930s." In *Work Engendered: Toward a New History of American Labor*, edited by Ava Baron, 296–319. Ithaca: Cornell University Press, 1992.

———. *Rethinking the American Labor Movement*. New York: Routledge, 2017.

Fernandez-Stark, Karina, Stacey Frederick, and Gary Gereffi. *The Apparel Global Value Chain: Economic Upgrading and Workforce Development*. Durham, N.C.: Duke Center on Global Governance and Competitiveness, 2011.

Ferraro, Vincent. "Dependency Theory: An Introduction." In *The Development Economics Reader*, edited by Giorgio Secondi, 58–64. London: Routledge, 2008.

Foner, Philip S. *Women and the American Labor Movement: From the First Trade Unions to the Present*. Vol. 3. New York: Free Press, 1982.

Fonow, Mary Margaret, and Suzanne Franzway. "Women's Activism in U.S. Labor Unions." In *The Oxford Handbook of U.S. Women's Social Movement Activism*, edited by Holly J. McCammon, Verta Taylor, Jo Reger, and Rachel L. Einwohner, 729–50. Oxford: Oxford University Press, 2017.

Frank, Dana. *Buy American: The Untold Story of Economic Nationalism*. Boston: Beacon Press, 1999.

Frey, Bruno S., and Friedrich Schneider. "Informal and Underground Economics." In *International Encyclopedia of the Social and Behavioral Sciences*, edited by James D. Wright, 50–55. 2nd ed. Oxford, UK: Elsevier, 2015.

Friedman, Charles, dir. *Pins and Needles*. Music and lyrics by Harold Rome. Labor Stage Theatre, New York, 1937–39.

Friis, Robert H. *Occupational Health and Safety for the 21st Century*. Burlington, Mass.: Jones and Bartlett, 2016.

Gabaccia, Donna. *From the Other Side: Women, Gender, and Immigrant Life in the U.S., 1820–1990*. Bloomington: Indiana University Press, 1994.

Galbraith, John Kenneth. *American Capitalism: The Concept of Countervailing Power*. Boston: Houghton Mifflin, 1952.

Gamson, William. "Defining Movement Success." In *The Social Movements Reader: Cases and Concepts*, edited by Jeff Goodwin and James M. Jasper, 383–85. Oxford, UK: Wiley-Blackwell, 2015.

———. *The Strategy of Social Protest*. Belmont, Calif.: Wadsworth, 1990.

Gaventa, John. *Power and Powerlessness: Quiescence and Rebellion in an Appalachian Valley*. Urbana: University of Illinois Press, 1980.

Geertz, Clifford. *The Interpretation of Cultures*. 1973; repr., New York: Basic Books, 2000.

Getman, Julius. *Restoring the Power of Unions: It Takes a Movement*. New Haven: Yale University Press, 2010.

Gills, Barry K., ed. *Globalization in Crisis*. New York: Routledge, 2011.

Glenn, Susan. *Daughters of the Shtetl: Life and Labor in the Immigrant Generation*. Ithaca: Cornell University Press, 1991.

Glück, Elsie. *John Mitchell, Miner: Labor's Bargain with the Gilded Age*. New York: John Day, 1929.

Golin, Steve. *Fragile Bridge: Paterson Silk Strike, 1913*. Philadelphia: Temple University Press, 1988.

Gompers, Samuel. *Seventy Years of Life and Labor: An Autobiography*. Edited by Nick Salvatore. 1925; repr., New York: ILR Press, 1984.

Götz, Norbert. "'Moral Economy': Its Conceptual History and Analytical Prospects." *Journal of Global Ethics* 11 (2015): 147–62.

Gramsci, Antonio. *Selections from the Prison Notebooks*. New York: International Publishers, 1971.

Green, James R. *Death in the Haymarket: A Story of Chicago, the First Labor Movement, and the Bombing that Divided Gilded Age America*. New York: Pantheon, 2000.

Greene, Victor. *The Slavic Community on Strike: Immigrant Labor in Pennsylvania Anthracite*. Notre Dame, Ind.: University of Notre Dame Press, 1968.

Greenhouse, Steven. *The Big Squeeze: Tough Times for the American Worker*. New York: Knopf, 2008.

Greenwald, Maurine. "Women and Pennsylvania Working-Class History." *Pennsylvania History* 63 (Winter 1996): 5–16.

Greenwald, Richard. Review of *Fighting for the Union Label*, by Kenneth C. Wolensky, Nicole H. Wolensky, and Robert P. Wolensky. *Journal of American History* 90 (June 2003): 277–78.

Grigor, Talinn, and Romina Katchi. "Debris of What-Would-Have-Been: A Photo Essay Concerning Deindustrialization in Hyper-Capitalist and Post-Socialist Cities." *Journal of Urban History* 41 (2015): 294–306.

Guglielmo, Jennifer. *Living the Revolution: Italian Women's Resistance and Radicalism in New York City, 1880–1945*. Chapel Hill: University of North Carolina Press, 2010.

Gutman, Herbert G. *Power and Culture: Essays on the American Working Class*. Edited by Ira Berlin. New York: New Press, 1987.

———. "Work, Culture, and Society in Industrializing America, 1815–1919."

American Historical Review 78 (June 1973): 531–88.

Haberland, Michelle. *Striking Beauties: Women Apparel Workers in the U.S. South, 1930–2000*. Athens: University of Georgia Press, 2015.

Halbwachs, Maurice. *On Collective Memory*. Translated by Lewis Coser. Chicago: University of Chicago Press, 1992.

Hall, Jacquelyn Dowd, James Leloudis, Robert Korstad, and Mary Murphy. *Like a Family: The Making of a Southern Cotton Mill World*. Chapel Hill: University of North Carolina Press, 1987.

Hard, Anne. "Anthracite Country." *Nation* 121 (November 1925): 2–3.

Hareven, Tamara K. *Family Time and Industrial Time: The Relationship Between the Family and Work in a New England Industrial Community*. London: Cambridge University Press, 1982.

Harvey, David. *Spaces of Capital: Towards a Critical Geography*. New York: Routledge, 2001.

Harvey, Oscar Jewell, and Ernest Gray Smith. *A History of Wilkes-Barre, Luzerne County, Pennsylvania*. Vol. 5. Wilkes-Barre, Pa.: Raeder Press, 1909.

Hayden, Dolores. *The Power of Place: Urban Landscapes as Public History*. Cambridge, Mass.: MIT Press, 1995.

Hentoff, Nat. *John Cardinal O'Connor: At the Storm Center of a Changing American Catholic Church*. New York: Charles Scribner's Sons, 1988.

Herold, Ruth. "Mechanisms of Merger: The Implementation and Distribution of the Low Back Merger in Eastern Pennsylvania." Ph.D. diss., University of Pennsylvania, 1990.

Hobsbawm, Eric. *Industry and Empire*. New York: Pantheon Books, 1968.

———. "Religion and the Rise of Socialism" (1978). In *Workers: Worlds of Labor*, by Eric Hobsbawm, 33–54. New York: Pantheon Books, 1984.

Howard, Walter T., ed. *Anthracite Reds: A Documentary History of Communists in Northeastern Pennsylvania During the Great Depression*. Vol. 2. New York: iUniverse, 2004.

———. "'Radicals Not Wanted': Communists and the 1929 Wilkes-Barre Silk Mill Strikes." *Pennsylvania History* 69 (Summer 2002): 342–66.

Hutchins, Grace. *Labor and Silk*. New York: International Publishers, 1929.

Jacobs, James B., Coleen Friel, and Robert Radick. *Gotham Unbound: How New York City Was Liberated from the Grip of Organized Crime*. New York: New York University Press, 1999.

Jensen, Joan M. "Inside and Outside the Unions: 1920–1980." In *A Needle, a Bobbin, a Strike: Women Needleworkers in America*, edited by Joan M. Jensen and Sue Davidson, 185–94. Philadelphia: Temple University Press, 1984.

Jonas, Andrew E. G., Eugene McCann, and Mary Thomas. *Urban Geography: A Critical Introduction*. Malden, Mass.: Wiley, 2015.

Jones, Eliot. *The Anthracite Coal Combination in the United States*. Cambridge, Mass.: Harvard University Press, 1914.

Kashatus, William C. *Dapper Dan Flood: The Controversial Life of a Congressional Power Broker*. University Park: Pennsylvania State University Press, 2010.

Katz, Daniel. *All Together Different: Yiddish Socialists, Garment Workers, and the Labor Roots of Multiculturalism*. New York: New York University Press, 2011.

Keil, Thomas. *On Strike! Capital Cities and the Wilkes-Barre Newspaper Unions*. Tuscaloosa: University of Alabama Press, 1988.

Kessler-Harris, Alice. *Gendering Labor History*. Chicago: University of Illinois Press, 2007.

———. *Women Have Always Worked: A Historical Overview*. New York: Feminist Press, 1981.

Kim, Jeong-Hee. *Understanding Narrative Inquiry*. Thousand Oaks, Calif.: Sage, 2016.

Kirkby, Diane. "'The Wage-Earning Woman and the State': The National Women's Trade Union League and Protective Labor Legislation, 1903–1923." *Labor History* 28 (Winter 1987): 54–74.

Kitch, Carolyn. *Pennsylvania in Public Memory: Reclaiming the Industrial Past*. University Park: Pennsylvania State University Press, 2012.

Klein, Philip S., and Ari Arthur Hoogenboom. *A History of Pennsylvania*. University Park: Pennsylvania State University Press, 1980.

Kozura, Michael. "We Stood Our Ground: Anthracite Miners and the Expropriation of Corporate Property, 1930–41." In *"We Are All Leaders": The Alternative Unionism of the Early 1930s*, edited by Staughton Lynd, 199–237. Urbana: University of Illinois Press, 1996.

Laslett, John, and Mary Tyler. *The ILGWU in Los Angeles, 1907–1988*. Inglewood, Calif.: Ten Star Press, 1989.

Lawrence-Lightfoot, Sara, and Jessica Hoffman Davis. *The Art and Science of Portraiture*. San Francisco: Jossey-Bass, 1997.

Le Blanc, Paul, and Tim Davenport, eds. *The "American Exceptionalism" of Jay Lovestone and His Comrades, 1929–1940*. Vol. 1. Boston: Brill, 2015.

Leeder, Elaine. *The Gentle General: Rose Pesotta, Anarchist and Labor Organizer*. Albany: State University of New York Press, 1993.

Lefebvre, Henri. *The Production of Space*. Translated by Donald Nicholson-Smith. Malden, Mass.: Blackwell, 1991.

Levine, Louis. *The Women's Garment Workers: A History of the International Ladies' Garment Workers' Union*. New York: Huebsch, 1924.

Levine, Myron. *Urban Politics: Cities and Suburbs in a Global Age*. New York: Routledge, 2015.

Libonati, Michael, and Herbert Edelhertz. *Study of Property Ownership and Devolution in the Organized Crime Environment*. Prepared under Grant No. 80-IJ-CX-0066 from the U.S. Department of Justice, National Institute of Justice, to the Temple University School of Law. Washington, D.C.: Government Printing Office, 1986.

Lin, Jan, and Christopher Mele. *The Urban Sociology Reader*. New York: Routledge, 2013.

Louie, Miriam Ching Yoon. *Sweatshop Warriors: Immigrant Women Workers Take on the Global Factory*. Cambridge, Mass.: South End Press, 2001.

Love, Barbara J., ed. *Feminists Who Changed America, 1963–1975*. Urbana: University of Illinois Press, 2006.

Lowell, B. Lindsay, Jay Teachman, and Zhongren Jing. "Unintended Consequences of Immigration Reform: Discrimination and Hispanic Employment." *Demography* 32 (November 1995): 617–28.

Lynd, Staughton. *Doing History from the Bottom Up: On E. P. Thompson, Howard Zinn, and Rebuilding the Labor Movement from Below*. Chicago: Haymarket Books, 2014.

———. *Solidarity Unionism: Rebuilding the Labor Movement from Below*. Chicago: Charles H. Kerr, 1992.

———, ed. *"We Are All Leaders": The Alternative Unionism of the Early 1930s*. Urbana: University of Illinois Press, 1996.

Lynd, Alice, and Staughton Lynd, eds. *Rank and File: Personal Histories by Working-Class Organizers*. 1973; repr., Chicago: Haymarket Books, 2011.

MacGaffey, Janet. *Coal Dust on Your Feet: The Rise, Decline, and Restoration of an Anthracite Mining Town*. Lanham, Md.: Rowman & Littlefield, 2013.

Maines, David R. "Narrative Accounts." In *Sociology: The Key Concepts*, edited by John Scott, 111–17. New York: Routledge, 2006.

———. "Narrative's Moment and Sociology's Phenomenon: Toward a Narrative Sociology." *Sociological Quarterly* 34 (1993): 17–38.

Massey, Doreen. *Spatial Divisions of Labor: Social Structures and the Geography of Production*. 1984. Reprint, New York: Routledge, 1995.

May, Robert, dir. *Kids for Cash*. Documentary film, 2013.

McAdam, Doug. *Political Process and the Development of Black Insurgency, 1930–1970*. Chicago: University of Chicago Press, 1999.

McAdam, Doug, and Ronnelle Paulsen. "Specifying the Relationship Between Social Ties and Activism." *American Journal of Sociology* 99 (1993): 640–67.

McCammon, Holly J., Verta Taylor, Jo Reger, and Rachel L. Einwohner, eds. *The Oxford Handbook of U.S. Women's Social Movement Activism*. Oxford: Oxford University Press, 2017.

McCreesh, Carolyn Daniel. *Women in the Campaign to Organize Garment Workers, 1880–1917.* New York: Garland, 1985.

McGuigan, Maureen, producer. *A Shop on Every Corner: Memories of the Garment Industry.* Documentary film, 2008.

———, writer and producer. *Six Women in Labor.* Fictionalized drama, 2003.

McGuire, John Thomas. "Maintaining the Vitality of a Social Movement: Social Justice Feminism, Class Conflict, and the Bryn Mawr Summer School for Women Workers, 1921–1924." *Pennsylvania History* 76 (Autumn 2009): 393–421.

McKee, Guian A. *The Problem of Jobs: Liberalism, Race, and Deindustrialization in Philadelphia.* Chicago: University of Chicago Press, 2008.

Meinig, Donald W., ed. *The Interpretation of Ordinary Landscapes.* New York: Oxford University Press, 1979.

Meser-Kruse, Timothy. *The Trial of the Haymarket Anarchists: Terrorism and Justice in the Gilded Age.* New York: Palgrave Macmillan, 2011.

Milkman, Ruth. *On Gender, Labor, and Inequality.* Champaign: University of Illinois Press, 2016.

———. *Women, Work and Protest: A Century of U.S. Women's Labor History.* New York: Routledge, 2013.

Miller, Donald L., and Richard E. Sharpless. *The Kingdom of Coal: Work, Enterprise, and Ethnic Communities in the Mine Fields.* Philadelphia: University of Pennsylvania Press, 1985.

Mills, C. Wright. *The Sociological Imagination.* New York: Oxford University Press, 1959.

Minchin, Timothy J. *Empty Mills: The Fight Against Imports and the Decline of the U.S. Textile Industry.* Lanham, Md.: Rowman & Littlefield, 2012.

Montgomery, David. *Workers' Control in America: Studies in the History of Work, Technology, and Labor Struggles.* New York: Cambridge University Press, 1979.

Moody, Kim. *Workers in a Lean World: Unions in the International Economy.* New York: Verso, 1997.

Moore, Mildred. "A History of the Women's Trade Union League of Chicago." Master's thesis, University of Chicago, 1915.

Morgan, Ted. *A Covert Life: Jay Lovestone, Communist, Anti-Communist, and Spymaster.* New York: Random House, 1999.

Munts, Raymond, and Mary Louise Munts. "Welfare History of the I.L.G.W.U." Supplement, *Labor History* 9 (Spring 1968): 82–97.

Nearing, Scott. *Anthracite: An Instance of Natural Resource Monopoly.* Freeport, N.Y.: Books for Libraries Press, 1915.

Nelson, Steve, James R. Barrett, and Rob Ruck. *Steve Nelson: American Radical.* Pittsburgh: University of Pittsburgh Press, 1981.

Newton, Michael. *The Mafia at Apalachin, 1957.* Jefferson, N.C.: McFarland, 2012.

Ochs, Elinor, and Lisa Capps. *Living Narrative: Creating Lives in Everyday Storytelling.* Cambridge, Mass.: Harvard University Press, 2001.

Orleck, Annelise. *Common Sense and a Little Fire: Women and Working-Class Politics in the United States, 1900–1965.* Chapel Hill: University of North Carolina Press, 1995.

Page, Ruth, and Bronwen Thomas, eds. *New Narratives: Stories and Storytelling in the Digital Age.* Lincoln: University of Nebraska Press, 2011.

Palmer, Gladys Louise. *Labor Relations in the Lace and Lace-Curtain Industries in the United States.* Washington, D.C.: Government Printing Office, 1925.

Parmet, Robert D. *The Master of Seventh Avenue: David Dubinsky and the American Labor Movement.* New York: New York University Press, 2005.

Passerini, Luisa. *Fascism in Popular Memory: The Cultural Experience of the Turin Working Class.* Translated by R. Lumley and J. Bloomfield. Cambridge: Cambridge University Press, 1987.

Pennsylvania Crime Commission. *Report on Organized Crime.* St. David's, Pa.: Commonwealth of Pennsylvania, 1984.

Pennsylvania Department of Labor and Industry. *Pennsylvania Occupational Employment 2017–2019 Short-Term Forecast.* Harrisburg, Pa.: Center for Workforce Information and Analysis, 2016.

Perks, Robert, and Alistair Thomson, eds. *The Oral History Reader*. New York: Routledge, 2016.

Pesotta, Rose. *Bread upon the Waters*. Ithaca: Cornell University Press, 1987.

Phelan, Craig. *Divided Loyalties: The Public and Private Life of Labor Leader John Mitchell*. Albany: State University of New York Press, 1994.

Porta, Donatella della. *Social Movements in Times of Austerity*. Cambridge, UK: Polity Press, 2015.

Portelli, Alessandro. *The Battle of Valle Giulia: Oral History and the Art of Dialogue*. Madison: University of Wisconsin Press, 1997.

———. *The Death of Luigi Trastulli and Other Stories: Form and Meaning in Oral History*. Albany: State University of New York Press, 1991.

———. *The Order Has Been Carried Out: History, Memory, and Meaning of a Nazi Massacre in Rome*. New York: Palgrave Macmillan, 2003.

———. *They Say in Harlan County: An Oral History*. New York: Oxford University Press, 2010.

Portes, Alejandro, Manuel Castells, and Lauren A. Benton. *The Informal Economy: Studies in Advanced and Less Developed Countries*. Baltimore: Johns Hopkins University Press, 1989.

Potter, Gary W. *Criminal Organizations: Vice, Racketeering, and Politics in an American City*. Prospect Heights, Ill.: Waveland Press, 1994.

Potter, Gary W., and Philip Jenkins. *The City and the Syndicate: Organizing Crime in Philadelphia*. Lexington, Mass.: Ginn Press, 1985.

Raab, Selwyn. *Five Families: The Rise, Decline, and Resurgence of America's Most Powerful Mafia Empires*. New York: St. Martin Press, 2005.

Reich, Robert. *Saving Capitalism: For the Many, Not the Few*. New York: Vintage, 2015.

Rhodes, James. "Youngstown's 'Ghost'? Memory, Identity, and Deindustrialization." *International Labor and Working-Class History* 84 (October 2013): 55–77.

Richards, Lawrence. *Union-Free America: Workers and Antiunion Culture*. Urbana: University of Illinois Press, 2008.

Ritzer, George, ed. *The Blackwell Companion to Globalization*. Oxford, UK: Blackwell, 2007.

Roe, Maggie, and Ken Taylor, eds. *New Cultural Landscapes*. New York: Routledge, 2014.

Rosen, Ellen Israel. *Making Sweatshops: The Globalization of the U.S. Apparel Industry*. Berkeley: University of California Press, 2002.

Rosenfeld, Jake. *What Unions No Longer Do*. Cambridge, Mass.: Harvard University Press, 2014.

Ross, Andrew, ed. *No Sweat: Fashion, Free Trade, and the Rights of Garment Workers*. New York: Verso, 1997.

Ross, Robert J. S., and Kent C. Trachte. *Global Capitalism: The New Leviathan*. Albany: State University of New York Press, 1990.

Roth, Mitchel P. *Global Organized Crime: A 21st Century Approach*. New York: Routledge, 2017.

Rupert, William W. *Pennsylvania: Tarr and McMurry Geographies*. London: Macmillan, 1903.

Scarpaci, Jean. "Angela Bambace and the International Ladies' Garment Workers' Union: The Search for an Elusive Activist." In *Pane e Lavoro: The Italian American Working Class*, edited by George E. Pozzetta, 99–118. Staten Island, N.Y.: American Italian Historical Association, 1978.

Schillaci, Joseph. *The Ragman: The Garment Industry in Northeast PA*. Pittsburgh: RoseDog Books, 2013.

Schneider, Friedrich. "Size and Development of the Shadow Economy of 31 European and 5 Other OECD Countries from 2003 to 2014: Different Developments?" *Journal of Self-Governance and Management Economics* 3 (2015): 7–29.

Selekman, Ben. "Miners and Murder: What Lies Back of the Labor Feud in Anthracite." *Survey Graphic* 60 (May 1, 1928), 151ff.

Shackel, Paul A. "Immigration Heritage in the Anthracite Coal Region of Northeastern Pennsylvania." *Journal of Community Archaeology and Heritage* 5 (2017): 101–13.

———. "The Meaning of Place in the Anthracite Region of Northeastern Pennsylvania." *International Journal of Heritage Studies* 22 (2015): 200–213.

———. *Remembering Lattimer: Migration, Labor, and Race in Pennsylvania Anthracite Country.* Urbana: University of Illinois Press, 2018.

Sherman, Vincent, and Robert Aldrich, dir. *The Garment Jungle.* Film, 1957.

Shogan, Robert. *The Battle of Blair Mountain: The Story of America's Largest Union Uprising.* Boulder, Colo.: Westview Press, 2004.

Sifakis, Carl. *The Mafia Encyclopedia.* New York: DaCapo Press, 2005.

Silver, Beverly J., and Sahan Savas Karatasli. "Historical Dynamics of Capitalism and Labor Movements." In *The Oxford Handbook of Social Movements*, edited by Donatella della Porta and Mario Diani, 133–45. Oxford: Oxford University Press, 2016.

Smith, Adam. *An Inquiry into the Nature and Causes of the Wealth of Nations.* Abridged with commentary by Laurence Dickey. Indianapolis, Ind.: Hackett, 1993.

Smith, Richard Cándida. "Popular Memory and Oral Narratives: Luisa Passerini's Reading of Oral History Interviews." *Oral History Review* 16 (Fall 1988): 95–107.

Spear, Sheldon. *Daniel J. Flood, a Biography: The Congressional Career of an Economic Savior and Cold War Nationalist.* Bethlehem: Lehigh University Press, 2009.

———. *Wyoming Valley History Revisited.* Shavertown, Pa.: Jemags & Co., 1984.

Stanger, Howard R., Paul F. Clark, and Ann C. Frost, eds. *Collective Bargaining Under Duress: Case Studies of Major North American Industries.* Ithaca, N.Y.: ILR Press, 2013.

Staudohar, Paul D. *Deindustrialization and Plant Closure.* Lexington, Mass.: Lexington Books, 1987.

Stegner, Wallace E. "The Sense of Place." In *Where the Bluebird Sings to the Lemonade Springs: Living and Writing in the West,* 199–206. New York: Random House, 1992.

Stepenoff, Bonnie. "Child Labor in Pennsylvania's Silk Mills: Protest and Change, 1900–1910." *Pennsylvania History* 59 (April 1992): 101–21.

———. "'Keeping It in the Family': Mother Jones and the Pennsylvania Silk Strike of 1900–1901." *Labor History* 38 (Fall 1997): 432–49.

———. *Their Fathers' Daughters: Silk Mill Workers in Northeastern Pennsylvania, 1880–1960.* Selinsgrove: Susquehanna University Press, 1999.

Sterba, Christopher M. "Family, Work, and Nation: Hazleton, Pennsylvania, and the 1934 General Strike in Textiles." *Pennsylvania Magazine of History and Biography* 120 (January–April 1996): 3–35.

Stiglitz, Joseph E. *Globalization and Its Discontents Revisited: Anti-globalization in the Era of Trump.* New York: W. W. Norton, 2018.

Su, Julie. "El Monte Thai Garment Workers: Slave Sweatshops." In *No Sweat: Fashion, Free Trade, and the Rights of Garment Workers*, edited by Andrew Ross, 143–45. New York: Verso, 1997.

Tager, Sabrina. "Women in the Global Clothing and Textile Industry." Master's thesis, Duke University, 2016.

Thomas, Norman M. *Socialism Re-examined.* New York: W. W. Norton, 1963.

Thompson, E. P. *Customs in Common: Studies in Traditional Popular Culture.* New York: New Press, 1993.

———. *The Making of the English Working Class.* London: Victor Gollancz, 1963.

———. "The Moral Economy of the English Crowd in the 18th Century." *Past and Present* 50 (1971): 76–136.

Thompson, Paul R. "Life Histories and the Analysis of Social Change." In *Biography and Society: The Life History Approach in the Social Sciences*, edited by Daniel Bertaux, 289–306. Beverly Hills, Calif.: Sage, 1981.

———. *The Voice of the Past: Oral History.* 1978; repr., New York: Oxford University Press, 1988.

Thompson, Paul R., and Joanna Bornat. *The Voice of the Past: Oral History.* 4th ed. New York: Oxford University Press, 2017.

Tilly, Charles. *From Mobilization to Revolution.* Reading, Mass.: Addison-Wesley, 1978.

Tilly, Chris, and Charles Tilly. *Work under Capitalism.* Boulder, Colo.: Westview Press, 1998.

Tonkin, Elizabeth. *Narrating Our Pasts: The Social Construction of Oral History.* Cambridge: Cambridge University Press, 1995.

Tripp, Anne Huber. *The IWW and the Paterson Silk Strike of 1913.* Urbana: University of Illinois Press, 1987.

Turk, Katherine. *Equality on Trial: Gender and Rights in the Modern American Workplace.* Philadelphia: University of Pennsylvania Press, 2016.

Tyler, Gus. *Look for the Union Label: A History of the International Ladies' Garment Workers' Union.* Armonk, N.Y.: M. E. Sharpe, 1995.

———. *Organized Crime in America.* Ann Arbor: University of Michigan Press, 1962.

U.S. Department of the Treasury. *Mafia: The Government's Secret File on Organized Crime.* New York: HarperCollins, 2007.

Valletta, Clement L., "The Settlement of Roseto: World View and Promise." In *The Ethnic Experience in Pennsylvania*, edited by John Bodnar, 120–43. Lewisburg: Bucknell University Press, 1973.

Velie, Lester. *Labor USA Today.* New York: Harper & Row, 1964.

Waldinger, Roger. "Another Look at the International Ladies' Garment Workers' Union: Women, Industry Structure, and Collective Action." In *Women, Work, and Protest: A Century of U.S. Women's Labor History*, edited by Ruth Milkman, 86–109. New York: Routledge, 2013.

Wallace, Anthony F. C. *St. Clair: A Nineteenth-Century Coal Town's Experience with a Disaster-Prone Industry.* New York: Knopf, 1987.

Wallerstein, Immanuel. *World-Systems Analysis: An Introduction.* Durham: Duke University Press, 2004.

Warne, Frank J. *The Slav Invasion and the Mineworkers.* Philadelphia: Lippincott, 1904.

Weaver, Karol K. *Medical Caregiving and Identity in Pennsylvania's Anthracite Region, 1880–2000.* University Park: Pennsylvania State University Press, 2011.

Weiner, Lynn Y. *From Working Girl to Working Mother: The Female Labor Force in the United States, 1820–1980.* Chapel Hill: University of North Carolina Press, 1985.

Wilkes-Barre Record Almanac. Wilkes-Barre, Pa.: Wilkes-Barre Publishing Co., 1952.

Willett, Mabel Herd. *The Employment of Women in the Clothing Trade.* New York: Columbia University, 1902. http://archive.org/stream/womeninindustry500abbo/womeninindustry500abbo_djvu.txt.

Winefsky, Holly R., and Julie A. Tenney. "Preserving the Garment Industry Proviso: Protecting Acceptable Working Conditions Within the Apparel and Accessories Industries." *Hofstra Law Review* 31 (2002): 587–631.

Witwer, David. *Corruption and Reform in the Teamsters Union.* Urbana: University of Illinois Press, 2003.

———. "The Dress Strike at Three-Finger Brown's: The Complex Realities of Antiracketeering from the Union Perspective in the 1950s." *International Labor and Working-Class History* 88 (Fall 2015): 166–89.

———. "Pattern for Partnership: Putting Labor Racketeering on the Nation's Agenda in the Late 1950s." In *The Right and Labor in America: Politics, Ideology, and Imagination*, edited by Nelson Lichtenstein and Elizabeth Tandy Shermer, 207–25. Philadelphia: University of Pennsylvania Press, 2012.

———. "Westbrook Pegler, Eleanor Roosevelt, and the FBI: A History of Infamous Enmities and Unlikely Collaborations." *Journalism History* 34 (2009): 194–203.

Wolensky, Kenneth C. "Unity House: A Worker's Shangri-La." *Pennsylvania Heritage* 20 (Summer 1998): 21–29.

———. "'We're Singin' for the Union': The ILGWU Chorus in Pennsylvania Coal Country, 1947–2000." In *Chorus and Community*, edited by Karen Ahlquist, 223–47. Urbana: University of Illinois Press, 2006.

Wolensky, Kenneth C., Nicole H. Wolensky, and Robert P. Wolensky. *Fighting for the Union Label: The Women's Garment Industry and the ILGWU in Pennsylvania.* University Park: Pennsylvania State University Press, 2002.

Wolensky, Kenneth C., and Robert P. Wolensky. "Born to Organize." *Pennsylvania Heritage* 25 (Summer 1999): 32–39.

———. "Building the ILGWU in Pennsylvania's Anthracite Mining Towns: The Leadership of Min Matheson, 1944–1963." *Sociological Imagination* 31 (1994): 83–100.

Wolensky, Robert P. *Better Than Ever! The Flood Recovery Task Force and the 1972 Agnes Disaster.* Stevens Point, Wis.: UWSP Foundation Press, 1993.

———. "POWER: Collective Action and the Anthracite Region Water Crisis." In *Communities at Risk: Collective Responses to Technological Hazards,* edited by Stephen. R. Couch and J. Stephen Kroll-Smith, 230–61. New York: Peter Lang, 1991.

———. *Power, Policy, and Disaster: The Political-Organizational Impact of a Major Flood.* Final Report, Grant No. 8113529. Alexandria, Va.: National Science Foundation, 1982.

———. "Power Structure and Group Mobilization Following Disaster: A Case Study." *Social Science Quarterly* 64 (March 1983): 96–110.

———. "Toward a Broader Conceptualization of Volunteerism in Disasters." *Journal of Voluntary Action Research* 8 (October 1979): 33–42.

———. "Working-Class Heroes: Rinaldo Cappellini and the Anthracite Mineworkers." In *Storytelling Sociology: Narrative as Social Inquiry,* edited by Ronald J. Berger and Richard Quinney, chapter 18. Boulder, Colo.: Lynne Reinner, 2005.

Wolensky, Robert P., and William A. Hastie Sr. *Anthracite Labor Wars: Tenancy, Italians, and Organized Crime in the Northern Coalfield of Northeastern Pennsylvania, 1897–1959.* Rev. ed. Easton, Pa.: Canal History and Technology Press, 2013.

Wolensky, Robert P., and Edward J. Miller. "The Everyday versus the Disaster Role of Local Officials: Citizen and Official Definitions." *Urban Affairs Quarterly* 16 (1981): 483–504.

Wolensky, Robert P., and Kenneth C. Wolensky. "Local Government's Problem with Disaster Management: A Literature Review and Structural Analysis." *Policy Studies Review* 9 (1990): 703–25.

———. "Min Matheson and the ILGWU in the Northern Anthracite Region, 1944–1963." Special issue, *Pennsylvania History* 60 (October 1993): 455–74.

Wolensky, Robert P., Kenneth C. Wolensky, and Nicole H. Wolensky. *The Knox Mine Disaster: The Final Years of the Northern Anthracite and the Effort to Rebuild a Regional Economy.* Harrisburg: Pennsylvania Historical and Museum Commission, 1999.

———. *Voices of the Knox Mine Disaster: Stories, Remembrances, and Reflections on the Anthracite Coal Industry's Last Major Catastrophe, January 22, 1959.* Harrisburg: Pennsylvania Historical and Museum Commission, 2005.

Wolf, Stewart, and John G. Bruhn. *The Power of Clan: The Influence of Human Relationships on Heart Disease.* New Brunswick, N.J.: Transaction, 1993.

Wolfe, Julia, comp. and arr. *Anthracite Fields.* Oratorio, 2014.

Yarrow, Mike, Ruth Yarrow, and Douglas Yarrow, eds. *Voices from the Appalachian Coalfields.* Huron, Ohio: Bottom Dog Press, 2015.

Zappia, Charles A. "Unionism and the Italian American Worker: A History of the New York City 'Italian Locals' in the International Ladies' Garment Workers' Union, 1900–1934." Ph.D. diss., University of California, Berkeley, 1994.

Zieger, Robert H. *The CIO: 1935–1955.* Chapel Hill: University of North Carolina Press, 1995.

———. *For Jobs and Freedom: Race and Labor in America since 1865.* Lexington: University Press of Kentucky, 2007.

———. *John L. Lewis: Labor Leader.* Boston: Twayne, 1988.

———. "Robin Hood in the Silk City: The IWW and the Paterson Silk Strike of 1913." *Proceedings of the New Jersey Historical Society* 84 (July 1966): 182–95.

Zinn, Howard. *A People's History of the United States.* New York: Harper Perennial, 1980.

INDEX